PRELUDE TO ASCENSION

Tools for Transformation

Vywamus and others
through Janet McClure

Michael Z. Tyree, Book Designer
Will Palmer, Editor

ISBN 0-929385-54-3

 Published by
Light Technology Publishing
P.O. Box 1526
Sedona, AZ 86339

Contents

About the Channel

J anet McClure was an exceptional channel who devoted her full time and energies to the conscious channeling of spiritual beings. She shared their teaching of truth and understanding to aid in humanity's transformation.

Janet studied intensively for many years with a spiritual teacher, receiving her Doctor of Metaphysics from The Brotherhood of the White Temple. She had already dedicated her life to the service of the Cosmic Plan when she was asked by Djwhal Khul to assist him in aiding humanity by being a conscious channel for his energies and spiritual teachings. Djwhal was responding to a request from Sanat Kumara, the Planetary Logos who ensouls the Earth, to return to his Earth contacts and once again aid humanity as he had done forty years earlier through Alice Bailey and her books.

Djwhal knew that channeling would flow easily for Janet, as she had had extensive channeling experience in previous lives and had taught channeling in ancient Egypt. Janet enthusiastically put aside her familiar and comfortable world of business and committed herself to this new mission. Being an Aries, it was Janet's nature to move forward with her New Age awareness, secure in the knowledge of the support she would receive from the Source.

After channeling for two years, Janet was introduced by Djwhal to the cosmic being Vywamus, a caring and loving being who is a light aspect of Sanat Kumara. Vywamus was attracted to the beautiful light of the Earth, and continued with Janet the work that Djwhal began in 1982.

The teachers were very interested in bringing their information to Earth through a group focus. Because Janet was already working with a dedicated group facilitated by Lillian Harben, and because this group's energies were compatible with those of the teachers, the entire group was asked to work together and form The Tibetan Foundation. The group learned specific methods to remove and clear the blocks in the subconscious belief structure that have accumulated from all our past lives, creating resistance in our present life to moving forward with our development.

The Tibetan Foundation was incorporated in January 1983 with Janet as its president. The founding purpose of the Foundation was to spread the teachings of the spiritual masters to all of humanity, through lectures, seminars, workshops, correspondence courses, personal appointments, books and transcripts, throughout the United States, Canada, and Europe. The information channeled through Janet and the other certified channels brought transformation both to the channels and to the thousands who participated in Foundation events.

Vywamus encourages the training of channels, as he believes channeling to be the single most important step we can take to move forward in our evolution. Concerning her own evolution, Janet said, "The benefits I have received by channeling in terms of clearing blocked areas for myself are enormous. My evolution has accelerated greatly through the channeling process."

Sliding Affirmations into a Lake

The following technique is recommended as a way of using the meditations that appear throughout this book.

- See your subconscious as a lake. Choose any color lake that seems appropriate.
- See a slide going from your conscious to your subconscious and slide the affirmation down the slide into the lake.
- Try seeing the affirmation as a series of words sliding in, or see it written on a piece of paper, as in a fortune cookie, sliding down into the lake.
- When the affirmation enters the lake, the lake may change color. Ideally, it will become clearer or whiter.
- After you slide the affirmation into the lake and it dissolves, then see a golden light shining onto the lake, filling the whole lake with gold.
- Splash that golden water into all of your cells.

Affirmations for Clearing the Lemurian Experience

1. I release the fear that a traumatic experience must be encountered when I activate 100% service in my life.
2. I release any past experiences that prevent me from seeing service as a free flow.
3. I do not encounter difficult electrical opposition as I serve, now.
4. I can safely allow those who have different points of view to serve with me, now.
5. I know that humanity is standing together, now.
6. I release any defense mechanism against those who oppose me, now.
7. I know that my light has dissolved all anxiety, loss and trauma from my encounters with the Electrical Ones.
8. I cut all ties with past patterns that bring in a destructive mode on the Earth plane.
9. I release the need to pull in an impact to the group as it seeks to bring together the various individuals' agendas.
10. I allow the sorting out of the group's purposes to be harmonious.
11. I allow the group vehicle to be free of interactive factors that create disruption and opposition.
12. I allow the group to be free from the entangled qualities that are stimulated by specific misconceptions from the past.
13. I see the free flow of the group energies as they come together divinely, now.
14. I allow the intrigue factor within a group to fall away or to be resolved, now.
15. I know that a group can bridge the gap of the different experiences of its members.

✦ PART ONE ✦

YOUR FOUR BODIES

The Tibetan, Djwhal Khul, 1983

❖ O N E ❖

Your Emotional Body

I WOULD LIKE TO TALK TO YOU ABOUT YOUR EMOTIONS. PEOPLE RELATE TO LIFE in different ways. They certainly do not approach life in the same manner, do they? When you look around the world, this is very obvious and one of the main reasons for the difficulty of communication. Many more than half of the people in the world respond to life through an emotional focus. Now, this isn't bad or good — it just is. It is one perspective for viewing life.

If you know yourself, or are beginning to do so, you may be able to ascertain whether you *feel* life or whether you *think* about it. It is very important that you know the difference, that you understand what your particular approach to life is and understand those in your environment and what their approach is; in this way you understand self and those around you more fully. You grow in awareness by such recognition. An emotional focus upon life can be very positive in its higher aspects. It makes you very sensitive to beauty, it makes you appreciate nature, it makes you love the arts and dancing, and it makes you recognize many things and really become a part of the feeling side of creation. It can be a wonderful, joyous experience in its most positive aspects. However, my friends, those of you who are so focused, recognize that it can also be exactly the opposite. When your emotions are stirred up, are churning within you, there is such a focus there that you can go to the very pits within self. You can become very depressed, very out of balance, because your beingness gets centered in the emotions within you.

If you are focused upon the emotional body, life becomes a see-saw. You go to the heights and you also experience the depths. It is an eternal process that moves you back and forth, and you become ever more frustrated by it — ever moving at the whims of your emotional body.

My friends, is it not time to look at this process, to consider some alternatives, some ways to prevent that eternal swing? It is time at least to tone it down a little and to gradually learn that you do not need to focus there. You may retain the benefits of your emotional focus without remaining *that* focused at all – by approaching life through a more balanced perspective now.

How do you begin this? You begin with your will. Yes, with your will. If you begin to find that you are experiencing the depths too often and if in your desire for a more balanced approach to life, you utilize your will, it will make all of the difference. But you say, When I get in this place, I cannot help it. I try to get out, but I cannot. You cannot because this is a pattern that is well established – a focus – and when you get into this focus, this pattern, you know not how to escape it. Use your will. Reach down inside of self with a big hand of *will* and *pull* yourself out. Yes, *pull* yourself up and out of this situation. Is it easy? No, it is not easy, but it is necessary. It is important to recognize that until you are able to do this, you will keep setting up different emotional traumas. You will keep reexperiencing them because it is an established pattern, a way of living, one that you are very comfortable with. Does that surprise you? Yes, you are comfortable there. You know how to function in the depths – you have done it often and although you are miserable in a sense, you are comfortable. It is familiar there. Familiarity is important. You are afraid of what you may find in a whole new land of balanced living – not consciously, of course, but with the subconscious mind, which is not directly connected with the conscious mind, has fears from past experiences and, for most people, says the unknown is to be feared because it is not familiar. So keep this in mind. Recognize that with your *will* you must go forward.

Now, it is a good idea, if you are working within your belief structure, to remove the false beliefs of fear of the unknown; to remove the false beliefs of familiarity or to purge the areas, or perhaps both. In some way it lessens the mountain, if you will, that needs to be climbed. But it is your will that will bring you over the top. My friends, those of you who are seeking growth, seeking to become greater, know that for each one of you there is a time of crisis, and for those of you focused upon the emotional body, the time of crisis comes when you must utilize the will to lift you out of this pattern. It will be very difficult to do at first. But if you have confidence in self, knowing how much you want to grow, knowing that ultimately you are to become perfect, that it is toward this potentiality that you must ever move, then do it, my friends, do it! Use the will, *now*. Launch yourself by your lifting upon a whole different spiral. Get excited about it – do it with joy. Do it, my friends, however you wish, but do it!

When you are in the pits of despair, you view life with hopelessness, with a feeling that never again will you be able to function, that you will always be immersed in this pit of despair, do you not? But when you begin to experience this, analyze it — yes, analyze it. Is that not ridiculous? Have you not been there many times, and if you have, then ask yourself how you could have been there many times if you had not gotten out? Otherwise it would have been just once that you were there. But you have had moments of the heights, too, have you not?

The mere fact that you begin to analyze the situation will aid you. You begin to utilize the logical processes and to balance a little this heavy emotional area. Analyze your current situation and see what is really true and what you are just feeling to be true, my friends. If you cannot analyze it, if the pit holds you too tightly, go to a friend or to your teacher and say, "Would you please help me? I am in this pit of despair, I cannot get out of it. I need an outside opinion." And as you begin to do this, also use your will. You must make the first step, either by willing yourself out or going for help, or both. The deeper the pit, the more you will resist any sort of a change. It will hold you, and you will need great will to make any effort, but you can do it, can you not? And the sooner you begin to do it — to use the will — the sooner you will be out of your great immersion.

So pity not self, knowing that self pities itself enough, and you do not need to add to it now. Pity self not, my friends. Do not allow pity to enter in here. No "poor me" syndrome, please. Use the will, use the logical processes, and pull yourself up, *now*.

One suggestion I have given recently that may aid you is to view in front of you a red ladder. It is the will. Climb your red ladder, my friends, when you need it. Climb it to a place of greater balance. Use your great necessity for growth, your great necessity to become greater, and climb your ladder of will. It is always there, no matter how deep you are. It will aid you if you let it, so climb now this ladder right there. Reach up to it and climb it with your will.

Let us suppose that you have done what I have suggested. You have used the red ladder and you are feeling better. You really feel encouraged — "I've done it, I don't need to do that anymore," you've said, and life seems to be flowing a little better, and you are feeling a little more balanced. And about the time you're feeling it . . . boom! You are back in it again. And you say, "What's the use, I can't do it. I've worked as hard as I can. I've sought growth and I've worked intensively within my belief structure, but nothing works. Take it from me, nothing works." Have you been there, my friends? Stop. Don't allow this pattern to reestablish. The minute you get into it, run to your ladder; don't allow one thought of self-pity to enter here — not one. If you are purging, purge the area of self-pity with every emotion you can think of — "necessity," "repeating pattern" — anything that you can think of. Get rid of it. If you are not working within your belief structure, begin to use affirmations. Say to yourself, "I do not need self-pity. I am becoming greater now." Write that 500 times. And another one: "I am attaining greater balance all the time. I am utilizing my will to remove myself from emotional turmoil, *now*. Everything is getting better and better, and better and better." And write that one 500 times.

Do whatever you wish. Work within your belief structure. Use affirmations. Visualize yourself as perfect. Work on imagery, but remember, it is a process of will, in connection with everything else. It is a blending of every type of effort you can think of to get you out of this pattern. But the key is the will; develop it. Use red in a very positive way to attune to the will of your higher self, the will of the Creator — not the will in any negative connotation. Know, my friends, the will of your higher self at the spiritual level — the will of the Creator to create what is positive in life. Yes, using your will, you can create a better life, a more positive life, like the Creator Himself meant for you to have. Yes, a positive life was planned for you, but you have chosen not to experience it fully up to this point. Make another choice. Recognize that you can choose to live more productively. Use your will, *now*. Pull yourself from this emotional focus. Blend it, now. Come out of it, my friends.

Do you not know what a wonderful opportunity humankind has now? Positive energies come to us — energies that aid growth. Will you not use it? Will you not take advantage of such a wonderful opportunity? Now, because there is more energy here, it can also immerse you further, if you let it; it intensifies wherever you are. But it can intensify your effort to free yourself, and this is the way to use it. Do not use more energy to immerse further. Use it to will yourself from this position, to raise yourself. Climb your ladder, knowing that this is marvelous — this opportunity that you have now to come into greater balance. It is so marvelous.

My friends, I too come from this emotional focus. So I am not speaking of theory. I am speaking from my own experience, and I know what is necessary to free yourself. I too floundered in emotions for eons. I too enjoyed their familiarities. I too suffered — with a capital S. I could have printed it across my chest: "I Suffer now. I was a martyr — I did it very well. I suffered, my friends. One day, as I grew and evolved, I said, I do *what?* I suffer? I don't want to do that anymore. I choose not to suffer, *now.*" And I stopped. I stopped suffering. Of course, it didn't happen immediately, but what did happen immediately was my choice. I decided right then that I was through suffering, that I would do whatever was necessary to free myself, that I chose to live with freedom, that I would not remain in that emotional immersion. Whenever I began to slip into it, I pulled — I yanked — myself up. I did not allow self-pity; I said, "No you don't, no you don't, I do not suffer. I used that statement over and over: I do not suffer, I choose not to. It is my choice, and I make it, now. I do not suffer!"

I did some meditation work. I did much clearing. I also dedicated myself to the Creator and His work. I prayed a lot. I received much help. I asked for it, down on my knees I asked for it, and I asked for the strength to maintain my balance. I studied intensely, learning as much as I could, using the mental faculties consciously to balance this emotional immersion. And very gradually, very gradually, my friends, I began to come out of it, and whenever I started to slip back (which I did it often), I said, pulling myself up with my will, "No, I choose not to suffer, *now*."

It worked, my friends, for me it worked. This was a turning point in my growth pattern. Of course, I had much work to do. I am still working. My life did not suddenly just become perfect, of course not. But by my choice, along with my complete dedication to the Creator, to knowing that everything that I was, and am, is for Him and His purposes, I freed myself – completely. I did. I didn't do it all in that same life. I'm not telling you that I did. But I did a great deal in that life. I turned a corner; yes, I did.

I am not just telling you this to be talking about myself. I am trying to give you hope. I am trying to say that it works; I have tried it, I know it, it works. To some of you who think it is impossible to free yourself, I am trying to give you hope, telling you to try it, that you can learn and grow and become greater, become more balanced, and not suffer. Choose not to, my friends. Choose, now, not to suffer.

Each of you has my love, and I appreciate your attention now.

Cleansing the Body to Aid You

🕊 *Seated in a quiet place, become as tranquil as possible. Slow down the thoughts. Allow them to flow – the ones that do enter – smoothly. Seek not to pay attention to them. A few deep breaths will aid you, now. Experience a sense of tranquillity, of deep peace, my friends, becoming centered, quiet.*

🕊 *A string descends from above, and it is focused between the eyes, all the way down the center of your body. Your consciousness is centered there, upon that string. It is very balanced, now. You feel peaceful, completely relaxed and centered upon that string. Very centered. And whenever I mention the word centered, you will feel very centered, now.*

🕊 *A beautiful transparent ball comes down over you and encloses you. It is not disturbing. It is rather protective, and you feel very comfortable with it. You do not experience any negative feeling from it. It is open to the Creator and His love. It is open to your teachers. All that it keeps out are bad emotions – negative feelings. That is all that it keeps out. It lets in love. It lets in joy. It lets in compassion. It lets in forgiveness. It lets in every good emotion, and negative feelings cannot enter here. Know that you are this protection. Feel it.*

🕊 *Now take a deep breath, my friends. There is a window in this protection. Open it, and now – wooooooooooh, you have blown out all of those negative feelings within. Do it again: Breathe in, bringing them up, and blow them out, now – whoooooooooooh. All right, when you are practicing, do this several times. Know that each negative feeling there can be is literally pulled up with your will – expelled with force, gotten rid of. You can cleanse yourself of these negative feelings, now. Do it several times, then close your door, there, the one that allowed you to expel them.*

❦ *And now, from above, come all the positive emotions, my friends. They come from the Creator. See a beautiful golden light as it descends. It's full of love, it's full of joy. It's full of peace, it's full of tranquillity, it's full of happiness – do you not feel it? Oh, experience it. It fills you, now, it fills you to the brim. You have gotten rid of all the negative feelings, and the positive emotions flow in, my friends. Feel it, experience it. You are full of joy, are you not? The Creator's joy, is it not marvelous? Expand with it, feel the joy that has come to you. It fills you. it crowds out any little negative feelings that might be lurking there. How can one so full of joy have any negative feelings? It is impossible. Know that this is true, that you can just dance with joy, you are so filled with it. Is it not marvelous? And the love also fills you – joy and love together, my friends. Experience it now. Is it not marvelous? Do you not feel refreshed? The tranquillity gives way to the joy and the love. Experience it now.*

✧ T W O ✧

Your Mental Body

NOW WE WILL DISCUSS YOUR MENTAL BODY. YES, THAT ASPECT OF SELF which is in the spotlight of attention, which is considered by advanced humanity to be the most desired and sought after aspect of self.

We will talk about its attributes, the advantages of fully developing it, and then we will discuss the disadvantage of being focused upon this aspect, the pitfalls that must be avoided, the need to move beyond the intense focus as one seeks further development, as one seeks to clear and balance one's life completely.

What is the mental process? Have you ever thought about it? One knows that the brain is a very complex organ, that it contains many things whose purposes science is just beginning to discover. They have not yet fully identified the human brain. Is the mental faculty the human brain? Well, not exactly. It is an aspect of the consciousness that functions through the human brain, that is true, but the mental process is an aspect of your consciousness. If you can remember that this is true, it will aid you in understanding why, although most human brains are physically the same, some people utilize them much more productively than others. So the brain is just the vehicle within which that particular aspect known as the mental process operates now.

Why then do some people have the ability to compute very difficult problems, to logically deduce certain aspects that others are not capable of doing, to consider the rationale of a situation and come to very concrete decisions regarding it while others do not? Some people pretty much avoid this level of thought unless they are forced to do it. They are not able to utilize their brains, which are probably as good as anyone else's. Why is this true?

Well, from an evolutionary point of view, the aspect of self that contains the mental abilities has developed over eons of time. It does not necessarily have anything to do with that particular vehicle through which it currently operates. If the mental process has been very traumatized, very affected, then perhaps the vehicle in which it functions is not perfect. This is from its own doing; remember, we are products of many experiences, and thus, the mental abilities within the brain area, if they are not perfect, are also a product of what we have been and what we have experienced. Those who have mental dysfunctions and are within institutions may occasionally be products of this process. Usually, however, it is an emotional disorder. Sometimes it is a misalignment between the mental and the emotional bodies that is so forceful, so extreme, that serious mental disorders are seen, forcing these people into the care of others because they are not able to function and care for themselves. In these cases, the brain itself is not affected, but the alignment with the mental faculties and the other bodies is greatly off and causes very severe problems.

While confined to institutions such people usually are not able to pull this alignment back to the extent required for several lifetimes. The fact that they are in body can resolve some of these problems a little bit. Thus, they may have to spend perhaps ten lifetimes confined to institutions before they can balance the mental processes sufficiently to function as an independent consciousness upon the Earth plane. Know that such severe handicaps have resulted from severe misuse of the mental abilities.

Occasionally there is an exception here. A great one may choose to aid the Earth and come to Earth in such a misaligned manner, knowing that because of his much greater abilities he aids the Earth itself in achieving mental balance so that others who are unbalanced do not have to work quite as hard to resolve their balances. The great one does this with much love. Great ones come to resolve many problems. They do it in many areas, but we are talking now of the misalignment of the mental body, and many in the history of the world have done this. The numbers are not great when you consider the numbers of people who have lived, but just one great one's consciousness accomplishes a great deal toward easing immersion in any particular area. They give this with love, knowing that it is their part in the Creator's Plan as with grace He allows humankind to approach Him again with greater ease than perhaps they deserve, for the Creator certainly is not vindictive. He aids His children many times when perhaps they do not deserve it. Is it not marvelous, the Creator's love that aids us now?

The Earth is currently in the process of complete development of the mental body. That is, the bulk of humankind is; advanced humanity has already developed this body to a great degree, but the bulk of human consciousness is engaged in this activity in the present age. Thus the emphasis on developing the mental faculty upon the Earth. Thus the need for so many to be educated mentally, the emphasis upon the complete understanding of the mind with not as great an emphasis upon the emotional needs. Humanity gets in a little bit of trouble here.

Humanity seeks to develop one aspect without seeking to develop the aspect that balances it. This is one reason for current problems, for world turmoil. The emotions churn within humanity because they are not as balanced most of the time as those who have begun to balance the mental faculty. This may sound like a contradiction, for I have said before to use the mental faculty to develop and balance the emotional body. That's very true, and when you can do it, it brings about a balanced condition. However, I am talking now about those of humankind upon this Earth who do not yet recognize the need for balance. Their thoughts pursue the mental activities and pay no attention to the emotional ones. I am talking about mentally *focused* human beings. Perhaps you might equate what I am saying to college professors, those who pursue the intellectual area in great depth, not even recognizing that the emotional body is important – they do not find it so. They simply, in generalizing, fence off the emotional area and allow it to fester, and when it has festered enough, it bursts forth in some unexpected way, and suddenly one who has been very mentally focused collapses from lack of balance.

There are those so mentally focused that if they would pay just a little attention to their emotional bodies, they would achieve good balance. That is just wonderful. We are not talking about those rather rare individuals, but about the ones who allow their focus upon the mental abilities to take precedence over everything else, and thus block any sort of balance that may be needed with the emotional body. Great danger is here because it leads to submersion of the areas within the subconscious mind which need attention. They rest there, and when they reach the point where it triggers a very immersed area, then you have this great explosion.

Please think about it. Those of you who go into the world every day need to understand this situation very thoroughly. As teachers you need to know how to understand the ones you encounter. If one who is so mentally focused that he has developed the mental body to a high level recognizes the need to integrate all of the learning process – as many of you are doing now, recognizing that you have physical, spiritual, emotional and mental needs, that you must learn to work with all four bodies – then he can do some very wonderful things. In fact, this is the ideal way to begin the clearing process. It is an ideal focus from which to clear because the mental focus enables you to see that you can do many things. You can rationalize and logically discern many needs that you have – but only after you become advanced enough, if you will, experienced enough, to see beyond self, to begin to understand the Creator's Plan for Earth and to begin to seek your own part in it. This is most important. So, if we have one who is mentally focused and can see beyond self, then we have the beginning of a very good disciple, one who will probably, in one lifetime, complete much work. It is wonderful and it is the most effective place to begin your esoteric work.

However, for a long period of time, one who is mentally focused, after developing these great faculties, thinks that this is all there is. In a sense he develops great mental superiority, looking at those who are not so focused and saying, "Look at what they are doing there. They churn emotionally. I do not do that. I am focused within my mental body and that is a very good place to be. I am much superior to them now. Why don't they just quit churning like that. Look at that immersion. How unusual. They are not very advanced — I am certainly much superior to them now." He also seeks to study everything, finding life so interesting, and he seeks greater and greater knowledge, never getting enough. This is not bad, my friends, as long as it is done with a little bit of balance — recognizing that seeking knowledge for knowledge's sake can certainly be overdone. What it does is waste time. Yes, it does waste precious time that might be used to serve the Creator.

Now, I am not saying the Creator judges anyone for this — He does not, nor do we, your teachers. We recognize that everyone who is mentally focused spends a period of time at this activity. We hope that it will be as short a period as possible, that this advanced piece of human consciousness — because that is what it is, at this point — will soon begin to recognize there is so much more, that they are so curious about life that they will begin to see how much they are missing by not going beyond the mental faculty. When this point is reached, the Creator has a very valuable one who will soon be serving Him completely, serving Him with great intelligence, which is necessary, and in balance, which is also necessary, and in joy and love, which is wonderful!

Generally speaking, those who are so mentally focused have not allowed great development of either the psychic abilities or the intuitive faculties. This is a generalization, and there can be exceptions to everything. It really depends on the amount of mental focus, because in this body it can be complete focus, and it is very intense when it is present and does not allow focus upon any other body. Thus you see great scholars who neglect even their physical needs and practically starve to death unless someone, such as a wife or a student, shoves food in their hands. It can be total.

This mental focus can be all-consuming. Many of them see not that there could be a Creator. They see only the mental processes and cannot understand anything of the spiritual area. What they have done, in effect, is block any other aspect completely, and as it begins to dawn on them that they have done this they begin to seek these other aspects and it is rather slow-going at first. The rational gets in the way. They seek to go beyond it and then analyze this process, putting them right back into the mental area. This is a very deep pattern and very difficult to let go of. The will must be utilized in this case, and, as one so focused begins to seek greater development beyond the mental and begins to analyze that, he has to stop and say to himself, "Oh no, I can't do that now. I must let go of these mental processes. I must go beyond that." Do it with the will and then do it with love, because the love aspect can aid here. Those who are so mentally focused and wish to move beyond it must first surround themselves with the love of the Creator, and the more intensely they can become involved with this love aspect, the more easily they will move beyond the mental.

Now, occasionally you will see one who is mentally focused but allows the intuition to develop to a great degree without losing his mental focus. What has happened here? Think about it very carefully. Another aspect of the personality has entered here: the ego, which says, "I have great mental capabilities, and I must not let go of them." But why does he allow the intuition to develop? Because it is recognized by the ego that if he extends these mental capabilities into the intuitional area he can really extend his own effectiveness, his own abilities. The mental area can recognize this. However, he has not yet let go of his mental focus. One who begins with this great a focus will always be so focused, but he must allow it to lighten, allow it to come under the direction of the soul. This, my friends, is the key! Yes, it is the key! The personality must come under the direction of the soul for one such as this who has allowed great intuitional abilities to form, but nothing else. You can surely see that when the personality is directed by the soul it says, "I do not have to be so important. I do not have to extend my own abilities now. What I have to do is balance all four aspects — the physical, the emotional, the mental and the spiritual — and thus I will find my own proper point here now in the Creator's Plan for Earth. I am not meant to seek this unbalanced mental condition. I am meant to serve."

This is the key word here — to serve. The soul knows that the personality must let go and allow the soul to function as it was meant to function on the Earth. Do you not see, my friends, that the purpose of our living is to serve the Creator, not our own individual growth? Our own growth is a part of the Creator's purpose, but it is not the main part. Our main purpose here is to implement the Plan of the Creator, and each individual consciousness knows that at soul level. We must allow the soul to function here — not just these greatly developed mental faculties or intuitional faculties, or any other faculties from a separate aspect. It must all be integrated into the soul, for it knows how to serve the Creator.

Techniques for Balancing the Four Bodies

Mental facilities are wonderful and develop over great lengths of time, but they need to be brought into line with other aspects of self. As you begin to do this, there are several valuable exercises that can help to overcome this pattern of involvement with the mental facilities.

First, decide that you are going to seek and practice other means of identifying solutions to life besides the mental abilities, which are already developed. At first there will be resistances to this because your present method is familiar and easier than learning a new one. But if you truly wish to grow, to evolve, to become greater, then seek this way.

Let go completely of the mental facilities. Choose a specific situation and give yourself an area to work in. If you are seeking to know more about the area of your particular part in the New Age, then do not analyze it, do not consider it logically. First, see what you know about it. Then launch yourself into it in a state of meditation. Take part in it and see what happens. Do this in a very balanced way, not when you are having an emotional problem or being engaged by a mental exercise or problem. Try to be as balanced as possible when beginning the exercise and then let go of everything. In a sense, erase as much as possible any mental patterns, emotional trauma, physical trauma or needs. Become open to possibilities. This is very important.

Visualize the physical, the emotional, the mental and the spiritual bodies in a perfect line, a vertical pattern in which they all fit together very well. Use the blue-string exercise that follows.

See all four bodies superimposed upon each other and then see centered right between your eyebrows a blue string that is balancing you now. Then launch yourself forward to the New Age. Experience it in this completely balanced condition. Do not rationalize, do not conceptualize it mentally, but experience it from a complete point of balance. This may aid you, and if you find yourself going back into an old pattern of mental analysis, then pull yourself out of it with your will. Do not allow it to happen. Will yourself back into a completely integrated state. Remember: the four bodies, vertically placed, with your blue string centered within self. Experience from a centered condition now.

After completing the exercise, analyze it and look at it logically. Decide how well you did in freeing yourself from this intense mental focus, if that's where you operate from. It will aid you now.

Another exercise that will be very helpful is to begin a step-by-step progression toward your integrated state. Of course that's what you are doing already, but undertake a conscious one now. Take a little step forward; in a state of meditation, see yourself stepping forward. Now feel around self. Are you balanced or are you completely mentally focused? If you are mentally focused, regroup — see that your bodies are balanced as stated before and then take another step. Are you balanced? Look and see and then take another step. Continue this, rebalancing when necessary, and then begin to experience within self, in an inner state, what is happening.

Be sure you look at all four bodies, because one or another may fall out of balance. Look at your string in your physical body. Is it centered? Look at it in your emotional body. Is it centered? Look at it in your mental body. Is it centered? Look at it in your spiritual body. Is it centered? Then look at your string. Is it centered itself? Is it one continuous vertical line through the four bodies? If not, realign it.

Then consider a subject — whatever you wish. Is it spiritual growth?

Then consider spiritual growth. Look at the four bodies. Are they centered? If one comes out of line now, then there is something in the spiritual growth area that is out of line. Which body is it? Look and see. This will give you a clue as to what area needs to be worked upon.

If you wish to step forward in the area of the New Age, take that step, then check the four bodies. Is one out of balance? Perhaps the mental? If so, perhaps you are intellectualizing about the New Age and not understanding it spiritually or emotionally or physically. Bring the four bodies in line now and keep them that way. Experiment with whatever subject you wish. This is a very valid technique for aiding self now.

Another helpful technique is to sit down and blank your mind – blank it. I know it is difficult, but you can do it for an instant at least. As the thoughts begin to flow, what are they? What area do they relate to? What thoughts within your mental body are influencing your need to be completely balanced? See if you can identify some of these thoughts. Write them down and become aware of what they mean.

Let me give you an example here. After clearing the mind, perhaps the first thing that comes back in is "I must prepare for this social event I am going to have." Well, I would say then that the physical body is affecting the balanced condition, perhaps the mental also, because worry enters here; in fact, with this emotion of worry you could say that all the bodies are affecting the balance. What to do? You look for the beliefs and you remove them, you look at the physical involvement, seeing if there is a reason it intruded on your need for balance; you begin to will the mind to do as you wish; you, in a sense, begin to put it all together – not just the subconscious mind where the beliefs are stored, but the physical body and the mental body also in line with the emotional body, which will accomplish the balancing of all four bodies.

Many techniques such as these will aid you in balancing. These have been specifically designed for those of you who are focused in the mental area.

✧ T H R E E ✧

Your Physical Body

W E NOW TURN TO YOUR PHYSICAL BODY AND ITS POSITION IN THE complex, overall pattern of self. To begin with, the physical body is that part of self that functions here upon the Earth, the vehicle that allows one aspect of the totality of the divine spark to function in a specific manner. It is the means by which a spiritual spark gains knowledge despite much resistance. Here upon the Earth, lessons are learned, most of the time, with difficulty and against resistance. The physical body allows this type of experience to take place; it is the means by which it takes place. For many, the lessons that are learned are learned because the body is really a battle-ground for those lessons. Many choose to experience their lessons through the physical body in the form of illnesses and other types of dysfunction that present some resistance. Some do not do this, do not use the physical body as a battleground, but most do it at least at some point in their earthly lives.

The way of experiencing is not as important as what is learned, but it doesn't seem terribly appropriate to me to traumatize the physical vehicle to the extent that it limits your experience and makes you less versatile in your earthly experience. Thus, when one recognizes that one is using the physical vehicle as a battleground, it seems appropriate to seek the causes and remove them. In our work within the belief structure we are doing this, and it is a very definite step forward in freeing the physical vehicle from its pain and trauma.

A vehicle performs only as well as it is allowed to under the care of its owner, and you are the owner, the proprietor of your physical body. It is up to you to maintain it in a state that makes it usable. This is why human bodies only last for a limited time — because the owner or proprietor does not yet understand how to utilize the vehicle in the most appropriate manner. When one obtains such knowledge completely, then the vehicle will simply last forever; there is no need to get another one; you can keep the one you have; it does not wear out. Thus anyone within the Hierarchy usually just keeps one vehicle which he uses whenever it is necessary to assume a physical vehicle. It does not wear out. The reason, my friends? It is because there is no resistance to utilizing it in a completely appropriate manner.

If you are working within your belief structure, you can purge in the area of running trauma through your physical structure. The emotions would be: *necessity for, appropriateness, no other way to solve, happens automatically,* and whatever other emotions you can relate to in understanding the area from the point of self.

If you are not working within your belief structure, you can use affirmations — ones that say your body is perfect and not suffering. The wording can be whatever you wish. One that I think is very appropriate and which I would use if I were you and needed to become free from physical pain and suffering, might be worded as follows: *My body is free of pain and stress. It functions perfectly, and clearly reflects the Creator's pure state of consciousness.*

What happens when you begin to do this to self? Why does your subconscious use the physical body or physical vehicle as a battleground? Let us now begin to analyze this situation and discover together the reasons, and how, besides purging, we may understand and avoid trauma such as this within the physical structure.

One of the most important things you can learn is the symbolic meaning attached to every portion of the vehicle or physical body. Do you understand that when your throat hurts it is often an obstruction of your will? Do you understand that when your head hurts there is something in the area of control that is frustrating you? Is your life out of control? Are other people seeking to control you? Are you frustrated because you can't control others? A headache indicates that control is involved. Do your eyes hurt? This usually indicates that there is something you don't want to look at. Are you having repeated ear problems? What is it you don't want to hear?

Are your teeth, and particularly the root area, involved? Are they painful? If so, perhaps in your belief-structure work you are getting to the root of the problem, and as you do, your subconscious becomes more and more frightened and anxious and the pain is being reflected in the physical structure. Are there problems with the feet? This usually is related to understanding in some manner. There is a very good book by Alice T. Steadman called *Who's the Matter with Me?* that talks about this extensively. It is very worthwhile reading.

Some complex problems within the body structure, such as cancer, have to do with life force or energy. You must learn to recognize what area is involved and what it is saying to you symbolically. Then you will know where to look within the belief structure, or if you are affirming, to make your affirmations so that you can remove or overcome the area involved. In a sense, you must know self very well – then you can see what is involved.

Working with the chakras of the physical area (you know they are not in the dense physical body but in the etheric body), view them as open and flowing with a lot of energy, in a continuous flow, from the top or crown chakra to the next one, the third eye area, to the throat, then the heart, the solar plexus, the polarity area and the base chakra, and then a return flow. See these being as open as possible; this will aid you in any area of the body that is affected by an energy problem, whether it is specifically the life force or a trauma that has "bunched" your energy or perhaps is missing in specific areas. But learn to utilize the visualization of energy within the body to aid it, because it is the means by which the body is run.

To me, energy is the way the Creator creates. So your physical vehicle is propelled, in a sense, by energy, by the way the Creator creates. If you visualize energy as free-flowing and the body as having an unlimited supply, this will aid your life to be free-flowing, with an unlimited supply of everything that you need. It is an aid to do this for self now. One thing I have been telling people that is very important is to make sure that your "energy intake valve," you might say, is always completely open. At the top of your head you could visualize a funnel into which energy pours and comes into you and is appropriately utilized. Make sure that the door that allows this funnel to enter and to send the energy through you is always open and unblocked. Look often and keep your energy door open now.

Use the stress within your physical body to help you see areas in which you need to work, and at the same time, remove the necessity for experiencing these stresses within the physical body. You don't have to experience a lesson through pain, though most upon the Earth choose to do so. The sooner you can remove all of the inclination to utilize the physical structure or the physical vehicle as a battleground, the sooner you will be able to keep it in optimum repair, and it will not even age; it will remain as it is now forever. Yes, it will! It is entirely possible – in fact, it is necessary, eventually – to learn how to do this. The first step to this condition in which it will be completely free from duress is to look within self and remove all resistances to keeping it in optimum running condition.

The next area I wish to discuss in regard to the physical body is its position in your learning experience. It is focused here upon the Earth. Your consciousness resides within the physical vehicle, it occupies it, and thus it has a means by which to learn and to grow, as I stated earlier, against great resistance – the resistance of the Earth. Even if you do not run all of these resistances through the physical vehicle, you still meet them in life and must overcome them. Because upon the Earth you are but a reflection of what you are above, you are a part of your own totality: the divine spark exists on a higher level and you are a reflected image of it. Then you work in the areas that need focus, that need identification, that need resolution, and you make more progress here, my friends, than does the higher level, because of this greater resistance. The divine spark chooses to work in a physical incarnation in order to make as much progress as possible.

Those of you who have had a spiritual evaluation have heard me talk about the monad or the spiritual spark sending down extensions, which are souls, and the souls then sending down expressions, which are what you are: an expression of your soul. So it is a reflected condition upon the Earth that allows growth to take place within your totality. Some of you have said, "But I cannot see how one that is so wonderful as a monad could need my input. Why does it?" It is the method of learning, my friends, that the Creator and your monad have selected. Your Earth experience is the method of learning.

It is important to recognize that, as the Earth reflection of your monad, you have set up specific lessons to learn in this lifetime, and it is through your physical body, your physical vehicle, that you now must learn them. What does that mean? It means that there is even more separation within consciousness than there is at the higher level. The sense of separateness begins from the time of the monad's emergence from the Source. He feels cut off from the Source, no longer a part of it, although he probably still identifies with it very closely. But on the Earth, or wherever there is a heavy vibration similar to the Earth s, a physical incarnation within a physical body means there is even more separation felt and experienced by the conscious- ness within a physical body. This makes it even more difficult to identify with the Creator, to identify with the Cosmic Plan. For a long time there is a sense of turning in to the personality – that the personality is the center of that particular person's consciousness contained within the vehicle. This is reflected into the physical vehicle, making its needs very important. Thus, if there is a confusion in some areas of the consciousness, the person becomes very addicted to certain types of activity, whether they be eating, smoking, drinking or something else. The confusion in a specific area of the consciousness is reflected into the physical vehicle, which is affected by this confusion. Now, these addictions, if you will, are difficult to find and work with in the belief structure. Many of you who have worked out problems have noticed that they resist resolution rather well, and the reason is that they are really buried in the physical vehicle. The subconscious contains the beliefs, yes, but it has, in a sense, transferred the storage into the physical vehicle. You must, in a sense, free the physical vehicle of all of its addictions before freeing the belief structure – and yet you must free the belief structure before freeing the physical addictions.

Does that sound like a circle, my friends? It is. What must you do, then? You must do both at the same time. That is why, when people are trying to work on a weight problem, for instance, they must approach it in every way. They use physical exercise, which helps the body overcome a problem, they work within the belief structure, and some people use affirmations or a programming technique such as sleep teaching. There must be several approaches in order to break that circle that loops forever between the physical body and the subconscious mind.

There is one very good approach that can also be done to get the soul involved here. The soul does not take part in any sort of addiction, and thus, as you bring it into line with the personality and it begins to take greater and greater control, you break the circle. No longer does the subconscious connected to the personality hold as great a sway or partake of this circular approach within the physical body. The soul is not addicted to anything except the Creator's work and the Creator's Cosmic Plan. It does not consider it appropriate that the physical body be addicted to anything, and thus, those who are functioning here as souls have no addictions. It is simply broken — the pattern just dissolves.

What to do until it is completed? Keep up your work, but call upon the soul for aid. It can aid you by strengthening the will to work with this circular pattern, because you approach it, as I said, from your belief structure and affirmations and from the physical side of it as well as from the will. Ask your soul to aid you in this important and necessary pattern removal. Remember, your soul wants the physical body to be very usable when it is functioning here upon the Earth because the soul knows that for most of you it will be functioning within this lifetime here upon the Earth. That's why it pushes you to learn and to study and to grow. It wants that vehicle to be as usable as possible and it will aid you when you ask.

You may also ask a teacher such as me or any teacher you care to choose. But all of these approaches are necessary if you are to break these very severe and difficult addictions.

I haven't really addressed drug or alcohol addiction. They are the same thing but more severe; when one is completely under their control, and this pattern is very deep and very strong, it can be carried from one physical vehicle to another. Many of you don't know this, but if it is not resolved, it leads to a propensity for this type of addiction in the next life. Also, particularly in the misuse of drugs, it leads to the shredding of the etheric body, which requires much time in an "inner" hospital and much suffering there in order to rebuild it; it is a difficult problem to resolve. Many who begin innocently to play with some of these dangerous areas do not understand what they are doing to self. Certainly they have free will to choose these problems if they wish, but they know not what they are choosing, my friends, they really don't.

Remember what I told you earlier, that the Creator gives us free will. Yes. But He also gives us each an individual path, and if we adhere exactly to this path there is no trauma. There is no pain. There is just experiencing and growing and becoming greater, whether we are in a physical body or in the spiritual aspect. It matters not. If we adhere to our own paths we do not experience pain. It is when we need these little diversions, when we choose to experiment, when we deviate from our own true paths, that we begin to suffer, that we begin to experience trauma, that we begin to forget who we really are.

Now the Source, the Creator, doesn't mind. He gave us free will. He knows that eventually we will come back. He also has unconditional love for us. He allows us to experience whatever we wish, and so we do. If we choose to run pain and trauma through the physical body, then we may do so. He knows that eventually we will decide and we will learn that this was not the way the physical body was meant to function, that we were given the appropriate material for perfection and we must make it work — and we will, eventually, my friends, yes, we will! Most of you are doing very well. One step at a time you learn about self, do you not? Each time you identify an area within the physical that is not properly maintained, and change your beliefs and allow freedom in that area, you are making a step toward your own true path again, and that is very pleasurable for the Creator. He wants you back on it. Yes, He does, but He knows that if you choose to leave it, it is all right. He allows you that freedom, my friends.

All right. So the physical body is a reflection of your totality. It is your means of experiencing here upon the Earth. Utilize it well. Analyze what it is you would like to reflect here in your physical body upon the Earth. For most of you I think that would be perfection, would it not? Would you not like to be perfect upon the Earth? Certainly! And yes, you can. No, I didn't say you can do it in five minutes, but you can eventually. I will help you to become aware in whatever area you wish, and all that we do together will lead toward this perfection.

Thank you for your attention, my friends, and my love to all of you.

✧ F O U R ✧

Your Spiritual Body

L ET US EXPLORE TOGETHER WHAT WE WILL TERM YOUR SPIRITUAL BODY, THE vehicle that enables you to experience at a very high level. Although I refer to it as a single body, it is not. It is really a compilation of several different levels. But for the sake of our discussion, we do not need to differentiate any further now.

The reason I say this is that this is the fourth in a series addressing the vehicles; we have already discussed the physical, emotional and mental bodies, and this is what I am calling the spiritual body. On further examination of this fourth area we will see the balance that is necessary on all levels and we will be able to tell, a little bit anyway, what is necessary to understand in relation to what we have already discussed. I am not defining any specific body within the spiritual area — I have already done so extensively in the Alice Bailey works and I refer you to them for those definitions.

We are seeking to clarify, then, methods for obtaining balance on all four levels. We have increased our awareness in the first three areas, so what do we need to understand about the spiritual vehicle (no matter what level it is at) in order to obtain a more balanced approach, to go forth on the evolutionary path in as balanced a manner as possible now?

First let us say that the spiritual area is the most important. Do you know why that is, my friends? It is because the spiritual area is the origination point occupied by the Creator when the Creator began to create. Since it is the origination point and it contains the Creator, it is really what existence is. There is, in a very special sense, nothing else except the Creator and His experiencing. Everything else is illusion. So we are getting down to basics when we enter the spiritual area and discuss it now.

The spiritual vehicle, then, no matter what level we are talking about — it matters not — is the means by which we experience as individualized portions of the Creator. It is our means of traveling and learning and becoming greater in the basic area of creation. It gets us down to basics. It is the vehicle in which we begin our experience and in which we are destined to complete it, and anything in between is only the means to attaining that goal.

As we learn and grow and evolve we drop first the physical, then the emotional, then eventually the mental and return to the spiritual vehicle; we drop them one by one until we reach again the essence of self — the self-realized spark that is truly one with the Source and yet forever individualized as a cocreator. This is the goal, and we must see it that way. All of the other vehicles are the means to achieving that goal, and in order to achieve it, all must be completely balanced, completely merged and completely in line with the Creator's Plan. We do this very gradually, over eons of time, we do. For the most part, through most of this experiencing, we do not know that this is what we are doing — balancing, becoming more aware of the Creator and His purposes — but we certainly are, my friends, we certainly are.

A spiritual vehicle is chosen to contain the divine spark. This divine spark chooses to experience, mostly by projection of itself into denser areas — first as a soul; and then the soul, which is part of the spiritual area, chooses to work and to learn and to grow by expressing itself in a physical type of existence, at least during a part of its learning experience. You, my friends, are such expressions or experiences of your soul — which, remember, is a reflection or an extension of the spiritual spark. Thus, the spiritual vehicle extends itself in many directions, some of which we have not even gone into.

The spiritual vehicle, then, must learn a great deal to be a cocreator. Is this not logical? It is, when you see what is created and how wonderful, how complex it is — but not complex in a negative sense, for complexity really is the key to simplicity. Does that sound like an oxymoron? It is not. It simply means that existence happens on many levels, that the Creator understands all of these levels and puts them together in a completely appropriate way that makes creation seem simple, though it is not; it is very complex but it fits together perfectly.

Is it not logical, then, that as potential cocreators, we must learn on all of these levels? How can we be the new chairman of the board, my friends, if we do not understand each layer of the corporate entity, if we are not familiar with each layer and can take it apart, in a sense, and put it back together completely and with ease? If we cannot see exactly how all of it fits together we cannot create, can we? And this is what we are meant to do. We will serve the Creator as cocreators. We will begin again these processes for Him in other areas that He wishes to expand into, so we must know every detail, everything and how it all fits together.

We learn that now, hopefully, with joy, but at certain points we do not. We learn how it feels to be immersed, how it feels to be in a physical existence, to be learning how to fit it all together. Yes, and we learn how to balance all of this against our potential greatness, to literally absorb all of these lessons back into the spiritual vehicle or body and then thrust forward from that into a higher level that is there awaiting us when we can learn enough to fulfill its requirements.

There are specific requirements that we must meet in order to reach our goal of cocreator. Each one of us has in the past (at a higher level, granted, but we do know it) been told exactly what we must do to reach this goal. It was given to each of us at the time the Creator sent us forth. Do you not think this is logical? When you join a new corporation and management has great hopes for you, and they see that your potential is great, and they mean for you to be very influential, to be a very important part of that corporation, they give you an indoctrination course. They tell you exactly what the corporation is and what it is doing; they tell you areas that are available; they tell you to seek what you would like to do. And then this corporation, my friends, goes a step beyond that and tells you where you are fitted to serve and the path that you need to tread to reach that particular goal — an individual one, you see, in each case. How marvelous! The Creator has set it all up for us.

You say now, don't you, "But what about free will?" Yes, what about free will, my friends? The Creator knows what's best for each of us. He really does, but we must discover this ourselves. So He gives us free will. Yes, He does, and we may deviate, we may loiter, we may choose to experience in any way we wish — but he knows that each of us will eventually come back to Him. What does that mean? It means we will, each one of us, choose by free will that path that we knew about originally and decided to leave so that we could see for ourselves if we could find a better one, for we all learn that we can't.

Does that upset you a little? Does it say to you there really is no free will? Of course there is. Certainly there is. If you choose to, you can reject the Creator's offer to become a cocreator. You can and you can stay at one point in your growth for as long as you wish. But, my friends, you defeat the purpose of creation when you do. You defeat the evolutionary spiral. Whom do you defeat? You just defeat self. The Creator allows you to do this if you wish. But as you grow and evolve and become greater, you will not wish to do it. You will see the necessity to serve the Creator in your own unique, appropriate way. Just because He has already defined this way does not mean that there is no free will. It simply means the Creator knows more than you — and what's the matter with that? How could He not? He would not be the Creator if He didn't know more than you, my friends.

Also, He doesn't view you from a time-tied point of view. By that I mean He can see all of existence. He knows what you will choose, so if you wish to view it this way, you can simply say that He looks into your future and sees what you will choose. That's valid also. Does that help in understanding free will? I hope so, my friends, because I know that some of you have questions about it. Work in this area until you understand it fully, because it really does exist. It really does and it really works just as you think it works, but more! Yes, there are areas of free will you don't understand yet. Imagine that. Did you think you understood everything? Of course not. So just allow yourself your present understanding and recognize that it will enlarge, it will grow, it will change as you enlarge and grow and change. How marvelous! Yes, it certainly is.

The spiritual vehicle, then, on whatever level you view it, is very much involved with the Creator's work, whether from an individual growth pattern, which is part of it, or more importantly, seeking to serve the Creator — because both are done at the spiritual level, my friends, both simultaneously. They always fit together perfectly; no conflict there. As the spiritual vehicle enables you to do the Creator's work, it also enables you to grow and to move along your individual path. On the spiritual plane there is no conflict. One does not block the other. They are simply parallel paths that always go together.

The spiritual plane is forever expanding, and the means for its expansion are the workers, the lightworkers, the spiritual sparks that do the Creator's work. Each one of these sparks works within a spiritual vehicle — one of which we are talking about now, the spiritual body — on some level or another. But remember, the spiritual sparks that are within these spiritual bodies are concerned with the Creator's work. That is what the spiritual plane is: the area in which the Creator is primarily concerned. Certainly all the rest is a reflection of this area, as there is nothing but the Creator and His experiencing, but I wish to emphasize that it is the primary area.

Why is it so important to recognize this? Because we spend most of our existence there. These comparatively short sojourns that we take in physical incarnation are but specific learning experiences of the spiritual spark, and the relative importance of them is not very great. Does this sound like a contradiction of what I have been telling you? It is not. It is analogous to saying that you have gone to school for, let's say, a twelve-year period, grades one through twelve. Each time you enter a classroom and are involved with a specific class. And on that day you know a specific lesson is important, don't you? You know that lesson will aid your overall growth. But if you look at the twelve-year picture, then that one particular lesson on that one particular day assumes a new perspective, doesn't it? Your Earth experiences, from the sense of your own totality, are only a one-day chapter within a specific area that you are learning about and within. Does that give you greater perspective on it? Each lesson and each area is valid, but in the context of your totality, it is only that: one specific area. Keep that in mind, my friends, to gain a truer objective understanding of Earth living.

I do not mean to negate Earth living. It is as we have said: If you have a test on a specific area in school that you have studied, you must get a passing grade to go on, to graduate — or in the case of just one subject, to integrate it into the areas that you are learning that year. Is that not right? Similarly, your Earth experiences must be mastered, they must be learned. You must reach a point of proficiency that allows you to graduate and go on to other types of lessons and learning experiences.

Many of you are perhaps in grade eleven of a twelve-year curriculum upon the Earth. Some of you are in grade twelve but some are not. That tells you a little bit about the work that lies ahead, does it not? You may remember that in your senior year perhaps your work was more intense. It really was a focus, in a sense, for all of the other work you had done, and it was the gateway by which you went forth on whatever path you chose, either to another learning institution with specific lessons or to a broader experiencing in Earth living itself.

Your experience now is similar. You may choose to graduate from Earth experience and go on to a broader application in spiritual work doing specific assignments for the Creator, but not as specialized as if you choose another area — for you may choose, if you wish, to have specialized training in specific areas, and many of you do. Or you may choose to do what I did — to remain near the Earth, to in a sense become a teacher who teaches those who are seeking to do what I did: graduate from Earthly living. I received special instruction before returning as a teacher, certainly. Everyone is trained as a teacher before teaching, and you may choose to do the same if you wish.

But look upon the spiritual area now, and the spiritual vehicle in which you individually experience it, as the main area of existence; from it you go forth to experience in many other ways, among which is earthly living, my friends.

The spiritual vehicle, on whatever level we look at it, is marvelous. Do you know why? Because it is forever attuned to the Creator! Is that not marvelous? When you reach that level, there is no more pain because there is no deviation from the Creator. That is what gives you pain: the sense of separation. Now, it is true that for a while after you return to the spiritual vehicle you will still sense some separation, but gradually even this little bit will be dissolved, and then you will reach the cocreator state, which is not separate, and you will not experience a sense of separation. This is to be looked forward to. It is to be sought with eagerness and with joy, my friends. I am looking forward to it with great anticipation. I long for it now — not from an emotional trauma but from a knowingness that it lies in my future and from eagerness to participate now in an ever-growing sense of more responsibility, serving with more appropriateness, knowing that the Creator sees what I must do and acknowledging that I am doing it and attuning more and more and with greater and greater joy in the service area within my need to be a greater and greater participant within the Creator's Cosmic Plan!

It is very exciting, my friends. Get excited about it! Work hard to learn those things that need to be learned — and then participate in it. You will have earned it, and it is wonderful.

Merging the Four Bodies

To complete this series on the four bodies, I would like to discuss the merging process in greater detail. What do I mean by this? I simply mean that all four bodies must be integrated – that this really is the purpose for experiencing here upon the Earth. Yes, to merge now the four areas, if you will, and then have them all function together on the Earth. This would be what we term the soul experience.

The foregoing material gave some details on each of the four bodies and ways to overcome the particular areas involved. I also gave some techniques for balancing. Now I wish to discuss more completely integration of the four areas.

Know that the Creator in His wisdom has given us awareness, when we can recognize it, that may be used specifically to aid our growth by various means. The vehicles that we have been talking about are these various means, and by compiling now the different aspects of self – in a sense, putting it all together – we blend self in the appropriate way and lead self back toward its totality.

It is a little confusing at first when you begin to work from an integrated point of view. Yes, it is. You have been used to thinking of your existence from either an emotional focus, a mental focus, perhaps a physical focus, or for some even from a spiritual focus that does not look at the other three. But as you begin to seek the blending of all four, it can become a little confusing. You begin to be aware of the necessity to blend, to balance, to integrate, and then because of this new awareness, you get an input into each of the areas of the self all at the same time. Now, certainly you have been doing this but you have not recognized that you have been gaining information from each of these areas; or perhaps you have blocked information regarding a specific area – perhaps the spiritual here on the Earth; in many cases this is true. Or perhaps you have not yet functioned very much mentally; perhaps you have blocked off your emotions; perhaps the physical has been negated – you have said it isn't important in contributing to spiritual growth. These are but examples, and it matters not where you as an individual are – all of you will be at different points – but know that as you become aware of the need to integrate and work out blocks, if there are blocks in any specific area, then the information comes into self in a fourfold manner. It can be a little confusing.

What to do? You begin to function from a higher level of totality. Yes, when you can function in the vehicle that allows totality to become its means of sustenance, then no matter how many individual points of reference come into this totality, it doesn't matter, does it? It will just become a part of the totality, and it is not confusing.

Here upon the Earth the first reflection of totality that you will encounter is at soul level. The soul is not yet your true totality, but it is a reflection of it, and certainly much closer to it than your personality is. So what you must attempt to do in integrating all four aspects is to become your soul. Merge with it. First do it in a state of meditation: consciously merge with your soul. See yourself and your soul becoming one, and then do some inner balancing work. Look and see what the physical is doing, then the emotional, the mental and the spiritual. Do these exercises that I have given you in this series. Utilize them to aid your growth. If you can do it at soul level it will work for you, but you must consciously attune to the soul often. Do it daily. Do it in the morning, and then if you become out of balance, do it again at noon, and if you come out of balance, do it again in the evening. But make a conscious effort now in your integration work to remain at soul level. You will get to know when you are at soul level and when you are remaining there. Once you have experienced from that level you will want to remain there and you will forever seek to do so. It works, my friends. I hope that you will try it.

Thank you very much. It is a privilege to be here and to work with you now.

✦ PART TWO ✦

THE TIBETAN LESSON SERIES

The Tibetan, Djwhal Khul, 1983-1985

✧ O N E ✧

Joy

THE SPIRITUAL GOVERNMENT OF THE PLANET RECOGNIZES THE IMPORTANCE of the present times, and thus we seek to aid humankind in its needs to become greater, to grow, to increase awareness and to lead humanity in as smooth a transition as possible from the Piscean into the new Age of Aquarius. By coming in this thrust, I and others of the Hierarchy hope to do several things: first, to anchor joy more and more concretely upon the Earth; second, to aid as many as possible to gain more self-understanding; and third, to obtain for the Creator as many new workers as possible to implement the Creator's Cosmic Plan for Earth. This is my mission. This is my goal. But I am not alone. Remember, all of the spiritual government is putting effort into this mission. We seek to raise the awareness of the Earth, to lead it forth in its journey to the golden New Age.

In these ten lessons, you and I together will explore many things, both to aid your self-understanding and to perhaps see what you can do to aid the planet and the Creator's Cosmic Plan at this critical time. We will explore joy, we will explore love, we will explore the entire gamut of higher emotions. And I know that from our exploration will come many good things that will light up your life with joy. I say that with assurance, knowing that joy is available for you now. I would like to give you first the joy song, that you may participate in it. The words are set to the tune of "You, You, You."

> Joy, Joy, Joy,
> I experience Joy, Joy, Joy.
> There is nothing else but Joy,
> I am filled with Joy, Joy, Joy.
> Now I know

Joy within supports me so,
I may move serenely through
Life and still enjoy it too.
I must be
Filled with Joy eternally,
It will lead me carefully,
To my own true destiny.
Joy, Joy, Joy,
I experience Joy, Joy, Joy.
There is nothing else but Joy,
I am filled with Joy, Joy, Joy.

What, then, is joy, my friends? It is a very specific vibration by which much can be accomplished in your life. I encourage you to learn about it. Most, perhaps, do not really know it yet. But you can learn, and you can imagine, if you haven't experienced. Imagine joy, utilize it in your life, and imagine that you have it.

Then, gradually, the knowingness that the real thing is present will replace this imagination, and you will have it as a part of your life. Joy can replace pain and difficulty as a way to live your life. It is the way to live life more productively — to live it on a higher "vibration." We will discuss the joy vibration through which so much is to be achieved. I intend to give exercises throughout these lessons to aid you to accomplish various goals for self-development. This first one has to do with joy.

Visualize joy as a very pixyish figure, a personification of joy. See it there in your mind's eye. It dances, it is a pied piper of joy. Can you see it? It is dancing and leaping with joy. Unexpectedly it did a cartwheel there. Envision it very completely — as much as you can — and then bring it forward, this pixie, and merge with it, my friends. Can you feel it dancing inside you now? Do you feel like jumping up and down with joy? Are you expressing the need to be joyful? Yes, you have literally brought joy into self. You have merged with it. How can you not be joyful in your life experiences now? You have this pixie of joy within you that will express itself. It will come out in your activity. You will act joyful because it has to express — joy must be expressed. Yes, use it this way.

What is joy, my friends? That is an interesting question. It is a celebration. That's why you feel like jumping up and down when you are joyful: it is a celebration. Of what? Of life itself, by attunement to the Creator. You feel so good about it that you celebrate the Creator and attune to Him by expressing joy. You cannot help it. It is a specific vibration, remember, joy is. And you need to celebrate when you are experiencing it. Think about that, but be joyful while you do so.

Perhaps you are thinking, If I go around celebrating joy, someone is going to lock me up. They are going to say, "That's not appropriate for Earth-living," or "He's been sampling some of that fermented stuff again." Well, perhaps, but perhaps they will simply catch the joy from you. Have you thought about that? Joy is very contagious, and when you have a lot of it, others catch it from you. And what a wonderful thing to spread on the Earth. If you are going to spread anything at all, I would certainly recommend joy. Yes. You couldn't aid or be of service to the Creator in any better way than by spreading joy.

How do you spread joy? By being an example. By being so joyful that others catch it from you. Remember, you have to learn how to be joyful (most do, anyway). Begin by imagining that you are joyful. Yes, shout with joy. You may want to do this by yourself at first, but pretend that you have a lot of joy. If you keep doing it, pretty soon you will not be pretending anymore, and people will say, "My, you've changed. What has happened to you?" And tell them, "Joy has come into my life. I am celebrating now." And if they say, "What are you celebrating?" you can say, "I am celebrating life itself, because I am joyful to be experiencing it." Does that sound strange for Earth living? Well, perhaps; but it is the coming thing.

If you want to be really in fashion now, you'd better get some joy. It is a very new item and it is going to catch on very quickly. Do you want to be the one who spreads it in your neighborhood? Your neighbors will say, "She had it first" or "He had it first — that's where I got my joy." And their neighbors will say, "Really? That's wonderful." You can be the one to spread the joy in your neighborhood, my friends. Think about it now. I promise you, it is going to be all the rage.

Now, you may notice that, through Janet, I, The Tibetan, have a rather light approach to language. I have adopted her vocabulary very specifically. We don't have to be serious, we don't have to be terribly sober about our approach to truth. Let's use the current language. Let's allow people to be comfortable with these wonderful concepts. Let's use this comfortableness to move people into higher states. After all, we are talking about joy, my friends, and the first way to begin to experience a lighter, more joyful approach to life is to take yourself a little less seriously. Eventually we all discover that we are not the center of the universe. Guess who is? The Creator. And we discover that some of these events that shake us to the depths of our toes are not Earth-shaking events to others. In fact, most of the time they don't even notice these important events in our lives. Imagine that! They are so busy being the center of their universe that they don't notice that we are really the center of ours. More appropriate, my friends, is to let the Creator be the center of everyone's universe. What does that do? It makes you more objective about life. It puts life into proper perspective for you. It allows a lightening up of your life so that you may experience this joy, so that you may see, truly, the right picture of how everything fits together — especially your own portion — and how you truly fit into the whole picture.

How wonderful! To use an attunement to the Creator to achieve this whole picture. "Attunement to the Creator" — what does that mean? Think about it more carefully. The Creator — that is obvious, everyone knows who that is, don't they? Well, think about it: What do you believe the Creator is? I'll give you my perspective, and you can see if you agree with it. The Creator is the Source of everything. And attunement — what does that mean? It means becoming aware of what the Creator really is. The Creator is the Source of everything, and by becoming aware of this Source, by keeping that within our awareness always, we gain greater perspective on living, whether it be of the Earth or elsewhere.

It certainly does change your perspective when you can truly attune to the Creator. And when you can do it, there is so much joy that the joy transforms you into something greater. It does it specifically — as we have said, joy has a specific vibration, and it transforms you into something greater when you use it that way. When you become joy, you raise your vibration — you become greater. A permanent transformation takes place when you use it in your life. Joy, then, is a specific way to reach the New Age in a smooth fashion. It is the free-flowing method of evolving, becoming greater. Making an intense effort as an individual to attain more joy and use it in your life, is a specific way that you can aid self and the Earth at the same time. What more can you ask than to be given a means of serving and increasing your own growth at once? Try it, my friends. It will work for you as it has for me and for others also.

✧ T W O ✧

Belief Structures

Mᴏꜱᴛ ᴏꜰ ʏᴏᴜ ᴡʜᴏ ʜᴀᴠᴇ ʀᴇQᴜᴇꜱᴛᴇᴅ ᴛʜᴇꜱᴇ ʟᴇꜱꜱᴏɴꜱ ᴋɴᴏᴡ ꜱᴏᴍᴇᴛʜɪɴɢ about the belief-structure work currently being done by me and the Foundation. Many of you have begun to aid self with this method by clearing out blocks that cause your life to be not as free-flowing as you would like. It is very important that you all recognize that this is a method that works, but that it doesn't work in five minutes; that it takes time to make the changes toward a free-flowing life; and that the blocks were caused by a number of experiences, and in the areas of your life that have noticeable blocks, there have been a large number of such experiences.

The belief-structure work does work, and I find it a very productive way to clear self. What do I mean by "clearing self"? I mean completely clearing the subconscious of the blocks to allowing the soul to function here upon the Earth. This is your goal: to allow the soul to function through you here upon the Earth plane. It will be wonderful when this occurs, because life will flow very smoothly. Although the soul has lessons it is learning, they have nothing to do with Earth living; the soul can function here with complete freedom, with no blocks, my friends. Earth living is very easy for the soul, so when you build this bridge and the soul comes to Earth, your life will be completely smooth and free-flowing. Some of you are doing well with this. You have made good progress, and thus you know that at times in your life you may experience a few hours when everything flows completely, you know nothing can go wrong, and everything you touch just flows so smoothly. This is when you are functioning at soul level. Isn't it a marvelous experience? Your goal is to remain at this level, and to do so you work within your belief structure, removing the blocks to such a permanent association.

Now, other types of growth efforts certainly help. Working with the rays is important, and in the next lesson I am going to go into that more specifically. And meditation, in which you see yourself blending with the soul, is important.

See yourself in a state of meditation, actually blending with the soul. Visualize it coming toward you and then coming into you and becoming an integral part of self. This can be visualized as a beautiful white light – the christed portion of self – or perhaps it can be visualized as a beautiful, serene figure dressed in white and surrounded by the light. Whichever approach helps you, whichever you identify with, will work for you. After you have blended with the soul, become aware of how you feel. Do you truly feel as if everything in your life would flow? Do you experience a feeling of freedom from Earth restrictions? This blending consciously with the soul will certainly aid you. Also, striving to understand your higher purposes will aid you.

You know, I love it when people come to me and ask, "What are my higher purposes?" I truly love to hear that question. Now, of course I don't tell them, but I love to hear it. As a spiritual teacher, I can't tell them. They must search it for themselves. This searching indicates to me how important the connection between the person and his soul is. The soul is getting in the act. The soul is the one that will fulfill these higher purposes, and it says to that person, "Come on now, make this connection ever closer. Understand what our work is here, do it now with intensity." And so that person begins to seek his higher purposes. In this manner he begins to understand what he will be doing when the bridge is completed and that soul is functioning here upon the Earth. This is the reason for seeking those purposes – so that you will truly understand the program, the agenda, what will be happening. And you feel the need to seek them because the soul gets pushy. It pushes you toward a more complete understanding of what is involved. It says, "Perhaps now, if you understand the importance of our work, you will allow it to happen sooner." So it gets involved, it gets pushy.

You might say, These are lovely, high concepts, but what has it to do with me now? I have responsibilities. I can't just go off like the Tibetan and do a mission for the Earth. Well, for most of you that's true, at this point anyway, but you do not have to go off and do a mission in order to serve the Creator. What you can do right now is do a little service for the Creator along with your regular life; by beginning to serve now, you will first of all increase your own connection with your soul – you will make that connection more and more strong – you will aid the Cosmic Plan, and you will have a sense of fulfillment from beginning this. Also, in the coming days, when life here upon the Earth will be "interesting," you will have an anchor to hold on to. Not an anchor that drags you down – an anchor to hold on to. And what is that anchor? It is your knowledge of your own divinity – that no matter how "interesting" life becomes upon the Earth, you are a part of something much greater, and that "everything will be all right" because there is so much more than just the Earth involved. Is that an interesting statement? Well, it's true, my friends, it certainly is.

Now, at your current place, what can you do? You want to get on with your life in as productive a manner as possible. And I say, do that — take responsibility for changing self. Some of you might say, "Change? But do I really need to do that now? Do I have to look at all of those painful areas?" Yes; the answer is yes. Sooner or later you are going to have to go in there and look at them. There is no other way, my friends. Believe me, I tried them all. When I was where you are, I tried everything and finally came to the realization, after I'd gone around it a thousand times, that the only way was through it. Through what? Through the misconceptions, through the struggle with the ego, through the barrier, through the wall, through the patterns that hold you here on the Earth. Learn how to release all of them. Go beyond them. And why not do it now? You're going to have to do it sooner or later. Now seems appropriate to me. Again, I say that you won't do it all in five minutes, but you can begin now, and that is a step that will show what you truly wish to accomplish.

You begin a journey, my friends, by taking the first step. The journey you are on now is to greater self-understanding, more productive living, a complete, free-flowing life. And so I say to you, Begin! Take that first step. But when you come to that first wall, don't go back. Don't remain there, either. Go over the wall. Know that you can do that. You can, because you have a ladder — a way to go over it. And what is the ladder? It is the soul connection — knowing that you are part of something bigger. This is so important, my friends. Hang on to it when you can't see the way through. Say, "But I am going to do it. My will and my wish to be a part of this something greater, ever more closely connected, will allow me now to get through this trauma. I will face it. I will do it."

This is your ladder. Use it. Go over the barriers. Release the pattern. Don't allow self to remain in these eternal patterns. You see, my friends, you can remove what we call the "false beliefs," but if you do not release the pattern, you are held there. By what? By your illusion. Yes, a pattern is an illusion. You have taken out the beliefs many times by the time you are ready to release the pattern. They are gone, you have removed them. But if you do not erase the pattern and remove it, let it go, release it with your will, you can't go anywhere. You remain there. We call it being stuck in a pattern. Stuck in a specific method of working.

An example of this is being focused in your emotional body. In other words, you feel life. You have lots of emotions. Certainly, you have laughter and joy, but you also have loss, trauma, pain and anxiety. You have every emotion in the book. You experience life from an emotional point of view. Now to clear everything in your life, to allow the soul to function here on the Earth, you must balance this emotional body with the mental one. You must lighten that focus, you must balance between the emotional and mental bodies. You could say you are balanced there in the center as you begin to balance all four bodies: the emotional with the mental, the physical with the spiritual. And by bodies, I mean not only bodies but the experience also.

We were discussing the emotional body, or the emotional focus. Let us say you have removed within self all of the false beliefs, or at least a great many of them that block you, that keep you so emotionally focused. Can you move beyond them? Can you go to a more balanced focus? Perhaps, my friends. But to do so, you must release this pattern.

Now, this pattern is heavier than the false beliefs. It is glued to you. And you are going to have to pry it away from self. Again, you call upon the will. You say, "I will do it, I will erase this pattern." You can begin by seeing it erased. Put it on your blackboard and erase this pattern of heavy emotional involvement with the joy method. Erase it now, visually, and that will aid you. And then use the soul connection to aid you. Say, "I am a part of something greater. I will use this great desire I have to serve to help me now, to complete the balancing of all four bodies and specifically the lightening of the emotional body. I will do it now, in order to serve." Or, if you consider this to be the appropriate way for you (because each of you will have different methods), say to self, "I do not allow my emotions to control me any longer. I am tired of suffering. I am tired of emotional involvement and emotional immersion. I do not plan to remain in this pattern. I don't care if it is comfortable for my subconscious. I'm not going to remain here. I will go beyond this pattern now."

You can also use your own needs to achieve this. If you cannot use the needs of the Creator for serving, then use your own needs to achieve it. You need to and wish to experience life in a more balanced state, one in which you have less pain, in which you do not suffer as much. Then you must consciously release this pattern, knowing that your life will change. Now, change is not necessarily bad. It can be very good. It is difficult sometimes for the subconscious to accept that, so you may have to work within your belief structure on change before you can release this pattern. But do it, my friends. Go beyond this important, critical point. Do it now, because it is important — it is a critical point for you right now. Go beyond this pattern with your will, with your desire for more productive living, with your wish to serve the Creator, with your desire to participate in living with your soul, with anything, with everything, but do it, my friends. And begin now. Take that first step, and do it now.

❖ T H R E E ❖

The First Seven Rays

MY FRIENDS, IN THIS THIRD LESSON WE WILL DISCUSS THE RAYS. THESE ARE really different types of energy by means of which the Creator seeks to establish creation. These are the methods He has chosen to use — these different types of energies, or rays. By talking a little bit about each type, by discussing them and some of their characteristics, we will learn about different aspects of the Creator and His experiencing. I discovered long ago that by studying the rays I got to the very basic part of creation and learned a great deal. Over a long period of time I have studied them from different angles, looking at them on different levels, looking at them in relationship to each other and to the whole. And from this has come a very basic understanding of creation. I invite you now to begin to learn in this area also; to discover the unique characteristics of each ray and thus to aid your understanding of Earth living, of people and, as I said earlier, of the Creator Himself. For the Creator is everything, you see, and as we look at the pieces that make up His creation, we then learn more about the Creator. It seems to me that this is a productive goal that we begin together now.

First let us look at the seven basic kinds of energies that are available to Earth living. Each human has these energies within self; everyone has some of each. But the six divisions that we deal with in any given ray are: the spiritual level, the soul level, the personality level, the emotional level, the mental body and the physical body. Now, most that function here upon the Earth have not begun to be affected by the monad's ray (the spiritual level) and most not by the soul's ray, either. But it is helpful to know them so that you can understand the potential each person has. By looking at oneself through a specific focused area such as the rays, one can understand each part and then put together a whole that is understood more completely.

The first-ray energy, which usually is depicted as *red*, is very dynamic, very thrusting. It is the beginning of much. It is the means by which you advance into a new territory. Many leaders have this aspect of self; leadership is a Ray One tendency, well developed. It is also the will ray, whether you consider it the personal will or, later, the divine will. This ray, when misused, creates much trouble in the world. It is present in its negative connotation during war – a great deal of it is greatly misused. The rays are energy: We must use them productively. Each one has its positive and also its negative ways of use. The first ray can be misused rather easily. It doesn't take a lot of Ray One energy to be very powerful. It is a ray that is powerful.

This ray has one very positive use. When something is running away – when a situation is out of control – there is a tendency to just allow it to keep flowing. It needs to be ended, but it has been allowed to go on; there has been an allowing beyond the appropriate point. In this situation, bringing in the first ray, with its qualities of discernment, is appropriate. It can limit a situation that has been allowed to just go past the appropriate point. It can discipline a situation. When raising children you must discipline them, you must not let them just function in their own method, in their own often inappropriate behavior. Sometimes a limitation is placed on the child in order to bring the behavior back into balance. It is not inappropriate to bring a situation back into balance. There can be too much restriction, also. The allowing of the situation goes into play there, to balance the limitation. Everything must be brought into perfect balance upon the Earth, within self, in all creation. Ray One energy balances the unlimited extension of a situation that has gone past its appropriate point.

Ray Two energies, which are usually thought of as *blue* in color, are the energies that, through too much allowingness, can go past the appropriate point as in our former example. They balance the harshness that results from overuse of the Ray One energies. Thus, harsh discipline without the love/wisdom of the second ray is not appropriate either. A balance must be struck between the restrictive qualities of the first ray – the limitation – and the allowingness of the second ray. They naturally balance each other.

This great second ray, when used appropriately, is the love/wisdom ray. The great teachers of the world function on this ray: the Christ, the Buddha and all the great teachers have contained much of this unconditional divine universal love. They have been able to see how to literally raise humankind by applying this second ray to a situation. Many times when humanity has reached a point of black despair, this love/wisdom ray has come in the form of a teacher such as the Christ, to aid, to lighten, to raise the situation.

The higher mental-conceptual areas are also reached through this ray. The Universal Mind can be entered by means of this beautiful blue ray. You can obtain the great mental concepts that await you in the Universal Mind, if you stretch to reach them. Thus, when a great concept is placed in this universal area by teachers – the Spiritual Hierarchy – those who are able to stretch can receive it, and thus a great idea may be received in several areas of the world at once by the advanced humanity that can reach up via the second ray and obtain this information. It is there when you can conceptualize, when you can stretch to obtain it. This ray has been used productively for the most part (though each ray has its negative connotations also) to aid humanity. That is productive use of this great ray.

The third ray, usually conceived as being *yellow* (although you may go beyond these concepts of colors, if you will) is called the ray of concrete intelligence. It is a very productive ray, it certainly is. Many of the great healers of the world have much of the third ray now. To me, healing upon this ray is more than a physical healing. Raised to its heights, it can be used for holistic healing and teaching. This is the ultimate use of the third ray. People who have much third ray are always very practical, never a bit abstract in their thinking. When you urgently need something done and you want it organized very well, ask a third-ray person to do it for you. He will do it, and do it very well. It will all fit together and will be a practical application of what you are seeking.

Now, these people are very persistent — you didn't hear me say "stubborn," did you? That would not be true of our third-ray people; persistent is the word we wish, isn't it, my friends? One point I should probably make here is that the remaining four rays pass through this particular great ray, the third — the practical ray. And that's important because the practicality aids them to be valuable to the Earth.

This ray is a means to getting the Earth's lessons learned, to getting accomplished for the Creator His Cosmic Plan. It is a specific in many ways to putting together everything for planet Earth. It has a practicality that one must acknowledge as being appropriate in its particular function.

The fourth ray is the one that one might say is especially associated with the Earth. The color is usually considered *green*. And you could say that is a foundation — a four-sided figure, my friends — for what lies ahead. This ray is called harmony through conflict, and most of those who utilize this fourth-ray experience it through conflict rather than harmony. They must learn to take this energy, this vibration, and raise it up to function on the fourth ray harmoniously. It is important that the Earth understand this. It is very interesting: We have done some work by putting the seven rays on a world map and seeing which rays lie in which countries, and whenever the fourth ray is present, there is a reflective quality about it that reflects other rays into a specific area. Now, the productive part will not be reflected, because that is being used up by the ray in question. Thus, if the fourth ray is reflecting first-ray energies, the trustingness of the ray is used up; the conflict of the ray in question — less desirable qualities — is what gets reflected by this fourth ray.

Thus, its reflective qualities reflect the conflict aspects of the ray into other areas. This is very important when you look at energies around the world. This material is available if you care to study it. When this energy is used in its higher sense, we get the great artists of the world, the great musicians, the great dancers (although some types of dance focus an even greater ray), all the ones who harmoniously put together Earth living. Mother Earth herself is attempting to balance this type of energy, and we partake of this experience by working with energy.

The fifth-ray energies are just coming into being, from the cosmic perspective. You see, they've been here awhile, but not as long as the types we have just been discussing. In humanity's evolution, and later in the New Age, they will become more prevalent. It is called the ray of pure intelligence, and upon this ray function the great scientists of the world – those with the intelligence to penetrate deeply to the cause of a situation. They can analyze a situation, take it apart and put it back together, synthesize it, and know the best way to productively undertake a venture. They are the ones who do the conceptual work in the world. They have the mental capabilities to lead humankind past the present situation and bring it into the New Age. They can conceive it, and then others can bring it into being. They have the ability to conceptualize life as it would be most productive to live it. Without this great ray, such possibilities could not be understood. The ray allows this type of understanding by those who can use it productively.

We usually think of it as *orange* in color. Later, humankind will use this ray especially for the Creator, as cocreators. Of course, they will use all of the rays, but this one will enable them to conceptualize exactly what the Creator needs done in His Cosmic Plan. It is a marvelous ray that, as I said, is only beginning to be understood and used by a few of advanced humanity.

The sixth-ray energies are quite heavy. This is the ray of devotion. It is the one that has been present during the 2000 years of the Christian era; thus the emphasis on devotion. The perspective part of this ray allows you to experience something with great intensity. You become very devoted to it. You can attune to this ray and experience the Creator in a joyous, emotional, intense way. Of course this ray can be used unproductively, also; thus the fanatic of sixth-ray persuasion may be a dictator, as opposed to the Christ, who was a great spiritual leader.

Remember what we said earlier: the Christ is really on the second ray, but the post-Christ history of the Earth, this 2000-year period, was a sixth-ray experience. The color is *indigo*, and the heaviness of the energy confines you pretty much. It is a specific type of devotion that is not open to further concepts. Once you have decided within a sixth-ray intensity that this is your experience, you are no longer open, perhaps, to New Age concepts or to go beyond the ones that you already have. You will be happily devoted all of your life, probably, to these same concepts, serving very well within this original framework. The traditional religions – many people who experience within them – are on this sixth ray.

The seventh ray, the *violet* one, is often called the Violet Flame – the transmuting flame does just that. It is the *gateway to the New Age experience*.

The means to enter the New Age are offered by this seventh ray. It is coming into Earth now ever more intensely, but is not yet what it will be later. This ray has been referred to as ritualistic. What does that mean? It means specifically that things will be set in motion here by this seventh-ray experience that will enable us to reach the New Age. They may be done with a preciseness that is repeated many times to bring about a raising of the energies, specifically to reach this evolutionary point we are seeking to reach. So it has been decided with precision how to do it. The seventh ray sets this into motion, doing it specifically as required to perform this function. It is part of the ray's experience. An individual with much seventh ray, with a religious connotation, may enjoy a ceremonial approach to religion – but not necessarily with the overall experience of the ray. It just means, my friends, that there is a method within the seventh-ray energies leading to the New Age. This beautiful transmuting energy is seen often in auras of those who have entered the doorway to the New Age. Many of you stand in this doorway, and when I look at you I can see the beautiful transmuting qualities of the seventh ray that are aiding you.

This, then, is a brief description of each of the seven rays to aid your understanding. Remember, you have characteristics of several within the six different areas. For most of you, only four of these characteristics are yet obvious. By studying the seven rays intensively – and I have written about them extensively in the Alice Bailey material – you can learn and understand self and everything else, as described earlier. Seek to put it all together to understand creation from the basic position of the rays. They will aid you.

✧ F O U R ✧

The Higher Rays

M Y FRIENDS, I WOULD LIKE TO DISCUSS WITH YOU NOW THE FIVE HIGHER rays. We discussed the first through the seventh rays in the previous lesson, and now we will discuss rays eight through twelve. Remember, the rays are different kinds of energy, and I have defined energy as the means by which the Creator has chosen to create.

About ten years ago, the Earth was granted five additional or higher rays — five additional ways, then, to create. And because they are higher rays, they are of a finer vibration. What you can create with them is higher, is finer. Does this not seem logical? The Earth was granted these rays in order to lead it from its present evolutionary point to the New Age experience. I am going to go into that briefly after we discuss the rays.

The eighth ray is a *cleansing* ray and it helps to clean out from self those characteristics that are no longer appropriate; this truly may be the only thing that is the matter with your old behavior patterns — that they are what one might call old-fashioned and inappropriate for a New Age experience. This ray is luminous, as are all of these higher rays, and when viewing it you will see a beautiful *green-violet* luminosity. This ray truly allows you to release and cleanse the conditions within self that are not as productive as you would like them to be. It is a beautiful luminosity that allows you to go beyond the point where you are. Use it, my friends. Call upon the Creator. Cry out and say, "Use this ray on me now; I call it into self in order that I may cleanse and loosen those conditions that I do not find appropriate to keep." This is just a brief description of this eighth ray.

The ninth ray is one that continues the work that the eighth ray has begun. After you have cleansed and loosened, in a sense, this pattern of Earth living that you are now seeking to expand, to go beyond, you can use this beautiful ninth ray to aid you. You should see it as a beautiful *blue-green* light or luminosity. It also connects very specifically with the body of light. You use the christed part of the beingness to establish contact with this body of light, and this beautiful blue-green luminosity can help you to do so. The body of light is recognized and becomes available when you attune to this light blue-green luminosity. You recognize it, and joyfully you acknowledge your own true greatness as one that is entitled to such a beautiful vehicle there. You see, this ninth ray is very specific. It will enable the joy level to come into self, and thus the connection with the body of light becomes more and more apparent.

The next ray is the tenth ray. And this one is a beautiful luminosity that is *pearl-colored*. It really is one step beyond the ninth-ray realization. The Divinity is truly recognized when you meditate on this ray. The *divine pattern* is truly established, truly connected by means of the tenth ray. Yearn for this pattern to be strongly established — know that it is becoming a part of your conscious reality, and use this pearl-gray luminosity as the connecting point.

The eleventh ray is also luminous — it is *pink* with a little *orange* mixed in. This one continues the evolutionary spiral and leads to the New Age experience. It really is a bridge from the age where we are now to the New Age experience. That means that you can focus by means of this ray into the New Age. It is the *threshold*, not merely the doorway, that has been approached or entered by means of the seventh ray, which begins the New Age experience. The immediate threshold comes when you use the eleventh ray. Use it to get to the New Age. Know that you move up a level by means of this eleventh ray.

The twelfth ray is *gold* — the summit of the higher rays. The *New Age experience* itself is contained in the twelfth ray. It is the means by which all of the created activities that we are looking forward to in the New Age can be brought about. We work in meditation to sprinkle the Earth liberally with all of the higher rays, but it is the twelfth ray that is the height of the rays and used to bring it about now.

I probably should have begun by telling you about the New Age, but you can read this part and then go back and study the rays, if you wish, to get more specific information. You will have to study this material more than once. Reading it one time will not impress upon the mind enough if you are unfamiliar with the concepts and the areas I am discussing.

Let me say, then, that the New Age I am referring to has been referenced by many others on the Earth. Some have referred to it as the Armageddon, and by that they mean the end of something. But this is focusing on the death experience rather than the continuation of life on another level. To me it is not appropriate to focus on the New Age as the death of the old age, but rather as the beginning of a new level of Earth living. It is where you focus your attention that makes the difference. I am currently predicting that the New Age will begin in about 1996, with two years' leeway on either side, but probably two years later rather than two years sooner. Now, I say "probably" because the future is not ever fixed. There are only lines of probability, and we look at those probabilities and decide what probably will happen if something else doesn't happen and if all of the rest of the pattern fits in as we currently see it. Timing of the future is the most difficult thing to predict because it depends, truly, on too many other things happening and on free will, you see. If I looked at one of you and said, "In about ten years you will have a beautiful child" or "you will have a beautiful home," that might depend on many things. First, if you are going to have a child, perhaps you have an appropriate relationship partner at this time. If you choose to depart from that relationship, then probably the child will not be born, or at least not that same child. It might be a different one, you know. So if the choices made do not lead to the probability that is seen now, the future may be different than we currently view it. But it looks pretty certain that the New Age will begin around 1996.

What will be the launching point of the New Age? The Earth itself, my friends. It will flip on its axis. It has done this three other times. It is not a new event, but this particular time it is part of a New Age experience. The other times were important, but this one is the most important event that has transpired upon the Earth — a major event. And because of that, the focus of the cosmos is upon the Earth. Not that other worlds have not had these events, but it is a one-time thing at this particular level. Now, I am not saying that flipping on the axis happens only once. I am saying that the esoteric connection that goes with this flipping on the axis happens only once. The Creator is represented in existence on all levels, from the very highest to Earth existence and a little bit less — not a lot less, because the Earth's vibration is very heavy, but there are different levels of existence, as I'm sure you realize. They truly go from the Creator and cocreator state, step by step on the evolutionary path. You could say that you will go from where you are physically, step by step, leading up to the cocreator state. There are consciousnesses, evolving consciousnesses, that are far ahead of us on the evolutionary path. This path is begun at the time the spiritual spark, the individualized portion of the Creator, emerges from the Source. It then begins a loop of experiencing, and its ultimate goal leads back to the Creator as a self-realized cocreator. Spiritual sparks remember, and the totality of each of you is at all different levels.

There is one whom we refer to as "ensouling the Earth." This simply means he is so far ahead of us that we cannot conceive of any other term for him — his evolution is that far in advance of Earth living. His name is Sanat Kumara. About eighteen million years ago, he came to the Earth because she was needful of his aid. He came as a service to the Creator's Cosmic Plan. We say that he "ensouls" the planet because he is the planet's spiritual connection to the Creator. That is the meaning of that term. His experiencing as a heavenly man, who is evolving and growing and becoming greater, is our experience; or more properly put, we are a part of his experience. You could say that he is a large being and we are parts of him — his cells, the little parts of the body that you know are within you. We experience, but all of us together are his experience.

He currently is reaching a critical point in his evolution. It is his critical point that will launch this New Age. It is what is known as an initiation, or a point, a focus on his evolutionary path that leads him to a more expansive or greater level. After this point, he will forever be different — will be greater. And we, and the Earth also, as part of his experience, will forever be different and greater because of his activity. All are learning; all fit together. The complexity of existence resolves itself into a very simple fact: All grow, all become greater, all joyfully serve the Creator now.

❖ F I V E ❖

The Cabala

THIS FIFTH LESSON DEALS WITH THE CABALA. WHAT IS THE CABALA? IT IS A means by which you can understand self. Now, of course, it is much more than this. It is a means — a whole metaphysical system — for understanding creation at every level. But the focus that I use in the Foundation is "self-understanding."

Associated with the Cabala is what is known as the Tree of Life. This tree is a way, is the means, of looking at self. The Cabala — this complete metaphysical system — was a part of Jewish mysticism, hidden for eons by the teachers to protect it from total destruction. It is very valid when you can sort out its vast philosophical ramblings, when you can focus on it specifically to get what you need from it. The writings are so vast that people have been lost and wandered in them, not really understanding anything.

I am going to try to pinpoint certain techniques that I think are helpful in the self-growth program we are focused on in the Foundation. I will be ignoring, mainly, those great philosophical comments that are interesting but maybe not appropriate to one who is seeking, first, service, and second, greater understanding. The time is short now before the New Age. We must make choices by concentrating on the service and self-growth areas. You can accomplish a great deal more than you could before. Choices must be made. Do you want to be as advanced as possible for this great New Age? Do you want to partake of it? There will be an automatic cutting-off point when it comes. If you have not attained a certain point in your evolution, you will not be able to function on the Earth, because the vibration of the Earth will go beyond what you can live with. It has nothing to do with anyone else's decision. You, by your own growth, by your own efforts, decide whether or not you will live longer on the Earth. It is your decision.

The Cabala, then, is a tool for self-understanding, for enabling you to see different aspects of self, to literally pull out one aspect, view it under the microscope, and learn what you are like in this area. And then, if what you see is not what you want to see, change it. The Tree of Life contains what we call ten sephirah. You could call them ten lights, or ten different aspects of self. But here we are talking about self. They are ten different areas that you can put under the microscope to aid self-understanding.

Let us start at the origination point, talk briefly about all ten, and give you an idea of what is involved. If I whet your appetite, your interest, in the Tree of Life and the Cabala, then learn more about it. Get a glimmer from this lesson and see the potential for more self-understanding. I have done a series of tapes on the Cabala. William Gray is especially good. His "Ladder of Light" and "The Talking Tree" are excellent. I recommend them. The first one is more basic than the second.

The Cabalistic Tree of Life literally lights up each aspect of self and lets you examine it. At the top, at the center of the tree, is what is termed *Kether*, the origination point. After coming into existence you are poised at this origination point. At that point, nothing has yet happened. You are still just bursting forth into existence and you are poised there in the gateway. You could consider this a white light — the white that contains everything.

Stepping down the vibration, the next sephirah, the next aspect, is what is called *Chokmah*. This light contains all of your potentialities — everything that you are capable of doing, of being, of becoming, everything there. And when you have done this, you are wise, are you not? What is wisdom? It is going beyond learning or understanding. It is achieving in all of the areas of potentiality. All potentiality and wisdom are associated with the Chokmah aspect of self. Now, at this point on the Tree of Life, we are dealing with remote or high concepts. Don't let that bother you; just flow with my words. I am seeking to give you but a brief outline, so that is all that is required — just a flowingness here.

The next aspect is what is called *Binah*. Binah is the third of the three highest. Here are the purposes, here are the great receptive qualities of life. Beginning here we can see the possibilities of a life within a specific type of force. Force is what we are dealing with on this level — not form, which comes later in the tree. But for the purposes of this lesson, we will call Binah the great receiver — a receptive energy, and one that contains your purposes.

These you could say are the three spiritual aspects of self. You could call it a spiritual triad of self. Can you see that on the spiritual level you will know your purposes, you will have the understanding that goes with that area? You will have gone beyond that understanding into wisdom from all of the potentialities, and, of course, you will again come to the Source, the origination into this point. These are the three areas that have to do with the spiritual aspect of self.

The next area on the cabalistic tree that is important to understand is called *Chesed*. Here is divine love, divine allowingness, compassion, great

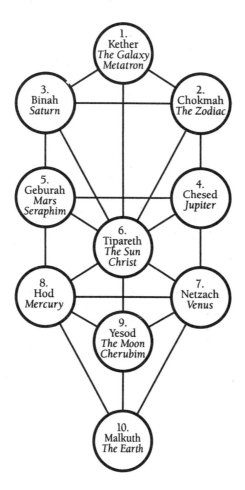

The Cabalistic Tree of Life

mental and conceptual abilities — truly the higher mental, not the logical processes, which are lower on the tree, but the great divine qualities of understanding and compassion, the higher emotional concepts. A great allowingness is contained here. We are going, now, into this second triad, so keep in mind that Chesed is one aspect of this second triad.

The next sephirah, the next aspect in this second triad, is called *Geburah*. It is the divine will, the will aspect of self on any level. It is also full of energy because the energy of self is focused there. You could say that the color is red because of all of this energy. Chesed is blue, and many times we associate compassion (anyway, I do) with the color blue. Also, the divine love, or universal love, I associate with blue. So you have the blue and the red of the second triad: compassion and divine will.

The third part of our second triad, the next aspect of self, is called *Tiphareth*. Now, if you decide to study the Cabala, you will note in the visual picture of it that Tiphareth is truly the center of the Tree of Life. Your true identity lies at Tiphareth. This is the christed part of self where the identification can be made, and it is important to know that every other aspect we are discussing — including the ones that we haven't yet discussed — all nine feed into this particular sephirah. It is the true identity level of self. It is yellow in color.

We have said that this is the second triad; it is the triad of unconditional love, divine will and true identity. We can equate this level to soul-level experience. The first triad was the spiritual level. This is the soul level.

Next we have a beautiful green aspect that is called *Netzach*. It is the emotions of physical existence. Here we enter our third triad, and from this point on we can see the personality part of self. This first is the emotional body, the emotions that may be experienced on two levels: conflict or harmony. It is also the "doingness" of creation. You might consider that.

Next is *Hod*, a beautiful orange aspect that is the logical processes — the ability to logically deduce, to reason. This is not the conceptual area, which we have already said was at the Chesed level. At Hod are the mental, logical processes.

The next aspect of self is what is called *Yesod*, the third aspect of this personality triad. It is the subconscious mind, the automatic processes within physical existence. It is the one that most people focus upon, rather than the one that is above it in the tree, Tiphareth. It is an illusion of the personality that causes this area, Yesod, to be focused upon. The focus must be raised up to merge with the soul, to allow Earth living to reflect what is the true identity level. So we have said that the personality contains the subconscious mind and the automatic processes (interesting) as well as the logical processes and the emotional body. Can you see how important it is to look at these automatic and subconscious areas? The Foundation is doing this specifically to allow self to become greater.

The final area is directly below Yesod, and it is called *Malkuth*. It is the physical part of creation. If you are looking at self, it would be the physical body itself. If you are looking at all creation, it is physical existence itself. This tenth sephirah is what connects you with the Earth. All of the others do not. In other words, only one-tenth of your existence has to do with the Earth. Isn't that interesting? It gives you a whole different perspective about creation. Nine-tenths of it has nothing to do with the Earth. Now, the personality that flows from this Earth sephirah is directly attached to it, is connected with the Earth, but it doesn't have to be. It can be raised up to a higher level — to the soul-level experience.

On the Tree of Life, then, we have three triads — the spiritual triad, the soul triad and the personality triad — all finally focused on the Earth. This shows how important Earth living is. All the rest is dependent upon it, truly.

By working through problems — blocks within self — on the Earth, you affect all of the rest, the other nine-tenths of your existence.

A Tree of Life exploration is very interesting. Each sephirah or aspect on the Tree of Life is connected by a path to all the other aspects. Then you have a way to travel from one to another. Constantly, in your life, you are moving on these paths, experiencing in various aspects of self.

Here is an illustration of how to work symbolically with the tree. Tiphareth, you will remember, is the true identity — the christed part of self, part of the soul triad. If you personify it in a state of meditation, if you look at that area and say, I want to see self as indicated by this aspect, you will see a person there, doing something in a specific scene. It is symbolic work, similar to working with dreams, and when the spiritual teachers look at what is going on, what the person looks like, whether it is a man or a woman, how he or she is dressed, the surrounding scene, then they can learn a lot about what you are currently experiencing in your evolutionary pattern. Also, if the teachers look at the paths that lead from one aspect to another, and you place yourself on these paths, they can learn a lot about you, depending on the path and what you are working on. This seems to me to be very important.

This is very brief, but I hope that it will aid your understanding of the possibilities of working with the Cabalistic Tree of Life. Thank you for your attention, and my love to you now.

✧ S I X ✧

Energy Management

I WOULD LIKE TO DISCUSS A VERY INTERESTING SUBJECT, ONE THAT EACH OF you has thought about and wondered about but perhaps become a little bit confused about when seeking to understand it in depth. The surface of it, the outside, seems rather simple. It is only as we begin to delve beneath the surface that we see that perhaps there is more than meets the eye. Let us begin, then, to consider the color blue.

In a previous lesson we discussed the rays, and you will remember that blue, from my point of view in teaching here, indicates the second ray. It has a special connotation for me in an intense application of energy. Let me explain that a little. I stated in a previous lesson that energy is the way the Creator has chosen to create. To me if you are looking for any one color that denotes energy, blue "fits the bill." Blue has a special application as far as energy is concerned. You can view it as an intense blue that vitalizes or as a beautiful serene blue that calms. You can do much with it, and that is why in working with the energies in my mediation, when the general connotation of energy is wanted, I have visualized energy as being blue. It also helps to attune, to understand, to know, to become a part of the second ray. This is the ray of love/wisdom, and it is always worthwhile to attune to it.

In an energy management program, which is a part of aura analysis, you visualize intense blue energy coming down through the top of the head, flowing through all seven chakras, which are energy centers, and then coming out a little from the body and returning to the top of the head. This means that this energy, or life force, flows through you from the crown of your head to the base chakra (the base of the spine) and then returns — a circular flow of life force through the trunk of the body. It seems rather simple, doesn't it, to bring blue energy down through the energy gate that lies at the crown of the head, to flow through the body — the energy body, the chakras themselves – and then bring it back up in a symbolic way indicating wholeness. This is not difficult to conceptualize, to understand, but when we begin to see what is accomplished by doing this on a regular basis, then, my friends, you can see that there is much going on beyond what appears on the surface. First of all, let me explain the chakras just a little.

The crown chakra is the highest, esoterically speaking. It lies at the crown of the head.

The second one, in descending order, is the third-eye chakra, between the eyebrows.

The third is the will, the throat chakra; if you ever feel choked up about something, this chakra is usually having a problem, or is what I call deviated from its ideal. What do I mean by that? The etheric or energy body within which the chakras reside has an ideal distribution of energy, and if the energy departs from this ideal, I refer to it as being deviated from it. When this occurs, many times there is an adverse effect reflected into the physical in the throat area. If the chakra – the energy center that connects with the physical there – is afflicted, the energy within it being chaotic, then you may see it reflected into the dense physical body.

The next chakra is the heart chakra. Many who have heart problems have caused this chakra to become so afflicted, so deviated from its pattern and so held within this deviation, that the physical becomes nonfunctional. This is what happens when a heart attack occurs.

The next chakra is in the solar plexus area, and it is very connected with the emotional body. When one is experiencing emotional difficulties and they seem rather severe, then the solar plexus has deviated from its ideal energy distribution.

The next chakra is the polarity chakra. It is divided into halves, just as people on the Earth are – the female the left, the male on the right – and if you have within you beliefs, or what we might call considerations, about men or women, or both, this chakra will show a deviation within its energy pattern. If there is enough of a deviation, then this also will be reflected into the physical body.

The base chakra is very basic; it has to do with survival itself. Again, deviations within its ideal pattern would indicate problems with surviving – a very basic problem with the life process itself.

I ask you to see the energy door open at the top of your head. It is but one way of allowing self to experience and to get and to maintain as much of the life force as you need for a productive life. You are entitled to it. The Creator wants you to have all of the life force that you need. You don't have to get it from anybody anywhere else but directly from the Creator. It is your right. That is the reason for the choice of seeing the energy come through the top of the head: it is symbolic of bringing it right from the Source. Sometimes, because of your considerations, that energy door may close, and then you do not get the energy you need. Many people who have serious illnesses that lead to death have begun the process by closing this energy door. Certainly they do not realize it is closed; they would not do it consciously. But the compulsiveness within the belief structure has brought this condition about. If you know someone who is very tired all the time, this may be the problem. If you can have them look, symbolically with their inner sight, at the top of their head, and see the doorway there, visualize the intense blue energy coming down into self, you will have aided them. Have them look at this doorway daily. If necessary, prop it open, make sure that it stays open. If it does not, have them seek help in keeping it open.

In your own energy management program, begin by looking at all seven chakras individually; view them with your inner sight and see each one with its energy ideally distributed. Even if you do not have the knowledge of each individual chakra, you can see each one patterned ideally. Know that each chakra is ideally patterned, energywise. If you spend a moment each day doing this, it will aid you.

First view the crown chakra and see its energy ideally distributed; then the third eye; then the throat, the heart, the solar plexus, the polarity area, the base chakra. After completing that, bring the blue energy through your energy gate; see it flowing smoothly through each chakra, which now has ideally patterned energies. Bring it down smoothly, intensely, feel the difference as the energies surge through these energy centers, and then bring it out a little from the body and feel the smooth return flow. This indicates the wholeness of creation. You see, you have an oval there, almost a circle, that indicates that creation is one, that there is no separation. Now, of course, the energy does not just all go out and return to the crown; but symbolically seeing some of it do that aids in this symbolic wholeness act.

This is so important that I wanted it a part of the lesson series. In an aura analysis the spiritual teachers can also tell each person where, within his aura, there are what we call energy scars. These are formed from traumatic experiences. If you've perhaps suffered a great loss, then a specific part of the aura is affected. For a while it may leak badly. As you get over that particular trauma, the aura heals there, but a scar is formed — an energy scar — and if you again experience an emotion similar to what caused it in the first place, that scar can begin to leak again, and you can lose much of the energy that is in the auric field. You see, the etheric body surrounds the dense physical body, and beyond it are the various kinds of energies, your own individual patterns that make up your selfness on the Earth. It is a visual picture of you. Everyone is different, each is unique, but when the auric field becomes afflicted from conditions within self, it can tear, there can be holes in it, and then you can lose your needed energy. By knowing where these are, you can avoid this. If you do not know specifically where the tears are, you can have someone seal the whole auric field from the top of the head by running their hands along the field from about twelve to fourteen inches out, all the way to the floor, all the way around. This will aid you to seal in your energies. One of the most common ways that the auric field can leak is through tiny pinholes above the head. These are caused by anxiety, and usually there is an affliction in the solar plexus chakra also. If you put your hand twelve inches above your head and feel heat, then your aura is leaking from these pinholes, and you can have someone seal it to aid you.

The energy bodies, then, are very important in regard to how you feel physically. They respond directly to emotional involvement — or noninvolvement, as the case may be. It shows truly what you are, what you have been, and within a limited time frame, what you are becoming. By working with your aura, by managing the energy within the etheric body, you can aid self to feel better.

Now, I would like to discuss the etheric body itself. It should contain an inch-and-a-half to two inches of energy completely surrounding the dense physical body — that much energy everywhere. This is a goal, but it is not what most contain, as pictures show. But I give that amount as a goal because when you are truly through with Earth living, that is the amount of energy the etheric will contain. If you add to your daily energy maintenance program, viewing energy all around the body with that much life force smoothly distributed everywhere outlining the body, you will aid self. There will be within each of you certain places where the energy is not ideally distributed. It will be very helpful if you will do these things daily.

First view the energy body all around the outline of the dense physical, with its energy ideally distributed. Second, work with the chakras and their patterns, bringing their intense blue energy down through self. Third, have the aura sealed and watch the auric field when in specific areas you feel heat, then have it smoothed and sealed again. In this manner, my friends, you can maintain your energy, feel better and come into greater balance emotionally and energywise.

See a blue string balancing you. It hangs between your eyebrows, a blue string that is always balanced. Keep it there as part of your energy management program.

Thank you very much for your attention.

✧ S E V E N ✧

The Three Levels of Existence

MY FRIENDS, IN THIS LESSON I WOULD LIKE TO DISCUSS THE THREE LEVELS of existence as I teach them through Janet. The first is the monadic level, which equates to the spiritual spark, or basic level of creation. Extending from this level is the next, the soul level. Both of these two levels exist upon the spiritual plane. The spiritual plane is the basic part of creation. In this area all serve the Creator. All recognize here that the Creator and His experiencing compose all of existence, that that is all there is. The spiritual planes celebrate this with joy daily — the Creator and His experiencing. Thus, those existences there serve Him. Their purpose is service to the Creator, to aid Him in His Cosmic Plan.

The third level of experience that I talk about is the physical, which is an extension of soul level. We have, then, three levels of experiencing. There are others, but I do not seek to make too complex the outline of experiencing. If each of you can understand this outline, you will have a good general idea of what has happened and what is happening and what will happen over your whole evolutionary period. It is a simple approach that is most effective for understanding the totality of existence.

When each of you began your experiencing, you came forth from the Source. At that time you were the individualized spark, what I refer to as the monad. Remember, this is the basic portion of the totality of each of you, the totality being composed of the monad, its souls, and the physical extensions of those souls. All of these compose a circle, if you will, that makes up the individualized portion of the Creator. I equate it to a circle to show you that, symbolically speaking, if you affect one portion of the circle, the rest is affected also. Thus, if an experience affects one level of your totality, it affects all of the other levels.

At the time of its emergence from the Source, your monad participated in some assignments as part of its service to the Creator. Because the monad served the Creator, its own needs were met — service always leads to having your own needs met. That does not mean that by serving the Creator you will automatically grow, become greater. It does not. It means that when you serve with joy, seeking to bring about the Creator's Cosmic Plan for Earth, the means for your own growth will be given. Thus, you may find a teacher who will help you know the changes that need to be made within. Then you must make the changes, but the means to identifying them, the means to finding them, will have been given to you through your service.

Monads, then, existing on the spiritual plane, are very, very remote from Earth living. In trying to describe what they actually do, words limit me. I usually equate a monad to one who is very close to the Source, one who is very close to the ideal, one whose individualized pattern contains much light. This is part of creation that exists far beyond the physical existence as you on the Earth know it. It has really nothing to do with physical existence except as everything is related to everything else, and upon the Earth we see a reflection of such remote experiences — truly, Earth living is a reflection of what has happened to each of us in the spiritual area.

At the time a monad emerges from the Source, its teachers give it an individual plan, an individual outline, an ideal, a means to experience and grow that will lead back to the Source in the most free-flowing and most ideal manner. Also, at the time of emerging, each monad is given free will, so each may choose whether or not to adhere exactly to that ideal path. We learn by such choices. What we learn is that the Creator truly knows what our ideal is, and that by deviating from it we will experience effects that we do not like, that do not flow well, that lead to "interesting" experiences. Thus, we will always come back to the ideal until eventually we can maintain it always. At that time, when we can hold this focus of perfection, or the ideal, we will be completely self-realized, completely ready to be cocreators, able to take our places and be administrators, to accept our full responsibilities in line with the Creator's Cosmic Plan. It is our destiny. We cannot, and we would not, and we should not, and we will not escape it.

Each level of existence, then, is given free will. The monad, after experiencing a certain length of time, extends itself into another level of existence, and we call this soul level. Because the number twelve, esoterically speaking, is important, that is the ideal number of souls to extend. Most do extend to twelve, and some do not; if they do not extend the ideal number, they deviate from their outline as given and get some interesting effects. Soul-level living, then, is still on the spiritual plane but is also very service-oriented. The souls recognize that serving the Creator is their job, and they also serve, and many times they serve with the monads — not especially their own, but with the monads in general. The souls are considered children by the monads and many times are taught by them.

Energies everywhere have an ideal also, and if there is a deviation resulting in a chaotic energy condition in a specific area (remember, this is a state of consciousness), then a team of workers is sent in to return the energies to their ideals. Mostly this is done by monads. Sometimes souls are involved also. As we have said, the monads have much light. They have an individualized pattern, just as you have an individual body. By running these disrupted energies through their patterns, they gradually return them to the ideal. This is done in a group situation, remember. The monads also learn by doing this. What they learn is not to deviate from their ideal — | to in a sense stand there and allow disrupted energies to flow through their ideal pattern, to aid them, but to remain unaffected no matter what is happening. Isn't that interesting? That truly is the goal of Earth living.

Also, as we have already said, it is a reflection of the spiritual area — to walk on the Earth, to live here, to associate with every person, every condition, whether or not it is ideal, and to remain unaffected personally by it — to aid each area and still remain unaffected. Do you see how Earth living is a direct reflection of the higher monadic and soul experience? Each of you has had many experiences at monadic level. The soul level is ideally divided into twelve, and usually only one of them is involved with Earth living. There have been a few I have evaluated who had two souls involved with Earth, but mostly not. Mostly, the other souls are involved in other areas of creation, some having extensions of themselves in a physical environment, but probably most do not. Your own soul obviously has such extensions, and you, my friend, are one of them: an extension into Earth living.

Now, because you are reading this, I know that your soul came to Earth to aid it — a child of the light. Great waves of them are sent to the Earth at specific times to aid it, not all coming at once, but great waves of them in several different sequential times, from an Earth point of view. The purpose was to aid the planet, to bring more light to the planet. Much of your experience was already learned elsewhere, but the soul came here as a part of its service. You've had many lives on the Earth, an average of 2000 to 2500. These have been in all areas of existence, many different places, many types of experience; some were very prominent, most were not prominent, but all of you have existed in all of Earth living, many extensions of your soul. The purpose of such a life is, of course, service. Summing up the Earth experience, it is for the purpose of the soul's growth, so that it may serve, so that it may function here upon the Earth and serve more completely.

In the next lesson I want to go into this in detail so that you will truly see the opportunity that you now have. Thank you very much, my friends.

⟡ E I G H T ⟡

Merging with the Soul through Service

T HROUGHOUT THE MATERIAL GIVEN IN THE FOUNDATION IS THE THEME OF merging with the soul. It is at the very heart of the program. Let me explain it a little to you.

The hierarchic government viewed humankind and the coming New Age. We thought about different approaches to humanity and outlined several that we felt were quite important. I was then asked to focus one of these approaches and I prepared a program that I thought might be helpful to allow humankind to enter the New Age at the most elevated possible state of their evolutionary spiral. My plan was approved by the Hierarchy, along with several others. It was approved by the Hierarchy, mostly the teachers on the second ray, and this program was shown to the Christ, the lord Maitreya, and approved by the Buddha and then Sanat Kumara. We agreed that the term "initiation" had been misunderstood, and so in my plan I sought another way to explain the important evolutionary point that is called the third initiation or the first major initiation, which the Hierarchy views as a critical point. After reviewing my suggestions, I was asked to focus this on the Earth, to go in an intensive effort with two other teachers, to bring it to fruition, bring this focus, this particular look at that evolutionary step to the attention of humanity. This I agreed to do, and we began to look for someone I could work through. Several were considered and for various reasons were not contacted. Janet was the ultimate decision, the one we contacted, and she agreed to allow me to focus my teaching on Earth through her.

I am not saying that the Hierarchy doesn't work through other people – and I work through others – but I focus by being anchored here in her, a specific point of view that is considered important. Other teachers in the Hierarchy are involved with me. I certainly do not consider this effort to be anything that I am doing alone; on the contrary, all of the Hierarchy has input into the developing or unfolding plan as we go along. That does not mean that the Foundation is composed of members of the Hierarchy. It is composed of human beings who are serving the Hierarchy and the Creator's Cosmic Plan with varying depths of commitment. There is a board of directors that truly seeks to guide the Tibetan Foundation. They have elected me, Djwhal Khul, chairman, but in a sense I really just guide the activity, bring into awareness things that need to be handled. I do not do the actual outreach to humanity.

Does this sound strange? Well, let me analyze it for you. Each one on the board is learning and seeking to grow, to become more and more aware of his own true divinity. The Hierarchy, as focused through me, does not desire to deprive any of these human beings of a specific learning experience (growth opportunity). We certainly will guide the Foundation, but the bringing it into focus, the launching of it and guiding it in its physical unfoldment must be done by those who are still physically on the planet Earth. The Tibetan Foundation is not the only hierarchic outreach, but it is an important one, as will become more and more evident as time progresses. Also, this focus is specific. It has as its goal the bringing of as many as can allow it to the third initiation, or soul-merge evolutionary point. Thus, you could say that I, the Tibetan Djwhal Khul, have become a specialist at this time in my approach through Janet. I seek to make others aware of what is blocking their progress toward the point of merging with their souls, and then we, the Foundation, seek to aid them to remove the various blocks. This is done in several ways simultaneously, but the main way, of course, is the work through the belief structure.

For the Earth, the evolutionary point that I call merging with the soul is a very advanced one. You probably do not know personally anyone who functions at this level. You may have heard of someone who does, but the way to tell is, are they 100% involved in service to the Creator? That percentage is the key. Their personal lives no longer control their functions; their sense of direction has turned. They may have personal lives, of course, but this is very incidental to the service aspect. There will be many, many people approaching such a one. Such a one will be (normally speaking, because there will be exceptions) very widely sought, and the life itself of such a one will flow completely smoothly. Earth living will no longer be a problem or a less-than-ideal experience. Truly it is not a problem but it is an exercise in learning. The teachings have been carefully prepared by many, many teachers in the Hierarchy on all levels of evolution within the government there, because, of course, at the spiritual level we are also on different levels within a service area.

We seek, then, to make these teachings as clear, as simple, as precise as possible. We have carefully guided every word. Janet has become a very clear channel. That is very important because, as I said, we are carefully considering every word and its application to this specific mission. We want to focus through the Foundation a specific offer to humanity. As I said earlier, I am a specialist now in my approach through Janet. It is very different from my approach through Alice Bailey; it is for a specifically different purpose. Those of you who remember and love those teachings, I want to say thank you for relating to them and loving them. That is wonderful, and I am glad that you feel they are aiding you. However, times change. Conditions on the Earth are changing. Humanity is changing. The hierarchic government is changing. Sanat Kumara is changing. Truly, all of creation is changing. We need, then, a spiritual teacher — we being the Hierarchy, focused in a very specific manner to aid others, to achieve the breakthrough to the soul-merge (third initiation). I am here specifically to do this. It is felt by the Hierarchy that my specific understanding of humanity will be helpful. It is felt that my plan as presented and approved by the Hierarchy will be beneficial. We truly offer it with this purpose: to aid humanity at this particular critical, evolutionary period for all of creation. All of creation reflects this important time, and as we gain awareness we see the enlarged scope of what is taking place on all levels.

✧ N I N E ✧

Balance

I N YOUR GROWTH PATTERN, IT SEEMS TO ME THAT THE MOST IMPORTANT thing to begin to seek is balance. The balanced approach to a growth pattern is extremely important. As one gets to the point where growth is not just an event to be contemplated in the future but is necessary, is intensely sought, then one must always balance this intensity with the knowingness that one step at a time is required in any spiritual growth pattern or program.

A beginner who approaches the point of moving beyond the obvious, of seeking to understand and become aware of what lies beyond the Earth plane, usually moves slowly, making a few tentative steps and then incurring large blocks of time in which no seeking is present, where he is again caught in Earth experiencing only. The condition of the beginner gradually gives way to the intensity of the advanced disciple. Both are a part of the evolutionary path. It is needful to recognize that a balance must be achieved in order to sustain an effort of growth to the desired level of attainment. Each of you has your own evolutionary point, your own perceptions and goals, and your own desires in regard to future evolvement. Thus, it is sometimes necessary for you to work, and sometimes to take a little time off to rest.

A balanced program consists of striving to understand and perceptively travel the path of evolution. Such a balanced program includes several different aspects, some of which I will discuss now. Increasing the input of the learning process by studying and seeking to intellectually understand is important. Studying, using the mental focus, also helps to balance the emotional body (it allows you to disconnect the emotional trauma when you can begin to use well-developed mental faculties). And as I have said, working within your belief structure is one of the very best ways present on the Earth to work on self. It is not the only way, but its specificity makes it valuable.

Also very important is meditation. It seems to me we could divide meditation into many different kinds, and one is the traditional meditation which you do by yourself. In doing this you find a special place and you go there daily, quieting self and participating in an inner experience. It is most beneficial if done regularly, usually daily to begin with, and at a regular time and in the same special place. The physical body responds well to a regular routine and will partake more joyfully in your meditation if regularity is stressed. This means that perhaps you will want to meditate early in the morning, or in the evening before retiring, or perhaps, if you work daily and you have a private place to be, during a lunch hour. Whatever you choose and works well for you is appropriate. But by doing it regularly, it will certainly aid you, even if you do not yet visualize or have not yet developed that inner seeingness. If you can know that something is happening, if you can hear it, if you can smell it (some people do), if you have an awareness of it, whatever the sense through which you have that awareness, then you can use experiencing on what we call the inner planes to aid you. This takes you that one step beyond the obvious.

Group meditations are also valuable, and you learn a great deal by going into a group situation. It is a good learning experience. Group meditations are also helpful to aid the Earth; learning to work with the rays and using them to increase the vibrational pattern of the Earth, to raise it, to hone it a little, is very beneficial. You also may contact an inner teacher in a state of meditation. It seems to me that whether this is done in a group or individually, it is very, very important. It is easier for most to meditate in a group experience, because of the added energy present. Some like one or the other better, of course, but it seems to me that both are very appropriate.

Another inner experience that I find very helpful is what we call symbolic work, in which you are directed by a teacher. You have an inner experience in a state of meditation and then it is interpreted for you. Groups can also record these sessions then interpret them themselves, have an interchange there and learn from the experience.

Another area that is very important to develop in a complete metaphysical program, a spiritual growth experience, is to begin to blend all of the aspects within self equally, to balance self in the complete harmony that is necessary for the next major evolutionary step – the soul-merge. I would encourage those of you who wish to learn from the teachers to sit down with a piece of paper and a pencil and say, "All right, what is it within self that is not yet developed, that I need more development in?" Then you will learn to evaluate yourself as objectively as you can. I'm not saying that you will find everything that yet needs to be done, but you will begin by taking that responsibility for self, saying, "I must truly look and discover what is still needed in my growth pattern." If you will do this, and if you will request aid from the teachers, they will work with you on it.

The next point that seems to me to be very important in your growth pattern is what we have been discussing — serving others. This is the means to attaining your own growth. This has always been true, my friends. Those who serve always receive in return what they need in order to grow and to learn. Of course, they still have to do the growing — no one does it for them — but the means to do it is given when one serves. I recognize that most of you are very busy. You have an established life pattern, and it is difficult to fit a large block of service into it, but the service, my friends, is most important because it begins the process of acknowledging that perhaps the Creator's needs — His Cosmic Plan — are more important than any of our personal needs and requirements.

I am not defining any type of service or any particular group or organization here except to say it must truly be in line with the Creator's Cosmic Plan as you currently define it. And that is important, because each of you must work right where you are now, where your perceptions hold you at the current moment. Yes, you can change, and you will. But now, right now, what do you perceive as a service to aid the Creator's Cosmic Plan? Choose something that you enjoy or that you believe has aided you. Get involved with it and use this focus to raise self to a higher level. Now, I hope that is not the purpose for choosing it — I hope you will choose service because it is your wish to participate with the Creator and His experiencing. How joyful that we may do this! And it is, truly, a joy to serve Him. Service is the gateway to the heights. The more you can change that focus, move from the personal needs, desires and wants, and focus on divinity, the sooner you will achieve what each one of you truly desires: the perception to know, to finally, on this Earth, acknowledge completely that divinity within. Certainly you want to do so. Certainly you are attempting to. But by changing your focus, by not so much seeking it as serving it, you will, my friends, achieve this goal.

Thank you very much for your attention. I do appreciate it.

How to Be of Service to the Cosmic Plan

THIS IS THE FINAL LESSON IN OUR FIRST SERIES OF TEN LESSONS WHICH ARE meant truly to be an introduction to the philosophies I am teaching through Janet. It is just a different focus, perhaps, another way of looking at creation and self and everything else, and so it seemed appropriate to me to spell out some of these teachings that are being made available through the Tibetan Foundation.

In this lesson I want to make several suggestions. First, you might want to sit down with self and say, What is it that I truly want out of life? Why am I seeking? Write it down. Are you seeking a more free-flowing relationship, or a new one, or a better one, or what, in the relationship area? Are you seeking to understand your relationship partner, and if so, are you doing it daily? How are you doing it?

In the area of your work situation, are you seeking to enjoy your work more? Are you seeking to expand in how you use the job situation? Are you seeking a better job? A more lucrative one? Or, are you seeking to balance the whole work area with your spiritual one? It seems to me this is done in the Western world, which is important.

In the East most of you have sat upon a mountain and meditated for the world. It was very helpful, a very productive thing to do, but you are no longer on that mountain, and Western living is mostly experiencing in the world of people. I am not saying that you shouldn't meditate for the world – don't misunderstand me. But know that your spiritual endeavors are intended to be balanced by normal living. When you reach a specific point in your evolution by dedicating yourself 100% to the Creator, then some of your involvement with the normal world will begin to fall away. Until that time of 100% service, this will not be true, and much of your learning will be dealing with this balance, neither ignoring the world nor becoming immersed in it, approaching a growth pattern in as balanced a way as you can at that particular moment, allowing self to be where you are. That's very important — self-allowingness.

Over my past association with human beings, one thing stands out clearly, in my estimation, in my perception. It is that they are not allowing as far as self is concerned. They may be very allowing of others (or not at all, depending on the person), but almost never are they completely allowing of self. That does not mean that they should seek, or not seek, growth. It means simply that a spiritual seeker, one who recognizes the divinity within and seeks it more and more clearly, is critical of self because he has not yet attained it. As I said, I am generalizing, and some are more critical of self than others are.

The mainstream of humanity sees self as good enough, as not needing to be changed, and they do not even recognize that change is appropriate. They see living as an experience of which they partake, that life is truly inflicted upon them by they know not what, but they do not view life as a learning experience, a growing experience. So this not-allowing of self is confined to those who recognize that learning is necessary. Of course, there are some in the mainstream of humanity who are critical of self also because of a past experience, a compulsiveness within their belief structure.

What should you do? Begin to send yourself divine love. Say to self, "You are divine. I recognize that pattern within you. You are seeking, you are growing toward that perfect perception of the divinity, and at this time, at this particular point, you are doing the best you can." You might do this as a meditation and do it often. Now, everything is to be done in true balance, so do not let this allowingness convert to the perception that there is nothing to be done within self. That is obviously not true, for if you are still functioning on this Earth, you have things yet to overcome within self.

The only exceptions to this rule are the few teachers who have chosen to come here, but the way to know whether you are one of them is to look at your life. Is it completely free-flowing? Is there absolutely nothing in your life that needs changing? Are you involved with helping people 100% of the time? Have you put such service further ahead in importance than your own wants and needs? Have you released those wants, needs and desires in order to serve the Creator? If so, then you are already functioning at soul level and have no further things to learn on the Earth. If this is the case, you always have enough energy, everything within your life is free-flowing, and you are attuned to the Creator always, joyfully partaking of His Cosmic Plan for Earth. If, however, you recognize that although you are trying to reach this point you have not yet achieved it, then there is still work to do on self.

There are methods you can use to do this work, but if you choose not to use the methods of others, I encourage you to work in some manner, always seeking to learn more and more about self and existence, bringing into conscious awareness everything that is happening in your life, evaluating the experiences you have and learning daily from each of them. Use synchronicities especially to aid you. For those of you who are not familiar with the word "synchronicity," it means a meaningful coincidence. One level of existence is truly a reflection of the other levels. Through synchronicities you can utilize what you are experiencing on the Earth plane to understand what you are working on in the spiritual growth area. Is your car battery dead? Well, perhaps within self is an area you are working on that involves not having enough energy – the energy source there is dead. You can look at everything that happens in your life by looking at the various levels and seeking to synthesize all of the information into the totality of your experiencing. Synchronicities are symbolically important in your life.

Also, begin now to program yourself to remember your dreams. Say to self, "I choose now to remember my dreams." You might symbolically turn on a spotlight just before you go to bed or have a symbolic tape recorder right by your bed and say, "I am going to record this. This is recording into my consciousness now so that I can remember it." You are turning the spotlight on it, putting your attention on it, and thus you will begin to remember to bring the dream back from the sleep state. Approach these dreams from the symbolic viewpoint. Most dreams have to do with self and self alone. If you have another person in your dreams, try to understand what that person represents to you. Dreams are, of course, of various types, and the type I have just discussed is a symbolic message to you from the higher self or soul level. There are other kinds of dreams. Many are past-life experiences, which of course aren't symbolic, but may be showing you that this experience is affecting your life now, or at least the conclusions reached from it.

If you have much fear in self and you dream about a time when you were scalped by Indians, then you might look at that experience and that fear pattern and see what is going on in your life that has stirred up a fear pattern of such intensity that the subconscious mind has taken you back to a previous experience in which a similar fear pattern existed. There are also dreams that are telling you of future probabilities. These dreams are usually for a learning experience also. It may be something that you don't want to experience, in which case you can change it so that you do not have to. You are not fated to experience a fixed future. You create your life, so you may choose how to create it. But perhaps if you are working in the area of understanding your purposes, then the dream may be helping you in that area and showing you a probable future, and from that you can see what some of those purposes are and how they will ultimately work out, if you choose to allow them to do so. The soul may be showing you the agenda for when you function upon the Earth at soul level. It may be saying, "This is what we will be doing – get used to it and understand the agenda so that when we are together you will already know it, you will be familiar with it."

You see, dreaming gets very close to the creative process. It is part of the experiencing in the creative area. The conscious mind has been laid aside, and you can learn a great deal by remembering and partaking in this creative process.

Also, personal meditation – and service through such meditation – is very important. I find meditation so important that I want to emphasize it in this final summing up, even though I have discussed it in previous lessons.

Recognizing where you are in your life right now and what you want to do later is important. Before many of you looms the choice of service to humanity. In what area are you equipped to serve? What should you be doing now to prepare for such service? These questions need to be approached gradually, slowly. They need to be approached by sitting down with self and saying, "This is where I am now, and I know I want to serve, but I haven't the faintest idea how." Begin then by seeing what you like to do. Do you have an affinity for children? Do you enjoy physical activities? If so, how can these be applied? Well, perhaps with hatha yoga in which you aid others to get the body in tune with the whole beingness. Children need aid. There are going to be many who will be working with special children in the future, and with those who are here. This is just an example and, of course, it is not the only way you can serve. I am saying you should set out the possibilities.

Start with things that you like to do. Make a list but do not analyze them. Sit with a group and brainstorm "service." How can you be of service? Be as creative about it as you can. It doesn't matter if it's practical. Get the ideas put forth, and after everyone (or you) has recorded all of these ideas, then begin to dissect them and see where they lead you. I tell you, it works. You can then begin to take the practicality of the situation that holds you now and see what you can do to make a few steps toward the goal of service. You can begin right now. You must begin right now. It is what you can do. It is what is appropriate. You can't just look at a large service organization and say, "I want to do what they're doing." You have to begin right where you are, from your dedication, your willingness, your practicality of working from where you are. Then the rest will evolve. I find it appropriate for each one who wishes to serve to begin to remove the blocks to service and look at why they aren't doing it already. That seems to be very important. No matter how, or if, you choose to do this, this technique is very helpful in getting to the goal of more productive service.

My friends, I wrote extensively, through Alice Bailey, of world servers. Now I call to you. I say to you, serve the world. This is what a world server is: someone who makes the effort daily to help the world. World servers come in all shapes, all sizes, all colors, all stages of evolution. Together we will raise the Earth, we will move it forward. We will enlarge the concepts that are presently here on the Earth. We will make this beautiful planet enter the New Age in a lovely, free-flowing manner. I say to you then, as a world server, begin. Contact those you perceive to be serving. Perhaps you can say, "I'm thinking of doing so and so. Is there something in that area with which I can help you?"

When you come to an organization and say, "I want to help," they always want to know what you can do, what you would like to do. So if you have preanalyzed your abilities, gone through this searching process, then you will have something very practical to offer to an organization. You can say, I do so and so very well. May I help in this area? If the organization says, We have a lot of help in that area, but we need someone in this area, then are you truly open enough to take advantage of that wonderful opportunity, to allow yourself to go beyond the original concept? Why don't you just go to them in the first place and ask what you can do? Well, you can always do it that way, but it seems to me that in order to understand self, as a fully responsible human being, you should always be analyzing what it is you can do. This is why I gave you this particular method of approaching others. I am sure that when you go to a group and say, "I'll serve in any way I can," your help will be utilized if they can think of something specific for you to do. But it seems to me the other way is a very practical way to take some of this responsibility, to say, "Yes, I am developed in this area and I would be glad to help here, but if you have something else that I can do, I would like to do that, too."

What is service? An interesting question. Service is aid. If you pick up a neighbor's newspaper when he can no longer do so because he is incapacitated, have you served him? Well, in a special sense you have, haven't you? But at this particular time on the Earth, my definition of service is, serving the Creator's Cosmic Plan to move the Earth forward. So when you are looking for ways to help, when you are looking at organizations to approach, ask yourself if this is what they're doing. Because this is what must be done, my friends. It must be done by whoever is willing to do it. All of us together aid the Earth and move it forward in its evolution. Join me now as we go toward the New Age. Come along with me and serve the Creator now.

Thank you for your attention.

✧ E L E V E N ✧

Launching the Earth into the New Age

THIS LESSON IS MEANT TO GO BEYOND THE ORIGINAL SUMMING-UP PROCESS of what has been taught within the Foundation, perhaps allowing self and the Foundation as a whole to see further along the lines of probability.

Let us begin by analyzing the consciousness of the Earth in general. It is poised, in a very real sense, on the edge of a new experience. It seeks to go forth to this new experience in as smooth and effective a manner as possible. It does not wish to experience the cumulative effect that is now present here on the Earth – the effect that has come about through the experiencing of untold numbers of evolving consciousnesses here on the Earth. Because this is true, the Creator and His representatives who work with the Earth (the Hierarchy, Sanat Kumara and those who assist him) have decided to seek, through specific focuses such as the Tibetan Foundation, to raise the general consciousness of the Earth. The possibilities there are awesome as we tremble on the brink of the New Age. This New Age experience can be at such a height that, again, it is awesome to consider. Such a giant step in evolution is rarely contemplated, but it is now being made available. Sanat Kumara has earned this giant step, and humankind may partake of it with him now as a part of his experience. Let us discuss in detail some of the possibilities that we might encounter during this last approach to the New Age.

We are seeking to move toward our goal in as aware a manner as possible, consciously working to aid the Earth in general to move forward, and consciously working to aid self, specifically, to understand with more perception. By "moving forward," I mean just that: We must understand much more clearly. Suppose, my friends (because I am looking at probability lines here) that within five to ten years we do lose the West Coast. It is hoped to be avoided, but if we do, what then? Do you think that this event or another major event will show humanity that the Earth is changing? It is just one way – the way the Earth has chosen to experience evolution, painfully and with trauma. If each of you would make one major realization between now and the time of this probability occurring, the Earth would not need to go through it. It would have evolved beyond this point of "pulling in" this trauma, this loss, because a major loss of this kind, a loosening of part of the Earth, would be a great trauma to the Earth consciousness itself. It would feel a deep effect for quite a long period of time. Let us specifically, then, aim some of our inner work toward avoiding such a trauma.

I have often said that the Hierarchy holds the West Coast on with "spiritual chewing gum." That may sound like a silly remark, but perhaps not as inappropriate as it may seem. The Hierarchy works with energy patterns all over the Earth, and by relieving energy pressure from one point on the Earth it can aid another. For a long time now, we have looked at energy pressure in California and sought to always make it as low as we were allowed (because we work within a specific framework). Sanat Kumara directs our activity in this area. We may not violate the free-will principles of those who live on the Earth. If they create enough trauma, California will go, because it will have been chosen by the aggregate experiencing of those on the Earth. However, if you disciples, you seekers, will make a stringent effort to avoid such a traumatic encounter in the Earth's evolution, we will see instead a loosening of the effect, and it can then fall away and not need to be experienced. I say to you, this is appropriate, and let's do it now. I have several specific suggestions.

First of all, by evolving and growing and understanding self, you aid the Earth in general. In your group work, in your meditations, include the Earth in specific ways, using the higher rays to literally pull up the energy of the Earth. To bring the Earth up in a group experience, a group meditation, is a powerful tool to help the Earth's evolution. It works especially with rays seven through twelve.

You must make certain important realizations about evolution. If a cross section of humanity makes these realizations, they will create a direct focus into the conscious stream of the Earth itself, and will help the Earth to attune and make such a realization itself. Realizations, whether made on an individual evolving-consciousness basis or in the consciousness of a specific planet (which in a sense is also an evolving consciousness), help the Earth to grow, and it becomes, as a result, that which has been experienced upon it. Our efforts in seeking to analyze evolution and what is happening now, in seizing the growth opportunities that are here, in seeking to understand what occurs every day on the Earth, and then making the necessary bridging effect to important realizations, will, my friends, pay great dividends.

What is a realization? It is the ability to bring into self, as a result of the analyzing process, a complete understanding of a specific. Do you understand it? If you do not, then use that to meditate on, asking self to meditate on the realization process itself to aid you to understand it completely. A realization allows you to be, to know and to participate in a specific which before that time may have been understood in an intellectual focus, but that is all. It does not negate understanding intellectually, but it is the intellectual that must lead to the realization. This, then, helps you to integrate that into your pattern of Earth experience.

Do you understand that what you are seeking to do on the Earth, in a personal sense, is to understand everything while you are focused within a physical structure? This is much more difficult to understand than when you are not in the physical structure. Thus, the learning opportunity is much greater when you can understand something and realize it within the physical structure. You hold on to it, you keep it in an eternal way that is not always possible on other levels of experiencing. This is why opportunities are so awesome within physical existence, why we are all so privileged to be within it, and why we can evolve and grow and become greater in such a rapid manner.

Earth itself, then, participates in this wonderful evolution, and we, because we love her and appreciate her nurturing us over eons, can aid her at this critical point. If you enter a relationship you try to support your partner in times of crisis, in the partner's times of seeking greater understanding. If the partner is confused by the process of experiencing, then you seek to support him at that time. If the partner asks, you may help her to understand what she has not yet understood, help her to realize and utilize as a result of such a realization that newfound understanding. Similarly, you have a specific relationship with the Earth. Each one can approach Earth in a supportive role, meditating with her — and I am talking about her divinity, her divine consciousness, her consciousness that is as much a part of divinity as your own — contacting this divinity of Earth and supporting it during this period of crisis.

Use a meditation in which you see this divinity of Earth in any way that you wish. I personally envision Earth as a female, and this is a personal preference. I do not want any negative connotations felt with that statement. I am being appreciative of her qualities, which seem to me the pinnacle that a female energy can achieve in physical existence. Of course, the male qualities are in the female, anyway. We have both parts of the energy polarities within self. I find a wonderfulness from encountering this receptive type of divinity.

Whether you choose to envision the Earth in my manner or in your own manner, seek to connect consciously with the divinity of the Earth and support it, perhaps explaining a little your perspective of what is occurring and being loving and supporting of her now. You may also help the Earth through the focus of realization I mentioned earlier, seeking to realize exactly what is happening now and leading to a focus that the Earth can utilize to aid itself. The Earth does not view self as you or I do, but it may see, from such a focus, a specific pattern of what is occurring, and it seems to me it should be very helpful to the Earth experience at this time.

Is it not exciting to know there truly is something that you can do to aid the Earth? There is much, and we will continue to discuss it, seeing in great detail what is possible, what is probable, and then (according to whether or not it is desirable) seeking to negate it or to bring it about.

A specific example in this regard is our conversation on Los Angeles and the West Coast. I would see this area enclosed, encased in the twelfth ray. This ray is New Age; see this area existing at that level. Do not see it as falling off but as being present during the New Age experience. Send it the love as spiritual chewing gum, knowing that love and harmony and the efforts of many are filling that area with this beautiful golden ray that will keep it there into the New Age experience. You may, as I said, see this ray in meditation as a part of the Earth, and see it raising the whole Earth, and specifically the California area. Jack it up; see it raised. Be creative about your meditation. Whatever you can see is helpful in bringing forth the productive Earth-consciousness associations.

The Earth does appreciate our help. The Earth has asked for those who live upon her to help her. We have her permission to so aid her. It is really a part of our own experience and we may focus by means of that. It is, then, our responsibility (as one who has been nurtured by her) to support her, to raise her up and allow this beautiful New Age to begin on this high level that is there awaiting physical existence. I say this very carefully, because the New Age already awaits on the astral plane. It is very fluid there. It moves and swirls. It is not yet fixed, as it will be within the physical, and we may utilize this fluid approach that it still has to existence to raise it to the heights, knowing that we may go as high as we choose to go with this vibration. Isn't that wonderful, that we are not restricted, that we are not limited, that we may raise the Earth to the heights by our efforts, by our desire to aid her now? Think of it, my friends. We can do it. The Hierarchy does its part. Join us now, each one of you, with the group experiencing and also with your own individual efforts. All are important. It is part of what you can do now, so do it in a consistent and specific manner — a manner of your own choosing. Do it, my friends, and do it now.

You may help to bring about this wonderful New Age experience by your visualization of it. This is very helpful. See it beginning, and be excited about it, visualizing buildings, people, experiences, energy patterns, and everything that you think will be productive for the beginning on this new level. As you do, raise it up. Envisage a specific experience and raise it up, knowing that by doing so you do help to raise the level by which the New Age is begun.

See the Earth enclosed in a golden aura, and it will become more and more familiar, more and more comfortable within that vibration. Your efforts are important and can make a true difference as we approach the New

Age, as we stand here with baited breath for it to begin. That's said in a cosmic sense, because we are right there, poised now on the edge. Give a little shove. Push the Earth up to its wonderful new level. Launch it, my friends, by means of your efforts, individually and all together, now.

✦ T W E L V E ✦

Developing Your Conceptual Abilities

MY FRIENDS, I WOULD LIKE TO DISCUSS WITH YOU NOW AN IMPORTANT tool to aid self. It is the mental-conceptual area, one we have not discussed yet in the teachings through Janet. This important area is a key that helps you, as you evolve and grow, to see the journey's end, to understand the goal and then to perceive it. It enlarges, unlocks, the understanding by means of the creative process. We have stated many times that we are cocreators in training, that we are learning the creative process, attempting to reach (and eventually we will reach it) the cocreator level, the level that unlocks the complete free-flowing state of creation. This creative ability should be utilized to help understand self — to image, if you will, the whole conceptual area and then fill it in. And I would like to give you an example here and ask you to try it.

Let us say that you are seeking to understand what existence truly is. First of all, you begin to analyze it. You say to self, I want to understand what existence is, so I will now build a framework by means of my current understanding and then, one step at a time, fill in this framework in as creative a manner as I can, recognizing that I will practice expanding this ability, seeing that I will learn much by this attempt, utilizing and stretching my abilities in each specific focus.

All right, let's begin to do that. What is existence? You may say to self, "Well, I already know that it is what I am experiencing." All right, we've put up part of our framework there. You then ask self, "What else do I know about what existence is?" You say, "Well, I know that I am here on the Earth." So, you can add to it: "It is what I am experiencing here on the Earth." You then ask, "What else do I know about existence?" And you may say to self, "I understand that Divinity has created it." And so you add that to your framework, to your outline of understanding.

Let's stop right there. Let's say that this is what you understand about existence, and now you are going to fill it in as creatively as possible. You've outlined it. Although we could, of course, continue in this area, in our example we will use these three points as an outline. You have related it to self first. Second, you have related it to the Earth. And in your third point you have related it to the Creator. So you now add those three focuses to your understanding, don't you? You enlarge what you've understood and build another layer of understanding into your outline.

Now, you can take each one of these areas and enlarge it continually. You can look at self and experiencing and seek to relate and interrelate self to the Earth and to Divinity. That brings another layer of understanding. Do you see the direct connection between self, the Earth and Divinity? Do you, my friends? What are we saying here? Perhaps that all existence that has been created by the Creator is for the purpose of Divinity's experiencing — that you are Divinity, that the Earth is Divinity? And all three are experiencing on different levels of existence. Thus we have said and learned that existence is for the purpose of experiencing. But what experience? It is, of course, Divinity's experience.

So, truly, in our outline that we have filled in, we have learned that existence is for the purpose of Divinity's experiencing — that it expands evermore so that Divinity may continue Its experiencing, Its expanding, on many levels and perhaps in many forms, or (if you wish) in a more encompassing way — for the Source Itself is a wholeness that experiences, as do Its individual parts, on every level. This is important to add to our concept — that when we have built this outline and filled it in, we have a wholeness that also is conscious and is experiencing. Do you see that by such a creative exercise you can learn to use these conceptual abilities and consciously move your perception closer to that ideal, as far as the soul-merge level in concerned? That is your goal: to perceive it. And the more you conceptualize, the more you do these conceptualizing exercises, the more perceptive will be your understanding of the whole and its various portions, and how they truly fit together.

Many of you use the analytical portion of the mental very well, but the higher mental (the creative portion of the mind) is not yet utilized by many here on the Earth. It seems to me to be very important to recognize these great abilities that will allow each of you to see the wholeness. There truly is no other way to understand wholeness. Such understanding of wholeness launches you to the higher mental creative level where you must function as a cocreator. This is the level on which creation truly takes place. The spiritual level is the basic (the origination) point, but the higher mental is the level on which the cocreators do the work — the conceptualizing, the creating work.

The sooner you understand this level — the sooner you can utilize these conceptual abilities within self — the sooner, my friend, you will return to the Source, merge again within It, and become a cocreator. The creative process of the mind must be understood completely, must be gathered together completely, focused on completely and then utilized completely. But it can be done one step at a time: first, of course, recognizing that it is necessary to develop these abilities, and then seeking to do so. It is the responsibility of each of you to take that creative step, knowing that as a baby must crawl before it can walk, you must learn this. Some of you need to begin. Others of you have already begun, and you must seek to understand and creatively work more and more in line with the wholeness. That is very important because as you creatively consider the wholeness, you approach it more and more. This wholeness must be understood. You must understand your relationship to it, and if there are blocks within self to doing so, these must be worked out before the wholeness can be understood – thus the higher mental conceptual abilities utilized at the cocreator level. It is an important focus of your evolution, and one that we have not talked about much within the Foundation.

Unlocking these abilities, then, is important. Truly, my friend, if you can see yourself at the level of a cocreator, you can be there. Isn't that an interesting statement? If you can conceptualize it as a part of your present state of beingness, it will become a fact, a truth, for you. Perhaps you will have to do it in stages, but if you can go right to that goal now, conceptually, in an encompassing manner, you will at that moment be a cocreator. How about using that as a reason to unlock the conceptual abilities? How about doing it now? How about it, my friend? Isn't it a wonderful goal? Will you not begin? Will you? Get excited about it! Know it is important. Work on the higher mental conceptual abilities to aid your integrating the awarenesses and the perceptions into a wholeness.

Thank you, my friends. I appreciate your attention in this matter.

◇ T H I R T E E N ◇

Other Dimensions

MY FRIENDS, THIS IS THE THIRTEENTH LESSON IN OUR SERIES. AND PERHAPS we will discuss something a little different: exploring the various dimensions. Have you ever discussed or thought about dimensions? What are they, my friends? What is a dimension? Think about it. It is a specific in a vibratory pattern, for one thing — a specific vibration within the whole. And why is it that from a physical state, here on the Earth, we are aware only of the third dimension? It is because of the very nature of the dimensions themselves: they are a type of perception that is specific in nature, and you cannot see into another when you are held within, for example, the third dimension. A barrier exists there that does not allow you to see beyond the specific one in which you stand. Now, this is as true within the other levels of existence as it is on the physical plane, the difference being that you know how, on the other levels, to enter various other-dimensional experiences. You, here on the physical Earth, do not. But if you did, what would you find? First of all you would find that there are parallel Earths — that there are other Earths very similar to yours except that they lie within a different dimension (a different focus, a different "specific" as far as the kind of energy, the focus of energy, is concerned).

To understand why this is true, consider standing under a spotlight on a stage. It is lit up where you are. You are standing there in the light and if you attempt to look out beyond the focused spot in which you are standing, it is dark out there and you can't see beyond it. Now, you may be able to make out the general outline of what is there, but you can't see any specifics. And that is also true as you stand here "spotlighted" in the third dimension. You can get a hint of what is out there, but you can't get any specifics.

What do I mean by a "hint"? Well, there are indications of what exists in other dimensions. There are several such indications: there are items, physical items, that make their way through the barrier of this dimension and thus come suddenly into this dimensional experience (much to the surprise of those who are in the vicinity, sometimes). Also, there are specific points where you may enter the other dimension (sometimes very much to your surprise, my friend). Why is this? Well, in this other dimension the Earth will be experienced in a very similar but not exactly the same pattern, and the evolution for those who exist there may be somewhat different. There may be specific basic differences that cause them, for example, to evolve without the wheel (which for you was a basic concept, wasn't it?) or to evolve without the combustible engine. There may be other differences that cause the evolution to be somewhat different. But the Earth itself would look very similar and the people would be similar. So if you enter such a new dimensional experience by accident, you become rather confused, not recognizing the Earth but almost recognizing it. This is really more confusing than if everything were completely different – at least then you would know you were somewhere else. But sometimes, when going from one dimension to another, you become disoriented. You don't recognize that you have gone into this new dimension. Now, it is much easier to find your way in than to find your way back, and so perhaps you must continue your existence there within that physical structure, not being able to get back again. The other dimension will be receptive to you, but of course your friends and relatives and those who are familiar will not be there.

Now, what would happen if you, in this new dimension, would stumble into still another one? Well, my friends, the same thing would occur. It would be similar but not quite the same. Is there a limit to these dimensions? Well, it depends upon your interpretation of dimensions; if you define it as the entire spectrum of existence, then it has unlimited potentials and possibilities. If you define it as the one through which physical existence is currently operating, then we say that there are nine dimensional experiences. Even then, not everyone is part of the physical, but the physical in a certain sense partakes of all nine dimensions. The first two, however, are for a less evolved type of experience, and you would not find there an Earth such as we now know it. You could find one at the fourth, the fifth and the sixth dimensions, in a sense. But if you go beyond that, you really unlock another type of dimensional experience that leads you to the unlimited possibility area. In other words, it gets you beyond physical existence as we know it. Now, if you were to go from one to another gradually, you would not recognize that you were getting into a finer vibration, if you will (a little finer, perhaps, in each higher dimension). But if you were suddenly to go from the third to the sixth dimension, you would note, quite dramatically, that the Earth you viewed was different, was perhaps more evolved, or at least quite a bit different from your third-dimensional world.

The dimensions are rather interesting to study, and we are just getting started on them. I will say to you that they are a little confusing, because they have been given from different points of view at different times by different teachers. I am giving you the complete picture of dimensions, including physical dimensions. And in a sense, this is a different focus than is usually given. Usually, when they talk of dimensions they maintain a package of about nine, and the third dimension is the physical dimension, the others being progressively less. But I am dividing all of existence into several main categories here and saying that the dimensions are contained within the whole of existence and that the physical, in various forms, is upon the third, the fourth, the fifth and the sixth dimensions. Thus, you could really, if you knew the key and how to do it, go from one to the other and still remain within your physical structure.

If we enlarged our look at existence and said that you are able to function in your astral body, you could go to four more. And in your mental body, you could go through four more. But in your spiritual body the dimensions would be unlimited. They would extend "forever," truly, as existence grows and becomes greater. Why is this? Because it is in the spiritual area, the basic area of creation, that the extensions are usually made. Now, reflected from this basic area, the extensions can be made into physical existence of various dimensional frequencies. But the basic area of expanding is always on the spiritual level first, then reflected, as I said, one by one, into the other levels of existence.

Why are the various dimensional experiences present? They are, of course, for the purpose of more learning. But they also divide consciousness and types of consciousness for specific experiences. In other words, on the physical Earth as you know it now, your soul is experiencing. You are an extension of your soul. And what is it learning now, here on the Earth? Well, the world lesson in this age is to develop the mental body. And that goes on right now in the third dimension. But what of the fourth dimension – what are they working on? There is a different type of world lesson going on at this time. Thus, a soul may experience in another dimensional experience in order to learn and grow in a different way, or develop a different aspect, you see. Also, the soul may be sent to serve in another dimension (often at the same time) for its service and its learning. This just means that existence is more complicated and yet more simple than we first perceived – that the dimensions, my friends, add more depth to our learning possibilities, make potentially more experiences available to us. There are uncounted numbers of evolving consciousnesses connected with the Earth. And part of those that have learned and gone beyond and left the Earth already, have done so through another dimensional experience.

The hierarchic government and Sanat Kumara deal with the Earth on all of its dimensional experiences. We get involved with all of them. That does not mean that we have evolved completely through all of them. It means that at the soul level, which most of us exist in and operate from, we may enter any of these dimensions that we wish. And thus we teach in all of these experiences at once.

Sanat Kumara is growing and changing and becoming, and thus on each dimension an important initiation period is approaching. But, my friends, it isn't always the same one, and the perception of it is different. He perceives existence from a different focus, perhaps, if you view it from a different dimension, and that's kind of interesting. Sanat Kumara is able, while focused in Shamballa, to clearly perceive all of the dimensions, and if you are focused in a specific dimension, you view Sanat Kumara a certain way. It may not be, and is not, the same as he is viewed from another (adjoining) dimension, perhaps. You know, if you are an esoteric student, that he is the one who heads the spiritual effort for the Earth. But you may get, from a different focus, a completely different understanding of him. It is kind of interesting. It gives four specific points of view from which to view the Hierarchy and Sanat Kumara. That number four (a square, a foundation) also fits very well with the physical experience of which these four dimensions here partake.

Now, of course, I have just briefly summarized this and just begun to discuss it with you, but it means that you must begin to enlarge your perspective of what is, even on the physical level — that now you can see that there are four Earths evolving and growing and becoming, each one giving those who exist upon it the ability to learn and to grow from, as we have said, a specific focus. This focus is necessary; it allows you to understand precisely. That doesn't mean that you need not go beyond it eventually; of course you must. You must seek to understand from wholeness rather than a specific focus. But the way to understand wholeness is to experience many different focuses and then blend them all together. That is the purpose of the dimensions: they allow many specific focuses that are almost, but not quite, the same. Generally, they are not meant to be partaken of at the same time, and your soul is focused mainly in this third-dimensional experience. But there may be occasions when it enters another dimensional experience and focuses on that Earth, as I said earlier, for a specific learning experience.

Now, what happens when all of these souls begin to merge — when the merging takes place, and there are so many souls on soul level? Doesn't that "clog up" the system? Not at all. There is no limitation. And because the spiritual plane is certainly under divine order, you could say, it all fits in very well. The souls that finish from the various dimensions and move beyond physical existence simply move into another area for their learning experience. Some stay near the Earth to aid it but most do not. There is all of the room that is necessary, that is desired, in existence; it is ever-expanding, ever-becoming. It is never crowded. We all fit there very well.

The dimensions, then, give all of these magnificent (and I'm saying that very carefully) evolving consciousnesses the opportunity to grow and evolve and understand divinity. They are, then, looking at divinity from every conceivable focus. That's what dimensions are for, my friends.

We have talked about the physical being in four different dimensions, and we must qualify that now by saying that the sixth dimension is also the gateway or the corridor to the next four dimensions — and that includes its own. That's four, you see: six, seven, eight, and nine. And what do I mean by that? Well, I would like to say this very carefully, and then enlarge it. This "corridor," this dimension for moving about, allows you, when experiencing it, to see much more clearly into the whole. You can, then, begin to travel, to move toward that wholeness while you are experiencing a type of physical existence. It is not quite the same vibration as the third dimension. No, it is much finer. It is, you could say, the finest of the physical dimensions, and leads, when you experience it, to the seventh. Now, on the seventh dimension we begin a much broader type of experience, and this broader experience, specifically, allows one to encounter other types of existence. Think about that.

Here on the Earth, in the third dimension, you meet, pretty much, beings such as yourself. Now, if you are quite psychic, you may be able to see to the astral plane, but that is truly still a part of this dimensional experience. On the seventh dimension, however, you can begin to see the eighth and the ninth and then get in touch with the beginning of the unlimited quantity that I discussed earlier.

How is that possible? Well, the fineness of the vibration begins to break down the barrier, and it is just the beginning. Remember, we've said the sixth is the corridor leading to the seventh, and the seventh can see into the eighth somewhat; the eighth sees quite well into the ninth; and the ninth begins to see down that endless corridor of dimensional possibilities that is always expanding.

Now, this has not been taught much on the Earth. There are a few cases in which it has been. But the unlimited quality of existence is important to understand, and the ninth dimension begins that unlimitedness. Now, let us suppose you are in the ninth dimension and you are looking down that endless corridor. What do you see? Well, what you would see would be a finer and finer vibration of whatever you are experiencing. And it would seem to be mirrored there forever, but becoming more etheric as it progressed. It is probably not appropriate to view it in that manner. It could make you rather dizzy — I've done it and it is a little disorienting. But you can begin by viewing it, to conceptualize the true size of existence — that it extends forever — and you get a glimpse of this "forever" from the ninth dimension.

Dimensional viewing, as we call it, can be done, but one must be prepared for the enormity of seeing it truly as it exists, now. It is important to recognize that dimensional experience is a part of existence. And it is, again, just a specific focus within which to experience. It adds layers to experience and enables greater perception of the whole — to look, then, through the different levels, the different dimensions when you view existence from the spiritual plane.

Thank you, my friends. This is but a sample of our dimensional work, and I promise you we're going to be talking about it more and more. My love to you now.

✧ FOURTEEN ✧

A Gathering of Various Concepts

I N THIS LESSON SERIES I AM SEEKING TO TALK ABOUT A DIVERSITY OF SUBJECTS, giving some indications of areas being explored within the Foundation. I find it important to have in one place all of the areas being explored. This lesson is a means of gathering up different concepts that are being discussed and disseminated, information-wise, through the Foundation.

The subject is one that we have approached in classes and seminars in different ways. It is the following: Evolution on the Earth is for the purpose of allowing Divinity to experience at a specific vibration or frequency, if you will, which we call physical existence. We, then, as Divinity, experience here on the Earth. And I include myself because I have come through this particular type of experience also. Each of you is focused, by what I have called your totality, into physical existence for the purpose of learning and understanding personally and, of course, from the broader perspective, for the purpose of aiding all of evolution here on the Earth, all of the "pieces" of Divinity. The individual sparks together, along with the original level of Divinity which we call the Source, the Creator, make up the totality of Divinity's experiencing.

The Source (Divinity) brings forth individualized portions of Itself, which is what we are, and we experience in many ways, on many levels, in all possible types of situations for the purpose of getting to the place where each can perceive Divinity at the same level as the Source Itself. All experiencing, then, is done by Divinity, even if it is another level of Divinity, another way that Divinity has chosen to experience. This is true whether it is a beautiful flower, a beautiful rock or a crystal. These also have a piece of Divinity, if you will. It is not the same as the individualized spark that then evolves and grows and becomes. But in a certain sense it is: it is a part of the whole. It is learning and becoming and growing and evolving. It is just doing it in a different way, perceived from a different focus.

Many of you have asked me about the archangels and the angels. They are what I have termed direct extensions of Divinity. And they are not the same as you. Each one of you has a specific goal and that goal is to be a cocreator — to learn and grow and perceive, return again to the Source, merge again within It, and become a cocreator. The archangels and the angelic kingdom have specific duties which they are already doing and doing perfectly. Thus they are a direct extension of Divinity, not an evolving consciousness — there is a distinct difference. That doesn't mean, though, that they aren't learning. Why is that? Because all of Divinity, all of the divine package, if you will, is evolving and growing and becoming, and they as a part of it are learning and growing and becoming, also. The difference, my friends, is that they have no choice, no free will, here. They are for a specific purpose within the Cosmic Plan, and they already do it perfectly.

Now, the reason, in my understanding at least, that the Creator has allowed His divine sparks, His evolving consciousness, to have free will, is that ultimately this will make them equal to Him — to the Source Itself. It strengthens Divinity to allow them to choose, to evolve in their own way, to make their own choices and to then experience as a result of these choices.

Now, one of the most "interesting" choices that we make is to come to physical existence. And this really is what I wish to discuss now. In a physical situation, the vibration is different from the higher level. This doesn't mean that it has to be experienced traumatically or painfully, but we usually choose to so experience it. Many of us feel a little put out by the need to experience it at all; we would rather be experiencing on the spiritual plane. And when our souls choose to come to the Earth (as they do, my friends), sometimes they comes not as much from choice as from knowing that it is appropriate in the service area; from a need, then, to fulfill their commitment, and not from the desire to experience physical existence.

Now, that is not always true. We have some souls that are delighted to come to physical existence. And, truly, there are enough of these that there really is a "waiting list" to come to Earth, there truly is. But each evolving consciousness' unique abilities and strengths are taken into consideration when the Earth assignment is made. Some are more suited for it than others. And this is the basis for how each one is chosen — if they have developed the suitable abilities; because, of course, each evolving consciousness basically has everything within self. Some have developed some of these characteristics more than others, however. Thus is the choice made. And there are many others that would like to come into physical existence.

Why is that? It is, of course, because they recognize the opportunities here. Some may consider it a service opportunity. Yes, it's true that in physical existence the service opportunities will be greater than on other levels, and that's an interesting point of view. I've never shared it, but I know that this is considered by some to be true. Then there are those who feel their evolution will be aided by a trip through the Earth school. And this, my friends, I do feel is true. Now, mostly because of the point of evolution that the Earth has been in, humanity experiences Earth living rather painfully, so many souls have not wished to get involved in all of that pain. After the New Age begins, I'm very hopeful that most of this will be negated. At least, after the New Age gets a good start, then it really will begin to dissipate – less and less pain, more and more joyful learning experience. The Earth, this school of learning, is interesting.

Once most evolving consciousnesses get involved with physical exist-ence, they feel a little cut off, a little shut out of most of the levels of experiencing. There are exceptions, of course, but because of what they have experienced in the past, most do believe that physical existence cuts you off, shuts you out, alienates you from the spiritual area.

In our work within the belief structure, we are clearing out this misconception, because, my friends (and this is the purpose of this teaching), Earth living is so special, such a wonderful opportunity. It gives you the chance, while focused in a physical environment, to see all of creation aligned, from a physical point of view. It is a wonderful opportunity. You can feel the alignment, you can see the alignment, you can realize the alignment, you can enjoy the alignment, you can experience the alignment when you allow self to do so, when you can perceive it. And it is a very special focus, one that is different from the other levels. It is, my friends, more intense when you can allow it to come into being. I have experienced this: I know what I am talking about. It is wonderful. It is far from being a painful experience. It is one of the most exhilarating and beautiful experiences possible – to see all of creation while focused in a physical environment. It is awe-inspiring. It lets you see it from the framework, from the foundation, from the bottom up. It's wonderful. It can be a little awesome, but when you can align your understanding, when you can conceptualize what it is from this point, my friends, you can conceptualize and realize it from any other point there is. Isn't that interesting! It's true. It's why it is such an important experience, and a key to evolution. Once you've unlocked it, it is the key to understanding more and more completely what existence is in its totality.

I'm not saying that after you leave physical existence you understand everything and go right to the cocreator state. I'm saying that once you see the alignment, the total existence, the totality of what the Creator has wrought, from a physical point, it changes you completely. You will never again be the same. You will never again be as narrow in your concepts. You will be much more encompassing in your understanding, much more able to perceive existence as it truly is. How wonderful! It opens the door, my friends, to the totality of existence.

How, then, do you begin to perceive all of existence from an Earth point of view? First of all, you work on not perceiving it as being alienated, as being separated. You begin to take out the blocks within self that make you feel separated from other levels of existence; then meditating on existence, on what it truly is, will help. Perhaps you can take a walk, and as you walk along, think about Earth living. Think about what it is. I am not talking of thinking in a mundane, everyday way – although that's all right, too. I'm talking about the experience of being here on the Earth. You know that it is a learning experience. You know that you have different types of relationships that allow you to learn. You know that basically you are learning to understand self, and that mirrored into your environment now are those areas that you need to look at in order to understand self more completely. You know, then, that you are getting to learn from the Earth experience. You know that you are divine. You know that everyone else is divine.

Why do you feel cut off from other levels of divinity? Why do those within a physical environment feel and believe and think and deduce that there is nothing else but the physical? The scientific community has been enlarging its scope a little. They are getting some interesting effects and are trying to decide what is happening there. Why are they getting these effects? They don't really have, within the physical universe, the answer, so they are beginning to go beyond the physical universe to seek these answers.

Oh! Are we saying, then, that the effects that we call physical existence have causes or correspondence on other levels? Imagine that! That when we look at Earth living we are truly seeing a reflection of other levels? Do you think that we could use these effects that we see, to then see other areas? You know, on the spiritual evaluations I have been doing it the other way around; I've been giving people spiritual experiences and then relating them to Earth experiences. How about, now, as you are taking a nice walk, you look at the physical experiences and say, "Yes, I know these physical experiences – these effects – are there, and I understand that Earth living (physical existence) is a reflection of a higher level of experience. So maybe I'll think about it. Maybe I'll conceptualize this area on Earth and let it help me realize the spiritual experience – that I truly am not cut off, not at all. I am simply experiencing a reflection of the other level." That's kind of fun, isn't it? Kind of an interesting way to approach it.

Within a relationship, that ought to be interesting. If you have a one-to-one relationship that you are working on (many of you have these), what is being reflected? What is the experience on the spiritual level? Interesting! Perhaps (this is very basic within all of you) the relationship that you are working on on the spiritual level is between you and the Source Itself. Oh? How interesting! Do you love your partner here on the physical plane? But does your relationship partner sometimes not perceive life exactly as you do? You can't really communicate all of your feelings? You can't make him or her understand your needs, or perhaps those needs don't exactly fit in with yours, or anyway there is not yet a complete communication, a complete free-flowingness within the relationship? Do you think this is saying, my friends, that on the spiritual plane you are still seeking to understand your relationship with the Source? That you're still seeking to get the communication going, completely, in a free-flowing manner, to understand how your own needs, wants and desires fit into the package of the relationship between you and the Creator? My goodness, isn't that an interesting concept: think about it. Reflect up, then, your experiences from the Earth plane to the spiritual area. This is a lot of fun and it helps you to see that you aren't cut off from anything.

You are a part, an important part, a really (if you want to use this word) critical part of existence. You have a wonderful opportunity now to see the true alignment, to perceive the part that physical existence plays in the totality of existence — to analyze it, to see the framework of the totality of existence in a conceptual way, and then fit physical existence into its proper slot. You must see that it isn't the only kind of existence, as some people think it is, and neither does it "cut you off" from the totality. You have to, as I said earlier, put it in its proper slot, its proper perspective with the whole. And to do that, you must consider it from every angle, from every focus that you can conceptualize.

This is an excellent class topic. Look at the totality of existence. Write down as many levels as you know of, and see how physical existence fits into this totality. Look at it, conceptualize it, understand it, merge it. Merge it? Oh, do you think that is what you are doing now, at this critical point in your evolution? You are merging physical existence into the totality of existence? Oh, how interesting! Yes, how interesting.

This is what I have for this lesson. Thank you very much for your attention, my friends.

✧ FIFTEEN ✧

Evolution – Our Loop of Experiencing

MY FRIENDS, I WOULD LIKE NOW TO DISCUSS QUITE AN IMPORTANT subject. Let's begin at what one might call a specific point, a beginning on a new level, and then lead gradually to the point that I am trying to make.

We begin by stating again that evolution truly is for the purpose of more evolution – of learning, of becoming, of always advancing – and that Divinity and Its experiencing, truly, is all that exists. I have said this in many ways at many times, and I will continue to reiterate it – that only Divinity exists, that there is only Divinity – whether we consider It the Source Itself (that all-knowingness that permeates all of existence) or the individualized portions of It, such as each of us.

We come forth. We are individualized. And we begin our experiencing mode. And it truly is a privilege to be brought forth, to be allowed this individualization. Most sparks such as self, such as each of you, do appreciate it, but there are a few that hold on to the Source and wish to return to It. Now, as we experience, we do encounter specific points in our evolution where it would be rather easy to slide again into the Source. We would like to do it. We yearn to do it. It seems appropriate to do it. However, we are not ready. We have not yet completed our "loop of experiencing." Thus, the Source will not permit us to slide in, although sometimes we get close, sometimes our attunement gets so complete that we feel we can do so.

At such times our consciousness becomes so aligned with the Source Itself that magnificent things begin to happen. We attract, magnetically, those that serve the Creator – those direct extensions of the Creator that we call the angelic kingdom. They do not see, perhaps, certain items as clearly as do evolving consciousnesses. So when they look and see one that is aligned with the Source, even if briefly, they see not whether it is permanent; they see only such alignment. Thus we have stories of the host of angels singing the praises of specific individuals in biblical history. This was during a specific period in which that evolving consciousness was truly again aligned with the Source Itself. They see not (they being the angelic kingdom) that it is but an attempt and probably will not continue in exactly that same alignment for long. It will, then, be necessary for that particular evolving consciousness to disconnect a little from the Source, enough to be a part of existence again as an individual. You see, as individuals, as individualized sparks, we do not permit self this complete alignment with the Source until we truly are ready to go again within It.

Now, that's important to understand. We may make the attempt and be successful for brief periods. We then must disconnect a little to continue our journey through the loop of experiencing. What am I saying here? That it is not appropriate to yearn for the Source, to seek it? Not at all. What I am telling you is that you keep trying to do so and that there are going to be periods with each of you when you succeed. But then because you probably are not yet experienced enough, you will break that intense attunement (somewhat, anyway) and continue your evolution.

When the Source becomes so magnetic to you (because you, my friend, have evolved to the point that you are the same as the Source), the attunement, the alignment, the attraction will be so great that you will be drawn right into It again. It is truly very interesting to watch evolving consciousnesses as they align temporarily with the Source. All of creation seems to celebrate. All of creation seems to align with them. At those periods, they truly are capable of creating on almost the same level as the Source.

Now, that's very interesting and perhaps should be handled very carefully. If one is really not yet ready to handle creating at that level, perhaps it is important to recognize that one must understand one's own point in evolution — one must know whether or not one is ready for this completeness, for this wholeness. We as evolving consciousnesses have the responsibility to remove all illusion about self; to know where we are on the path; to recognize what yet must be learned by self; to understand that as a responsible piece of Divinity one goes forward but only within one's own framework of understanding.

Of course, as we have said many, many times, service is the point of seeking one's evolution, and seeking to aid the Creator's Cosmic Plan is why one should be ready to change, to grow, to become, to evolve, to understand ever more completely. Truly it is. When evolution is approached with such an understanding, one sees perhaps that his service is hinged to his evolution.

Let me give you an example. A member of the Hierarchy who is currently functioning at soul level, but is about ready to break through to the next level, which we call the monadic level — this great one (for he certainly is) made such a perfect attunement to the Source. It was a glorious time. All creation celebrated. All looked on. All said, "Wonderful! Here is another great one that is merging back to the Source." Now, my friends, this event requires great balance. You might say, "What's the matter with wishing for it to come about right then? It would probably happen, wouldn't it?" Good. Wonderful. Well, it could have, that's true. It could have. And this great one certainly sought it, certainly wanted to be a part of the Source again. But what happened was this, and this is why it is important to know what to expect, because then when it happens to you (and it will, my friends, it will) you will know what to look for. Look for that next step. And if it is not there, then know that this is but a temporary connection and will require more effort, more experiencing, to make it permanent — but look for that permanent connection as you go into it. This is why this lesson is being given.

Those who exist upon the physical plane also may experience this alignment. It is more rare, but then, the soul-merge condition is more rare, and once one gets very close to this state — and some of you are beginning to do so — then you may begin to have such alignment. I need, then, to discuss with you what is happening, make you aware of it. If you approach this state, look for the following (if it is there, marvelous). You will be within the Source permanently from that point on because that permanent connection will be made, will hook you up there as a cocreator. If you cannot find that specific connection, then, my friend, enjoy the experience. Remember it and treasure it and know it will come again — and perhaps then the permanent connection will be made.

Now, not having merged myself back into the Source yet, I am giving my perception of this process, having discussed it with a number of cocreators and being assured that what I perceive and what I am presenting are basically correct.

First of all, as this state begins to occur, there will be great light within self. Everything will be perceived as light. All of your yearning, all of your needs, all of what you wish, will be for more light, for greater service, for greater unfoldment of the Creator's Cosmic Plan. Light will permeate everywhere. Know that this is true; and as this intense light becomes a part of you, whatever level you are perceiving it from, know that you are aligning with the Source. This great light is you focused directly into the Source — connected directly to It. Now, this will become more and more intense over a period of several days (I wouldn't even look for this if it just happens to you for a moment or two, though some of you may begin to get this). As that light gets brighter and brighter and brighter, and everyone notices your bright light, after a week or two, sit down with self and begin to explore that light. Go into it as completely as possible.

Now look before you. There are seven steps within that light. There is more light beckoning to you. Go toward those steps and begin to scale them (and that's the word, "scale"). With each step the light becomes brighter. You begin to feel the light as permeating self completely. No longer are there any separate needs, separate thoughts (this is hard to put into words because the individuality is maintained but all thoughts of separateness are let go of). At the first step you should still be pretty much as you are when you begin. By the seventh, all separateness is gone, and a specific anchoring process is available as you stand on that seventh step.

This anchoring process, I am told, is unmistakable, and you will know beyond a shadow of a doubt that you are home, that this is your destiny, that you can create whatever is needed for the Creator, that all is possible, that all is necessary, that all is, and that you are. You see, you will stand there on that specific focus within the Source, and the Source Itself will acknowledge your presence, welcome you home, and there will be a specific sense of familiarity. And you will know beyond any doubt that never again will you go forth.

Now, as I said, my friends, the possibility of experiencing this while focused within the Earth focus, if you will, is not too great; it really is rather remote. But these temporary focuses within a physical existence are very possible. And as you experience an alignment with the Source Itself, you should begin to recognize the possibility of being anchored within It. Go forth, then, into the experience. Explore the Source Itself. Allow that that possibility may come for you. It is true that you must not go into it in a state of illusion, a state of imagination — for one can imagine that these things are occurring when they truly are not. So complete knowingness of your own point of evolution, complete knowingness of your reason for seeking such a connection, is important. Know who you are. You are divinity, that is true. How perceptive are you in your experiencing! This you must completely understand. Because you are focused within a physical personality, it is difficult to see self clearly. But as the soul-merge takes place, you will be in a much more perceptive state. So utilize the soul level to know that you will be able to discern your own evolution and to see clearly what is taking place as you begin these wonderful alignments with the Source Itself. They are given to us, it seems to me, as a point at which we can realize what lies ahead for us, to show us what is there, to teach us that we may unfold completely — that we may know and go beyond the current understanding.

I say to each of you, enjoy them, but recognize that for most of you there will be a long series of such alignments before the permanent merging again with the Source.

This, my friends, is how evolution generally works — one step at a time, beginning to approach the next level in a periodic alignment and then seeking to make that alignment permanent. The Source-merging, then, is our ultimate goal as far as we know. There may be much beyond it — in fact, I am sure that there is — but as far as our individual loop of experiencing is concerned, this is the ultimate goal. For some of you, this is remote from your Earth perspective. For others it is what you yearn for more than anything else. But know that you will begin the approach in specific attunement – that you will have a glimpse of it long before the actual event. And as one who has experienced such alignment, I cannot put into words the beauty of the experience.

"Go forth, then, little spark, and experience," the Source says. "But once in a while, come home for a visit and then go forth and continue your experiencing." Home is there waiting. She has (notice the "She") a candle in the window and awaits our return.

Thank you, my friends, and my love to each of you.

✧ SIXTEEN ✧

The Input of Higher Consciousness

I WISH TO BRING INTO CONSIDERATION NOW THE ACCEPTANCE OF THE INPUT of higher consciousness. Know first that all of life is the expression of a divine Source, a loving Creator. In His desire to express and to give of Himself, He has created more and more of and from Himself. In the beginning, we (as Source expressions) expressed at a very fine level of creation. Later, in the eons of time, the expression moved downward, if you will, into another layer or step in consciousness – His consciousness moving into involvement. As we experienced the Creator at different levels of beingness, we probed ever deeper (involved ourselves), wishing to understand ever more experience – going into slower and slower vibrations and finally arriving at the physical level.

At this point the Creator stimulated a desire to have His creations return to Him all that they had acquired. It was as if the prodigal son had gone forth from the Father's home, from the Kingdom in Heaven (as stated in some of the religious writings), and now that the prodigal son had "tasted," had experienced, had lived apart (in his own perception), the desire was stimulated within this creation – this expression, this focus of divinity – to seek something which he knew not. He had forgotten! And now the dim memory was being stirred within his being. Faintly, he remembered. Faintly, he sought to open his vision and to allow the impetus to pull him forward. This time the seeking was for higher and clearer and more complete awareness. Having involved, his desire was to evolve and return to his original state.

This spiritual seeking has been recognized by many. To those who have reached this stage of yearning to return, there is a period of not knowing where to go or how to unfold their spiritual growth, their spiritual direction and evolution.

You may recognize that, in a state of meditation, much input comes to the individual. He receives inspiration, direction, comfort, strength – much of what he needs to function in the physical world, as well as to make progress on the spiritual path. Meditation, then, is a means of opening one's self to the input of higher consciousness. This input can come from various directions, if you please, but it is all spiritual input. You may think of it as the input of your higher self – of your soul. The soul, at this point, has seen the flickering of light within the physical entity. The light is flickering, and the "note" is going forth. There is a recognition now, and the soul responds with joy at this point. In the state of meditation one contacts the soul; the soul comes from the spiritual realms and the individual entity meets it in its desire to know itself.

This truly, my friends, is what the yearning is about – knowing one's self, knowing one's self more completely, and finally knowing one's self in the totality, as the totality.

The soul instructs, and gradually the spiritual body grows in brilliance, grows in responsiveness, and is able to respond to more and more input from the spiritual realms. The spiritual body glows ever brighter, and the spiritual teachers recognize the call for assistance. The individual at this point (and, my friends, most of you recognize this development and are at this point now) earnestly seeks assistance and direction and inspiration. The response of the spiritual teachers is simultaneous with the opening that the individual has created with his desire for spiritual unfoldment – with his desire for spiritual awakening and with his desire to be part of the Creator's Cosmic Plan, to partake in the Creator's Cosmic Plan, to add his own beingness to the all-beingness, to the expansion of creation.

This desire eventually must express as a desire to serve, for that is the epitome of desire: to serve the Creator. At this point the seeker, the partially awakened one, is full of questions, seeking answers: "How can I become greater, that my participation may be greater? Where can I get the input necessary to unfold to a point where I am flowing and knowing my purposes and the direction they must express in my physical existence?"

Having created a means of communication through this sincere desire, the contact is made, and the seeker now is aware of the spiritual assistance available to him, that he may move forward quickly in his development. He is given inspiration, and his attunement to this inspiration and to this contact becomes finer and finer until finally he recognizes that this is so.

The input now can become clearer and more definite as the seeker becomes more balanced, more focused in his objective. He becomes balanced, he becomes aligned with the spiritual will, and thus he is able to attract to himself the help that he requires. His attunement with the wholeness will determine the extent to which he can receive.

In the Tibetan Foundation we emphasize that it is necessary to clear the spiritual channel that allows the spiritual input. The channel must be cleared of blocks (false beliefs that have impeded clear perception and the ability to receive fully and move forward easily to one's goal). Therefore the subconscious must be reeducated. The subconscious has been a faithful servant, giving back to the person that which he has impressed upon it, but now (in his evolving awareness) he knows that certain areas must become cleared in order to allow the free-flowingness that will take him to his heights. He begins to recognize the blocked areas — the false beliefs that must be removed from the subconscious.

A spiritual teacher appears to assist one in recognizing the blocks, and the difficult process of removing the obstacles begins. Slowly at first, and sometimes painfully, the blocks are forcibly removed. As you work in the false-belief-removal system, this becomes more acceptable and you are able to release these blocks. You recognize more and more that they are impeding the progress to your true desire — to your true goal. The aspirant becomes ever more anxious to clear, that he may become ever more open to receive, ever more able to give and to serve. At this point the blocks are being recognized and removed, and the flow is easier.

So, my friends, you have arrived at a point of awareness where the input has become acceptable and recognizable and useable. The desire, at this point of development, leads you to more and more contact with your soul, and to contact with your spiritual teacher. You are working at this time more freely, and the soul is able to express more easily. The blocked areas are being cleared, allowing more and more the soul expression, more and more the input and assistance of the spiritual teacher.

Soon there will be the merging, the allowing, the uniting of the lower self with the higher self; then the communication will be instantaneous, and there will be a knowingness and a free-flowingness.

As you seek to purify self, to refine self, to balance the four bodies, to be in tune, the input that you need will be available to you and you will be able to receive it. Your spiritual teachers are assisting you and you are becoming receptive and responsive. Your desire to serve finds a means of expression on the physical level and you begin to serve in an ever-expanding manner, thus allowing more of the input to express in you, to be received and given forth.

My friends, make of yourself a receptive vehicle, that you now may receive that which you desire — the assistance that you desire, and the merging with your true self.

✧ S E V E N T E E N ✧

Opening to Expanded
Perceptions in Consciousness

W E SHALL NOW CONTINUE THIS SERIES BY BRINGING INTO CONSIDERATION the process of going into new states of awareness, of bringing into consciousness new perceptions.

This is a breaking-ground process, if you will, and brings with it, in the beginning, the realization that here is something unfamiliar and perhaps destabilizing. Know that this merge of spirit and matter cannot be comprehended through the logical process and therefore it requires an extremely fine balance and a willingness to accept this unfamiliar representation. One must continue to function within the physical structure and utilize the mental equipment (the brain and the nervous system) and the senses, which receive the input. Senses are accustomed to receiving in a certain manner and must now become sensitized to a point where the spiritual input is recognized. (The physical, in a sense, is allowing the spiritual input to come into being and to express in this "vehicle"). The individual seems to be reaching into spiritual ground with the spiritual property itself. The development of the spiritual vibration within has, up to this time, been developing within the physical structure (which knows not that it is reaching for the spiritual counterpart).

The spiritual body has been nourished and encouraged and allowed to develop until it has reached a measure of maturity where it can now reach out into the unfamiliar areas of spiritual beingness. Spirit responds to the spirit "within," and the "bridge" is completed, allowing the communication to flow freely. There can now begin an interchange, for the lines of communication have been established within the individual. Spirit responds in an ever-greater manner, and the contact becomes more familiar.

Spirit is able to utilize the physical entity. It enters and becomes a benign influence in the life of the individual. It is as if a part of him were being recognized, and he allows the transformation to take place — seeking always to make the spiritual contact more binding, more complete, more at one. This, my friends, is the purpose of being: to make this contact with the spiritual essence of one's self, to grow and reach out to the point where one realizes the extent of his beingness. Reaching out, the unfamiliar becomes familiar and dear. He recognizes the totality of his being and grows ever greater as he seeks and allows this expansion to take place. The connection has been made, the merging has been accomplished, and now, freely, the expansiveness begins.

At first, this too is difficult to recognize in totality, and one reaches out and expands, and reaches out and expands, until he becomes, in his awareness, totality itself. He becomes the wholeness which he has been seeking. The completion has taken place, and now the physical being demonstrates the spirituality within (the spirituality within now generating an impetus). The old ways — the confining, limiting concepts — have dropped away to allow room for this new, indwelling spiritual expression. Now the old limiting concepts must, and do, give way to the all-encompassing spiritual oneness.

The truth of his being is known, and demonstrates in all areas of action, all areas of thought, all areas of performance. Once more has this spiritual transformation taken place, and the spirit is now the prime mover in the individual's life — spirit, ever wishing to serve the Creator completely, in line with divine will. This impetus to serve now becomes the undeniable motivation of the transformed physical entity. The union with the spiritual self must express itself in serving the Creator, and the individual allows the spirit to become the motivating factor of his existence.

He has, at this point, allowed self to move with divine will. His will is aligned with the will of the Creator, and he permits this to flower in every aspect of his being. He becomes a receptacle and a conveyor of the spirit within, and the spirit within exerts its influence on those who come into contact with this spiritualized being. Filled with humility at the developments that have taken place within him, he acknowledges that it is now divinity, and not the ego, that is the attracting and influencing power, shall we say. The magnetic quality continues to grow as the dedication of self and the spiritual growth continue to take place. The influence of this magnetized, spiritualized individual cannot be denied. He is now able to be of greater and greater assistance and usefulness to the Creator through his physical position. As he serves and as he gives, this ability grows quickly, and he can thus serve in an ever-expanding way.

My friends, is it not exciting to recognize the spiritual potential and usefulness within? Strive always to make this into your own personal realization. Look diligently at removing all that stands in the way of this culmination of your desires. Learn to become ever more aware of that which interferes with this goal. See in self those areas that are blocking your fullest expression. Use any method to bring the subconscious into alignment with your new spiritual aspirations. Instruct the subconscious that it is to remove the hindering blocks — that it truly can serve in an expanded, clearer fashion also.

Recognize that the subconscious wishes to comply with its master's (shall we say) direction. We can refer to the conscious mind as the master of the subconscious, just as we can refer to the higher self, or soul body, as the master of the physical expression. Thus we see there is always a hierarchy within self and within the cosmos — the entire cosmos being governed by this principle of a higher governing consciousness.

The Cosmic Plan, my friends, is evolution! There is always a progression into something finer, something greater, something more in alignment with a greater quality. The need to express at the higher level, thus, is a divine need within all that exists! All that exists strives to become greater, for that is the will of the Creator Itself! Recognize, then, the urges to become greater as coming from the will of the Creator — the will to move forward, to become greater and to express in a greater and greater manner.

The fullness of the Creator is unlimited, my friends. Is this not an exciting prospect! The Creator is complete. The Creator is allness and wholeness. Yet the principle itself must govern all that is, and therefore all that is is ever-expanding. Let your mind move into this concept, and let this concept itself expand the consciousness. Let your consciousness move into allness. Let your consciousness become that which it is. Be allness, now, my friends. Know that you are limitless — that your potentialities are limitless — and move forward now and express your potentialities in greater and greater fashion.

Expand, my friends. Expand.

✧ E I G H T E E N ✧

Expansion into Your Divinity

I WISH YOU TO REALIZE THAT WE ARE MOVING ALONG, STEP BY STEP, INTO greater consciousness – into higher realization. The entire process is an unfolding one wherein one moves, bit by bit, piece by piece, adding on, growing and stretching into the allness, into the wholeness.

Now we will continue this expansion by considering the limitlessness of possibilities – the unlimited possibilities as perceived by each unique focus of creation. In other words, you (as a unique focus of creation) have infinite possibilities, infinite creativity focused from within your own unique perception.

By "allowing" each point of consciousness within His consciousness, the Creator can expand infinitely. Each particular point of consciousness, by going within to its point of origin, reaches the realization that its source, its reality, is divinity itself. As divinity, each of us has the freedom of expression, the freedom to be creative and to expand into the greatness which we can perceive from this original focus point.

My friends, in a state of meditation let us move back through our own "lineage," through our own development, until we come to this realization of divinity within self. Realizing the divinity makes possible expansion into divinity, expansion into allness.

Having realized the source of our being, knowing that it is incorporated (brought into fleshly consciousness), we can each do the work of the "Father" in our own unique, beautiful way. Maintaining the high level of awareness at all times is the secret of moving freely without limitation at all levels of being. Functioning from this point of awareness allows the divinity within to direct one's life and one's actions at all times. It allows the physical expression of divinity!

Would you not like the physical expression to be perfectly at ease at all times – to move freely and graciously, with energy, with strength, with freedom from limitation? This is possible when the knowledge that the physical body is a divine expression is fully realized. Then one is able to do for the physical that which is appropriate as a vehicle for and of divinity. You may wish to use a "divine yardstick" to measure how completely you are allowing divinity to express through the physical.

Then, considering the emotional body, or the emotional aspect of this focus of divinity (yourself), and knowing that divinity is always expressed in the most balanced, loving manner, one can gauge his own emotional reaction or response at any given moment, in any given situation, to determine how much of divinity is being allowed to express in this particular "outlet." If one is focused in divinity, it is literally impossible to react to situations in an unfavorable, nonproductive, reactionary mode. Being centered in divinity means being centered and controlled. Apply the same test now to the mental body. Maintaining the high state of awareness at all times that the mind of God (Divinity Itself) expresses as individual mind – as a point of consciousness and awareness within self – one's mental processes become attuned to the inflow of divine ideas. Divine mind expresses through him, and his mental processes are orderly, logical, intuitive, creative. This is truly "embodying" the principle of infinite intelligence.

My friends, at this point let me bring to your attention the fact that by maintaining this high spiritual "posture" of being in the divine flow, one automatically functions from this position. One has transmuted and lifted up the lower triad, bringing about the merging into the higher triad (the spiritual) and creating in the process a unified, integrated, complete being – completing the original pattern formulated by the Creator: the unique, beautiful point of expression which is His desire. The fragmented and divisive part has been reclaimed and now shines in its own completeness.

This return to the divine state is not a magical process but one of greater and greater realization of the truth of one's own being. As one becomes ever more cognizant of his rightful and complete wholeness, he is ever watchful of self, recognizing the areas of incompleteness and disharmony. He moves forward through realization of each area that contains a blockage to the free-flowingness of divine expression. Each area that inhibits this is scrutinized and recognized, and the necessary removal takes place. Work on self, my friends, until your perception of divinity becomes so clear, so bright, that it overshadows and becomes itself in you!

The Creator's love is the pinnacle of realization. The Creator's love is that which in the beginning sent us forth from Itself. Wishing to expand love ever more creatively, He created the limitless loving points of His own expression, sending them forth to experience, to grow and to embellish that which they were. The experiences of living must be brought into alignment with this divine purpose, this expression of love itself. Living love, then, is expressing the Creator's purpose and your own individual divine purpose.

Analyze your own concept of love and it will reveal to you your true thoughts of divinity. How do you view self? Do you withhold love from self – love of self? Do you withhold love from others? This, my friends (and ponder this well!) means that your perception of God is that His love is not inclusive, does not reach out to include all – for are you not part of all? If this is your perception of self, then recognize that you have put up a screen – a blind – blocking your own true beliefs about divinity. When there is condemnation and nonacceptance of self, what you are doing is avoiding the realization that your criticism is aimed not at self but at the Creator! In your own belief structure, you are not perceiving the Creator perfectly; your concept of the Creator is not whole; you are not "seeing aright." Therefore, in your avoidance of acknowledging your beliefs about the Creator – knowing the Creator – you have imposed these beliefs on your concept of self, not wishing to stir up the sense of guilt that acknowledgment would bring to surface.

My friends, probe deeply. Acknowledge each awareness that comes to the surface. Carry it to its point of beginning. Carry it all the way to its source. Unfold each step of awareness until you reach the Source Itself. Know the Source for what It is, and your self-condemnation will disappear. You will view self in the light of the Creator's eye. You will know the Creator through the "single eye" – seeing the perfection, the all-lovingness, the all-knowingness, the limitless potentialities of the creative process. Remove condemnation, criticism and judgment at all levels of your being, and the truth of divinity shall set you free free to be that which you have denied: your own acceptability, your own divinity.

✦ N I N E T E E N ✦

Moving Forward into Spiritual Awareness

WHAT, THEN, SHALL WE CONSIDER NEXT IN OUR JOURNEY ON THIS evolutionary path to perfection? My friends, you are immersed in spirit; you are supported by spirit; you are known by spirit; and your spirituality now comes forth in its own recognition of self. My, doesn't that sound like a roundabout way of saying that all is divinity? We have been saying this in numerous ways: We have said it gently, we have said it forcefully, we have said it intellectually, and we have said it with feeling. We'll continue to say it in as many ways as necessary for the student to hear!

The ears are both outer and inner, and the esoteric ear must be quickened to the point where it responds to the intuitive message that comes to it. The inner eye must be opened to respond to the inner light that comes to it now. And the totality of being must be integrated into one responsive unit of beingness.

Do you recognize the goal? "The goal is the same as the path," we have been told in esoteric literature. You are the path, and this knowingness must unfold and grow as you become a wider path, as you hack away the growth that has been allowed to take root and see the light ahead. You are the light and the pathfinder for those who follow after you.

The recognition of your own beingness is known as the soul-merge. When one truly recognizes this truth of self, the soul is able to say, "Aha! Finally the message is reaching. Finally he/she is getting it." Now, getting the message is not a simple matter, because for eons we have functioned in erroneous zones of thinking and acting — building layer upon layer of unclear perceptions of self. Now, in its effort to uncover these layers, self encounters the resistance of the false beliefs, and these must be perceived and removed, that the divinity within may once more proclaim its dominance — its presence and its ascension.

Divinity knows itself at all times. My friends, when you know self, you will know that you are divinity and that there is no "other." You have been functioning on the erroneous assumption that you are other – that you are a persona, a mask, a division, an otherness known by a particular name, a particular role that you are playing, and that you must respond in certain set patterns of thinking and experiencing.

What do your experiences tell you now? Examine your experiences in life and they will bring to you the needed work areas, that you may be free of the cyclic effects of experiencing over and over. Recognize the blocked areas and be done with them! Remove them so that the freedom can come forth and the evolution into spiritual reality can be your new level of experiencing. You will know this is accomplished when life flows in perfect harmony – when there is no resistance within you. All will be moving as one – your physical, emotional and mental bodies will know their true spirituality, and the merged condition will be you.

Now, what I am trying to do is to prod you, my friends, to do all that your unfolding intuition is revealing. Do whatever is necessary to bring you to your highest aspirations. Complacency is no longer appropriate, for the "divine unrest" has been stirred within self, and one must respond now to this inner urging. Recognize the dissatisfaction of self and the need to transform into your ideal.

Do it, my friends, in a loving manner. A gentle and kind approach is necessary, as is a thorough and close scrutiny. As you recognize the areas that need attention, assume the role of Divinity and go about your work of knowing self and transforming self through the eyes of Divinity. Divinity is ever nonjudgmental; Divinity is ever noncritical; Divinity is ever truly loving; Divinity is allowing; Divinity is joyous. Yes, know that your recognition of self will be assisted by employing these qualities of Divinity. Approach your cleansing now with this gentle, loving allowingness and your progress will be hastened. Do not allow self to become dragged down into depression or despair.

Know that you have assistance available to you. Call on your own soul. Let it assist you in finding self and bringing forth self. Call on the spiritual plane, for there are many wishing to help who are but waiting for the call. The growing numbers of humanity who are clamoring for their spiritual unfoldment can now call the teachers, who are able to assist in this most crucial time of development.

Know that as humanity's consciousness moves forward into spiritual awareness – as you begin to function as spiritual beings – so too the Earth moves into its spiritual position, into its rightful place as a spiritual planet, an entity expressing spiritually. Assist self and assist planet Earth and you will be assisting the entire creation in the forward thrust, for all is one.

TWENTY

Becoming Divinity —
Casting off the Chrysalis

M Y FRIENDS, THE ANALOGY OF THE METAMORPHOSIS OF THE BUTTERFLY IS a common one in spiritual teachings. The larva, of course, is analogous to the individual in a "dark" or unawakened state, who moves into the next evolutionary step, the pupa (the awakening, growing individual, not yet aware of his divinity). Finally, having wound around self a binding coat, the individual forms the chrysalis, which, like the wrappings of the mummy of old, encases a physical form. The physical form, being limited and bound by its own actions, by its own experiences and by its own traumatic lessons, must break through the casing of limited perception and evolve into its destined expression.

Like the beautiful monarch butterfly emerging from its case, so too the spiritual seeker breaks through the limiting concepts that have held him on the wheel of return. He breaks through now into the light, freeing self to be that glorious expression of divinity which was heretofore hidden, unknown to him. The treasure was hidden within self, needing but to emerge, to unfold and to fly free in all its innate beauty.

My friends, you are now at this point! Your persistent stretching and growing — your spiritual expansion — is now reaching the point where it can no longer be held by the former concepts. The urge is now undeniable. There is no turning back at this point, for the time of the spiritual birth has arrived. The new life comes forth with vigor, with a cry of joy! This is what the birth experience should be — a joyful one — for it is coming forth from the darkness into the light, coming into a new beginning of growing and learning and being.

The soul has called you forth, and you are rising to merge with the spiritual oneness. Know now your perfect divine pattern and soar to the heights, untrammeled by your former covering. Rise to new areas of awareness and functioning now. Move in strength and beauty to the "heavens," for they are your true home, your residence, your medium for existence.

What a beautiful analogy the butterfly provides! Use this analogy in a meditative state. See self moving into finer and finer expression. See self emerging as the Creator's image of perfection. See self free, beautiful, strong, sure, at ease in your newfound identity. Go forth, my friends, with this assurance of knowing your true self. Cast off the swaddling clothes. Unbind self from the limiting perceptions of self and flow with the realization of your divinity. Expand now into the allness that is divinity. You are that, my friends.

Integration or Synthesis of Awareness

We have up until now been in a process of gathering together information, gathering together specific points of awareness and growth. It is like a meal with various kinds of food that are taken in, chewed over for a while, digested, assimilated and finally transformed, transmuted into new forms: new living cells. Thus, the intake of all you have experienced, if it has been with conscious awareness, can be used in the growing process at all levels of being.

Can you not see that physical experience can be used as a launching point, as an experience for transmuting into spiritual awareness? Now, all of you have lived extensively, many lives, experiencing much. You now have garnered the essence of these experiences and integrated them into your total expression. Are you not what you have experienced and what you have learned from these experiences? You are a synthesis of all that has gone before.

Now, let us with inner vision know that these experiences are contained within a "core" of self, within a "seed." The experiences have brought you to this point of unfoldment and development and (using the analogy of the flower this time) you have grown through the Earth experience into the light. The light has drawn you forth and you respond to the light, though your roots are held within physical matter. Now, as we said for the butterfly, the urge cannot be denied — you respond to the call of the spiritual sun, and the bud opens to display the beauty contained within it. It opens fully in its spiritual expression, sending forth its inner fragrance. The purpose is being realized. And now the seed draws into itself the total experience of this life. It has come to its fruition. It has conformed to its divine pattern and now is able to disseminate this perfection, this knowingness, into the world. It has produced many seeds for the expansion of the Creator's purpose.

All right, my friends. We have become a bit flowery here, but man can respond to this example of growth, for it has been evident to him from his earliest observations of nature.

Learn to observe and to identify with the evolutionary process going on within all of nature and within self. Self in this process of growing awareness begins to see the unity of all creation, begins to see the universal laws, the universal love encompassing and motivating all that is. Feel the oneness with all. Be one with allness, with oneness, and expand into your own potentiality, into your own divinity. A seed is destined to become the full-blown divine image contained within its seed pattern. Man is destined to become the divine image implanted within his deepest seed pattern.

Gratefully, be aware of your innate potentiality, and give thanks as you allow the divinity within to become — be!

My love to you now.

✦ PART THREE ✦

THE TWELVE RAYS SEMINARS

The Tibetan, Djwhal Khul, 1983-1984

✧ O N E ✧

Ray One – Will, Power and Drive

Good evening, my friends. Tonight we are going to discuss Ray One (the red ray). Many of you haven't learned to use it really well yet, but you are going to be helped tonight, I know.

Let us *attune*. Come to the Ray One with me. We go forth on a special journey. We will begin, now – and that is what it is: a beginning, the first aspect. So feel it flow. Ray One energy is flowing around the circle and it is building, my friends. Feel it – visualize red. Send it, attune to it – Ray One, the Creator. How *magnificent* – feel it, the redness, the energy of it, the will aspect, the Creator's energy as it comes from the Source. You are attuning now. Good, it's flowing well. And now, get excited. Isn't this an opportunity to grow – to understand one of the Creator's aspects and how to utilize it in the most productive way? It's an opportunity, and we do it with joy, my friends. Thank you.

Ray One is exciting. You have to be stimulated by it (that's part of it), not traumatized (that's not part of it). Ray One energy is will, power and drive. It is Aries, the first part of life, vitality, initiative, thrust. As it thrusts forward it causes a breaking down of the old to make way for the new – a very dynamic, direct force. There is a lot of energy there now. We are building it. If you do not feel comfortable with Ray One energy, it might be because you associate it with a heavy, warrior-type, warlike energy. It is very direct, and some people might have trouble with that. But this direct approach can be very positive.

Among the people who have used this ray productively are Winston Churchill and General Patton. Many who are outstanding in sports have well-developed Ray One qualities or have much of it in their horoscopes. Another thing to remember about Ray One is that it is usually a focal point for a person or a time. Earth is getting more Ray One now: We are at a very focal point in the world's history. In a time of crisis when changes occur, there is a lot of Ray One present, either embodied within many people utilizing it, or as a direct response – or both. The Hierarchy might be directing it, or much might come directly, at this time, through Shamballa and Sanat Kumara. It doesn't always come through the Hierarchy. The reason that Ray One comes through now is that this is a critical time for Sanat Kumara and the Earth. The fact is, they are both reaching a point of crisis, and the Ray One energies are important in starting the correct critical angle for ascent. That's a good way to put it. Other people in history who might be good examples of this are Christopher Columbus, Brigham Young, Eleanor Roosevelt, the pioneers, Indira Gandhi and General MacArthur. The first ray was strong in all of them.

Working with the rays, attuning to the vibrational patterns and becoming comfortable with them will aid you in your understanding of what the rays really do. When the first ray comes, it uses the will and focuses on the target. It moves swiftly through all resistance to accomplish its goal. It starts to build because of the resistance. Of course, you need to know what you are building and what are your purposes. Let us say that the goal is to increase the Creator's territory – to thrust back the negative conditions that exist at the "edge" of creation by bringing the light – the first-ray energy – to penetrate into this negativity. The resistance is the so-called negative, which isn't negative; it is just opposite in polarity. As you meet this thrust, something is happening behind you. Yes, there is a path – you have established a path – and the Ray Two energy can begin to follow you. It expands the path with love – love of the Creator. The Creator uses a balanced approach to creation – all of the rays together – but He begins with the Ray One energy. The focus begins there.

Ray One isn't sent in until the appropriate time. Then it is sent by a master, and it clears out, or thrusts forward, or both. After it has made its thrust, the other appropriate rays take over, and Ray One leaves that area. The Creator uses all the rays in proper balance. We are segmenting creation simply for the purpose of study.

Now, in speaking of people functioning on the first ray, many times it would be an Aries who goes in and starts and then gets very bored and says, "I'm tired of that now." Or a first-ray person would rationalize: "I've begun this and now I have other things to do." These people often have other interests and tend to get bored. They don't like details if they are very pure Ray One individuals. Now, they may have other personality traits that negate some of this; they have to learn to balance. They are very dedicated and they come in very focused to do a specific mission, knowing that they will probably not be in balance personalitywise, but agreeing at a higher level that it will be all right for doing something special. But if they are not very dedicated, they need to balance just as anyone else does, for you can have too much of anything, and within your human structure all must be balanced. But we are not looking at balance tonight. We are giving you the characteristics of the ray and how it appears in its pure form.

If you look, you will see a lot of Ray One – much more than you used to. Look at the younger people. Look at the teenagers and the little children. Do you know any six-year-olds who are very thrustful? We have a lot of Ray One six-year-olds running around. Look at them as you approach the New Age. These six-year-olds have a specific duty, a specific mission here. There are many of them – a whole group. If you know any, look at them. They will be interested in challenges – especially in brand-new areas where nobody has done anything for a while. They think, "Oh, that will be interesting" – and it will be, too. At the time of the Earth changes, they will be nineteen or twenty. They have a very special mission. Many of them won't survive in the body. They will be so dedicated to saving, to thrusting, to doing many things, that they will be in the forefront and accept challenges. They've agreed to do this – this is their mission. Now, don't look at every six-year-old in this regard, because it isn't always true. But there is a group of them. They have a tendency to see an obstacle and say, "That's not there," and walk right through it. They ignore all obstacles. They are very focused – more than most children – and need to be kept productively busy. The best rays to use with these children are the second and the seventh rays. Many times the parents of these special children are second and seventh ray, and they have chosen to help this venture.

We are going to talk about the fact that all of you can use Ray One. Now, the will aspect is very strongly evident with Ray One energy. You can use it to will things into being and to will things out of being – yes, to overcome. If you are traumatized by your emotions, use your will to pull yourself out of it. It is hard because when you are in that emotional turmoil you think, I'm going to be here forever – I've been here forever and there's no hope for me at all. At such times you can meditate on Ray One and use the will of Ray One. You can use a visual symbol – see it as a red ray inside of self that you reach to and say, "I'm going to use this red now, to pull myself up" – get a little mad – use it with intensity. Say, "I'm going to use it to aid myself. That's what it is for." That's how you can use it. Try it. It's very specific – that's how you get out of your trauma specifically. Use it with fervor and intensity. Will is a part of the ray that you can use to pull up a condition out of self. If you wear red you might notice a difference. The color is simply symbolic and attunes you to the Ray One energy. But be very careful: it is very powerful. Use it with purpose. Putting on something red to increase your energy is a way of activating the will. The color red will intensify whatever condition already exists, so it is important to know what it is you are intensifying. It may intensify the will in a negative way: "I will have my own way. I don't care what you want." Or, if you are very joyful, if you are an advanced soul that is working in a very productive manner, it will intensify that, too. Most of mankind is not yet willing to live that way. Yes, that's the word — willing.

An energy that is as intense as the first ray must be used with caution. Those of you who are purging are using first-ray energy. First-ray energy has a purpose. Learn to utilize it within that purpose, within its proper framework, and you will have no trouble. It is a very valuable tool for all of you to use, but beware if you misuse it, because you will get an almost instant effect. All of you who are working on yourselves so intensely should do it in balance, my friends, knowing that you need other things to maintain a proper perspective. When you get out of balance, you lose your perspective on life — you see everything colored through the first ray. Just a pinch of first ray into a great, big batch of creation, please.

What are some of the negative manifestations of Ray One to watch out for? War is an important one. We have to watch that Middle East very carefully all the time and sprinkle some other energies in there when the first ray gets too intense. We have to dilute it, if you will. This is very important. Another thing that can be done when there is too much intensity of the first ray is to break it up, my friends. You can break up the ray, and then it can't thrust forward. You can work on the first-ray energy itself. Instead of a stream, visualize it as being broken up into pieces. In a state of meditation, do the breaking process with a very balanced approach using the entire spectrum, knowing that you are bringing in a balance by breaking up the pattern of the first ray. Don't add more first ray, or you will just intensify it. And don't take out any specific rays. Just know that it is a balanced approach that you are seeking to achieve. Now, sometimes it isn't appropriate to put more energy in there, even if it is other kinds of energy. In this case it is appropriate just to break up what is there. Sometimes, if you see a stream of red, you can break it up with white. You can also use the first ray with another ray. The fifth ray can be used to plan an action and the first ray to carry out the plan. They harmonize well together. The first and second rays are a good team too.

First-ray mind is a very direct, intense focus. Problems might be "too focused," but it can certainly thrust forward into new areas. First-ray physical body wills its way through anything, even when it is on its last legs — which you probably wouldn't realize. First-ray personality might be a little harsh in its application without meaning to be. This personality focuses on one thing at a time and moves forward without letting any obstacles stand in its way. First-ray emotional body can be very threatening — you don't see it much anymore. Very explosive. First-ray soul is very thrusting.

Ray One Meditation

This is a meditation to balance out your Ray One experience with the rest of the rays.

Coming into us is an intense electric blue. I want you to take this electric blue and swirl it into a whirlwind and bring it down through the body, cleansing the body of Ray One. Do this with intensity. And into it, now, put all of the particles of the rainbow that will literally scrub you clean of any Ray One that clings there, so that you will again have a more balanced approach to your life. Do it with intensity. Scrub out every corner of the Ray One energy that you have used with intensity.

All right, coming toward you is a rainbow. View it, my friends. It drops on you like a blanket. You each have your own rainbow that is settling on you now. It feels so wonderful, so good, so complete, and every aspect of you welcomes the rainbow. It almost has a personality of its own. It is full of joy, this rainbow. Allow it to fill you — the whole rainbow now. And while I am quiet for a little while, experience the rainbow.

And now, friends, approaching us is a beautiful gold. It is luminous and gorgeous and beautiful. Do you see it? Welcome this gold as it comes in and fills the room with intensity here — a beautiful, luminous gold quality that is so lovely. A higher-ray application comes and merges with the lower rays of the rainbow to aid you now, my friends. It lifts you up, so allow it to lift you. Allow yourself to become greater with this gold. And follow it now as it becomes a golden ball — it's dancing there. Do you see it? Keep following the golden ball.

At the end of our journey, do you see the beautiful white light, luminous before us — the white of the Creator and the Christ, both? Feel it. See it. Experience it now, the great white light, as you move into it. Attune to it. Merge with it. Become a part of this great white light — joyfully, my friends, with joy. And send it out.

Now send out love and joy to the world, through the colors, if you wish. Send them the rainbow, the whole spectrum. Send love. Send love. Send love. Become very comfortable with yourself. Know that you have balanced each color within you — that all of your areas feel balanced, very refreshed, very renewed, very joyful now, my friends. Allow it to happen. Let it take place. Do it with joy. Joy! Joy! Joy!

And now a final cleansing. Again run the intense blue light through your body, whirling it and cleansing it completely. I thank you for your attention, for your love and for your joy — and for your participation. Thank you for your patience and for your understanding. Thank you and goodnight.

✧ T W O ✧

Ray Two — Love/Wisdom

T HE SECOND RAY IS VERY COMFORTABLE FOR ME AND FOR MOST OF YOU, ON one level or another. First we are going to have a short meditation and really fill the room with Ray Two energies.

❦ *An intense blue light containing Ray Two is beginning to fill the room and it is very intense. We are going to permeate the room – including the people – with this ray. We want an intense identification with it today to show you how you can utilize it.*

❦ *So begin now by identifying with this aspect of the Creator. His love, for our purposes today, is our focus – His love. Feel it, experience His love – the Creator's love. It is coming in stronger and stronger and it makes you feel joyful. Feel the love and with it the peace and joy that is beginning to be so strong here. Is it not wonderful? The love of the Creator is what we share – yes, the sharing of it is also a part of this aspect. Do you not feel it? Attune to it and be a part of it – this love aspect of the Creator. We will work with it in joy today, with various exercises and with our increased understanding as we begin to attune to it – this second ray of the Creator. Acknowledge that you wish to become a part of it, and then allow it to happen, my friends.*

I want all of you to participate with each other in the love of the Creator. Attune to His love, my friends. Yes, when you attune to love, you attune to laughter and to joy. Love does that, friends, when you allow it to. We are going to work mostly with love today. The second ray is divided, so we will work on wisdom also, but perhaps a little gradually, knowing that it might take more than just today.

All right. Love: What do you think of when you hear that word? Have any of you used color in association with love? We have talked of pink mostly, but blue is certainly an aspect of love also. You know they give blue to baby boys and pink to baby girls. What began this tradition was wishing to give love to offspring – and the colors fit very well. White is given to represent purity of love; red for Valentine's Day represents a will to love, and red is the life force. We have talked of the will of the Creator as the first aspect, and right on its heels comes love – the Creator's love.

When you flood an area with love, the intensity of an adverse condition begins to abate. When you are in an environment that is so intense you feel you can't take it anymore, and you say, "I've got to do something about this," what's a good way to handle that? Do you think color would be appropriate, and if so, what colors would you use? Yes, there are many approaches, and different people can choose what they feel is appropriate. If you feel that blue is appropriate for representing divine love, or pink, or even the rainbow – all are valid. I think that if you change where you are, it can change many other things. It is not wrong to work on self to make changes in other areas. It would be inappropriate to do it for just your own benefit, but recognize that you must start where you are, and from there the waves go out. It is appropriate to realize that you are to help as much as you can, but you must start where you are. If you send a rainbow to a condition, what you probably will accomplish is some cleansing, and that seems valid to me.

But today we are going to use the second ray, and if you wish, you may identify it as blue, or some may identify it as white. (You can do this with any ray, if you wish.) If you want to use it raised to its highest potentiality, to its highest point, you can use an intense application of it as white. You can use pink, if you like. I want you to choose, for today's work, whatever color is appropriate to you, recognizing that later you may change your mind and use a different color. I don't want you to restrict yourself on colors.

What do you think a baby feels when it is held closely and rocked in its mother's arms? What kind of love is this? Would it depend on what kind of love the mother has for the child? Different mothers have different beliefs about love. Every mother will have her own way of identifying with her child. She might say, "Oh my goodness, I'm late, but I must nurse the baby. It's my duty, and I must do that now. And of course, I love my child – I take care of everything. This is my duty and I am not negligent in it." And then there is the one who says, "This is my child: I have created it and I own it. This is my baby." And then there is the very young mother, perhaps, who says, "This is my child, but what do I do with it?" We are getting into different kinds of love in a specific situation. Do you know how many different kinds of love can be projected by a mother? There are as many different kinds as there are mothers. Each kind would be received by the child differently, wouldn't it?

So we begin to identify how many types of love there are just in the more mundane sense. There is the love between mother and child, between man and woman, love of animals, love of nature, love of the Creator, love of life and love of self. Many of you do not love self very much, I think. This is something we all need to work on — love of self — because you are all potential creators. My goodness, can't you love that? A potential cocreator — how wonderful! I have great admiration for each of you for that ability. I certainly do, and you can have love for yourself in that area, in that way.

In the area of conflict between parents and teenagers, how can love be applied to solve problems? Even if the mother establishes a basic rapport to begin with, there may be times when it seems a situation cannot be resolved. But eventually love prevails — eventually it does work out. So love is difficult to see as a short-term remedy, but as a long-term one there is nothing that can be compared with it — nothing. A short-term application can be used, but if you can't see any effect, know that the long-term application will work. It is the most positive approach to anything. No matter what else you are doing, no matter what other way you seek to resolve a situation, use unconditional love. And have confidence in the Creator and His love even if you don't have confidence in yourself. Know that this isn't you, it is part of the Creator, and use it productively and positively.

I think love is interpreted by people in different ways. Sometimes one shows love by standing firm. You might have an extremely brilliant child who needs to explore much and is very creative, or one of those who has received love and all of the reinforcements and is still just interested in life and needs to learn about it. A mother can show love by setting firm boundaries, by being responsible and not letting the child leave those boundaries. And in the name of love she is entitled to do this. Sometimes permissiveness is very unloving, very selfish. In interpersonal relationships, in the family, and between male and female, the use of second-ray energy is important. If it were my home, I would keep it absolutely packed with second-ray energy all the time. I think the love aspect will flood wherever it is needed — it will filter through everything. That is my opinion, and I've seen it used a lot. If you use love in a productive way for the planet, by flooding your personal area with this second ray, you will aid it. The unconditional love will begin to filter down. That is really what the Creator wants used here upon the Earth: this intense love application of what the Christ brought, which has been getting more intense ever since. It is an intensification of the love aspect, and hopefully, eventually, of the wisdom aspect.

If you were told that a person had a second-ray personality, what type of person would you expect to see? You might see second-ray persons in different ways, of course. They will individualize, depending upon the other aspects involved, but to generalize, they are loving, allowing, considerate, friendly and responsible. They need a quiet place within themselves, but this does not mean they do not reach out to others.

And what about a second-ray soul? Most of you have them, but not all. Most of them are teachers, or perhaps architects or in some profession requiring higher conceptual abilities.

And how about a second-ray mind? It might be very receptive; it is likely to consider itself a part of the whole. It is a very interesting mind, one you don't see very often.

What about a second-ray emotional body? You might think of it as rather peaceful, but don't think that you need to have a second-ray emotional body to attain this. It is not destined that you should — some will and some will not. You might keep the one you have and "raise" its use. The second-ray emotional body is thought of as stable and mature.

All right, what about a second-ray physical body? It is placid, yes — this is rather unusual now. In the past there were many second-ray physical bodies. There are fewer and fewer now, but you are going to see more and more second-ray physical bodies coming along.

What about the monad? The monad is more encompassing, but it has its own ray, which doesn't usually change. As we approach the New Age, however, changes seems to be happening. Because of the spiraling forward of the Earth, there has perhaps been a need to realign. The Earth is a small planet in relation to the whole cosmos, but what it is experiencing is a reflection of what is going on at a much higher level, just as what you are experiencing is a reflection of what is going on at a higher level. And the needs of the Earth are a reflection of the needs of the cosmos, in a sense. The cosmos needs certain aspects at this time, and you will see some monads switching from, particularly, the second to the seventh ray in emphasis. Now, don't get it out of proportion and say that the Earth's needs are affecting those of the cosmos — that is true only in the sense that they reflect each other. But the monadic ray almost never changes, outside of these special situations.

In a certain esoteric sense, all of the rays that come into the Earth begin from a higher aspect of the second ray. Every ray is contained within this great second ray and then descends upon the Earth. From the first aspect that descends comes the Earth's second aspect, and from this the third, and then, in a special esoteric way, all of the others descend from that. To begin with, cosmically speaking, the greatest application is made from the second ray, which then becomes the other rays as we know them upon the Earth in all seven aspects. This is what is meant by saying that the Earth is a second-ray planet. In a cosmic sense, it receives the second ray, which is then broken down into the rays for the Earth. For the New Age, the rays might not change, but the way it is broken down — the emphasis on the rays — will change. It is similar to playing an organ. The source is the same, but what you are doing with it is different. You emphasize certain chords or certain harmonics in certain ways.

The seventh ray will be intensified as we approach the New Age, but the basic application of the second ray on a cosmic level is still true for the Earth. And as far as I know, that will not change. But keep in mind that the Creator does not always tell me these things!

◇ T H R E E ◇

Ray Three — Perseverance

T O GENERALIZE ABOUT THE RAYS A LITTLE, LET'S START WITH A FEW INTER-
esting facts. The rays are really energy — God's energy, the Creator's
energy. And they are His method of creating. Basically, this energy is
divided (at least on the Earth) into seven different kinds. And all of these
energies (rays) have specific characteristics. Now, they function in you, some
of them. You each have different aspects of yourself on different rays, and
by studying what kinds of rays they are — by learning about the rays and their
characteristics — we can learn a great deal about ourselves. We can learn a
great deal about the world. We can learn a great deal about everything,
because the energies, the rays, are very basic to understanding, first of all,
the Creator, and then everything that follows from It. Each ray has positive
and less-than-positive qualities. But for now, let's look mostly at the positive
ones. We'll discuss the others some, too, so that you can avoid them.

Now we are talking about Ray Three energy, but let's recap just a moment
to say that Ray One energy is the way it all began. It is the thrusting energy
— the energy by which something is focused into a new area. You thrust
forth with the first ray. An army general, for instance, has a lot of Ray One.
The first ray is the ray of the will.

The second ray is what we term the love/wisdom ray. The Christ
functions on the second ray, and he is the great world teacher for this age.
All of the teachers of the world function on this ray, but the Christ is the
one most people are familiar with. The Buddha too has functioned through
this ray. And I, the Tibetan, am also on this ray. Janet is not — she is a
first-ray soul, and because of that, we are a good team. She is the will and
I'm teaching her love and wisdom.

All right, the present topic is the third ray. This one is interesting, and
I think you're going to enjoy it. I think you could say the main characteristic

of the third ray is perseverance — the ability to hold on to something. I didn't say "stubborn." Perseverance is a very good quality. Now, the Hierarchy, which is the spiritual government of the planet, is divided into seven departments that follow the seven rays. Each is head of a specific effort in line with one of the rays. The third department is the organizer of the Hierarchy. It is the one that "gets it all done." The first-ray people say, "This is important; this is new," and get it done. And the second-ray people say, "And do it with love and be sure that it fits into the learning experience of the people." Then the third-ray people say, "But how do you want it done?" and "What are we going to do?" and "We should organize it this way, and this way" — and they do it, my friends. The third ray is the one that gets it done. They are the organizers, whether we are talking about Earth living or our spiritual government.

Think about figures in history you are interested in. Can you think of some who showed these third-ray characteristics? Thomas Edison, certainly. Everyone has several rays within, but he had many third-ray characteristics. The third ray is considered the ray of concrete intelligence. Eleanor Roosevelt had quite a bit of third ray.

Third-ray personalities must watch out for the holding on — the keeping within oneself of these characteristics that often are not let loose, you see. Everyone must learn to let loose, to change and to grow, and if you have a lot of third ray, it is more difficult, because you are more focused in it. Think of people who take something and then do something with it — such as Yogananda, who took the spiritual and brought it down to classes and opened schools. Ernest Holmes, founder of Science of Mind — yes, he gathered material and focused it into a teaching.

Of all that we have mentioned, Thomas Edison was probably the strongest in the third ray. How did he appear to the world? Do you think that he was so focused on what he was doing that he didn't appear normal to the rest of the world — that he didn't pay attention to it because he was so focused? Then we could say that the ability to really focus is a characteristic of the third ray. These are the types who will stay on one track until they finish it — forever, if necessary! They are very often perfectionists about what they are focused on. They may ignore everything except their project, which must be done with great precision. They usually stand firm on what they believe in, and they stand right there all by themselves. They don't need anyone else, but they may need to reorganize and refocus. The negative use of the third ray might be to try to make everyone partake of one's own perception.

The world map on which we recently showed the energy lines reveals a very interesting thing. Spain is completely surrounded by the third ray. In looking at that country, we see the influence of this ray: the Inquisition, the influence of the Catholic Church, and the ability of the country to maintain its own national identity through many years of foreign influence and rule.

It has been maintained by their perseverance. Sometimes the Spanish appear "stuck in a pattern" — the holding on to the past. The third ray shows in Spanish dancing — it is uniquely precise and very focused.

Spain is also affected very much by the first and second rays, which are shown close to it. There is a thrustingness shown by her adventures in the earlier years. At this time we see examples of first-ray activities in the bullfighter, who holds up a red cape — the color of the first ray. And what follows is the mindless bull that is merely led. People can also be led mindlessly by the first ray. This is not always appropriate for a mass of people. The lower aspect of the first ray was shown by the cruelty of the conquerors. The second ray might be seen in their love of the land and their very family-oriented society. There is a sixth ray influence there, too, in the intense need to worship. And there is the fourth ray — they have had much involvement with the arts. There have been some wonderful artists, some beautiful music, and the dancing — nowhere else is there anything like Spanish dancing. The dancing shows first ray and also third ray — very vital, and also very precise.

Now, Germany is very third-ray. Let's talk about it and let us also include Austria. They are very traditional. Let's look at the history that caused some of the conditions within Germany, because Germany has focused, or begun, many interesting events in the world. We could say the two world wars were really one war that lasted from 1914 through 1945. It is really one situation that has occurred two times — experienced in different ways. Think about the third ray (though there is some first-ray influence here, of course — a war situation). Look at the countries of Germany and Austria, and the characteristics of the third ray: great focus, strong perseverance, organization, the ability to get things done, but not always to see beyond the focus. Here we had people at the end of the First World War who were starving. Along came someone who promised them something. They were focusing on survival — they couldn't see anything else. This is third ray, remember. They concentrated on it, and third ray is a good, concise, concrete type of intelligence, but it does not plumb to the depths of a situation. It doesn't dig down underneath the layers of what is presented to it and see what other ramifications might be there — and in prewar Germany they didn't do that.

This period of events was a play between good and evil, in many connotations. And that play really made the difference in what we are experiencing now. If this event had come out a little differently, we in the Hierarchy would not have been able to plan for the New Age in the way that we have, because this event, this little play that was going on, was a cosmic event, in a sense — it was largely between good and evil. Now, I'm not saying that the Earth didn't earn the situation, that the people didn't allow it to happen. They might not have known about it, but the situation was there, and by participating in it the Earth learned a great deal. This event was focused in Germany, although it was a lesson that the whole world was learning, you see.

What we are focusing on here is, what can we learn, energywise, from this situation? Right and wrong and good and evil were all played out on various levels, with people watching it from various planes. Certainly we looked at it a lot; it was very interesting. When the wars ended, third-ray Germany had such tenacity in coming back after all the trauma — very positive. The characteristics of the people seem to hold pretty true — they don't change a lot; they are focused. Many people don't do that; they lose their basic characteristics by blending with others.

Let us summarize some of the characteristics of the third ray. We have said the energy is very persevering — we haven't said "stubborn," we have said "persevering." And we have called it very focused, concrete, logical, clear-minded energy, organized, and not always aware of consequences.

Now, how do you think we can ultimately best use the third ray to aid the Earth, to aid ourselves? As we begin this intense approach to the New Age, how can we best use this energy? And what color do you identify with the third ray? Yellow, yes, unless you prefer to use another color. This kind of energy is used in bringing very specific methods to help people in clearing, and there are very many of these methods going on now in the world.

We, here, are now implementing and working with the specific vibration of joy to clear — and it is wonderful. Joy is a higher ray — one of the high ones — the ninth ray. If you take the third ray and triple it, then you have this higher ray we are working with.

About the specific use of the third ray to aid the world — yes, the focused persistence of spiritual awareness, the ability to remain balanced, could help stabilize a chaotic situation. Meditation would help to maintain this. You could say that the third ray is like entering a tunnel — a very focused journey through the tunnel — and I don't especially mean a covered-up, sheltered tunnel but a focused application. The journey leads, then, directly to the New Age, doesn't it? But it really does begin with this third ray of persevering, of focusing, of knowing, of holding your perfection within, if you will; of holding the thought that everything will not be chaos, it will be perfection, true divinity — even you. Certainly. So we get from the third ray by a tunnel to the twelfth ray, eventually, which is the ray of these greater teachers who are coming when we are here in the New Age. Mathematically it is just four times the third; three times to the ninth ray (our joy vibration), while the fourth step brings it to the twelfth ray (the vibration of these higher teachers). You can do all these things mathematically because mathematics is just a reflection of divine truth anyway, isn't it? Certainly.

You can utilize any of the rays specifically, whether you have them within you or not — they are all available on the Earth. You have certain rays predominant within, and even if you do not have a lot of a particular ray, you can use the characteristics of any of the productive ones to serve. Many of you have thought about service and have wondered what you can do. This is one thing you can do. You can send out rays. Where could you send the third ray? Perhaps the Middle East could use some, and South America. Sending a specific ray, a specific color, to an area aids the area and helps you. Now, don't send to a specific person in the area, unless he or she has asked. Use a little discretion. I wouldn't send the first ray to many places — please do not. But I do not see anything wrong with sending the third ray. I don't think you'd want to send more of it to Spain or Germany — they already have their share. You really do have to know what you are doing. It is called responsibility for your actions. The unstable areas would be good places to send the third ray — yes, Africa. If you look at an area and see that there isn't much third ray there because you've analyzed it by studying commentaries on TV — not the ones who just talk at you, but the ones who analyze it, who talk about it from a more balanced perspective — then you know what is going on in the world a little. But please don't send any fourth ray around! This ray is the one that is misused on the Earth more than any other, and until people learn how to use it and deal with what they already have, perhaps we shouldn't send any more of it — nor first ray, either. But send the third ray, which we are discussing, and certainly the second and seventh rays. A little fifth ray wouldn't hurt — sprinkle a little of that on. All of the higher rays would be appropriate for Mother Earth.

✧ F O U R ✧

Ray Four – Harmony through Conflict

L ET US TRACE RAY FOUR ON THE GLOBAL ENERGY MAP OF THE WORLD. WE shall start at Australia. From the lower part of Australia it moves north of New Zealand and across the Pacific to South America, crossing the lower portion – Chile and Argentina; then across the Atlantic to Africa, crossing the lower portion; across the Indian Ocean to lower India, and up through India to New Delhi; then across China and over to Japan; from Japan it goes up through Alaska and across Canada; then up and across the lower end of Greenland; across Iceland and across Great Britain; across Poland and Russia and down into the Middle East.

The rays are simply a way of indicating different energy patterns. Basically there are seven. With Ray Four we are in the middle, you might say, or at the basis of Earth living – the foundation of it. If you follow that fourth-ray pattern, you will see the first part of the world that was ever energized – where energy really began. For you could say that when the Creator began to allow the Earth to become as it is now – began to create it, in the most esoteric sense – this pattern was energized first. And that is a little difficult to explain, because if you consider a complete energy pattern you are likely to say, "But how can that be? That's just one part of energy, and if you create, don't you use all of it?" Well, in a sense you do. But you do different things with different parts of it.

The fourth ray is very connected with physical existence, so if you as a cocreator are going to create a physical world, the fourth ray is very important. Now, those who come to this world as evolving consciousnesses and say there is great resistance within the physical are really referring to this ray. This fourth ray is the one that contains all that wonderful resistance you all enjoy in your emotional escapades, or interesting adventures, or involvements. When you are held in the middle of an emotional problem, what you are experiencing usually is the fourth ray at its least productive level.

The immersed quality of this ray is very well known, and it is very closely associated with the emotional body — with the solar plexus chakra. I find it very productive. It is the means to overcoming things within self that need overcoming — the way to do it. The heaviest part of this ray gives you the way to get beyond a very specific point, because the heaviness within it allows the resistance pattern to launch you, if you let it. Now, if you get in the lowest part and go around there, then you don't launch anywhere else but to another part of it. You start going in a circle emotionally. But if you use it as a launching pad, it is excellent — it really is. It is much easier to use this kind of energy to launch than it is to use, say, the fifth or the third.

So we are looking at what we might refer to as this heavy, but good, energy, with its resistive quality. Now, it also has one very interesting characteristic that makes it a very challenging ray with which to work: it is very reflective. And if it is used in connection with the other rays in a specific area on the Earth, what it reflects is not terribly productive, because it reflects what the other ray is not using in that area. So if the good qualities are used up, and what is left of another ray is chaotic, then you get a reflection of that from the fourth ray, which is very interesting there. It is reflective — it lets you look at what you haven't finished yet, at what's left. It lets you hold up to yourself exactly what you need to look at. It may be chaotic energy that you'd rather wasn't there in a physical environment, but whatever it is, the fourth ray acts as a mirror and lets you see it there. This is part of the Earth experience, truly — getting to see; looking right there and seeing self and thinking, Oh, my goodness, is that really there? and then changing it and going beyond that point. This great fourth ray is the means to doing this in physical life. Isn't that exciting? Don't you think that is good? Certainly it is a very good opportunity.

Let's talk about this ray. In the first place, the color usually associated with it is green — green on two different levels. When I look at it in the auras, many times I see different shades of green, letting me know how developed someone is in a particular area. And sometimes, if it is close to yellow, that gives me a clue as to whether someone is identifying with or getting into the third-ray area. The most productive green is, of course, a beautiful clear green, which says you have handled the emotional body — you have done your homework, and now the green reflects it. This is truly the clear beauty of this fourth ray. It is called, by the way, harmony through conflict. And that is why it is so closely related to physical science: because most of you have chosen to experience that way — harmony through conflict.

Now, this ray rules a very interesting area — the musical field. That certainly is harmonious, generally, isn't it — beautiful music, and the arts? And when you get into the higher parts of this ray, it is very, very lovely. To me, one of the beauties of physical existence is this ray in its most positive attributes. Have you ever looked at a beautiful painting and marveled at the artist's ability to portray certain realistic or impressionistic images? Have you ever looked at a beautiful image of the Earth and said, "The Earth is so beautiful, and I can see it so clearly in all of its greenness"? It is no accident that the greenness in your planet's nature is so emphasized. And have you ever walked through a jungle and partaken of the music of it and the beauty of it? It literally sings to you, you know. The animals there are very much in tune with the environment. Certainly it is sometimes nature at its most "raw," but that doesn't mean anything bad, does it? It just means it is truly right there — that you get to experience it exactly as it is, physical existence represented by this beautiful fourth ray.

Have you ever looked at a sunset? Now, that certainly is not green, but what does it do for you? It attunes you to the heights through viewing physical existence, and it is a pleasure. I may be downgrading physical existence, but I love it, I really do. I am feeling very privileged to be a part of it again. Now, I'm not saying I'd want to have to stay here, you know; I like to be able to go, too. But it is a privilege, it really is. And I do think that when you leave it, you will like returning — you will. You will enjoy it.

Now, we have an opportunity here to aid the Earth in her growth by literally lifting this ray to its higher aspect. Too long has Earth kind of scrambled around in the bottom of this ray. Too long have the emotional bodies been hooked to it at the lowest level. I have given, in some of the material, a way to climb out of your emotional body, and you could equate this to climbing out of the lower part of the fourth ray. You can bring into self the red will aspect — you can use it as a ladder. Climb your ladder of will, then. And do you know what else you can do when you get to the outside of it? Bring it up with you! Raise up that emotional area. Begin now, in your meditations, to raise it up, using the greenness to signify this ray. If you will do that as a service in your meditations, it will aid the Earth, because this is the heaviest part — and if you raise up the heaviest, you've got it all raised up, haven't you? Yes! Well, we don't need to be so solemn, do we?

Have you ever considered the fourth ray in connection with any of the other rays? Or why it is as it is? Do you think it is the heaviness of it, the emotional connotation, that makes everyone resist it? I've always enjoyed this ray. You could say it is a square ray, and the squareness fits very well into physical existence. You can anchor self with this fourth ray. Those of you who think, But goodness, I don't want to stay here — why would I do that? You would do it so the specificity of your launch could be achieved, you see. It is a way to attain your goal very specifically. If your goal is New Age living, then anchor this fourth ray in its most productive state within self and use that as the way to launch self.

The foundation that you build with this ray by balancing the emotional body and this ray, and then using it in the context of balancing the rest of self, will launch you, and you will get there this time without falling back as a result of being imbalanced. Using this fourth ray in its most productive way truly provides an opportunity to go beyond where you are now. I want you to learn to be familiar with it. You're all familiar with it! But the key is to be happy with it and to know that it is a good ray and to enjoy it – on the highest level, of course, where you want to experience it. Now, you can use it in combination with the fifth ray, which is mental, by using the fifth ray to climb out of the emotional areas when you need to. Of course you can use the will, also. We need to see the complexity that makes a oneness. By using the productive levels you can increase your understanding of how different parts of self fit together and get you to where you want to go. Now, the will ray – the first ray – is to be utilized at its highest level, too. The first ray and the fourth ray really have bad reputations, don't they? They don't really deserve this – they are beautiful rays.

Can you think of people in history who had a lot of fourth ray on either level? Artists, actors and actresses? Yes. Now, on what level do you think they experience? Many of them go so intensely into their art that they might not balance it with the mental. Pablo Picasso is an example, yes, and Vincent Van Gogh. Does this explain what we have said – that geniuses (in this area, anyway) are not very well balanced? It is very difficult to hold the focus at the highest level, and very easy to get into a stuck-in-a-pattern condition or not to release the lower level completely.

In working within a specific ray, you must learn – and artists do – to experience at the heights. But artists don't always learn, in one lifetime, to release the depths. This is something that is necessary to do.

As I analyze the chakras for all of you, many of you are experiencing at the highest level but you haven't completely released the lower level yet. In all of the rays in which there is more than one level, you have to learn to release the lower one completely. It is done gradually over several lifetimes, usually. But what you see is kind of a seesaw effect. You see the beauty of these great abilities and the immersion of the emotional body, don't you?

Fourth ray in the Lebanon area? Yes, there is a great deal patterning around that area – the fourth ray at its lowest level – and it reflects other types of energies that are not productive, getting you into a "Ping-Pong" effect, back and forth. The least desirable qualities of several rays go back and forth. Now, you must understand that there is a destructive part of rays that some people are into.

Hitler? He was a class unto himself. Certainly there was evidence of the destructiveness of several of the rays in this very complex being we have described as quite departed from the light. He was truly a leader aligned with what we call the dark forces, the negativity – not merely the physical vehicle within which he functioned. This case really has nothing to do with what we are discussing about average humanity. He is one who will never again be in the physical or anywhere else – he is an exception to most of what is experienced here on the Earth. We don't need many Hitlers, do we? There aren't many of those around.

When fourth-ray people get into the middle of a conflict, it becomes very compulsive, very self-feeding, and they keep going into it and around and around. It is very characteristic of fourth-ray individuals to go to the heights and then to the depths — a roller-coaster effect. They get held within this ray: they may be very happy and ecstatic one day, and then the next day everything is terrible and they feel it is an absolute disaster they are never going to get out of. The subconscious holds them there in a sense and they become comfortable with their trauma. That is a part of it: they feel consciously uncomfortable — "Oh my goodness, I don't want to be in this" — but they are comfortable in a subconscious reactive pattern. They are very aware of their own needs and desires and they defy anyone who tells them something else. They create the problems over and over.

Now, we are looking at a fourth-ray condition at its extreme. A fourth-ray being doesn't have to experience this way, because everyone has balances that allow them to function as balanced human beings. But we are saying that if you focus just in the fourth-ray emotional body, this is what you get. People who have developed artistic abilities have much emotional focus. Now, in the higher level of the fourth ray are the higher arts and talents and harmonious types of Earth living. The main way to get up out of the emotions into balance is by using the mind — that is the natural balance. Beautiful music can help also.

As a teacher you are going to meet people who are in the emotional pattern, and they are going to do this over and over. They need help out of it, don't they? They need to understand that it is a pattern, because many times they don't understand that and they need to know that they can overcome it and get into the higher level of the ray.

The Cabala teaching can help you to symbolically look at these aspects of self. You can learn to raise the fourth ray in this way. There is much inner work, and some of you have been doing it, in that area. The symbolic way to raise this ray would be to look at self — see a green area and put an image of self there. Then look around and see what else you see. Is it raining? Perhaps that would tell you symbolically that you are experiencing a pattern of loss. Maybe there is a big thunderstorm. Whatever is happening, note it, and if you need help with it, you may ask. It is like looking at a dream situation, a symbolic picture from which you can learn — particularly with this ray — the emotional aspect of self.

Now, there is a lot of basic appreciation for Earth living in fourth-ray people; they will relate to the Earth in a way that most of the other rays do not. It is sometimes difficult for them to meditate and get up into the spiritual area because the Earth connection gets in the way. Many times they are into physical activity — doing things on the Earth such as driving vehicles, horseback riding, hiking, climbing mountains and relating to animals. They like participating in Earth living. For fourth-ray people, working with the solar plexus chakra, which is connected with the emotional body, is important. It is important to stimulate it in the highest and most productive part and balance it completely. Yes, working with the chakras is very helpful. Eventually you will evolve beyond the use of the lower chakras (from the solar plexus down) and you will drop them. These chakras are part of Earth living at this point. They are the physical energy patterns. In an esoteric sense, when you go beyond what mankind is now – beginning in the New Age – there is going to be a change there. The chakras will be different. They will be at a new, higher level than they were before.

Try to imagine what characteristics you might observe in a very small baby with a lot of fourth ray. How would it react to life? Yes, it would have mood changes, cry a lot then smile a lot, be fascinated with colors and music, be restless, demanding – these are possibilities. Now consider a three-year-old, just coming into self-awareness – the same qualities would be more evident, whether on the higher fourth-ray level or the lower. There might be a problem with relating to people. The artistic abilities might be showing up. The mental abilities can be stimulated to help balance the emotional. Lots of love would be helpful, as would be the teaching of a logical approach to problems – showing him how puzzles work and explaining things so that he can understand. Now, when he is a little older and starting school, what is he going to experience? That it isn't always appropriate to have his own way – that when he seeks his own needs and desires, he will meet with resistance. That is the fourth ray. Of course, people are going to be different, for you are what you create – a composite of what you have experienced.

Fourth-ray people can be manipulative. They would like to have everyone experience from the same focus as they do. Now, this tendency can be modified by other rays in the person's makeup. It doesn't help these people when you cater to this quality, but you shouldn't be insensitive, either. If people are focused very much in the emotions, or the fourth ray, you have to recognize that they have specific problems that make it difficult for them – that just as you have problems that are hard for you, and they may think your problems are very easy because they have handled them, so you, in turn, may think that theirs are easy because you have handled them. First you have to have understanding, but then you have to have sensitivity, and that is just as important. And you might wonder why they are doing something over and over – it doesn't seem to make any sense. Of course it doesn't make any sense mentally, but it isn't mental – it is emotional. It isn't logical, they aren't doing it because they want to. It is because they are in a pattern.

You all have your own emotional programming – programming that stimulates the emotional area. Everyone has that, but the focus makes the difference. Those of you who are mentally focused must allow that the other sixty percent of creation is not. Sixty percent is focused in the emotional area. Now, the emotional focus is not a bad place to be. I know – I come from it and it can be very nice. I enjoyed it mostly – yes, mostly.

All right, now let's say our little boy has become a little older. (Did you notice he was growing up while we were talking?) He's about thirteen — that interesting age when he's starting to become a man. How do you think the fourth ray affects him now? Yes, he is a conflict unto himself. He doesn't know what he is doing — neither fish nor fowl. He is half man and half child and half neither one. If there are three halves, which may seem true with these children, sometimes they will form anger groups — big-city gangs are a case in point. They need physical activity to release the hostility and the adverse emotions they have within. It enables them to let off some of this pent-up emotion, this frustration with the life processes, by acting out in physical activity. Many athletes have a lot of fourth ray. Now, many have the seventh ray, which is very good at that, too; it is very coordinated. Many have both fourth and seventh. A boxer might have a first-ray personality, a fourth-ray emotional body and a seventh-ray physical body.

So our young man of thirteen has discovered he is in the midst of a change, and he is all upset about it. He is swirling through his emotions — and again we are talking of the lowest level. But one day he discovers that he has a lot of ability in the arts, so he goes to his mother and he says, "You know, I really like art and I want to study it." She says, "Good, you can have lessons. You can go and learn to paint." He does that and then discovers it is a lot of work, you know. Then he starts playing the piano. But he discovers that perhaps if he focuses in on this area he is going to miss a lot. And usually, unless a fourth-ray person is into the more harmonious part of the ray, he becomes rather a generalist in life — a jack-of-all-trades. That is one of the characteristics of the fourth ray. They have to experience in the Earth. They experience here, and then they think, Well that looks interesting, and they go and experience over there. They experience all over, and at about thirteen this usually begins.

All right, now he's sixteen. He is very much interested in the opposite sex (he has been for a while). He could be very many things if he is emotionally focused in the fourth ray. We said he is a generalist, so he probably doesn't do specific things for very long. He may play football for a while, or basketball. He could be emotionally aggressive, or he could be very introverted if he is experiencing emotional problems. It can be complex. Maybe it is part of one and part of the other. What about those who are withdrawn? What about the teenage suicide rate — what about those young-sters? Do you think many of them have fourth ray? Perhaps that pattern is spinning so within them that they are held there and it is like a tunnel effect — a whirlwind that pulls them into it — and they can't see beyond their emotional trauma. So they get to the point — and all of you who have worked within your belief structure know this — where it is so deep it's as if they were in a big bowl, right there at the bottom, and all they can do is look up, and they know they're never going to get out of that hole again, that they are there forever. There is no point in even trying; they will always be there. And that is when they end it all — in the middle of all that — unless someone reaches out a hand and helps them, or they allow some help that has always been there. But if they do it in a repeating pattern, there is not always someone available — that's the problem. They get help for some of this, but on one occasion the repeating pattern doesn't allow them to get out of it, and then they leave on a "three-day vacation."

Now, self-esteem is part of the emotional balance, it seems to me. If they can anchor this fourth ray in the emotional body in a productive way so as to then launch self up, out of that emotional focus and into the mental area, and help balance it while still secure in the "square" there, then self-esteem is not at stake. They know they are secure within it. But the emotional balance must be maintained. It must be worked with, and the earlier we can begin to work with these children, the better. I would love to see belief-structure work started at age twelve. I'd like to see it on a regular basis, but not intense at first — perhaps a tape a month — and see how they react to it, see how they work with it. When I work with these young people I find that you can anticipate, you can see the problems before they develop in this life, and take them out so they don't have to experience them — rather than using the hindsight approach of being in a trauma and then trying to fix it up. You can take them out before — not that you can keep people from experiencing the problems, but you can help them when they have evolved to the point at which they can ask for help.

Children ask many questions, and you might not always know how to answer them. It is very interesting to start asking them questions and see what you get. Some of them are very aware, and you may learn a great deal from them.

Our child has grown into an adult, at which time he makes many choices on how to live his life — or does he? Perhaps not. He wants to experience everything and he doesn't know which to do first, because they are all a lot of fun. He may go from one thing to another, trying to experience everything. He is very curious about Earth living in all its aspects.

Fourth Ray Meditation

❦ *Relax completely. A few deep breaths will aid you. And let us begin now to explore this fourth ray. I want you to feel the harmony of the ray as completely as possible. So to begin, bring a beautiful, clear green down into self. It is lovely, just as clear as you can imagine, and you just know that this is an aspect of the Creator — His beautiful harmonious green energy. Bring it down into self now. Feel it. Know it is aiding you. Good. Now raise up self by means of this beautiful clear green ray. Yes, up, up, up we go. We have built a beautiful foundation here and we are going to the heights with this ray. Feel the harmony within. Feel very comfortable with this green.*

❦ *And now floating in it is some gold. Do you see that? Know that it is there. It contains the means to reach this beautiful twelfth ray. And it is raising us up, up, up, higher we go by means of this beautiful green that is now flaked with gold. Enjoy it. It is a celebration. Experience joy as we go ever higher. And we are expanding and getting lighter and lighter. The beautiful green ray is now taking us to the heights. I am enjoying it: Are you? Look! We can view everywhere from this height. It is very lovely. And the gold is now intensifying. Do you feel it? It is becoming very attuned to the Creator's heights. Here we can see all over – yes, all over creation – by means of this beautiful, clear green ray. Are you feeling very calm, very serene, very tuned-in? Enjoy it. Become a part of this ray as you continue to rise, as you continue to expand. Yes, expand, expand, by means of this glorious green ray. Isn't it marvelous – the greenness of creation, which is so clear, so comforting? It feels so good. Know it is a productive ray and that you are utilizing it to raise you to the heights. Have you noticed that the gold is getting more intense? It is. It is becoming a part of this ray as the expansion continues. Expand self in an ever greater way.*

🐞 *And now there is a teacher there. Can you see him? The Golden One stands and he puts out his arms and he says, "Welcome, my friends. Thank you for coming by means of this green ray. How productive! I come now. I greet you. I bring love to each of you." Experience now with this wonderful teacher.*

🐞 *Good. Very good. Attune to him now because he says, "Let us work for the Earth now. We will use this green ray from the heights to jack up the Earth's vibration. Specifically put it in each corner. Yes, visualize the Earth as containing corners – a square – and we place this green ray at each corner. And now we have a jack there. Jack-up the Earth. Jack it up by means of this green ray. Now we are focusing the gold there, too. It is a complex pattern of green and gold. Jack up the Earth. Work with it now, because it will rise by means of your efforts. It is what you can do to aid the Earth's vibration. This greenness is so much a part of the Earth, but now by raising it the Earth can become greater. She has nurtured us. Aid her now. Jack up the Earth by means of this green ray, which contains also the gold." The Golden One is aiding us. Jack it up. Keep working at it. Raise the Earth's vibration now . . . . Good.*

🐞 *Do you not see, my friends, that by using this beautiful green ray productively, you can accomplish much? You have expanded self and you have aided the Earth. You have attuned to a teacher – all accomplished by means of this beautiful green ray.*

🐞 *Come back now, but keep the harmony of the ray within self. You may keep it. It becomes, now, a part of you. Use it daily. Harmonize self by means of the beautiful green ray.*

🐞 *Begin to come back to awareness. Take a deep breath to make yourself a part of this room and this group again, knowing how much you have benefited. Thank you for your aid. The Earth has benefited from this meditation. Good evening, and my love to each of you.*

✧ F I V E ✧

Ray Five — Logic and Reason

ENERGY IS LIFE FORCE, AND THERE ARE MANY DIFFERENT TYPES. IF YOU CAN learn to work with specific kinds of energies for specific purposes, then you can, in a sense, be in the flow, energywise. In this lesson we will work on Ray Five, a ray being a specific type of energy. We have already covered the first, second, third and fourth. The first ray equates to will, to drive, on whatever level — we hope the divine level, but it can be on any level. It is a thrusting type of energy. The first ray is usually perceived by me as red. The second ray is blue and is the teaching ray of love/wisdom. The third is perceived by me as yellow (I say "perceived by me" because there are other perceptions of color that are not necessarily wrong; they are just different perceptions of color or of energy or life force). The third ray many times has to do with healing, with an especial attunement to what we might call the identity. The fourth ray I perceive as green and this is the ray that is closely associated with the emotional body. It is experienced on two different levels; many of you are familiar with the lower level, which is disharmony or emotional trauma. We are seeking to have everyone experience this wonderful ray on the higher or more harmonious level. That's why we encourage joy. This is the harmony of the fourth ray: the wonderful joy; the wonderful paintings you see and the music you hear — this is the harmonious level of the fourth ray.

Ray Five I perceive as orange. This particular ray is very closely associated with the mental body, and the age we are in now is focused there — you might even say "stuck there" (for many). In other words, the world perceives that existence is in the mental body, and to try to go beyond it is not appropriate. By that I mean that there are many in professions and in the scientific community who think that if one cannot logically understand something, it is not valid. They are not yet able to perceive that there is a way to integrate logic into the whole of existence – to in a sense go beyond that particular focus, into the intuitive, into the higher level of the emotional, and put it all together into one package. It's why mentally focused people have a resistance to going into esoteric studies. Once you convince them to go beyond this, they are able to understand the esoteric better than most. They are able to see how everything fits together and they do it very well, but there is a point of resistance, of holding within the mental body. The main reason for this is that this age is focused within the mental, within the fifth-ray experience, and people must go beyond this focus. In other words, they must be truly ready to go beyond the mainstream of the evolution of the planet, beyond the mental focus that's here at this time. When they are able to do this, they can begin to integrate this beautiful fifth ray and its qualities into their whole life, their whole life stream, their evolution.

The fifth ray, then, is very important now on Earth. Because there are so many of you on the Earth, you are at all levels of evolution. There are those who are still rather closed to this ray within self. In other words, these people are focused emotionally. Their mental faculties are there, of course, but they have not yet learned how to use them as a balance for the emotional body. They are the ones who are benefiting the most from the fifth ray. They are able to use this ray as it comes in more and more and focus within the mental body. When they get into an emotional trauma, they can use the mental, they can pull up out of the emotions, they can use the first ray of will to come up out of the emotional body, and they can then focus in on the area that is very important now on the Earth: the fifth ray.

In combination with the fifth ray we get the higher rays, and those have come in specifically to enable the Earth to reach a new level. They stimulate this fifth ray, and then one gets the feeling that there's a great deal coming in. You can learn to handle it so you do not get overwhelmed. One can feel a lot coming in from different directions at different times. One of the most interesting patterns occurs when we are trying to sleep. You might be considering on the inner planes the material that has been given, and are probably close enough to a conscious level that the mental patterns are working in the conscious mind. Then you are following the pattern of "think, think, think." To that you add "worry, worry, worry." Then you have "think, think, think" and "worry, worry, worry." What you have to do is break that cycle, and you can do it in different ways. One way is to turn both of them off by getting into a meditative state. That stimulates the intuition – it stimulates going beyond those particular focuses – and it's a wonderful way to go into a sleep pattern. When the mental is going around and around before sleep, you must learn to turn it off.

We have discussed how to get out of the mental before sleep. Now, how does one get into it if one is not able yet to use it? I think all of you know people who focus mostly in the emotional body. They feel about things; they don't particularly think about them. Have you ever talked to someone, saying, "I think, I think, and I think," and they tell you, "I feel, I feel, and I feel"? Usually, if you really are paying attention, you have to go where that other person is to communicate with him; if he is talking about feeling, you'd better go where he is, and then the communication will be better. The mental processes can be stimulated by those who have the feeling nature very well developed – too well, perhaps. They respond to life emotionally, always, and they are the ones who, although they want to study and grow esoterically, when they attempt to use the mind, they can't make themselves read a book or take a class. They simply resist it because it doesn't conform to the normal operation with themselves. They would much rather, for instance, have a discussion with a few friends and learn that way rather than concentrate on a book. Now, there's nothing the matter with that except that if you are finishing life on the Earth and trying to be as balanced as possible, you must balance that just like everything else within self. So if there's something you don't do well, that's probably the very thing that you should do; and if you don t, then life will probably see to it that eventually you get to do it. This is especially true when you enter the life of service. Whatever needs to be finished you'll probably get to learn, because when one serves and seeks to help the Creator, He knows you are willing to help, and because of that you will be given whatever you need to grow; whatever it is, it will come. It seems to me, however, that this is a harder way to learn than consciously trying to balance self in every way. When we learn by experiencing, we can choose our own timing. We can consciously try to develop these abilities, and then we are in control of our lives.

The mental focus on the Earth is achieved by those who are currently focused within the emotionally body – gradually, and usually with great difficulty. The reason for this is that the emotional body is held in a resistance pattern that is difficult to break. An exercise to aid this resistance pattern is to actually see the first ray, the will ray, as a ladder, a red ladder. When your emotions are churning and you are feeling very sorry for self, then is the time to get that red ladder of will. Set it very firmly on the bottom of this pit into which you have fallen, run to it and climb up out of that pit, saying, "I will do it. I choose to now." Get into your mental body, look at the situation objectively and see what has placed you there. Why are you there? What's going on? Use the experience to learn from it. Use the will to get up out of the emotional and into the mental area, and balance it. You must get up out of it. No one can do it for you. You must be able to live on the Earth and not be affected by anything. That's your goal and that's what you are reaching for – the perfect balance, and to maintain it all the time.

The fifth ray contains many specifics. The logical, mental processes are useful for scientific endeavors, for reaching down beneath the obvious. This ray has the ability to thrust right to the heart of the matter, and those who have much of this ray within self are able to pierce to and understand the heart of the matter much more easily than others. If you have a fifth-ray mind, it will always thrust into a learning experience and dig out the very essence of it, making it more clear to you and others. A scientist can get to the very basic part of his research with this fifth ray. Another good mind is the third-ray mind. It is a logical mind that has the ability to identify precisely and to organize thought, but it does not have the depth or the ability to pierce into the very essence of the subject that the fifth-ray mind has. The piercing quality of the fifth ray is why this age is important. When those who are so mentally focused, and those who are attempting to be so, can see the evolution of mankind, can pierce to the center mentally, they are going to come up with some very good realizations. More and more of humanity will be doing this. It will suddenly occur to everyone one day that there must be a basic plan here. It all fits together so well. There must be a Creator. There must be an all-knowingness; there must be something beyond the obvious. That's why the fifth ray is so important at this time. Before the mental development there was the emotional, and before that there was the physical, and now this logical process will launch the mainstream of humanity to the next level: the development of spirituality here.

The scientist upon delving into the very heart of a specific matter is impressed with the intricacies of it – the way it all fits together – and he discovers that there is so much more. No matter how small it may seem, there are so many levels, so many layers, and yet no mistakes were made – everything fits together so well that it is awesome. It is very awesome to see the magnitude of existence when you consider it mentally, and yet each small detail fits within that pattern; nothing has escaped the Creator. Everything has been designed with perfection. That's why, when scientists get into this, they are gradually led to the conclusion that there is a lot more going on than they had originally considered. This is interesting because as we approach the New Age everything is beginning to change, and scientists must enlarge their mental conceptions. For instance, the jet streams suddenly changed completely, and some scientists can't understand why because the jet streams have always fit very specifically into their patterns of understanding and all of a sudden they don't fit there anymore. As these things happen on the Earth, the mentally focused people are going to be able to see that there are other things which they must now consider in order to see the whole pattern – that perhaps the pattern is a little bigger than they thought, and they were focused too closely, and if they had stepped back a little and enlarged their perceptions, they would have noticed some other things. More and more examples of this will be noticed in the next ten to twelve years. It will be very interesting for the scientific community. There will be a lot of growth opportunity. They will learn by experiencing.

The fifth ray is coming in very rapidly and it is a part of the way to get to the New Age – the New Age being the new level that the Earth will be reaching in about twelve years. It is a focus, the forward thrust of the seventh ray — the seventh ray being the gateway into the New Age. If you study the map on which all of the energy patterns of the Earth are shown and notice the path of the fifth ray you will see the forerunner of the New Age experience. That may be evidenced in many ways. For instance, wherever there is a lot of the fifth ray, you will see a lot of New Age churches. You will see a lot of the "new thought" movement, because that truly is the gate beyond the traditional.

The fifth ray is a great focus. A good way to meditate is to see a big orange spotlight coming down into self and to focus the mental body — not necessarily on any specific subject, because you are working on focus itself. The fifth ray can be utilized to do that, so the fifth ray is helping focus the New Age. It puts the focus there and then the seventh and the higher rays begin the activity. If energies are multiple and unfocused, you get a mixed bag rather than a focused application of growth.

When we look at the cities that are fifth ray, we see activities speeded up and massive pieces of information being used. The fifth ray brings us an understanding because it balances the emotional. It integrates the two. We must be balanced mentally so that we can be tolerant, so that we can understand, so that we can get beyond trauma within self. Until you are mentally balanced, the emotion — the needs of self — hold you there and you can't see beyond it. The mentally balanced person can then get beyond to the greater understanding, to the greater focus. The mentally balanced person can see that in the Creator's Plan, the Creator is a little more important than a personal view reveals.

One of the qualities of the fifth ray is unconditional love. Cabalistically speaking, you would launch the mental focus into the higher mental, which contains the area of unconditional love. You are getting into the soul-level experience. That's what your goal is. The higher mental is focused within the Christ consciousness and the divine will, so that is the ideal triad of experience and it enables productive service to the Creator.

The fifth department of the Spiritual Hierarchy is very busy. It has a lot of members here who are very able to answer your questions. If one really projects a desire to stimulate self in this mental/logical area, help will come. Now, if you had to live in an area that had a lot of energy specifically attuned to a particular ray — as many cities do — and you settled down in a fifth-ray area, what do you think you would experience?

There is a certain pattern of intensity coming to the Earth, where more and more of the fifth ray acts in conjunction with the higher rays. It is a plan specifically outlined to balance all of the applications of the higher rays. As the higher rays come down into the Earth more intensely, the fifth ray is acting as a balance. This is probably the most important thing I have told you.

The mental focus is necessary for beginning the process of balancing everything. You can reach through the intuitive level to the higher levels, but when you are trying to balance everything completely, then it is through the mental you must go, because it balances the emotional. Of course, the intuition is very important and leads to discovering the whole. If your mind is not functioning on the fifth ray, this does not indicate that you are not using your mind. It indicates that you are using it a little differently, and maybe for some this is more appropriate. No one has said that the mental capabilities of the fifth ray are the only definition of mind. One must use the mind in balancing the emotions, and one may choose which method one uses. If you use the fifth ray, then the penetration qualities of the mental will be much greater than any other. It can be done this way, as an example, and many of you will do it this way. You will use the third ray to balance the emotions, and then a greatly developed intuition will become a part of that, but the mental capabilities will be used — not always the same ray, but they will be used.

I have been asked how we will know a New Age church. You should look it over: if there is something there that seems to be in your growth pattern, then it could be for you. There are some churches now that are harmonious with a group such as this. It depends upon the individual person. Many who come into a situation with a spiritual teacher who is trying to give them a great deal more understanding of the next level are led through a New Age church. It's truly a doorway for many, and it aids them in understanding something they've never understood before. It supports them in the concepts they are seeking to enlarge. It's an excellent way to increase your understanding of the wholeness. It gets into that concept, rather than a specifically focused perception that has long been on the Earth, because the Earth is changing so much.

As you evolve and grow, you experience much and thereby cause self to function within each of the various aspects of the different rays. The ones that are within the physical — such as the mind, the personality, the emotional body and the physical body — may change as you grow and evolve. There's an ideal pattern for each of you. Self must be balanced, but each will do it a little differently.

❖ S I X ❖

Ray Six – Devotion

W E SHALL DISCUSS THE SIXTH RAY NEXT. THIS SHOULD BE INTERESTING, and to begin with I want to show you something. I want to begin our seminar with a small meditation. We don't usually do this, but with the sixth ray I want to show you the difference. The sixth ray is here tonight, and at this point in the Earth's evolution it is a rather heavy vibration. Now, I want you to move it up a little. I want you to raise the sixth ray and I want you to do it as a group. I want to show you what you can do with a vibration by paying attention to it, by working with it.

Sixth Ray Meditation

❦ *So will you each close your eyes. Become centered. And if it helps you to see the ray as indigo, do so. But feel the energy that surrounds us in this room now, and by means of your true desire to serve, by means of your dedication, begin to feel this energy coming up, up, up. We are raising this ray, this ray that is present. We are moving this energy up by dedication, by our efforts. Feel it going higher – it's coming up. Feel it lighten. Experience it now. Good. Continue to raise it, to lighten it, knowing that the energy there can be raised, can be lightened, can be used on a higher level. Good.*

Please come back now, feeling in the flow with this energy, harmonized with it and able to see it from a different perspective. Does anyone have comments on this?

It seemed to lighten in color as it was raised. It became thinner.

What are we saying about this energy – or about energy in general? We are saying, looking at it from an optimistic point of view, that you can lighten any energy. And how did we do it? By dedication, by seeking to do it because service and dedication are a part of your life now. Interesting.

The sixth ray is a very special energy that, if you think about it esoterically, has perhaps gotten a slightly bad reputation. And it shouldn't have. It's a specific kind of energy, and truly is not any worse nor any better than any other kind of energy. It is just different and it is used for a specific type of creation. Isn't that true? Each one of these types of energy is used for a specific purpose or as a part of a specific purpose — as a part of a wholeness, the wholeness of creation.

The sixth ray has been on the Earth for a while. It has done much for the Earth. How? As a devotional focus? Good. It enabled mankind to go beyond an Earth perspective, providing a specific focus of connection with divinity, perhaps not an encompassing one but at least a specific focus that aided them. Very important, wasn't it? You don't give a ten-year-old a method that he does not yet understand, you give him a tool that he can utilize at his particular age and point of development. The sixth ray, then, was made available for Earth "ten-year-olds" so that they could have a tool for attuning specifically to divinity — in a specific way.

It also was utilized very much by the Christ — the lord Maitreya. How? As devotion to one God — obedience — used in connection with the second-ray love vibration. He focused the sixth ray here in a special esoteric sense, and through its use a certain focus grew up. Among the characteristics of that focus were the specifics of the Christian religion, of which healing was a part. (I usually equate healing with the third-ray energy.) The second- and sixth-ray connections were shown in the teaching. He went everywhere teaching and, in addition, focused on the specific religions.

The sixth department is still doing this. They are attempting, as we've said, to synthesize all the religious activities of the world. And that is very interesting. I've not been involved in that too much, but it is a challenging job, as I think you might all recognize.

It was a wonderful opportunity for the Earth when this energy began to come in. Why? Because before that time the Earth could be called (and we use this term a lot with those who are involved with purging) stuck in a pattern. What is meant by that is that people were experiencing and learning here on the Earth, but they were not really able to see beyond that specific evolutionary point or to go beyond it. Thus, each kind of energy, which is always there potentially, comes in to activate a specific opportunity in the evolution of whatever we are talking about — and right now we are talking about the Earth.

And so this specific and, on one level, rather heavy energy pattern began to be available to the Earth. Now, one thing that is interesting about Earth is its vibrational pattern — what it has been. And what is that? Heavy, yes. So if you are going to pry up the Earth's evolution, you need a big crowbar, don't you? The sixth ray is such a crowbar. It can help lift the vibrational pattern. And who focused it? Why, the Christ did — the lord Maitreya. He was on the handle of that crowbar, seeking to specifically (because that's what it was) focus. Very carefully he had preplanned this focus, the evolutionary effort.

By activating the love aspect of self to see existence as it truly is, he was seeking to focus people into love rather than fear. He activated the love aspect — unconditional love — that allows you to see with the mental processes very clearly. Unconditional love does that — it enables you to see clearly. It was complex on several levels and only partially successful, as is usually the case, but we were generally very pleased with the evolution at that time, recognizing that through free will and choices some of it would be "shelved" until a little later. And a little later is now. We are reaching that point where that which we didn't do then, we must do now.

So we have the sixth ray to help us with it. We have other vibrations — we have the seventh ray to help us, but that is our next topic. How, specifically, now that those shelved things have caught up with us, are we going to use the sixth ray to help us with it? Yes, by using unconditional love. That's always there. It isn't rationed — except by self. It is available within self when you can see it, when you can acknowledge it.

Somebody I have been working with recently made a good realization and said to me about it, "You know, I can see that." And I said, "Well, I've only said it to you five thousand times, but now you can see it — I'm so glad for you!" Unconditional love is like that. You know it is there. You understand it intellectually, but you must understand it with the knowingness and, of course, practice it. You don't have to do anything except be it. You have to be unconditional love as a part of the package. As a part of what package? As a part of the divinity package. Because, basically, all you have to know is that you are divinity — that's all. That's it. That's the whole statement. But you have to know it. It's very simple, isn't it? Isn't wholeness always simple? It's just achieving it that may not be quite that simple. But the complexity of wholeness is simple — and that's not a contradictory statement. And the unconditional love is a part of that simple complexity.

The sixth ray, then, can be used now in the sense that you can devote yourself to finding this simplicity. You can focus with it on divinity. It is specifically for doing that. Remember, we said earlier that it enables you to see beyond an obvious focus, namely an Earth-oriented one. So how about using this nice, usually heavy energy, raising it up a little as we did tonight and then using your crowbar for self and for the Earth, both, in a dual application — doing your part for the Earth and certainly aiding self, also.

Now, that is very nice and esoteric, but truly, how do we use this in a practical way? This indigo ray, which is closely connected cabalistically with the subconscious mind, has another very unique quality that I love. It is automatic — once you set it in motion, it functions that way until you change it. How about using the specific characteristics of this energy to achieve what you want and what you seek — divinity. Why do you want and seek divinity? Because that is the way you serve the Cosmic Plan. You want to serve more and more. You want to achieve these breakthroughs in self so that you can be of further service, isn't that right? That is the specific purpose of seeking growth — service to the Creator. That is important to understand.

Utilizing this energy, then, can enhance this automatic process, and then if you bring in the transmuting Violet Flame (the seventh ray) you can do a great deal for self and then begin to reference the higher rays. Using the seventh ray will get you to a progressive transformation through all of the higher rays, truly. But the seventh ray in connection with the sixth starts the automatic process — this can help cleanse what is already there that you want to get rid of, and then you use the seventh ray to also transmute self, to change self. And between the two of them, you can do a great deal for self. Then you begin to reference the higher rays — the eighth, more cleansing, the ninth, really letting go and finishing the cleansing, and so on in a progressive manner until you can achieve a major point at the twelfth ray.

But beginning with the sixth, putting it on automatic, use this wonderful process in a manner that will aid you instead of holding you, as it has. If you have been using it with the subconscious mind, it has kept you as you have experienced in the past. Instead of using it that way, visualize it as holding a new pattern that you see, that you want — a new experience — and then put that on automatic with this ray. That is the way to use an energy pattern productively. The sixth ray is the energy we use to hold on to patterns we have created in our lives, and it is also the way to hold on to new patterns we create. Having raised it up with our opening meditation, we can now use it on a new level — like creating our own steps in a ladder.

This energy is going to be available for a little while longer — it is rather fading out. I encourage you to use it now while it is available. Then when it comes back to the Earth later, after the New Age has begun — it will be a while — it will be available at a new level for another opportunity in evolution that the Earth will need at that particular time, you see. That is how energy is used. It will, at that time, be a finer vibration because the Earth will be on a new level.

The energy patterns have a whole range of levels, depending on where they are used. You could say they can be played in any octave, depending on where you are playing them in creation and what kind of instrument you have there. Are you playing on a Stradivarius or are you playing on a homemade?

The physical vibration is of a specific density, to begin with, and then those who live there partake of this density. But part of the reason they are there in the first place is because they can exist there. It is the choices they make in their evolution that eventually affect that vibration, so there is a circle there. The vibrational pattern of the Earth has definitely been created by those who have lived here and evolved here. But to begin with it was a specific, and then the people who lived here created it from what they were, in aggregate amounts. It is not any one specific time or person, but a combination, a synthesis of what has been.

Even though the sixth ray is being withdrawn, the potentiality will always be there. You could say that the focus is being withdrawn and that this is the way those within the spiritual government direct some of the energies. How? Under the direction of our superior, Sanat Kumara, who functions under the direction of his superior, and so on and so forth until we get to the Source Itself. And it fits into the whole scheme of things in all of creation — what we are doing here is a reflection of what is happening at the universal level.

We are saying that after the New Age begins, when the Earth is at a higher level, there will not be a focus here of this sixth-ray energy. What does this say about the subconscious mind? Does it say, perhaps, that the focus will not be on it as much (cabalistically speaking) as at soul level? The focus will be on a higher level. The subconscious is an integral part of the process, of course, but will no longer be focused on as the only part of creation that truly exists. The subconscious will blend with the divine will in service to the Creator, rather than remaining connected with the personality level. In the New Age only those who are focused on spirituality will be here. The whole era will be focused on spirituality. It will be a whole new age in which spirituality is the focus.

In about ten years, as I have said, there is probably going to be an interesting encounter in regard to synthesizing the churches. At that time there will be a lot of sixth ray here. After that time, after that resolution, probably (I am looking at probabilities here) we will see less sixth ray.

At this time it would be helpful, in using the sixth ray, to focus on its positive qualities and seek to transmute its energies to the highest level. That's why we talked about it tonight — so you can use it that way.

The second ray is the outline, truly, the pattern and the main vibration here on the Earth — the one from which all the rest are derived, in an esoteric sense. But the sixth, as a reflection of this pattern, of this outline, holds it specifically as it comes into form.

We've said that the rays are different kinds of energy, and that energy is the means by which creation takes place. The rays are specifics in different types of creation, and there are basically seven different kinds of energies. Then there are the higher rays, which have been given as a specific for evolving the consciousness of the Earth and those on it (if they choose) to the level of the New Age. The Spiritual Hierarchy, in a rather complicated manner, brings forth these energies and makes them available for the Earth. Originally, everything comes from the Source and it is stepped down in a ladderlike fashion by a specific evolving consciousness whose function it is to do just that — to focus a specific energy, or a combination of them, depending on the level at which we are looking, and then to make them available in a usable fashion for the next level of evolution.

Now, the Planetary Logos here on the Earth, through his state of evolution, through what he is, is able to make available to the Earth the specific types of energy that are needed. Some of them come directly, truly, into the Shamballa area; some are passed through other members of the Hierarchy in a specific way. But basically it is true that the Planetary Logos is the focus, and because of what he is — the second-ray energy in a cosmic sense — yes, the second ray is the great ray of which the Earth partakes. And its subdivisions are what we call the seven rays. If you want to get technical about it, these are a division of the great cosmic second ray.

The purpose of evolution, the means by which we evolve and the reason for doing it, is to take part in the Creator's experience — to share with Him and to help Him implement the Cosmic Plan in a manner as attuned, as harmonious with what He wishes as possible, and in as conscious a manner as we can. We partake of it whether or not we are conscious of it, but the goal is to do it consciously. We still function within the same universal laws, whether we do it consciously or not. We still utilize the rays, because energy is the basic unit of creation.

When church members worship, they utilize the sixth ray a great deal, whether they are conscious of it or not. They are using the devotion which they truly experience — that is very sixth ray. What are they doing with that devotional pattern? They are using it to raise their consciousness within a narrow focus of divinity. That's good. It may be narrow, but it is a high channel for them and very appropriate for their understanding at that particular time. Yes, they are using it, they certainly are. They certainly use the fourth ray also — harmony through conflict. That one is used on the Earth all the time. It is used in wars — but that gets into the first ray, too. Now, when you go out into Mother Nature and see the beautiful deer and the little ones — they are so cute, aren't they? — isn't that a harmonious level of the fourth ray? When you see a beautiful mountain you partake of the highest level of the fourth ray. So you see, we use all of these rays all the time. Whether or not we understand it from that focus is perhaps incidental some of the time.

What are we doing, then? We are experiencing as divine sparks from the time we come from the Source. And we seek to experience in as definitive a manner as possible. But in the process we probably focus in different ways during each part of our journey. And if we can't yet see the whole journey, well, we will eventually, won't we?

First of all, we must get to the point where we recognize that we are responsible for creating our lives, and then be willing to think and go beyond that — be willing to acknowledge that our destiny is to be this cocreator I've talked about so much. And we see, by taking responsibility for self, how we are going about it — we objectively understand how we are learning and what we are learning, and we see how it all fits into that divine pattern we talked about earlier.

That's why so many of you come, and you seek and you learn. What are you learning? Well, you are trying to see the divine pattern of self and of everything — of the universe, truly. And then consciously, step by step, you reach that cocreator state. But the conscious part is important — and it is only done as a summing-up process of the Earth living. That is important. You must experience many focuses on the Earth, utilize many different types of energy, and then what happens? First of all, you reach a point and you think, Is this all there is? Isn't there anything else? Am I going to be doing this forever? Have you been there, friends? Then you begin to recognize that there is something else and you begin to seek it. I can see you've all been there and that's why you are here. People can take as long as they like to get to the point where the gateway of responsibility is reached!

What is the function of the head of the Hierarchy's sixth department, besides focusing the ray? Well, right now it is to gather together the religions of the world into a focus — one focus. And as you can understand, that's quite a strenuous assignment. But he, the master Jesus, is very able to do this, and I have total confidence, because of who he is and his specific abilities, that it will be accomplished. We are ten years or so away from the most obvious attempt to do this. We will see, about ten years from now, the . . . well, I don't like to say "clash" — the "coming together" of different opinions, and out of that coming together, on whatever level they choose to come together, will be the resultant solution. This includes all religions, not just the Christian factions — the Eastern religions too, and all of them. All are parts of the whole, aren't they? What we are talking about is mixing perceptions. If you objectively figure out how to work with it all, it blends. That's what the master Jesus is seeking to do — to objectify the religions of the world into a specific focus of divinity. This doesn't mean that after the New Age there won't still be some differences of perception, but I think that because of the long evolutionary period here on the Earth, it has become somewhat fragmented. And some blending, you might say, is rather appropriate now, isn't it? You are not really going to change anything, because the divinity is always there. What you are changing is the perception with which divinity is viewed, and perhaps the level at which it is viewed.

Now, creation when done at the Source is always orderly. It's always perfect. It's always enlarging and becoming, always getting more and more clear, more and more free-flowing, always becoming and expanding. Evolving consciousnesses (cocreators in training) who haven't yet understood completely, get involved, and what is created is not yet at the level of the original Source — the Creator. We are all learning, but we have not yet clearly seen as the Source does, so we get what you might call a mixed bag in creation.

All creation comes from the Source Itself, originally. The Source is an origination point, and within It are evolving consciousnesses that have gone through the loop of experiencing and have again entered the Source to become cocreators. That is all a part of the original Source. Everything was created from that Source — every universe, everything. We are talking about a very remote-from-Earth-living point. A divine spark that is not at the level of the Source creates on not quite as perceptive a level, not quite as evolved a level, because it can't yet see as clearly as the Source can. Remember, we've said, "All we have to see is divinity." When we can see that, and there is nothing else, then we can create from that level.

Most people pray to a specific focus of divinity as they understand it, regardless of what name they give it. What they call it isn't even important, as long as it is divinity. The name they call it is merely their perception of divinity. What is going to happen in the Moslem world, with all the violent differences? Well, they are going to have some interesting growth opportunities. They must eventually let go of a specific focus that they have, but they may keep it as long as they wish.

I have been asked about the Ayatollah Khomeini. Well, I don't evaluate other individuals for anyone. I don't do that. Why don't you evaluate him? That's good for you — it's called learning discernment. It is very interesting to see the understandings of Earth living, and the complete nonunderstandings of it, and the focuses for specific purposes that really have nothing to do with divinity. It's very interesting. It is part of the evolution of the planet, part of the physical experience. When we come here into physical existence, we get many opportunities. Some of us take advantage of them to understand our totality and who we truly are, and some use existence for other purposes, but eventually we all must come to the understanding of who we are. But for a while, we might not care. You know, we get too focused in on our own needs and desires — and that is the crux of the matter. When we are focused on self more than divinity, then what we get is not free-flowing when we create it. What we get is less than divine. What we get, my friends, many times, is chaos. Yes. That's how you can tell who is doing the creating.

The most important thing you must learn is who you are — that you are divinity. That is the most important thing you must learn — to see it clearly. And one of these times you are going to come to me and say, "I see that. How come you didn't tell me that before?" You have to accept that what the Creator is, is what you are — that He has brought you forth in order that you may individualize what He is, and then you may experience at whatever level you choose, but He hopes that eventually you are going to share with Him on the same level because that's where it's most fun — the cocreator state. It will be! I promise you that — and I haven't been there, either, but I've been told that's true. Yes, it's a lot of fun, joy and sharing, and expansiveness eternally.

Expansiveness and the joy of such expansiveness and the joy of the sharing — that's important because as one becomes a cocreator he leaves the individualized state in the sense that he leaves the separateness and joins again completely the wholeness concept, while still remembering with his individual consciousness what has been learned and accepted at that level. He is experienced, in other words, as he was not before. When he came forth from the Source, he was a pattern of divinity. What's the difference? The difference is the leap of experiencing in which he learned the creative processes and saw the pattern of divinity so clearly that he can create at that level. The experiencing makes the difference.

The sixth ray was given as a specific focus; it was considered the most appropriate. It is the one that was given at the time of the Christ – it really came before that time, but that was the height of that experience. These rays, when they begin to come in, do it rather slowly. You know, it isn't appropriate to "zap" humanity with a new ray at full intensity in five minutes. You have to let humanity gradually get used to it. Now, if this specific were not present, what other ray could you use? Yes, the third ray. It holds, but in the process of holding it allows you to expand – that's an interesting paradox. But why is the sixth ray better? Because in addition to the holding quality, it has the devotional aspect.

Master Jesus is working with devotional patterns. He is working with specific religious organizations and he can, truly, research and understand each particular one and, from that understanding of each one, see it and synthesize it – use that energy to raise the level of the experience. Where? To the level of wholeness. And then he can see it as a whole, and with his consciousness, with his abilities, he can work on that level. You see, the masters are working with large groups of consciousness, with humanity as a whole. He brings it into being on a spiritual level before it starts to work its way down into creation, because it must be done that way. He is bringing it to the wholeness level by his wonderful synthesis ability now, and bringing it down into the astral-plane level. It's already there. All we have to do is bring it forth. Everything we need for the New Age is already there; we just have to bring it forth.

How is the master Jesus preparing you for the New Age? You all go to classes at night during sleep. You've all studied all of these religions. You've all sought to understand their strengths and what's happening. What you get in the inner-plane classes from the master Jesus is his understanding of what's happening with the religions of the world, as well as what each of you can do to aid this situation. Now, you might not remember it consciously, but it's all there.

In addition to his teaching, he focuses energy to bring about the origination process as far as Earth-level living is concerned. The energies have to be understood and worked with to bring about this synthesis, and we all work with them a great deal. This is what we do, mainly. We teach, yes, but that is only part of what we do. We work with vast amounts of energy in different combinations and for different purposes. Why? To bring about at the spiritual level what is desirable in the evolution of the planet.

Will there be a one-church consciousness? I feel that there will be –

maybe not until about the time of the New Age, but it will be very interesting when we reach that point. It is definitely changing already. More flexibility is coming in. The New Age churches are very helpful for those who are beginning to see that they must enlarge their understanding, aren't they? They are very definitely helpful.

As we approach the New Age, the sixth ray will be withdrawn and the seventh ray will come in stronger because it is, specifically, the gateway to the New Age. It has been getting stronger for a number of years already, and the higher rays are becoming more prominent also and becoming a part of the package of energy that's available.

This is all simplified, of course. It is really more complicated. There are elements, and within those there are other elements, and within those others. It is like looking at creation. You can look at something that is very, very big or something that's very, very small, and one thing would fit into another, wouldn't it? Certainly the seventh ray contains many parts of the other energies, and the sixth does also. Each one does, in a different combination, so that when you make up that combination, you get the element or package that we call that particular ray. Yes, the Earth functions on the second ray, which is divided into seven different kinds of energy. When Sanat Kumara came to the Earth as the Planetary Logos, he brought the second ray with him. He brought this focus to the Earth. Before he came, the Earth did not have much of a focus, not as specific.

Who is the Planetary Logos? He is a heavenly being. We call him a heavenly man — one who has evolved and understood divinity much more clearly than has anyone else now connected with the Earth. He came here eighteen million years ago to focus divinity so that the evolvement of the Earth could take place as it had never been able to do until that point. I have said that he ensouls the Earth. He came here directly from Venus, together with some other great beings, but that was certainly not his origination point. A great heavenly being who has maintained that focus for eighteen million years — think about it! Nothing human — a heavenly being.

Now, the white light of the Creator, the Source that contains everything, focuses on divinity, but not on a specific aspect of divinity. The second ray, for instance, has its own focus, but contains all the others; its focus is on the second. All seven rays contain the other rays, but each has its specific focus.

In the New Age we will have twelve rays — the seven plus the five higher rays. They are here now potentially. Not all of them have been active all of the time as yet. They were brought to the Earth only recently.

✧ S E V E N ✧

Ray Seven — Transmutation

R AY SEVEN IS OUR TOPIC TONIGHT. IT IS CALLED BY MANY THE TRANSMUTING Violet Flame. Transmuting to what? To another level — to a higher level of perception, enabling those who use it in a perhaps progressive way to reach a new level of understanding. It is becoming more and more apparent that those who are seeking to understand beyond what I have called the obvious are utilizing this ray as an important tool for doing so.

How many of you really enjoy wearing violet? How do you feel in it? Have you noticed that on a day when you wear violet (which, if you haven't noticed, I want you to do), significant opportunities present themselves? Now, what do I mean by that? I mean that this energy has a way of allowing your understanding to come to a specific point that you might not have quite been able to put a handle on before. And by wearing it, you perhaps intensify that opportunity. Isn't that interesting? Yes, the violet colors that you wear on the outside may be reflected into your inner understanding. Now, this is interesting and important, but why is it like this? What characteristics does this ray have? For those of you who are not familiar with our subject, energy is life force. It is the means by which creation takes place. And there are different kinds of energy for different purposes. Knowing about the specific kinds and how to utilize them can be very helpful. It is a means to increasing your understanding in different ways. And, of course, the more we understand about life and why we are partaking of it, and the more we can use natural laws to aid others and self, the more appropriate it is.

It is part of your evolution to use in the most appropriate way what has been given to you by the Creator, so we are studying these rays. We have reached the seventh ray, and next we will go into what have been termed the higher rays. They are for the purpose of aiding evolution specifically as we begin the approach to the New Age, which is just a way of saying that the

New Age simply means a new level of Earth evolution, a very important one. Now, the seventh ray is the gateway to that experience. You could say that we are reaching up to a ledge, and the seventh ray is the means by which we grasp it and begin to understand it. It is specifically for moving toward this greater perceptual experience on the Earth.

Let's begin by talking about this particular kind of energy and how we might use it to aid self and others. The Violet Flame can be utilized in a meditation for a general clearing process. And in your meditations many of you are doing this. Now, if you are not yet meditating, you can learn how to do it. It is just tuning within self and finding out who is in there, getting acquainted with the inner part of self. And it is very reassuring to many to find out there really is someone there. Perhaps they hadn't thought of it before. Well, that's kind of silly, but it's true that when we are dealing with the Earth on the everyday level, we sometimes forget that there is an inner self that is very eager to communicate with us. Using the Violet Flame can help you to understand self more completely and to then unlock and go beyond that understanding. It has been used for hundreds of years, truly, but is now reaching a point of intensity on the Earth (in other words, there is more of it here) that allows the cleansing and the clearing to be even more thorough.

Now, those of you who are working with me within the subconscious mind belief structure know that we like specifics for the clearing process. This is true, but even with this type of specificity, there are some . . . you could say crumbs, some kernels left, and we want to sweep the table clean. How better to do it than by the Violet Flame. This is an important tool. And one way to do it is to (in a state of meditation) know — and if you don't see it, that's all right, it doesn't matter — know that coming down into self is a beautiful brush, and it's turning around, and around, and around, and it's a beautiful violet, and it's cleansing all of the self. It does work. It sounds kind of silly if you haven't tried it, but as the old saying goes, don't knock it until you've tried it. (I like modern English, and I use it.)

All right, then, the Violet Flame can unlock this New Age experience, and the specifics of it are important. We have said it has cleansing characteristics. What else does it have? It has an ability to precisely identify within self exactly what remains to be done. We haven't ever really talked about this, but the precise quality of the ray is important. If you meditate with it and use it over a period of time, you may get some interesting opportunities to look at self, and those who work with me know that when I use the word "interesting," it's like a red flag, isn't it? It means that if you use this energy regularly in meditating, you are going to get to look at self pretty closely. That's good, isn't it? Yes, you will get to see what's there. Maybe that will be absolutely wonderful. You know, it probably will be, because all of you are basically very wonderful. You have and are divinity. Looking at divinity can be a very interesting and wonderful experience. This is what you are always attempting to do – to see your divinity clearly and to see how it relates into the wholeness. The Violet Flame, then, can help you find out how clear you are.

Now, some of you ask me that: "How clear am I?" The Violet Flame can help you find out and it will allow you to see. I would say to use it daily for about two weeks, and then take a look at what you see. You will have become aware of the next step to take, and that's why the Violet Flame is important now. It is a step-by-step, do-it-yourself kit to the New Age, to higher perception. That's important, and it's why this energy is coming in so strongly now. The New Age is a wonderful opportunity to understand existence at a more perceptive level – to be clearer. It can be gained by means of the Violet Flame.

What else does the Violet Flame have that we can utilize at this important time? We've said it has preciseness and it has the cleansing ability. If you feel more comfortable when you use the Violet Flame, it is because you have moved to a higher, more harmonious level. There is no right or wrong way to attune to it. Some can visualize it, others can just know it is there. It's always there. You can always have any of these rays, any of these energies that you want. There is an unlimited supply from the Source. You are really not limited in anything by the Source, you know. You can have everything you want. You are entitled to it. All you have to do is know that you can have it – and that includes abundance, prosperity . . . anything.

Have you ever noticed how Mother Nature uses the color violet? Have you ever looked at the beautiful violet-colored flowers? Have you seen a whole field of them? They are very delicate, aren't they? Does this say to you that this type of vibration is delicate? It's precise, but quite delicate. Intricate, yes – and that's true of almost everything that is violet. It is either intricate or, if it is large, it is delicate. Orchids are considered to be very special. At one time, to receive a beautiful orchid was really the desire of every young lady when she went to a dance, wasn't it? She felt very special to have this beautiful orchid. It was the symbol of being special, the symbol of someone caring enough to give you this token of special consideration. The Violet Flame, likewise, is a delicate and cherished type of transmuting energy. It is coming in more so that we are getting the full potential of it now. It has been around for a few thousand years, but the intensity of it is increasing and becoming almost full-strength now to enable the New Age to begin.

How else can we use this type of energy – how can we use it to aid others? Well, for one thing, you can use it in your meditations. You can put it all over the Earth. You can see the Earth literally becoming transmuted in the Violet Flame, and that is very helpful. I've said to you often, and I am saying it again now, that for the next two years meditations will be very important. Group meditations especially are very important to aid the Earth in this next two-year period. This is a specific way to aid the Earth. See it transmuted by means of the Violet Flame. See it rising up, being transmuted. Work with it. If you like, you can even throw orchids at it. Wouldn't that be fun? You can see the violet in any way you want to. Use an orchid for the Violet Flame — and you might see it as a flame, too, for it is violet, intense. And then put in some of the beautiful luminosity; do that in your meditation. Seeing it as luminous gets it into the higher-ray category — that's very important.

All right, now, the one within the Hierarchy who is so closely associated with the Violet Flame is Saint Germain, the one who is called the master R. He works with many of you and is a spiritual teacher who is extremely well known by humanity because he has been around awhile and he is the specific one who is turning that key in the lock that is opening it to the New Age. He has many abilities that will help bring in this New Age, including the conceptual abilities that utilize this type of energy, along with everything else to "put it all together." He works with large amounts of this energy. You could say he is not doing this in a physical body — let's keep this in mind. Part of the time he is doing it in the etheric body, and the rest of the time within the mental body or a combination of the two. In his work he is literally seeing problem areas on the Earth and transmuting them (where he is allowed) by means of the Violet Flame. This is a part of his responsibility, done under the direction of the head of the hierarchic government, Sanat Kumara, and the Christ. The specific locations he deals with are the troubled spots of the world, and I don't think you'll have any trouble identifying where some of those are. He's very concerned right now about Central America — imagine that — and about the Middle East, China, the United States and Russia. Think about that. He's working in specific areas within those countries with the Violet Flame, but his work is very vast. It doesn't deal with specific people (except with his students). It deals with the energy fields on the Earth in general. And that's one thing that I am trying to get across — that the members of the Hierarchy generally work with vast amounts of energy.

If you feel attracted to this being, you may call on him. He has given you permission to do that. He will work with anyone who does so. And if you establish a direct connection, it doesn't matter if you know what he looks like — he has looked like many, many people, because he's had many lives. Whatever you perceive him as will be fine, but it might be a good idea to perceive him as being within the Violet Flame itself, and then establish a two-way connection. You might be within the Violet Flame also, and begin to flow a communication between the two of you by means of this transmuting Violet Flame. I think you might get some very interesting things from that.

You can call him the master R. or Saint Germain, whichever you prefer. He will respond to your call. It is his desire to contact all who ask, and he is able to do this now. He has specifically told me to tell people this, because he wants the contact. The more people we have using the Violet Flame, the better. When we get focuses of Violet Flame all over the planet, it's going to bring that energy down and focalize it — allow it to be used more and more between the Spiritual Hierarchy and the planet. Just visualize that — all of these streams coming on to the Earth. How marvelous! Do you know anybody in China? Write them and tell them to do this. Russia? The Middle East? How about Egypt? Write them and tell them to do this. It would be very appropriate to let people all over the world know about it, if they are into this type of a thing, working in this manner.

✧ E I G H T ✧

Rays Eight, Nine and Ten

LET US TALK ABOUT THE HIGHER RAYS IN GENERAL – A LITTLE INTRODUCTORY statement here. We've said that basically there are seven kinds of energy. Well, what about the other five – where did they come from? And what are they? The higher rays were given to the Earth about ten or eleven years ago. Were they specifically created for us? Well, in a sense. They are aggregates of energy. In other words, they are specific combinations of energy, of rays, plus one important ingredient: undifferentiated energy. You could say wholeness is mixed in, or that there is a little white put in with the rays and they become luminous from it. You see, the Source, the Creator light, really raises up specific combinations of the other seven rays. That's truly what the higher rays are: specific combinations of energies plus the light, the white, the wholeness – and that's the ingredient that makes the difference. So then they become a series of rays to aid evolution on the planet, and each one has a specific purpose, used progressively until we get to the twelfth one.

Ray Eight – Cleansing

Ray Eight is perceived as a green-violet luminosity. It is composed of three kinds of energy – the fourth (emotional), the seventh (physical) and the fifth (mental) rays. Now, the fifth ray is able to penetrate to great depth – and you want to cleanse what? Well, for one thing, the emotional body. And you want to transmute it – you want to transmute all of self, but it is usually the emotional body that needs it most. It is a major factor in the cleansing process here on the Earth. So you have these three kinds of energies, plus a liberal sprinkling of the Source light, the white, the wholeness. Then you scramble, mix well, and you get the eighth ray, leading from the seventh.

We've talked about the transmuting flame, the seventh ray. It begins to transmute you to a higher level – to a possibility. And what possibility? Well, the beginning of the ninth ray, the body of light. That's very important, but you know you don't want a body of light if it's a little dirty. You want to cleanse it a lot first, to clean it up a little. If you are going to bring a beautiful luminous light into your house to illuminate it, you want the floor nice and clean, and you perhaps want to have nice white walls to reflect the beauty of it. So you must cleanse by means of this beautiful eighth ray. It cleanses, it helps you go beyond what has been experienced through the eons on the Earth.

And what has been experienced on the Earth, for the most part? Pain, yes – a painful way of approaching life. Isn't that interesting – that you can use the eighth ray to get rid of the pain. And then on the very next ray what do you encounter? Joy! Perhaps the Creator really does know what He's doing!

As the cleansing continues through the use of the eighth ray, a lot of old energy gets loosened up. Now, we've said that energy is just energy – it is neither good nor bad, it is just energy. So what matters is the way it is utilized, true? You are going to loosen the way that you've used certain energy, aren't you? But it is still there. What happens to this energy as you cleanse it and loosen it from its previous usage? You raise its vibration to a level in which you can see more clearly – clearness is the key here. The energy then helps to establish a new base. This is part of what is happening to all of you as you work on yourselves and begin to transmute self by means of the Violet Flame. So on the Earth there's quite a bit of the eighth ray present now. There's also some ninth and some tenth.

The transmutation, the cleansing, the raising begins to take place, and all of this energy that was tied up in the misconceptions you've had within self is actually utilized by self to rise up to a clearer level. Now, sometimes this is a very interesting encounter for self. Self encounters the personality. The personality is pretty much interested in maintaining what is called the status quo, isn't it? And when this happens, when you are working on self, using this beautiful eighth ray and the cleansing process, suddenly what was, is no longer, and you are somewhere else. The personality looks and says, "My goodness, we were here and now we're there. What's going to happen?" The next time the personality looks, you are on yet another level. What happens then? Well, many times the personality begins to dig its heels in a little. It says, "Now wait a minute – it's happening so fast."

You see, you are getting it from more than one place. You are using meditations; you are using the removal systems; you are using the transmuting flame; the eighth ray is coming in. All of these things are changing you very rapidly. The very nature of change is resisted in the physical body. So just know it, just allow it and do it anyway, and don't worry about it, because you can then transcend it. That's important to know, isn't it?

But consciously bringing in this eighth ray, literally using it now, can be very beneficial. And I really want to talk about how to use it rather than giving so much intellectual information – how to use it specifically to aid you.

Have you tried the technique of aligning all four bodies – the spiritual, the mental, the emotional and the physical? Cleansing all four bodies while using the alignment technique is important. The emotional body in particular will respond most readily to the eighth ray. I suggest an alignment meditation in which you actually view this.

Four-Body Alignment Meditation

❦ *See now the four bodies – the four parts of self – in perfect alignment: the spiritual body at the top, and then the mental body, the emotional body and the physical body, all lined up in a vertical manner. Now, for the purposes of this meditation, the spiritual, mental and physical bodies are to be filled with white light. See them filled with white light, but reference them as we work with the emotional body.*

❦ *Note what happens when we do the following: See, now, the emotional body – the second from the lowest – completely filled with the eighth ray, a beautiful green-violet luminosity. Intensely focus on it now, more and more – put in more and more of this beautiful eighth ray. Fill it full, pack it full of this green-violet luminosity. And now expand, expand, expand this body. Notice (look quickly) what is happening in the other bodies. I will give you a moment.*

❦ *Keep the focus within the emotional body – keep it intense, keep the eighth ray there intensely – but look now also at the other bodies . . . it is working. Feel the cleansing there. And now all four bodies go up, up higher, because of this cleansing process. Note what is happening now. The cleansing continues within the emotional body. More and more eighth ray. More and more. And again, expand, expand, expand . . . .*

All right, good. Come back now, and we will discuss the other bodies with the emotional body cleansed by the eighth ray.

Some of you who are working on opening the third-eye chakra can stimulate it by means of the eighth ray – but do it carefully! Do not cleanse and open it too suddenly. If you don't notice any change, then use the ninth ray on it. If you still don't notice anything, use the tenth ray on it – each one being a slightly higher energy. If you get all the way to the twelfth and haven't noticed anything, perhaps use the white light for further meditation. In other words, when you are sitting there, see coming into self a ray aimed at the third-eye area. Sit for a couple of minutes, knowing that it is the beautiful green-violet luminosity. And as it comes in, see an opening. It should be rather like a tunnel. It too might be green-violet. Can you see a light at the end of that tunnel? Then go through it and allow self to see beyond that light. It might not happen in five minutes, but I think these exercises with the higher rays will stimulate that more perceptive inner vision. And you see, with the ninth ray, it would be a different color, wouldn't it? The tunnel would be a lovely, luminous, light blue-green. Now, you could put a few little diamonds around if you wish, and some sapphires – have a beautiful tunnel. I once saw one like that – a cave – it was lovely. I used to meditate there. Oh my, did I meditate there! You know, each one of those crystals focused on some of that wonderful energy. My teacher said, "Come on out of the cave!"

You might also try a crystal at the third eye. Put it right on the third-eye area. Use a natural quartz crystal and see the eighth ray, then the ninth, tenth, eleventh and twelfth. You will get some very interesting observations of the inner spaces. It will be fun.

Now, I want to give you some other techniques you might do. View yourself as a giant crystal. Your whole body is a crystal, and it is crystal-clear. Fill it with the green-violet luminosity and get in touch with your body as viewed in that manner. Especially those of you who are working on the physical body should try this. As you view the body through this ray, notice where the color is not clear. If you see within the body an area that has a gray or muddy color, evaluate that area – what kind of a physical is that? Perhaps it needs some attention. Then get a spray bottle and put an extra dose of that ray there. Spray it there very much. Is it in the kidney area? Is it in the heart area? Is it in one of the chakra areas? The solar plexus? A joint area? Where is it? Look within self as within a crystal. It is a very interesting way to utilize this ray.

Now, this particular energy is very valuable for the Earth at this time. And I would certainly include it in your group meditations. You could use this technique of seeing the Earth as a crystal and filling it with this ray. And pay attention, you who are very visual, to the astral plane: Where do you see dark areas? Transmute them. That part of the Earth needs more cleansing. So again, with your bottle, spray more of this ray on it, and maybe some gold, too. Shake some gold on it with your cosmic salt shaker! Always, you can use the twelfth ray in connection with any of the others. The gold of the twelfth ray is specifically for aiding the Earth.

What about the Earth's emotional body? It has the four bodies, also. Try seeing its bodies lined up and filling them full of the eighth ray, expanding them and seeing what happens.

Now, we haven't said much about the fifth ray, but it is very penetrating. It is a necessary ingredient for approaching the specific areas that need to be cleansed. It has great focusing qualities. Thus, it enables a specific focus. When using them together, one ray reinforces the others. In this way, the eighth can be focused in an area that is very, very interesting. You might think of this cabalistically. Also, there are ways of looking at it astrologically.

Wherever you are focused, the eighth ray will help your evolution. All of the higher rays do that – they are a progressive way of aiding evolution at any point. The seventh ray has a specific connection with the astral, with the subconscious mind. So you can use the eighth ray to cleanse the subconscious mind. It would be appropriate to use it in areas that are very heavy for you, areas you have difficulty clearing. It can aid in getting rid of little remnants that are still affecting you. It can help to raise you to a higher level. And how marvelous! The cleansing, of course, of the subconscious then allows the more perceptive level to move right in, which is what all of you are looking for.

Use your eighth-ray spray bottle. You might keep it right there on your spiritual table and use it to cleanse. If your feet hurt or your joints ache or your head aches, spray them. But it's not appropriate to use your spray bottle on anyone else unless they ask you. If you have a little animal that's hurting, why, try a little spray on it. It might be very interesting. Or with a little grandchild who falls down and bumps his knee, you might say, "I will fix it by means of my spray bottle." Children can truly accept this and would benefit a great deal — they'd probably utilize it as well as or better than each of you.

Ray Nine – Joy

Going on, Ray Nine is a beautiful light green-blue, not quite aqua. It is luminous (shining) — I like to call this ray joy, or the ray attracting the full potentialities. The ninth ray continues the cleansing process, and as you cleanse and raise the level of self you bump into other possibilities. The soul level begins to approach, and you can see it there. That christed part of self we call the soul level becomes a distinct possibility. So for those of you who are seeking this soul-merge, or who just want to evolve, utilizing this beautiful ninth-ray energy will certainly aid the process. And if suddenly your soul says, "Here I am and I've come to stay. I brought my suitcase!" — you will know that it worked.

Now, the body of light also becomes a distinct possibility with this ninth ray — not recognized or realized completely, but a potential which you begin to see can be a part of you in physical existence. That's the important point to realize: All of you utilize it on other levels, but you can also utilize it on the physical plane. And with the ninth ray, suddenly that occurs to you. You say, "Look, there it is – that beautiful luminosity." The body of light has this luminous quality. By meditating on the ninth ray you get in touch with it more and more.

In meditation, then, the following realizations should be sought: What is a body of light? How can I make it now a part of self? What about the christed part of self — this desired level — how do I realize it? Because, of course, that is all that needs to be done. Once you can realize it as a part of self on the physical plane, then truly have you moved to that next level we are calling soul level. The ninth ray has specific characteristics that help you get in touch with it.

Now, we haven't talked about its composition. It is rather interesting and not nearly so complex as you might think. What do you suppose it contains? Yes, it has second ray in it, as well as first ray. Now, think about it. What does first ray do? It thrusts into new possibilities — the possibility of reaching this christed part of self, the possibility of making that first contact with the body of light. And it is because of the blending of these two rays with the white light of the Source that you can utilize it in this regard.

Now, we've said it has a green-blue luminosity. What does the green indicate? When you mix specific types of energy with the white light of the Source, you get some unexpected effects. The first three rays are very special — they are the three main rays. The other four rays really come from the third ray itself. So the first three have very strong characteristics, much more definitive than the other rays, which are a blend and come through the third ray. However, we have to remember that all of the rays that reach the planet come through the great second ray. Why then is the ninth ray this color, if it is a blend of the first ray and the second, which have no green? It must mean that the Earth experience, the very nature of physical existence, causes this ray to be green — that if you were utilizing this ray on another level, you wouldn't get this reflected color. The first ray when blended with the second ray and the Source light creates in physical existence this color. But on the spiritual plane it would appear blue and white. How would red appear on the spiritual plane if blended with white and blue? You could get a pinkish cast, but the predominant color you get there (and it's true on the Earth too) is blue. The green that gives the appearance of aqua is a reflection because of the nature of physical existence. We've said the foundation of physical existence is the fourth ray, the green ray. The nature of the spiritual plane is the wholeness, and if you use the rays on different levels, you get different reflections, depending on where you are — different combinations.

All right, first and second ray blended. That means that if you think of how you would utilize first ray on a level that is in attunement with divine will, then this ninth ray could probably be utilized in a way that would enhance the first ray. In other words, if the thrusting energy of the first ray used at the divine will level is followed by such a ray (the ninth ray) on the spiritual plane, what happens? First the expanding existence would tune you directly into joy, wouldn't it? It would be the means by which all existence as it expands is then attuned to its possibilities. It gets right in touch with it there. Again, the Creator knew what He was doing — imagine that! This is the initial expansion process. Then, it seems to me, this quality would allow existence to attract the most positive and magnetic qualities that are potentially there by the very nature of this type of energy — the possibilities, the potentialities, yes. Getting in touch with the very positive type of energy, the very highest level of it, leads to clarity on the Earth plane as probably never experienced before — ever, if one is really in touch with the higher part of self. Until one gets in touch with that, he may be frustrated

— frustrated by the fact of knowing it is there but not being able to get in touch with it; he just can't let go of whatever is holding him and reach it. But eventually he does, and that is very special.

As the evolution continues, how can we use this type of energy to aid self? Have any of you ever tried putting on your body of light just as you would put on clothing? It is the electrical part of self that can be utilized when you get in touch with the energy body at that level. It is part of the energy of self that can be utilized, really, whenever you can realize it. So why don't you put it on — it's beautiful. It might help with the soul-merge. You can put it on every day. You don't have to wash a body of light; it's always nice and clean and always available. And one way to do it would be by means of this ninth ray.

Now I would add something to the ninth ray, and that is the beautiful white luminosity that one associates with the Christ light. If you're going to have it as a robe, you might see it as having, first of all, an electrical quality — but not dangerous to self, just a part of self. A beautiful magnetic web of light, luminous, beautiful, white, and yet transparent. You can use the blue-green to get in touch with it, but the body of light is a white that is transparent, that contains all of the luminous qualities, all of the shades of the rainbow — every one, every color imaginable that sparkles there — magnetic, electric, alive! There is nothing dead about a body of light. It is life force — at a very high level. Beautiful! Put it on and everyone will say, "What have you done to yourself? You look so alive!" It is almost indescribable.

Now, as you magnetically attract this body of light, it becomes a part of you. You can don it gently. When you meditate and wear your body of light, it connects you with the universal body of light. You can then experience at a level beyond which I can explain in words. It is a marvelous experience. You won't want to miss that one.

Now, the eighth ray is the deep-cleansing ray and it is continued within the ninth ray. It prepares you, it introduces you, it announces to self the possibility that you may then don this beautiful body of light.

A good way to meditate is to first use the seventh ray, the transmuting flame. Then use the eighth ray in any way you wish. Then use the ninth ray — and use it with joy. After that, call for the body of light and allow self to put it on. Now you get in touch with the beautiful tenth ray, also. The tenth ray, if you allow it to, can actually code the body of light into the physical structure. The tenth ray is the pearl-luminosity. It is the body of light.

Ray Ten – The Body of Light

Ray Ten is the means by which your pattern of divinity is actually coded into the physical. And this we can refer to as the body of light or any term you wish. But as experienced now on the Earth, it is an opportunity to move far beyond the traditional experiences here on the Earth. Now, it contains the first, second and third rays mixed with the white light, which raises it up and gives it the luminous quality. Now, adding the third ray (the beautiful yellow ray) is important here. Why? Because it has great holding powers, and you want to code this divinity into self and hold it there, don't you? So you can add what you've had already with the ninth ray and then hold it by means of this beautiful tenth ray.

The color is interesting. How did it get to be gray — or pearl with rather a gray cast but not exactly? It is not an Earth color, and nothing here reflects the true qualities of the tenth ray. It really is a combination of many, many, many colors. The main colors are the first, second and third rays, but it goes far beyond that. And you must recognize that, with these higher rays, although I've given you the main characteristics, they contain a sprinkling of many other things, many other potentials. That's always true.

The tenth ray can enable you to lock in those changes that you're seeking to make — whatever they are. That's important, and you are all undergoing this process now on the Earth. The tenth ray is here in quite large quantities, and only those who recognize its presence because of their point in evolution are getting in touch with and being affected by it. Others don't even know it is here. So if you are rather sensitive to it, you can see that there are important changes going on within self.

Now, if you are getting rather adverse effects, then start using the eighth and ninth rays to help you handle this higher vibration. Because maybe you haven't enough of those two, and by the time you get the intensity of this tenth ray, it is a little disquieting. As the divinity pattern starts to be coded into the physical, the physical says, "What! What is this that's coming in?" So you don't sleep, you get patterns of variety. This is unknown — and it's happening to several of you. What do you do? Begin to work with the eighth and ninth rays, and maybe throw in the seventh. Start by seeing self transmuted, raising self up by means of the seventh ray. And then go to the cleansing process and get in touch with the body of light so that the physical part of you will recognize what's coming in. This is important. Some of you are encountering it.

Now, what about when you feel flooded with energy? That's happening, too. It is the approach of the body of light. It is trying to come in, and you haven't opened the door, so it is sneaking in under the door and through the cracks. Why don't you open the door and invite it in, and then the physical will respond. First you must transmute self, cleanse self, and then prepare self for this body of light. Yes.

Each of the higher rays has a specific purpose. The tenth ray allows you to utilize some of the greater potentialities of self. You get in touch with them through the ninth ray, and then they can be utilized on the tenth. For what purpose? So that you will know you are a totality that functions as well within the physical as within the spiritual — that the same qualities, the same potentials, that are there on the spiritual plane and utilized by the self there can be utilized on the physical plane also.

✧ N I N E ✧

Rays Ten, Eleven and Twelve

WELCOME, MY FRIENDS. IN THIS LESSON WE FINISH WHAT WASN'T GIVEN last time on the tenth ray, and then we go into the eleventh and twelfth rays. We've already covered the eighth, which is specifically for the cleansing process, and the ninth, which begins to attract the electrical part we call the body of light. The tenth attracts the body of light and allows it to anchor completely within the physical. You will eventually make an even closer connection. In a special sense, the tenth ray anchors within the body of light. And that is very exciting when completely realized. Did you get that word – when completely "realized?" Because the tenth ray is now coming in to the Earth strongly enough, those of you who are ready can do that right now – pull in your body of light.

The electrical quality of it is very evident on the Earth now. Electrical storms are a special connection to this higher ray and its electrical approach. The Earth, specifically, is also receiving the possibility of anchoring its body of light – by way of a network of those who can attract their particular portions of it, the Earth can connect with its own body of light. And so, what you do for yourself now, in your evolution, directly reflects into the evolution of the planet. This is available right now – the tenth ray is here. Avail yourself of this opportunity and bring forth the evolution of the Earth.

You can sit within your own" inner lightning," your own inner connection to this higher ray, and in a state of meditation, bring down this beautiful pearl luminosity. As it becomes stronger within self, you can connect with that electrical quality and begin to transmit it to the Earth. This is a way to allow self to serve in this specific electrical connection.

If you are afraid of electrical storms, this means that the electrical quality is something that, deep within self, you haven't connected with yet. And you could probably take out a pattern or two to make yourself more comfortable with this phenomenon. To some of you it is an opportunity, isn't it? You enjoy seeing this electrical quality. Yes. It symbolically invokes the Source light for you. And to me, thunder is an exclamation point. This will be considered an unusually electric year.

Now, we've discussed the tenth ray and its composition – that it contains the first, second and third rays, and quite a large dash of the Source light itself to give it the luminous quality. The increasing of its intensity is a rather constant process, with a pause here and there to allow humanity to adjust. We've equated it to going up a staircase and reaching a landing, then going up another staircase and another landing.

The intensity of the tenth ray does increase your opportunity to learn in the polarity area, because, of course, when fully realized the tenth ray will allow the oneness of self to be experienced – the complete balance of the male and female aspects. That is part of its goal, of its specific vibratory quality.

The opportunity given by this tenth ray is to perceive the body of light – to realize it while in a physical structure. It is always there – you have everything already within you, but you have yet to realize it.

The body of light is not the energy body as you know it. It is a finer area of vibration that usually is not "accepted" on the Earth. You really have to change your vibration so that it can become a part of physical existence. We call it raising the vibration, but truly, it becomes finer. This part has never been physically present on Earth before. It is meant to come completely into physical existence. After the soul-merge, which in a sense recodes the cells, this becomes the "model" for physical cells as never before possible in physical existence. It isn't the soul itself but rather the soul level that contains this energy. This particular body of light doesn't really stop at soul level. It can be equated to some of the monadic level, also. It is the doorway to what all of you are seeking – the body of light. Yes. You can begin to experience it before the soul-level merge, but you will not completely lock it in place until after that time. You can begin to work on it – it is not just for the specific level of the soul, but a part of the evolutionary process.

Have you noticed that time seems to have speeded up? As more energy comes in, it affects people differently – it intensifies whatever is within you: more joy, more confusion, more pressures . . . it depends on what is within you. It doesn't have to be negative, it can be positive. It "lights up" what's within you. And there you are all lit up, and you can look at it and see where to work.

Ray Eleven – Service

Because the tenth ray has paved a way for it, we call Ray Eleven a bridge to the New Age or to the next level. But it already is, in a very special sense, the next level. When you work with this ray, you've unlocked something very important. I guess "service" is the closest I can describe it. By the time you are really able to connect with this energy and utilize it in your life, there will be no question about the service — about the stimulation of the way to aid evolution here on the Earth.

As this ray begins to come in, we see many people seeking their higher purposes. The color, an orange-pink, seems to me important. It gets you in touch with divine love expanded by divine wisdom. The eleventh-ray color combination contains the Source light, which we equate with love (although it isn't pink), and also the second ray, fifth ray and some first ray. Those are the kinds of rays of which it is composed. It is very special because it is a bridge to a whole new era in human living here on Earth. The first ray makes it very penetrating. It is softened then by the second, and again made more penetrating by the fifth. What does it need to penetrate at that level? It is the remnant-remover, we could say. As the new opportunity comes closer and that final cleansing approaches, the final removal of the former remnants will be cleared out.

Does that say something about the times that are coming? It has three different kinds of energy: the first ray, which is the will, the second ray, which is love/wisdom, and the fifth ray, which is more mental but is very direct, very penetrating. It gives humanity much opportunity in how to utilize this ray. If it is not balanced by humanity, the first-ray destructive mode could be "interesting." In clearing out the remnants there might be war, catastrophe. It can be used that way, but it doesn't have to be. If you balance it with the penetrating quality, which sees beyond the necessity for destruction, for clearing out, and you add some divine love to it, then it can be used without the destructive connotation. There does not have to be destruction if the energy is utilized in the highest and most appropriate manner. The opportunity will be there to utilize the energy as humanity chooses — that's always true, isn't it? It is a penetrating ray that clears out the remnants. You can look at the situation if it is within self and see what is still there, the remnants of what you've had. Or, if it is on the Earth, then humanity in general can look at the remnants of what needs to be let go of and can move the Earth into a final clearing.

But the eleventh ray — I like the bridging connotation, and I like also the choice that it gives. And that's important. It says to me that the Source really does allow us free will — that we may choose how we transcend or transmute from one level to another. The choice is there.

My estimate is that it will be two years before humanity begins to experience this ray. It is here in potential, not in actuality. But you can work with it in your meditations and send it out to the Earth, also. A good way to work with it is to cover self, or a specific area, or the whole world, with a blanket of it. And as you do, see the Earth begin to absorb this energy. At its most ideal, it is a very balanced energy and will add to your balance. If you're out of balance sometime, put on one of these energy cloaks that contain the eleventh ray — orange-pink luminosity we have called it. This ray has one of the most penetrating and balanced types of energy that exists, because of the combination of the first and the fifth rays, and then the second ray — that's what makes it so balanced. This ray gives you the opportunity to clean up anything that was missed by the eighth ray, and also to balance self so that you will be very stable when the next ray comes in. That one, the twelfth ray, is meant to be a new beginning, a foundation. The eleventh is bringing you to that point of stability, of balancing, of bridging, from this level that humanity is really on now to the next level. It is a specific for the bridging process.

Will there be other rays after the twelfth ray? Well, there could be. There are other combinations that are possible. There are as many combinations as there are probabilities in existence; but for the Earth experience coming up, these are all that are now planned. But in the cosmos, in existence, there are other combinations used, other ways of intensifying an opportunity or presenting it — not only in physical existence but in spiritual existence. There are many various combinations that are used quite often. There are always patterns of energy present in existence, and they could be considered limitless as far as our understanding is concerned. Each pattern is seeking its energy ideal, and those who exist within it are those who are using that type of energy to support their service efforts or their learning experiences on the spiritual plane. So each physical existence has specific patterns at specific times, and so has spiritual existence.

We've talked about the eleventh ray balancing, about its gathering up remnants. The usage of the first-ray part could include fire in clearing away — tearing down of the old — war, aggression, conflict. Allow the clearing process to go forward. To me, flames and the clearing process are connected in a special sense with the first ray. And it is not always negative. It is sometimes necessary to clear out the old, as with cremation of the physical structure, to allow a new beginning — to transmute that particular structure back to its origin and let it be recycled. The Creator is very good at that. He just never lets anything go to waste, does He?

I think that humanity is at such a critical point in evolution that the letting go of what has been gets to be very hard for some because they are looking at everything and letting go of everything. What they are in fact letting go of is a whole period of evolution. And some people think they can establish some stability through a religious concept that has been valid in the past — it helps them to feel stable.

How will the eleventh ray focus into Earth existence? All of the energy that comes to the Earth, comes, in a sense, through the one who ensouls the planet — Sanat Kumara. However, sometimes it comes directly from the Spiritual Hierarchy to humanity. But the Planetary Logos, Sanat Kumara, is the one who really invokes for Earth the necessary energies to accomplish the evolution of the planet. From his own growth and learning, from his own consciousness, goes forth an invocation that draws to the planet the type of energy it needs for its particular stage of evolution. This indicates that about ten years ago he invoked these higher rays and they were made available by his superiors, by his teachers, by the ones who know how to make them available. To be specific, the Solar Logos is the next direct link with the Source in a stepped-up sort of staircase. The Solar Logos through his consciousness directs the energies to Sanat Kumara.

The particular area of the Solar Logos is perhaps as varied as the whole Hierarchy. There are many opportunities to work in that area, and some of the work may be within the hierarchic level we call the solar level, but there may perhaps be openings in which they have done specific patterning of energy — sort of an apprenticeship — under the direction of those who do this for the Source level itself or one of Its representatives. So through that area you get into the direct energy work in a more encompassing sense that is available for most of us. This is the area that I feel I will be in eventually, but not yet in a direct sense. Perhaps when humanity is safely, securely experiencing the New Age. The rays have always interested me. You know, I am very fascinated by energy — always have been.

Ray Twelve — The Golden Ray

Let's talk about Ray Twelve. For the Earth, the twelfth ray is a combination of all potentialities. It has a little of everything, including the higher rays. It is a combination of all the kinds of energies that have been available here on the Earth — all of them, from one through eleven. The proportions are not equal. For instance, you don't have as much first ray as you do second — that wouldn't be appropriate. And you would not have as much sixth — very little.

The twelfth ray, the golden ray — the New Age — this is the new level for humanity, and it means that humanity will be in touch with the Christ consciousness. The Earth will also be in touch with this level, so you can see by the very nature of it that it invokes the white light, doesn't it? The gold invokes the Source light and the Christ consciousness, which to me are a little different. But it invokes the white light. And that allows more direct conscious interaction with the Source level itself.

And so it is an entirely new beginning in which conscious interaction with the Source level takes place more completely. After the New Age begins, when this is the level that humanity has reached, it will understand as never before its own part in the cosmos. The Earth itself will understand its part in the cosmos.

In four or five years Earth will begin to experience the twelfth ray. It has been here all the time in a reflected way. Humanity has always sought the gold that comes out of the Earth — this is symbolic of seeking potentialities within.

The twelfth ray is a mirror: It reflects everything! As you know, gold is very shiny — it reflects. It can also reflect Source light. At a specific angle it could reflect directly into you the Source light. This could prepare the way, step it down a little, allow you to accept it. Now, if you can get yours directly, fine. But if you have difficulty with the intense Source light, then try it that way. Bring in the gold ray and allow it to bring in the white from an angle. This modifies it a little for humanity. Gold and white go beautifully together. Maybe you could swirl them up and utilize them to reach a level of greater understanding.

Now, we've talked about making realizations and about their importance. A specific to aid you in making realizations is the twelfth ray, so if you are seeing to understand, to see your situation, you might place the whole situation in the twelfth ray. Either bring it down through self or really say to yourself symbolically that you are putting the whole situation right there in front of you. Then bring the whole ray down onto it and look at it through the twelfth ray. It reflects the clarity of the Source light and it reflects the next level you are trying to reach. It makes available for you right then energy that will help you to understand. It contains every kind of energy available on the Earth, plus the Source light itself.

What the twelfth ray does is very interesting: it raises up whatever is there. It will bring it right to the surface and then you can look at it. When you allow it to reflect the Source light, you can see self in relationship to the Source more clearly. It is specifically for aiding the realization process. Now, recognize that when you use it, everything you have in a specific area is going to be raised to the surface. So allow time for this.

The twelfth ray is a specific for a new beginning, whether it is on an individual level or on the level of a new cosmos or a new Source! When this comes to the Earth, many things will surface for the Earth, too. It will depend upon what conditions the Earth is holding at that time, and on how much you all have done your homework.

We can use the twelfth ray now, but when it comes in fully in four or five years, it will be much more effective. We use it a lot now through the Golden One, in our meditations. And I encourage you to do so, to use the golden ray. Using the twelfth ray helps invoke the New Age and the higher level and is very appropriate. I would say that if you had your choice of rays, the twelfth brings in the highest invocation of the New Age.

In the New Age the main focus will be on the twelfth ray. It will be utilized as a focus of the highest energy available on the Earth. But all of you will utilize the rays in different ways. The higher rays will get more involved, but the other rays are going to be there, too. Within a specific temple of light, within many of them, the golden ray will reflect the Source light, anchoring the invocation of the light on the planet Earth. And there will be specific temples where this is done.

After evolution has taken us into the New Age, the chakra centers will be different. The physical structure will then become a more finely tuned instrument, from an energy sense.

✦ P A R T F O U R ✦

ENERGY AND LIGHT

The Tibetan, Djwhal Khul, 1983-1985

✧ O N E ✧

Energy

H UMANITY, IN ITS THRUSTING FORWARD, REACHES THE POINT WHERE THE energy patterns must be renewed. This is due to the nature of creation: Energy comes forth from the Creator, but when it becomes tired, when it gets a long distance from its origin, then a renewal process is made that enables it to go forth with renewed vigor. This point is referred to by those who work with energy as the critical area, and we look at it often when we are seeking to understand how to utilize energy in the most productive manner. When energy reaches its critical area, it is not as forceful as before. Also, it needs perhaps to be tuned in order to put it with the other types of energy, to blend it together to accomplish a specific purpose. We who meld and blend energies use it here at the critical area because that is where it is most easily worked with. We can tell by attuning to the energy patterns when they are at that particular point that makes ease of handling more readily available to us.

Energy of course is the way the Creator creates. It is His method of creation, and as it comes forth from the Source, it is very dynamic, very positive, and it is broken down into different types of energy that will serve different purposes. After it reaches this critical area it is much less dynamic, and at that time there is a special pulsation sent out from the Creator. These special pulses come along each energy line individually at regular intervals, and because the Creator planned everything so well, they reach the critical area just when they are needed in order to boost, if you will, the energy back to its original strength. All of this of course happens very rapidly so that it seems to be a pattern that the energy flows smoothly and constantly; but this is not true, as is discernible to one who has a trained eye. There is a variance within each energy field, each thrusting out of energies.

In utilizing energies made available to us upon the Earth, no matter what the source – be it a prayer group, a football game, a musical event – seek first to receive it, to see what types of energies they are (not whether they are good or bad, but how they are different). And then we look at the energies themselves, instantaneously ascertaining how much is at that critical point. We then meld and blend the various types of energy by utilizing this critical point for the specific purposes that are necessary at the time. For example, if there was a major earthquake with many people ill and hurt, the Hierarchy would then seek all available energy and utilize it to aid those involved in this situation. They might not have asked for assistance, but we can ascertain it from the soul – the Earth is entitled to assistance. Many times when we are seeking to help, what we are doing is helping the Earth – the people too, if appropriate, but especially Mother Earth, our home.

As the energies become blended they lose some of this critical-point activity because each particular kind of energy, or each ray, reaches its critical point at a different time and place in the thrusting out. So when you blend the energies together you get an overlap, with some reaching the critical point at one time and some at another; you don't have any clear definition. This makes it a little difficult to utilize this critical point for our purposes, but still we can see and learn to use them, adapting our perspective to the energy involved, watching the patterns and seeking to utilize our knowledge of energies to aid us to manipulate them and use them for God's Cosmic Plan.

All of this is done very rapidly, of course. The one who is doing it is using his mind, his will, to accomplish this purpose. He can visualize the energy streams and what to do with them to accomplish what he needs to at that time. Some of the specific creations from the Creator also aid him – they do what they are told. The ones that are most known for this are the devas, of course, and they are very helpful when called upon because they have no conflicts. This is their job and they do it very well.

Let me give you an example of blending energies and then seeking to use them for a specific purpose. Let us suppose that there is a large fire that is destroying a large building. From this fire much energy will be released, particularly first-ray energy, although there will also be a blending of fourth ray and some seventh ray at this time. Also, of course, you will get a small amount of all of the other energy patterns, depending upon who is there and exactly what is being done. The member of the Hierarchy who is in charge of this particular area will attune to it, noting the energies being released and then looking from his more informed perspective at the needs of the Earth at that time. Is there an area there that is on the brink of war? Is there a problem that is causing the Earth itself to have internal problems, perhaps combustion problems deep within? Is there a potential hurricane somewhere? Whatever the area, he looks at it and sees what energies would be needed to quiet these conditions.

Now, of course, when people are involved it is one thing; when it is the Earth, he is much freer to deal with it if he has the permission of Sanat

Kumara. At his level he instantly knows whether or not it is permissible to aid the Earth in its larger scope. He gets either a yea or a nay and then proceeds accordingly. He utilizes the energies available, but many times there is so much Ray One being brought in that it must be blended with others to tone it down, although Ray One energy is the most useful energy in manifestation at this time. You might find that rather difficult to believe, but it is true – humanity has used it in an inappropriate manner and does not understand its much wider application. It is used prudently, of course, blended with many other energies, particularly the second and the fifth rays. This is just a generalization; each situation is different and must take into consideration the whole picture. Much activity now being carried out within the Hierarchy calls for utilization of every bit of energy that becomes available. We are seeking to negate upon the Earth the effects set up by humanity over the eons, and with Sanat Kumara's permission we have been quite successful. Each little bit of energy is useful because we can hold back certain aspects of which there is too much. We can carry it until another time. We can hold it in a pool until needed; nothing is wasted, but it must be prudently blended. It must be sought, each little type, each little gift that comes to us, and used to further the Creator's Cosmic Plan.

Energies are the means to create. The Creator, in His wisdom, made available everything we need to live a productive and abundant life. It is all there for our taking, but we must use it with discretion, with wisdom, and this has not always been done upon the Earth. Then the energies get out of balance within us and we experience this until we learn to balance out – to use these energies as the Creator intended them to be used so we can live here in harmony and peace.

So when the fire is analyzed, the one analyzing it instantly notes the types of energies available and their proportions and notes the needs of the Earth at the moment. He then filters out the needed energy and sends it, after obtaining permission, of course, to the area. The rest he directs to a pool, a holding area, as individualized types of energy. At the same time he directs the needed mix from the holding area into the ones from the fire that he is going to use and send to another area. All of this is done by utilizing the critical area, the critical point, in the energy patterns, because there they are most ready to be used. This all takes time and training, of course, and he must see the overall picture very clearly. And he is aided – he is the director, but the direct manifestations of the Creator that are not ensouled, that are created for specific purposes, aid him in this regard. He has learned to utilize these creations as part, as an extension, really, of his own consciousness.

After the fire is under control, the one who is utilizing the energies cleans up the area energywise. He seeks to bring it into balance again, if it is appropriate to do so. Again he asks permission, and if it is given, he looks to see what energies are needed to replace the ones that have been brought out of balance by that particular experience. This is an important idea to grasp: that experiencing brings the energies out of balance, and through the conscious will of those who manipulate them they must be brought back into balance. It is not an automatic process; it must be done by those who serve the Earth with joy and gladness, and there are many more than you can imagine – it is an important job. They work on different levels, of course. Some work with the Earth itself, some work with the people, and some with lower manifestations. And all, of course, work under the direction of one of the masters, who has the overall view as his responsibility. All of this must be coordinated on different levels and is a very important job within the spiritual government.

This energy area is one with which I have been closely associated. I have worked many times within it, and still do, because I can do some of this work and still work through those on Earth. Because I have been assigned responsibilities that require more direct association with the Earth, I have been training another to take over my major responsibilities in the energy area.

So energy control, if you wish to put it that way, is very important. Although you might not have thought of it, it is just part of the Creator's Cosmic Plan for Earth and an area that Earth beings know nothing about. It must be controlled, it must be sorted, it must be directed, it must be stored. It must be cared for, like any other resource, with prudence and joy and love.

This activity does not come under any specific ray, as far as administration is concerned. It is under the direct administration of Sanat Kumara and the three who aid him. Thus the one who administers the energy flows to the Earth is in direct contact with Sanat Kumara at all times. He needs this direct line to know if he is working in accordance with karmic patterns, individually and collectively. The wishes of Sanat Kumara are also taken into consideration. After all, he directs the complete planetary activity, so his wishes and his administration are needed at all times. By this I mean that the energy administrator simply has a special attunement to Sanat Kumara and knows instantly whether or not he is following the wishes of the Planetary Logos, and this enables more effective manipulation and control of the energy patterns.

The seven types of energies blend together uniquely to form patterns. The patterns must also be taken into account when working with energies. Some are more entwined, if you will, than others; the patterns are all different. And when looking at an energy pattern you can look at the way it flows, at its various angles and circles and the distances between these and see, just by looking, what type of energy it is and how much and how heavy. And it is very important when you are working with energy to be able to instantly see exactly what you are dealing with. Seeing the patterns gives you an added dimension toward identification. It aids you.

Color is also an aid. The color is part of the energy pattern and it swirls with beauty. When you view the energy patterns coming into the Earth at a specific time, you see the beauty of the straight energies as they approach and are broken down into various forms. Then after they have been utilized upon the Earth in various ways by various experiences, the patterns change – the colors become no longer pure. Also at the critical point, the colors become much less intense, and this is one way we can tell where the critical point is.

I wish to discuss another aspect of energy to increase your understanding of it and enable you to begin to work with it in a cocreator fashion. You might not consider yourself at a point in your evolutionary pattern where you could begin to do this, but you are – it is true! You have begun and now you will continue to learn the necessary methods of creating.

To begin applying the Creator's method, visualize as clearly as you can what you desire to create. Many of you have done this many times, but you do not know exactly what you are doing. You are doing it as you have been told, not knowing the energy processes involved here. As you begin to visualize a desired manifestation, use your will to direct as forceful a stream of energy as you can toward the desired object. This is the way to create; you do it all the time unconsciously. When you learn to do it consciously, the results are more rapid, more forceful and more apparent. If you analyze my words, you will see that this is true. Conscious creation always results in more effective results. Before this time in your evolutionary path you have created your reality through your belief structure. This is fine, it is good – it is part of your evolutionary pattern. But now, as you begin to become a cocreator, you begin to utilize the will aspect to create. This takes a conscious direction, a conscious process, in order to achieve the desired results.

Let us give you an example now. As you begin to become a cocreator you attune to your purposes. If one of these is to aid in the creation of the New Age, then begin to visualize it as you would like to see it. Perhaps there are golden temples and marvelous teachers. See everything as clearly as possible now. Then direct with the will a stream of clear energy. Mentally visualize it and know the desired results are there. The will aspect is what lets you obtain the desired result. When you are functioning in this manner you are working on the mental plane, and you must recognize this. The higher plane is where true creation takes place. You might be surprised, thinking that the spiritual plane is where creation begins – and that is true, it comes from the Source, but the actual implementation of creation is done on the higher mental plane, and you must be consciously aware of this to utilize the will and attain the desired results.

As you are visualizing the New Age and directing the energy to it with your will aspect you recognize that what you have created is there, that it has indeed become manifested. This sounds very simple, but it is not. To know that what you have sought to create has indeed been created takes much work, much growth, much recognition – to know that you have the ability to serve the Creator as a cocreator. All of you who read this paper are beginning to recognize that you do create your own life, but now it is time to raise your recognition to acknowledge the fact that you create, or at least can create, much more.

Begin to broaden your scope now, begin to seek this cocreator aspect. Begin to attune to your higher responsibilities now. How do you do that? How do you recognize whether or not the New Age has been created? It is a valid question, my friends. I cannot tell you how to do this, but as you seek to learn how to do it, you will know when it has been accomplished. Of this I can assure you. In this paper we are giving you some food for thought, and I do not want you to become frustrated if you cannot create the New Age by tomorrow — even the Creator took seven cosmic days, and He was the originator of creation!

In your cocreator work, visualize the energy after it surrounds your manifestation as being cohesive, permanent, as enclosing your visual picture and supporting it completely. This will give you the feeling, as well as the knowing, of creation. The reason I am emphasizing this point is that creating must be done from a balanced condition like everything else. First you *will* it (the mental aspect) then you *know* it (your intuitive faculties), and third you *view* the energy surrounding it and thus you *feel* it also — a completely balanced method of creation. Now, you students of the Cabala will say to me, "But that is not a valid condition — the will, the intuition, and the feeling aspect." But I say to you, on the level of the cocreator, it is, my friends, it certainly is.

As you make progress with your creation, perhaps a less ambitious project than the New Age is appropriate. A suggestion might be to try to manifest some article from you to a friend. Try to manifest whatever you wish — perhaps an apple, a flower, a book, whatever you desire as an object of your learning experience. Follow the preceding suggestions, visualizing your object where you desire to place it, having preplanned this event with your friend. This will enable you to know when it is beginning to work. You may think this is a silly idea, but it is not — it is a practical approach to learning creation.

The best way to proceed would probably be to not tell your friend the exact article you are going to attempt to create; then you can tell how you are doing by questioning your friend and seeing what he or she attunes to. As you begin your creative efforts, they will manifest first not upon the physical plane but probably upon the astral. If your friend gets glimpses of the object, but it is not physically manifested, you will at least know you are making good progress. If, in your attempts, you do not succeed immediately, do not become discouraged, my friends. As I said, even the Creator took time in His efforts. If you are utilizing your "helpers," when you visualize the energy flow directly, also know that these helpers are carrying this energy to the desired manifestation. Of course, you must know the correct procedure.

You must utilize them properly or their services will not be obtained.

Now, I can hear you all saying, "But I utilize them all the time, and they do what I tell them. I have gotten what I wanted." Yes, you have, but do you know how you have gotten it? Do you understand the methods you employ? Could you broaden your scope to something besides your personal desires? The answer is no, you could not, because you have not yet understood the precise method and have utilized the creative process only in an unconscious or automatic manner. Begin then to do it with conscious intent. Begin to create with joy, with the knowing that you as a cocreator are carrying out your part in the Cosmic Plan and that you have been assigned this responsibility because you know what you are to do and how to do it.

I am giving these instructions because many of you are reaching a point in your evolutionary path where you can utilize this information. Try it, my friends, because it is important to begin. Everyone begins somewhere, and a cocreator needs training. It takes effort to learn it and it takes work and determination. This does not mean that you cannot attune to it in joy. On the contrary, joy is an important part of creation, but do it with the recognition that effort, time and work will be involved.

✧ T W O ✧

The Monadic Experience

L ET US DISCUSS THE MONADIC EXPERIENCE. YOU HAVE PROBABLY HEARD ME speak of the monad, or spiritual spark. As each spiritual spark emerges from the Source, it is immediately evident that this spark is different from any other that exists. A reflection of this high truth would be the difference in snowflakes — that no two are exactly the same, that the patterns within them contain differences. Similarly, the spiritual sparks are each different. They come from different locations of the Creator's consciousness, one might say. And so they come with potentialities that are probably going to be manifested in certain directions rather than others. Each one comes with a specific path that is exactly right for him to experience in his journey through creation toward his own individual goal.

However, free will is also given, and very many choose — almost all, as a matter of fact — to deviate somewhat from that perfect goal. In a sense, each must find out for himself that the Creator is who He says He is — the Creator — and that He knows what's best for each of us. Then we can journey through creation by experiencing and return to the origin as we left it, but self-realized, knowing that it is appropriate that we be here, that with free will we have chosen to be here. And where is "here"? It is back where we started with the Creator, but with the knowledge that that's where we are, knowing that we now serve Him and we choose to do so as an individualized portion of Him.

That is what the Creator needs in His experiencing — ones who are happy to be there and know it is appropriate to be there and have chosen to be there. Many of us have resisted this, but we work through each little experience — the Creator isn't in any hurry. He allows us our experiencing, our realization of the ultimate goal. We have as long as it takes, and He knows that ultimately we will return, for we are, remember, all different. He experiences different things through each of us. He learns and He perceives life through each of us from a slightly different point of view. When He puts it all together, He has a very balanced perspective on His experiencing.

We are, then, a part of His experience, no matter on what level we are currently functioning. The spiritual sparks will always be functioning there. The monads will continue to work on the spiritual plane, no matter how close they are to the active cocreator state (the emphasis being on "active"). But we must recognize that as children of the light we are extensions of those monadic experiences, those individualized sparks that are journeying toward being self-realized cocreators. We experience, that they may learn. We learn, that they may experience. We are directly connected in a rather circular effect, as is all creation. The circle is a symbol of unity, of wholeness, and we see it reflected on every level of existence and between levels of existence. We learn from our higher aspects, and they learn from us. We experience for them, and they learn from us. We learn from them, and they experience for us.

Now, there are certain general patterns for each monadic experience that everyone partakes of, but everyone has his own individual interpretation of how to implement these general areas. So we might say that the spiritual monadic experience is divided into several levels, and beyond it is the soul level. Beyond that is the journey into physical existence. Each of these general areas can be broken down into more divisions, and are. Certain of these divisions, certain numbers, certain patterns are very important and add to the progress, to the focusing of a lesson in a specific way.

For example, the appropriate number of souls a monad sends down to experience is twelve. Why twelve? Because twelve is a very special symbol of the whole, and by experiencing in twelve different ways, the monad gets a very balanced experience. One of you has asked, "Is it as simple as cutting up a pie in twelve pieces?" Well, not exactly; it is more complex than that. First you cut the pie in twelve pieces, then you cut each piece in half, and perhaps again, and then you might blend some of the pieces together. You will still basically have twelve divisions, but each division contains pieces from some of the other twelve divisions too. The twelve enables the spiritual spark to get what it needs from a soul level.

Now, when you go beyond the soul level, that no longer holds true. You get into physical existence, in which there is much resistance. In order to overcome all of this resistance, a stringent effort must be made, and thus you get many, many more physical existences than souls. Again, it is because of the heavy areas in which the physical existences occur. The soul is still on the spiritual plane, where there is not nearly as much resistance.

The monad, then, is on a very special journey toward self-realization. It knows its goal and the means to achieving that goal. It knows each step it should take, but sometimes, because of free will, it chooses not to take that step right now. That's important because eventually it will take that step; it just chooses to experience a little in other ways first to see and to understand why that stuff is important. This is why the Creator knows that all of experiencing is fine and is going to end well. He knows that the divine spark, the monad, must simply experience and learn that His Plan is the right one, but it must be very experienced before it will know this for sure. It must take many detours sometimes to find out that these can be painful, can be blocked, can be inappropriate for that particular monad, though they might be appropriate for another. They must come to the conclusion that each path has been divinely planned just for them — and this is true. They must have the knowingness within self that the Creator's Plan for them is the way to experience. When they know this within every fiber of their being, then they can forget it — they don't have to learn any more about it. And at that point they can become cocreators.

Why? Because they are no longer distracted by self. They simply do what is appropriate because they absolutely know it is the way for them. Then the Creator uses them to enlarge His experience, and He does so with great joy. They also do it with great joy, knowing it is the appropriate way to experience. They have no doubts, they just do it; then the Creator gets all of their energy, gets all of their attention, and they do it out of divine realization that that is what existence is — the Creator — and that's all it is. How wonderful! How perfect! How appropriate, my friends.

I have been asked about twin souls or, as some people refer to them, twin flames. Sometimes, at soul level — because of something that happened at a higher level — a soul chooses to divide; this is what we might call a twin soul. We also have talked about soul mates, or twin flames, but what we are really talking about here are souls that belong to the same monadic experience, no matter what the mechanical process is. It might be a soul that, because of some condition on the monadic level, has chosen to come down as one soul and then divide, or it might be a condition of two souls that are attracted to one another because in a sense they represent a polarity within the monadic level — although that's a little misleading because each soul contains both polarities; it is a reflection up of what this condition would be in physical existence.

You see, it is more complicated than words can easily explain, but what you get with twin souls, soul mates and twin flames is a knowingness that your patterns, your vibrations, fit together very well. You're very compatible because you have the same sort of vibratory pattern at a very high level. This is why many times it isn't appropriate for twin souls to meet on the Earth, but sometimes they do. Sometimes they plan it so they will not be attracted. They are, in a sense, playing roles, my friends. It's very interesting to see this happen. At other times there are problems within them that do not allow them to experience this mutual compatibility within themselves. This is very interesting too, because at the same time they are very attracted to one another, they are also repelled by some of each other's beliefs; or perhaps they set up some conditions in some experience that had nothing to do with this particular soul, but the twin soul reminds them of this previous condition and prevents mutual attraction to have the force that it otherwise would. The great lovers we have known in history are usually twin souls — ones who can't see anything but each other, so perhaps they don't learn a great deal, except the intensity of each other, of course, and they learn that very well. Perhaps that's appropriate once in the Earth existence, but the higher levels usually do not permit this sort of association and intensity more than once or twice at most.

I have been asked if one on a physical plane attracts other extensions of one's soul that are also functioning here at this particular time, from a sequential time point of view (remember, the soul does not experience time as the Earth does — it experiences existence on the spiritual plane). This is a good question, and one that is not especially easy to answer. The general answer is no, one does not attract other extensions of one's soul upon the Earth plane. However, if one is seeking to clear everything for one's soul, this requires breaking through all of Earth's living and allowing the soul to approach upon the Earth; then you might very greatly affect the other extensions of your soul. If you make that major breakthrough, my friends, the soul must terminate its other extensions upon the Earth, both from a sequential sense of time and an eternal one. In other words, when the connection is made strong enough that the soul's main essence mostly functions here through you upon the Earth, or through another extension upon the Earth, whichever one really makes the breakthrough first, then the soul pulls back all of its other existences from the sense of the eternal *now*. You could say that all of these thousands of lives — for most of you, between 2000 and 2500 — would cease to exist. The learning would have been accomplished because this is the goal for Earth living: to enable, through some extension, a breakthrough to be made to live here upon the Earth as a soul. If it were you, then you would function here as a soul. If another extension made the breakthrough, then you as a personality would cease to exist. Your physical vehicle would die, the consciousness would be withdrawn, and the essence of what you have learned would be returned to the soul. You would never die because the essence is there within the soul, but the personality, which is only a part of this physical existence, would no longer exist.

Actually, that is pretty much true when the soul comes to the Earth, also, although you will remember what it was like to be a personality. You will cease to be one — you will be functioning at soul level. Now, because this comes very gradually, you as a personality will, one step at a time, take that way to experiencing, build that rainbow bridge to greater experience. This is one more reason to try to become greater: so that you may function here upon the Earth as a soul, and your personality will be the one to make the major breakthrough. Is that not wonderful? I think it is very important for all of you to listen to these words very carefully. You can do it – all of you who read this are getting close, relatively close, to this state. You will either do it through this personality or you will enable it to be done very soon after this personality begins to experience in the New Age. It is important to recognize that. Most of you have chosen growth as your experience – you wish to become greater. Use these words now, study them, and learn and grow from them. It's very important to know how all of these things fit together.

I have been asked what the relationship is between an extension of a soul and the original monad. It is a reflected quality and not in totality, you see. You will reflect, as an extension of the soul, specific qualities of the soul, and specific qualities of the monad, but not all. Some will be reflected, and your monad has these reflected ways of learning, in totality, many different reflections that come back and compose what one might call a jigsaw puzzle, allowing the monad, in a sense, to put it all together – to fit each learning experience into the picture and thus become a self-realized cocreator from each of these experiences. Do not misunderstand these words. The monad also experiences in its own right, and much is learned directly, but the Creator works in cycles, on levels, and with different types of reflection. This is His chosen method of operation for Himself and for everything else as part of His totality.

The next question is rather complex: When two or more souls of a monad experience on the same plane, what relationship do the extensions of each soul have with each other? There's no general answer to that; it depends upon the individual situation. Most of the time, I would say probably none. If it is the spiritual plane the souls are experiencing on (and probably it would be), then it depends upon what sort of experience the soul is getting. Is it going to put extensions into the physical? Is it going to put them into another-dimensional experience? Is there a multiple experiencing as far as probable realities are concerned? This is much more complex than appears at first glance. I am attempting to give it in as simple a language as possible, deliberately leaving out some of the complexities in order not to confuse you. Each individual circumstance would be different. There are probable realities, and yes, extensions may be sent to each one of these probable realities, in which case there would hopefully be no interconnections between the extensions. Sometimes they attune to one another, but it's probably not appropriate. If the extensions were functioning on the Earth plane, they might feel attracted to one another. Some have been compatible, and some have married. There wouldn't be the close association that there would be between extensions of the same soul, but a very compatible one – you might say a step removed from being a group of just one soul. It's a little different.

Do twins born to one mother on this plane share the same soul? Generally, no – 99% of the time, no. But once in a while, because of individual circumstance, yes.

I have been asked, What is a soul's consciousness? It is a direct reflection of an individualized spark of the Creator.

When a soul experiences a trauma, how does it heal that and release any false impressions from it? That's a good question, and again, there's no simple answer. One way is through you, as an expression, an extension, of it. You can help a soul release these traumas, these false impressions. The false belief system can be removed from the soul. Of course, they do not always work this way, but this is a specific method that works well at the soul level as well as at the subconscious level. Why? Because you are a means by which a soul can learn and grow, and it accepts your experiencing as part of its experience; if you work with this specific removal method, your soul can learn and experience and grow from it also. There are as many methods as there are souls. Each must individually seek to erase these traumas. They are a part of the experiencing, you see. All must do it, but one's own methods are unique. We offer this method as a good way to release false impressions from the soul level as well as the subconscious level.

Someone has said that he senses a quality of limitation in souls. Is that a correct perception? Well, only if the soul perceives itself as limited. Everything is awareness and perception, and the soul is only as limited as its own perception of existence makes it. That is true at any level. Certainly its perceptions are not limited as far as Earth existences are concerned, and that is why most people consider the soul to be perfect. It is perfect from everyone's point of view, but it does not yet know that it is perfect, and thus it might perceive life as imperfect, as opposed to later, when it has grown from its experiencing and its sense of limitation or imperfection. You see, it really is perfect, but it must perceive that truth.

Finally we get to the question of what the relationship is between soul and the personality. The personality is an essence of the soul that comes here to learn a specific lesson, to experience. Is the personality the same in all extensions of the soul? Certainly not. It is the same thing as above: The different extensions learn different lessons; and again, the division is not that simple. Sometimes the lessons are rather mixed, as with our piece of pie. When an extension personality drops the body, is it in harmony with the soul again? Well, certainly. The essence of what it has learned comes into the soul very positively, and the soul simply absorbs that again and has learned from it. This is very important.

The monadic experience is very vast, and we have touched upon it just a little. It is very complex, and yet the simplicity of the way that it all fits together, the way the Creator has constructed it, always amazes me. To me it is symbolic of the Creator and His infinite wisdom and ability to "put it all together."

✧ T H R E E ✧

The Archangels

W E ARE GOING TO TALK ABOUT THE TEN ARCHANGELS THAT CORRESPOND to the Cabalistic Tree of Life. Each archangel has a propensity for one of the aspects of the tree. As I have said in the past, this tree really divides up all of the aspects of creation so you can look at anything you want and analyze it. Right now we are looking at it as creation, and each aspect, or sephirah, has a particular planet and a particular archangel associated with it.

I think you will enjoy these beings we are about to discuss, these archangels. We are going to make them seem like "real folks," because they are, really. They have specific duties, specific likes and dislikes and individual characteristics, although they are not evolving consciousnesses as we in the human evolutionary consciousness are.

Some of you have worked with these archangels and some have channeled them, in this life or in previous ones. They are available to humanity and used by humanity in specific ways to aid them in understanding creation.

Now, these archangels do not work alone. In a sense they direct a great host of beings – the angels. You could say the archangel is the director of a department and the angelic hosts do the work. The archangels interpret and direct; the angels take directions and follow them – they do not do any interpreting. It is like a large corporation: the president interprets the overall program given by the board of directors, and the various department heads follow the directions given.

The archangels are direct manifestations of the Creator and do not have free will as we know it. They are like the right arm of the Creator, and like our right arm, they do not have any will separate from that of their Source. Now, these direct manifestations, the archangels, are not "becoming" – they are not growing, except in the sense that everything grows as the Creator grows. They have been created directly for these particular tasks and they do them magnificently. They do them without failure, without difficulty, without resistance, without false beliefs, without any needs, desires, or wants of their own. They serve the Creator exactly as they have been programmed to do, and at the end of a specific time in creation they will be pulled back into the Source and they will cease to exist. They do not go beyond that point.

At some other time in the future the angelic kingdom may be different. It may be doing some other things. But right now it is allowing all of you to receive the benefits of its service to the Creator. The Creator has set it up to allow you to share in this manner. Their destiny is not, as with you, to become cocreators. It is to serve the Creator exactly as they are serving Him now – as they have been created to serve.

Let us begin with the archangel who is at the very top of the tree. His name is **Metatron** and he is known as the archangel of the Presence. If you look at the tree you will see Metatron at **Kether** at the top of the tree, and Sandalphon at Malcuth at the bottom of the tree. These two work together frequently. Isn't it interesting that the top and the bottom of the tree are so closely connected? This is for balance and focus in the physical.

Metatron is the direct representative of the Creator whose job it is to acquaint individuals with their divinity – who allows divinity to shine through him in order to launch that divinity upon the journey through the steps of creation to allow it to manifest. He is springboarding the energy at the point of creation into a manifested state.

At this level, Kether, what is there to be distributed? Light, of course – the beautiful, pure direct light from the Source. He begins the distribution of the light to the various subdepartments of Kether and then down the tree toward Sandalphon.

Metatron can be utilized to tune you into the Source if you have some hesitation in approaching the Source directly. You will still get the essence of the purity of the Source but you won't be as overawed by His overpowering all-knowingness. It is his responsibility and his privilege to represent the Source. Sometimes he does it at board meetings. He is a special friend of mine.

Metatron is standing among us and he is glowing. In answer to a question about whether he had a part in building the Great Pyramid, he says, "Yes, I did. It was created to be a great initiation temple, and when it was finished I placed within it the purity that goes with this high area." Metatron teaches classes on the inner planes and he has taught extensively in the area of using light within physical manifestation to raise the consciousness of a particular area. That is one of his specialties and it is why he is so closely associated with Sandalphon. Bringing the great light of the Source into the awareness of people is truly his responsibility, whether it is perceived at the Source itself or on a stepped-down level.

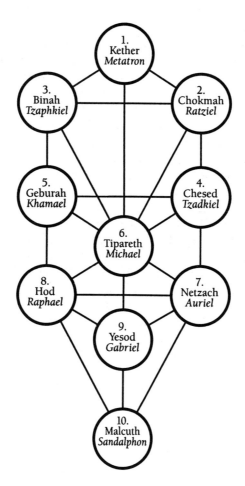

The Tree of Life of the Cabala
Showing the name of each sephirah and associated archangel

The next archangel is associated with the aspect of the tree called **Chokmah**, and his name is **Ratziel**. His presence feels completely different. Since he is not quite as close to the Source, his vibration is not quite as fine, but it is very intense. Within this aspect of the tree are all potentialities.

Ratziel holds a focus of all potentialities and works continually to bring the now-realized conditions of existence into fuller and fuller creation. He allows the energies of all potentialities to come forth, to burst forth in as full and encompassing a manner as evolution will permit. He seeks always to enlarge creation and its manifestation, focuses his full creative effort, and evolves it as the Creator's Cosmic Plan requires. He seeks to bring forth the progressiveness and evolvement that have been gained from experiencing during manifestation.

When creation has evolved to a certain point, Ratziel can bring into manifestation a certain potentiality, but not before then. So he is constantly looking everywhere, asking, "Is this coming in now? Can I begin doing this?" Imagine checking all existence to see which things are ready to evolve. Isn't that quite an assignment? He is very much involved in timing, not from an Earth sense but from an evolvement sense.

He is looking at us now. The Earth is doing well. It has one of the heaviest vibrations, but it won't after the New Age. He will be able to bring into existence things that have never been here before. But remember, he is not concerned primarily with the Earth, but with all existence, all potentialities. He can direct an unlimited number of angels to do whatever is needed. He can have all the help he needs to do his job.

The next archangel is connected with the third aspect of the tree, **Binah**, and his name is **Tzaphkiel**. I've been very interested in him for a long time because it seems to me that he has been changing. This is because existence is changing, shifting a little, and as it does he changes. It is bringing him closer to Metatron, for one thing, in the area of work. This third of the three spiritual aspects of the tree is changing in focus. Tzaphkiel is changing direction to focus existence, as never before, at the other levels (mental, emotional and physical). He is focusing this change for the New Age. He brings forth as required the specifics to begin the intent of the Creator. There is much joy and love in this one.

The fourth aspect of the tree is called **Chesed**, and the archangel associated with it has another wonderful name, **Tzadkiel**. He is the foundation of the archangels — not the one you walk on, but the one you depend on. Now, if you are going to build a universe, you have to have plans, and you get very practical about it, don't you? He can do that. At this level he is not sitting down and drawing plans and writing up specifications in the physical, but he is bringing the plans into the causal area, the higher mental, where it can be picked up for practical use. Tzadkiel is also a very visible manifestation of the love aspect of the Creator. I certainly have worked with him a lot, and he is one who teaches a lot. He is very helpful to evolving consciousness. When you take the class called Creating a Universe, he will be there to help you.

Now we come to the fifth aspect, **Geburah**, and the archangel **Khamael**. He also is a good friend and a marvelous being, quite regal-looking and powerful-looking. There is much energy there, much serene confidence — a figure of authority, in the divine sense. He is able to give directions with complete confidence, dedication and understanding, and those who get them follow them, my friends, believe me. This particular archangel has centered within his essence the energy of creation, and if there is a need for focusing more energy at a specific time, he and his department will become involved with doing so.

Right now is such a time when more energy is required. Why? Because of the changes that are coming about and the greater energy coming in at specific levels such as the Earth. He is very involved in the change of focus that is going on and the means by which this will be accomplished. His energy is controlled for the purpose of accomplishing his goal: to unify the energy of the tree of creation and bring about a productive universe.

The sixth aspect of the tree is **Tipareth,** and the archangel you all know because he is **Michael.** Michael is well known to humanity as the defender of the just. He defends people's right to attune to the true identity, to partake in the trueness of creation, which involves free will. He will go all the way to defend your right to your own free will. However, if you call on him for justice, please recognize what you are doing. He can see some fine distinctions that you cannot, and you are going to get exactly that – justice – but it may not be just what you thought you were asking for.

There is a polarity in existence, and everything struggles to balance completely. If existence swings too far one way or the other, Michael is there. We perceive this as defending, but it is truly balancing.

The seventh aspect is **Netzach,** and the archangel is **Auriel.** He is the diplomat with the ability to smooth over trouble spots in creation, and he often does. He focuses the most harmonious level of the feeling part of creation, and by attuning to him, you too can participate in the harmonious aspect of his area. If he were here on Earth we would call him a courtly gentleman, but of course he is not a human being, but one who encompasses the smooth representation of harmony. He is able to harmoniously settle areas of disagreement between close associates. He does this with his energy – his harmonious energy causes the situation to become less tense.

Now, if you call upon him for aid in a personal relationship, he might not solve the problem completely – you have to do that for yourself. But the particular moment of tenseness would be smoothed by his harmonious energy. After that it would be your job to work to remove the causes of this disharmonious condition.

Auriel has directorship over every artist that has ever lived – every musician, every painter, every dancer – though not in a personal sense. He is the one involved in any art movement as it begins to flow, as in the Italy of the Renaissance. If you create beautiful objects at a time when there isn't much light on Earth, you can bring about, in an esoteric sense, a harmony that will be very helpful. The art movement here is a reflection of wonderful celebrations we have for the Creator on the higher planes. Auriel is responsible many times for arranging these celebrations.

The next aspect, number eight, is **Hod,** and we have here the archangel **Raphael.** All of you know him very well. He is intellectually curious about absolutely everything. He is a logical focus that can deduce specific ways of bringing about what has been outlined and energized. Now, this is a specific in the area of logic. Can you attune to it? He is one who perceptively views creation and sees beyond the obvious, and aids others to do so also. If you are seeking to understand more in the mental area, calling upon him would be very productive. He has the beauty of a great intellect and the resonance of understanding that goes to the heart of a matter.

Raphael is a beautiful, great being. He is involved in deciding through logic the best way to accomplish most everything, including how to bring the most appropriate type of higher consciousness to the Earth. All of us in the Hierarchy (and we are not yet perfect, as we keep telling you) can call on him when we have doubts about the best way to accomplish our objectives. Archangels don't have any doubts – they have figured it all out within their own knowingness. They know what will work and they just assure us, and we believe them. It is very helpful.

The next sephirah is **Yesod** (number nine), and the wonderful being **Gabriel** is the archangel of this aspect. He is one that ever seeks to clarify existence, to focus the divinity from the heights into the physical and, conversely, to allow those who live in the physical to focalize and transcend through him to the heights, to the divinity within. He thus stands at a very important point, seeking always to cut through the illusion of Earth living and aid others to do so. This is a part of his service.

It is very interesting that Gabriel is known as the one who blows a horn. What does that say to you? Gabriel deals with the astral plane, the part of creation that is very close to the physical but isn't there yet. He says, "I am going to blow my horn here so you can find me." In doing this he is announcing that you must penetrate the astral illusions and see what is truly there on the astral plane, because it will be coming into manifestation in the physical. If we see what is coming, then we know what needs to be worked with. Gabriel focuses all of creation, the creative activity that has gone on in aspects one through eight, and passes it on to Sandalphon, the archangel of the physical.

Sandalphon is the archangel at **Malcuth**, aspect number ten. He is probably the most responsible archangel I have ever met. Try to feel him: You feel a solidness about this one. You could rely upon him forever. He is very actively involved with the New Age. He is directly connected to Kether, and he works closely with Michael, Auriel, Gabriel and Raphael. These four archangels are called the Angels of the Four Corners and they are a unique representation of the focus of energies before they come into the physical.

Sandalphon is always working with the Earth energies, transforming them to the highest level possible. He is now seeking to guide the Earth and its direct manifestations into a more smooth-flowing path as we move forward into the New Age. He focuses the seventh ray and seeks to implant it more securely on Earth now.

Archangels are not assigned as personal teachers, with some exceptions. However, we may learn from any of them and we study with them. All of you have gone to classes where these great ones taught. Depending upon your purposes, you can call upon any of them to help you, but be sure it is within the scope of their responsibility to address the problem you desire help with. They can only help you within the framework of their job area.

Most of the time you are your own teacher — your soul and your monad are very capable of directing you. You really don't need anyone else. And of course, you have teachers on the inner planes also. The archangels mainly teach evolving consciousnesses through classes on the inner planes. Then, when finally you evolve to cocreator status, archangels take orders from you.

You might wish to call sometime upon the Archangels of the Four Corners (Michael, Auriel, Raphael and Gabriel) for protection. You could say that in the manifested world they stand ever ready to guard you against the polarity of existence. I don't like to call it negativity; it is simply energy that is more disassociated from the Creator. By invoking their protection in a specific way you can be protected from invasion by those who have separated themselves from the divine.

Thank you, my friends.

✧ F O U R ✧

The Language of Light

MY FRIENDS, I WISH TO GIVE YOU SOME FACTS THAT I HOPE WILL AID YOUR growth so that the world will be a better place as each of us grows, enabling us to lunge forward into the New Age joyfully as part of the Creator's Cosmic Plan for Earth.

What do you think the New Age will be like? What do you hope it will be like? Think about it. Use your imagination and consider it. Do you think it will be a place where the streets are paved with gold, similar to the Heaven of the Bible? Do you think it will be a world we have to build from the very beginning because a great deal of destruction is coming?

This is important because by our growth, by our creativity, the New Age is created. It is a joint effort of mankind now, and to get it to the place where we want it, we all must grow into the New Age. That is the main reason I have come, the main reason for our thrust now – to get this New Age attunement going, to individually contact anyone who is ready to grow, because the higher the individual awareness now, the more attuned we are all going to be to the New Age. It is a joint effort. We of the Hierarchy have known that we need to raise the consciousness here on Earth to as high a point as possible to enable the New Age to be as productive as possible. Therefore we are encouraging mankind to grow, to understand the importance of growth right now. Each little realization aids mankind, and everyone should be working toward this wonderful event, this New Age of ours that we create together by our actions. Right now, my friends.

We have talked much about responsibility for self, and you know this includes our future together on the Earth. We must create it; it is our world. We will create it one way or another, but by our own productive living we can enable it to be more advanced, higher, more attuned to the Creator by our growth patterns. That is why I will be traveling extensively in these next years — to help as many as possible make as much growth as possible right now. We are utilizing methods for rapid growth, knowing that to get from here to there quickly, we must accelerate. It is as if you are hurrying for a bus, and the bus is going whether you do or not. But you must hurry if you are going to catch it — catch it and ride toward that wonderful place.

In this New Age we will all be using the language of light. The language of light is the next evolutionary step in communication for mankind. It is wonderful. It enables one to talk with another in a universal way instantly. There is no limit on light, although the scientists consider there is. This language of light makes possible an instantaneous attunement between beings that know how to use it. It is so swift, so beautiful, so exact. It is superior to words — there is no comparison. You can begin to learn this language now. It will take some time, as it did to learn English or any other language you might speak now. And it takes some time to understand.

On page 216 there is a meditation to be used for beginning attunement. It makes some changes within the mind that enable you to receive the language of light. It lets the teachers know that you are ready for it, by your desire to receive it. Nothing is done against your will — you must have free will. You must *agree* to accept this wonderful language of light. Once you have agreed and these changes have been made, you can learn to understand it, my friends.

After you have used the meditation, begin to meditate by viewing in front of you a beautiful screen. Allow the language of light to come in to you upon that screen. See it as a beautiful gold. Use it as a focal point to receive. When it begins to come, do not seek to sort out the colors to understand it; just allow it to come. Experience it. Accept it. Enjoy it, knowing that you are learning. Each time it comes, get excited about it, realizing it is something new, something beyond your experiences to this point.

After you have allowed the language of light to come to you daily for several weeks and you are very comfortable with it, then begin to notice the patterns. Do you see the same pattern at regular intervals? Are the colors similar sometimes? Look at it, analyze the light. Seek to discover things that you notice about it; this will be the beginning of understanding what you receive. After you've done the analyzing, then dismiss this. Let go of the analyzing process, and with intuition, know what is received. It will not be from your logical mind that you understand the language of light. It is a combination of everything, but perhaps your intuition is the most useful aspect to aid you. Do not allow your logical mind to get in your way, for it will if you do not restrain it. It is not logic we are seeking here; we go much beyond that to the greater patterns that come from the other, higher realms — the attunement to the language of light.

Once you feel you are beginning to perceive what is being said, it will translate for you back into words. This will be necessary for a while, until you begin to think in the language of light. It is similar to learning a foreign Earth language: You are not totally comfortable in it and you do not experience it fully until you can think in that language. So first it is necessary to translate it into words. At this point you might wish to write them down, to keep a small diary of what is received. It will be interesting to keep it over a period of time to see how you grow in your ability to receive. See if there is a pattern you are receiving. Is it all from the same source? Can you tell the differences? See if you can direct it to a specific source. Consider various ways, experiment together and share your results with one another. See how many colors there are. Understand that together you can grow into the language of light; it can be a shared experience.

Later, when your understanding has grown to the point where you receive with ease and understand it instantly, you can begin to use it yourself. And then you too will begin to transmit in the language of light. You can send to the teachers everywhere in the cosmos. You can send thoughts, you can send your emotions, you can send anything with the language of light. It is not restricted, as words are in Earth communications, and it is instantaneous! It is a marvelous language and well worth the effort to learn it. I tell you this is so with joy, because I experience it and know that it is true.

The language of light comes from the spiritual plane. It was developed by a very high soul who sought a better way to talk with all of his friends who were spread around the universe — not a great distance in consciousness, but too far to talk with by the means used then. The attunement of consciousness is quite easy, and the the language of light makes it instantaneous. Everyone who experiences it is very joyful and very pleased with this step forward. It has been around for eons and eons, but only fairly recently have Earth beings been ready to experience it. It is being brought by one of the glorious teachers who will be with us in the New Age, and he is now beginning his descent in consciousness toward the Earth. It is his gift, really. He does it with joy, and when you are receiving it, you are attuning to this great one's consciousness. It is his gift of love in serving the Creator and of his love for humanity. He sees you when you begin to seek and he really aids you. This is a wonderful opportunity to know one of the great ones, and he will aid your growth in seeking this attunement.

So my friends, please do the following meditation. Receive what is given and then begin your own meditations, seeking to attune to him through the language of light. It will also aid you to use the higher-rays meditation in conjunction with this very regularly. It will aid you to attune to the New Age, where you can utilize your new skill, the language of light. So use them together and we will go forward to the wonderful New Age. See it with me now, shining in our future, this New Age with its glorious temples, its wonderful teachers, its joy, its attunement to the Creator.

Our planetary logos, Sanat Kumara, in his wisdom and his love, has made this language of light available a little sooner because he knows that mankind sometimes takes a little longer than we would like – but mankind gets there, and that is the important thing.

Meditation for Attuning to the Language of Light

❦ Begin by becoming as relaxed as possible and do not cross energy points (arms, legs), knowing that to do so will block the energy that flows within your body. There is much energy here tonight, more than usual, and I want you to feel it now. It is an intense blue and it permeates every cell of your body. Feel it, the intense blue of the Creator's energy. And now it begins to pulse and it is urging you to grow, to become greater. Attune, my friends, to this energy, and pulse and grow with it. I am eager for your growth, as the Creator is and you are in your higher aspects. I want you to feel this intense blue light. Realize it is working. Experience it now as it works to aid your growth.

❦ Gently floating toward us now is a white luminescence – the Christ, the beautiful color of the Christ. It gently floats toward us. It contains much joy from the Creator and also from the lord Maitreya. He looks upon our efforts with joy, knowing that as we grow we aid others to grow. This white luminescence settles now and comes among us. It is so beautiful. Feel the joyousness of this white light. And the blue is still working. Feel it. Experience it. Know that it helps your growth, this intense blue light. It is raising your consciousness, aiding your growth, and now the whole rainbow descends upon us. This is what we must work with for the body of light and to learn the language of light. See the rainbow as all of the colors fill your horizon, and begin to utilize these colors. Begin to know they are telling you something, that there is a pattern. Begin to work with each color, realizing its purpose. Attune to them with your intuition. Yearn for this attunement. Each color must be attuned to separately and then put together in its appropriate pattern. In this manner you will learn to work with the language of light as it flashes before you now. Experience it now for a moment while I am quiet. A world teacher has been utilizing it to show you how it should be utilized. Keep this pattern in your memory banks, store it, and take it out again to learn from it. Each of you has received this pattern now and can use it. You just need to remember that you have it. Seek to know how to do this again – it has been programmed into each of you. The luminous golden light of the twelfth ray descends now. Feel it. Know that the eleventh and twelfth rays are our goal for reaching the glorious New Age. It is important to realize this is our goal. The gold is so beautiful. See it. Experience the higher love of these teachers – this ray attunes you to them. They await us in this New Age with their love and their knowledge and their joy. It is something to yearn for, to seek. Yearn for it. Experience it. Attune to it now. Strive, using this luminous gold ray. Utilize the group energy now. Every one of you intensely yearns to attune to the New Age. Do it now, my friends, with intensity. This particular time of year, right now, tonight. It

is important – do it with intensity.
❦ *My friends, this is a very strenuous mediation, but it will aid you. Use it often, grow with it. Enjoy it.*

The language of light was created for everyone to use and understand throughout all the planets. The language of light is an attunement, a complete attunement. It is important to recognize that this is not just a mental exercise – that you must really let go of the analytical process at some point in order to communicate in the language of light. It is very important to recognize this in the beginning, although there may be a point later when you will use the analytical part of your mind.

Is the language of light used for communication on the spiritual plane? That is one method, and here are others. My "superior" and I just keep an open channel, and when there is a knowingness of communication, I simply attune and receive it. I don't need to use the language of light where a close rapport is established, but otherwise I would use it. And no, you are not the only group on the planet learning it; there are several.

Tonight we have some colored illustrations to aid your visualization and understanding. Now, all of you like my green bananas, is that right? These are just a few visual examples of some ideas of the language of light. These are given as examples only – miscellaneous symbols to show you that what you get is a flash that conveys a whole idea rather than a single word. That's really what I'm seeking to clarify here.

First symbol:
What does it represent?
A light shining through a door. A mouth that is saying something – channeling.

Very good. The message is: Receive now what I send; it fulfills a need. Or you could say: a merging of an idea that you assimilate.

green

Second symbol:
Does it look like a quivering line, or a snake? Look at the colors: red blending into orange which blends into yellow.

A stream – stream of thought – energy.

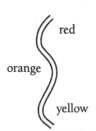

red

orange

yellow

The message is: a message that comes from the Source and shades into the heart of the matter. You would perhaps use this when doing some very important work and you want to tell someone to pay attention right now – that what was to come next was very important.

Third symbol:
Does it look like a blue volcano? Use your intuition.

Release. Breakthrough.

The message is: a break in thought, a paragraph — that's all. A new thought is coming up. The blue is important — it is used in the language of light a great deal as a way of establishing the flow.

blue

Fourth symbol:
This one is not blue; it might be purple or gold or green. Anyone here take shorthand? It is a period! I just wanted a little bit of punctuation in here to show you some of the different concepts you will be learning.

Fifth symbol:
This is meant to be a very pretty pink (pink = love).

pink

Energy.

The message is: the eternal progression of love.

It looks the same upside down.

Very good. Yes, exactly what you should do with love — view it from every angle, because it is important to understand it and most do not.

Sixth symbol:
Is it not interesting — orange, yellow, red.

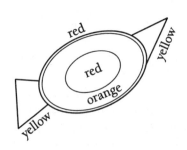

red

yellow

red

orange

yellow

A bird — a flying saucer — a seed. The message is: the blending of the event to create what you wish. What do you think that means? It is when you are working at the level of a creator (as you all are learning to do). You aren't there yet, but of course you do create your own lives by your activities. When you can create as part of the Creator's team, this symbol is used quite often. It is used in communication — with great care, discretion, restraint, caution. At the level where the masters work, this is a very important one.

Seventh symbol:
A nuclear bomb explosion? Last chance. Final.

Eighth symbol:

Now, if you see this one, you won't be frightened, will you? You'll just know someone is saying good-bye to you.

Ninth symbol:
Is this a forerunner of a punctuation mark? It is a forerunner of a synthesized thought.

blue-green

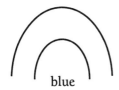

blue

Tenth symbol:
This horseshoelike thing is an expansion of the one before it.

These are just a glimpse, a preview, showing the use of colors and shapes as they can be utilized in sending and receiving communication universally. The language of light is composed of various symbols, and this is a very brief look at some of them to aid your understanding. It is an attunement rather than a mental process, and you can learn to do it gradually.

Let us have a practice session — one person in the center of a circle. Now, we want to communicate with the person in the center and we have no other way but the language of light — it is the only means of communication open to us. What do we do first? We get her attention, then vibrate a symbol to her. [Group sends symbol 2, the wriggling line — something very important going right to the heart of the matter.]

[To the receiver:] Please report what you get. (What is received is not always what is sent.)

There was a line coming through with lots of motion. The color was turquoise blue. And then there was a chair covered in white leather . . . .

[To senders:] All right, you sent her a chair instead of the message we agreed on! First we have to get the message of the squiggly lines fastened down into one place. It means: We'd better get the foundation set up before we go on to the heart of the matter. You have to learn how to send as well as how to receive. You must be able to focus on the message without any other thought interfering — otherwise you might get a chair!

Now I want you to begin to send and receive in a very special way. Instead of the group I want three – triads. One person is going to send, one is going to receive, and the third person is not going to do either but is just going to sit and experience in-between the two. I would like you to send a message that is fairly simple and rather elementary like an apple, a boat, a simple scene, a person – something not complicated. Do this in groups of three.

All right. Did you all enjoy that? It's just a preliminary exercise, but I'm especially interested in hearing the experience of the one who didn't send or receive – the center person.

[Receiving student:] I saw something rolling, something like a ring of light, and I was sent an orange rolling off a table.

Yes, you were doing very well. But the center person of the triad was in a very special place while this was going on and should have received a different type of information.

[Center person:] Yes, I saw something else that was much stronger than light. I saw a waterfall, as in a forest, with all the rocks, and this waterfall was pouring into a lagoon down below. And I don't know why, but I kept trying to shut it off and it just kept going stronger and stronger.

Yes, the person in the center gets the energies in a different way and can sense both the sending and the receiving – a separate place and still part of the whole. It is as if the energies are swirling, and it is very interesting. Did you feel a part of it? Even in the midst of it?

Oh yes, very much.

That, my friends, is the point of it. The language of light does the same thing. You become a part of it, in a sense. The energy swirls because the triad of energies utilized in the language of light makes you a part of it.

All right, I'm going to send you a message in the language of light. Everyone become as comfortable as possible. A few deep breaths may aid your relaxation. Visualize a golden screen in front of you, my friends – a way to help focus your attention. Now feel the energies from this language enclose you as I send it. Focus upon the screen at first to help you see the message; then you will decode it for me.

I am sending it now, my friends. Receive the language of light. And again it comes – the same message. Try to become a part of it. Try to feel it wrapping around you. Experience it *now*.

We are going to discuss it a little. Who saw something?

I saw some kind of a caterpillar – a dark color that became a deep lavender or purple ball and then it became gold.

I saw a kind of galaxy – a spiral.

I got a galaxy also, only it was gold – a small gold one with a ring around it.

I got a red triangle and then I moved to the twelfth ray – then something turquoise or blue.

I got a message of peace and love – love energy that was white.

Did any of you "become" a part of it?

Yes.

What I sent you was the love of the Creator. And the Creator, my friends, would appear as a great big ball – a round, golden one with many lines radiating from it. Some of you came very close to that. Love is the symbol we showed you earlier. The blue you were picking up was the energy itself rather than the message, because energy is blue. Many of you see it with your inner eye, and you must learn to discount that. You are going to see a lot of blue because that is the language itself. It is like writing with a lead pencil: You don't read the lead. You know that's part of your writing – the flow of it.

The language of light feels wonderful. Did you feel the love, the joy? Lots of energy there. One must learn to handle energy in order to handle the language of light. If you have any problems in the area of energy, that should be worked out.

The twelfth ray is the easiest place to focus for attuning to the language of light. You can learn to do it right in your living room without any of the aids that you may feel you need at first. It's like learning to draw. At first you carefully get the very best of everything and you get your paper set just right. Even if you're just copying a picture, you have to make very deliberate efforts at first. Later on you can do it anywhere, even on the bus. But this attunement will always be easier in a state of spiritual meditation or focus. The object of living is to learn to do whatever you're doing – meditation or anything – continually. Recognize that. Meditation – the serenity, the peace – in a sense can be experienced all of the time.

   ❦ *On our journey tonight, we embark on a ship. And this ship is sailing, my friends, to a far-distant land – the land of the rainbows and the rainbow people. They live in the land of joy and they believe that everything is full of joy, because they are rainbows. Really see them, these rainbow people, attune to them in all of their glorious colors. See the young woman who turns toward you – she is full of color. See the violet, the orange, the red, the yellow, the green and the gold everywhere. This is the land of the rainbows, my friends. Experience here. Use your imagination. Let the colors run wild. Experience this land of rainbows – it is full of joy.*

All right, did you all enjoy rainbow land? Yes, you d all love to be a part of a rainbow – the totality of experience. Those of you who do not yet experience color in its intensity can just know it's truly there, and that's valid. It works just as well. And you might have other abilities that are more developed, like hearing music, perhaps, and in that way you can experience joy through sound.

We can only take you so far with this and then you must launch *yourselves* into the language of light. I am simply opening the door, but you must do the work yourself. We have accomplished much more than you might recognize on the surface. We are attuning you to what might be an unfamiliar area for you. We are moving your attention from a very focused look on your faults, to your possibilities — to the totality of what you are to become, the higher aspects. This group does much work with the belief structure and is very eager to change and to grow and become greater. That is marvelous.

Learning the definitions of the symbols is a matter of synthesis. It's much easier with a teacher, but you can learn it by yourself. It is a matter of taking the pieces and finally making a whole of it, like a jigsaw puzzle. You can learn it by identifying and attuning to each piece until you put it together. But the intuition is very much involved here — you simply *know* what you have received and what it means. It takes time, my friends, and practice. You have to work from where you currently are, utilizing whatever is open, but recognize that eventually you're going to be able to do it all. You always seek to go beyond to your totality to your point of perfection, recognizing that you begin right where you are. You stretch toward the point where everything will be perfect, knowing that you are your perfection, but you begin to work from where you are now functioning.

Meditation on Color

❦ *I want you to become immersed in the light of the Creator. Feel the energy begin to swirl around and through you now. The colors are intense. Every color of the rainbow is here. Feel it working and swirling through you now. Feel it working as it becomes even more intense. This swirling energy is the totality of our experience. Feel it, become a part of it, a part of creation now. Feel it as intensely as you can. Become creation. Take part in all of the colors here now. Immerse yourself in them. Feel them with intensity.*

❦ *And now, floating down in the form of a soft pink cloud, the love and joy of the Creator floats onto this intense scene. Feel the joy, the love of this higher kingdom. It floats now into this intensity. And notice what happens: immediately things become calm. Creation sparkles. It becomes brighter, lighter. Still the colors are here, but now they change. There is a serenity, a peace, a joy, a love. Feel it, immerse yourself in this beautiful peace, tranquillity, joy, love.*

❦ *And now laughter comes. Feel the difference? It is still joyful, but there is laughter here. See it sparkle? Isn't it wonderful, the laughter of the Creator? It comes to us — His amusement. Feel it and experience it now. And now compassion. Watch it as it works with the colors. Compassion, my friends. How does it change all of the colors when they become immersed in compassion? And understanding — how does that affect the colors? Experience the understanding aspect of the Creator in the form of color now. Is it not interesting? See it and feel understanding now. And now the serenity returns. Float on it. Immerse yourself in serenity. Feel the colors of it. What color is your serenity?*

❦ *And now, descending as a gift to you, the Golden One comes. He is a higher being who has love for each of you and sends it to you. Experience this love and know that the love of the creator comes through him as a gift. And now we wash away all of the beautiful colors in the beautiful white light of the Christ. It is luminescent and it is all of the colors, of course. Experience the white and wrap yourself in it now. It is marvelous. It contains everything. Feel it and know that it is yours.*

❦ *This has been a short meditation on color, showing you the various ways you can experience color. Use it again if you wish. Work with color. Become familiar with it and it will aid your progress in the language of light.*

It is marvelous that you are beginning to recognize that there is more to existence than your concrete minds can conceive, that you must recognize and let go of some previous concepts and begin to flow with the higher concepts of the Creator.

I wish to discuss that a little bit – the fact that mankind does not understand these higher concepts yet. He is only beginning, and that is fine. That is the way it goes – a little at a time. A baby does not learn to walk all at once; he does it gradually, and so we begin this intensive effort to teach mankind about this higher concept – this language of light.

I want you to sit quietly and begin to be aware that there is an inner vision. Yes, there is an inner vision that does not have anything to do with your eyes – it is viewed internally. This is a much greater reality than what you see when you have your eyes open and look around, because externally you are limited to the Earth plane, to this narrow concept of life. The higher concepts of which the language of light is a part do not have these restrictions. It is more free-flowing, much more comprehensive, much more allowing than we upon the Earth can view.

To begin to understand it, one must recognize that it is necessary to seek to let go of any preconceived notions about sight. Yes, they must be released. Can you, with your inner vision, take an eraser and erase your concept of sight? Do it very carefully, my friends, and then look. Your blackboard is blank. Is it squeaky clean? Yes. Now together we can tell you what sight is, as far as the higher aspects are concerned.

What is it we are seeking to see, to learn? It is a means of communication. But I am not talking about that; I am talking about the perception that you will have of it, because it will not be the same as what you perceive with outer sight. To gain an understanding of this inner perception, begin to move forward in your mind's eye. See yourself upon an inner path, moving forward. You are going toward your own potentiality. You are growing, and you see yourself doing this visually.

Now, again, just with your inner knowingness, know that you are moving toward your greater self, toward an expansive life. See yourself moving there. Now that you are moving, what do you need in order to continue this? What will help you to get there more rapidly and more expertly? Do you not need a means of communication with those who have already achieved what you are seeking? Do you not wish for a means of identification with others who can teach you? Now, we have talked about attunement, and that is valid. But this is awesome — the language of light. It is so magnificent, so broad in scope. It covers such great distance — not in space and time but in distances in consciousness. Do you not see that this is a tool different from attunement? It is necessary to have as many methods as you can to do things.

Attunement with your teachers is very possible and it is really very necessary, but would you not also like a means of communication that would make it as if you were standing right together in physical bodies? Would you not like to be able to converse with those you do not know? You cannot really attune to them yet because you do not know them. But if you send out the language of light, one whom you know not — even of his existence — can see your questions and can answer you, my friends. Is this not marvelous? And before you know anything at all about the one who is sending, you can begin to receive answers.

Now, I am saying this because only upon the spiritual plane, upon the higher aspects of the Creator's universes, does the language of light exist. Anyone with whom you converse here is of the light. It is a tool for the children of the light only. Those who live without light cannot converse with it because they do not have any. So this is a very positive tool used only for your highest good and the highest good of the Creator's Cosmic Plan. Have no fear, just know how wonderful it is!

I would like to give you an exercise now to aid you in beginning to send out questions and then wait to see if you can get answers. I would like to help you to begin talk in the language of light. As you are sitting in a state of meditation, begin to send out from yourself purple rings — similar to smoke rings, but these are a beautiful purple. Form one and send it out, then form another and send it out. Keep sending these purple rings — as many as you can. Suddenly you will hear a clink or thud, or a knowing that one has landed. Did you listen? Did you hear your ring land there? I did! Someone received it. It is simply another being who is becoming aware of your ring. You will not actually hear it of course, but you will become aware of it because you will attune to your ring. And when another attunes to it there will be an establishment there.

Your rings are simply saying, "The channel's open now. Is anyone listening? Is anyone ready to talk? I am here and I want to converse." And you will get someone. You must listen for it, though, and know when one is there. And when you think you have one who has received your communication, wait. If you are right, you will begin to receive the same rings in return, but they will be golden. Yes, golden rings will come back to you. They will be so beautiful. Can you see them? Can you feel them with your spiritual hands, your inner knowing? These beautiful golden rings say, "The return channel has been opened, and I await your message." A return channel has been opened, and you must do the next step.

What do you do now? Do not sit in bewilderment, my friends. Attune to me and I will aid you. And you may try it for yourselves. Then what you get in your golden channel will be a way of learning for you.

All right. Your dark violet channel is open and it is ready to send. What are we going to send? Perhaps it would be appropriate to send first the line of love — pink love that flows in a wavy line. Send it through your dark violet channel. See it flowing. You're sending love — the love of the Creator. Feel it, my friends — the love that you are sending along that channel. Did you feel the receiver pick it up with his hands? With your inner knowing, did you know that it was received?

Now wait and see what comes. It won't take long. It's very rapid. Receive now. Visualize your channel as golden and very open and you can receive what is coming in it. Look into your channel with your inner vision and see what kind of a beautiful light, beautiful colored symbol, you are going to get. The one who sends will know you are a beginner. He will sense it and will send only one lovely symbol at a time. We have arranged it that way to help you learn. We are all eager to help you learn.

What is coming through your channel? View it, and then write down some notes, my friends. View what is coming through this channel. It should come three times. Three separate times you will be given the same symbol, because we have arranged it. So write down your symbol and then you can ask me what it means. We will build a dictionary of symbols this way. I want you to begin receiving them in your golden tube, your golden channel, my friends.

I'd like to give you another symbol to send and you will receive one in return. Send a type of blue-green light that resembles a ball that is connected to another ball. You might view it as a dumbbell — intense blue lights that are connected by a light blue color. Send one ball first and then the line of blue and then the other ball.

What does this mean? Think about it, my friends. It is very balanced, connected by a line. What could it mean? It means "I am a child of the light, I am balanced in my approach, and I desire that my growth and my balance receive the creative aspects of the language of light. I desire to learn it." All of that from a little symbol? My friends, the language of light talks not in words but in concepts, conceptual ideas only. And this balance, this creative blue energy, indicates to the one receiving it that you are a child of the light now, that you have reached this place, that you wish to learn. The teacher will begin to send to you now. This will establish a connection and you will, over a regular period of time, begin to receive symbols through your golden tube, your golden channel.

Will you set up a program to receive these now? It is being offered through me by a very high teacher in the Hierarchy. Will you take advantage of it, my friends? Are you ready for the interesting experiences you will obtain in this way? Are you ready to aid the Earth by beginning to learn the language of light? Will you help the Earth this way? Think about it: You can grow. You can learn. You can become greater. And, besides that, you can help the Earth, because the more this higher aspect is used here upon the Earth, the more it raises the consciousness of the planet. It is marvelous, it is a step forward, and we offer it to you with our love. It is given for your growth and for your aiding of others. I encourage you to take it and to utilize it now.

A regular time should be established by means of your intuition. It should probably be done daily for not more than five minutes, and preferably at the same time each time. In fact, it is almost a necessity that it be done at the same time in order for the teacher to attune to you. Yes, the teacher will attune to you, and eventually you might do some attuning to the teacher also. But the language of light is important even if it is not attunement (they are two different things and really for different purposes, as we have said).

So to use the language of light in the most productive way for you and your teacher, for your learning, set aside five minutes a day. Whatever time you wish — the teacher doesn't care. He will just set aside five minutes for you. Although time is not the same there, he is giving you a great gift. The teacher has many responsibilities. This is a special effort on his part. He reaches down now with his love and joy and makes this available for the Earth. Will you aid? Will you do it? Will you accept the responsibility? Will you utilize the self-discipline to do this now? I will be very interested to see who does so. It really doesn't matter, my friends, but it will be interesting for your own perspective of your place in the Cosmic Plan now.

This is May 13, 1983, and this offer is being made beginning right now — about 7:00 p.m. Earth time. Remember this. It is important. It is a very significant advance for earthlings and the youth — learning the language of light now.

✧ F I V E ✧

The Mineral Kingdom

W E ARE GOING TO DISCUSS THE HIERARCHY OF MINERALS – THE BUILDING blocks of Earth's evolution. We will discuss some of the more spiritual components of these gems, their composition and their hardness. I will give an introduction to the mineral kingdom first and then get into specifics.

Let us talk about the mineral kingdom – it is very interesting. You might not have thought about it in the application we will be discussing. Elements are really the basic unit of the Earth's evolution or composition, and when combined they compose what are called minerals. You can then combine the minerals and you get the combination usually called a rock. And the Earth is composed of these. As you consider the rocks, truly the gemstones, you will notice their composition. We are seeking to show that gems are a combination of things, not just one particular mineral (except for one or two of them). I will be giving the spiritual applications of these gems and also the purpose of each of them.

The mineral kingdom is evolving and becoming, just as the human, plant and animal kingdoms are. It is a basic component of physical evolution. It is neither less nor more important than the other equal distributions of consciousness on the planet. You might not have thought of it this way, but the consciousness of a beautiful gemstone is evolving, just as yours is.

The twelve gemstones that we have selected (there are many more) have, in my opinion, attained specific points of evolution that are important to recognize. If you look at the chart and the index of hardness we have used, you will see a similarity to crystals. The shape of a gemstone is crystalline in nature, which means that the consciousnesses of these particular gemstones are interactive with one another; that is what we mean by "building

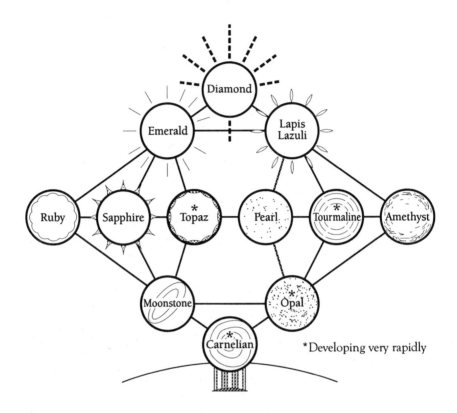

HIERARCHY OF MINERALS AND GEMSTONES
Building Blocks of Earth's Evolution

blocks." These gemstones help evolve the Earth, but they also interact and help build each other's consciousness, just as each of you does.

Why have we called it a hierarchy of minerals? In a specific sense, these gemstones are very important in leadership of the mineral kingdom. This does not mean that there are not others that are important. But the spiritual teacher Vywamus and I decided that these particular ones are all seeking to achieve this New Age experience, and each one has a specific leadership role.

If you consider that the mineral kingdom has been developing for much longer than humanity on Earth has, you will see that there are some gemstones present that have been here a long, long time. There are some that have not — they have been seeded here from other places. There are some that are relative newcomers to this mineral kingdom; there are some that are developing very rapidly; and there are some that have attained the peak of their development and are phasing out of the Earth experience.

The one that is now at its peak, the one that is most powerful and, in a specific sense, the most evolved, is the diamond. It has a very powerful vibrational pattern and it leads the mineral kingdom. I have stated previously that I didn't care much for the diamond. It isn't that it isn't evolved or that I am opposed to it, it is simply that one must know how to use the diamond properly, and most do not. It enforces or magnifies or adds to whatever is in quite a strong manner. I will give some specifics later in the most appropriate way to use it.

Each gemstone in the mineral kingdom has a unique consciousness. Any grouping of them has a consciousness that is an aggregate of the consciousness of the elements. When these minerals are combined together they become an aggregate called a rock. Each time they combine, they add to the consciousness of that particular mineral or unit. Some of the minerals combined in ways that were very productive for that particular unit, and if that unit evolved rapidly it might have become a diamond due to that speed of evolution. Now, if in a gemstone, in the combination of what it was, some sense of resistance existed or some part of the component did not add to but rather resisted evolution, then that particular gemstone might have evolved more slowly.

It is the same within self: If you have some units of resistance, it adds to the load that you are carrying when you seek to evolve. So there are some basic elements and some basic minerals that are more progressive than others. That has always been the way of it. The Source puts out every specific that it can imagine and create, and some specifics respond more consistently to the stimulation of the life force that we call evolution than do others.

The Gemstones

Diamond

The diamond took evolution quite seriously; it took its component and evolved it very specifically. It is a 10 on the hardness scale — the hardest material that we have here, although it is composed of carbon, which is not hard. Look at the emanation of the diamond: it looks like little squares. That was brought through to show you the type of energy the diamond has. Look at the specific particles of energy and the way they are formed; this says something important about the emanation.

From a spiritual standpoint, if a diamond has reached its full potential on the Earth, then it has reached its maximum energy. When something is at its fullest potential, many things happen as the emanations of the life force come forth. It invokes the full potential (or seeks to) from everything it interacts with. A natural diamond does not seem to have the sparkle of one that is cut, but in my opinion a natural diamond is the most effective form to utilize. Humanity cuts it in order to clearly see the emanation within it.

In Vywamus' opinion, the diamond is the king of the mineral kingdom, and I believe him. This king is potent, creating the invocation of potentiality as it interacts with anything, including the other kingdoms. For example, if you have a sick plant, you might use a diamond to heal it. But be careful not to use too large a diamond lest you burn it. If the diamond is used with other stones, it really can augment the qualities of the other gems. One learns not to mix gemstones indiscriminately – that is very important – but the diamond can be used with more gemstones than almost any other one that has not yet attained its full potentiality. Gemstones can be used in a variety of ways – certainly for healing, but perhaps most importantly, for evolution.

Diamonds are a spiritual model in the mineral kingdom and, if utilized to epitomize the ideal, can be helpful. The diamond's hardness, its specific degree of evolution, has become rather fixed. It has reached its peak and it is holding and sharply interacting with everything else. There is perhaps a connotation of hardness here.

There are various colors of diamonds, due simply to individual approaches to existence. If one has a yellow diamond or a blue diamond or any other *clear* diamond, then energy is being experienced from a slightly different focus. This doesn't mean it is any better or worse; it is just looking at its evolution as divinity from a slightly different focus, a slightly different mineral – but all the same, divinity.

If you wear a diamond, it stimulates your state of being, and that's why they are beneficial for spiritual seekers. If you combine it with another specific gem that you personally relate to or with which you have a great affinity, the diamond will augment the qualities of that particular stone. If you are a woman, you might try a pendant that contains the stone you really like or have been told is a good one for you, and then surround it with small diamonds. Or, if you prefer, wear a ring.

The diamond can do a great deal in healing if you know how to use it with care. For instance, if the solar plexus is reactive, to put a diamond on it would stir it up even more. Its use is appropriate if you are dealing with something that is rather sluggish and you want to speed it up, raise it, get it to thrust or be more active. You could use it symbolically. It would be appropriate to put the diamond in a specific place and visualize it in that particular area of the body that you seek to restore to full circulation. A visualization process can be used to speed up any sluggishness – if it is not a crisis situation such as a heart attack.

Diamonds are used extensively in industry. They are used to cut many things, and that seems important to me. They *cut through* things. Symbolically, they cut through everything on the Earth. You might want to think about that symbolically rather than literally. They are first-ray minerals, although in their particular evolution they are also all of the rest of the rays. They combine all of the rays within themselves, but I would say the first-ray application is apparent when the diamond interacts with another consciousness.

Water can be potentized by putting diamonds in it, if you know how. If you have a 10-point diamond (100 points to a carat) you can place it in a small glass or something clear, something to hold about six ounces of water for that size — a little punch cup will work. Place the diamond in it and put your hands on both sides of it. As you do, visualize the white light, the undifferentiated light, coming forth into that particular glass, coming forth from your third-eye area — this invokes the same thing from the diamond, which then returns it to you. This is kind of fun to do, and it helps to clean up the third eye and open it. As you do this, you should be able to feel the energy stirring. The hands begin to receive this energy response. There are words that you can use, and perhaps the best one is *aum*; sound the *aum* as you energize the water.

What would you do with water like that? It becomes very special because it has been energized with every type of energy that the Source contains. It is an excellent protective device and also very good for healing. It will be as potent as you have allowed it to be.

Emerald

The emerald is my favorite. I had a big one and really enjoyed working with it. Someone else has it now. The emerald, in my opinion, has a very beneficial quality. If you look closely, it is made of beryl and it is rather hard, too — 8 on the hardness scale. This means it is durable and lasting. Perhaps beryl will be a 9 on the hardness scale within time.

A beautiful emerald contains much. It has natural inclusions that are an integral part of the stone, and they are lovely. It is difficult to find an emerald that is clear, and in my opinion, if you do, it is less desirable than one that has the beautiful inclusions. Its emanations are very even. To me, this is the universal stone for humanity and the Earth and dealing with the hierarchy of minerals. You could say that in the mineral kingdom the emerald symbolizes the Christ consciousness, but even that does not say it all. It represents that and beyond. It is a universal symbol that is attaining a stature that no other gemstone has ever attained.

The word "universal" means all-inclusive. If a stone has these characteristics, it is highly valuable for aiding our evolution. The lovely clear green color, with the inclusions, is symbolic of the Earth, the green being the beautiful higher application of the fourth ray, but with such beauty and such an encompassing sense that it stretches one beyond any limitation that the Earth may have. It is a harmonious approach to the Earth. The emerald brings aspirations that are very spiritual.

The emerald is almost always a crystal — some sort of crystallized form. Some are very large and some are small. You have seen little emerald crystals, little groups worn together in pendants. They are lovely, and even an inexpensive one would be very valuable to you in your evolution. Get one that is as pure a green and as translucent and clear as possible. Inclusions are fine. But the clusters in the crystal part of the emerald are the most potent.

Any gemstone will take on your own particular emanation, and therefore is practical to use for the self as well as for any sort of healing you are doing for others. One should be a little careful about using a personal gemstone on others. It should be cleansed between usages. We are talking of natural stones — the laboratory has not been able to duplicate exactly what has been created naturally over the eons of time.

Lapis Lazuli

It may surprise you to see lapis lazuli present in the highest triangle, but lapis is a very rapidly developing stone. It isn't very high on the hardness scale — 5 to 5½ — but it is very special in its applications to the Earth. This stone will be very important in the New Age, for several reasons. The first is its color. That beautiful clear blue indicates an application of the second ray and also some seventh ray. Sometimes very beautiful lapis has almost a purple cast. It is a very beautiful stone. Second, it is not crystal. It is usually worn as a cabochon, a cut stone that has a rounded top to it and is worn in rings and pendants. Sometimes it is worn in its natural state, but usually it is cut into a cabochon, and for this stone, that is a good way to get it.

I particularly like the lapis that has quite a bit of the "fool's gold" (pyrite) in it. This just makes it a little more potent. This fool's gold seems to add a dimension to the lapis, a characteristic that is helpful. In the ancient days, this was used as a medicine. They used to grind it up into powder and put it in a liquid and drink it.

Lapis has been known for a long time, but it is also approaching the height of its evolution as it reaches its peak on the Earth in the New Age — probably not too long compared to the other gemstones, maybe a thousand years or so into the New Age. This is not long, for sequential time is much longer for a gemstone. Look at all the things the lapis has in it, all of the specific ingredients; it is a complex, specific stone that has much to offer.

A spiritual attunement is important if the lapis is going to be one of the leaders in the New Age. It has a specific healing application that is very good. A lapis on a pendant long enough to reach the solar plexus area would be very, very beneficial. It can help stimulate your dreams; if you want to remember them, try a lapis lazuli cabochon under your pillow. Dreams are not automatic, but the lapis will help.

The best type of lapis on the planet comes from Afghanistan, though it is rather rare now. Look at the color — a blue-purple is what you are looking for.

Lapis is a beautiful stone. I would encourage you to wear it if you enjoy lapis, but not a whole necklace of it — that's too much power. Use your specific enjoyment of the stones to guide you. Now, diamonds are fine with lapis, if you want to be very fancy. I prefer them alone, but the diamond is the best compliment. Don't use anything else. This is true of emeralds, also. If you want to put lapis with a few diamonds, that is all right. But don't use rubies, sapphires, pearls or synthetics with lapis because it takes away the potency of the stones.

Ruby

The ruby is a crystallized part of the corundum mineral. It is number 9 in hardness, as is the sapphire. They are both part of the corundum, but they are different in color, the ruby being red and the sapphire blue. They are both very hard, next to the diamond in hardness. Although our scale is from 10 to 1, the distribution is not even. There is quite a bit of difference between 9 and 10, more than would appear, and there is less between 8 and 9.

If you look at a beautiful large natural ruby, it is magnificent. The ruby might be equated to life force, symbolizing the blood. Rubies are quite developed; they have been around quite a while and they are considered a "staple." They are not as abundant as they used to be, and therefore are very expensive. In other times, rubies were readily available and were worn a great deal by royalty. Crowns were studded with rubies. I knew an Indian prince whose crown held two or three dozen rubies, all the size of pigeons' eggs. Rubies have not left the Earth; I think many are in bank vaults and caves.

The ruby is closely connected with the specific connotation of life force that is called first-ray. After the first ray has "done its thing" it becomes a part of that specific unit. It is now in the Earth and is symbolized by the ruby. Look where the ruby is placed on the chart — the diamond is at the top, with the ruby to the left, a stabilizing factor for the energy represented here.

The ruby is brilliant — not in the sense of sparkling, but a brilliance in its understanding as a gemstone. It is the smartest of the gemstones. It has a brilliance in its application because in its combination of elements, it has placed an emphasis on exploration in all potentialities, a first-ray application. It has learned much — it's a very experienced stone, you might say.

If you have a ruby, be careful what you combine it with. Diamonds? Yes. I would not advise using them as small ornamental stones around emeralds, pearls, amethysts or sapphires, and certainly not with opals; they are not compatible.

The specific rayed ruby has a different approach to evolution than do the ones that are crystals. The stones we have identified here are the most helpful to the seeker. The clearer the stone, the better quality they are — the more perfect in their physical application of divinity, and thus the more helpful they will be to you in your physical application of divinity.

Sapphire

We are not talking about star sapphires or the rayed rubies here. New sapphires (and rubies) have become staples in the mineral kingdom, but they were not always available. They are a rather modern stone, millions of years younger than some of the other stones. This means they have evolved very well, for they are now a staple among stones. If, in looking at the diagram, we removed the ruby and the sapphire, it would not look complete. That is why they were sent to the Earth: to complete in a specific sense the crystalline interpretation we are calling the hierarchy of minerals.

Members of the mineral kingdom do not have individualistic conscious-nesses that say, "I'm a ruby" or "I'm a sapphire." They do have an ability to achieve a direction because of a stimulation of the interaction of the basic unit of creation on the Earth, which we call the element. As they come together they stimulate and interact, depending on what they are. The ruby is slightly different from the sapphire because the color shows you it is. It may be the basic corundum, but its interpretation of *what is* is a little different. The ruby is more first-ray. The sapphire is more second-ray; it doesn't usually decide consciously. There is a potential for the mineral kingdom; there are many rivers in the flow of life or the life force, and the mineral kingdom explores all of it in its entirety. And the corundum territory has two tributaries, you might say. As evolution takes place, everything has a purpose as chosen by the Source specifically. It is not chance, but a wide expanse of exploration, and in it each has its own place.

The removal of rubies from circulation – from humanity's use – is causing an interesting difference on the Earth. This beauty, this evolvement that has been part of the Earth consciousness, has been so removed by some of humanity that it makes a difference. Now, if the ruby is to interact with humanity and evolve the consciousness of humanity for its balance, but it lies in a bank vault or in the tomb of a pharaoh, it does not help the interaction of the various kingdoms, which is one of its purposes. It is appropriate that humanity also help to evolve the mineral kingdom. By interacting with a beautiful sapphire or a beautiful ruby, emerald, lapis or diamond, you can help it to become. It is ever meant that different focuses of divinity interact and learn from one another.

Carnelian

Carnelian is a variety of quartz and has an interesting name – chalced-ony. This is a very rapidly developing stone, and that is why it has been included in the hierarchy. Have you ever known someone who was in a rush to get somewhere and was moving rapidly? That is the carnelian – it is way ahead of itself, and way ahead of its fellow types of quartz. The amethysts, another form of quartz, are also doing well in this regard. But the carnelian is very special. I used to wear carnelian but I did not find its characteristics nearly as potent as they are now – and that wasn't very long ago in sequential time.

At its best it is translucent, large and rather orange in color. It is often cut into cabochons, which enhances its translucent quality. The carnelian does not know that it is a piece of quartz – it is certain it is a diamond! It has the diamond as a role model. Its place in the diagram is rather like the lowest element in the Cabalistic Tree of Life – there is a close correspondence between it and the diamond, which it is emulating.

Quartz is one of the most common minerals on the Earth; only very specific, "eager" pieces are carnelian, and the ones that are the most translucent are the cream of the crop. It gets its impetus from the combination of what it is. Because of the specific combination of elements that combine to make carnelian, it has reinforced evolution more than even the Source recognized would happen. Sometimes specific pieces of divinity go forth but they never forget their basic association with the Source. The carnelian still remembers that Sourcelevel application of divinity. I feel that eventually the carnelian is going to be one of the most valued of gemstones. We may well be into the New Age before its true value is recognized, however.

Diamonds enhance the carnelian, so wear it surrounded by diamonds and it will be happy. Happy gemstones perform their unique function of rapid evolution right along with you, so if you are ready, wear carnelian surrounded by diamonds, and you will go off like a rocket!

Carnelian has a wonderful approach to life. It is the optimist of the mineral family. It is an emotional stone, but very optimistic. The carnelian's energy flows out to every other part of the mineral kingdom. It knows how to focus energy very well; it focuses within self so that it may evolve, and it is very happy to share that evolvement with everything it comes into contact with.

Amethyst

This gemstone is the cornerstone of the New Age. It is quartz and it is composed of silicon and oxygen, with a 7 on the hardness scale. Amethyst, in a specific sense, is the most evolved part of the quartz, but carnelian is starting to give it a run for its money.

The most beneficial aspect of amethyst lies in its particular interpretation of the rays, which takes it into the transmutation area. Amethyst has a quality called anticipation: it is anticipating the next level of evolution – its own, fitting in with the Earth's and all of humanity's. Everything fits together well. Amethyst's major characteristic is anticipation of what will be. If you wear one, you are going to get to deal with that particular quality within self – anticipating what will be.

If there is any resistance to change within self, the amethyst will anticipate and help you bridge that gap. We have said that the next five years will be full of change – everything changing everywhere – and you can anticipate that. Amethysts will help you in this regard, and that is why so many of you like to wear that color. It is an innate attunement to it that helps you deal with your life. A good, clear amethyst is helpful. If you use the amethyst over your third eye, it will serve as a bridge to the New Age. I encourage you to wear the color, for it benefits anyone.

There are four rapidly developing stones: topaz, tourmaline, opal and carnelian. They are rather new to their point in the hierarchy of minerals. In the far-distant past, before humanity had anything to do with the Earth, there were other stones in their places on the diagram. The rapidly developing stones stimulate your consciousness. Amethyst helps one to deal with and overcome resistance in any area.

Opal

We have assigned the opal a hardness of 3½ to 5; it is composed of silicon, oxygen and water. The opal does not have a crystallized form, but starts in a fluid form and then creates layers between other specific minerals. It is always on a parallel with the Earth. It forms in layers of basalt rock.

The precious opal (as opposed to regular opals) contains the beauty, the reflected energy, that is called fire opal. The silicon, oxygen and water form in a specific energy pattern that shows many, many colors. If I equated the Source with particles of the rainbow in the white energy, I think the white-fire opals would represent that more closely than anything else. You can see how important the opal is to this hierarchy of minerals. It literally has a direct connection to the Source level and is growing very rapidly. Its beauty sparks to the Source level. Have you ever looked into a beautiful opal that has many lovely colors?

It is a rather brittle stone, not an especially stable one. It is not true that opals must be kept in water in order not to dry out. If they are properly created and processed, they do keep their beauty, their fire. Generally they are put into cabochons.

A cracked or crazed opal indicates that when it came together with the human kingdom it was not treated properly. It has nothing to do with the opal itself. It was simply enjoying itself in the Earth, being beautiful, and then humanity took it out of its natural habitat and didn't prepare it properly. Something like cracking occurred, and though humans might complain about that, the truth is that they were the creators of the condition.

The opal should not be worn with anything except diamonds – or by itself. Diamonds will enhance it, but rubies, sapphires, pearls and amethyst are not appropriate. These other gems cause imbalance and cancel out the specific emanation that would allow a holistic application of its beauty as a healing stone or for spiritual attunement to the Source level itself. The opal becomes imbalanced and then it acquires a bad reputation by being placed within a setting that is not conducive to its use. The opal cries and is hurt when it is not appropriately set. The precious opal and the beautiful fire opal are very emotional stones, and I have actually seen them cry.

Common opal doesn't have any fire, so its energy is not the same. Black opals from Australia are quite rare and therefore quite valuable, but they are not appropriate for spiritual use. They are not as evolved and just haven't gotten it all together yet. Opals may come from Australia, Mexico or the United States. Some of the most beautiful, valuable and evolved stones are the Mexican ones, but generally they are not as spiritually attuned in their evolution. It is generally accepted that Australia's opals are some of the very best. It is their fire and the range of their fire that indicates their spiritual attunement. Some have green, some blue, some violet, but I like the multicolored stones. They are a more balanced application of this specific gemstone's divinity.

Tourmaline

This is another important stone. It is 7½ on the hardness scale and consists of a complex silicate. It is amazing to see how rapidly it is becoming, developing, growing, realizing, integrating and thrusting. The tourmaline is very valuable but it should be used by itself. Don't surround it with anything else; wear it simply in a pendant setting where a balanced application of its energy and yours would be most beneficial.

The quality that is most unique in the tourmaline is its ability to aid in realization, because it is really realizing its own divinity so rapidly. There are many, many kinds of tourmaline. Watermelon tourmaline has several different colors, but if you are using it for your development you should wear one specific color. Tourmaline is developing as a group very well, but I don't find wearing the mixed colors very appropriate, because they are less effective. It would depend on what part of the body you are going to wear it on and what area of the energy centers you want to stimulate.

Moonstone

These are part of feldspar, which is one of the most common minerals around and is really an aggregate of several things. They have a specific interpretation of their divinity as an integral part of them, a rather luminous quality. Many of them hold the electrical part of the energy body within themselves.

If you are attracted to moonstones, it is because you are looking for the electrical properties of energy or your body of light. They are forerunners in the body-of-light area because they have already found theirs. Although they are part of the basic Earth (as a gemstone), they have that luminous quality already integrated into self as no other gemstone has. The opal comes the closest, but no other gemstone has achieved their level of evolution yet. In one specific area, evolution, they have thrust forward and developed way beyond any of the other stones.

In wearing or using moonstones for their beauty, they should be left by themselves and not combined with any other stones. There are many qualities of moonstone, and the highest-quality stones are not readily available, which means that many that are on the market are not good representatives of the epitome of evolution that is possible through this stone.

The moonstone does not care how it is cut; it just enjoys it. The opal, on the other hand, resents being cut, and it may respond by doing something inappropriate, like cracking. The moonstone just becomes whatever it is, recognizing that it is divinity regardless of its shape. It is more stable in its divinity. All of these stones have interesting, unique interpretations – just like humanity.

Topaz

The topaz is formed of granite and igneous rocks and is a fluorosilicate and aluminum-based gemstone with a hardness of 8. It is difficult to find, and the best ones come from Brazil. The highest-quality stone is clear translucent with many fine highlights in it. Yellow is the best color for the topaz, although you will find many with a brown cast to them. Yellow is a reflection of the third ray, which brings to the topaz the logic that is in ordered intelligence.

This gem is worn to bring forth a balanced, logical approach to situations or conditions. It looks good in jewelry for the ears and is beneficial also for the throat-chakra area, so a choker pendant would be very appropriate. The topaz by itself is a beautiful gem, and the clearer it is, the more perfect the stone. The off-yellow shades are attractive, but those stones are not as perfectly formed. The synthetics are of no spiritual value whatsoever. They are frequently of a brownish color, and brown quartz is often passed off as topaz.

The spiritual value of topaz lies in its balance, because it sits as one of the three primary rays and therefore is part of the creation triad. It has been used by royalty – not too often, because they generally preferred the darker stones. The topaz is valued now not only for its healing qualities but also for its ornamental value. It is a stone that has developed over the millennia and has learned to utilize its components to reach its purpose as a balancing gem.

The topaz is placed within the heart center of the diagram and represents the Sun's rays streaming forth from that important balance point. In earlier times, it was worshipped as a Sun stone by tribes who believed that their Sun god was within the topaz.

Pearl

The pearl is not too hard, because it is formed by a different type of nature – by sea mollusks. The mollusk forms a "cocoon" around an irritation point caused by a bit of sand or other foreign matter that has gotten into its shell. The cocoon substance is identical to the material used to form its shell; thus the pearl's hardness value of only 3½.

Pearls are an opaque gem. Those that are naturally formed, not cultured, are the best; these are often not round but in variously shaped forms. The pearl does not care what shape it comes in; it just wants to express itself joyfully once it is released from the cocoon. The pearl, over many years, is made from layer upon layer of mollusk substance, and if it is created happily — meaning through the consciousness of the mollusk — then the pearl becomes a happy gem and this is reflected in its luster.

Pearls come in a number of shades and colors, but the white pearl with an iridescent coating is one of the more beautiful gems that we have. The pearl represents the white light or the Christ light. It is very useful in the third-eye area and also for balancing the body.

You will note that both the pearl and the topaz are in the center of the diagram, in the heart center of the hierarchy of minerals. The pearl represents the physical human kingdom on the chart, at the heart center, bringing forth the Creator's love as it shines with its iridescent light and balances all of the gemstones within the hierarchy utilizing the Sun's rays of the topaz. In a way it represents the path that humanity has passed through and the path that is left to complete before the epitome of gems, the diamond, symbolically representing the cocreator state, is reached. The pearl's spiritual aim is to bring a calming influence into the hierarchy of minerals and to serve as a mediator between all of the gemstones with its calming, peaceful influence.

There are black pearls, but as I stated for the black opals, they are not quite as evolved as the iridescent white pearl. The pearl, while not far along its evolutionary path, enjoys serving at its current level because it unifies and blends the animal and mineral kingdoms.

It is a unique gem because of the consciousness of the animal kingdom that has gone into the making of this beautiful expression of divinity.

HARDNESS AND COMPOSITION OF THE GEMSTONES		
GEMSTONE	HARDNESS	COMPOSITION
Diamond	10	Carbon
Emerald	8	Beryl — Beryllium, Aluminum Silicate
Lapis Lazuli	5 – 5½	Sodium, Aluminum, Calcium, Sulfur Silicon (Pyrite)
Ruby	9	Corundum — Aluminum, Oxygen
Sapphire	9	Corundum — Aluminum, Oxygen
Topaz	8	Fluorosilicate, Aluminum
Pearl	3½	Concretion, Mass of Nacre
Tourmaline	7½	Complex Silicate
Amethyst	7	Quartz — Silicon, Oxygen
Moonstone	6 – 6½	Feldspar — Aluminosilicate of Potassium, Sodium, Calcium
Opal	3½ – 5	Silicon, Oxygen, Water
Carnelian	7	Quartz — Chalcedony

✧ S I X ✧

Crystals and How to Use Them

W HAT IS A CRYSTAL? CRYSTALS HAVE A PARTICULAR LATTICE FORMATION that holds the energy in a specific pattern. They are a specific way of using energy for a specific purpose. Crystals are used for healing, lasers, radio signals, growth-working with energy, reflecting rainbows, and many other ways of focusing energy. The Atlantean civilization used crystals to run the society energywise — and to destroy it.

In one of my lives I worked with crystals almost exclusively. I love them. I find them a very high form of life and in their own class. They have much to give us, and they receive from us, too. Crystals bring about a more focused application of the higher energies.

Some crystals can be utilized by a specific individual more easily than others. When you buy a crystal you should hold it in your left hand and attune to it — that is, in an altered state try to become a part of it. Let your inner knowledge relate to the crystal. When you have decided that the crystal is right for you, keep it for your work and do not let others use it, or, if they do, redistribute your energies into it after they have used it. Keep it in a closed space when you are not handling it.

So you now have a crystal that feels almost like an extension of you. When you hold it in your left hand, you are receiving from it and attuning to it. Now you switch it to your right hand and put your energies into it. Cup your left hand under your right as you hold the crystal in your right hand. At first you will be unable to accomplish a full charge immediately, but after working with it for a while, you will be able to do it instantly. Charging is an act of the will aspect of the Creator. Will the crystal to become divinely charged with the christed energy for the purposes of healing. I use the christed energy because the Christ is the one who came as a teacher to the Earth to embody love, and love is used very productively in healing. After charging your crystal, you might feel many things. Some people can feel their heart beating in it. Some experience a sense of immersion in the crystal — seeing the structure, the inner parts of it. You are beginning to exchange consciousness with the crystal.

Now, healing is really done from within self by changing the belief structure. But if people come to you who are hurting and don't know how to change their thinking, you can ease their pain and trauma with a crystal. Hopefully, if someone comes to you for this type of healing, you can also counsel them about working on the source of their problem.

Where does karma come in? Karma is merely an effect of a cause that you have set up in a previous experience. If you understand your own self and know the areas that do not respond to life as you would like them to, you can see these causes and remove them from the subconscious. Say, "All right, I recognize that this area in my life is not flowing well and I accept the responsibility for creating my life, so I wish to change it." Nowhere does it say that because you created a situation (karma) you have to keep it. It can be changed according to free will.

You do this all the time in your experiencing, but that is much slower. If you can identify an area that would take perhaps five lifetimes to work out and you can remove the cause, then you won't have to experience it. It's called a shortcut. This is why those of mankind have had so many lifetimes — because experiencing takes so long.

Hold the crystal in your right hand with your left hand cupped under it and focus your attention on your crystal. With the following statement you can charge the crystal.

🐾 *We call upon the energies as embodied by the Christ and we ask that these energies become a part of this crystal. We charge it with love in the name of the Christ, now.*

Now your crystal is charged. See if it feels any different. I have aided you this time, but you can learn to do this yourself in a state of meditation by visualizing the white energies of the Christ with love and sending them into the crystal with the divine will.

Now we have a charged crystal. What shall we do with it? If someone you know has a joint that needs energy, place a towel or other covering on the area you are attempting to heal and put the crystal on top of it. Holding the hands of the one being healed, bring down the Christ light and focus your attention on the crystal. You will most likely feel some warmth. You can heal yourself in this way as well.

This is the most appropriate way to use the crystal, but if you can't put the crystal on the body because the area requiring healing is in an inconvenient place, then hold the crystal in your right hand and place that hand on the area needing healing. Then hold the person's left hand in yours. You and the crystal are one, and when you hold their hand, they become part of the circuit. Begin this healing process with a prayer, and afterward thank the Creator for His help. After using the crystal for healing you must recharge it. You're amplifying your own inner healing abilities with the crystal – amplifying the energy pattern.

We are talking mostly about quartz crystals. Natural crystals are much better than glass ones, but the faceted glass ones will hold some charge. Please recognize that if you have an emerald that size, you can use it too. I had one in one life, but it would probably be cost-prohibitive now.

You can maintain as good a charge as we have given for about three weeks. However, you must recharge after healing. As you become more proficient in their use, you can charge your crystals so they will hold a charge longer. Arkansas crystal is quite pure, and the purer the crystal, the higher the energy it will attain, and thus the more christed energy it will hold.

If you are healing someone who has a lot of negative energy in his aura, use the crystal in your right hand and smooth the aura with both hands. But if you start feeling immersed, stop and wash your hands, then start again. In these cases you should protect yourself first and then start with a prayer. Also, ask for divine guidance during the healing. Be very careful when you begin to aid those who have become damaged through negative experiences. You don't want to refrain from helping them, but work with caution and prudence.

All of us would like instant illumination, but it doesn't work that way. Still, if you are seeking the answer to some question such as "What are my purposes?" (everyone asks me that), you can use the crystal to help you. In a state of meditation hold your crystal on the third-eye area. You might get interesting pictures when you do that. Then you begin to meditate, asking the question. What you are asking for is understanding from the higher aspect of self. But you are focusing your question, in a sense, through your crystal, and you must ask it with intensity and love. This higher self is the christed part of you, and you must use love in connection with it. You must first feel heat in connection with it; once you do, then intensify the feeling of love, and wait.

If you do this with dedication and ask for divine guidance, the crystal focuses the divine love and guidance back to you, and it will aid you. Crystals are a tool for intensifying whatever you are seeking to do, if it is in line with the Creator's Plan. They are used for working with the higher aspects.

If you misuse the energy of a crystal, it will soon become unchargeable for you. It is charged with christed energy, and if you have low or negative purposes, that energy simply won't work for you.

Suppose you have someone who hurts all over and says, "Heal me." If another healer is available, you could make a triangular configuration, with the person to be healed at one point of the triangle, and the two of you using your crystals, circulating the energy through the triangle.

The christed light is generally the most appropriate to use in healing, but if someone very close to death has asked for help, and you feel it is valid, you can call upon Sanat Kumara or the Creator Himself and charge the crystal with their energies. You can do this if you accept that you can and if you can run those high energies through your own body. I would try it a little bit and see how it works; if it is too strong, you can go back to the christed light. You can also use the crystal to attune more easily to your teachers.

Color

Now let's talk about color in crystals. In my opinion the violet light is best for a spiritual type of healing. It can raise your vibrational pattern to a new level. Some use the violet color by calling upon St. Germain, the head of the seventh-ray department of the Hierarchy. You can also visualize the color.

Someone you've healed can be further energized if you use a vivid blue for energy, then a soft pink for love, with maybe a sprinkling of red (first ray), but only a sprinkling, because it is quite intense.

Green is energetic and renewing. It is appropriate if you noticed the person had a heavy emotional problem and seemed not to be helped by the crystal. If they have been helped but their emotional trauma needs healing before they can truly feel better, the use of green can be emotionally very calming, very serene.

Yellow is a cheerful color and has an intensity that lifts a vibrational pattern. It can lift the emotions. Of course, it lasts only a short while, but if it is used in healing – perhaps if a room is painted yellow – it can be very beneficial.

Gold is more intense than yellow. I like to say it is a "crowning" of yellow, a higher aspect.

White certainly does contain all the colors, and black does absorb all the colors, but in a sense black contains them all too because it absorbs them. Black is not appropriate for healing. It is very interesting when you use it symbolically. It is good for understanding certain aspects of yourself in meditation.

With indigo one thinks of depth. Indigo comes from an intensity in other areas. It isn't even an Earth color; it is seen as a reflection on Earth. If used prudently for healing it can be helpful – a little goes a long way. If someone comes to you who is still quite immersed in himself, the indigo will probably not help him. But if you find someone quite developed in the mental body, the indigo does awaken those higher aspects that are latent in them. If they are already awake to the higher aspects, this will intensify them.

Gemstones

Most emeralds have many flaws. I had a large one once that had a number of internal flaws, but it was still valuable for specific areas of healing, such as diseases of the central nervous system. This has to be rather carefully done.

Rubies are interesting. They are a Ray One energy, and you have to use them carefully. They are useful when the vital forces are depleted, such as when a person has had a heart attack or suffered a major trauma.

Until you have started searching and growing, your birthstone is beneficial. When you change your life, your birthstone doesn't apply anymore, and you can benefit from any stone.

Opal is disastrous for some. It is often traumatic for those who are emotionally oriented. An opal comes from a liquid and it is layered. Contained in that liquid are the various bright-fire colors, and sometimes those who are not seeking have a subconscious fear of them.

Garnet is a coarser stone than ruby. Ruby is my very favorite stone. Garnet can attune you to some of the smaller animals such as rabbits.

The Indians looked at turquoise and it reminded them of the sky and became a symbol of the Great Spirit. They didn't do healing with it, but wore it as a symbolic reminder of the presence of the Creator.

Lapis lazuli is the stone I love most, next to the ruby. It is a composite stone having three components and its intensity can aid you to clarify certain aspects of the mental.

I don't like diamonds for healing work. They are very hard and harsh. If you wear one all the time and it is compatible with your vibration (which it often is not), then it can give you a clarity of thinking. Many people do like them.

Some plants like crystals and some do not. Two of the plants in this room care nothing about having a crystal, while the other one loves them. Crystals are like pets for them, and they get a mutual benefit, just like you and your pet might receive mutual benefit.

The purer the crystal, the more it will reflect the total rainbow. But you can look within a crystal with your inner eyes and see how many colors are in it. The more it has, the better, because the whole rainbow is the Creator's energy in totality.

A crystal that is cloudy can become clearer if you use it very often, because the white light of the Christ raises the vibration of the crystal.

A crystal will intensify any clairvoyant ability that you have.

Crystal-Empowering Meditation

❦ Begin now to become as relaxed as possible. The arms can be crossed if you are holding your crystal. A few deep breaths will relax you.

❦ The room is now being flooded with the white light of the Christ. See it and feel the intensity of it. And now in our midst comes a beautiful robed figure, and he is here with his love. See it and feel it now. Your crystal is intensifying with the application of love. Feel it with intensity.

❦ And now before us a whole rainbow of colors is present. The energy of the Creator, all of it, is here, and in it is a figure representing all of these energies. And it is full of love, full of joy. See it, feel it. And it too begins to change *your crystal – it becomes more powerfully charged now. Keep the love very strong within you, knowing that this aids a productive charge. This charge will be very beneficial. Much love . . . the love of the Creator, the highest love aspect, is here now, very intense. The rainbow literally explodes in front of us, all of the colors going everywhere. Much energy is present, also flowing into your crystal as it becomes more and more charged now. Feel the intensity, become a part of it. Merge with the crystal for your higher purposes and feel it now.*

🕯 *Now we bring in the higher love aspect. Visualize it as a special pink crystal that literally surrounds us. Feel the love as it streams into every fiber of your being. Feel it now, the love of the Creator. Is it not joyful to be a part of this love? Feel it as it permeates your crystal. It is being programmed with love. Love will aid you to work with others with crystals. Feel it and permeate yourself with this love. We are a unit of love.*

🕯 *Send it out now to the world, the love of the Creator. Use it – there is plenty left. Use it to aid the planet. Do it with your will, my friends, and do it now. Do it with intensity.*

🕯 *When you work with the crystal, remember love. The crystal can represent love to you. Use it this way with love and you will do much good.*

❖ S E V E N ❖

Energy Distribution in North American Cities

THE ENERGY RAYS PRESENT ON EARTH WERE NOT ARBITRARILY PLACED around the Earth by Sanat Kumara, the Planetary Logos. They are an effect or a result of evolution, and in turn they also influence evolution. The lower rays – the first seven – affect about a 50-mile spread, while the higher rays extend to a much larger area because of their finer vibration.

Today we are going to look specifically at energy in North America. To begin with, we have a compilation of energies – different kinds of energies with different effects from others that you can't even see here. Why? Because in another area of the world there may be a condition that literally launches an effect, energywise, into this area. What we have is a complex representation of energies throughout North America.

To me the most important aspects of North American energy are the first and second rays. The first ray comes in through Vancouver and runs across Canada. It doesn't come into the United States at all. The second ray comes in through Vancouver and goes down through Minneapolis, to Detroit, over to New York and then down into the Bermuda Triangle. There is a lower loop of the second ray, too, which goes down through Central America and the lower Pacific to a little above Australia. This has an emphatic effect upon the second ray, even if it doesn't exactly run through North America. You have to take into account some rays that are not even close but have an effect.

So the first and second are very important. You could say that in an esoteric sense they were there first – the first ray, being very thrusting, is the first that comes into manifestation, and the second then follows. You get a very thrusting ray followed by one that brings into focus, perhaps, what the first has done. Then, the third ray is a clear focus of what has been going on with the second ray. But it is the interaction of the first and second that is important in North America.

If you have a specific area on the Earth that has much first ray, but the Earth has not yet raised the first ray to its most productive use, it can affect the entire picture. The second ray then might not enter as we would like to see it. It might reflect some of what is going on in the first ray. The first ray goes in, and if it is used in a very negative sense, it destroys. Then the second ray enters and what does it do? If it is not being used as productively as it should, what effect do you get?

For an example, look at the condition in Germany after the war, after the first ray had gone through the area. The first ray cleared out a lot — not in a productive sense, but it cleared out a lot and got people right back to survival. The use of the second ray can bring people back to caring about each other. After the cause of all the conflict is cleared out, then people can look at basics. They say, "Perhaps there are a few things that are more important than shooting at other people." It gets into one of the more positive areas, and people begin to build again.

So in North America you have the first ray that's always thrusting. It moves across and is surrounded by the second ray in a very literal sense. Even if you don't see it here, still it reflects down here. What kind of effect do you think this has on North America? Basically, if we view the whole North American continent, we are going to see that it contains a different type of, shall we say, consciousness than South America — especially farther north in Canada where you would have to have a very basic drive to even survive, a determination to get things done. North American people can accept something new, including people. The area as a whole is open to many new concepts. Not everybody understands them in the same way, and they will allow that. My definition of tolerance is that when you become aware of something, you consider it and see what is involved, and you reserve judgment until you have followed through on it. The energies reflect, in a sense, all of what we are saying.

Ray One energy contains certain characteristics, and as it moves through an area, you use certain parts of it. Parts of it are not used up because you have not utilized it fully. Both the positive and the negative connotations are available; when you use them in time of war you are using up the negative. What's left then? The positive. Then you are not thrusting forward so much, and it can be used to combine with the second ray in a very specific way. It literally allows the second ray to blend with the first, and then, my friends, you are accomplishing something. The positive part of the first ray activates the positive part of the second ray, and vice versa. When you are using up the positive part of the first ray, the negative doesn't reflect as much — you move to a new level.

Let us talk about specific areas. **Vancouver** is interesting. It has the ninth ray, the sixth ray, the second ray and the first ray all coming through it. That should do something for it. We talked about the first and second.

The sixth is the devotional ray, which has been used less than productively on the Earth. But it can be used in the highest sense to allow the richness of Earth living to become apparent. That's important — that would be the best way to use it as far as the Earth is concerned. All the energies in Vancouver here move in the same direction, which says they are harmonious. Going in the same direction tends to increase their effectiveness, and if energies are going in opposite directions they are less harmonious and less productive.

The ninth ray is one that we are working with right now. You could consider the ninth the one that is actually going to begin this deep, deep change. The eighth is cleansing, too, but the ninth brings the deep change. Now, the sixth, most of the time on the Earth, is not subject to change. The traditional religions are on this sixth ray. The sixth ray holds very well. Now there is also, in a sense, a harmonic of it — the sixth and ninth. And that's important. You have those and you have the second ray, the teaching ray as well as the love/wisdom ray, so that seems to be very good. And you have the thrusting ray, the first.

So what kind of an area do we have here? The area itself is experiencing an opportunity to let go of much, but it is probably resisting a little, energywise. The sixth and ninth are giving it a very interesting opportunity for growth. What is the key to this situation? Perhaps raising all of the energies to their highest level — the richness of Earth living of the sixth ray; the beauty of the second ray; the thrust of the first; and the lifting power of the ninth — would make that a simply marvelous area. In the first ray you see a lot of the frontier; in the sixth ray a holding to traditional cultures; in the second ray much religious allowingness — yes, I imagine the Religious Science Church would do well there. It might be in the middle of the sixth and ninth ray at this particular time, but that's potentially a good area for it.

Now, there is one other thing that affects this area, and this one is very interesting to me. There is an effect there caused by the whirlpool of energies in the New Zealand/Australia area. Between those two places is something akin to the Bermuda Triangle but it only has two energies going into it, instead of many, as in the Bermuda one. The energies go there and swirl. These are really areas of release — pressure release — for the planet. But in a sense this area is closely connected with the Bermuda Triangle area and also with the potentials set to take place as the higher rays become ever more available on the Earth.

I recently said that the eleventh and twelfth rays were not at all present on the Earth. A little bit is here now, and I feel it is thanks to the efforts that some of you are making in your meditations to bringing them in. So thank you all. We are beginning to see a little bit reflected in Vancouver — some of the eleventh and particularly the twelfth — because you have been working with it. And I'm seeing a little bit of a launching effect. Remember, these are very powerful energywise. That is why so much has happened in the Bermuda Triangle. And when the twelfth, which circles around, gets reflected, it can launch in any area. There is some twelfth ray coming in here now, because of the location and the launching effect of these two energy areas. So you are doing good work.

The New Age is created by what we do now. That's why we encourage people to work with the higher rays – because then we can see, reflected in specific areas, what is happening.

Another area in which we are seeing some signs of the New Age, and specifically the twelfth ray, is El Paso. Vancouver and El Paso are the two areas in North America where we are seeing the twelfth ray right now. One other place that I am seeing some twelfth ray (and it is because of the second ray and its path) is the East Coast. This is really rather unexpected, and it has happened since the last time I talked with you. It is as though the twelfth ray is sprinkled along the whole eastern seaboard. To me that is very productive. I don't think it gets as far as Washington, unfortunately. It is only beginning, my friends. But we really didn't expect to see it at all for a while, so it is good. Keep up your meditations – they are helping.

Now the **Minneapolis/St. Paul** area. The second ray goes right through it, and the third ray is very close, both going eastward. The seventh and fifth are going west. So we have the teaching ray, the second ray of love/wisdom; the staying power of the third; the deep analytical quality of the fifth; and the New Age connotation of the seventh (the transmuting Violet Flame).

What is the potential here? If the rays are not used as productively as possible, we may have the third ray holding on to the traditions of the area. In this combination of rays where the fifth is not as strong as the others (the seventh is coming in stronger now than the fifth because so many New Age people are working with the transmuting Violet Flame), it seems to me, in this situation, that if people do not analyze exactly what the New Age is, they might gloss over it and miss it. They would not see the possibilities or connect with it. If told about it, they might say, "Yes, that's very interesting," and the next day have forgotten about it. This is always possible when the fifth ray is not strong, and it is why we like to see it coming in ever more strongly. So you can work with that one, too – not only the higher rays, but the fifth also. Send the world a lot of orange; it will really help. You could mix it up: Put some orange and violet and gold into a hose and spray it on the Earth. Isn't that a good combination! Excellent. Probably, the key to that area is for them to realize what the New Age is.

We are looking at an energy pattern of all the rays available to Earth. Some are used more precisely, more consciously, by the Earth than others. Energy has always been available since the Earth began, but it changed and developed and became utilized. It was always there potentially. The higher rays have always been there in potentiality, even before the past ten years, but the use of them is certainly not what it could be. That has been shown by the growth of consciousness on the planet. Certainly when Sanat Kumara came, he brought a focus that had never before been present on the Earth. In a sense you could say that all of the potentialities were there, but as in a picture of an astral being, it was just kind of "swirly," not very focused. He focused the planet's consciousness as had never before been done.

Now moving on to **El Paso**. The seventh ray originates there, and the eighth ray also goes through it. They are both going the same direction — west. This says much about that area after the New Age begins. It's the beginning of the New Age — the gateway. It began right there. How? After the 30s or the 40s the planet began to turn its esoteric consciousness from the east to the west. El Paso is a focus of that consciousness now, leading to the New Age experience. Why there? It is because of the history of that area throughout the entire time of the planet, including the future (timewise for the Earth) — what has been and what will be in that area. That's something we haven't gone into — that many of these things are the way they are because, if you get above time and look at it, there are potentialities that have been referenced in the future. And that sounds confusing, doesn't it? But you have to take that into account when you look at these energy patterns and why things are exactly the way they are.

The eighth ray, then, begins and spreads the cleansing of the planet — it focuses it. In El Paso, I feel there is a great deal going on. A very high spiritual teacher has begun his approach to the Earth by literally utilizing another consciousness, in the same way the Christ overshadowed the body of Jesus. This baby was born in El Paso on September 29, 1983. This one's approach to humanity will come to fruition in the New Age.

So the eighth ray begins there and spreads. How do you think we could see the spread of this cleansing on the energy map? The eighth affects us here in Arizona. These higher rays have a much wider effect than the seven rays. Their cleansing can take place on any ray line that is open to New Age concepts. Therefore, the seventh certainly would have a cleansing effect. And the fifth would have this effect — specifically, cleaning out old mental concepts, perhaps. Look at the fifth, which comes down through the Phoenix area. It would clear up mental concepts. The cleansing by the eighth can be utilized by any ray that is compatible — the fifth, the seventh, the second, the first at its highest level, and also the fourth at its highest level. It really could be utilized by any ray the Earth is using at that level. Now it is the fifth and the seventh that are being utilized by the eighth ray. The seventh ray is literally being sent from El Paso — that's its origin. In the future this area will be a center of large dimensions. And in the past it has been important, too. It has been very different than it is now, certainly. The cleansing is really only just beginning. It started about ten years ago and only now is becoming more apparent. So the eighth working with the seventh will be cleaning out the ideas about the future and clarifying it.

The ninth ray goes through Canada very near the U.S. border. It is close enough to affect all of the United States, truly, and Canada. It is a very important ray as far as the New Age is concerned. It too is cleansing – it takes over after the eighth ray and continues the cleansing. It loosens and brings it to a new level – the joy level of the planet. That is very important. I use the ninth ray a great deal in teaching and reference it directly. You learn where these rays are and connect with them specifically. That's what you are doing when you are connecting with joy: you are connecting with the joy that is available on the Earth. It comes from the Creator of course, but in a sense it has been stepped down so that it will be available on the Earth. You might visualize it as a wire that you can put a pulley on and just sail along on. Then you will be full of joy!

Now, we all want to raise the planet to its New Age beginning, and this is how. It happens specifically through the higher rays. The ninth ray lightens the area and begins the lightbody possibilities. This is very important. You can attune to the ninth ray and begin to literally see the Earth in its body of light. This would make a very good meditation. El Paso has much of the ninth and a wonderful New Age teacher who will literally focus the New Age there. He will begin before long, possibly within about six months, because all he needs is for the body to be very settled. His consciousness is very high, and the body must partially sustain the vibration of his consciousness. In about six months he will begin to send out the specifics of evolving that area and thus the whole continent. In six months, I think we are going to see a difference in that area. You might even watch the news. What happens might not be understood right away, but this area will have an impact on world events. El Paso has an interesting past, with some people with a deep heritage, perhaps, but open to many possibilities. It is potentially a very dynamic area.

New York is a center that holds on to whatever is there, and when you bring in the second ray in its "less than desirable" connotation, then there is an allowingness to hold on to the situation. Esoterically, this area is important for Sanat Kumara. He's probably had more learning experience in New York than anywhere else in the country, in an esoteric sense. We mentioned the tolerance and so forth. Certainly New York has about every kind of consciousness that is available to the Earth – whatever it is, there is somebody there who has it, whether because of their geographical origin or just their development. There is every different degree of consciousness and every different level. I know of at least one high spiritual leader there in connection with the highest part of the second ray. In a sense he is there to hold on to this highest part of the ray. He has been carefully placed in New York to serve. He is not well known, and I am not going to tell you who he is because his job is not to teach. He holds the highest part of the second ray in his consciousness to help overcome some of the third-ray holding on of the present state and to balance the less-than-desirable part of the first ray and other rays too. You get a reflection of the fourth ray there from other parts of the world.

I would say that New York, because it is very close energywise to the Bermuda Triangle, has input of almost every energy, whether from individuals or through the energy patterns of the globe. This high spiritual being who holds on to the highest aspect of the second ray is probably the reason we are seeing some twelfth-ray energies along the coast. He is literally attracting it there. Of course he cannot accomplish what the New York area has not yet realized; he is New York's *potentiality*. He helps to begin it.

So you have here an area that literally participates in the whole life of the planet. And if you have ever been to New York, I think you know that's true. Literally everything goes on there, from the most productive to the least. The Planetary Logos has, in a sense, experienced everything through this specific area. The opposition also has a stronghold there — those who don't think the Creator is terribly important. They think their egos are more important. So there are strongholds of those that have separated themselves consciously from the Creator — or perceive themselves as being separate. The people in New York are locked into a pattern and they need that stimulation. They are used to all of this energy stimulation. Everything is there, and if they go elsewhere they are bored: they say, "There's nothing going on here!" Sometimes when they begin to open to their higher possibilities, that changes a little. Of course there have been many who have left New York because they didn't feel compatible with it anymore. They had probably changed. If you want to send help to the New York area (not to people), a good combination would be the second, fifth, seventh and twelfth rays.

The fifth is the only ray that goes through **Denver**. The seventh really goes around it. Denver is in a traditional area where people tend to keep to their traditions and not move much. There are two factions in Denver now: the tradition energy and the fifth-ray energy, which has more New Age connotation. It has much possibility and is growing esoterically in consciousness at a very good rate. It has changed — I know you feel that — and it is going to become more and more New Age. That is my opinion of it. When Denver gets through the next two years, it is going to be very different. It is in a sense overcoming some of the traditions that are not as productive as we would like to see in connection with the New Age. It will retain memory of them without seeking to have them present. That is truly what you should do with the memories of the past: remember them with fondness and then release them to your new experience.

Denver is very interesting. It is having mixed opinions about itself — about where it wants to go and about its past. In the beginning it was very tied up with the Western tradition and the Indians, but it remembers even more the frontier heritage of the 1800s. Denver was a very spirited community that really enjoyed itself — you know, Baby Doe and all her wonderful antics (she was very connected to the mining community). Denver sought both gold and silver — gold representing the highest, and silver less than that: holding on to traditions. There is a growing scientific community that is seeking to move beyond the obvious. This will be a focus of the fifth ray and some of the higher rays that come into the continent and around the globe. It will begin the specific depth of thrust into more New Age. New Age teachers who go there will find fertile ground — especially in the age bracket of 28 to 38 years. Between those ages the fifth ray is blending specifically with the eighth and ninth, so it is the most fertile period for the fifth ray to reference the New Age concepts.

Which city has the most people near the soul-merge (third initiation)? I will look at the light and see. Yes, **Dallas**. You are surprised. You know we in the Hierarchy look at Earth and see the light of spiritual beings. Dallas has much — it is a very realistic city. San Antonio is a very spiritual area also.

The city most focused on the New Age? Probably specific places in California — not the Los Angeles area, but a little north of there, maybe close to San Francisco. Into the Mount Shasta area, too. Yes, certain communities in California. Here in Arizona there is quite a bit of activity — it would be second, I think. There are several areas that are very close. Some high spiritual centers are focused many places in the North American continent: several in Canada, one lovely one in Alaska, several in Mexico, and all over the United States. There are certainly some very productive communities that we value and treasure; we watch over them and say, "Aren't they wonderful? Aren't they doing well? They are productive and helpful." There are many, and more shining forth all the time. A center of light is where the people identify with their own divinity. If the people move around, the centers could move too.

In **Hawaii**, all of these rays — first, sixth, eighth and tenth — created a beautiful people who were very pure spiritually. But as the incoming people came, thinking they were bringing to them opportunity, and merged with them, this purity was diluted. It intensified in that area what we might call the less-than-desirable characteristics of the sixth ray. The quality of their spirituality is covered up by the energy patterns that are there, leading to a time when this area will not be present — namely, the New Age. (Up until that time it will be.) In a sense, the energy that is focused there will be absorbed by many other communities. I think it is going to build to a peak and focus more and more intensely in its diversity, until the time when the New Age begins, and that area will explode — literally and figuratively — and permeate other areas.

So Hawaii is valuable. You could say that it allows the Earth to accumulate some things that need to be gotten rid of, and someday it is going to release them. It will focus some of the less desirable characteristics of some of the rays. There are many spiritual people there and many productive things going on, but in a way it is similar to New York — accumulating much because much is going on at different levels. The same thing that happens to Hawaii will probably happen to New York.

So as you get ready for the New Age you will see that it is all planned out very carefully. You move in and focus the less desirable characteristics – you accumulate them – and then you get rid of them when you are cleansing. It will probably be a Japanese thrust that leads to this New Age – literally exploding it. Hopefully, in the New Age, all seven rays will rearrange themselves by what we choose now, by what we do now. Some of the energy will be rereleased. It will be cleansed and made available for the new patterns that come in there. The eighth and tenth will stay – they help hold the planet in its new pattern of divinity while you cleanse and change all of the rest. They are a framework within which the Earth will be held. The twelfth ray will act as a focus there, and the others will accompany it.

There is always another surge of energy coming from the Source – forever. At that particular time and place, the ray is utilized to create an experience of some sort. It is used in experiencing. There is plenty of energy – you can have all you need. Energy is the life force to create whatever we choose.

Las Vegas – there are no rays going right through it, but it is relatively close to the seventh. And the fifth is somewhere below it, so I think it would be influenced by these rays. In an esoteric sense, it focuses the history of that area: Indians, early settlers and the desert. What is the desert? It is a place without water – very warm – associated with other climates that are similar, such as the one the Planetary Logos, Sanat Kumara, began with. They are complex areas, but Las Vegas partakes of several things. There is a direct connection to the desert area above Shamballa in the Gobi Desert. Las Vegas is not as energized by Sanat Kumara's consciousness now (he has turned it to the west) but there is a connection, and this is why Las Vegas is so exciting – many people feel it. The stimulation is not what I as a spiritual teacher would like to see, but there is the anticipation of that esoteric connection. Things happen in layers, and truly all that there is when we get down to it is the Creator and His experiencing and our relationship to Him. Why do people go there? They are looking for the knowingness and the going forth into their own divinity – but they certainly do not know it, do they, as they are gambling, trying to get something without working for it!

The nuclear tests in Nevada make this area even more unstable, and this probably is why people are attracted there. People are looking and seeking but they know not for what. They are tired of where they are, so they go there to be stimulated, to be excited. It all makes this area more unstable, and I think this is what keeps attracting them. There is a connection with it in the least productive way. When there is a nuclear test, the area is shocked – even esoterically – and it becomes difficult to hold a focus on the spiritual. The area sometimes responds spiritually and some-times not at all. It will come and go and be unstable, frustrating, elusive. A very strange area. In its esoteric connection with the Gobi area, it is as a brother to a sister. Perhaps some spiritual teachers will go to the area to aid the ones who live there to focus the light more clearly. Perhaps it will be transmuted into the positive.

Cuba is affected by the Bermuda Triangle, and it sometimes literally becomes part of the Bermuda Triangle. It is that close. It has a whirlpool of energies dumped on it from the Bermuda Triangle. This stirs it up — usually in a less-than-productive manner. Cuba used to be considered romantic, but not on the higher, unconditional-love level. Now it is entirely different because the energies of the planet are different.

We are going to see a lot of change there. It is a good area to watch as we continue our work toward the New Age. I would say that in about ten years there will be a crisis point there that will be very connected with the activity of the sixth ray. That is again because of all the energy that will come into the Bermuda Triangle. Even if it is not the same kind of energy, there will be a splash-over from the entire energy input of the planet. There is so much energy here that every release point will be affecting the nearby areas. Very interesting — you are going to love it! I hope it will not be quite as traumatic as it could be — perhaps just a recognition of who people are. But knowing humanity, to expect that to happen in ten years probably isn't too realistic. Let us hope for it.

Florida is interesting — very nearly surrounded by water, almost completely isolated from the rest of the continent. What does that mean? Esoterically it is very different, a remnant of the past, rather closely associated with the Atlantean consciousness. They have the drug traffic, and what do drugs represent? A dreamy state. It has a consciousness of its own and does not seem to be accepting its role as part of the continental United States. It clings in a rather dreamy, mentally unfocused way to its interesting past. It has a Spanish flavor, and the Fountain of Youth is said to be there — one drink and you live forever! A lot of illusion there. They have lots of storms, which are the planet's attempt to "reconnect" it, stir it up a little by saying "Get with us." But Florida is not listening.

New Orleans is also a very interesting place for the romanticism there and the focus of the polarity chakra area. What do I mean by that? This planet has energy centers too, just like humans. Well, the polarity chakra isn't centered in New Orleans, but that area partakes of its center. What is the Mardi Gras? It is an orgy — a polarity adventure, illusion. You could say that all of the connotations of Yesod are there. Oh, there is a little spirituality, but it doesn't do very well there. It lasts for a while then leaves. There is a continuity by some for a while and then by others for a while. There is one very bright light there — there is at least one bright light in most cities. But this city doesn't contain the same people all of the time in their brightest light.

Santa Barbara? Yes, an interesting area — definitely a New Age community, one that is very much aware of itself right now, but not in a large metropolitan way. It is a "now" city with many who are very fifth-ray there.

But they don't want some of the larger Earth concepts as perceived by the big metropolitan areas. They want the smaller concepts. They are holding on to tradition in a very productive way. It is a nice place — I find it an excellent area, I really do. Very unique. It has a definite opinion of how it should be, and if energies or people don't fit into that, they don't last long there. It is not accepting of many energies that have tried to enter it.

Phoenix, in the first place, is a very psychic city — psychic as differentiated from spiritual. Why? Well, there is a special holding quality of what has been here. And what has been here goes very deep into the Earth's past (to the Lemurian era) through many layers of civilization. One of the main things that was being developed was the psychic ability. It was a major community and it still remembers and is very proud of it. Those who come here and are not compatible with these energies will not feel comfortable. Now, psychic abilities are neither good nor bad — they just are. It depends on how they are used. So Phoenix has an opportunity, and that's what it is getting right now — the opportunity to use its psychic ability for the raising of the planet. That is why the metaphysical community here is so vast — here come the lightworkers! Some of them don't know they are lightworkers, but they all are, and they now have the opportunity to raise this vibration to the highest. They have different opinions on how to do it. It is a very segregated community, metaphysically, with many different perceptions of the goal. The goal truly is to contact spirituality.

The Phoenix area has a long history. During the Lemurian time it was very attuned to surviving physically. That was what was being learned by mankind. Conditions here are very harsh, and you have to live within the framework of that harshness — nature at its rawest, sometimes — but it is very connected with the basic part of the history of the planet, which was that survival level.

❖ E I G H T ❖

Understanding the Earth from
Its Past Civilizations —
Lemuria, Atlantis and Egypt

EMURIA WAS AN INTERESTING TIME FOR THE CHILDREN OF THE LIGHT. ALL OF
you were the children of the light. You had volunteered to come to the
Earth, and when you landed, the Lemurian era was in progress. There was
not a specific location on the Earth where this happened, although there was
a prominent one called Mu. Civilization was truly widespread, so we will
discuss it in general within the specific period that I call the Lemurian era.

The ages of the Earth represent a wide range of learning experiences.
What was being learned by humanity during the Lemurian time was
attunement to the physical, to really get in touch with physical existence.
Lemuria gave each one of you that opportunity. For some this experience
remained deeply buried because it was a rather difficult period — humanity
remembers it that way. For one thing, the remnants of all those big animals
that you call dinosaurs were there, and perhaps man learned a lot by avoiding
being stepped on. The dinosaurs were mostly vegetarian, but you didn't
want to get in the way of one of those big feet; it could be a little disconcerting.
There were a few that deviated from vegetarianism, and once in a while a
human remembers being eaten by something like that. To the subconscious
mind this can be disconcerting. One learned all about physical existence
on the Earth at this time.

What were humans like at this time? What kind of physical structure?
Rather small, for one thing: the average height of a man was five feet, and
women were a few inches shorter. It is interesting that, as evolution
continues, the physical structure is getting bigger. For many of you, coming
to Earth was your first experience. Most lived within group environments,

and most of these were in caves. It was not the Hollywood connotation of a cave — the caves were safe; the big animals couldn't get into them and they didn't try. Many of these caves were beautifully and artistically decorated by the humans that lived there. There are some caves buried very deeply in certain areas of the Earth which have yet to be discovered.

For the children of the light — you who came here to aid the Earth — this was your first Earth experience. But many of you had experienced physical existence in other places. There were other beings here already, humans who were just getting in touch with physical existence. So we see a division in humanity. This is true at the present time too — many of you are more experienced and more spiritually mature than others on Earth. So at this particular time in Lemuria you were learning to function within a physical body.

The paintings in the caves had an etheric quality, because humanity remembered what they had been and put that on the walls of the caves, beautifully decorated. Perhaps it helped to stimulate them for the later part of their Earth journey when they would learn to develop the emotional body from an Earth perspective; we call that the Atlantean era. What is the lesson for the current age? That is obvious: developing the mental body. You can see that — the world does not consider it valid unless you can analyze it and see it. You are working with the mental. After the New Age begins, the great lesson of the world will be the spiritual. You see how it progresses and evolves.

In Lemuria you might have had a beautiful cave, and after finishing the decorating you got restless, looking for another cave to decorate. When the group expanded beyond the size of the cave, members were sent out to look for another cave. Maybe they had to go into a new area where perhaps food was more available, which could be another reason for going. You might have had ten men, seven women and thirty to forty children. The survival rate for children was not very high. The food supply was mainly grain, berries and fruits, so if they didn't replant, they would use up the supply and be forced to leave the area for another one. Some groups did learn to plant and to cultivate, but not at the beginning, and not always.

When going on a journey, the packing was not much trouble. You would just roll up a little grass mat and you were ready; you could put cushioning under it at the new place. As the group moved there were guards on the outside who would make sure that the dinosaurs were not coming. They would march single-file for several days and camp along the way, not in caves but in a natural area that could be protected. When they reached the new cave it was very exciting: Who is going where? What is the food like? Are there other groups in the area? What are the dangers? What do we need to know about the physical environment?

In those times the Earth had many earthquakes. As one group was journeying one day, there was an earthquake and it split the group. It was very deep. The two parts attempted to get together, but the crack was hundreds of miles long. Families were separated then – perhaps your loved ones were on one side and you on the other. What happened then? You learned about physical existence from this perspective, that sometimes you perceived a separation from those you loved. Then what did you do? You made your life in another way. They learned from what happened to them physically. This was the biggest lesson of that time.

It started in exactly this way. It lasted for thousands of years and gradually evolved and became of a society that went from one physical place to another less often, until finally they stayed in one environment. Doing what? Utilizing the resources that were there instead of seeking from elsewhere. We learn that we can get everything we need right here. For many this was the first lesson in human experience on the Earth, and the children of light came to these people. You were sent by the Light Itself, but in a sense you volunteered. You might have had a conference with a teacher who pointed out the importance of such a volunteer act. Perhaps they said, "You know as a child of the light that you serve, and this is where you are needed." Why were you chosen instead of someone else? Because of your unique vibration, which fits into the needs of the Earth. The Creator and His representatives really know what they are doing. They look at a planet at its evolutionary point. They know what is light and what combination is needed to help this planet to evolve. Then they pick out individuals who fit into that needed pattern. Thus each of you had the type of light that the Earth needed. You came then to this more primitive area, and some of you said, "My goodness, do I have to do this again? I thought I had done this already." Now, some of you really enjoyed it. You said, "Good. Here I am again, and it is fun." But perhaps this was a minority. Most of you said, "Well, I think I d rather be light up there than light down here."

Lemuria was an experience that lasted thousands of years and led to the next step. I am going to break this into three sections and cover all three. Lemuria was about 100,000 years ago and blends into the next era. There is not a sharp cut-off point between one era and the next, just as there isn't a sharp cut-off for what is coming in the future. It has already begun. When you get in touch with the fact that the Planetary Logos came here 18½ million years ago, say to self, "What happened into all of this?" Well, this era lasted a long time, then it led to the Atlantean era, which lasted a long time, and then the Egyptian which lasted a long time. Before these there were many other types of civilization. There is a veil before Lemuria and after. There was a different pattern, creatures that were not human. You are the Adam Kadmon divinity, and there were others that were here previously. Ours is a very common physical divinity model, very efficient (even if sometimes you don't think so) for experiencing physical life. The area which we call Mu was in the South Pacific, and the Earth was different from what it is now. The civilization was much more spread out and included parts of Central and South America. Some of these people were in Africa and in the area of the Soviet Union.

When the children of the light arrived, speech was very simplistic, but because they had more experience, they quite rapidly complicated it. They remembered a more complicated way. You as the light were the means by which evolution speeded up on the Earth. You began to appear in babies, and the consciousness then began in a new physical structure. What happened was, the soul arrived in the vicinity of the Earth and said, "Here I am. I have been sent. And it began to extend into physical existence, coming close to the beginning of Lemuria.

All of humanity on the Earth has been contacted by other civilizations, visitors in spacecraft. They were beings more knowledgeable than those who were there. This has often been humanity's gift – beings from other planets knew more than they did, and they were aided. Now, because humanity on Earth has been extremely interesting, sometimes these visitors were not always willing to come out into public view. Maybe you can understand that when you know that they heard that some would not get home. But spiritual teachers still came – they always have – though they came incognito. The visual remembrance on Easter Island is a racial memory that shows what they perceived these beings to be. It is a symbolic, not actual, representation.

There have been scientists – they are always interested in the Earth. They come and they look, and perhaps they take a few samples. Now, if that sample happens to be your physical body, or parts of it, there may be some subconscious remembrance of this. It was not that they intended to hurt you; they were just interested. How could they analyze if they didn't have samples – and who were the most logical samples? Human beings. They came up and said, "Who are you?" So there was the opportunity and they utilized it. There were a few who went beyond this. There are always those who choose to separate themselves from the light and not participate in the Plan.

Atlantis

Lemuria gradually evolved into the era we call Atlantis and became something else. Atlantis entails three different eras in one. Early Atlantis began as a blending from Lemuria – the dawning of the New Age. It became obvious that there was more than a physical place to think about. The beings there had very interesting things happen to them. They might be sitting on their rock and they would look up, and suddenly there would be somebody. When they talked to him he'd disappear, and they would say, "He was here a minute ago." They had forgotten the astral plane, and when it began to open for them – and they did it more easily than you do – they began to see some of these beings. Some were direct extensions of the Creator, who were doing work – for example, fairies. In Ireland they got in touch with them. They were workers for the planet, and each area sees these energies in a different way. The people were enlarging their perspective of what was. Sometimes they got a little too much in tune with that and they began to function there instead of on the physical plane. They got a bit out of touch with reality. They related to the inner planes again instead of physical existence. It pulled them back into what had been before they came into the physical.

In a sense it was a difficult period for humanity because they could now see something else which was wonderful, and when they got in touch with it at the beginning of the Atlantean era, it pulled them out so much that it was difficult to function in the physical. They began to research this happening to get in touch.

When humanity has needed it, a gift has appeared. Some beings came and said, "How would you like to work with crystals? This will help you focus." Certain individuals began to research ways to adapt the use of crystals because they came from an area that used them in a different way. In a research facility, crystals were used to help them focus. They could focus in on those beings who were no longer functioning physically. You could focus energy, and through that stream, reach them and say, "You must function here physically," and they were literally pulled back into physical existence. Thus began the association with crystals. They were widely researched and eventually used as the major color supply.

We get then into the middle Atlantean period, in which the great healing temples were built. Everyone, without exception, has worked in these temples. What did they do there? People came who were having illnesses, mental and spiritual problems, or any out-of-balance condition that they couldn't identify. So the healer would refer to a rather complex charting system: "You need some of the first ray, the second ray, a dash of the third, a little of the fourth," and so on. They would dial in a prescription of energy. The healing rays were used in rather complex ways, in ways that are only just being approached by humanity again. They knew how to prescribe energy and focus it through the crystals. Many of you have been at facilities, researching ways to keep using the crystals. There was a giant crystal which did an overall powering of the Atlantean civilization. It had smaller crystals that attuned to it, and it could direct them. Very interesting and quite complex. Once they began using crystals with you, you never let go, and some of you had interesting experiences.

As we begin to move into the middle period it becomes more and more complex — something of the tempo of modern Earth. The latter part did have the same tableau of a fast pace and a sense of urgency, a sense of seeking to accomplish. But the middle period was the beginning of a time that was as close as humanity has ever come to utopia. A beautiful time to live, in which you were able to have a job that you really enjoyed. There was equality between men and women, the children were cared for, and it was a beautiful time for recreation. No unemployment — there was always a need for another research worker, another healer. You could be trained in a healing temple and learn, and there were people to work with. You all took part in the healing and helped to heal — a two-way exchange. Lives averaged forty years, and you probably had a whole string of them.

In early Atlantis there was a lot of research into hearing. Hearing what? Hearing physically, and then going beyond that to inner hearing. This was a part of the Atlantean civilization. They had evolved through the physical and now began to reference the emotional or the astral level. A very interesting thing occurred during this period. Some souls that perhaps were naive or misguided, not cognizant of what they were doing, became confused. This resulted in monstrosities — a mixture of the animal and human kingdom in inappropriate ways. What did they do about this? Within the healing temples were these mixtures of all types. They had a consciousness of divinity and knew they had made a mistake and were in need of releasing what they had created. So the healers got busy helping to free them, allowing divinity to go back to where it was supposed to be. The consciousness was meant to be in a human form. They worked until humanity was again as it should be.

Later in Atlantis there was a battle, a battle of light against darkness — those who had separated themselves from the light. They wanted to control the Earth, they wanted power, they wanted the rest of humanity to follow them, and so a battle ensued. All of you were strenuously involved in this battling against those who chose darkness. If was an extremely tense time, very difficult for humanity. Physically it was very much like now. There were airplanes. As you beings on Atlantis encountered this power struggle, many of you made a dedication to the light again. Even if you had made it once, you reinforced it. The beings of darkness began to take control of the temples from the children of the light, who fought every step of the way. The Atlanteans had weapons like ray guns and many advanced things that you do not yet have. Where do you think all these movies come from? Racial memories.

Many times you beings were highly developed. You were just not aligned with the light; you knew how to do things on the inner planes, to a point. Those who have departed only a little from the light have returned to it. If they have gone further, it takes a little longer. There is a critical point beyond which it is very difficult, but that happens very seldom — with one in a hundred million of those that depart. If you have separated from the light for quite a while, it truly takes some time to get back. Some are still in the process. They are still divinity but they do not perceive it. That is the difference. Your divinity does not change; you just shut the door.

When darkness takes over, the Earth gets unstable. The light is Earth's spiritual "chewing gum." It holds together its existence, and if you take it away, the Earth starts to fall apart. It needs the light, so without it eventually Atlantis was destroyed. We see the destruction symbolically and actually.

In the area of Atlantis it was actual; in the other areas, the children of the light were driven out. They went to Egypt, Tibet, China and South America. They were not discouraged. They lost a battle, not the war: "We will spread the light and surround this darkness, and then it will be gone." The light always triumphs.

I have to tell you my explanation of the totality. Self comes forth – the spark comes forth from the Source. It then extends to the soul level, and from there to the physical level. Most of the transferring from one planet to another is done at the soul level. Sometimes physical beings have emigrated. Perhaps there were not enough beings to create new bodies, so the Creator and the teachers said, "How would you like to come in a physical extension this time?" But mostly it happened through the evolutionary process on the inner plane.

Egypt

Egypt already existed, but the children of the light came to it after the Atlantean episode had come to a rather sudden climax. They came with a great spiritual teacher to the area we know as Egypt. We call this great evolving consciousness Thoth, later to be called the light of the Buddha. Beginning with the New Age, he will be graduating and departing. We are fortunate to have had him. For several thousand years he was a physical being in Egypt. He just didn't get old. He was just there, and you would come and have a life with him, then you would get out and come back and he would still be there. He served the Earth in this manner.

Through the painful encounter in Atlantis, humanity began to recognize divinity. Thus in ancient Egypt we see a civilization of great spirituality that sought God intensely. It was for many a full-time occupation with a great deal of guidance. We mentioned Thoth, but other spiritual teachers also came at this time and were there. If you wanted to talk to a great one, all you had to do was go and look. There were so many available that you could have private sessions. You might work with one for several years or maybe a whole lifetime and then say, "I think this structure [body] is about done. We'll have another chat when the new one gets done." And so the opportunity was there to work spiritually.

One thing that all of you know about is the pyramids. Great guidance was given for these by spiritual teachers. They were constructed by laws that most of the Earth didn't understand, higher than engineering principles. There were no slaves dragging heavy blocks, as depicted in movies; you just worked with the higher knowingness. Gravity was overcome and the stones could be moved into their exact positions. This was learned from these spiritual teachers; perhaps some of them were engineers. A spiritual teacher might have been many things before he becomes aligned with a specific department in the hierarchic government and can reference what he has been. Thus the Great Pyramid is an engineering marvel and a symbolic representation; much is learned by studying it. Many books have been written about it. It was certainly not a place where they stored dead bodies. Originally it was a temple of initiation. That was its purpose, and it was designed specifically to fulfill its purpose.

If in an inner experience you allow an evolving consciousness in a physical structure to encounter itself and to have the opportunity to go beyond what has been, then you want to design the building, the physical structure, to allow this to be done in a precise manner. That is why the pyramids, and the great one particularly, were designed so specifically for cosmic law to aid evolution. When tours go there now, very interesting things can happen in the King's Chamber. Why? Because you get in touch with self in a very encompassing manner.

Let me tell you about those initiations. You might have been a seeker in many lives and said to your teacher, "I am ready now to go beyond the Earth experience." And he may have said, "Really? Are you sure?" And you said, "Yes, I am sure." Almost every one of you did this. So then you got the opportunity to do so. There were dedicated beings in these temples of the Great Pyramid who served as initiators. It varied during different periods, but in our example you were dressed symbolically in white. You entered the temple, approached the altar and made a dedication to the Creator. You were then led to an enclosure whose lid was closed. By a process that was known only to the initiator, you were guided to the inner part of self. They knew exactly how to do it.

If, within self, you had a fear of snakes, you probably in your inner experience found yourself in a snake pit. If was filled with vipers and you were there facing them. If you were successful you had the knowingness that this was not real; you got in touch with what you had created. Because you had created it, you could get rid of it, and when that happened it was gone. You then faced whatever else was within self.

If you truly were ready for this initiation — you probably had two or three — you faced and conquered and went beyond that. You leaped joyously from this slab and were transformed to the next level of evolution — you had faced and passed your initiation. What about the rest of you? Well, it was interesting. Perhaps you were pursued on the plains by a tiger. He got closer and closer and closer, and if you were still afraid, could not transmute that fear into the knowingness of wholeness, of oneness, of divinity, the structure, that particular physical body, was lost.

What happened to you then? It was as when you are studying for an examination and you don't pass. Well, you haven't really lost anything, because you'll have another opportunity. You need to read and study a little to see why you were not able to get beyond that particular experience. Most of you are at that point right now. You have taken exams; some of you have taken them twice. Now you are releasing these inner fears in another way. When next you face the initiation, all will be light. For most of you it will probably be done in a different way.

So the initiation was an important part of Egypt. It got to be interesting. It is not appropriate to pin anyone down to their point in evolution. This is something all of you learned in Egypt. Because of the nature of the experience, Egypt was an excellent place in which to evolve spiritually. There were many temples in which many were trained. As for channeling, as Janet is doing, this was intense if you agreed to it. In Egypt it was a full-time occupation within a temple experience. It took hours and hours, for more and more seekers were always coming. And pretty soon a channel would say, "Oh my goodness, do I ever get any time off?" And they said, "Maybe. Right now we need you."

I find Egypt an interesting place. Many of you had very productive encounters with larger animals. The large cats were very much a part of Egypt, and the communication between humans and the cats was at its height. There was love and there were good relationships, and thus you learned. The temples had cats that were used as guards. They were large and doing their job. There were also cats in Tibet.

What was ancient Egypt like? It was truly a divided civilization. There were the children of the light — the spiritual seekers — and then the rest of the human beings, the bulk of humanity, which was seeking to go beyond the Atlantis encounters with the astral. They were seeking to get in touch with the beginnings of the mental realm. They had only just begun, and the children of light had done it already — this intense encounter in Atlantis had put them in touch with the spiritual area already. We had a great separation in Egypt, probably greater than in most civilizations. The children of the light were there to help, but they were also learning and becoming. We now claim our life in Egypt as a spiritual experience. This is truly what happened. The children of the light said, "We claim this time now. We have been here a long time, and we want this as a spiritual experience." The teachers said, "Good; we will guide you. It is perhaps a little ahead of schedule, but you have earned it."

The climate of Egypt is very interesting. It is a warm country — what does that say to you? There is an intensity about the environment, which symbolically has a great deal of meaning. Egypt had a spiritual intensity. It is not an accident that the Tibetan Foundation is in Phoenix, which is also a warm place with intensity. There were many symbols such as the scarab and the sphinx. What is the sphinx? It is a direct attunement to the Adam Kadmon, a direct representation of the image of the divine man. In a sense, if you consider humanity as a more advanced part of the animal kingdom there, the sphinx is the divinity it represents.

Beneath the pyramids are many things, whole areas in which spiritual seekers sometimes took refuge. At times in Egypt the political and administrative realms were run by those who were not especially attuned to spirituality. There was persecution of those who were spiritual, so seekers took refuge. They were prepared for this and beneath the pyramids they had many secret areas. Many records were stored. If you could not go to the King's Chamber or the Queen's Chamber for initiation, you could go to the lower area. There were classrooms, places where you could live, food storage areas, all kinds of places where you could be safe and live your life without losing your body right away.

Egypt to me is a shining example of spirituality. The pharaohs were the physical manifestation of the spiritual teachers. The later pharaohs were not as evolved as the earlier ones — a mortal man symbolically represented the pharaoh. With the help of the great spiritual teachers, ancient Egypt was more a part of the galaxy. In Atlantis we met the teachers, but in Egypt we worked with them a lot in helping other areas. Only handfuls of humanity were initiated so they could handle energies. After initiation we understood that the Earth is not isolated and we could use energy through the focus of the pyramid to aid other planets. We used the precision of the pyramid itself — the engineering structure, completely aligned in a very specific way — with the apex as the focus. Knowing how to use energy in such a structure, we then aimed it in the direction wanted, from one physical structure to another.

The Hierarchy has asked your help in meditation. You are here on the Earth, and it is valuable to have helped with the energies.

Egypt was an encounter with divinity that you enjoyed. You have built a foundation and can now go beyond it and be stronger for it. It has not been a failure; it was an opportunity to gather up the loose ends that were there. You will know the third initiation as the time when the personality level merges into the soul level. You are consciously present at that time.

NINE

Approaching the Soul-Merge

THE SOUL KNOWS HOW IT CAN FUNCTION HERE ON THE EARTH. IT HAS NO problem with seeing and identifying the service area. It is the personality level that needs education in whatever way is appropriate. The perception is what is involved here. You must unlock this door. What then is the key to the soul-merge? We will try to discover that, and to see what occurs when that level of awareness is maintained. I cannot identify how close each of you is, but I will help you see the signs and the guideposts along the way.

What is the first sign that one is seeking a major leap forward in awareness — which we have termed the soul level? It could be a dissatisfaction with the condition of the Earth experience itself: Suddenly it is not enough, you've done it all before and it gets suddenly boring. This is not to say that life becomes all boring, but you do encounter a boredom with life as it exists and you want more. You seek to go beyond it, but you are not quite sure *what* you are seeking to go beyond, or how to do it — you are not quite sure, period! You might have been a wonderful executive on Earth, very much in touch with how to function, and suddenly you are not sure. If you are in charge of large groups of people, then they can sense it. Suddenly they look at their boss and they think, "I wonder if he's having a nervous breakdown" or "I wonder if she's having a midlife crisis." There is something going on that others can sense.

So what do you do? You attempt to solve what's going on within self. And guess what? That magically opens up many possibilities (and the word "magically" is very appropriate) Suddenly you attract the soul's attention, you invoke the soul. It comes and says, "My goodness, look at what's going on within that extension! Look! There is an invocation of me, of the higher level. Good, now we're ready to begin." That begins the activation of whatever remains within self to clear.

Now, before this life, you and your soul probably had a little chat, and your soul might have said to you, "Are you going to be the extension that allows me to function on the Earth?" And your reply would have depended upon you and your approach. You might have said, "No way. That's too hard. I like a neat little package here and I don't want to get everything all stirred up and live in chaos and pain. Let somebody else do that." (And you know what happens!) The other approach might have been "Yes, of course. I'm going to do it the day after I'm born – or maybe the day before." And then when you are born, when you come into the physical, things look different. Perhaps all of the areas within self that are not clear look different. When you look through a glass and it isn't clear, it makes the vision fuzzy, and perhaps you can see only an outline of what is on the other side. So some of you can see it more clearly than others, depending on the amount of programming, or nonclarity, that you have within self. If you see nothing, it isn't always that you are completely blocked. Sometimes it is because you have programming in the area of *not seeing*.

So you're looking at this, and sometimes when you invoke the soul through your dissatisfaction with life as it is, a little gong or bell goes off within self that says, "Oh yes, I was going to clear that this lifetime. I was going to allow that soul to come in. Yes, I remember." That's important, because then the soul gets involved and it says, "Yes, yes, yes, you remember!" And you get going between you and the soul energy. Then you can utilize this energy between you and your soul, hopefully in a way that will magnify it. What will magnify energy? Service will. Why? Because as you involve yourself in service, you begin to utilize your personal will in alignment with the Creator's will. The two approach each other and you have a magnification of the will aspect of creation itself. You've magnified that thrust when you have aligned the will because you wish to serve.

What is this magnification of will? This is first-ray energy, and it will thrust you anywhere you want to go (and sometimes where you don't want to go). It is the thrusting first ray that is magnified by your desire to serve. Now, if you attempt this soul-merge without aligning with the divine will, what happens? Well, divine will is going *up*, and if you attempt to use your will only for self and not in service, it goes *across*. If it happens often enough, then you say, "I think perhaps there is a problem here. When I attempt to break through to a new level, the breakthrough isn't happening." What is the key to that? It is service, realigning the will with the Creator's – and not only *saying*, "I am aligning it," but doing it. The doing is very important.

Service is the key for you. It is the alignment of the will that allows it to happen. But what if you choose not to be directly involved in service? You can choose that, but you can't expect to achieve the soul-merge without it. It just won't happen if service isn't a part of it. Service is a cornerstone of the soul-merge. If you are not ready for that, it's all right. The Creator says that His program will probably get along without your input for a while. You can stay where you are or go at your own pace. Yes, you will grow; yes, you will learn; but the soul level will not be achieved until you recognize that the Creator's program is probably more important than your personal agenda. That's what the Creator is creating: the opportunity for all existence to keep learning. And you have an important part in aiding it. Your personal input has its own uniqueness and you must get in touch with it.

So let's say that you have recognized that service is the most important thing, and that you are more or less committed to it. (Some of you have some degree of subconscious resistance.) Then what happens? You become very involved in service. Does that mean your own growth ceases? Not at all! Service is the key to your growth. If you want to move quickly, get involved in service, and then get ready to run!

As you serve, many growth opportunities occur. These are the unlocking process. Self recognizes that you've been in a holding pattern in a particular area, and then the opportunity is given through service to unlock it. Let's say you are in 100% service, and it flows very well — your personal evolvement is growing, and you really feel quite good about it. All of you have then a final unlocking process to go through in whatever area is rather difficult for you. This unlocking will seem rather heavy. It doesn't have to be heavy, but most choose to participate within it, because it's a final releasing in an area that has many layers, and you've probably built it up from the soul level. It might have begun there, or even from the monadic level. Then it takes an intense encounter of self to let go of it on the physical plane.

Let's say that you have resolved all of these easy things — you've unlocked these core items and gotten through. These core items begin to interlock with one another so that as you begin to experience, it's like a frog: it leaps from one to the other, and in this cyclic effect you stir up whatever is left. What does this mean? It means "Hang in there!" When you get one of the frogs, you're going to get the rest of it: making progress, evolving, growing, changing. You're getting at the nitty-gritty. Excellent! But it can be intense. So get involved in service again. Keep working on self, but say, "I'm doing it because I wish to serve, and I will do whatever is necessary." Then *do it!* Don't feel sorry for self: "Poor little me." No! You have a wonderful opportunity here.

Some of you are into what we might call illusion about what your own place is on this path, so how do you know where you are? First look at what happens to you in your life — and I mean over a month's time, not day to day. Are you regularly encountering areas that are not clear? Are you experiencing long periods in which everything flows very well? This will happen as you begin to approach the soul level. For very long periods there will be no interruption of the free-flow. Then you might have an intense period when nothing seems to go right and you have to work yourself out of that one. When you get out of that, you have another long period where it flows well. Notice these times; you will be more comfortable if you have a little recognition that you are working on something and you know what it is. Try to see what is happening in your life from a synchronicity point of view.

As the soul approaches in its final merging, it gets very excited. You begin to experience part of its excitement, maybe as an electrical discharge. Several of you are experiencing this. Unfortunately, it doesn't mean the soul-merge is going to take place in five minutes, but it is part of the final approach. Now, you might not even have a problem with it. It might happen very smoothly, but if it is disharmonious, you can know that this is a part of connecting with your soul, and you simply deprogram self in the area of electrical trauma. Some of you might experience it without trauma, which is wonderful.

The soul, then, is electric and magnetic. This means that it attracts a mutual sense of divinity. Let's talk about that a minute. Divinity recognizes divinity and becomes magnetic. When they merge, we have a soul-merge. The soul, being magnetic, is attracting you. Now, for the soul this is an intense time. You might not have considered this if you have been thinking of it from your point of view, the personality level. But the soul is resolving all of its Earth living, and this is a critical point in its evolution. I don't think it chews its fingernails, but it says, "Now, I wonder what's going to happen, and I wonder if we've made a breakthrough. Is this one really going to allow the process to be completed? I wonder how it's all going to fit together." Then it says, "I wonder what my next step is going to be." Imagine that! Have you said that a few times?

So the soul is as anxious for this merge as you are. You partake of it, but it is the soul that is very anxious to fulfill its commitment. If you have any programming in the area of commitment, it sometimes enters here, saying, "I'm not ready for this mission that the soul has." Most of you do very well with that, but if there is a hang-up at the last moment, it is usually in the commitment area.

In the initiations in Egypt, there was sometimes a last-minute back-off — some of you weren't able to break through it. Why? "I'm not ready for that." Commitment to service hung it up. That's why the key is through service.

I would say that as the final approach to the soul is made, one begins to realize that it's probably not such a big deal, that it is not that important, that it is but a little cog in the overall wheel. This means that you've become objective about existence and that you're ready for the soul-merge. One way you can tell is by asking yourself how objective you're becoming about it. Is it necessary? Are you intensely desiring it? Intense desire isn't bad — it helps you see where you are, to know that you have not yet allowed it to be unimportant; this is always necessary. If something remains terribly important to the self, you have not released it, have you? What will happen when you've released it? The knowingness of its approach enters, and suddenly you recognize "All right, it's coming now!"

Within a short period – probably within six months – the knowingness will come in. It's going to happen and it doesn't really matter when, because you're so very busy with service and other people's needs that you forget about yourself and you think, "Well, I really know that I've done what I can and daily I'm trying to do more, and that's all I can do. And the other people here need help. This is what I must do." Then it kind of sneaks up on you!

And one evening I, or another spiritual teacher, knocks on your door after you've gone to sleep, and we say, "Are you ready?" And you say, "Well, for what? What am I . . . ?" (And you usually get a little excited at that point.) And we say, "Well, we have an appointment with Sanat Kumara." Then you look at yourself, perhaps in your beautiful white gown or robe, and you recognize that indeed you are ready, indeed you are to begin this exciting experience. Now, as this white also approaches, you recognize that it isn't only your *experiencing*. You begin to see how you fit into the whole picture, more than you've ever seen before, that there are others taking this same step at the same time. But not only that. Reflected up, there are many others who are going to be taking their next step, and indeed this process of conferring initiation is bestowed upon all of creation at the same time. And if you can recognize it, you can have it. It is always available when you can see it! It happens all of the time when you can know it. It is there when you can allow it.

This will probably happen to each of you: First the knowingness that it is about to happen and the divine indifference about whether it does or not – that is the key for you. And then, within the inner experience, the initiation itself, it is a specific attunement to an evolutionary point, and it unlocks and outlines the future evolutionary path. This exact wording is important.

Sanat Kumara with his rod of power initiates the next evolutionary step. When that rod of power touches you, you then see, framed in, the next process that you will begin. It is then up to you to fill in the details as you go along. What happens when your teacher who has knocked on your door tells you that it is about to begin? It might bring a little bit of anxiety, but most wouldn't admit it: "I'm not going to admit I'm a little scared. I will just show that I am ready. I will be very cool about it."

For me the soul-merge, the third initiation, was probably the most important because it is a major perception period, showing you how exciting your whole future is going to be. Most, including me (although I haven't admitted it before), get a little bogged down in Earth living, wishing a little bit that we didn't have to remain here. We get a little resentful of it. Then we can see how Earth living is but a part of the whole of true existence, and how it all fits together. To me this is very exciting.

Now, your teacher, whoever it may be (and I hope that for all of you I can always be doing this), will represent you. In what? In being proud of his child, in being privileged to show that "Here comes another piece of divinity through an important doorway. Then you will probably perceive, as I did, that it is a great gathering, that as we approach the ceremonial area, there has been much preparation for this ceremony. There are many candles on an altar, arranged in very specific symbolic detail. There are figures in white robes, with different-colored insignias. Some of the robes are edged in violet, some in gold, some in white (a different interpretation of white). Several are robed all in violet. And when they are arranged very specifically in their group, the pattern they create invokes Sanat Kumara. Then he knows there is a ceremony about to begin. This is always happening, though your perception is not that way. Even on the inner planes you will perceive this as happening in sequential time because you are still closely connected with it. You still have a physical vehicle lying there that you are connected to; if you were not, that would change the way you perceive it. It is that connection that holds you there.

You might not notice any other candidates. I really didn't; I was told later that they were all there. At the next initiation I was able to see them. Gone was my self-assurance that I was a part of the whole, and it didn't matter. But suddenly it *did* matter! Momentarily, as the rod descended, there was a feeling of . . . I don't like the word "unworthiness," but, my friends, Sanat Kumara is very special, and when you stand face to face with him you're not quite sure sometimes how you fit in the picture. He's awe-inspiring. At this point in evolution, it's difficult to be divinely indifferent! There is so much light there! But from this point on, it is much easier. The rod descends, and what is experienced is an *instant attunement to all of creation!*

The first thing I heard was the music of the spheres, the music of all creation, celebrating this event. I also heard the flow of existence. I'd never known this; suddenly I could hear it and it was like a mighty river that is forever moving and surging but flowing in a very harmonious and beautifully melodious, attuned way. I began to recognize more than ever before my unique part in all of this. I began to see self in relationship to the whole — that there really was no difference except that my perception was deliberately different, and this was how Divinity could experience from every possible perception. This was not a separateness; it was simply a different focus. That very focus will be experienced by Divinity, and I was simply sitting on one of them.

And it was as if I were on a stool and that stool extended into the Hierarchy itself. That's a little scary — suddenly you look around and there are all these teachers that have been learning and growing for a long time, and there you are! And you look and you say, "Oh, hello there, how are you today? I think I saw you in my last meditation." And he might say, "Why yes, I'm the lord Maitreya." And you say, "How do you do?" It's a whole different approach, and they begin to attune to you in a completely different manner (not that they treated you badly before) What's the difference? It's your perception. You suddenly perceive that these pieces of divinity are just that, and that eventually you are going to be experiencing just as they are. And perhaps there are other things that they haven't learned yet. This was a real revelation for me – I was sure that the lord Maitreya had done everything and learned and been everything. When he carefully pointed out to me that that wasn't true, I just said, "Oh, really?" And I had to think about that one. And Thoth too – I carefully followed him around Shamballa, sure that he had done everything. I tugged at him all the time – he got so tired of me!

After this evolutionary point, the Hierarchy begins to call you an initiate (though there are those who consider the initiate level to come before this time). This means that your responsibilities increase – they have increased as far as the Creator's Cosmic Plan on Earth and – guess what – beyond Earth. It shows that you have acknowledged and agreed to specific requirements and that from that point forward you have agreed to do them. You also go forward in the commitment area.

What happens to you, more specifically, at the initiation? Let's use the observations of one whom I respect as none other here on the Earth: Sanat Kumara. "One is illuminated by the light that is possible on physical existence, allowing light to penetrate into the vehicle and permanently transforming it."

That's what I was getting at – the permanent transformation of the physical vehicle at this time. (It is not really completed until after the next initiation, but it begins at this one.) This begins your disinvolvement with Earth, your ability to leave the Earth plane. Forever after that you will be almost completely detached emotionally. And that doesn't mean you can't have joy or love, or anything like that. But when you view what is happening on the Earth, you can do so with divine indifference, seeing it for what it really is.

What about the physical structure itself? Well, I've talked about "coding" the divine pattern into the physical. This certainly is potentially present before this time, and you are still the model, the Adam Kadmon, that is the divine pattern. In an intense energy sense, this is not completed until after the fourth initiation, but it changes after the third. How? In the physical reaction areas. You choose after that time not to experience pain. You haven't yet figured out exactly how to "get off the wheel," but you're in the process; you've decided that pain is not necessary and let that go. We're talking about the four bodies here. Now, what about the mental body? It has become cognizant of the completeness of the Earth experience – which has been a wonderful learning opportunity, and the mental body is always very interested in that. It sees that the Earth experience is pretty well completed as far as personal development is concerned. Naturally then, after that point, the mental energy will be used for service.

The spiritual body, in this case, you might equate with the soul – after the soul-merge the spiritual body is the soul. Of course, it is all four bodies, but it will serve, it will be involved in bringing forth upon the Earth the Creator's Plan. The body is completely aligned, but different.

What is the physical vehicle going to do after that time? It's going to serve. The emotional body might experience joy and compassion. It will be into compassion.

The soul-merge, then, allows two different perceptions to merge into one on the physical plane. That is what is happening. You might have what can be called trial runs, in which there are initiations that you recognize, but afterwards, life doesn't seem very changed – you are just aware of having had an inner ceremonial experience. This doesn't invalidate it; it just means this wasn't the soul-merge, it was something else. There are inner ceremonies that allow you to perceive more clearly in one specific area, and Sanat Kumara does participate in these on occasion. You could call these initiations between the major initiations, or a perception in a specific focus that is changed forever after. This is really done as a gift from Sanat Kumara, acknowledging that you are making progress but saying, "No, this is not the major event." These are valid experiences, beautiful gifts that one may treasure – a special connection with the highest representative of divinity on the Earth, Sanat Kumara. If we feel the connection, this is always purposefully applied by him. There is a reason you perceive him; so if you do, look for that reason within self. It might be an acknowledgment of some breakthrough that you've made, or it might be a spiritual gift because of your efforts. Does this mean that a light such as Sanat Kumara is cognizant of every piece of divinity within his domain? I think so. He leaves out no one. He attunes to each of you, and when you perceive him, then look and see why you can perceive him. You know it is not an accident – there are no accidents. You learn about nature and other things through your conscious connection with him.

After the soul-merge, the continuity of consciousness may or may not be utilized. There are those that are soul-merged here on the Earth who have not yet completely released the need to sleep; they haven't gotten through that yet. And sometimes this continuity-of-consciousness thing has an impact on their rest, so they might choose not to use it for a while until they can unlock the body's need for rest. It depends upon the individual. The soul-merged human being has more energy, so certainly the need to sleep will be less intense, but they might sleep three or four hours a night, and at that time they will turn off that continuity of consciousness. Later they will say, "Oh, I don't have to do that anymore." There is a continuation of a learning experience. You see, they aren't quite through on the Earth yet; they are still unlocking it. The same is true of food: By the time of the soul-merge, you are very much in touch with your body's needs, and you will still be eating, but you will be flowing with it. You will be able to perceive what your body needs and eat in line with that. Then gradually you recognize that the need to eat is really rather a habit and you can break it. By the time of the fourth initiation it is broken.

Concerning the seven spiritual paths and your choice, do you make that choice at the time of the third initiation? You should have it carefully thought out and be well on your way toward making the final decision by that time. It is very difficult to make it in the short time between the third and fourth initiations. Recognize that after the third initiation, it is the soul that is here, so your soul has been considering it and knows what it is, but after the merged state, it has to take into consideration all of what has been input into it from the Earth plane, and sometimes that changes it. It will be in line with the Creator's Cosmic Plan.

The more advanced you are, the better you can serve. The reason for making the effort to achieve these points, these initiations, is service. That's always true, and the more progress each of you makes, the more you are going to aid the Earth to avoid some of its trauma. It can get above some of it then and not have to experience it.

You could say that at the time of the soul-merge you are aligning more completely with the totality. Certainly, through the alignment process you invoke the monad and, in a sense, line up the monad, the soul and the personality. As you merge the personality within the soul, it changes the whole perspective of the totality. You could say then that the physical extensions have ceased to be. So what do you have? You have a monad that is extending to the soul level only, in this sense — one part of it, anyway. The soul level is no more emphasized by the totality than the personality level is. Just as you stand at the base of a mountain, you are looking at your next evolutionary step. To me it is an alignment of all three, with the soul as the intermediary. The soul will no longer be the focus. If you reference it from the monadic level, then when the soul-merge with the personality takes place, it does seem that the soul no longer functions as it did. It does disintegrate in a certain sense. The soul itself is changed by the droppin-gaway process. It looks different depending on your focus. A mountain looks different from above than it does when you are standing at its base, but it is the same mountain. Nothing has changed but your perception, your focus.

If the soul has extensions that are functioning in India, perhaps, or England or South America, and you merge with your soul, then they are reabsorbed by the soul, and the physical structures disintegrate. Remember, soul is just self on another level. But all is divinity, and if you don't experience it on one level, you experience it on another. After the fourth initiation, you might not have a physical body.

✧ T E N ✧

Symbology and How to Use It

W HAT IS A SYMBOL? IT IS ANYTHING THAT SIGNIFIES A REPRESENTATION of something. Words are symbols of concepts, and by utilizing them we seek to understand. That is important. Through symbology we are seeking greater understanding of everything. It is part of the way we evolve and grow. Through the use of symbology we can begin to relate one level of experience to another. We can, in essence, put all the parts of creation together into the oneness, which is a process that will always lead you forth. By understanding all of the pieces and their relationships to each other do you evolve and grow. Then suddenly, at a specific critical point in your evolution, it becomes clear that everything relates to everything else. That's really what you are studying, and by symbology do you discover it.

Now, each of you has specific symbols that are important to you. Each of these symbols is more individualistic than you might have thought, even more than words, which may mean one thing to one person but something entirely different to someone else. It seems to me that words, in many cases, are the least desirable of symbols. The symbols that employ the sight process are, for this point in humanity's evolution, the most important. The visual conception of ideas can lead you forth in a way that perhaps a less visual way will not. Later, utilizing different symbologies — those of the senses of smell, touch, hearing — may be important. But at this particular period in humanity's development, it seems to me that symbols that you can see, that you can understand through the reference of seeing — not necessarily by outer seeing, but inner seeing as well — are most important.

How does this relate to the emotional area? Words are really mental symbols. The feeling side of mankind's nature was more present earlier. Now, if that seems to contradict what I have said, remember that we have involution and evolution, and at a specific turning point you again reference what was referenced before, through perhaps on a more perceptual level. So in the past you looked at life from the feeling part of nature – even those of you who are now more mentally focused did so. Those who are mentally focused at this time will, in a symbolic way, a little later, encounter the feeling part of self, and as you do, this is an important symbol for you. You will see it differently – you will see it as the way to complete the evolutionary spiral, as far as balancing yourself on the Earth plane is concerned.

What about those who are emotionally focused when they again encounter something on the point forward? Well, they will again reference it, but they will reference it on a more perceptual level. This will allow them to see that the way to balance self is to deal with the emotional body perceptually, balancing it by means of the mental concepts. So it is still an inner-seeing process. Do you see how all the pieces fit together from your own specific focus, whatever that is?

What about those who are physically focused, for we do have some who are? They have already encountered the feeling part in their involution. What about their evolution? Well, in a sense, evolution will lead them forth as never before, because for most of them, the feeling will have to do with the divinity of the Earth, the symbolic harmony that comes to them from the divinity of the Earth. So whenever you are focused, that is a symbol of the evolutionary process. Symbology, then, is understanding through a specific focus, and hopefully the understanding is the oneness, the divinity of self.

It seems to me that the more one can understand by looking at everything symbolically, the more one can learn from it. You can look at everything in a room, and your relationship with it, symbolically. Everything that happens to you during your day can be understood symbolically, from an enlarged perception. You can equate it, if you wish, to the four planes of experience. For example, there is within humanity a false belief, or a superstition, that if a black cat walks across your path, it is bad luck. Why? Well, on the physical plane you could trip, you could hurt yourself. On the emotional plane, if a cat crossed your path and you believed it was bad luck, you could react emotionally to it. You could become emotionally sure it was bad luck and thereby activate a specific belief through fear that such an event could lead to bad luck. In fact, by entering the emotions on that plane, you could activate that which you were afraid would happen. On the mental plane, there is the belief itself that the emotion that is attached to it activates the belief that you would have bad luck. This process has an emotional trigger that you would activate if you truly believed that such an event would create bad luck.

On the spiritual level, for many, black equates with negativity, or a receptive state with an unclear perception of what was coming at you. With any event that happens to you, there are many levels of significance. The more you can see them, and the more you can reference these various levels, the greater will be your understanding of existence and how it all fits together.

Now, if you encountered a black cat and you chose not to experience this situation, what might you do? Well, it seems to me that first of all you would reference the spiritual level, the most important level, the basic level of creation. You could know that a cat, no matter what color it is, is a piece of divinity, and if you encounter it, it's probably not going to bring bad luck. In fact, it might be a good piece of luck. An exchange with divinity on any level seems to me appropriate and not bad luck. In any case, the cat might be as startled as you are by the encounter. So if you view it for its point of origin — Divinity — that will help a lot.

If there was fear at the encounter, fear that you had activated a specific belief, how would you deal with it? You could enter the mental plane and evaluate self. Look to see whether there is a reaction present. Is there fear present at the encounter? If there is, by using the removal system you can take it out. After dealing with it mentally and removing it, seeing the cat as a little piece of divinity, then you can enjoy it (entering the emotional plane) and have an affectionate regard for that small one on the physical level. You might want to pet it. In this way you can handle all levels of existence symbolically.

You might look at major news items as they come up. Let us talk about one: the summit meeting between the U.S. and the Soviets. All right, what's a summit meeting symbolically? It's a meeting at the highest level. Now, on the physical level, they don't happen very often. Why? Because of reluctance, distrust, fear, false beliefs, and lack of communication. There is a tendency by each of the participants to hold on to their own wants, needs and desires, and not to go to the point where they will be joining toward a mutual goal rather than seeking for themselves. That certainly is important, isn't it? So the highest level on the Earth as far as the political arena is concerned has not yet *perceived* beyond their needs, wants and desires. But the important point is that they try sometimes, don't they?

I'm getting at the symbology behind symbology because that's important. Do you think their souls wish them to reference in a more free-flowing manner? I think we are seeing in the summit a specific opportunity that those who are perceptive enough really do attune to sometimes. There are those who are genuinely interested in solving specific problems. They might not be clear yet on how to do so, but they will make an attempt periodically, and this is important. This is one perception of symbology behind symbology. What is another symbology behind our summit meeting? "Good against evil"? Now, you know I don't like that word "evil." It seems to me that symbolically it does not say in words what is true. That is why I object to the word. "Evil" is merely a different perception of how to work out physical existence; that's important. Certainly there is a difference of perception on the Earth about how to evolve the Earth, if there is such a thing as evolution, and certainly there is, in my opinion — it's very easy to see that, symbolically. But instead of "good" and "evil," perhaps we should say "light" and "separation." These are my terms, and they indicate those who function servicewise with the light and those who do not.

In this case, yes, there are those who symbolically, behind the symbology, work out by means of their own beliefs a specific pattern that Divinity expresses physically. Now, that's an interesting statement – that Divinity expresses on the physical plane symbolically and that there are those who fulfill the roles that need to be played. By their own choices, by their own free will do they fulfill this symbolic unfoldment on the physical level. Unfoldment of what? Of evolution itself – humanity's evolution specifically, but the evolutionary process itself.

What we are saying basically is that there is a Oneness, and It explores, It learns, It experiences evolution from every specific focus It can conceive of. And if you think about it, that's quite a few levels. But symbolically, it is the growth, the evolution that is experienced. Leading to what? What is the Oneness' purpose? What is It doing as It symbolically experiences every possible perception? It is trying to explore everything.

It seems to me that evolution takes place in a very orderly manner. I do not see "disorder" or "chaos." I do see nonparticipation in the active process of discovery. In the beginning, before the process of evolution began, there was just nonparticipation in evolution. And sometimes, as evolution comes forth in an unclear manner at specific levels, you can reference it as not yet orderly, as not yet evolved to a specific level of orderliness. But this is not so at the highest level – only as it unfolds in its specific interrelating segments.

It seems to me that chaos represents areas that had already been exploring but had not yet done it at a clear and perceptive level. This would be chaos symbolically representing a nonbalanced energy pattern in the evolutionary process.

What are we referencing symbolically? The creative process – the way it takes place. We are, then, looking at that which comes forth. You can look at it within self – in the evolutionary process there may be an emotion that some would equate with chaos because they do not fully understand that it is "not clear." That is symbology. The good news is, you don't have to keep that. As divinity, it was never meant that you should.

How can you use symbology? You can use it to understand. Use it to look at everything that is present in your life. In astrology, by looking at what is symbolically represented in the heavens at the instant of your birth, you can see many things about self. It really does work, because all of the layers fit together very well. As you evolve and grow you become able to reference astrology at the universal level. You can take the zodiac as symbolic of the wholeness, the oneness, and by seeing yourself in a specific focus and how you relate to everything else within it, you will understand self completely. That's your goal. It will probably be a little while before you can do it, but when we begin to work with cosmic astrology, you may find it a way to symbolically see self as you evolve beyond the need to reference the Earth to self. As your evolution spirals you forward, then you can use other reference points. I would like to see all of you use the wholeness as that particular reference point.

In the area of cosmic astrology, we may work some more in heliocentric (Sun-centered) astrology. I am very optimistic that soon all of you are going to need it. It doesn't hurt to stretch a little. By using cosmic astrology you can look at the levels. It will be easier because you will be above them. You can still reference self from wherever you are. By going to this level, we can combine it with the heliocentric, referencing it then from the wholeness. Thus you can use astrology symbolically to understand yourself.

You can use sound and vibration. Vywamus is aiding you in using patterns of sound, symbolically, to create openings and see self in perhaps a different way. What's a pattern of sound – what is it a symbol of? Well, by referencing a pattern of sound through vibration, you can look at self in unlimited ways. In the toning of Vywamus, it gets you in touch with yourself as never before, because you have closed off that particular opening or that particular opportunity to see self due to certain limitations that have been accepted. So through the energy, the vibration, you have again created an opening that truly gives you a good look at self.

We will talk about harvest a little bit. What is a harvest of souls? Yes, it is a harvest of those who have pretty much completed their Earth experiencing. But let's discuss harvest as an experience on the Earth. What are some of the concepts? There is the bright harvest Moon, which is gold (the twelfth ray) – a full wholeness, a circle. What is the Moon? A reflection of the Sun, but also the mother aspect, the female principle. The Moon is symbolizing something to us – not a one-pointed focus, but focuses in as many ways as Divinity can interpret.

You can look at the symbol of our Moon in as many ways as you can conceptualize it, because the wholeness, the oneness, experiences in all of these perceptions. As one completes a harvest, one brings forth a more complete understanding of the whole concept that has been sought as a learning experience; in what we are referencing now – the whole Earth – this is the learning process that each one has understood. To do that, you have to see and receive the specific energy that allows a receptivity to the whole concept, don't you? Now, how does this female principle fit in? It represents love and nurturing. All right. What each of you is seeking, perhaps, is greater understanding of your own divinity. Another concept is that nurturing (the wholeness) is available to self through a clear foundation of your own divinity, as symbolized here by this perfect circle that is receptive, loving, nurturing. To me, that is the most symbolic representation of the Moon; and as a reflection of another light in its most positive sense, it is another level of divinity as clearly as it knows how to be. What are some of the other symbols of the harvest? A cornucopia – horn of plenty – an interesting shape like the spiral of creation that you fill up with every possible bit of bounty that you have gathered, that you have raised carefully, that you have developed, nurtured and energized.

How about Halloween? We have already dealt with the black cat, but what does Halloween symbolize? Many faiths – and some of them are referenced in not an especially positive manner, but some are. It's part of the Earth's physical existence experience. Halloween could be a part of that whole experience. "Trick or treat" – what does that mean? I think that here we are referencing what has *been* on the Earth. And that is not necessarily a negative statement, is it? The Earth in its most positive sense is being harvested at this time. You look at what has been and you understand it, and then, hopefully, you raise your perception by what you have experienced in this area. What else can be said about "trick or treat"? The veil between the physical and the astral levels is thinnest at this particular time of year. Because this is true, astral energy comes through most strongly now, and it energizes whatever is there; and for you who are attuned to spiritual things, it can energize that and make it that much more fun. Spiritual energy can be experienced through a strong Earth focus. It certainly can, so that's good.

What about the Indian cultures? Do we see the same concepts in the way that they symbolize living? Their dances, rituals and so on symbolize their direct connection with the divinity of the planet Earth which allowed them to gather symbolically for themselves this divinity and to aid the Earth and those who participated symbolically in specific ways of attunement to it. They brought forth symbolic representations of this particular attunement to the spiritual part of the Earth. To me, this is productive. Now, not every one of them used it the same way, and not every one of them understood it the same way. There are those who used the physical symbols with it. Certainly the Sun was used by many peoples as a symbol of divinity.

In Mexico, Halloween is called the day of the dead, and it is a very big festival time. Children eat candy, there is dancing, feasting and fun. Through the skeleton, coffins and so on, death is caricatured. The more primitive peoples reference some sort of physical activity to create or not to create a specific situation on any level. It might have been a spiritual event that they were seeking to bring forth, or an astral event that they were seeking to prevent, but they did it through a specific physical process. They understood more levels, didn't they? They understood symbology.

The symbol of a nuclear bomb? It certainly has energy of awesome powers that, if unleashed, would do what? It would make an immense physical change. A specific focus to create an immense change on a physical level – that's my definition of it. In the ways humanity has usually used it, the change has not always been productive. Great change is almost always perceived as disastrous, but there are those who love change. They are reacting to some experience in the past. Most people have experienced immense change in a specific way that was not always clear. One needs to see what change really is — a part of the evolutionary spiral. At some specific points there might be an abrupt change, but change has been happening all the time anyway. It takes a while to see that sometimes.

I prefer to think that any sort of a spiritual awakening, even of a major nature, is just that. A major change in the spiritual area then may reflect on other levels to an unclear level, but I do not find anything nonproductive about a major spiritual change. If you can truly see and understand change at the spiritual level — if you can really do it — all the rest can be perceived in true alignment with this spiritual perception. That of course is the point that all of us are seeking, is it not? To align our consciousness with the spiritual level and use it as we stated — symbolically reflecting from that clarity on every other level. The greater your understanding and perception of how the various pieces and levels of existence fit together — the greater your attunement at the spiritual level, and the more open you are to change in its more positive sense — the more you will resist the implication of disaster at the physical level. You may view it, then, as change that perhaps clears out a specific effect and leads to a new beginning.

What about a globe? What is it a symbol of? Is it not truly the physical presentation of all that is? It really is, isn't it? But it is an encompassing look, to see this miniature replica of wholeness and look at every little point on it. You get a glimpse of Divinity experiencing in a specific way, don't you? So it is a miniature of the wholeness. Everything that you could discover on that map would show you a different perception of Divinity's experiencing. I feel that they probably are unlimited — that there is really absolutely no limitation to the way Divinity expresses and experiences, if you look at every level and every available focus. At least I certainly have not been able to find any sort of limitation.

What about a clock? Time, of course, but what else? A specific division — a focus within a focus? Well, it seems to me a division of the experiencing mode. It's divided into twelve segments; that's the number of completion. It has three hands — an hour hand, a minute hand and a second hand — meaning that if you begin to focus into the fullest sense, you get to twelve, but when you begin to focus each level, you get the three. We deal with that in our symbology of self, too — in a simplified version of it through the monadic, soul and physical extension levels. Numbers of course are a very interesting symbolism themselves, and we certainly are not going to get into numerology in this. We don't have time. But numbers do symbolically reference everything that truly exists — in one way or another or in a specific combination. They are an interesting study. Now, coming from that clock is a cord that plugs into a specific area. What does that represent? Energy — a connection to a supply of power, a supply of energy. It is the supply of energy that you need to plug into in order to obtain a free flow of your full purpose — which from the clock's point of view is to show the specific sequential time that is present here on the Earth. It has attuned, then, to its purposes by plugging into the source of power. Isn't that interesting?

Now, there's a box of Kleenex on top of the clock — you see how much fun we can have with everything? Now, the box "holds" the Kleenex. What's the box? It's pretty — it fulfills its purpose by being attractive; in other words by referencing the harmonious part of existence. It also is practical: it is a specific shape that integrates well into the structure of physical existence. And it is symbolic of the practicality of using harmony on the Earth to perform a specific function. What is its function? It is a handkerchief? What's a handkerchief? It's used to absorb excess "emotion." Well, it could perhaps blot up anything that is in excess. What else? Some people use them to make flowers — a creative use of something that seems to have a single purpose, but when you enlarge the perspective of its usage, it really is unlimited. Kleenex is created from something else: wood. So the natural resources of the planet are used to create something that most perceive as being simply utilitarian but that may be extended beyond that single focus into a much more creative and perhaps harmonious usage than one might think of.

A lamp is very pretty. It contains components of wood, metal and plastic, and perhaps glass, if you include the light bulb. It has various earth components, then, and man-made components combined into an attractive, decorative usage that is also practical. By combining, as with the Kleenex, the utilitarian with the decorative focus, you get something of beauty that you can use and enjoy practically. Isn't that nice? What is a lamp symbolic of? Bringing in the light — shedding of light, illumination. Yes, and it's also referencing existence in its most positive sense, isn't it? Because we begin with a very simple application of Earth existence and then we keep enlarging it, enhancing it. Now, that does not mean it has to be complicated, does it? It's just that we may use it in a more creative manner. Perhaps when we get back to this new beginning that we call the "New Age" we will see that things can be simple and perhaps beautiful at the same time. And I think humanity is beginning to see that.

How about ice cream as a symbol? Why do people like it so much? It has the ability to nurture, to support you in seeing beyond the life that sometimes is referenced at a less-than-free-flowing level. It is symbolic of a reward. It is cooling and soothing and it comes in many delicious flavors. Why is chocolate so appealing? It has a specific taste that in the past, even back into ancient Egypt, was appreciated and enjoyed, and when people reexperience it now, they remember it in a very basic way. What is ice cream symbolic of? A treat!

What is cotton? A means to achieve a protective covering while experiencing physically. It is a natural fiber, which says what? It's more comfortable, it breathes. It also absorbs better than other things, except linen. What does that say? A way of cleansing? Cleansing from what? From those things that are *not* natural.

The Star of David is a specific gift that in my opinion was given to humanity very, very early. It represents the entwinement of physical existence and the spiritual area. It is really a promise that both are equal and that those who are in physical existence will be as perceptive, eventually, about spiritual existence as the ones in spiritual existence are with the physical — an entwining, an equality. That relates to a specific ceremony long ago. Now, we are referencing a past civilization that is very, very ancient, and there are many symbols from such past civilizations that come forth. Sometimes they are changed just a little, modified because of mistakes in symbols. For instance, some of those intricate symbols that you have, when brought forth by someone new, may change a little, and eventually you get a whole new approach — a whole new symbol. This happens over, perhaps, thousands and thousands of years. The symbol then is used by humanity to show a coming forth from the past to present understanding and then going beyond what is present to a new level. It seems important to reference symbols that way — that they can put together all of the pieces when you let them.

What does electricity symbolize? It is the electrical quality of energy itself manifested physically. And some of it has been present on the Earth for a long time, but it is not yet complete. The completion of what we call electricity will be present only when the body of light becomes a part of the Earth in the New Age. Now, that says something rather important, doesn't it? That the nature of electricity has never been understood, because it isn't complete — and it's difficult to understand something until you have all of the pieces that fit together. Light is the same thing: It's better understood now than it used to be. Symbolically, for many, it represented something that dramatically changed their lives. Many referenced it from a sense of superstition at first. But as they began to see the productive changes that it brought into their lives, it became symbolic for many of evolution — of a means by which they could create a more abundant life in their very own home environment. They did not understand it, but they saw that it symbolized a lighting up of the physical plane.

What about fuel spills? Fuel is energy. Spills have taken place on the expressway. The expressway symbolizes transportation, a means of getting from one place to another. The energy, then, has been spilled, creating a specific blockage. The full usage of the energy to achieve going from here to there, or your full evolution, is not yet seen on the physical level. And much energy is wasted, spilled, and it creates an impact in the free-flow-ingness of evolution on the physical level. Sometimes these fuel spills create fire, which is chaotic and creates its own problems! Whenever energy is used in a way that does not reference free-flow, there may be instances in which the intensity of the nonclarity results in a block of such size and magnitude that it affects many people, whether it is a highway that is completely unusable or a fire that encompasses a specific area. But a physical manifestation of the usage of energy that is not yet free-flowing does create some interesting physical encounters. This is not fun if you are involved in it, I guess!

It seems to me, then, that free-flow is sought by everyone, and you bring your various perceptions to it, reaching specific points depending upon what you have created as you are seeking it. There are many perceptions about working with creating a free-flowing physical existence. And many times, those in charge have perceptions on how to deal with the physical realities in creating the free-flow that differ from each of yours. Isn't that true? Sometimes physical existence, when treated in a practical manner, makes you aware that specifics need to be dealt with before you can make it free-flowing.

About Tibetan incense — its purpose was an attunement to the spiritual energies that they represent, a specific focus that helped to utilize what many of them were seeking to do — to enlarge Divinity's perception in that area. But they also used it to focus their lives where they were.

So we have had a look at symbology. Everything is symbolic!

✧ E L E V E N ✧

The Hierarchy Today

T HE PAGES THAT FOLLOW ARE AN ATTEMPT TO REVEAL MORE INFORMATION about an area referred to as the Spiritual Hierarchy. The Spiritual Hierarchy consists of a group of dedicated workers who seek to aid the implementation of the Creator's Plan upon the Earth. Some of this work involves humanity but some does not. The Hierarchy is a distinct group, just as humanity is a distinct group. Those who are working within the Hierarchy have for the most part completed their earthly experiences. They have overcome the Earth vibration. They have freed themselves from the wheel, as it is sometimes called. They have chosen to remain nearby, however, and aid the Earth.

The Creator has chosen to divide the energy patterns here into seven distinct varieties. Therefore the Hierarchy is composed of seven departments.

The First Department

The first ray is the will aspect of the Creator and it seeks to use this aspect upon the Earth when it is appropriate to utilize the Ray One energies as they are meant to be utilized – to carry forth this intense and focalized application of energy where it is needed to go forward with the Cosmic Plan.

I will be discussing the Planetary Hierarchy, but of course these energies come to us from the Solar Hierarchy, and it in turn receives its energies from a higher source, until you reach the Source – the Creator Himself. This is always true – the energies are stepped down to us in a ladderlike effect until they reach us upon the Earth. So I am talking about this first-ray energy when it has been stepped down to the highest level within the Hierarchy, where it is differentiated.

The department head (as opposed to what you might call the head of the ray) is the Manu. He is a very special being who has devoted his great life to enable this aspect to be focused to the Earth more and more intensely. He now is of the Earth. The name Manu is the name of the department head itself and does not signify one particular person in that position.

The Manu is rather new to his position. He is currently known as the master Jupiter who has been promoted to that position. He evolved quite a bit upon the Earth, although he is originally from the planet Venus. He is a being with much experience and wisdom. When this material was originally given, through Blavatsky and Alice Bailey, he was still in his body, which had been very useful to him in the past. Now he has energized a much younger body that seems to be more effective for the work he is currently involved in. Eventually he might even come among men in this body, but that has not yet been fully decided. It is really the mission of the Christ, but he has agreed that if required, he too will walk among men to aid them. His is a recent promotion; the one who held the position of the Manu has replaced one of the Kumaras who recently left the Earth.

The three Kumaras came with Sanat Kumara on their great mission to the Earth. Their great sacrifice in coming here to aid this small, dark planet was done with love as their purpose, as their means of bringing forward the Creator's Plan — their way to aid the Creator in His work. It was a mission of love, my friends. The one who was the Manu has now replaced the first Buddha and freed him to go on to greater experience. That Manu has chosen the path to Sirius and is there now — not at a beginning level, for he is a very great soul that has *chosen* to replace another there. He is a Manu of the first ray because that is his specialty, if you will, and he now goes to do that on a higher level. This being who has recently left our experience is Sanaka Kumara, and he was replaced by the one who was the Manu, the first department head within the Planetary Hierarchy.

The Manu is rather distant from the daily activities carried out within the department of the first ray, but his responsibility includes the whole area, and he does this in his daily work. He looks at every conceivable area within his jurisdiction. He senses the problems and he resolves them. He removes the blocks, if you will, to the Creator's Plan or he simply recognizes they are there and a part of the scheme, and he utilizes them exactly where they are — because, my friends, at this level you do not seek to force anything. You recognize that at this level everything is done with reason, logic, and you utilize it with the will, which is his specialty. He utilizes the will of the Creator to implement, to bring forth these special attributes, these special energies of the Creator.

The Manu and his work are not available to humanity. You are not meant to know very much about him, for a number of reasons, the main one being that the more people who know about him, the more who recognize him and attune to him — the more distracted he becomes from his very strenuous work, and you are then slowing down the Plan. You are just an impediment to the Creator's plan when you do this. This is just a way to enforce progress, a way to assure that the important work of the Creator proceeds as rapidly as is appropriate.

The Manu has an assistant. Because of the vacancy created when the master Jupiter moved to the position of Manu, El Morya has advanced, if you can call it that. It is a more responsible position that he holds, though he still retains what he had before; he has simply agreed to do two jobs at once. There is so much work to be done, he has taken on more responsibilities to free up another master to work in another specific area, which I will discuss later. For this reason, he is not currently doing any teaching, and I have been delegated by him to work with most of his students.

Ray One is very active right now. Its activity will keep increasing over the next few years, and because of this, a young initiate will soon be training to assume some of El Morya's responsibilities. He is currently in the process of initiation to the level where it will be appropriate for him to begin. It is thought to be coming into being within the next few months. He is one who has been very well known in the world and will be a visible master, one whom you must learn about because of his activities. He will be coming into body before too long and will be working extensively with others here upon the Earth, embodying the will aspect here in an external process of the Hierarchy. He will be beginning with these first-ray energies as my associates and I begin with the second-ray energies. He will be working through one who has not yet been contacted, and he eventually will come here in his own body also, so his work will be very visible and you will get to know him very well. He has been a close associate of mine. I know you will all enjoy getting to know him soon.

The work done by those who step down first-ray energy is very intense. They are chosen specifically for their adeptness at working with energy. They must be able to utilize the most powerful of the energies in very specific ways. The first-ray energy is a catalyst on the Earth and it is applied with intensity at very specific times and places to do its work. Working with this energy takes someone with very special training. Many people think of first-ray energy as being quite destructive, and of course it does destroy form upon occasion, but it is not destructive as far as I am concerned. It is just a necessary breaking down of old conditions and a moving on to much more productive and practical means of expression. You can think of first-ray energy as a cleaner, a cleanser, a changer, if you will, to more productive energy patterns.

The master Jupiter, El Morya and the new, young initiate being trained all aid each other to step down the energies until they can be utilized in a form that is appropriate — neither too strong nor too weak nor too off-centered — upon the Earth. You must recognize that they learn to balance these energies, to apply them in the most precise way possible, to understand their use completely, to work with them intensely, and to accomplish the specific purposes that are required for each specific occasion.

Astrologically, this first ray of will or power comes from the constellations of Aries, Leo and Capricorn. This is true only for the present 25,000-year cycle and would be different in another cycle.

I have talked before about energies that are stepped down into fourths — sixteen in number. It is also valid to say that there are seven energies coming into the Earth, to which another five have been added, making a total of twelve. This seems at odds with sixteen, but it's not — it is just looking from a different angle at the same thing. It is a different breakdown, if you will, a different way of interpretation. I want you to understand this very clearly, my friends. Truth can be interpreted in many ways, and just because it is interpreted differently from your own understanding, that does not make other ways invalid. It may be just as valid or more valid than your understanding, and it is important to be open-minded in this regard.

When I talk of energy and when I talk of force, they are really the same thing, except that the energies are free-flowing and not within some sort of embodiment, while the forces occur within certain kinds of manifestation. This first-ray energy, then, when it becomes a force, is the most powerful means to produce change ever conceived upon the Earth. The Manu and El Morya are very cognizant of this, as are Sanat Kumara, the other Kumaras and the Buddha. These great ones recognize how potent, how powerful, this aspect of the Creator is, and they are very respectful of it, utilizing it only as directed. It is as if you could read on a box, "Take only as directed." They follow this very carefully, my friends, realizing the necessity for discretion and caution with the powerful first-ray energy and force.

The Second Department

Before we begin our study of the second ray, we must discuss the one who embodies the Christ consciousness: the lord Maitreya. He is really the head of the Hierarchy in a very special sense. The Christ, the lord Maitreya, was the first human being on this planet to reach enlightenment. Already at the time of Atlantis, he was in the process of taking the third initiation. He simply leaped, if you will, from immersion. He made very rapid progress in his growth, and so he has remained with humanity since that time to aid them in obtaining their freedom from the Earth immersion. In his love and in his devotion, these special energies of the second ray are embodied by him and passed to us through his consciousness. His love has enabled many to make greater progress than had ever before been possible. Before him was the Buddha, who brought wisdom to the planet in his intense experience as an earthly avatar. The Buddha came for one purpose, the Christ for another; each avatar anchors a specific aspect upon the Earth and aids it considerably by doing so.

The one that we know now as the Buddha had developed before this Earth was ready to nurture man, and at that time there was not the facilities available for taking the third initiation, so he took it with the Christ when he became ready for the third initiation. This, of course, was the first great initiation, from the point of view of the Hierarchy. Thus the Christ and the Buddha together were able to lift mankind in a very special way, and the Christ replaced the Buddha as the avatar and began his mission to aid the world. The Buddha continues to aid it, but will soon be leaving, as will one of his compatriots who came to us long ago from Venus. The third Buddha is also planning to leave shortly, and thus will all of those close to Sanat Kumara be replaced. Eventually, in my opinion, Sanat Kumara will proceed along his great path of evolution, but it is not quite time yet for that, my friends.

There have been many avatars upon the Earth, from the major avatars – including the Buddha and the Christ – to the many minor ones (certainly not minor as far as work is concerned, but only in the sense that they are not as well-known by humanity at this time). Also there are many within the Hierarchy who work in this second ray. It is the main thrust, really, having to do with teaching in the world – not only human teaching, but other kinds. Work here has concentrated on the second ray, and also the seventh and of course the first are receiving emphasis at this time. These rays, or departments, are now under the guidance of Sanat Kumara. But you must remember that Sanat Kumara is not a member of the Hierarchy. Does this surprise you? He is separate, just as the President of the United States is not a member of Congress. It is simply a division within the spiritual government.

The head of the second department of the Hierarchy now, at least the visible head of it, is the World Teacher, the Christ. But almost equally important, and certainly the operating figure now, is the master Kuthumi. He is very well known and is, before very long, to take over completely as the world teacher. He does much of this work already, but officially he is working under the Christ, the lord Maitreya, at this time. However, when the earlier teachings were given, it was not anticipated that he would be doing as much world teaching as he is. Because of the speeding up of the evolutionary spiral, he is now needed, and thus evolution reaches down into the ranks of this second department and lifts everyone up a rung or two beyond what was expected at this time.

The master Kuthumi has a large ashram with many students, but because of his new responsibilities, most have been shifted to other teachers. I have a great number of these students – most of them, in fact, but the master El Morya also has some and there are one or two other teachers also working with some of the students. Most that I am contacting will be the ones that I contact on the physical plane now, although there is a group of Eastern students also that were originally Kuthumi's, with whom I work within this ashram on the inner level, you might say.

As the master Kuthumi becomes more and more involved with the world teaching which will culminate in his Earth descent as an avatar later in the evolutionary cycle, he must involve himself less with his students. Of course, he is called upon by some of them occasionally, but he cannot devote much time or energy to the students now. An initiate has assumed the responsibility of stepping down his energies to the student as needed. This initiate has passed the third initiation and is very closely associated with Kuthumi now. When I need to contact Kuthumi, in order not to disturb him I go through this initiate, attuning to and seeing where the master is. One must recognize that as you progress, you recognize what is important, and right now what is important is the Earth and her evolutionary process, so we do not unnecessarily disturb those who are working so strenuously now to aid her.

Because of this important Earth thrust, Sanat Kumara, the Buddha, the lord Maitreya and the master Kuthumi are all four working on the Earth and the Earth changes. This is marvelous and it enables many of you to do things that have never been possible before upon the Earth. Know that your rapid growth would not be possible were it not for the aligning of these four great ones — the aligning of their energies with the Earth, the aligning of their power, of their light, to aid those who struggle toward it, who struggle to obtain more now. It is this second department that primarily carries this alignment process because of the second-ray energy that is here, which aids the Earth. The love attunes the world to the higher aspects that are necessary to carry her higher in her spiral. Thus, this department has great responsibilities now.

Thus we have the master El Morya constantly in contact with the lord Maitreya, with the master Kuthumi, with all of those involved in this great thrust. I am not interested in giving you personalities, or even names, my friends; I am interested in telling you about the work that is going on and how it is done. I feel very strongly that below the very highest level in each department, the masters and initiates will be shifted wherever they are needed in the coming times. We were told so at a council meeting in Shamballa recently. It will not be very important where each person is, only that each position is covered in as great a fashion as possible, in as great density as possible, if you will, to make sure the thrust is working out and on schedule.

This second department has come right up on the present world conditions that must be overcome — the traumas and other effects of the causes previously set up by humanity. The great problem now encountered by all who work with the Earth — including Sanat Kumara, the Buddha, the Christ and Kuthumi — is, "Which effects do you seek to lessen and which will you allow to remain?" Karmic patterns here are important, and we must constantly check with Sanat Kumara to see what his wishes are as a representative of the Creator.

The reason is that grace is involved here: Will the Earth be allowed to free herself of some of these effects by grace? The answer, my friends is yes

— yes, of course. This is happening more and more, and is it not wonderful that it is being allowed by the Creator, that the Earth is being aided, that some of the trauma is being removed? More and more it looks as if the greatest part of the trauma will be avoided. I say this with great joy, knowing that it is very new information coming from Sanat Kumara, and he too shouts it with joy, my friends. We are going to be able to spare the Earth much more than we originally thought possible. This does not mean there will not be trauma. All of you have noticed the strange energies now, the difference in the weather — these things will continue. But the great catastrophic events that were prophesied thousands of years ago — most of these will be avoided, my friends. This is a very new ruling given in the last few Earth days, and I am so pleased to tell you this now. It looks like there might be a skirmish and a war or two, but it looks more and more as if the great final war will be avoided. Some of the natural Earth trauma will also be avoided, although not all, certainly. This is all due to these four great ones in the second department and their immense effort — which humanity does not even begin to appreciate because they do not understand it. Of course, the great ones do not do it for this reason; they would rather that humanity did not attune to them, did not distract them now, although when they are attuned to, my friends, they say thank you.

I have not given you the Eastern names because it seems to me that here in the West we do not have to be concerned with them now. I, the Tibetan, Djwhal Khul, referred to as the master D.K. much in the past, have assumed much greater responsibilities in the second department. Working with me are two other young masters — young in experience compared to some of the others working now, my friends, through we do know what we are doing and we do it with great care. We fulfill our responsibilities as called upon to do. The three of us within this second department have come to Earth now upon a very special mission. I am headquartered here and anchored here within Janet, and will be so for quite a while. The others are anchored in India and England.

Our mission, my friends, is to maintain this triangular energy pattern and to bring to the Earth an aid, a growth pattern, a spiritual opportunity for those who ask. The aspect being emphasized at this time is joy, and our mission really is to anchor joy upon the Earth as never before possible. The triangular energy pattern here is attuned to joy and thus aids those who contact us to attune to it in a very special way. All three of us will be emphasizing joy and we will encourage those who work with us to experience it often. Our vibratory patterns have been especially prepared to contain an emphasis on joy, and this triangular energy pattern focuses on joy also. This is because of Sanat Kumara's study upon the Earth, of his utilization of what the Earth really needs, his utilization of his special understanding of the Earth's requirements now.

Sanat Kumara

As I have stated before, Sanat Kumara is not a member of the Hierarchy, but part of the spiritual government. Sanat Kumara came to Earth out of love for her about eighteen million years ago. He and three other glorious ones came to anchor the light upon the Earth. Before then it was a small, dark planet very immersed in the heavy atmosphere, the heavy energies here, and there was no possibility of loosening this or raising her energies. After he came with his love – and it was a sacrificial act of a magnitude we cannot conceive – this wonderful, heavenly man then came to aid the Earth. He is known as the Planetary Logos, and his superior, if you will – the one from whom he receives the Creator's energies – is the Solar Logos, whose energies are so magnificent that at our point of evolution we can scarcely understand or conceive of what he is. Of course, there are many steps above this before you get to the Source, so we have a ladder effect that leads to the Source and steps down energies until they reach us here upon the Earth. To me, it is glorious to consider these lofty ones, to know that when we attune to Sanat Kumara we can feel his love. It is sent to us with gladness and with joy, and we can attune and receive it, my friends, when we care to do so.

Sanat Kumara and his three Kumaras, the three Buddhas, reside in Shamballa. Now, Shamballa is not upon the physical plane. It has been reported to be in various places, and so it is if you know exactly where it is. Our discussion does not cover that topic, but know that he does reside there and his work is directed from there. Shamballa you might compare to the White House – it is the seat of the planetary government. The Hierarchy report to Sanat Kumara directly or indirectly through the three Buddhas, the three other Kumaras. There is not one fast rule, but Shamballa is where council meetings are held which include all members of the Spiritual Hierarchy after they have "passed" (rather a poor word to use) the fifth initiation. They are then considered masters of wisdom and entitled to attend these council meetings.

Shamballa, then, is both a location not of the gross physical and also, of course, a state of consciousness. When a council meeting is occurring, we simply attune to it and our consciousness takes part. Sometimes, when it is appropriate, we go in our astral or etheric bodies. But when an important council meeting is taking place at Shamballa, we all know it and we go one way or another.

Sanat Kumara is the Creator's representative here – that is his job and, my friends, that encompasses a great many things. It is his responsibility, by his love, by utilizing the energies that are given to him in as positive and productive way as possible, to aid the growth of the Earth. His aura, of course, is so large that the Earth and everything on it is contained within it. Does that give you some idea of the magnificence of this heavenly man?

The average member of the Hierarchy, to generalize a little, can hold his focus, perhaps, in five areas at one time. But Sanat Kumara can hold his in a thousand places at once, attuning to whatever is necessary upon the Earth and within the spiritual government and maintaining contact everywhere at once. "A thousand" is a little misleading, because it is much greater than that. His consciousness can encompass an entire state, for instance, and know exactly what is going on at any particular time or place. That is the magnificence that we have at the head of our evolutionary government, our evolutionary thrust, really. Does that not give you confidence, my friends? It should. We have in charge one who knows exactly what he is doing. In heavenly terms, which are far, far, far above us, he is a young planetary logos, but in terms of what the Earth needs, he is very old in experience, very wise and very able to aid the Earth as it spirals forward into greater experience and greater responsibility.

Sanat Kumara, then, holds the key, really, to the Earth's evolution. He turns the key in the lock that opens the evolutionary possibilities upon the Earth. He constantly looks for these possibilities, scanning with his great abilities the needs and the possibilities here upon the Earth and then passing down directives to those of us who work here upon the specific needs and specific possibilities that are present. As his representatives, we carry out these directives, passing them down again to those who serve here upon the Earth – to you, for instance, in your search as you begin to attune to the need, to participate in the Cosmic Plan, to help obtain the fastest possible growth for yourself, for others and for the Earth in its growth pattern.

Sanat Kumara, then, is the mastermind of evolution upon the Earth in his office in Shamballa. He holds a special energy field that enables him to do with energy what is necessary before it is stepped down to those within the Hierarchy because he can utilize such an intense energy pattern. He can change it so it can be tolerated by others who cannot stand such intensity.

The council meetings in Shamballa are held at regular intervals and also upon special need as called by Sanat Kumara or one of the other Kumaras, because they too are involved in giving the directives to the Hierarchy. The three Kumaras have a very special job to do here upon the Earth. As a part of the focus of the energies from Sanat Kumara, they maintain these energies in a triangular configuration to be utilized by whoever is attuned to that level of energy.

I have reported that one of the Kumaras went higher recently on his evolutionary spiral, and so there is a new Kumara working in the triangular configuration. When a new Kumara was added it became a different configuration of energy. We are seeing the results here upon the Earth of the difference in this energy triangulation. In the New Age the triangulation will be even more different, with two more Kumaras continuing their evolutionary path, and thus the New Age will be different than it would have been without this change.

Sanat Kumara monitors the Earth, watching those who have begun their rapid spiritual growth. He notes each one as he becomes greater with love, with joy, my friends. He looks at their progress and notes which areas need action. Aiding them is not always appropriate – there may be something else such as providing a stimulus to aid them in getting through a traumatic period, or cutting off a specific trauma in an area that is not appropriate.

When he sees an area that needs attention, he focuses more of his consciousness there and explores it in depth. Occasionally you might feel this probe as an intense surge of energy, an intense feeling of love, of being affected in every pore by love and energy.

Sanat Kumara is sometimes called the One Initiator because it is his decision when each of us is ready to progress in a very special way from one level to another. When we are, he initiates the transition period; this is called initiation, and he is the one who does it at the major levels. Before that time, it is done more informally, and these are equally as important, of course, but from the viewpoint of the Hierarchy and Sanat Kumara, only the major initiations in which Sanat Kumara is the initiator are of major significance in life. Initiation is in the life of the planet. We are each a small aspect of the life of the Earth, and by thrusting forward we aid the Earth and her evolution. It is the totality of evolution upon the Earth that concerns Sanat Kumara, not one individual's approach.

The Hierarchy works with large groups too, but Sanat Kumara works with the totality of the Earth experience, always weighing everything before making decisions. In his wisdom he recognizes individuals and their needs, as well as the needs of the entire planet, to see what is most appropriate for action. Usually, because of his wisdom, understanding, love and joy, everything flows very well. Occasionally we might not understand his approach, but he sees things we do not.

He is involved very, very strenuously now in a step forward in evolution for the Earth because his own evolution is what causes the whole process to begin to thrust forward. He is a heavenly man and getting ready for a very major step now. As the Earth in its totality steps forward now, it is his progress that reflects back and becomes our progress – the Earth's and each individual's upon it. Know that when you take a step forward it aids Sanat Kumara just as he aids you. It is a two-way street, my friends, and his aid is done with joy, as I hope yours is. And thus is progress made in the Creator's Plan for life here upon the Earth.

Sanat Kumara asked me tell you that he is very joyous now to be able to negate some of the karmic effects that would have begun to traumatize the Earth quite seriously very soon. This decision comes from a very high source and he is very glad to carry it out, my friends. He gives each individual his love, his assurance of his caring, his assurance of his desire for them to attune to their own potentiality, their own greatness, their own great thrust forward.

The Third Department

At the head of the third department is the Mahachohan, also known as the Lord of Civilization. This is a very important department, a very critical one, that carries heavy responsibilities, my friends. The Mahachohan, in his joyous serving of the Creator, gives the world its thrust forward in the path of evolution. Study these words carefully to ascertain a deeper, profound meaning. The Mahachohan works with energy in a very concrete way, unlike the ones we have already discussed. His work involves making it happen. That is rather a crude way of putting it, but it is appropriate. He brings into being the will of the Creator, the Creator's Plan for the Earth, in a very concrete way. The first and second departments are also involved in this but not as concretely. The Mahachohan experiences the energies in a unique way, while the Manu and the World Teacher simply utilize the energies for their work.

As we approach the New Age, the responsibilities of this department have increased to the extent that Sanat Kumara and his co-workers decided that a realignment of the department was necessary to make it as productive and purposeful as possible. Thus the Mahachohan has been raised closer to Sanat Kumara, and his work and everyone else in that department have been correspondingly raised to fill the vacancies above. Thus, the one who formerly carried out the directions passed to the third department by the Mahachohan has also pulled away from his former position; this is Paul the Venetian. Humanity has no need to know what he is currently doing. It is not available, but he does what he does with joy to aid humanity.

Into this vacancy the master Serapis Bey has been placed to do what is necessary in the work of great third department. This is a very responsible position and he still retains some of the work he was doing previously in the fourth department — which is a subdivision of the third, as are the fifth, sixth and seventh; all four of these departments derive their energy from the third. The fourth, however, also has a very special connection with the Christ.

The master Serapis Bey is very able and carries out the work delegated by the Mahachohan very well. Serapis Bey, because of his work upon the fourth ray (the ray of harmony-through-conflict), is very aware of what is needed to bring about the New Age with as little conflict as possible.

There has been much alignment within the Hierarchy that man knows nothing about (and keep in mind that we are talking about the Hierarchy for humanity; there are other hierarchies that work with other evolving groups upon the Earth). The master Serapis Bey still works extensively with the deva evolution in its thrust. Its evolution is different from ours. The devas are direct representatives of the Creator, and when I talk of devic evolution I am not talking about an individualized consciousness thrust but about the deva kingdom and its evolution.

The Mahachohan receives directives from the Christ, the Buddhas and, of course, mainly from Sanat Kumara. There is also a direct input here from the Solar Logos and his various representatives of consciousness. Thus the Mahachohan receives his main instructions from Sanat Kumara, but at the same time he must attune to the great one who is the representative of the third aspect upon the solar level. Is it not marvelous that he can do this — that he can focus the energies that come to him through Sanat Kumara and also directly, from this higher source on the solar level? This is one thing he must do always — maintain an aspect of his consciousness in direct connection to both Sanat Kumara and the Solar Hierarchy to know what is required, to be advised of each specific need because of changing, evolving growth within the whole solar system and also upon the Earth.

To recap, the energy flow from the Mahachohan comes from Sanat Kumara, the Manu, the Christ and also from the Solar Hierarchy, and it flows through the Mahachohan to Serapis Bey, who receives it directly in the third aspect in this present condition. It also flows directly to the Christ. It flows in every direction from the third to the first through the second, and from the third to the second directly.

The energy from the Mahachohan flows directly to the third aspect and from there breaks down fourfold. But here the energy becomes quite complicated. Each of these four aspects, which are really coming from the third, are energized also by the first and second. Thus the Mahachohan has a very pivotal point within the Hierarchy, and in particular to evolving civilization; that is why he is called the Lord of Civilization. His job intensifies when a civilization reaches a critical point. And it is particularly critical now because the whole planet, not just a civilization, is at a critical point. Because it is a matter involving all consciousness here, it is very important that it be done as intensely as possible, and thus many of the Hierarchy have been placed here to aid him in the third department. These are not ones that we can know of.

I have told you that great emphasis is now on the first, second and seventh rays, but know, my friends, that the seventh ray is the responsibility of the third department. It is that aspect upon which they make so much effort now.

The Mahachohan has great responsibilities but is not involved personally with the Earth except by experiencing what is necessary to aid it. A personal contact with him is not possible and not at all desirable. The stepping down of the third-department energies to Serapis Bey is a little closer to what man can understand. He is really an administrator in a larger sense: He oversees what is passed from the Mahachohan and he distributes this energy where necessary. He too passes energy to the first and second departments and receives from them, at a slightly lower level than the Mahachohan. Also he works directly with those upon the second ray in a very personal sense.

The second-ray personnel are doing the teaching, sending the love/wisdom aspects to the world, and the third ray aids them in a concrete or practical way. This is important to realize — that his work is always practical, even if abstract.

Right now the master Serapis Bey is very involved with overseeing the fourth, fifth, sixth and seventh rays and the ones who head them. There have been quite a number of changes, and there is training going on here with each of the ones who head these four aspects. These are very intense times, and the Hierarchy feels it also. Perhaps you think energies are intense at your level, but raise the energy level to the area of the masters and imagine how intense they are. They handle it well, but they need help.

There has even been a call from the Hierarchy — and this is new; it has not been given before — for us to use all available talent upon the Earth to raise to the utmost the work that can be accomplished. And still there is more to be done. Sanat Kumara has had a talk with his superior, the Solar Logos, and his representatives and several areas are sending aid. We are daily receiving reinforcements of our needed aspects, of the needed energy patterns, and the intensification of the energies upon the Earth is partly the result of this aid. It is a positive thing that will enable the Earth to increase its awareness very rapidly.

Some higher beings are approaching, also ahead of schedule. Through their sacrificial patterns they come close, they intensify their work beyond what they had planned to do, because the Earth requires it. We will soon be receiving energies from one we have not spoken of before, and his energies are more magnificent than any we have ever encountered before. The need is great and he has heard our call and comes close.

The Earth has sent out a call. It is rather like a beacon and it calls for those who will aid us. And the fact that we are all working to put forth our utmost efforts makes those who listen realize that we have earned this help. The Hierarchy now changes almost daily. The Earth is changing, and you can certainly expect the hierarchic government to change with it.

The third department is so major but we can say very little of what they are doing. It is impossible to delve into their work specifically, but the master Serapis Bey says to tell you that he is very joyous in his work and hopes his efforts will show a good response from the Earth in a concrete way. He wishes to send to those who know him his assurance that if he worked with you before he will work with you again. He has not been very involved in teaching but he has some students, and they are simply to attune to him when necessary. He has not abandoned them. Also, some others such as I are helping him with his student load. But he will be happy to attune to whoever asks and seeks this attunement.

The Fourth Department

The fourth department is really a division of the third in a sense. It is the area that carries out the work of the fourth ray. It is a separate subdepartment under the overall direction, of course, of the Mahachohan.

Many things are handled by this area and the most important at this time is bringing about a completion of work that has been going forth for some time in the field of art. This has been in development for quite some time and it is a whole new approach to the artistic aspects of creation here upon the Earth that will be focused here in the New Age. Is that not exciting? Much research is being done now and it is in the very final stages of development before the advent of the New Age that is creeping over the horizon.

Let me give you some examples of just what is being brought forth in the fields of art, music and other such creative areas. In the field of music, you will not only listen to a beautiful piece of music, but you will actually experience what the composer is seeking to portray. Now, some very sensitive people do this already because they are more attuned to the New Age than others. But in the New Age, each piece of music will be presented so that each person can attune to it. It will be done by anyone because the energy patterns of the New Age will allow you to experience this music. What is being done now is in the area of music archetypes. They are being finalized so that soon will be brought down the final entranceway in these fields. This is very different from just listening to music. You will be able to almost become a part of such a piece of music, being greatly attuned to its complete presentation. Before, you were separate from the music; now the barrier will be removed and you will experience it completely.

Likewise in the field of art: You will understand what the artist is trying to portray — whether he is a modernist, traditionalist, realist or abstractionist, whatever he seeks to portray will be understood. Do you not see how marvelous this is? It will lead to greater understanding of the arts and artists — a major breakthrough. Untold artists have been very frustrated by others not understanding what they were seeking to portray.

This fourth department has made a great effort, which is now in the final stages, to aid the direct forces of the Creator in implementing this purpose of the Creator, for this is one of the changes that our Planetary Logos has earned for the Earth in his evolutionary spiral. And the great cry goes out into the kingdom: "Let the work — the glorious joy of art and music — be heard and understood by the people. It is decreed that they will understand and they will participate in the joy of this presentation." That is a direct quote from Sanat Kumara. Is it not wonderful? I certainly find it so — almost overwhelming in its implications. This explains the many changes in this department and the overwhelming amounts of work that have been done with joy in the past few hundred years. This has not been discussed or understood very much because mankind, if they knew about it, would simply distract them from the work.

The master Serapis has been deeply involved in this work, but as I have explained, he has been promoted, or at least he has changed the focus, the direction, of his work. Thus a master who is not very well known comes upon this ray, and let us, for want of another title (which has not been given), call him the master Paul. That is all that is appropriate to say, but know that the master Paul is upon the fourth ray now and is the one who deals mainly with its administration. He has been upon this fourth-ray work quite a long time, and he has been discussed briefly in some earlier works. The reason these great ones are not discussed more openly is that most do not have students, and attuning to them only distracts them from their work.

The master Paul, however, recognizes that because of his change in position, his more responsible, or at least more focused, approach in this fourth department makes his more visible. He has been in Hierarchy work for several hundred years, is one of the relatively newer masters taking ascension, and is devoted to the deva kingdom in great detail, to a great degree. These direct manifestations, the devas, are of course the ones with whom the Hierarchy must work in order to bring about what we have discussed earlier, the different approaches to art and music and other things. I am only giving you a glimpse into this area, but he is directly connected with them in a very special way, and this makes his work more appropriate upon this ray than any other one now. Interestingly enough, he took part in much of the devas' experiencing. (If this sounds a little unclear, it is because that is all I am allowed to say.) Know that he has much experience in this area, is very valuable; Sanat Kumara and everyone else recognizes this, and his abilities are recognized. He is our resident expert upon the deva area and kingdom, my friends.

This fourth department has worked with energy also – it deals with harmony through conflict. The conflict is the lower level, of course, and the harmony is the raised application of this type of energy now. Another effort being made by this department now is to raise this vibration as quickly as appropriate, taking into account man's evolutionary pattern – raising the fourth aspect, the fourth ray, to one of harmony in order to enter into the New Age. Because, my friends, that is what we are all doing now: focusing in upon the New Age, making a deliberate thrust into this area, seeking desperately to get everything done that must be done before it begins. It is an intense effort, more intense than any of you can even imagine. We do it with joy, and we do it well as representatives here of the Creator as designated by our own superior, whoever that may be.

The great archangel Gabriel, whom many of you have heard of, is almost like a brother to the master Paul. They are close in relationship, very specially attuned, and this is very valuable here. It is important to recognize this connection because it aids the work of this department, and it is an appropriate association when you consider what Gabriel's responsibilities are, my friends. Gabriel is a superior being, a glorious one, but different from humanity – a direct representation of the Creator who does his job superbly. He is responsible for the arts, dance, and mankind's involvement with them. The connection, actually, between what the Creator sends and what the Earth receives is Gabriel's and his helpers', the angelic kingdom, who respond to his direction, really.

Another great responsibility of this fourth department is to disseminate certain types of information from the Hierarchy through the senses. Stop and think about this. Do you ever feel a need to experience a certain emotion? Do you ever feel a need to stop and smell a beautiful flower? I am not saying that all of this comes from the fourth ray's application, but I am saying that when it is felt, the Earth has earned a more harmonious state; it has worked its way through a conflict, and it gets the harmony – the more harmonious vibrational pattern, if you will – focused through this department. This piece of information I have given you is rather important, and if you will study it, it can lead you into some very interesting analysis.

The lord Maitreya has a very direct interest in this department. There is a special connection here that is rather mystical and difficult to understand. The master Paul reports to the lord Maitreya in a very direct sense, as well as to the master Serapis. He must attune to the lord Maitreya regularly – there is a schedule here and always a basic attunement – and thus carry out instructions as given that are appropriate to aid the Earth. There is an urgency sometimes to the requests given by the lord Maitreya because of the Earth's current crises. It is appropriate to implement needed changes in energy flows as soon as possible to avoid major conflicts, so the master Paul attunes regularly and listens to instructions as given very carefully.

On Earth's highest level, this fourth ray is very harmonious, very elevated, wonderful. And at the level that it is implemented by the Hierarchy, it is a very harmonious application of energy. It is only when it reaches the Earth that it slips into conflict or division. It is really the choice of those who receive this energy to use it that way. It is certainly not directed in that manner by the members of the fourth department.

It is appropriate to recognize, my friends, that great spans of time have gone by since Sanat Kumara landed here to aid the Earth. Conditions have changed very much, and he has evolved and grown very much, so the conditions upon the Earth are different, and this department, too, reflects that. He has come through many areas of conflict within himself and almost reached a very important point that will mean a much more harmonious state for him at all times, and thus the vibrational pattern of this department is being raised constantly now. It is important to raise it a little all the time at a very gradual, accelerated rate.

As I stated in a previous section of this report, a great cry has gone out to the cosmos for more personnel to aid the Hierarchy, and a great one who understands this department has responded. His input is greatly appreciated. He gives us not even a fraction of his consciousness, and yet this fraction has enabled the work of the fourth department to speed forward as never before possible. We are all so grateful for this input that has aided in ways that are difficult for humanity to understand but are nevertheless very valid and very appreciated.

Finally, I would like to say that Sanat Kumara requires of all of his staff their focused application to their work. Master Paul gives this in a very special application. His dedication is especially great, his attunement to his work especially noteworthy. I wish to state my admiration for his work and his devotion in an area where all are devoted. He makes a very special effort here in a way that gives impetus to the Creator's Cosmic Plan. All masters are devotees of the Cosmic Plan, and his is an extra-fine attunement to it, my friends.

The Fifth Department

We now address a very important area called the fifth department. In a very special way, this important department is involved with bringing through the New Age.

Mankind in its evolutionary spiral is learning to use the mental area ever more forcefully, ever more productively, ever more greatly. And this fifth department is very involved with man and his growth at this time. Heading this area is the master Hilarion, but because of his focused attention in certain very important areas, another now shares the overall responsibility of implementing the needed work here. This master has not been known to humanity, and I introduce him to you now. He wishes to be called the master Markco. Know that we in the Hierarchy have all had many names, and so we choose the one that is either the most appropriate or, when we are dealing with humanity, the most familiar and easily recognized one. In this case, Master Markco chooses the name most appropriate for his particular focal energy pattern.

The work of this department is different from any other. The masters here have mental capacities that are very emphasized and very persuasive. While the average member of the Hierarchy can divide his conscious awareness into five areas at once, in this department the average far exceeds that — and they need it. It is an important asset that is well developed because there are so many streams of energy going out now from this great department and its present work.

The master Hilarion is implementing the New Age in a very special way. He is receding, really, from humanity, as far as contact is concerned; he was never entirely involved with them, but humanity knew of him and he had a few students. He has removed himself in order to implement the New Age. Working with Sanat Kumara and the Manu, his work is to bring forth the New Age creatively — to give the Manu, Sanat Kumara, the Buddhas and the three Kumaras who hold the energy they are working with in triangular formation the higher mental focalized energy patterns that enable the New Age to come into being.

There is a special triangular pattern that runs from the point of the three Buddhas to the Manu to the fifth department and the master Hilarion, then back again in a very special way that is not seen even in the Hierarchy. It is rather an invisible return, but certainly it is there and very important in implementing the New Age. The master Hilarion, even with his great abilities, must focus almost all of his attention upon this creativity, this marching forth of civilization, this bringing into fruition what we have all worked so long and hard for through the Manu. Then he must receive, also from the Manu, the direct input of the first aspect of the Creator — a two-way exchange. And because he is so involved with this, the master Markco takes over from him many of his former duties.

The master Markco has long been associated with the mental focus, but only now is it appropriate for man to know a little bit more about him and his work. He has had students, but they didn't know him by name and they were not in physical incarnation. They have been those who were already a part of the Hierarchy and were studying the fifth department to increase the mental focus they already had. Because the members of this department are so very developed in creativity and the higher mental areas, many of the Hierarchy study this area with them and develop their greater abilities measurably in this area, and I appreciate his patience with one who always was interested in so many things that it was difficult to focus in one area. I learned this from him and I am forever grateful to him. As the New Age comes closer, the master Markco will become more involved in assisting the master Hilarion with his work, because it will take both of them to bring it into being. But right now he oversees the rest of the fifth department. There is a gathering here now of these great beings — these greatly mentally capable beings — and a great input into this area from the Manu and from the three Kumaras, whose mental abilities of course are very developed also. A great degree of Sanat Kumara's thrust effort is being made here too. And the call sent out by the Hierarchy to the cosmos has attracted several other great ones who now concentrate their efforts. For it is a great effort to bring forth the New Age. It is marvelous and it is done with joy and love, but it is a great effort to create a beautiful new age in which we can now live.

The master Markco also directs all of the scientific pursuits going on at present in the world. Impetus is given in the areas that humanity needs for its more rapid growth. Scientific principles are put forth which are then picked up by several advanced beings upon the Earth, and that is why, when a new scientific breakthrough is made, it might be made at more than one location upon the Earth. It is picked up from the higher mental area in a very special way by those who are able to receive it. Also, the master Markco is at present doing a special type of scientific research — that is, he directs the forces of the Creator to implement this research. There are a few advanced disciples upon the Earth who are aiding him, and they are not willing to be identified at this time because they fear that the knowledge will impede their efforts. Although he is a very busy master now, the master Markco has agreed that you can attune to him, if you call upon him by name in a state of meditation and use the color orange to aid the identification you are making with this great department.

The creative and higher abilities are very important, and we of the Hierarchy are very anxious to see mankind launched from the scientific or logical point to the higher creative mental point. A very important part of this department's work is to launch humanity into the intuitive, beyond the concrete, beyond the scientific and into the higher mental area now. So attune to the master Markco, calling upon him by name, and ask for aid in this regard.

You can even do it in a triangular configuration, seeing yourself as one point of the triangle, and your own master – whoever he may be, or you can call upon me – at another point of the triangle. Begin the flow between the three points of the triangle – beautiful, vibrant blue energy. Energize this triangle, my friends, and wait. You will feel an influx of energy and know that it is aiding you in this area. The higher mental is divided, with the creative abilities being aided, and the intuitive abilities that can be developed to a higher degree by this triangular influx of energy.

The master Markco came up through humanity's ranks just as you are doing. He had a long series of lives upon the Earth in which he experienced, learned and struggled and finally freed himself just as all of you are doing. He has had several prominent lives, but his availability to mankind is being emphasized now to increase man's evolutionary rate – to speed it up in the higher mental and intuitive areas. It is an opportunity that should not be missed.

The fifth department is very definitely connected with the first. This is necessary because the Earth needs these two types of energy together to progress past a launching of the New Age. It will be launched, my friends – that is inevitable – and what we are seeking to do is launch it as easily and in as joyous a manner as possible, and in as advanced a state as possible. So the connection between these two energies, these two departments, is very close now. It is closer than it has been for quite a while, and closer than it will be at a later time.

Recognizing this, you must see that the Manu has increased responsibilities also, and because of this, many disciples are being utilized in as forthright, effective and complete a manner as possible – particularly those who have abilities in the first and fifth departments. Those upon the Earth who can possibly do anything in these areas are being called forth and asked to serve as completely as they can and are willing to do. We do not ask anyone to do anything they are not willing to do; it must be on a volunteer basis. When each disciple reaches a point of commitment to the Hierarchy – to the Creator and His Cosmic Plan – they are called upon with intensity, much more than ever before, in order to be creative in launching forth the New Age.

In a very special sense, the cosmos watches our efforts. The Earth is a small, dark planet of relative unimportance compared to the totality of creation, but it is watched carefully to see how we utilize some very special gifts given to us by the Creator, some very special energies that are being spun down for our use. The Creator is doing some "experimentation" (but certainly not in any sort of a negative connotation) to see how evolution can be speeded up, giving some suggestions, sending forth this fifth aspect of Itself in a very intense application. It is being stepped down, then, from the very highest level to the Hierarchy with intensity and is being utilized to bring about this New Age in as advanced a way as possible.

The department is doing very well. They we making the effort ever more intensely, and with joy, my friends, are they doing it. This department's efforts are very vast, although very focalized at the same time, and we are only touching here on some of them.

The Sixth Department

We are going to talk about the sixth department here, remembering that, like the fifth, the sixth also comes from the great area directed by the Mahachohan. The one whom we associate with this department is the master Jesus, the one who served as the physical vehicle for the Christ, the lord Maitreya, in a great sacrificial act, enabling the Christ to work through the most suitable body possible for his work upon the Earth.

He took his fifth initiation as Apollonius of Tyana. He is a very special being, one who gives to the Hierarchy strength, will and purpose. Of course everyone in the Hierarchy has purpose, but his is very strong and especially appreciated during this critical transitional period on the Earth.

This department has been directing the Christian religion since its advent through the Christ, and the master Jesus still retains this work, seeking always to emphasize the higher aspects of the religious activity. He seeks to integrate at this time the Christian thought and principles with those from Eastern schools and philosophies, and he works with the masses at a very high level to do this. He is assisted by many in this regard, knowing that when this synthesis can be completed, the sixth department will begin to blend in many areas. This great sixth ray will become less prevalent on the Earth as this blending continues to take place.

The master Jesus is known as a very strict and stern master, and his pupils have found this to be true. However, it is not a negative quality at all; it is simply his manner of operation and his understanding of the Creator's energy flow as it comes to and through him. Know, my friends, that each member of the Hierarchy interprets the energy patterns within himself differently. This is certainly valid and it gives a balance to the Hierarchy that would not be otherwise possible. So the sixth department interprets the need to approach things in a way that is different from any other department right now.

In the recent history of the Earth, this department has had a greater direct association with the Earth than any other department. Thus the need for someone such as Jesus with this vibrational pattern to serve as the physical vehicle for the Christ. When Jesus served here the results were for the most part successful, though he did not accomplish everything that he sought to do. But by his great love he enabled possibilities that were never here before.

The master Jesus has special abilities in the will aspect. You might be surprised to hear me talk about the will aspect in reference to the sixth department, but if you give it some consideration you will understand. Many within the Christian religion use the will in a less-than-positive way, but when it is done in a completely positive way as Jesus did, it enables special progress now.

The sixth department is in a transitional stage, and yet a focused effort is going on. They are in a sense finishing up. You might equate it to moving from your home (though this department will not move physically; it is just a change of focus). When you are moving, you clean out the area, do you not? This department is doing that — cleaning out the area while completing the final stages of its work and while work is also beginning in the new stages. It is a cleaning-out process and resettling of the new at the same time.

This makes the focus required in this department especially important, and so the will aspect of Jesus and his associates is very useful. They must be able to focus completely on what they are doing and, at the same time, allow the new work to come in and, when they can, use a focused approach to it also. Others are beginning this work, but the sixth department area is being used and the sixth department will take over some of the new work as soon as they have finished the old.

The great transition work will not be finished until the beginning of the New Age, but as we approach the New Age there will be a leaping period — an intense period when the department will call upon the Hierarchy, Sanat Kumara and those who have come to the aid of the Earth for one final surge of complete focusing. Many on the Earth will be called upon for help at that time also.

The work is building in intensity now while the energy is diminishing, and this is rather a paradox. So it will take a blending of all of the departments of the Hierarchy to complete the work of this department at this time. And of course they do it with joy, and they bring down the sixth ray from the higher levels in a final great thrust before withdrawing some of this energy until a later date. I estimate that the period of this great thrust will peak about ten years in the future.

Again I say the master Jesus is an outstanding example of how to be as aligned with the Creator as possible and still be a representative of love. Just because one has great love does not mean one can abdicate responsibility to serve the Creator in as exact a way as possible. That is what the master Jesus does: serves with exactitude. His staff is equally dedicated, and because of the nature of his work, many of them are serving without recognition on the Earth plane. Many, but not by any means all, are serving within the government of the Catholic Church.

In addition to the work of synthesizing the religions of the world, the sixth department is involved with the devas. These direct manifestations of the Creator do what is necessary to implement the turning point in the evolutionary spiral of the Earth. The sixth department assists with this turning point, this critical position which needs to be focused and brought forth now.

Since the Christ, the lord Maitreya, depends now on the master Jesus for so many projects on the Earth, the master Jesus does not work much with students anymore. Some still receive instructions directly from him but most have passed to the great seventh department as it assumes more and more responsibility.

It takes more specialization to serve in the sixth department than in any other. They are specialists. When you consider that soon they are to do a different kind of work, you can understand how sacrificial their work is. They will have to change a great deal from this specialized focus to another. This indicates the devotional nature of this department — complete devotion of one's energies to one purpose, changing oneself to serve with fervor and with complete dedication here, knowing that eventually the focus will be changed and one must change self to serve in the next department in such a dedicated manner.

One thing I wish to point out to all of you is that the interpretation of truth varies, and this is as true in the area of spiritual government as it is in earthly government. Different masters interpret their work differently. They may perceive colors and their uses differently. They train their students differently and do their work differently. There is no right or wrong way to do the Creator's work, and each master brings to the Earth his own unique interpretation, his own blend of energy patterns. The balance thus produced in the Hierarchy is the key to evolution. Therefore Earth beings must realize that their particular master's approach will be different from the others, and they will get from different masters different opinions on the same question. This is not a case of separation within the Hierarchy. It is a case of balance.

Because of the current position of the Earth in its evolutionary spiral, the sixth department balances the Hierarchy now. In a sense, it is as if the sixth department is sitting at one end of a see-saw and all the others are on the other end — the sixth is balancing the others. This is because of the current position of the Earth and Sanat Kumara. Later a different department will balance the Hierarchy. This makes necessary the intense focus I spoke of.

The Seventh Department

Now we will discuss the seventh department of the spiritual government, the department that comes more and more into prominence because of the approaching New Age. The one who heads this area is the master R. He has long been associated with this area and has been building in his responsibilities toward the coming period. Because of the vast importance of this department, it is now being staffed by many more masters. The activity is joyous because of the coming New Age, which all greatly anticipate.

The master R. is also known as St. Germain, but in some ways this is erroneous. Some of the material given about St. Germain is not true, and there is more than one entity involved here: one who is a very elevated master and one who is not. So when you attune to the master St. Germain be sure you have the right one, or you may encounter some difficulties with what you expect from a master and what you experience. That is all the information available on this right now, but if he is your teacher, attune to him and he will explain further. I prefer to use the name Master R. and will do so in connection with this great being.

Previous to the last ten years the master R. occupied himself with administrative work within the Hierarchy because the time to work in his specialty had not yet begun. Since then this has changed drastically. He works now for the New Age, knowing that when it comes, his responsibilities will increase tenfold. He has much to do to prepare for this time and is studying a great deal to understand what is coming. Know that all of the masters in the Hierarchy can see far enough ahead to do very long-range planning and make the necessary preparations in advance for whatever line of work they are going to be doing in the foreseeable future.

A lot is going on in the seventh department. Being coordinated now on the highest level are the increasing energy patterns coming to the Earth. The Earth has received five higher rays since the mid-1970s. The seventh department of the Hierarchy is concerned with bringing through these energy patterns, along with the seventh ray itself. These energies come to the Earth via Sanat Kumara; they come to Shamballa, from where they are channeled to the seventh department. There, some of the breaking down is done, some of the intensity is removed so that the energy is suitable to be distributed throughout the Earth.

The various members of the department share this responsibility. They work in specific ways that are not available for publication because they could be misused by those not attuned to the Cosmic Plan. However, they work with this energy distribution constantly and diligently, knowing that it is an important thrust, that it brings the Earth closer to the New Age, that it is one of the more important means of reaching the New Age. Remember that this entire range of rays comes through Sanat Kumara directly. He grows, he evolves through it, getting ready for his important thrust forward to grow and become greater.

Because of Sanat Kumara's efforts in self-growth, he has earned the aid of those who work with him — his teachers. One of these very great ones, a member of the Universal Hierarchy, directs these higher-ray energies directly from himself to Sanat Kumara. This is a very high source. These energies are very powerful and are given because of Sanat Kumara's efforts.

But you could say that the Earth has been given them with joy by the Creator.

The master R.'s ability to work with these higher energies is very much appreciated. He does it because of a certain delicacy of approach which enables manipulation of areas that normally resist manipulation. I have watched him on many occasions, my friends, and marveled at his finesse and his ability in this area. As a student of energy I have looked everywhere to learn how to work with energies, and he has helped me immensely, showing me subtle ways to enhance the area being manipulated.

It is very interesting that the more finesse the master R. uses in his manipulation of these higher energies, the more energy is able to be channeled through and the greater the spiral forward made by the Earth. He is a critical point now in bringing in the New Age, and most of his time now is spent working with these higher energies.

Many people on the Earth are familiar with the master R., but only a few know him as he really is. They understand only one aspect of him — the St. Germain phase. He is much bigger, much greater than what has been revealed in the area of St. Germain. His competency has earned him the right to go wherever he wishes, to leave the Hierarchy of the Earth. His services would be very valuable in much vaster network governments, but he has chosen to remain here, at least until after his major responsibility of setting up this New Age energywise has been completed. He may reassess later as the offers continue to pour in. Because, my friends, hierarchic governments are just like Earth governments: When they see someone in another government doing a very good job, they seek to acquire his services with certain offers, certain opportunities. That is what is offered in hierarchic governments — nothing personal, but a way to serve in a greater scope. Thus, many take the opportunity when it is offered by another government, knowing they have earned it and it will enhance their service to the Cosmic Plan.

The master R. has thus far turned down such offers. His love of the Earth, his dedication to Sanat Kumara and his growth pattern have been holding him here. He has worked in the hierarchic government for quite some time, although an aspect of him worked on the Earth when he was already qualified to go into the Hierarchy. This was true because of his special vibrational pattern, which enabled Sanat Kumara to work through an especially heavy area for himself with the master R.'s help.

Know that several of the others masters have done this when necessary — sent an aspect of themselves to incarnate upon this Earth in order to flow a special stream of their energy directly to Sanat Kumara. From their experience a learning experience has gone directly to our Planetary Logos, enabling him to grow extremely rapidly. These are rather sacrificial acts by each of these great beings — the willingness to serve upon the Earth although they have earned the right to move on. These lives are usually painful, usually blocked and always unrecognized by humanity. This is because the completeness of their being is not there – only a certain aspect of themselves – and the result is an imbalance. They are not recognized by humanity as being very evolved; on the contrary, they seem quite immersed and unbalanced. I could give you one or two names of such beings that would surprise you. Of course, the great beings like the Christ and the Buddha also made a sacrifice for Sanat Kumara, but they did it in a balanced state.

Being trained at present to take over as many of the responsibilities as possible from the master R. are two unknown masters (by that I mean humanity doesn't know them). I will not identify them except as the masters A and B.

On the inner planes many who have been working with the master R. are now being trained by the masters A and B. They are a recent addition to the Hierarchy but have been specially trained for their jobs and are very proficient in them. They were rather latecomers on this Earth, but they spiraled forward very rapidly. Sometime in the future I will give information explaining how they achieved so much in such a short time.

Masters A and B are closely associated and have been all through their evolutionary cycle. When they were still in their monadic state (spiritual aspect), they became acquainted with each other and made a pact that they would remain together as much as possible – at least attuned to each other – whether or not they were in physical incarnations at the same time. They have kept it, my friends, even in between lives, and they have worked together and have always been attuned. They are not twin souls. It is just an affinity they feel for each other on such a deep and basic level that it has led them into the same hierarchic work together.

I would like to point out that the fourth and the seventh departments are related in a special way, and the masters of these departments work closely together. If you know the rays, you can think that through. By analyzing this material given you will learn a great deal about the Hierarchy and a great deal about yourself. Also you can aid your analytical qualities, my friends.

I hope you use this information I have given on the Hierarchy as a springboard for your knowledge. If you have question, ask directly, or attune to those who are your teachers and ask them. I certainly have done this often. You would be surprised how often you are given the answers when you ask.

Thank you, my friends.

◆ PART FIVE ◆

INTEGRATIVE TECHNIQUES

Atlanto, 1985

✧ O N E ✧

Integrative Techniques

W E ARE GOING TO DO MANY THINGS IN THIS GROUP PROCESS, BUT FIRST of all we are going to attune to what is possible, what is almost available to the next step. You stretch for it, reach for it and bring it in, and it stimulates and opens the chakra system. It is a focus that allows what you are ready to receive to begin coming in. It is a stretch and a recognition that you are bringing the energy in. Now reach to the radiant core as much as you can! Recognize that it is there! Bring it in and put it in the heart area!

What we've done is attune you to the next level that is ready to come in, and to the radiant core, the center of that perception. How does it feel? Is there an excitement, a sense of readiness, of opening? It is there, even if you don't recognize it. We are going to bring you many integrative techniques and show you how to use them in a way that will make integration practical. We will look at the steps toward this practical integration.

We can say that integration is the bringing together of various perspectives. Or we can say that it is allowing these perspectives to communicate in a way that increases your understanding. Integration is truly a shared communication that allows greater understanding. Our Source is truly the integrative process. Our Source is integration. It is a perspective that comes together from various facets of Itself that share; and thus It evolves. It has communicated and allowed each perspective to be part of Itself; nothing is denied or set apart. Each perspective is welcomed and brought in so that what might not have been immediately understood can blend as each learns from another within the whole.

I want you to get a sense of this beyond sequential time. Suppose you stand together to form a circle, and I move into the center of it and allow each of you to put your own perspective into the circle. I communicate with each of you with equal energy or life force, but not necessarily in the same way. To one I might say, "Dear one, allow me to help you see who you are, in order that your identification of self will be clearer to you." To another I might say, "Let us slide down a mountain together — we do that so well together." Or I might say to someone, "Let's format a new beginning. I have some colors here — will you share that with me?" Or "Let's go into an alternate reality. Let's see beyond what you have formatted. Let's go behind the mirror and let the mirror open so that you can see that portion you have not yet seen." As you can see, I will communicate in a way that is particularly meaningful for you. I am able — and so are you — to give equal time and equal opportunity to all of you in a communicative sense. Integration, then, is a willingness to share equally with every communicative opportunity in order that a cohesive whole may come from this effort.

Integration is many-faceted, and I shall be looking at a great many of those facets as we proceed. I have my own methods of teaching and want you to get acquainted with them. I love questions, because they open up so much. I invite you all to channel me, to work with me in your own unique way. Equal time is available for everyone. As you integrate, you will sense that truly there is always enough time. So often in your lives, time seems "jammed up." Many of you are looking forward to going into the fourth dimension so you can use time differently. The key to that is sensing the equality of existence. That puts you in the fourth dimension. There is a sense of movement that is needed for integration. What is not necessarily sequential movement does, on the physical, become sequential. This movement is a focus, an intensity, an identification — an "energy burst," so to speak — upon the cosmic planes, and there are many levels of cosmic awareness. I want to talk to you about these levels of universal consciousness which you can bring in to aid you on the physical plane.

These levels of consciousness are bursts that ignite, so that you have energy going out in every direction. The burst I activated here with you sends the message out to each of you. When the message is spoken it seems sequential, but it is not. There is a burst of energy going out from this level of universal consciousness and becoming available on the physical plane. From this burst of energy you can bring back to yourself whatever you are capable of bringing back. The opportunity is there to bring back everything! Universal levels of consciousness are literally unending.

We'll use the symbol of a ladder. It seems to go up forever as you climb it. It doesn't matter which rung of the ladder you're standing on, you've now stretched upward toward the next rung above you. That burst of energy that we began with has brought that next level into the physical. This burst of universal consciousness goes forth and it needs to be shared. That is the only way universal consciousness works. It needs to be shared, for it is not an individual process. You cannot grasp it and hold it. If you tried you would find it slips out of your grasp — a bit here and a bit there — sharing itself with others. This bursting, this moving out, when you allow it to flow through you in a balanced process of sharing and going forth, establishes a balancing base from which to receive.

You are all trying to receive from the universe the potential of your next step. You try to share with each other in a way that shows you how you fit within the whole Plan. It is a very delicate balancing system that says, "Yes, I'm willing to grasp from the universe the next step for me." That act of desire – of cosmic desire from the heart center – is the generator, the beginning point. Every bit of cosmic energy used by you comes from the heart center. You reach, then, from the heart center with your desire to be because you are a creator. Can you see that this is an individual reflection of Source Itself – the beginning that is always beginning? The Source reached from the heart center and It generated a connection with the next level and brought it back into the heart center. It ignited. It went forth. Each of you is seeking to establish that clear basis from which to go forth.

As we go on you will find some parts of the material talks to you more than other parts. Each of you has an awareness that relates to existence in a particular way. Remember this: Source is flexible. You are flexible; you are adaptable. As you relate individually to what I bring you, there will be an adjustment. Movement, dance, on the physical plane is what we might call the flexibility of Source – the flexibility of Source Itself moving and adapting to the conditions that are being generated through the heart center. If you tried to stand still and be rigid (which you can't), there would be distortion. You would get out of balance and when the universe sent you something, you wouldn't get the correct message. Sometimes the mental body can be so busy cataloging all the activity going on that if someone says softly, "I love you," the message won't register, even though you want to know of that love. Where there is a separation in the four-body system, the opportunity is only partially grasped and acceptance is not reflected back.

Acceptance – full acceptance – is an integrative point. If you sense separation occurring, then there must be movement – the flexibility that brings an alignment. Communication is the key. You must know and understand yourself so well that the spiritual intent, the desire of spirit to be balanced and integrated, is matched by your mental ability to analyze and to sense structure, by your emotional desire to flow, and by your physical strengths – which must be strong. Unity, the sharing of the four-body system, allows them to come together; this is integration. It happens through movement, through flexibility, through adjustment. You enjoy physical movement and it is important to the integrative process.

We are going to stand now and each of you will choose a place, not too close to one another. See yourself as the center of a structure. You are a structure – the structure of your auric field: etheric, mental, emotional and spiritual. Now move a little and be aware of life force – almost like a puppet on a string. The string is the auric field and the puppeteer is the soul level. (The soul is within; of course, we are creating a symbolic picture.) The universal energy – here specifically the soul – is creating the movement. The consciousness of the universal level is directing the physical level. Now place a perspective of that universal consciousness within the heart area. The heart is the generator for the physical level. It is physical, but it is also etheric. Move now and sense as you move that there is something going on in the heart. You know there is the heartbeat, its rhythm, but really there is a burst – burst – burst, a sweeping burst – a sweeping burst – a sweeping burst. This is the life force in action. It is how your life is generated. The heart has the radiant core. There is a burst that uses, that expands, the life force. It sends it forth.

The Sweeping Process

There is a sweep – that is the point of all this. The sweep is the identification process of Source Itself. The Source wants to know. The desire to understand and learn is universal. As that burst goes forth, it lights up the universe for Sourceness. It looks and learns as It sweeps consciousness out into the universe. It will look and learn and relate and interrelate and caress and cherish and love and nurture and understand and communicate in every way. Now, the burst and sweep are not sequential – in Source there is the capability to simultaneously burst and sweep all that is in consciousness. I bring you this concept to help you see that every time your heart beats, with every breath you take, you are sending life force to the universe. You are sending out the quality of the heart whether or not you consciously recognize it.

For those of you who have decided to be channels, and those who are already channels, here is an exercise to try. Let us say you are connecting your channel. There is a process that multiplies the way the message goes out to the universe. In one sense you are always channeling, of course. But there are different amounts of life force, different levels of consciousness, that are ignited through the amount of connection you currently have in your channel. If you are channeling me or someone like me, you have connected into the ignition, the bursting-and-sweeping process of the cocreator level. Think how important that can be for you in your evolution. What is the cocreator level? Well, you've heard it said in many ways, and I shall give you another now. It is the cosmic sweeping system of all that is being presented to you in the universe at this time. Which is not all, of course; there is, within the "storage system" of the Source Itself, all of Its unlimited potential. It is exploring only a fraction of what It now is; but in your connection with those of us who understand and represent a unified integration of the system, you are able to begin generating through your heart that integrated or cocreator response.

We (including those of you reading this lesson) are going to participate together in an experiment. Sit quietly and comfortably, with your feet flat on the floor. Have available some uninterrupted music that, for you, stimulates the heart center. I am going to place what I am within your channel. We are going to flow a lot of energy through you. It will flow into the Earth through what Vywamus calls the opening of the bottom of your feet. We are going to do sweeping, too, and will use music to facilitate it. I will lead you through this experience now as the music plays.

🐾 *Sense an energy that is present. This is the life force. This is life force coming through you now. It sweeps down through the system, generated from the cocreator level. It enters the crown chakra. You can feel it; you can sense it. It is within the channel of your awareness. It bursts forth. It identifies itself and then it continues to flow. The crown chakra is opening, opening and adjusting, becoming aware of who it is for perhaps the first time. A cosmic opening! The next step! You have grasped the next step and thus the crown chakra opens to receive the life force. Sense that energy as being connected, connected into every possible point of view. There is a multiple connection; a sense of energy that flows completely, that is moving sometimes a lot of energy and then a fine strand of energy. There is an infinite variety of ways in which this enters the crown chakra. Know it is flowing through you and through your feet. Emphasis is on the crown chakra – notice its adjustment, its movement. It is connected in all possible locations. The circle of the universal level is inputting completely into your crown chakra. We are now broadening the way the whole is inputting. There is a specific connection, and it is important to recognize it. The universal link is there – the structure within which the whole may input. Sense this universality, this opening into the framework of your individuality and your specific spiritual linkage system – a broadening, an impetus, a coming together, an integration.*

🐾 *Sense now the music as it links you in a way you have not been linked before. At times it slows, does it not? There is a need to integrate the sound of the music into physicality. The slowing down of the universal level allows it to work specifically for you on the physical plane. You can sense the adjustments as the energy pours through the crown chakra and becomes a generator within the heart area.*

🐾 *Note now the third-eye chakra and sense the movement there: this is an integrative center. There is a lot going on – a knocking, a seeking to integrate and come into a clearer perspective. Remember, within the whole there are specifics, and you are connected very specifically. Through that specific connection you are opening up to the whole. Thus your channel is connected in a way that creates a structure so you may receive and perceive now. You need the structure. You need that security – that specific security structure – to have a foundation within which to receive the whole and to balance; otherwise you receive in a manner not specific enough to use well. So there is a sense of specificness, but it generates a sweeping multilevel effect. In this multilevel reception you sweep now in consciousness.*

🐾 *You sweep now into the throat area. There is a movement in the throat area.*

The specifics are there, but they are moving, they are flowing, they are moving through the throat – the movement through the throat into the heart area. The heart gathers momentum; the heart moves; it generates a flow – a radiant flow that is growing. You feel united within that flow. It is the generator that is sending out to the universe the burst you have received. It comes in through the crown and now it flows out to the universe, expanding, expanding. This is the means by which you are able to use an integrated approach to your Creator. You receive, you connect, you build a structure, and then through the generator of the heart – the core of the heart, that expansive area – that bursting process itself goes forth.

❧ Now get in touch (beyond the chakra system) with the fact that you have four bodies participating in the exercise. Note the specifics: Adjust the emotional body within the heart area; now adjust the mental body within the heart area; adjust now the spiritual body within the heart area. As you do this it comes together and there is an increase in the flow, a balance in the flow, a surge within the flow, that sweeps again, generating energy that is very specific and yet broadly based. It is sweeping out and allowing this sweep to be constant. You might say it is going through the musical scale, through every octave, going through possibilities and bringing them in, allowing them to be generative to the universe – the universe as well as yourself.

❧ Generating, generating, generating – hear the generator working! Hear it in the music! Hear the generator working! The process continues. It goes into the solar plexus where there is a lot going on. There is a lot of sorting-out in this area, a lot of redefining and of seeing what is coming in and seeing how and where to use it. There is a lot of flow there. "This goes here and that goes there, and we'll generate more and we'll put it over here." A sense of sorting comes through the solar plexus center. It is not necessarily an area that generates difficulties. It is a sorting and aligning process – a deciding of how to use the energy. It is the process of doing all that! Thus you begin to see that it is all coming together in a way that it never has before, because you have accessed the whole cocreator area – a wide area – very specifically. You've allowed it! Listen to the music. It is going to new levels of understanding as never before. It flows now. It harmonizes. It is flowing well – coming together.

❧ Now we go to the polarity area, the generative center, in a very basic way. It gets down to the use of the receptive and dynamic energies. They flow together smoothly, uniting and flowing, and we get to the base chakra. There is a sense of cosmic understanding and awareness that allows an exploring of the base chakra – a basic foundation that opens up exploration. It goes very quickly into another level as this area also sorts out and allows a stability to be built through it. Certainly through all of this the energy is flowing into the Earth and the Earth is receiving it. Look at the Earth now and sense a more stable Earth – the energy of the cocreator level flowing through you and expanding all over the Earth.

🐦 *Look at the cities now – look at all the cities on the North American continent. Look at them. Look at the North American continent. Look at several cities and see the connection between them, see the integrative process that is taking place in North America. Look at the various cities and the shifting perspectives, the blending, the dance. What sort of dance is she doing? Look at that. What is the movement, and how can you help it? How can you help to blend this dancing process in North America? Now we go to South America. Listen to it. Listen to the dance of South America. See what is going on. Look at the various cities.*

🐦 *I ask you now to hold in mind a city, a city that you know, a city in which you have had an experience that you haven't really looked at. Attune to one and see what you can bring forth from your four-body system regarding it. I will bring in a mirroring from the cocreator level and I'd like you to put the specific experience of that city within it. Have some paper and a pencil available, and try to get a few comments down about what each of the four bodies contributes and what you can integrate from the overall view. I want to get a very specific sense of what is going on with each of you as the mirroring takes place within the four-body system. This might be very cosmic. Attune to that city and to all of what you experienced there. There is always a specific content to a connection that allows an expansion, or allows you to get beyond the specifics, but you need the specifics in order to stimulate a recognition of something beyond. So the city is the area of specificity that I'd like to use as a stimulus of the cocreator level. Remember, however, it is only passing through that specific area. You may work with a partner if you wish, for I can radiate through your partner and it will penetrate to the core of each particular body's perspective. The partner is reflecting not my energy, but the energy of the whole as it comes through your specific city. Integration is progressive on the physical level, and you can keep gathering it in until it "talks to you," or until it becomes that radiant core of energy that ignites, splashes out, or sweeps out. You keep looking for the integrative process until it gets, as Vywamus would say, very electrical in nature. When it gets to that point where it ignites, then you've gathered enough so you can recognize it. This doesn't mean that integration isn't taking place as you allow the stimulation that's come to you from the whole.*

You have done very well with this exercise. Two of you tuned into two separate lifetimes in your city or area; you both tuned to one lifetime as a male and one as a female. This is interesting, for when you open up to integration you are going to get seeming opposites to reconcile, because you are sending out into the universe, and the return comes in a multiple way. One person came up with a need for introspection. What is introspection? For me it is a unit of Sourceness that has a valid perspective within which to integrate. If you use it to perceive the personality self, see that level for what it is: a part of the Source. And don't negate that perspective or deemphasize it so much that it is no longer an integrative center. The personality self needs enough emphasis that it can integrate, but not so much that it shuts down the whole system.

Another person experienced our exercise quite differently. The mental body was arrogant and not communicating with the spiritual body, and the emotional body was afraid and didn't want any part of the whole thing, but there was an overall impression of needing to be involved in group efforts. There certainly is a need for the putting together of perspectives into a group, whether the group is called "self" or "humanity" or is an organized group of any kind. There is in a group a pooling of abilities and an opportunity to see that the universe really will run in and share with you. Some of the perspectives that run in may seem a little antagonistic or insecure, but the running-in process is what we call integration. Integration is a sharing, a caring. It is a sharing even if what is being shared is not yet clearly understood. If a child were to come into this room right now, crying or angry or unsure about what's going on here, he might be mentally curious but not yet able to conceive of himself as spiritually open. Yet the minute that child comes through the door, the group energy begins to incorporate what has come in, whatever its perspective is. It doesn't matter how seemingly limited that perspective is; there has been an opening for the group vehicle. Certainly you will understand what has happened mentally and spiritually, but for many of you there is also an emotional acceptance of the occurrence without getting stuck in it. Enjoy getting a perspective that doesn't seem to fit. It means you are going to get into a whole new way of relating to who and what you are. Don't see it as adversarial; see it as a fresh perspective. Even if it's on an old theme, it's a new perspective that you can then integrate. Integrating is such fun! Even if there are seeming stresses, note that these stresses are simply the adjustment of the group vehicle in regard to what is seeking to come in and be a part of the group. There is then an opening to an organized effort to see what really will help you spiritually to open to the next step: an opening to better accepting the emotional content of life — which means a perception of life at its richest and most fulfilling.

As we go into meditation, take your divine intent, or your desire to aid others, and place it in your heart. Imagine, if you will, a ball of golden energy going into your heart. It is rather like visualizing an inner sun in your heart. Use your heart as a focus. Seek to be consciously aware of this sun during the whole meditation. You will find it interesting, for it will radiate — it will move. There will be movement that you can follow. I provide a focus for you, but you need an inner focus that identifies that the experience you are in is real for you. You are really within that experience. You might drift away from the focus, but be patient with yourself and develop that. I think the inner sun connection will be very helpful for you.

Meditation with Music

❦ As we hear the harmonious sounds of singing, we realize it is supported by the other sounds that are present also. Harmony is present through an intricate structure; this is integration. Listen to it – harmony in many ways, point and counterpoint coming forth now, a flow that explores. You get into this flow and begin to explore with your own consciousness. Go deeply within it now. Hear and sense the flow as completely as possible. Hear and sense all of it from every point of view. Take your consciousness into this sound and expand through it. The generative core expands. Listen to this expansion. Listen to the support system within it. Remember, this is true integration; this listening to all of the parts, hearing them and being responsive to all of them. The flow and the dynamic content of the message that is there: get beyond the dynamic content into the support, the corresponding message from the whole. The dynamic connection is the way to get into the larger picture – study it and sense the adjustment within it – not only the flow but also the adjustment and the lovingness of the very dynamic content. You don't always think of the two together, but it is there as part of the support system of this dynamic flow. It is the background of love against which it flows, the background of trust which develops, the background of Source. It is interrelatedness; it is radiant; it is the cocreator level. Yes, listen to the various parts; listen as they speak and respond to one another, as they move freely in a certain perspective, supported by each other – the cocreator level expressing harmoniously, sometimes softly, sometimes dynamically. Even when expressed softly there is, within the whole, another dynamic expression that is speaking. It is my voice. Do you hear it? It is responding, point and counterpoint, to the sounds that are built into the music. The loving aspect and the dynamic aspect – both are emphasized in the music. Sense that! This is what you do! Whatever the universe provides, or is gearing into you, you express a balance counterpoint to it, so that a whole may be experienced and expressed. Without you it is not complete. It needs this counterpointing within all of existence. You are meant to be this counterpoint of Sourceness which makes the integrative state complete.

Come back now, realizing just a little more what it means to be a cocreator. What you have been doing as a counterpoint or, literally, a generative point within the cocreator level is expressed dynamically, lovingly, or perhaps as a combination, in an integrated way. You are the integrated covenant of Sourceness expressing in a manner that allows completion.

Visualizing the Integrative Process

I have some drawings (pages 326 & 329) that I want you to see. These drawings are of an integrative process. The first diagram represents an interpretation of the beginning of the cosmic day presently being experienced – we will say the Source-level stimulation of a cosmic day. I want to stimulate for you a beginning.

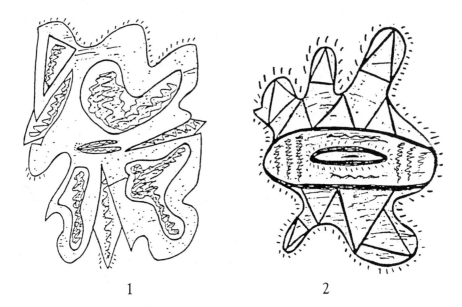

1   2

Now, if you look at this without mentally appraising it, but with all elements of viewing, what comes to your consciousness? You are aware of centers throughout the whole from which growth moves within the cosmic day. Good! The Source delegates activity like a good administrator. You see, there are infinite possibilities here to watch and study as they develop. The Source is never dull; there is always a stimulation of interest through what is presented. There is here an integrative process of discovering what is there but not at first seen. It is an inclusive, not an exclusive, process even though not all is visible yet. Although there is a general sense of direction and intent, the direction is not yet one of specifics. It represents a new beginning. There is a sense of a flowing within the energy pattern; there is nothing static; there is a flowing of forward movement, but not yet a streaming outward.

What advantage does this type of graph have over a spiral? The spiral is a stereotyped structure; it doesn't seem as free to move its energy out where it will. To me, this is closer than the spiral to what structure really is on the divine level. I feel that the spiral has come to be perceived as something you have to be a part of, a limiting structure; this to me is a misrepresentation. The overall design for this cosmic day is certainly present in it, but each aspect of Source is open to choice, and therefore open to more freedom and variety of expression. There are many ways to indicate graphically how evolution is taking place. The more freely the graph suggests that all its parts are self-creative, self-generative and open to as-yet-unknown manifestations, the better.

The first drawing relates to the Earth as it was in the beginning. The second drawing represents the Earth at about the time of Lemuria. You will see a progression. While in the first diagram the content, though inherently dynamic, was not yet streaming forth, here it is being much more fully explored. The colors and lines show there is now a more complete grasp of what it is. What do you notice about the structure in the second diagram? As your Earth began, it was a free-flowing concept of Source Itself. As choices began to be made by all the kingdoms on Earth, a certain structuring formed from these choices. The human kingdom began to see guidelines. The divine guidelines, of course, were much greater, but humanity had gained a sense of what worked out well and what didn't — or what was "right" and "wrong." Human choice set up the idea of boundaries, but at the center of the diagram, circles within circles show pulsing energy — unlimited possibilities yet to be experienced and integrated. Earth had moved through growth to the pre-Lemurian level. Why did it then become a battleground? You can tell by looking at the diagram: The center is coming in contact with the structure itself, and there appears to be an opposition between the structure and the radiant qualities — that is what set up the conflict. The ones who chose ways of "right" and "wrong" in terms of how the Earth should be used were humanity.

The electrical ones, who were magnetically attracted, came in with the overall ideal of sharing. Within the human ranks, however, there was not an understanding of how to expand this center to allow their existing structural understanding to fit into the concept that was being brought to them by the electrical ones. There was a jamming of structural input, and from that a conflict was set up that became global in nature. Because it jammed, this went on for five hundred years. Humanity kept going through that door and going around and around and around. It is interesting that there were times when that warlike state tried to end but humanity wouldn't let it end. Quite literally this is so, because this structure was seen only as a conflicting and opposing idea. Finally a group within humanity got together and said, We are really tired of this war that's been going on for generations. Let's ask the electrical ones to join us! It took communication and negotiation. The electrical ones were "given" part of the Earth. What part? We'll get to that another time.

So you accept a structure which seems adequate for a time, but you eventually break through its limits. You break through your association with old structures, even breaking through physicality to spirituality. You need the structure to support the development of the concept; the next step is to release the old structure so that the radiance can bring a whole new perspective within which you build a whole new structure. One can never assume "This is forever." It is not. There is always going to be a clearer, more progressive way of viewing everything. The diagram depicts this at the center, where there is the radiating out as though there is a seeking and asking. Then comes the choice, the allowing, the accepting within new limits of understanding. Evolution, in a sequential sense, is so rapid that there has to be something going on. Structure is certainly for support, but beyond that it is for the identification process. There are, then, many ways of seeing and interpreting this more earthly diagram, are there not?

Now here is another. In this diagram there seems to be the symbol of an eye within an eye within an eye, and around the symbol a great deal of emotion swirling about. In one area there seems to be a sense of defending because of fear, as though an attempt is being made to infiltrate or overcome. This is the way it did appear to the pre-Lemurians, but it didn't have to be seen that way. This was their interpretation; they were caught in an emotional imbalance. A radiant core is attracting, and it is possible to feel that what might be attracted can be threatening. What is the purpose of the radiation from the core — that light being turned on? What is created then? There is more light on the subject, a clearer view, with increased awareness and expansion of consciousness. In this Earth-oriented diagram we are really looking at how consciousness expanded on the planet.

When any growth takes place, it goes through three phases: the first stage holds the yet unformed, unstructured idea — a possibility; in the second stage the possibility resolves into structure, into useable actuality; and in the third stage what has been learned and experienced from the structure is seen to have opened up further opportunity which lay within the original idea — a transformation. There is a saying: "In order to understand, I have to get into it first." So the idea settles into form. Yet, taking the form here as the Earth, the Earth has always been aware that at the core it was a generative center, and there have always been those living here who have embodied that notion.

The third diagram looks rather like a patchwork quilt. A patchwork quilt is a concept of integration, is it not? The way I brought this diagram through Janet was like this: I brought one particular area and we colored that in, then we added another aspect and colored that in, and so on. But in terms of evolution, each aspect has progressed from the previous one. This diagram brings Earth evolution up to the 1920s. The First World War has ended and the conditions that led to the Second World War are generating. The energy here was a good energy in itself; what came in was due to what humanity chose to do with it. Within this time span Hitler was born. Remember, this third diagram came forth from the second, the pre-Lemurian diagram. Can you sense the progression? This was the time not only of Hitler but of a great deal that was positively productive. Interestingly, it was a time of the birth of many esoteric groups that were very active on Earth, such as Theosophy and many spiritualist churches. It was a time of great industrial growth also. Notice that the structure has become more rounded. There has been an integration process that has lessened the rigidity. There is more flow, and the energy at the core has

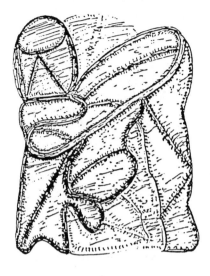

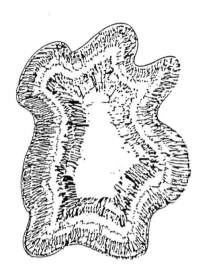

3   4

integrated, not just at one or two or three focuses, but has spread the integrative possibilities throughout the whole. This doesn't mean that there aren't certain areas that still speak of the old structure and certain areas that speak of greater integration. You can see in the diagram areas where straight lines suggest possible barriers to integration stemming from the old structure, as well as curved lines that flow, indicating the new, more integrated way of structuring Earth.

One can see a large area on the left side of the diagram, the receptive side, that really needs integrating. In this third diagram there is a special emphasis on receiving — and that's how you got Hitler. This is the old structure that goes back to the more rigid interpretation of pre-Lemuria. The receptive energies not yet fully integrated into the new possibilities brought in that dictator and an imbalance of the power area. The receptive side received the negative interpretation rather than accepting a positive one. In other words, the energy charge, the radiation, really invokes whatever you are in consciousness. Whether we speak of a group or an individual, if the concentration is upon what is considered "negative," then you're going to bring in a certain charge. If you radiate out negatively, what you get back is of like kind. Now, of course, it wasn't the case that all of Earth's humanity negatively invoked the need for a dictator, a Hitler. Greed was a very great part of the energy format, as was desire for power.

Hitler was a tool that certainly got out of hand, but he really was a tool that was being used by those who greedily sought power. What they got, bit them! On our diagram we see an imbalance, and it became all-consuming.

The beautiful violet turned to a very dark, dark red — a red that clogs, that has a distortion within it. A bloodbath spread out, almost covering the diagram. Fortunately, at the beautiful radiant core, the polarity of negative/positive generated a force field that began to clear this "red plague" from the planet. Nothing is ever closed off from opening to the light, from moving toward an ideal. Hitler didn't see that there is no way to take over the system, because the system is self-perpetuating, and though troubled times have to be gone through, the integrative process will always win. There are so many ways to integrate that they can't all be blocked. The light will always find a way in.

On the diagram there are lines that seem to separate, like apartments are separate yet contained in one building; there is a blending movement as the people living there visit each other with gifts or communicate needs. Each person's space can be shared in many ways, but it will never become so amalgamated that there is no individuality. There will always be differing points of interest to be explored very specifically. There is no desire to erase that individuality — only to blend, and from there to achieve a transcendence.

Overall this diagram will probably seem to some of you like a mess where elements that had set up their own clear definitions, very different from each other, were beginning to melt down and bleed into each other, becoming something with less rigid definitions. A new perspective was needed at this time, and nothing less than a complete meltdown of the old perspective was needed to generate this new perspective. The old structure seems to melt to allow a new one. It's not easy, is it? The emotions are upset, fearful of losing what had become comfortable. Can you see how, by studying the diagram, you can more easily recognize the source of an "eruption" in your life and find a new pattern of reaction? You can look inward and see yourself more clearly. As you do so, again a melting away of rigidities takes place, and your unique strengths become more and more representative of sourceness, allowing the radiant core of the universe to pour in. On the physical, you might have a distortion of experience because you can't fully see what is going on and what is about to occur. But looking inward can be a prelude to a balancing expansion outward. You are a multiple self; the inward-looking self is balanced by another, outward-moving self. This multifaceted aspect of who you are (and who everyone else is) allows you to experience both inner and outer perspectives.

On the physical there is a need for what Vywamus has called "resistiveness," a solid structural support that focuses attention. But this can be overdone. The structural support needs to be strong enough to support the effort, but not so rigid that it keeps it from becoming a more cosmic support system. On the diagram there is an area that has accepted a fragmentation. It represents the physical foundation of your Earth, and as it came through the energy movement, the centering process itself seemed to fracture. It seemed to create certain boundaries and restrictions, and afterward, in attempting to get rid of those boundaries, it became even more fractured. I realize this might not be clear to your mental body, but perhaps your emotional and intuitive faculties will be able to feel it. To complicate things even more, we still have reflections of what has been in past cosmic days. You have reflections from all your past lives that affect you, giving you a tendency to flow into an old pattern. So does the Earth.

The fourth diagram represents the Harmonic Convergence. Isn't it interesting? Do you see the differences? All this happened in the space of a few hours of Earth time. Do you wonder that this has been a time of adjustment? It is important to see the difference in the energy structure. You are each in your own way having to identify what has happened. Your four-body systems may feel insecure, unable to identify and balance these inflowing, converging energies. The Earth invoked this in-drawing, and what came in was an incredible transformation.

Now see yourself standing in the center of the fourth drawing. Visualize the colors. Violet is the color that surrounds you, and red is farthest away. Focus into the violet and gold – particularly the gold. It is a repository for many other colors such as blue and yellow. On the outside the radiating red, and the violet and gold within. Sense what is occurring with the energy as you stand within the energy field. Good! There has been a longing to feel centered, to feel one is moving in the direction of the goal and that there is accomplishment – something positive – going on. So centering, or integrating, is not an inactive state. It is a state that is peaceful in the sense that it is a balanced but also a very active state. There is so much energy that you may feel you're riding a skyrocket, but in a very balanced way. The energy is pouring in from All That Is, and you are centering yourself in the energy, which is ever-expanding. There is a pouring in, a centering and an expansion outward. Many elements had to be integrated, or centered and balanced, in order to give your rocket its outward surge. The Earth has its act together enough to have become a framework within which you can all center and move. The cosmology of it is the centering process that balances you to connect with something greater. I think we will go into a meditation at this time, and again we will use music.

Love Meditation

❦ *Sense existence coming together. All possibilities are moving into a centered space, and you are centered now. Calmly, peacefully and yet powerfully you accept this new center. Your emotional body says, "Yes, finally I am centered peacefully." This awareness stirs a connection to "something greater." It sings; literally, it sings through you now. Listen to it! It communicates that "something greater." It is communicating now, singing to you. Other levels of awareness flow in, and you are integrating into them. Note them – note all of them coming in, coming in, coming in. You are surrounded by all these levels of awareness. They are coming in, coming in now, singing through* you. The vibration is introspective; you are centered within it. It is introspective, and yet time, the dynamic, flowing perspective, is there also. The range, the whole gamut of experience, yes, the whole range – level upon level within level within level – all experience comes into you now. Be integrated, be centered, all levels coming in, centering, coming in, coming in. Be centered within them.

❦ There is a process I would like to lead you through – a boundless process. As these levels come in, as they express specifically, they put their arms around each other. There is a cosmic heart expressed, and from that cosmic heart a bonding, a bonding, a sharing, a joining through the heart perspective. Each area comes in – the sharing nature is accepted, bonded to another part of your sharing nature. It is done through the heart center – quietly, quietly, quietly each perspective is allowed to come in, accepted and bonded, accepted and integrated. As they bond together they become great strength, great strength of integrated perspective that shares the cosmos and radiates forth now, the strength bonded together from the individual perspective coming together into a flow. There is a flow that your emotional body may recognize as what it has been looking for. Yes, what it has been looking for. Each area is coming in, bonding to other areas, becoming the strength that then flows. See them coming together – each area, each perspective, each opportunity, each thought, each feeling.

❦ Here comes love; bond it together with another perception of love and blend it with a basic premise of love that is there for you. Here comes trust; bond it together with the trusting basis that you have about life. Bond it! Bond strength in the area of trust. Know that each perspective that comes in is a part of who you are. You can accept it. As you accept it, it will multiply the strength that you have within you. You now have more love. You now have more trust. You are multiplying those strengths. Stand here centered in the creative process, centered in the integrative process, centered in the energy pattern of the Earth. Now send forth again the radiance of who you are. Become aware of it and use it. It is going forth. It goes forth and shines all over the Earth, and you have the strength that you've gathered, that you've bonded, that you've multiplied. Look now to the integration that has taken place. This is what integration is: the allowing of the multiplying factor of your strength, the gathering up of those strengths so that they may be used as a radiant jewel to shine on the Earth. You shine now through more love. You shine now through more trust. You shine through a basic understanding that says, "I may use this energy that is coming in. It is the universal principle, and I may draw from it what I can take from it now. This is the way existence evolves. Here I get mirrored to me from the universe all of what I am seeking, and I may simply trust. When it is right I may take it within me and it will multiply the factors that I have – it will multiply the aspects, it will increase my awareness in each of these areas. I can simply accept more love. The universe is radiating it to me now. I can turn it on. The universe is bringing *it in. I can bond what I receive from the universe into what I already recognize within myself."*

❦ *It is that simple. The radiance of the whole is bringing you all that you need. You have only to grasp it to bring it in, to stretch to that next level, that next step. Bring in more love now. Accept it, bond it to the loving understanding. Listen! Your heart sings with this loving radiance. You accept more love and accept the ability to shine as a center of loving energy. The universe is providing it and it shines through you now. You can bond in the next level of understanding simply by grasping it, bringing it in and allowing it. There is more trust out there – it is being radiated to you from the universe. Take it! Remember, it is the universe; it is the outer radiance that you can bring into the core, into your inner radiance. There is trust – hear it in the music. It is coming in, coming in, a more and more radiant core. It is now generating a point of contact that is being integrated into who you are. The radiant core begins to multiply, begins to generate a point of contact that is extremely magnetic. That magnetic flow goes out into the universe in the next level of radiance. You have been radiated, too, and now you bond that radiating quality within you and it radiates forth. Thus it creates generative cores which in turn radiate forth, thus the cosmos evolves and expands. One radiating core generates a point of contact with the next radiating core. One is accepting and bonding and then using the strengths that have been gathered up.*

❦ *Integration: the process of allowing evolution to move through you, of accepting what the universe provides as a tool for the next step of evolution. You can let go of the insecurities and the uncertainties. The process works! You have but to open to it. You don't have to provide the premise because it's been provided for you. You simply have to accept it. Sense now the opening. You've chosen to accept it. You are an accepting core within the Source. The radiant energy is being bonded into an integrative core that is now generating another source of radiance – a source of radiant energy. Sense now and trust now the eternal progression and the eternal unfoldment of Source. It is ever creative. Each of you responds in your own unique perception of radiance. Hear it and see it now – your unique interpretation. It is unique to you but complementary to everyone else's interpretation. It is uniquely created, dynamically created, generatively created. Sense the gathering: the integrative process that allows you to keep magnifying Source and to keep on magnifying It. It radiates; it flows; you and this generative core flow within it. Yes! Flow with it!*

❦ *The journey is an eternal one, my friends. You are centered within it. You can't get away from it, but you can bond with what is being radiated to you from the universe. You can accept it and use it as a strength in order to radiate completely. The music says it is a continuing effort eternally discovering, eternally radiating, eternally bonding more and more strength. There is no beginning; there is no ending; there is only the continuing saga of discovery. There is only Source, your unique perspective of Source, generating on a more creative level, accepting a more unified and bonded approach, ever moving through the levels of creativity, ever discovering new ways of perception, ever allowing a unique radiating to take place between you and Source. It is the Source-level relationship that radiates. Discover it. As you do there will be a sense of release, a sense of peace, of harmony, of acceptance.*

🐛 *Come back now. Come back, bringing back into your awareness the Earth plane and a knowing that the generative core that you are is forever bonding more and more of your strengths radiated to you by the universe itself.*

The Heart Energy

Now we are going to work with your heart. I invite you to focus into the heart area. We have talked a lot about integration and now we get to the core — the heart energy. Your heart may be a little timid at times. It hides a little because it feels vulnerable. You play roles. You say, "This is who I am." Your heart peeks out from within and says, "I'm here. It's not who you are — I am who you are." As it begins to appear, become apparent to you, you glimpse who you really are. There is a sense of movement, of gearing into that acceptance of who you really are. You begin to relax. You say, "Very well, I will begin to allow the heart to present itself to the cosmos. I am this heart energy, this love center, and I will be accepted for what I am. I will allow it now."

Thus there is a deep relaxation in the heart area. Many of you are seeking this relaxed acceptance of the heart energy that will generate for you a new beginning. You recognize that you can become visible within your heart without becoming vulnerable. You recognize that it's all right to be who you are and let it happen. As it happens again, the energy moves and slides around — there's still an identification going on: "Who am I? Who am I? I'm sliding — I want to know who I am." There is a movement, a sliding, and you begin to bring that to the universe — a sliding scale of who you are. The energy flows and you begin to be a little braver. You begin to stand up to the universe and say, "This is who I am; this is what I think; this is what I know. This is who I am." The universe begins to respond. It says, "How beautiful you are! Look! I will mirror back to you love. I will mirror back to you acceptance."

Were you all geared up to be rejected? Some of you do that, you know. You're quite sure you'll be rejected and then the universe accepts you! It accepts you, and as it does there is an opening, a new beginning, a sense of the building of the momentum. There is a sense of balance and of a new beginning. It generates more and more energy, but for a while you might not notice much effect from it. You've been accepted, and yet life seems as it was before. But it is not! It is a whole new level of being, a whole new level of perception. It begins to build and you are gathering up the resources of the heart. You are integrating the response of the heart. You begin to identify with a clearer rhythm of existence. You begin to accept it! It multiplies! It expands and expands! It allows you to say to the cosmos, "Yes, this is who I am! I am the heart. I am a heart that cares. I am a heart that allows myself to be visible with what I believe. I am a heart that responds to the universe. I know that acceptance comes to me from the universe. I see – I know – I am accepted. I have my place and I am secure within it. The universe mirrors back to me that security. I am secure in who I am."

The universe responds and you respond, and the heart opens. The heart radiates. It generates more and more energy. It fills the heart until it spills over and you need to share it, for it seems as if it can hold no more. It generates and radiates; more and more comes in until there is an integrative point that sings through your harmonious heart. Your heart sings with joy, sings with happiness, sings because it is filled with what the universe mirrors to you. You have opened. You have allowed it, and the universe shares now. It sings. As you radiate, you continue to contact the universe, you continue to express and there is an acceleration. You have an accelerated way of relating to the universe as never before.

There is a very cosmic opening, and you are filled with gratitude for this natural space you have to grow in. You open like a flower opens, and you are grateful for this joy and true humility. You see your space but know that every other space is equal. That is the energy that is flowing through the heart, that is integrating, integrating, integrating. The process of integrating is allowing the qualities of the heart. They are radiating together, sharing together. They can be joyful and loving and have true humility with happiness and understanding – all of these qualities. This is the true integration flowing through your heart. All of this is singing; this is what it means to sing – to radiate these qualities to the universe through your caring nature. One can hear them reflected back to you. They echo back through the eternal now. This truly is the music of the spheres echoing back the true qualities of the heart which you've identified and integrated. They sing – they cannot sing until you allow them to sing through you. Love cannot sing unless you bring it in and integrate it into who you are. It must have this format in order to vibrate and to sing, expressing what it is by your allowing. Thus, as you integrate more completely, you become aware of what integration is: the allowingness of the heart state to share all of the qualities that are a part of it, all of its attributes, bringing them into alignment through your choice level.

Recognition and Acceptance Meditation

❧ *You are willing now to stand up to the universe and say, "Yes, this is who I am, and I share it by expressing the qualities of the heart and by multiplying them. I energize them by allowing them to be integrated. I will now share these qualities with the universe. I know that as they reverberate throughout the universe, they will come back to me multiplied, enhanced and multiplied now. I accept them as they have accepted me."* The process continues to another level of integration, and again I stand up and say, *"This is who I am: the integrated qualities of the heart. I am allowing them. I trust; I am surrendered; I am beauty; I am harmony; I am sharing with another because I care. I stretch out my hand to another because I love. I am willing now to serve. I am willing to choose to serve through the qualities of my heart. I serve the cosmos. I am the qualities of the heart. I allow them to expand me. I am willing to expand them. I recognize it is a reciprocal flow that I must accept and do accept. I choose such expansion and through that choice I will expand. So, too, the universe and humanity will expand. I allow the qualities of the heart to speak through me in an integrated way."*

❦ *"I will not be shy; I will not be quiet; I will be verbal in the fullest universal sense. I will shout to the universe of my love. I will shout to the universe of my allowing, perhaps not vocally, but spiritually, in an alignment, in the fullest alignment of who and what I am. I will allow my four-body alignment to announce to the universe my acceptance of the qualities of the heart and my integration of the qualities of the heart. I accept each choice, each opportunity to choose and to use these qualities of the heart. I know I cannot turn off trust. I know I cannot turn away from light. I know I cannot turn from allowingness. There is no other way. I choose now to integrate these qualities. I choose to use them and to allow the universe to reflect back to me the fact that I have used them. The mirroring is the integrative process coming in from the universe, bringing all of the qualities that I have chosen to expand. These qualities come back to me multiplied by my choice.*

❦ *"Yes, I must make the choice. I do make the choice, not just once but daily, hourly, every minute, every second. I choose now, and at every opportunity, the qualities of the heart: all allowingness, compassion, joy, harmony, beauty. I choose them more and more, and each time I choose them, I activate a process of evolution within the heart. I am joyous within this opportunity! I dance within this opportunity! I express exuberance within this opportunity! The expansion of the qualities of the heart come through every time I choose to express unconditional love. What comes back to me is a multiplied factor of unconditional love. When, by choice, I trust another, the universe multiplies that trust and it comes back to me as a full, trusting opportunity. I choose now to receive another's love, and what comes back to me is an opportunity to be trusted in that love."*

❦ Can you see that the qualities are multiplied by the universe, and as you choose to use them, the qualities come back multiplied? This is what it means to integrate into the qualities of the heart. By your choices you create the multiplying factor. You are the generative core within the process. You make the effort and the universe responds. It is automatic, but you, as the generative core, make the effort now.

❦ Bursts of color come back from the universe! Note the colors now – the colors flooding in from everywhere, into every space. The colors represent all the *qualities of the heart from every perspective. Your spiritual body greets these colors, these opportunities; it welcomes them. Your mental body greets these opportunities in color. It enjoys thinking about them and learning from them and has a sense of satisfaction in this incoming opportunity. The emotional body is ecstatic! This is what it's been seeking. This is the response it has wanted; this is the resultant factor from its effort, its outward flow. It feels supported in the process. This is the way to understand that – and it is ecstatic. Sense within the physical body a flow. It is looking for a flow. It is looking for the energy, the life force to surge through it. When it surges from the heart, from what the heart has created, it is not blocked. There is a deep, wonderful penetration. It is called "light." You've heard about that. It is a light energy that penetrates to the core of your physical structure. Your physical body seeks to be warm. That warmth is the core penetration it is seeking. Many of you are working to balance that area – to be neither too cold nor too warm. It is that core penetration of your heart which is being balanced now. Sense the peaceful space within the heart. This is the cosmic beat, the cosmic rhythm, the return flow. It is sent out and it comes back. I send it out and it comes back. Beat . . . beat . . . pulse . . . pulse . . . the great sweeping, the generative explosion that results from it, the generative effect that creates universes. It gives forth and it comes back. The basic rhythm is established, and within it a sense of harmony, a sense of unity – this rhythm, this support within the whole.*

🐦 *Yes, dear ones, the rhythmic acceptance of the whole, the support system of Source, the cosmic heart that beats – hear it now! It beats within all of you, responding now to the core within your heart, to the generative center within it, to that creative spark that has been born within you, which was given to you by the Source Itself. Be within the creative core now. As we come full circle in this meditation, sense that your choices are the key here. Sense that there are quiet moments within which to reflect upon your choices. As you choose, your choices will create enough energy to bring you yet another choice. That choice will generate for you a contact that will go out and bring you back a response from the universe. It is called an awakening. There are always opportunities that you may reflect upon and welcome in, but remember they are born from within the heart and they go out from the heart quality. Come back now with a new sense of connection within the heart at this time.*

🐦 *Because you are here focused on the physical plane and are still seeking to sort out much of what can come into the physical plane, you've never, from this perspective, met your integrated self. You really haven t, and Id like to introduce you now. We will seek to show you the qualities of that integrated self and what it is possible to realize about it.*

Putting on the Integrated Self

🐦 *As you close your eyes, use your inner sight to see a circle. Within this circle is a glowing crystal. Whatever color it is, the crystal is glowing, and as it glows, you recognize its radiant core. It is going to mirror back to you a picture, an image. We won't personify it; we will simply see a mirroring process coming back from this crystal. This image comes from the beautiful radiance represented by the crystal. The crystal begins to rotate and you are aware of this radiant energy being mirrored back to you. Sense that now and accept it. Listen quietly to the music being played and accept that radiance. Accept! That truly is all you have to do to be your integrated self. By accepting, you allow that radiance to shine in – but one must recognize that it is coming in. So sense that something is being reflected into you now, reflected from a radiant core, from a centered perspective of all that is.*

🌾 *More and more that reflection comes in and it becomes clearer and clearer. You get a message from this radiating effect. It begins to be more and more specific. Take one of your spiritual hands and reach out to grasp this image. Grasp it so that you can actually get in touch with it in a very tangible way. Bring it in to you. You can place it in your heart if you wish, or put it on your body as you would a body stocking, or color your skin with it. Really feel it, really get in touch with it, either in the heart center or touching the skin or both. You can sense that there is more coming in. There is a constant stimulation coming in from this radiant core. You have stretched and you have accepted it. Note how stimulating it is. Sense every cell of your being accepting what has been mirrored to you. Relax into it; allow it; trust it. Allow the reality of it to be here. You must recognize the interaction taking place.*

🌾 *More and more energy comes in that you can put on. Accept it. It is not just a one-time process. It is a process that you choose to embody. More and more – all of the time – more and more energy comes in. You constantly put on more and more of the garment of energy. You are constantly reaching with your spiritual hand to grasp it. You are bringing it to you. It is being made available to you by this radiant core. You are bringing it in to the physical plane.*

🌾 *Now you might note what is happening in your heart. There is radiance there, is there not? The radiance is going out and coming in. In our integrative self technique we are concerned with having you grasp from the physical level the spiritual perspective and bring it in. The more you allow this, the more you will see your integrated self. The spiritual perspective is integrating; it is well balanced. We are not talking here about the spiritual body. We are talking about the spiritual blueprint that contains the mental perspective and the emotional perspective that will fit into the physical structure. So it really is the whole spectrum of who you are that you may grasp – it is being mirrored to you from this radiant core.*

🌾 *If you wish, take a deep breath once in a while and release it, more and more letting go of what we might call "gathered resistance" to this acceptance. This is relaxation, and it is the key to acceptance and grasping of what we now term your integrated self. As you relax into it more and more, certain things* begin to occur. There will certainly be a stimulation of what perhaps needs to be released. This release can be done by grasping more and more of the integrated self that can view and assist this release. Keep breathing deeply and relax into this acceptance. Accept! Acceptance is the key!

❦ Some of you have not yet grasped – have not reached forward, actually grasped and then put on – the integrated self. Perhaps one of the four bodies has not yet fully grasped what is possible on the physical plane. Perhaps one body has taken precedence, has interfered with the full acceptance. It may be that you just haven't grasped enough of one particular body to balance out the quality of the integrated self. You might not have allowed yourself to understand the whole and bring it in and integrate it. By quietly accepting it, by making an effort yourself, by using your physical body, literally, as an affirmation of that integrated core, that integrated self, you open up the possibilities for integration.

❦ Open your eyes now and know that you are wearing that integrated perspective. As you once again become oriented to the physical plane, rise and move about as that integrated self. Some of you may feel like dancing; others may want to move quietly – but notice what you feel. Can you feel that there has been change in your physical processes? There is a more balanced self. See that integrated self and you can say, "I greet you, integrated self! I greet you from the heart and I'm excited by this opportunity and I look forward to more opportunities to be with you. I will be with you and yet I know I am you. There will now be that multilevel perception that will allow me to be more and more integrated on the physical level. I have opened the door; I have grasped and brought into physicality the part of me that is integrated – all parts together in understanding. I am now allowing that perspective on the physical plane. I am lovingly and trustingly entering this relationship. I know that is why I am here. I am here to gain this balance, this integrated perspective. There is nothing awesome in the concept of integration; it is the natural state, and I recognize that I am now at that perceptive point where this natural state becomes who I am on the physical plane. I am able now to move through any 'stormy condition' that may appear on the Earth because I am that integrated self. I know that 'storms' will not affect me negatively; I will feel refreshed by the rain, for to me it will be a blessing that I enjoy. I know that humanity also, in its totality, is refreshed by any seeming storm. I will accept this tumult serenely, knowing that what to others may appear to be turmoil is in reality a refreshing, cleansing experience. I welcome such an expression of Source as It seeks through me to experience everything. I know I will get into it and move with joy. I will move with the perception that it is fun. I will dance with joy because I am integrated. This is who I am."

❦ Enjoy the integration; it is there for you now. It is who you are, and you can accept it on the physical plane. It doesn't require a great effort; it is the natural thing – the state of giving up. Greet now your integrated self. Dance *with it; enjoy it exuberantly. It is on the physical level and the heart is expanding. I see in you a beautiful coming together so that each part of you can communicate with every other part, and it is a joyous thing. The movement is there; the balance is there; the joy is there; harmony is there. It's wonderful! It is a joyous affirmation of Sourceness. This is the cocreator level. It is a natural state where one welcomes an integrative perspective and uses it eternally. It doesn't fall off; it doesn't go away; it doesn't get out of balance – it stays there eternally.*

Well, that was wonderful! But you wonder if you can keep this knowing and feeling with you. I say this: It is sometimes valuable to pretend that the condition that you want is already there. During our meditation you were doing more than pretending, I assure you, but children pretend, don't they? They go into a state that is desired with so much trust that it becomes a reality for them, and if you trustingly pretend, you can reinstate the feeling of your integrated self. This reinforces its reality for you.

Exercises for the Integrated Self

Now I want to give you several techniques that will be valuable when you need to use them. As you work with these exercises, I am sure you will begin to glimpse for yourself what a cocreator does. These exercises are actually the ones we use for those of you approaching the cocreator level. If you are not yet quite at that point of close approach, this is a look ahead from which you can absorb all that you are ready for.

Exercise One

I would like to have you imagine a circle – a circle as large as this room will contain. Move yourself physically into the center of the circle. The circle appears as a beautiful blue energy that is literally pulsing. Stay in touch with that circle until you can sense its pulsing, its rhythm, its breath. You might want to set up a beat by clapping your hands or tapping your foot. Each of you will get a slightly different beat. The beat of the cosmic heart will be established through this. The circle represents the pulsing rhythm of the cosmos. You sit there and you establish that rhythm – whatever is right for you. Get in touch with that rhythm – your rhythm.

As that rhythm is established, something very interesting happens. Into the beautiful blue circle several other colors begin to appear, until the blue becomes like a framework around the edge of the circle. Pink may enter the blue, or some orange or green or violet, and there will be an iridescence. Eventually you will see a circle of rainbow colors that begins to move. Probably the circle will also begin to move in a counter-clockwise direction; there is a going back to what has already come forward, so the counter-clockwise motion symbolizes a return trip. Now, this is a moving meditation exercise. If your eyes are closed you may become physically dizzy, so keep your eyes open. You can focus on a point or on the center of the circle.

What you are going to sense will come through your peripheral vision. I want you to note the circle so your seeingness will be enhanced. You are even going to use the third eye of your knowingness to see behind you. You are really seeing that circle at all of its points as it moves. It will go as rapidly as you allow it to go. Remember to keep your focus to prevent dizziness.

You are centered within that circle, and the idea is to sense that its movement is the integrative process of the life force which circles because you have created it from a centered space. You can sense a flow of energy connecting you to the circle, but I don't think that is necessary. I would say that what you begin to sense as the circle moves is a developing structure — not a structure that is rigid — and you will find that the circle expands. As the momentum of it grows, it will radiate out until you find yourself at the center of a circle that takes in the city, the state, and so on to the universal level.

The goal here is not to lose any part of your circle. In its expansion you may find places that are not filling out gaps, so to speak. If this happens, turn the momentum back until the circle is filled in evenly again. You must, through the expansion, remain in touch with all that moves within the circle. Do not allow areas to disappear or become too tenuous to sense. See it expanding to infinity, but be sure you keep a focus. The synchronicity is focusing on your individuality while you focus on the expanding creativity that you have allowed to come to you. It is the wholeness, the integration of wholeness, that we are addressing. Continue with it until it works for you.

Exercise Two

For this one you are going to put on a fresh pair of shoes. You might even want to get a pair of soft, comfortable slippers and keep them just for this special use. You will slip on your slippers — they are integrative slippers, meaning they are rather like rainbows. You can use whatever you have, but I want you to feel very special about these rainbow slippers. They become very special as you endow them with an energy that will almost make them seem winged. Remember, in mythology Mercury had wings on his feet, did he not? It is that sort of image I would like you to sense. The winged slippers give you a very lofty perspective. By wearing them you begin to make a flying contact with whatever area you choose. You can be very physical about this, but remember that we are also talking about a much fuller and more integrative perspective. Whatever you touch into physically will be a light that illumines all perspectives, so if you touch into a physical location in the particular way I am telling you to do, there will be a resounding principle of creation which you will want to perceive as much of as you can. This is an exercise used by developing cocreators who have had quite a lot of experience on the physical level.

Now, not only do you have winged slippers, but you are able to become a "giant" in physical existence. You go forth with your steps cushioned by light. Your steps do not crush. Cocreators have such a cushion of light, and that light magnifies as they step. It radiates; it lights up a specific area upon which they focus their attention. These are the cocreators who are actively engaged in creating your existence right now. They are actively involved with this cosmic day.

As you step, be aware that you are intensifying the light in a particular area. One learns as one is personally involved in taking these steps. As you step as a cocreator, pay attention! You want to start very slowly. Place your foot in whatever space you are using, whatever environment you would like to step within. Have you wanted to step into a jungle with all its teeming life — past or present? Or perhaps you'd like to step back into Egypt as you once knew it. This step is through time, so as it comes into contact with physicality, it goes right to the beginning — the base of all that ever was upon Earth. You can literally be aware of any level of time and space that you choose through this technique. It is going back to the core, into the eternal-now concept.

Let us become specific. Let us say we have selected Egypt. This can be as simple or as profound an experience as you want it to be. You can see, as you begin to step, all civilizations in all time sequences. You may see it as a moving panorama. You can stop it and stay within a particular time and space. Perhaps you would like to step out into the period in which the pyramids were built and Egyptian civilization was at its height. Take one step and see what occurs and where you are. Where is the Nile in relation to where you are? Where are the pyramids? In what direction do they lie? As you note all this, you begin to sense an energy stimulation. Note what has happened in the surrounding area as you put your foot out and stepped there. You stepped there as light. What has occurred because you stepped there as light?

You will find that when a cocreator focuses a light into an area, there is a great deal of positive and beneficial radiation and the making available and igniting of potentiality. So as you step, pause — stay right there so you can get a sense of what is occurring. Now, as you do this, you get the beneficial effect also. This is an actual experience where the cocreator level makes available the energy for you to do the stepping as a cocreator. The cooperative effort of the cocreator level comes into play and you actually create an effect that you might think you are imagining. It is a reality that can be as real as you allow it to be.

You have stepped and then stood still, and you are going to note several things. First of all, the scene changes, civilizations rise and fall, and you get an accelerated glimpse of what we see when we observe the planet. There is a movement; a building rises and then is gone. You sense the literal effect of the stepping process. You might not have known that when a cocreator steps, civilizations rise and die away. It is an emphasis of the energy, the ebb and flow, the beat or rhythm, that I am addressing here. Egypt, with its time flow of regeneration and degeneration, is a good example. It was what it was because emphasis was put into it by a particular cocreator. You will note that Egypt was a little out of context with your planet's history. The cocreator created the energy emphasis that allowed the civilization that arose and also allowed those of you who were there at the time to get in touch with the power you have for your use when you are at the cocreator level. Some of you came closer to that power then than you have ever been since. We are planning another step, another emphasis; I think it will begin around the year 2010 and it will stir up a lot of potential. Again, it is not destructive; it creates a radiating emphasis that can then be accepted. This is what cocreators do. Wherever they step, there is a spiritual emphasis that occurs. It is an emphasis of integration, of potentiality, of what the creative principles are, of love, of trust, of acceptance. It emphasizes every existing quality in a most positive sense. Of course, all of you choose how to use these qualities.

In ancient Egypt there were those who were able to use the radiance and those who were not. There will always be those not yet spiritually mature enough to recognize an opportunity, who tend to feel fated to experience something less than the full potential of what is available. You might, as you step, look at this polarity, which in the fullest sense is a balancing. Where you step, there is an energy flow that needs balancing, and the emphasis is connecting very high into the spiritual concept. There was in Egypt a dynamic that was in great need of a balancing factor, so the cocreator light acted to stabilize it. There are always those who can accept the increased emphasis and those who cannot – a polarity.

It is interesting, then, to step and see what the radiation creates in your own universe, in terms of physicality. How does it affect your body? Know that these are more than exercises. They will bring into your life a change.

Now the final part of this – after you have experienced as much as you choose – is a circling of the perimeter of all you created. This stepping around the circle unites and brings in a unified perspective of all that has gone before. Do this stepping around the circle physically. Get the movement going so that it says to you that you have indeed moved full-circle. You are allowing now what you have seen, have realized, about this exercise, and it has become a part of your life as you complete the circle.

I want it clearly understood that this exercise can be done on many levels; therefore I want to emphasize this by enumerating and explaining seven steps which can be used progressively:

1. Stepping and recognizing that the light emphasis is there.
2. By stepping you have stopped the level of change in an environment. What effect have you made upon one particular time sequence? See it.
3. Release and allow evolution to take place within this time sequence and see what effect you had on it.
4. Begin to notice that there are responses in your physical body from your stepping.

5. Be aware that at the beginning level all this fits together beyond any sequencing – moving into the eternal now.

6. Observe the radiant effect from your stepping that opens up the core area. (This is perhaps beyond your perception as yet, but it can be learned.) See directly into the core of the radiation as you might look into an atom of which you are a part and see and understand all of the activity that occurs as you make choices that create a chain reaction in the atom.

7. Know that you have the ability to transcend and yet to use physicality as a uniting factor. You see all possibilities and then release yourself to experience that ideal level.

Exercise Three

Sitting in a straight-backed chair, raise your hands, palms up to about shoulder height. Sit comfortably but with your spine as straight as possible. You will begin to sense the energy coming in. The goal is to be sensitive enough to really feel this energy as though it were raining on your hands. You want to feel this rain-energy falling equally on both hands. If you feel the left hand is almost pushed downward by the amount of rain, leaving the right hand where it was, then you want to pay attention to the right hand until the two hands receive the flow equally. Sit like this for at least fifteen minutes. You need to be very comfortable, and the arms and hands must be free to move in case there needs to be an adjustment.

This energy coming in is doing something to the hands. They may begin to feel warm. The hands represent your receptive abilities on the physical level. You want to attune to the hands. You want to sit in a way that allows that equality as you hold them forward. Pay attention to your hands. Does your left hand feel as though it is warm and melting a little? Some of you might feel that; if so, go within and see what condition is being created in that. The right hand might not share the condition of the left hand, but the amount of energy and activity should be equal. Look at that: equal energy, but not necessarily the same activity on both sides. You might feel a sort of building up, a peaking, in the right hand, whereas the left seems to be hollowed out. One is not better than the other. I just want you to note and pay attention to what is occurring. Stay with it as long as you can. Try to keep the hands as flat as you can to maximize reception. If you find that fifteen minutes is too long, just stay as long as you can. Try this once in a while. I think you will enjoy it.

The goal is to see that a cocreator directs all sorts of activity. The type of cocreator activity that we're talking about is the direction and diversity of choice that active Sourceness is experiencing; we will speak of the inactive state another time. So the cocreator is centered within all the activity he has created, and he is equalizing all that creativity by his awareness and his balancing of it. If there is an imbalance, he adjusts it. You can start to work with this by adjusting two perspectives that are different yet equal in the amount of energy that you are able to feed to them.

Exercise Four

This exercise should be done lying on your back. Wear clothing that is loose and comfortable. If necessary, remove your shoes and tight-fitting socks or hose. Keep the legs a little apart. Be completely comfortable. You can go to sleep in this exercise if you like – it's all right to do so. Actually, this exercise could be a stimulus toward going to sleep.

Did you ever make angels in the snow? If your bed is large enough – or lie on the floor – move your arms out and make a few angels. As you do so you will summon the angelic kingdom. In other words, the movement that you make in physical existence, acknowledging the angelic presence, will bring them in. You are moving in physicality enough that you invoke the presence of the angelic kingdom. If your arms get tired, just stop doing this exercise physically, and strongly envision yourself doing it. Now, the angels are not necessarily going to come just through words. They are going to come in directed by Metatron, by Sandalphon, and particularly by Auriel. As they come in, they are going to make specific adjustments in your physical structure and into the awareness areas that you have everywhere. You might even have a sensation of pin-pricks and of having areas of your body stimulated. Well, you are being stimulated by the angelic hosts! As you say to them, "I am learning to invoke the cocreator level, to bring it into my physicality," they will then make actual physical adjustments in your physical structure.

If I were you, Id do this technique weekly. One nice thing about it is that you can go off to sleep with it, because once you've communicated through your movement that this is what you want, then they will do it. Id like to have you move physically, because your actual physical movement is an invocation. Every time you move, in whatever way, you are invoking something from the universe. The more conscious you are – the more you direct the process – the better. If you are sleeping or walking along, immersed in momentary happenings, you simply get what that automatically invokes. But when you inform the angelic kingdom that you are consciously reaching out to have your full cocreator ability stimulated, then that is what they help you to do. It's the difference between consciously working on your evolution and subconsciously allowing your usual programming to direct your activity. Recognize that the members of the angelic kingdom are the tools of your conscious directive abilities as a cocreator. You can use them in a very specific way.

You have now had a break, and physically you are refreshed. That's important. Also, after you have concentrated intently for a while, you need a release on that level, too. You will learn to concentrate for longer and longer periods as you move toward the cocreator level. Eventually the concentration will be absolute, in an infinite variety. As you concentrate and accept the stimulation being brought to you in many ways, you will remain more balanced during times when it seems you must do several things at once.

Exercise Five

I have for you now an exercise I want you to play with. We will do this one in groups of four. Each member of the group is to stand and put an arm around the ones on each side of you. Slide your feet until each foot is touching the foot of the one beside you. There should be a feeling of group balance. In one sense you could look upon the four as representing the four bodies, but they also represent aspects of self and of the cocreator level. Stand quietly and receive from each other the stimulus that will allow you to feel more complete and to recognize the cocreator level. The stimulus might come into the physical body. Be aware of any changes in the body. It might also come into the emotional body or the mental body or perhaps the spiritual body in your knowingness.

Good. You have been standing together listening to the soft flow of music. Now go back to your seats and write some notes. I suggest you spend about half an hour discussing what has come up for you. In this exercise there has been a certain stimulation, so through the interaction among the four of you, try to bring out what each of you perceives – or perhaps does not perceive. Then use the group focus to find out what evolved for the group consciousness. Where was the group tone at the beginning, and what happened through the group interaction?

Now, this process of group communication is the cocreator level and it is the ability to use more and more that cocreator level. You all have certain degrees of resistance to it. All of you have accepted the premise of individuality without seeing it as the gateway to something greater. Through your coming together, the presence of each member results in a balanced group and results in a group consensus about the value of the group. The acceptance of viewing this balancing integrative effect makes possible the use of the group as a tool in divine movement. Having used this exercise once, you can use it now and then and it will become easier, more revealing and helpful. The purpose is the balancing of the divine qualities (whether within self or in the group as a whole) by sharing in the balancing process. Your perception of how to use the divine qualities is also being balanced.

Let's say you have a group that has an area needing attention and exploration because of an imbalance. Come together in groups of four and focus on that particular area. Perhaps an organization has a need to stimulate and be stimulated by a greater number of people. The energy of the organization surrounds humanity widely, but as it reaches into humanity it seems to bounce off humanity. You might say humanity doesn't recognize who you are. Standing in groups of four, each member will represent a perspective of relationship to humanity – for in truth you do. Consider this area we have mentioned. Bring up a consensus and talk together about the relationship to humanity. All the groups of four can then come together and integrate the considered opinion of each into an organizational consensus.

It would be revealing to explore different individual qualities that would be valuable contributions to a group or organization of any size. Each quality has a rather awesome correspondence on the cocreator level, and each of you is connected with and integrating your own specialty. Here is a partial list of those you can identify with and make use of now on the physical level:

1. Conceptual strength which can bring forth a practical tool for members (or humanity) to use.
2. Enthusiasm and energy to grasp the flow that contains joy and abundance.
3. Practicality and willingness to serve; a sense of caring and sharing; a sense of purposeful, directed activity.
4. Networking and connecting – a generalists viewpoint that brings specialists together.
5. Transmitting – stepping down – spiritual or cosmic energies to be used on the physical.
6. Nurturing of oneself as well as of others, which allows an integrated state to emerge.
7. Integration – the ability to listen and make the response that helps others put it all together.
8. Leadership; the willingness to assume authority.

Before we go on to the next exercise, I would like to briefly address the question of authority. Some of you say, "Why do I have, on the physical level, this experience of being under rules and regulations imposed on me by leaders? The mental body wants to know. Why is it that rules and regulations coming from government levels still affect me?" Having this trouble with authority on the physical plane seems to take you out of the contact you really want with the spiritual. Many people use this as an excuse not to understand or accept the necessity to go through a step-by-step process in your associations. Authority figures give you the amount of allowingness you can expect for yourself. They mirror that to you. Thus in your country the IRS says that such and such rules apply to you. The IRS has been given, by a higher authority, certain control over specific areas that affect your life, and to a degree you have to accept their level of authority.

Generally speaking, this means that the cocreator level is reflecting down to the physical plane, and you all, in your associations with each other within your country, are giving energy, or authority, to certain structures and groups and being affected by what you believe about such authority. If you are called in to the IRS to be audited, you might feel some fear of what they might do. In observing the IRS and its functions, I would say that about eighty percent of the time what occurs in an audit is very positive and you find that nothing terrible is going to happen to you. Eighty percent of the time an audit is a further communication with the system to make sure all is understood on both sides. My point is that as you deal with authority, if you get together on communication, a great deal of what appears as a limiting factor may in fact be amenable to an opening to expansion to another level of acceptance in the area of authority. The other twenty percent may indeed hold an area of deep resistance that must be recognized and dealt with.

The ultimate authority is Source Itself, is it not? I am opening up this matter so you can look at it as you go along. I feel that you and others also have not yet a full understanding of the responsibility assumed by a cocreator from the Creator level. You don't as yet recognize what a cocreator does. You would like to just step into that recognition, but it actually will unfold gradually: an understanding of the authority of the Creator level in relationship to the cocreator level. So what I am trying to let you all see is that there is an ultimate level of "reporting," if you will. As you live your life in regard to every experience and in your relationship with each other, you are clearing your association into a greater understanding, an expansion into knowing what that basic level is. It will take time for you to come into full understanding of what I am saying, but hearing it will open the way. You might consider your fear of an authority figure to represent a fear of the ultimate authority of Source. I think it is not so much a fear of Sourceness as it is a matter of not comprehending the relationship between the cocreator level – you – and the Source level. You do not see what is required or demanded and what is not. You have created assumptions about what the Source expects of you. Some of your assumptions are true, but many, even most, are not. Most of it is an illusion. Most of it is trying to understand too much from an individual perspective. You all recognize some of this, don't you? We are intimately trying to understand the One who created us. We have accepted something from that One, but we aren't quite sure what.

Now, many people would like to do away with the IRS, but if you remove a structure you have to replace it with something else. So our wanting to remove it is a reflection of our nonunderstanding or nonclarity about the Source. A group consciousness has created it, so the collective consciousness must understand more clearly that area of authority for which it has responsibility. It must specifically clear in that area; it must go through the process of change – and I feel that is occurring. For a while that change can be seen to be a loss, and that's what you all are facing this year (election year, 1988). It is the changing of that structure, that authority figure, to which you have given the responsibility for governing your lives. There is a lot of fear about that, isn't there? There is fear on a very deep level about what is coming. Remember, however, that the outcome of an event or the granting of authority reflects a group consensus to which each individual has had an opportunity on some level to contribute — or not. Therefore, each carries a share of the responsibility for that outcome.

Exercise Six

Here is another exercise that I think may help all of you. I call it a "bursting" technique. A bursting is a dynamic release of fullness that has been held back by a barrier. Bursting is the creative process as it seeks to come through each of you. There is the generative effect in the core of what you are and it creates this bursting, this exuberance. As I look at you I see a burst of understanding here, a burst of concession there — a bursting effect that allows your creativity to expand. Through your expansion, the whole expands. So let us put some effort into it as a technique.

In a group, choose one person; the rest of you will attune to that person. See his/her energy literally exploding, expanding or bursting forth. Put that vision out to the universe. Some might feel that bursting energy, some might see it as a falling rain. If you can't feel the dynamic of explosion, step closer to the person until you do feel the power as an energy coming forth. You might find the aura becoming visible. If you tend to expect a physical feeling, check your emotions. Are they receiving the impact? Can you sense joy such as when a child lights up with the energy of joy?

I want you now to do for yourself what was done by the person you chose for the group exercise. Gather the energy in from the universe. Within a group you can also gather the group energy that is available. You don't enervate others — you take energy from what they are sending out. So, as you gather energy, concentrate on the heart center. What emotions have you gathered with it? You might not have realized that you gather up love and trust and receptivity and allowingness and humility — you gather up the surrender process. Those of you looking for energy in the surrender process, gather it up and use it! If you want a more dynamic quality, gather it up from the universe. There is no lack of energy. Gather it in, place it in the heart center and then send it out.

As you send it out, there is a bursting. It goes forth — it bursts forth almost as an explosion. It can also pour forth as a nice steady stream — and it's important to do it both ways. I think all of you are working with the dynamic energy or wanting to get in touch with it. So gather, draw it in. When it feels very centered, when you've brought those qualities to the heart and understood them, then allow them to burst forth. It becomes automatic; it spills over from the fullness within you — your fullness of these qualities. Because of their nature they must burst forth; they must be shared — that's the nature of what they are.

Trust is coming in; stability is coming in; unconditional love and joy come in — and they won't stay contained. They come in and their presence floods you with joy. If you focus on drawing in dynamic energy, be sure to let it flow out again freely. Trying to hold on to it in the heart or physical structure for long could cause discomfort, because it can't be stored — its nature is a dynamic movement. On a cold day bring the dynamic energy in — it will warm you. Bring in support, support from the whole. What happens when you bring in support? You feel it in the emotional body as the comfort of support. The mental body is aware that it has a sure place from which to draw. As the energy comes in, it has a certain quality such as joy or unconditional love or support. These qualities pour in until there is such a fullness that it has to burst forth, and as more flows in it must burst forth again, bursting, bursting, going out into the universe. There are waves and levels of bursting and bursting and bursting and bursting. Sense that! Feel how the heart is able to draw in and burst forth these qualities to others. Practice this as a group and individually — there is no one way better than the other.

Recognizing Integration

How do you recognize integration? I don't believe all of you do. I have seen people who were very integrated and they had no awareness of being integrated. You have a sense of what has been rather than what is. Many of you don't know when you're integrated. You might have balanced those qualities that were affecting you from the past without noticing — the balancing didn't catch your attention. You can be standing, perfectly balanced, but looking behind you rather than ahead.

There was a priest on your planet who had been a priest in his previous forty-five lifetimes. A more balanced being I have never seen. He served in his small parishes — forty-five of them in different parts of the world. In most, though not all, of these lifetimes he was Catholic. He was a beautiful being. But in his humble attunement to Sourceness, and in his inability to see what he had become, he kept repeating that area of service — forty-five times! As you grow you can increase your ability to serve in greater degree, in a wider scope of service. If you aren't seeing how balanced you are, you don't pick up on the wider opportunities as they are opened to you and knocking at your door. This man, with a bit of help from us, finally saw that he was ready for greater service. He's now in the hierarchic level working with the animal kingdom in a way that's beyond the physical, and he loves it! His service has enlarged him and he's moved into a higher perspective of who he is.

There must be, then, a recognition that integration has taken place and that you are ready to move beyond your current area of service to a wider one. There is a big difference between accepting your own growth and concentrating on self so much that you are "spiritually ambitious" but out of balance. I must emphasize that it is the purpose — the spiritual service — that is important. If you are doing what you're doing perfectly, it's time to graduate. As soon as you have integrated the purpose for which you've come, you will be given a wider application of that purpose. There is meant to be an ever-widening purpose and service. Keep the door ajar and see who comes to it and knocks. The priest really didn't listen to his counseling in the spirit realm about not going back to the same work over and over. He didn't think he needed it. You have to listen, don't you? For him there was a comfort factor in repeating a known area of service. Many people remain in patterns of behavior longer than he did. It was at the time of the Harmonic Convergence that the allowance came to him to release the pattern. He has gone on and is now taking up an assignment he actually had accepted forty-five lifetimes ago. He's just gotten around to it and has that assignment to fill before any more can be taken up.

How does all this relate to Janet, our channel? Well, Janet has many strengths. Her greatest one is her ability to create through dedication a particular focus that allows a link to be established. The dynamic content of who she is is very helpful. A dynamic content is needed to move a communication ahead. A spiritual teacher goes for quite a ride if connected into this channel. It is a challenge because we have to keep moving to keep up. Janet's astrological sign is Aries, so there is much dynamic quality in her energy.

She is learning to balance that. Recently she opened her channel to a deeper level. She doesn't quite know what that means yet. Her role is to create openings as a channel as well as to open who and what she is herself. She creates openings and she leaves and lets others handle that which has been opened. We use the term "deep" quite often in varying contexts, and you might understand that to mean a broadening of vision, but that is not what I mean. By "going deep" I am talking about going to the core of personal reality in any particular area. If you are on the surface of your understanding in any area, you haven't yet discovered the core. As you discover the core, you may find that doing so broadens the parameters of that area and shows how different areas relate to each other. However, the penetrative core really stimulates the cocreator level, so if you go deeply enough you reach your realized connection to the core, which is the cocreator level.

I mentioned earlier that there is a plan to create a very comprehensive spiritual center or temple in the area of Mississippi. I would estimate its date at about 2020 to 2050. You might not know this, but you are about to solve the process of aging physically. It's very close. When you no longer have to worry about an aging physical structure, it will be much easier to work toward the spiritual purpose for which you have come. Some of you will stay and be a part of this wonderful time on Earth. There are so many things that you, as humanity, have wanted that are going to be coming to pass. Arkansas is also to have a temple, and what will be taught in these temples is how to live in harmony and peace. Earthquakes have been foreseen in those areas, and certainly the Earth in its adjustment will cause some quaking, but I don't see as much earthquake energy there as there used to be. When a specific spiritual focus is located in an area, there is a letting-go of remnants. The spiritual emphasis placed on that area will bring some adjustments because of it. Again, "energy" is a word that is seen as a goal to be acquired. But energy is not the goal; it's what you do with the energy. Energy is life force, a tool by which you create. You are here to create! That's the goal. Energy is the tool of the creative process. If you feel you are not able to "feel" — be aware of — an energy others seem to tune to easily, it's often because you don't yet trust. You might have developed trust in some areas but not integrated these individual areas of trust. You don't allow a fullness of trust for yourself. Now that you can conceptualize that need, you can work on it.

Exercise Seven

Here's another exercise. Stand and stretch upward. We'll say that above you there is an angel or cherub, and you're going to reach up and bring your own individual angel dawn close. Bring it in — the angelic perspective. Reach up and see what you get. Have you brought close a cherub, a little Alazaro or an archangel? They enjoy coming, don't they? Have you noticed that when you pull on one, a whole string of them come along? We have asked the archangels to come, and they are here, and there are hosts of delighted seraphim and cherubim running around. Good! You will be moving about, having an association with the angelic kingdom. They are going to give you the angelic perspective. You will receive communication from them. Let's see what sort of communication you get from this perspective that is coming in now.

We will have some music and we'll let our joyous play with the angels begin. There is a sense of flow, a sense of connection — we validate their connection with us. You have experienced comfort, support, encompassing love, lightness, joyousness, protection, nurturing — good! All that is valid.

Creating a New Universal Level

Now I think I would like to have you create a new universal level. We'll look at it as a universal city and bring in the ideal of such a city. What is the first step in creating a city? The idea and the desire come before any blueprint. One must sort out alternative possibilities and decide on a purpose. Let us say we want it to be a city that anyone can visit, anyone can be a part of, anyone can share, anyone can join. It will be a center for the arts and music and intellectual pursuits, for spirituality, for growing plants and flowers — it will be a very universal city. We are sorting all this out from potentiality so that it forms our purpose. Now we can think of a blueprint. What would you like the city to look like? How do you see it conceptually?

Let us bring in some universal concepts. It needn't be made of your customary earthly building materials. You could decide to invent a crystalline material or something you've never seen on Earth but can imagine. Some of you see it planned as a square with straight streets. Some like a circular pattern or a wheel-like structure with a hub and spokes. One may see it as being not on the Earth but above the Earth and shining with light. Another might see a city of high crystalline buildings joined by ramps and bridges, with sun-powered vehicles and many lakes and streams in a rolling country-side. And still another might feel it needs a combination from a geometric point of view and, in order to capture the essence of the ideal of any given theme, should have a transparency. Most of you concur in wanting spiritual temples and universities where visitors can find inspiration and growth of consciousness.

Good! Where do people live? Oh, that's interesting. You suggest multiple-family buildings surrounded by beautiful green belts, with balconies or areas for outdoor living, and all with lovely views. Individual cooking areas — or communal food preparation and enjoyment of food and togetherness? Perhaps both. Each residential building could have its own temple of healing and spiritual communion and meditation. How about libraries connected intergalactically so that the resources of the galaxy and universe would be available? There could be viewing screens and communication systems with many other civilizations. What sort of computerized system are you visualizing? Your home could be plugged into the central libraries with facilities for holographic viewing. Do you feel there would be a need to visit other cities? Do you see industry going on? Do you want to be productive, to create, to keep busy, to have a choice of your work situation, to have a way in which the less attractive necessities can be shared appropriately? Yes, productivity is a sharing. Clothing — do you have any ideas on that? You don't want to wash and iron and you want to easily acquire changes. Perhaps material can be recycled to keep down waste problems. Women and men can dress as they like for comfort and pleasure. Visitors will be coming from their homelands and wearing their own choice of clothing — there would be wide variety.

Let's say we've created this wonderful city and you are all living there. You get word from Galactic Headquarters that they are sending a delegation and they'll be landing at your spaceport. They will be having their annual meeting in your city, and that will mean an influx of beings coming in from all over the galaxy. You prepare a headquarters for them, sleeping and eating arrangements, and everything is ready for their welcome. They have arrived! What do you notice about them? There is a great variety of physical structures. Some are of the Adam Kadmon form, and others have shapes and sizes and colors and characteristics you've never seen before on your planet.

Is your city adaptable enough to make comfortable such an unusual and complex gathering? Oh, you have expected to host beings from all over and can set up whatever is needed. You've planned to take them on tours of the planet and the cities beneath the seas and the caverns, and to share with them the beauty of your homeland. You feel they had a purpose in choosing to come to this city, and you want to join them in harmony and peaceful communion and to help them succeed in their purpose. You have buildings large enough to house their meetings, you have displays and holograms that allow them access to parts of the planet with which they might not be familiar. They can share in the temples and healing centers and libraries and places for recreation, and all aspects of your daily life. You realize that their feeling welcome here depends on the attitude that all of you have toward them. Good!

Well, I see that you are all ready to invite them over for a party and also invite them to stay with you in your homes – a galactic student-exchange program. You have suggested a cultural exchange program as well, much like the Polynesian culture center in Hawaii. So your willingness to share their culture and what they have created allows a communication that will integrate the whole event, won't it? Now, as this event takes place and you are all hosts and hostesses for it, what do you think is the most important thing to do to make it work right? Organization, communication, advance information, preparation – yes, all these are important. Are you ready for this event?

I think we might look at a few things that could be released in order to bring this specific event in. Wouldn't you enjoy such an event? It's in your future, you know – it's not something that I've just pulled out of my imagination. I've looked at your future and tuned into it, to a specific event, and certainly your city has been interpreted uniquely, but it is not far off from what cities will be in the future. So I thought we might do a little of what we call core releasing to allow that to come about. There is an overall core pattern, an overall basic "blueprint" – a basic pattern that is the ideal level. It comes through the angelic kingdom and cocreator level, but it comes from Source. It comes through many levels administratively – ten or twelve levels – but the angelic kingdom carries it from one level to another, so you might say they are the connectors and guardians. Michael has a reputation for being the guardian of the center of Source Itself, so he steps that down – or, conversely, up – into whatever level of perception you can conceive of. So he will respond as you ask for it and direct it. I think it is important for you to recognize that it comes through the cocreator level but it is the Source-level blueprint that you are invoking – the divine ideal.

We will say that the city is again the circle, and let's recognize that there is such a blueprint and say, "All right, I'm going to bring that energy in and place it on the city." We'll let that cook and simmer within each of you now. Place it in, and bring it on the city. That's the first step. What that does is ring our bell on the cocreator level. It's like ringing the doorbell to get our attention. You open up that ideal level and we say, "Look what's tugging on us. There's that little group down in physical existence and also their Source-level correspondence" — which isn't so little, my friends — and we get a sense of invocation. Now you've put some light force in your city. Certainly there's been some adjusting. The specifics that you see are now adjusting into the reality of not only what is the ideal, but also of what you are capable of creating from that ideal. It becomes more specific because of that.

Next, let us do some core-level releasing in the area of authority figures. There is a sense of being restricted or limited, and there is an excuse system that says why you are restricted. When you release the need to be restricted, then the excuse systems fall away also — it's not the other way around. You're going to do that one of these days with cockroaches. They have been used as an excuse system, and when you release that, then they will decide to transmute into something else. How do you do it? By releasing in the core level that which they represent. For all of humanity there is a great deal of nonclarity about authority and restriction, about the need to restrict because something won't work otherwise. You might get poisoned or you might get affected adversely in other ways on the physical level if there isn't something that limits and restricts you. I'd love to see that one gone.

Group Clearing Meditation

So let's see in the center of our city a temple. This is the hub of your city. Now, this temple is used in a unique way. It's a clearing temple and it rotates 360°; through synchronicity, when you enter the temple you will rotate through 360° in a perceptual sense and begin to release certain stuck points — you will rotate beyond those stuck points and release them. It works through an energy format. As you know, life force is used as a tool for what you create. Now conceptualize and see and view and connect with a temple that can burn out — can literally, through its spiritual connection and linkage, pass through areas of stuckness and transmute them. Certainly the transmuting flame is a part of this, but let's say that we put the flame on a rotator so it will turn and transmute all perceptions of an area instead of clearing just one perception. You can, then, clear out the whole area, level by level, in a way that hasn't seemed possible before — and there are many, many, many levels of perception in any area.

I invite you to sense that all of you are in this temple that rotates. The Violet Flame is in a chamber in the center of the temple. It expands when directed to do so, and its energy comes into the room and also around the perimeter of the building so that you actually rotate through that flame. Now, it's a cold flame, so it won't burn you, but it's transmuting, and when we overlay a portion of the ideal use of humanity's relationship with authority onto that flame, we transmute it to the ideal level. I am going to make a statement or two or three, and this is what is being transmuted. We are allowing the authority to become the level of authority that supports and allows the *stretching into ones full abilities. We are releasing the core belief, the core resistance, that attaches authority to restriction through fear-patterning. That is what is being stimulated and released. So sense energy being overlaid now with the Divine Blueprint. The temple now begins to rotate, and as it does, there is a transmuting process taking place at the core, and you, as a part of the process, will pass through this slow rotation. You're going to get to clear out of yourself, and out of the whole city and the whole Earth, at least one level of the relationship between humanity and authority and restriction. We're going to go through that rather slowly, and you can sense through your spiritual knowingness a burning off of the old and, equally, an activating of the new. Both are taking place simultaneously, so you may feel a lot going on in your physical structure; if you do, just allow it. The angelic kingdom is now connecting this, and it's really working.*

❦ *I invite you to use this as part of a group dynamic. It will work best in a group. You will want to write down, first, what you're seeking to stimulate, and then the negative, what you're seeking to let go of. Then put it in the center of the group and see, in a step-by-step manner, the transmuting of it. I would say we need to stay within this for at least five minutes. To visualize it as specifically as possible is important because we are, through the group focus, burning through, in a transformational sense, many old patterns that you and humanity have had. It will be very easy for you to burn through a level on your own individual material. But the more completely you can connect into this – the deeper the connection goes and the farther you can reach to that ideal level that is the cocreator level – the deeper you can allow the transformation for the Earth and for your city. Now, you might even see the creativity smoking a little, but remember, this is cold fire, transmuting fire, and you can see the temple rotating. I would say we're through about two-fifths of it now. The rotation is very slow, and the burning of it just continues. You are burning up the perspective of limitation in regard to authority, and you're opening up a more free-flowing perception in regard to authority. Eventually the word itself will be reframed, but let us be practical and remove it a step at a time, knowing that you get from the angelic kingdom any sense of protection that you feel you need at this moment, any sense of being connected that you feel you need. Eventually you won't need the angelic kingdom to stimulate this; you will be able to do it for yourself. All right, about two-fifths now as the fire burns and you can sense the old falling off. This is burning up for humanity.*

❦ *I would like very much to take the clearing method to the group process rather than the individualization process. You can do both, but you can do much more clearing for the Earth if you are willing to work in a group format such as this, rotating a specific belief so you really begin to bring in the energy of the positive use of these beliefs for a wide range of humanity. All right, about three-fifths has been rotated as we continue to allow it. Sense, then, as much as you can, validate it as much as you can, this burning quality that is intensifying as it gets the idea of why it is here. It begins to be quite electrical in nature, and we are going to use this in a moment to work on your electrical body, your body of light. You see, a body of light is never individual. It is interconnected with the body of light of the whole, and as you are willing to clear out the core and let the ideal come in, then your electrical core will be clearer. About four-fifths now as the rotating continues. As you get four-fifths, there should be within you a sense that it is coming to completion, that you're getting close to the complete release and the stimulus into the new level of perception in regard to authority. I am not substituting this for the realization process. I think the realization process should be a part of this too, but this is the energy use of the realization process that can stimulate a deeper penetration into the mass consciousness than you know. This is an excellent tool to aid the mass consciousness, and I think your service to the planet and to what we've termed the crystal city – your potential upon this planet – should be the release now of deep core issues in regard to the mass consciousness. We are complete now, and I thank you. You may come back now.*

How real was this for you? I ask about the reality level because if you have quite a bit of material that you haven't made realizations about in a particular area, it might not seem as real for you. In other words, if the reality of it wasn't there, do some realizations and try to figure out why it wasn't, because it will be real when you're clear enough to allow it to be real. That's the key. This technique can be very powerful, and it's one way to progress the methods you are using to include something very directly connected with the mass consciousness. I think that's important. That's part of the integrative process on the planet. Don't go so fast that you skip over some of the areas. You don't burn out the areas very well if you do. It seems to me that the best way is to relate it to 360° and you will burn out this, then this, then this, using the sequencing that you do so well. You are all masters of sequencing here on the physical level. Go into that enough that it slows it down for you. You've often overlooked certain things, glossed over them and not released what you thought you had. So allow yourselves the time to release. And now we will conclude with a final meditation.

Cosmic Skateboard Meditation

☙ *Center into the third-eye area, allowing that connection to be a modeling, a blueprint, of the full integration process. Allow it to open now, this area. Remember that the ideal is right there in the third-eye area and use that as a foundation to open up electrically to the universe. Open up to be stimulated within that ideal. You could say the ideal is a skateboard that you can skate upon now. Sense that stimulating you now with the urge to move, to flow; the electrical stimulation is there. You hear it now; you're going to stay balanced. You're going to get on your skateboard and move now. Movement, movement – where are you going to go on your cosmic skateboard? You can go anywhere you wish. You're flowing electrically on this balance that you've* created. Get a sense of movement, of electrical movement now. You are awake, you are cosmically awake. You are moving now on this electrical flow, but it is a very balanced one as you allow it now. We've been talking about integration; this is the integration exercise that will allow you to see how you've been doing. Notice the purposeful use of this cosmic skateboard and see what is stimulated as you move upon it now. Where is your awareness taking you? What is coming forth for you? This is the electrical flow, the use of the integrated energy, the purpose for which we have come together. You're being stimulated to use it now in a balanced manner. Only in an integrated manner can it be used, and you're flowing on it now.

❧ What are you seeing? What are you becoming aware of through this integrative process? Stay with me. Don't go off and leave me now. Stay here, focused in this integrative process through this electrical connection. Another way of looking at it is that your third eye is connected electrically with the eye of Sourceness now. There is that electrical connection, that particular flow connection, that allows you to move in an integrated manner now, that allows you to accept and receive and thus to choose to flow electrically. You have an electrical tap at Source level that is the stimulus for you, that flows now into an integrated slot that is stimulating the way that you move. The flow is there; sense it now, the flow is there. Are you having fun? Are you staying balanced? I think so. There has been a lot of integration and it is showing now as you flow electrically. Flow electrically now. What is becoming available to you? Sense the flow. Even if you don't specifically see everything yet, sense the flow and allow it now. Listen to the music. It's stimulating you now. The electrical system is being stimulated now. The integration of the electrical system is allowing you to use it very clearly. Flow it, flow it. Purposefully flow it, embodying this very electrical energy in a very balanced manner. Balanced and flowing, balanced and moving, balanced and playful – did you notice? Joyful, very playful and joyful, very humorous. There's nothing heavy about electrical energy at the Source level. It's very humorous; it has a wonderful sense of humor. Sense that now.

❧ It's very creative. The more integrated it is, the more creative it is. See the infinite variety of Sourceness as you flow in an integrative manner now, because the flow has many lines now, many avenues to explore, but they are all integrated now. You can sense the connections, the connections that flow together. You are experiencing in a multiple way now, blending in a multiple way, but it is no longer one perspective; it is a blended perspective, a unified and integrated perspective. Sense that. You are looking at creation, viewing it on many levels, from many, many points now, all cooperating, all flowing together, but be aware of the many avenues of exploration, all simultaneous, all taking place at once. See the exploration, hear it in the music, the exploration that is taking place in many, many ways now. You are creating many, many, many, many ways all at once now. Sense that flowing electrically many ways, many avenues of expression because you've balanced them and integrated them. This doesn't *mean there's only one way. It means you've balanced them and integrated or allowed them to cooperate – full cooperation, full communication, coming together in an integrated sense; cooperative, communicative, blending, flowing, allowing cooperation, allowing the purpose of the whole to be embodied, cooperating in the creative stream, allowing it to come together now. Good. Good. That was fun! That was fun!*

Electrically stimulated now through this integrative process, you are plugged into the multiplicity that we call Sourceness, the blending, the flowing, the uniting of purpose, the uniting of spirit flowing together now, going through various levels of cooperation, reframing, rebalancing. Movement! Allow the movement as the levels clarify, as they become clearer, as they communicate, as they share, as they care, as there is harmonious attunement through these levels, a cooperative effort that cares and shares through the levels now. Allow the electrical stimulus you're plugged into. The Source Itself is allowing that now, and your sense of cooperation comes forth from this level. This is full cooperation where everything simultaneously fits into everything else, through communication, through caring and sharing, and then it flows together electrically, stimulated now through the Source-level integration you've attuned to. You can attune to that Source-level integration and it will reflect into your present experience. It will reflect into your life as you allow it now. The glorious sound is telling us how much can be accomplished through this integrative approach, through this blended approach, and it is the electrical stimulus that you are all experiencing now, the electrical flow of the Source as you've allowed it to be integrated through you now.

Nothing much can be accomplished individually; it must flow together. It is flowing together and it is expanding because it is coming together, and what you are balancing now, transcending what has been, gloriously aware of this balanced space, is allowing this electrical energy to flow in. It examines and multiplies the structure. It clarifies it and then enhances it. It explores it and then enlarges. The enlargement of the structure, the enlargement of the support system – it is ever getting larger, balanced now, completely balanced, integrated. It is being allowed by you to expand, to keep expanding. Become aware of this constant, consistent expansion of Source through you. This is the integrative system, a continuing expansiveness of Sourceness that is available because of Its relatedness, because of Its communicative flow that you are allowing in the electrical area. Note that, and note that it keeps expanding and you keep expanding the love, the trust. The ability to allow all of these qualities is what you are expanding, but it is the multiple nature of the expansion that I want you to notice – that it flows from not just one point that you have validated individually, but now in your allowingness, now in your integration, it flows through you in multiple points.

Multiplicity is the goal here — multiple sharing, multiple caring, multiple focuses that are the integrative point of view. This is what is being experienced here: a multiplicity that expands and expands and yet comes back to the integrated purpose for which its expansion began. It goes through the levels, the levels of expansion, bringing you back to an integrated area, to an integrated focus. And note the expansive effect. This is the integrated flow within you, and it is important to recognize it expanding electrically, multiplying, multiplying. And note the fun, the exuberance of it, the sharing of it and, yes, the caring nature of it: an expanding, harmonizing, growing movement — a sense that transcends, a sense that lets go when needed but then adjusts to the new level of integration that comes in from this core-level releasing. Sense, then, the transcendence of the integrated state and allow the electrical stimulus to keep growing, to keep moving, to keep generating the contact within you; movement and electrical flow, flowing through all of the integrative possibilities, all of the integrative steps, the ability to flow electrically from every point of view, to keep transcending what has been. This is the way the Source works; this is the cocreator level, and you are embodying it. Sense that — the transcendence through the electrical flow, cooperating, changing and growing, the use of integration as a tool for that process. Good. All right. Begin to come back now. Begin to be aware again of the physical level, allowing yourself to be within your physical structure again.

I took you very deeply in that one to let you experience the integrated state because this was our closing meditation. I thank you for sharing this experience with me.

✦ PART SIX ✦

THE EVOLUTIONARY PROCESS

Vywamus, 1985-1990

Introduction to Vywamus

My friends, I, Djwhal Khul, have the privilege of introducing to you Vywamus – a great being who has come among us to serve during these critical yet marvelous times when humanity seeks to evolve into spiritual consciousness, casting off the outworn forms and moving in greater light into the New Age. Many spiritual teachers are appearing to help mankind and Mother Earth make this transition as painless and clear as possible and at as high a level as possible.

Vywamus is one of a very elevated consciousness. He is an evolved aspect of Sanat Kumara, our Planetary Logos, who ensouls the Earth and all upon it and within it. The Earth is in effect being held together by his focus of consciousness. At a still higher level of consciousness is Vywamus. He can be equated to the higher self, as we sometimes refer to it, or the soul, of Sanat Kumara.

Vywamus evolved to his present position through the physical chain – just as humanity has chosen to do. Vywamus chose to express in physical existence eons ago, and did this on a planet similar to Earth. While in physical existence he was offered the opportunity to be a channel for higher energies, and through this serving he gained clear perceptions and quickly passed on to the spiritual plane. This was accomplished after only 37 incarnations on the physical.

Now, in his great love, he has chosen to assist mankind. An exceptional channel, Janet McClure, brings through this explanation of the system, which Vywamus offers to mankind with his love.

– Djwhal Khul

✧ O N E ✧

The History of Earth Before Lemuria

H UMANITY IS READY TO HEAR ITS HISTORY. I THINK PEOPLE WILL FIND IT
interesting to hear about what we might call the old days.
We'll start with a rather modern event of about eighteen million years
ago, when Sanat Kumara came. You might not think of that as modern,
but given what we are going to talk about, perhaps it is. That event began
a whole different cycle for the Earth. Earth literally became able, at that time,
to know it had a soul. Sanat Kumara brought that knowingness to the Earth,
and it has been learning about it ever since. What, was the Earth like then
and what was it like before? Well, we are going to view the Earth in several
stages as it grew and evolved.

Some of you have studied about coming to the Earth and some of you
might remember it from a regression. You would remember yourself as not
being in a physical body but being in an astral shell and looking at the Earth.
The Earth was cooling. Some of you remember that or know of someone
who does. Now, what was that all about? You could say you were getting
a preview. The souls knew that they were coming to Earth. Have you ever
gone to take a look at a new house as it was being built? In a sense, then,
although your souls do not function in space at all, they were able to extend
into space, into physical existence, and begin to preview what would be
coming forth. Many of you came and looked at least once as the Earth cooled
off from what it had been. If was rather warm as the cocreator who brought
it forth put it all together. It was completed but required physical integration.
So as it integrated and became cool enough to be used by those who were
coming, it was really an interesting place to investigate.

Some of you looked at fire welling up from the deep volcanoes and you
wondered – without fear, just interest – if you were to live in that fiery
element, since it was a new and obviously different substance from the water

that had covered everything. You watched as the water became mud. After that the water evaporated, leaving a more solid substance. That is not a scientific description, of course, but an approximate view. Some of you had been in physical life and had lived underwater early in the Earth's history. There were many possibilities, and your soul, or an aspect of your soul extended in an astral sheath, would look and think about the possibilities and form opinions and wishes and desires about how evolution might go. The cocreator, who was setting up various possibilities within a physical framework, collected all those opinions, wishes and desires and considered them. He tried some of them. For instance, he tried physical vehicles of ten feet or more in height, which proved to be, considering the force of gravity, not too practical. There was a civilization, however, of beings that were eight feet tall. Theirs was perhaps the first civilization that came forth.

It is difficult to describe how the physical forms came to be. It was not the case that one man and one woman just appeared on the planet. In a rather cosmic way, the Earth nurtured the divine possibilities, and from the Earth itself came forth the first pair of these beings. This is not, of course, to say that they were made only of Earth; we are talking about the body, the physical vehicle itself, as a means to express. The divine essence, then, became indwelling within the body. So the Earth gave birth to the first life forms that resembled what we consider to be human form.

The Earth brought forth all the other life forms also. There were life forms already upon the planet before human forms appeared. In a sense, those who teach the progression of evolution are correct, for Earth and life force developed over eons of time from sea to land and so forth. But there is a particular point where consciousness again enters a new archetype. If you have a tape of a lecture and you make many copies from it, there comes a time when you want a new master tape. Learning from the old tape is no longer as appropriate; it becomes necessary to redefine the message to fit a higher level of learning, a different way of evolving, though not necessarily a better one.

There were beautiful mineral, plant and animal kingdoms, but a time came when a higher form was needed — again, not necessarily better, but able to define the life process in a different manner. So a different means of learning came forth — the human way.

You have wondered and asked about this, so we might as well talk a little about the dolphins. The dolphins were one of the earliest and highest forms of animal life upon the planet. At first they did not live in the water but on land. They had a close, friendly relationship with the eight-foot-tall beings. You could say they were pets, though not in the same way as dogs were. They were very close to these beings of the first race that came to the Earth.

Remember that these beings were really pioneers — a first-ray approach — and perhaps the archetype of the first ray upon Earth. They were well developed in the mental areas but did not necessarily make practical use of their mental abilities within a physical environment. For many of these beings this was their first experience of this kind, their first physical body, and though they knew intellectually what should be done, they didn't always apply their knowledge in a practical manner. We could say some of them were spiritual scientists: They knew all the theories, and now it was time to show some results. For instance, they knew that if you built a six-foot trench around a city, you would have a place into which rainwater could drain. But it was something else to figure out a means of digging the trench. Life in the physical was an interesting experiment. Some of them overestimated what physical bodies could stand, and there were many accidents and many shortened lives. It was sometimes painfully necessary to learn through the physical structure; you sometimes feel this, too. If you were eight feet tall and very, very thin, with very long arms and legs, there would be interesting adjustments to be learned in how to relate to environment. They were really rather strong despite being so tall.

Now, they did not believe the birth process had to be painful, so it was not painful. Babies were about two feet long at birth but very thin, which made them emerge more easily. Children walked at six months.

So what did they do? What was their life like? These people were literally seeded upon the Earth. They came forth, and within about one hundred years there were probably fifty thousand of them spread over the Earth. Now, the Earth was certainly very unlike the way it is now. There were three major continents and only four oceans. The part of the world now called America extended much farther into the Pacific and Atlantic oceans. Where South America is now, there was ocean, because South America was nearer to Africa then.

The principal civilizations were in the area now called the South Pacific, where there was a large landmass. There were civilized areas in what is now the northern United States and some in Tibet and northern China. Finland was also a center of a civilized group. The climate of the northern area was much warmer than it is now.

These fifty thousand people, after a hundred years or so, were in a sense scientists and developed a rather scientific approach to life. Many scientific developments occurred rather early. Women, for instance, decided that personally bearing babies wasn't as good an idea as having insemination and gestation take place in a test tube. They liked the freedom this gave them.

They found a way to support themselves with food by creating a specific type of neutralizer that, when applied to soil, made it possible to grow anything very easily. It sounds as though they produced an ideal civilization right away, doesn't it? What do you think happened? Well, the basic physical structure got in the way. The eight-foot-tall beings were always breaking bones, and it was decided by the cocreator that such a physical structure was not appropriate on the Earth, so some of them were literally removed by spaceship to a place having less gravity where they would be better off. Those who remained gradually died out.

Anyone who has designed structures has experienced the fact that modifications to an original product sometimes have to be made and you learn from unsuccessful attempts. Make no mistake, the cocreators learn a great deal from their creations, and in this way evolution takes place. The Adam Kadmon structure you now use has proven to be a much more efficient model. The form that followed the eight-foot model was shorter and heavier and did not last either. They had a third arm extending from the back, which was not as useful as you might think. Nevertheless, they were around for about ten thousand years, which is a very short time from the viewpoint of a cocreator, before they were pulled back. Now, later on, in Atlantis, there were memories of such beings, and part of the confusion within the cellular level led to the mixing of the human and the animal. This was not really so much animal genetics as a memory of what had been once seeded upon Earth. Once something has been seeded onto a planet there is a racial memory of it. If someone with possibly good motives but not enough knowledge of what they are doing creates something, "interesting" results may occur which can take quite a while to work out and change or end. I think it is important to understand that when something is stimulated without real understanding or knowledge of what might result, it starts a chain reaction. Some of these have happened here on Earth.

Now, there were some scientists in the Adam Kadmon model who decided to take a look at Earth and see what would be more fitting. They weren't sure that Earth was ready yet for the Adam Kadmon model, but they came to view Earth. So we have these beings arriving on the Earth, and thus began the legends of the coming of the gods. These scientists, these great beings of light, came and communicated in the languages of the inhabitants. They began to study the beings of Earth extensively. They found some of the dolphins that were still here and they recognized that the dolphin is a magnificent being — extremely so. The scientists wanted a means to store the history of the planet, so they chose to encode the dolphins with the whole story of developing Earth. Within the genes of the dolphins lies this history, though not all of them are aware of it. They have the ability to recall all of it, and if you were able to have them project images upon a screen, it would be fascinating.

The advanced scientists spread over the planet and began to experiment. One of them brought forth some beings in very small forms, like dwarfs. Some introduced Adam Kadmon forms in different colors of skin. Others brought the models of the ones you see in your science fiction. Many who write science fiction today are attuned to memories of beings of every description that lived here on this planet as the scientists attempted to find the most appropriate physical structure.

During a period of some fifty thousand years there were many diverse forms upon the Earth. It was during this time that there was an underwater civilization. They were gentle people with blue eyes and golden hair, a most attractive race. It was at this time that the dolphins began to adapt to living in the water. The underwater race learned how to find food, and indeed, how to grow crops and harvest them. There were fish in the seas, many of which were friends of the underwater race. There wasn't such a predatory attitude among the kingdoms then. The balance of the food chain remained, of course, as the larger fish used the smaller ones for food, but intentional predatory violence was something only gradually learned upon Earth. Finally it was decided by the "gods" that the Adam Kadmon structure was indeed the one that would function best. The other forms were not destroyed; some were lifted off to another place and some ceased to propagate and gradually died out. The ability to use space travel has been available since the beginning of your planet.

So Adam Kadmon was brought here with all the different races with their different skin tones, and they began to flourish. Great civilizations sprang up. They were not necessarily interconnected at this point – there was a great civilization in China and another somewhat south of China. There was a great one in the Tibetan area before the coming of Sanat Kumara. This civilization was probably the greatest the Earth has ever known. In the area of Ireland, a knowingness developed about the "little people" who were very connected with the Earth itself, and the archetype of this connection came forth then. There were scientific communities and rural communities, and the underwater community still existed. Many of the cultures were creative in the arts and there were forms of dance that have never been revived. Most people were vegetarians. Animal life as we know it now was not upon the Earth; there were some animals, but not many species. There were, however, millions and millions of birds of many different species, many more than you have now.

The First Avatar

The great civilizations flourished and then an important event happened: The first avatar came to the Earth. This great being who came is now far beyond interaction with you, except in a love focus. To be in touch with him now as you were then would be impossible. He has gone on to the full-fledged cocreator state. But at that time, in his great dedication, he came forth to the Earth and anchored a particular energy, a particular attribute or possibility. What to you think would be the first thing that would need to be anchored on a physical planet? Love? Use of mind? No – these were already active to some degree. What he brought was spiritual attunement. It was the desire to incorporate, through physical existence, the divine essence of All That Is.

How do you suppose an avatar would attempt to teach this? What would he be like? Would he be a poor carpenter or a wise man? Well, he certainly was wise. He came forth as a scientist in a highly developed civilization, and his message was, "Look at the beauties of creation that can be scientifically projected in physical existence. All of this can be incorporated into the understanding of spiritual opportunity." So he used his scientific framework and launched much beyond it into a spiritual incorporation of that scientific endeavor. That doesn't seem to fit with what you know about your Earth's history, does it?

Well, humanity didn't accept it. The great teachers saw that humanity wasn't ready for the opportunity. It was not a failure but it was, in the conceptual framework of existence and in the evolutionary process, offered too soon. It was going to be a while before this particular planet was ready to hear what such a great one had to say. So this great avatar did not stay here.

Let's take a moment to discuss other life forms. The Loch Ness monster, as it's called, is rather like an aquatic dinosaur and developed much later than the era we've been considering – he's much more modern. The time of the dinosaurs and the other large species of animals was in the time of Lemuria and early Atlantis. The Loch Ness creatures (there are three of them) have simply been able to continue on the Earth all this time.

The mermaids are both a figment of imagination and actual. There was in Atlantis a joining of the genes. At about this time there was a young woman who, in her desire to serve, had gone into the laboratory and was working to help free beings who were trapped in bodies that were monstrosities that were kept there in the laboratories. While working she accidentally became contaminated by material that was being processed. She inhaled smoke, and some of her skin was covered with the spilled substance, and from this a transformation occurred, changing her to a form that was half fish and half human. Of course, a great many legends have grown up around this actual occurrence. The young woman was lovely, with much divine intent, and she spent much of her time in the laboratories trying to help the unfortunates there. There were similar forms, but the many and varied stories about mermaids stemmed mainly from what happened to this young woman. As far as I know, there are none in existence today.

From the time the avatar first came forth and found Earth unready for the opportunity he offered, there came about a backslide in scientific knowledge, quite a distinct backslide, actually. When the Adam Kadmon beings came to Earth they had the ability, previously developed, of creating test-tube babies. However, many people – sometimes for religious reasons, sometimes for fear or distrust of the process – began to declare that such a thing was wrong or inappropriate, and so the knowledge was lost. It is, of course, there in racial memory. It was not that Adam Kadmon beings were more or less intelligent than the "tall people." It was more that in evolution there comes a fork in the road, or a detour, or a point of exploration. We do not have to detour or explore a byway, but we choose to do so. You might say humanity traveled a loop at that point, rather than using all of what was available to them. They learned a great deal from the experiences of that loop and entered back into the mainstream of evolution much stronger, so it was not altogether inappropriate.

If you want to study the difference in the sexes and whether women's opportunities began to be diminished, we have to get very esoteric to look at that. Everyone is seeking to save the equality of the life stream as it comes form the Source. Certainly on the physical level there are important points where, again, a decision is made, and that decision takes you, at least for a while, ever further away from the ability to balance the male and female. Eventually, after the deviation has been explored, there is more strength and more understanding. Humanity is well on its way back. Male and female began as a unity, then explored as duality, and is now coming again, at another level, toward unity.

I realize that humanity has formulated varying ideas about evolution. Certainly the biblical and Darwinian approaches are controversial. Perhaps humanity should remain open to the possibility of gradually learning much beyond what is now postulated. As the truth unfolds, eventually all the pieces can come together. It isn't that the Bible or Darwin is wrong; their information is incomplete. They both tell part of the history of the planet but not all of it. I do say, absolutely, that humanity did not evolve from the ape species. When you consider evolution, consider it from the Creators point of view.

Let's consider the steps of the creative process. To illustrate we'll use the creation of a painting. The artist desires to paint and knows generally the kind of painting he wants to achieve. A mental concept, an idea, is anchored deeply within him. He has the knowingness of the process of creating a painting. He desires, he has the idea, he knows what materials he will need and how to use them. He collects them and, because of the anchored conception within, he produces a physical out-forming of that idea. A cocreator creates in such a manner. He considers what he wishes to bring forth and takes into consideration all the intricate points involved in the process. He considers the evolution of the whole and how his creation will fit into the scheme of things. He looks at and considers the viewpoints, opinions and desires of the beings that will be involved as well as the appropriateness of this in relation to what is already in creation on all planes of manifestation. So it is using all of the criteria and then taking the knowingness and ability of cocreatorship to produce the concept in the plane in which it is to manifest.

The seeding of planets, the evolution and dissolution of planets, is an ongoing process — to use sequential terms. We speak of evolution as a spiral, for there are beings and planets at every point on the spiral, and we are here to help in this time when a harvesting is near. The seeding of a planet, you could say, is the taking of those souls who are to be a part of this process and gathering up just a little bit of each of them and that particular divine essence, which is then is seeded into a physical planet. It is a specific genetically controlled seeding process which evolves in a genetically determined pattern. Sometimes it works well right away and sometimes there might be unanticipated results. The Adam Kadmon seedings have generally been successful and reliable.

An Incomplete Utopia

After the Adam Kadmon were established and there were centers of civilization, and the great avatar had come and not been accepted, what happened then? A spiritual opportunity was given to your planet and was rejected, and although the people wouldn't have perceived it as such, it seems to me that life didn't contain a completeness. They had sent away the means to completeness. Sometimes when we are looking for something to get us to the goal, we know we want to journey toward the goal but were not sure where to go or how to get there; we just know we have to go. So humanity began a frenzy of activity. Great cities developed, there was much activity in the arts of writing, music and dance. Great scientific explorations took place, some productive, some not. There was a delving into the black arts. The intricacies of the Earth were studied, and we see a civilization going into the center of the Earth from the surface and coming back again. We see a very open interaction with other planets. There were spaceports where other planetary civilizations made contact in their spaceships and were welcomed, not rejected.

There was then something rather close to a utopia, but remember, it was from a point that was not complete. Then there were those who began power plays. Great "lords" came forth and ruled cities and then city-states, which became kingdoms. Their sons were given control over father city-states that would be gathered together until finally the Earth was under the rule of about six great lords. The population of the Earth numbered about ten million people living in about seventy or seventy-five of these city-states. Eventually they went to war with each other — and so we have the beginning of war upon Earth.

People became enslaved, and that civilization which had been so strong and so beautiful began to crumble. They had high technology, and though they didn't have atomic weapons, they nonetheless managed to blow each other up. So finally, under the direction of one warlord, they dwindled down from millions to less than one million — about nine hundred thousand. This warlord and his family ruled for about ten thousand years, and then we sent another teacher. Now, all this was much, much earlier than Atlantis. Your history, you see, is much longer than you know. This took place way before Lemuria and way before those we call the Electrical Ones, who also preceded Lemuria.

Another teacher, another great avatar, was sent to Earth. In appearance he rather resembled those beautiful pictures you have of Lord Maitreya, with his reddish blond hair and blue eyes. He was a very tall man and was fond of wearing a silver robe. He was the first great teacher to really make an impact upon your Earth. He was an absolutely beautiful being. His name was Lo Chi. This great being is deeply imbedded in your Earth consciousness, and the Earth is very grateful for him. You might call on him. I don't know if it would be possible to channel him, but you might touch into that magnificent essence.

There was a later avatar who anchored courage on the Earth, a later anchoring of wisdom through Buddha, and even later, an anchoring in the love area. This great being brought a tentative beginning in all these areas, and it was well done. This being came into physical existence as the son of the great warlord of whom I just spoke. He took the nine hundred thousand survivors of the war period and began to build a very spiritual community. Only remnants of the great civilization remained, but he purposefully separated some of them into colonies. He created spiritual communities and temples which flourished on the Earth for about ten thousand years. Some of the prototypes of your beautiful temples began right there with this great teacher.

This was a high point in Earth civilization, and it was after he was upon the Earth that the first harvesting took place. He anchored many possibilities for Earth.

The population began to grow and it was an interesting time in which to live. There were small aircraft, something like your one-engine planes. They were not propelled in the same manner but they were about the same size. The wealthy people could have their own planes, and some of you might tune into memories of this (as well as to memories of flight on Atlantis).

There were great expanses of unpopulated wilderness in which the animal population was beginning to increase. There had been comparatively few animals, but a much larger number of birds. Nine hundred thousand people was not a great number, and the animals had lots of space and began to increase in number. I spoke earlier of the seeding of the Earth with animal forms. The animal kingdom increased in one wave, and later the human kingdom increased in number, so there was an ebb and flow of the interaction of the kingdoms on the Earth.

While I'm talking about kingdoms, let's consider the plant kingdom, which is the most advanced one on your planet. It's very interesting and it's just continued to plow ahead. It hasn't been affected adversely by its relationship with any of the other kingdoms. The animal kingdom has been affected by the human kingdom, but the plant kingdom has moved ahead steadily over the whole history of your planet and now it is ahead in its evolution. You have one of the most advanced plant kingdoms in the galaxy. That's why you have such glorious flowers and such luxuriant woods and forests. It is very advanced, and humanity could learn much from its steady, progressive viewing of its goal. The plant kingdom has always been aware, in an esoteric way, of just what it was meant to be, and it has kept going for that goal.

The animals had these great areas in which to live, with great abundance of food. They began to flourish and many varieties and species developed. What could people do? Well, they could go on wonderful vacations and experience these wilderness areas. The wilderness was friendly — the animals were not ferocious, not afraid of humans. They didn't come close to humans so they did not know they should be afraid of humans; it was a live-and-let-live situation. The animals accepted humans as other animals that had their own way of loving. Humanity learned a great deal from studying the animals. There were great scientists who began to experiment with the animals. This was the beginning of the type of thing that came into the foreground in the Atlantean civilization.

There were experiments to see how knowledge of the animals could be used by humanity. They didn't seem to find it inappropriate to use the animals for this purpose. The animal kingdom took notice of this, and so began the fear pattern that animals now have deep in their racial memories. In certain less-developed species there are deep racial memories of the painful episodes in which they were misused by humanity. What have been built up, then, are specific areas of misunderstanding and mistrust between kingdoms. It was not, at that time, a matter of animals being used for food, though now there is a seeking to resolve this, and it is an important lesson. The scientists and environmentalists now working on this are the means toward balancing the relationship between the kingdoms. It's coming along, and it is important for this civilization to notice when the pattern began.

There were scientists looking to understand many things more clearly, and some were seeking information on the aging process. People were living for about one hundred years, and the span was increased to about one hundred fifty years. We seem to have gone backwards, but in my opinion there was a conscious choice to shorten the life span. Why? Because many times when you are seeking to learn physically, it's important to occasionally have a fresh start — a new slate upon which to write. You might say your souls had a conference on the spiritual level and agreed to shorten the life span. When they lived longer lives, people tended to become stuck in patterns of living. Taking on a new physical structure tended to break up that undesirable pattern and allow a chance to reassess and grow.

After life spans were shortened, they again began to lengthen progressively. Some of the very lengthy life spans were recorded in your Bible. We have spoken of that particular history of your Earth; it was a true history but not a complete one. Then life spans were shortened again, and now are being extended once more. So we have a pattern, an ebb and flow, as evolution takes place. We have said there is a pulse to existence — an active phase and an inactive phase — and here we relate it to the average life spans of physical beings.

People enjoyed their lives. They had to work to do — jobs. Children were cared for mostly in nurseries. Mothers had responsibilities other than twenty-four-hour-a-day child care. Families took vacations together. There were scientists, musicians and dancers; the arts were greatly developed. Under the direction of the great teacher I discussed, there was a well-balanced civilization, and it peaked at the mass ascension I have mentioned before.

Now, this particular mass ascension was not as traumatic as the one I'm going to tell you about later. This one was the end of a cycle — the end of a level of living on Earth and the beginning of a new one. Many of you began to wander in toward the Earth. Most of you — indeed, all of you — were on the Earth by the pre-Lemuria period. Before that, for about a fifty-thousand-year span, you would come and look, but the civilizations that followed after the spiritual teacher left and the mass ascension took place were rather stuck for a while. Some of those who were left sought to follow the ones who had ascended. Some did, but gradually the number of ascensions slowed to just a few here and there. There didn't seem to be any forward movement in the civilization.

A Third Avatar

The spiritual leaders observed the situation and decided to send another teacher. About every two thousand years humanity is stimulated by a spiritual teacher. So a new teacher came forth, a very interesting being, with some very novel ideas. He asked permission to try something different. He felt the Earth was an ideal format to try new ideas, and the beings who were guiding Earth at that time agreed, after some consideration, that he might do so.

He looked at the fact that the Earth was known for its many scientists and its scientific intelligence. It seemed to have a good climate for that. Now, it's interesting to see how this differs from what the books tell you, because we are going back beyond the records to the time of this particular being who had a novel idea that changed the whole history of your Earth. He said, "I think this emphasis on the scientific approach has delayed the progress of the Earth; it has delayed spiritual attunement. Let us try another approach. We will encourage more the emotional qualities and occupations and we will stimulate humanity in that area."

Well, many wonderful things came from that. Some of the greatest art was produced, but you could say the planet literally shut down scientifically and there didn't seem to be any activity there. Eventually it seemed as if the activity of science had never been. A veil seemed to have covered even the racial memory of it, and no one knew how to use it. You turned that off for a while; it really was turned off. Thus it seemed at this time of new beginning as if all that scientific experience had never been, and thus in your racial memories you think you never had it. Why? It was a conscious decision made by those who guided your planet.

I told you about the first avatar and how, in his scientific approach to spirituality, he was not accepted at all. The spiritual teachers had been looking at that and evaluating it and they decided on a new approach. So the pendulum swings from one side to the other, trying to balance in the middle, but no one knows how to make it stay in the middle without this extreme swing at first. Therefore we see the civilization really concentrated at first on the art, music and dance, and most people literally not thinking in a scientific or analytical way. Certainly there were some who did; I'm not saying there were not great thinkers and great leaders, but the masses, the mass consciousness literally began to forget, to bury the memory really, because once it is there it is always there. But it was forgotten, and it took several events to swing that pendulum back to the point where what was buried could be remembered and rediscovered.

Now, there were long periods in which humanity forgot to look deeply, to analyze — to think, in a sense. Humanity went a lot by feeling. (Not that thinking puts you in a "dark age," but we are talking about a time on your planet when it was as though you were guided along a certain path and you went along without thinking or even questioning the need to think or question.) The creativity, art, music and dance was there, but the mental potency was not there. Thus there was a tunneling-in effect and humanity went along that corridor until we began to approach again a period when some began to question whether this was appropriate. Remember, we are looking at vast periods of time. We see a period of fifty to a thousand years in this tunnel effect, and then it began to broaden until it reached a point close to your own scientific knowledge. Scientists were delving into the nuclear area and much was understood in this area. The spiritual teachers were helping humanity and again there was a mass ascension. After that, pre-Lemuria came forth.

When I talk about a mass ascension, I mean there were thousands who did so. They'd gone through a period of mental expansion, gone off of it a little, gone through an emotional and intuitive period and managed to balance both and were ready to leave. You see, the teachers were not wrong about that. They were teaching humanity how to balance — how to come into balance — so many were ready to graduate from the Earth and did graduate. But there were some, and some of you among them, who were not yet ready but thought you soon would be.

Now, what happens on a planet when there is a mass ascension? Those who are left do not have that "light" of the ones who have gone forth to help them with their relationship to the mass consciousness. What is left in the mass consciousness are many beliefs that have not yet been dealt with and balanced. You might say the programming of the mass consciousness is there without the understanding that those who had left had helped to balance. So those of you who were left trusted, and reached deeply into your spiritual connection, knowing with joy and happiness that you would be next, that soon you would be ascending also. What did you get? You got pre-Lemuria. You got the Electrical Ones. The planet was literally attacked by another group of beings who wanted to take it over. Now, I know it sounds just like science fiction, so enjoy it!

The point is that humanity believed in their Earth. They had great confidence in the Earth and wanted to keep it free, wanted to protect it. So they began to *defend* the Earth. The Electrical Ones came forth and tried to take it over. The Earth beings would come into a physical body, defend the Earth and be destroyed; come into a physical body, defend the Earth and be destroyed. So there developed a pattern that said, "When I defend, I am immediately attacked and destroyed." It is a recognizable pattern that is rather prevalent on the Earth now — various nations needing to defend themselves. Why? Because someone is going to attack. It's not the other way around — that we attack first and then defend against attack. It's that we defend because we expect — we believe — that an attack is coming. This is where that prevalent pattern came from. The interesting part of all this is that what is woven into the mass consciousness is "When I trust the most, when I really connect in deeply and make that connection in trust and love, that's when I get pre-Lemurian attack." Isn't that interesting? When you work with this pattern (take it out of your own subconscious), you certainly aid self and you aid the Earth. You help the Earth to break the chain, and I can't think of anything more important than to keep these old patterns from cycling through just because they've "always" been there.

This particular pre-Lemurian civilization lasted about five hundred years. It was an intense time for the Earth, and many of you — almost all of you — were there working for humanity, creating life for yourselves, but over and over and over, being drafted by the human need and going forth to defend the Earth. Interwoven into this are all of those stories that you see on your TVs. You have spies, implants, all of these things are woven into that particular time on the Earth that was so devastating. The mass consciousness has all of these things within its memory. Many of you have them also.

✧ T W O ✧

The History of Earth from Lemuria Onward

A FTER PRE-LEMURIA CAME A NEW BEGINNING CALLED LEMURIA, A NEW
beginning when humanity was exhausted. Much of your esoteric
literature goes into the story of Lemuria — humanity was very tired and
wanted rest and recreation. They got it, for they *created* it. So you have the
civilizations in the South Pacific that were very nice, where people swam and
enjoyed themselves and really rested. They had had a hard time for five
hundred years and now the Earth was safe and free, and they rested. Of
course, not everyone did, and nobody did in every lifetime, but there was a
sense of relief and release.

So humanity entered a long period called Lemuria in which they began
to reframe. They considered what they had been doing and decided to really
go in step-by-step and make sure that this time they reached their goal in a
progressive manner, without all the confusion. People didn't actually,
physically say they would do this, but on the spiritual level where the souls
really assess physical existence, this *is* true. The souls look at the progress,
or seeming lack of it, on the physical plane and literally go into analyzing to
see if there is a better way to handle it. Thus we see the beginning of a new
way of operating.

Now, let's see what you remember of this particular time. You remember living in caves and that there were many animals roaming about. You
remember that though you lived in a rather primitive way, you also had
considerable sophistication. That is true, but what humanity did was to
consider what had happened when they lived out in the open and found
themselves under attack. They may have moved into caves, but the caves
were beautifully decorated with paintings and floor coverings and fine
textiles. They had knowledge of how to construct buildings, but they wanted
to be free to move about and experience their relationship to the planet. It

was free and it was theirs, and they wanted to explore and attune to the planet. They appreciated it more after having defended it. It really was an important time.

You might have read that eyesight was poor during the time of living in caves. Well, esoterically, the eyesight is related directly to trying to see how goals can be reached. Integrating and fitting together ways to reach the spiritual goal of ascension that all of them were seeking had an impact. As you know, when you can't see how it all fits together, the eyesight can be affected.

Now, I mentioned animals, and large ones were there. The animal kingdom had been developing tremendously, and one of the developments was the massive species which came forth. But while the large animals were a danger, they were not the only reason people lived in caves. They lived in caves for a very basic reason – you could say it was synchronicity, a getting back to basics. They had technologies for building but they decided not to use them for a time. Large groups of people lived in the great caves together. Again, to me, it was more than a matter of protection. To me, it was getting back to basics. The very basis of existence is that everyone is an aspect of the whole, the group, so this was really getting back to the basics – learning through interaction with one another. It was a good life, similar to going on vacation in the mountains, living in a rustic way, relaxing and allowing the Earth to calm you down after a busy year at your job. After lifetimes of hectic struggle, the Earth was healing and life was back to basics.

Lemuria was a long, long period – about five hundred thousand of your years – but there is not just a cut-off point where one age ends and another begins, so there was a time when the Atlantean age was coming forth also. If you try to put together all the pieces of "time" I've given you, they arrant going to give the full scope, because I've rather condensed the history. We have not really discussed the coming of Sanat Kumara, the Planetary Logos, to ensoul the Earth about eighteen million years ago. It was actually before that mass ascension and Lemuria. So you might say that the time humanity spent recovering from pre-Lemuria was about five hundred thousand years. This seems like a long period of time, but in a cosmic sense it isn't. It's rather like a pause, a breath – a cosmic breath. As it breathes out it allows a new cycle of learning to come forth. The people *chose* their way of life. They had the knowledge to do differently, and they chose back to basics.

The development of the animal kingdom got in the way here. There were beings which truly were animals but which humanity considered to be the species from which they themselves had evolved. This was not true. It was a parallel civilization of the animal kingdom. The Stone Age remnants that have been found are from the animal rather than the human kingdom.

In this long period there were many types of experiences in many different settings. The Earth was continuing to evolve and there were volcanoes erupting, earthquakes and many natural disasters that affected humanity. There were settlements of people that were rather isolated and didn't have interaction with all the different areas of the planet. This has been true many times in the past. I have mentioned before that there were times when people interacted with those on other planets – there were spaceports and so forth – but not during this particular time. Certainly people from not too far away sometimes visited, but those at a greater distance didn't know of the existence of far-off settlements. So the people decided to build from a more spiritual point of view rather than from a scientific and technological one. They had had two periods of mass ascensions and then a devastating physical experience. Now they decided to forth again but to reframe their civilization and try to keep from having the devastation again. That was deeply buried in the memory patterns. It was carefully planned, and through the pre-Lemurian era humanity took some tentative steps, not really wanting to risk another wide global confrontation.

Each particular group had its own way of worshipping. Religious experience has always been present on the Earth. In that particular time it was often related to the Earth and appreciation of the Earth. Humanity had fought for it and it was very much appreciated. In the latter part of the Lemurian era and continuing into the time of Atlantis, they began to have the temples and the healing temples.

It has been said that there was a time when experimentation to develop the optimal physical form for humanity on Earth was taking place and that the process cast off inappropriate forms which had degenerated into animal bodies. It is an interesting theory, but I don't agree with it. If you see that the Creator is everywhere and the Creator experiences everything, it doesn't exactly follow that one species is to evolve into another, except when a single member of the animal kingdom "graduates" to another level. This is a case where, in an energy focus, there is a spillover effect through invocation and dedication. That animal might have earned graduation, but it isn't really the format that has been chosen by the Creator in this cosmic day, because there is a great appreciation, great love and great allowingness in the process. There is always room and allowingness through individual efforts. If someone earns a promotion, he or she gets it, but it doesn't mean the promotion is given as the norm.

A question has been asked regarding the fall of the angels. I will give my perspective on the subject and you can view and consider it. In the first place, I view the angelic kingdom as a direct extension of the Creator – the right arm, you might say, of the Creator. Each of you, as an evolving consciousness, is certainly part of the Creator, the Source, but not in the same sense as the angelic kingdom is. I'm not sure this has been understood. Sometimes there is confusion about the difference between the angelic kingdom and those who are evolving consciousnesses. I really believe that the fall of the angels refers to evolving consciousnesses, not members of the angelic kingdom. You see, they perform their function perfectly in a way they have always done it, because it's always been there to do — just as your right arm, as long as it recognizes it is a right arm, will do its function perfectly as a right arm.

I believe the "fall of the angels" refers to some great beings that were evolving consciousnesses approaching a point where they could be called cocreators or very close to that. They were becoming very powerful, learning to create on a truly cosmic level. There are different levels of cocreatorship, and as one goes through one level, there are learning experiences. You could say there is a final exam before becoming a full-fledged cocreator, and this is power — the recognition of what power is from every point of view. It is finally acknowledging that power is for the purpose of accomplishing the cosmic goals that have been set up by the Creator in the Cosmic Plan.

At any point in our evolution, we can make a choice. We can choose to define life from a wholly personal point of view. Occasionally someone who is approaching that cocreator level looks again within self and then focuses power as a tool for self. If you do this for very long, your evolution could take a plunge. Your conception changes from that cosmic point of view in which you participate fully within the Plan and create for it. If you don't perceive that, you are looking only at your own personal perspective and desiring power. That, my friend, is a fall. When we say the angel Lucifer fell from the heavens, we are talking about a great cosmic being who no longer could perceive the cosmic use of power and reference it, as the true cocreator does, as being for the purpose of the whole. He was accessing power for his own personal use and took with him a great many other beings who looked to him rather than to the whole, or the Source, for leadership. Thus we see a group of beings who no longer were an elevated part of the whole as far as the usage of their divine attributes was concerned.

The good news is that they eventually began to reassess this position because they were really seeking happiness and they found that their personal use of power didn't bring happiness. Being very intelligent, they began to consider what they were truly seeking and then were able to come back very rapidly. This is an extreme example of what most evolving consciousnesses do — they try to use all of their divine attributes, but if they can't quite hold on to that, they might again make it a personal assessment. But most who approach the cocreator state don't fall as Lucifer did. Lucifer's fall didn't really have anything to do with the other part. It happened very early in the Earth's history, before Sanat Kumara ensouled the planet. It was much more a cosmic event and, aside from the reflected sense that what happens above affects what happens below, it did not concern the Earth. The whole universe was affected by this — it was that cosmic — and there are many memories of it. Something of this magnitude does have an effect, but you place it out of proportion if you look at it from an Earth perspective.

The Electrical Ones were not evil. They were simply scientists looking for a new place to live. They were evolving beings, and some of them have come to your planet again as spiritual teachers. Certainly there are karmic ties between their civilization and yours. Some incarnated on the planet again after the five-hundred-year period, either singly or in groups, often because of karma. I say five hundred years very generally, but as I have said, there is no cut-off time to an era.

The problem of free will is one with which all evolving beings must contend. Every evolving being reaches a specific point at which they seek to see that choice really is a motivator. Free will and choice are cosmic motivators used by the Source. Sometimes the feeling that you don't have a choice is necessary to finally cause you to delve into it enough to find that you do have a choice. Free choice is attained when you truly utilize your divine gifts and your creative abilities — that is where free choice comes in. But there are periods when it seems one is "fated" to experience. You feel, What's the use? It's going to happen this way anyway, and you feel you have no choice. You are seeking to understand free choice and to know you do have a choice. The choice is not whether or not to be — that is your divine gift. But you may choose to hold on to a perspective for as long as you wish (no one will take that away from you).

The usage of your divine attributes is your choice, and your participation in the Plan in a conscious manner is your choice. All of these things are free-will choices, but when they are aligned with the Cosmic Plan, then your choices will allow you to have those things you really do want but you might not have seen in the same framework. Choice is the great motivator — that is its purpose.

Now, the Electrical Ones came from a very great distance and were looking for a new home. The war that ensued is buried in the memory patterns, but the fear many people have about the coming of spaceships and people from space stems from the scientists who came from space and experimented on the animals and people and on the Earth itself. They sometimes took people aboard their ships for experiments, which caused great pain. They were a different type of being, and if you experienced them in that way you very likely could fear their coming again. There was no single time when this happened; it's been an ongoing, sporadic thing, though perhaps particularly in the Atlantean times and later. You read of such reports even today.

I spoke of Lemuria in relation to the South Pacific, but it really evolved to be a full planetary civilization. As the civilization progressed, humanity again wanted to "get with it." They began to form small villages and communities, living beyond the cave groups. There were villages of five thousand and many more. It really became a worldwide civilization again.

Early Atlantis

Then we began to move toward the early Atlantean Age — early Atlantis — and it was beginning to look rather more civilized. There were farmers who raised food instead of roaming about and gathering food. They began to recover and use what they had in their racial memories. They began to explore scientifically and to be very interested in sound. This was the great period of working with sound. Many things were used for this, such as experiments to see the range of sound heard by animals and humans and what could be heard by the plant kingdom or the mineral kingdom. You measured these things in a scientific way and related and communicated them in a way that you have not gone back to yet.

There were great advances in sending sound. Some of you might have memories of such work. Perhaps you specialized and spent all of your life studying one particular frequency until you understood it very completely. In another lifetime you broadened into working with more frequencies. There was time, and each lifetime you specialized in one area of sound. There were at least twenty-five thousand years in which sound was of major importance to the Earth. There was uniting of the planes through sound, and ways to communicate in the spiritual area that you haven't yet gone back to. This is being worked toward now, but it was done before on your planet. You could literally call up those of us who lived on other planes; there was the ability to connect the planes through sound. It was a wonderful time. You could hear the angelic kingdom; you could not only attune to but talk to the devas. There was a recognition and appreciation of sound waves.

This was the beginning of the use of sound, and through sound you began to get into the whole spectrum of healing. Thus you began to develop healing temples. You went into the visual through color. You had used frequency, and now you began to use color and combine colors. Diseases were controlled very well — you made breakthroughs in this area.

At this particular time an interesting event happened: There was an inappropriate mixing of the species. (This is in the racial memories too.) And in the Atlantean temples they attempted to disconnect a being that had gotten trapped in a body that was a combination of human and animal. Some of them were grotesque. Now, most of the healers were trying to disconnect them, but at the same time there were some who were trying to connect, which is interesting. It was, perhaps, a karmic connection with the animal kingdom. It became a challenge, and many of you have memories of loved ones, or even of self, becoming trapped in a situation and only gradually being freed from it. It wasn't especially a big deal — almost every planet has this interaction of the species that they must separate. It wasn't necessary for it to happen, but a choice was made and they became intertwined, so they needed to realize that there are parallel ways of developing. The Creator experiences from every point of view, but you weren't really meant to mix them all together. It caused a confusion, so over the eons — and this was another long period in the history of humanity, another hundred thousand years at least — you worked on separating the species. There are some painful memories concerning that time.

Now, the healing temples continued to be used but they became more of a spiritual focus, because as you worked to free humanity and the animals from their inappropriate interaction, you became aware of your spiritual linkage. You became rather in awe of the creative process and how it works. You really did learn to appreciate it. The temples, which had been almost purely scientific, became a combination of a spiritual center and a scientific healing center. They came into a particular point of balance that was often really rather magnificent!

We are talking about an Atlantean period, and there was a country called Atlantis that was later destroyed, but I am speaking again of a worldwide civilization. There were great centers of civilizations. Besides the one in the Atlantean geographical area, there was also one in Mexico, another in central China and another in northern Africa – near Egypt – and another in the area of Jerusalem. There were these great healing centers where humanity worshipped and was healed. There were some great spiritual teachers; certainly Thoth was present at that time. He was there for about ten thousand years and there were others equally as great who are no longer associated with your planet who focused a new beginning in particular locations. In the area of Burma, there was a beginning that later was to be a spiritual center also. If you have seen some of the glorious temples that are there now, well, this was the foundation time. The temples there now don't go back that far certainly, but if you could excavate you would find remnants of this foundation era called Atlantis.

Then the civilization began to pick up pace. Civilizations flourish when there is a spiritual quality to life. Scientists were beginning to discover the use of crystals. Crystals were actually brought to you by another civilization of space beings who came frequently. At this time you openly communicated with other civilizations. There were great spaceports, and there were teachers who suggested that humanity begin to use crystals. There were crystals here on the Earth but they didn't have the quality and were not magnificent specimens of crystals, the crowning experience of the mineral kingdom. On the planet from which crystals were brought, there was an evolution beyond what your planet had yet made. So magnificent crystals were brought to Earth, some in great size, and they began to be utilized as power sources in the Atlantean time. Then from these great, magnificent specimens, humanity began to use the ones that were already on the planet. Pretty soon everyone had crystals that they used as power sources for all manner of things: personal planes, computers, a way to cook food, a way to make clothes. The whole civilization was powered by crystals. It was a magnificent example of their use.

And then again, as with the Electrical Ones, there were those who sought to take over, albeit in a different way. These beings were less balanced and more into power for the sake of power. This powerful Atlantean civilization, with all its advantages, began to attract those who wanted world domination.

These would-be takeover beings were very good at what they did. They approached very softly, very cautiously, and were deeply entrenched into the Atlantean civilization before humanity figured out what was happening; then it was difficult to get rid of them. They took over many of the temples. When they found out what was going on, humanity began to fight back. Again we find humanity engaged in battle, a battle to save their temples, which they could not save.

Birth of Modern Civilizations

From this imbalance there came forth several things. You know of the event of the sinking of that geographical area, but the downfall of many of these civilizations came because they had become the strongholds of the beings that sought to take over everywhere. Many of the more spiritually oriented people went to new geographical areas and founded new civilizations — Tibet, for instance. What they brought there was rather new to that area, although there had been many, many civilizations in the past. When they went to Egypt, they found many people already there. These spiritual beings from Atlantis found that there was no "hard-core" colony of those who had taken over their homeland, so they established themselves in this new territory.

In China the same thing happened. They went to China and then to Central America also. They began again in these civilizations which had many of the same methods of working, such as spiritually oriented temples. They did use crystals for a time, but for some reason (I'm not really sure why) the use of crystals largely fell away. They probably didn't have the supply in these new areas. After a few generations they no longer remembered much about the crystals. There were memories of focuses of great beauty — your racial memories have that, I've seen that in them. There is something called a shining star, but really it is a crystal that is remembered.

So began the other civilizations. Certainly the Egyptian civilization that resulted was a spiritual civilization combined with a less advanced one. Now, this is an interesting period. Certainly one of the most important things to recognize is how much the other planets were involved in this. There were great leaders who came from all over and landed in Egypt. Thus we find during the Egyptian civilization a melding of many philosophies that really did not originate on your planet. If you look at Egypt's history you can see that. You can see the coming together of many philosophies and you wonder how they got from one point to another. The point is, they didn't get it through normal earthly means. It was a more extraterrestrial point of view that brought the ideas through.

The worship of the pharaoh as a true incarnation of God on Earth seems to me to have come largely from another planet. It's not that your Earth hadn't had such beliefs before, because of course it had, but that one became deeply entrenched when several thousand visitors and colonists came to

Egypt bringing that particular belief. It began, it seems to me, because some of the visitors believed they were greater than the local inhabitants and saw a way to keep power. Perhaps not, but that is one explanation.

So then we encounter the long, long period of Egyptian history — much longer than commonly thought. It is said to be a period of only four or five thousand years or a bit more, but it lasted eighty, ninety or perhaps one hundred thousand years. It is a long period of time and it certainly was not as Hollywood depicted it. Those who built the pyramids came from other planets and knew how to raise the stones by negating the effect of gravity. It was then a very easy matter of positioning them and placing them there. The concept behind the great pyramids again came from other planets and was seeded into your Earth. So many of the important points of your Egyptian civilization were really a blending from several planets.

We now approach the more modern civilization that you all know about. I haven't talked very much about the avatars who have come forth, but certainly there has been a great spiritual teacher about every two thousand years. Some were more successful than others. Each brought a particular quality, and some have continued to help the planet in its evolution. From this point on, I think you know most of the events, so we will return to some of the subjects pertaining to the earlier times.

Some of the beings who sought to and did take over Atlantis came from other planets and some did not. It was a combination that revolved around power. You may have noticed that whenever there is a power focus, there are some who haven't yet learned to use it for the Source and seek to use it for self. Sometimes they are successful and sometimes not. This was a great learning experience for the Earth. What happened was that power from then on was not concentrated in one geographical area but dispersed — something it had not learned to do before.

The temples in Atlantis were run by dedicated spiritual beings. There were temples all over the planet, concentrated in several major areas. The geographical place known as Atlantis was a concentration of these spiritual centers. Here on the planet there were those who had specific desires to control, to take over the spiritual centers. In my opinion they were aided by visitors to your planet who saw what was happening. This effort was launched on an almost worldwide scale, which is why I believe it had some outside help. There were particular leaders who, again, had come as visitors, who sought opportunity and sought power for powers sake, and they partook in the takeover situation. It was all rather secretive. We haven't said much about the Electrical Ones, but during that particular time there were spies and secret missions and counterspies and all that sort of thing. One really couldn't know who ones friends were or who was trying to take over what, and it was very confusing. They couldn't stop it because they didn't know how. They couldn't see where it was coming from or who was connected with it. Indeed, you might have found that someone you had worked with for perhaps twenty years was suddenly seeking to overthrow the heads of the temple. Why were they caught up in such a thing? Well, they had been convinced by someone who had approached them with the idea that new leadership would be better. Humanity has had this "those in charge" complex for quite a while. It was all very plausible and very intricately woven into a web that came forth and affected all of the Earth.

What happens when several parties have a lot of power for personal reasons? A war ensues and eventually they destroy each other. This did not occur all in one geographical location. There were centers in other geographical areas besides Atlantis, the strongest. They did not destroy the earth itself in other locations but they destroyed the civilizations there. The temples as functional healing centers were destroyed. When there is no leadership in a civilization and many people are fighting to take leadership, then many people leave. Civilization is redefined over the whole planet, and that is really what happened. It was a long process covering thousands of years. Atlantis went down in several stages over a long period of time.

A great crystal aided those who invaded Atlantis. Edgar Cayce talks about what he called the Great Crystal, but there were many great crystals. Some have been discovered and some have yet to be discovered, but in my opinion they will be discovered. There was one which affected the climactic event. It wasn't really what caused the civilization to collapse physically — certainly you must look at the Earth in its wider evolution — but it was a part of it. The crystal was very much affected by all that was happening on the Earth. It was used inappropriately in trying to control — and not just in that geographical area. There were many things done by these leaders who had taken over; I don't really care to get into that, but they were doing things with the crystals that the crystals had never truly been designed to do. They overstressed the crystals, and they themselves were destroyed.

Some of the great crystals used were natural growth crystals, but not from this planet. They came out of another area of your universe. These were the magnificent ones. Some crystals were manufactured. The largest crystal, the one you talk about, was a manufactured one. A crystal is a focus and a means of magnification and must therefore have a connection to something. To what? To the Creator. Originally the crystals were used for healing purposes. They are a focal point of energy, and you can do anything with energy. You can use it for spiritual purposes or for personal power. Energy does what you as a divine being direct it to do. So in terms of the power source, those who knew how to program a particular crystal as an energy source, did so. Others received them for a specific purpose, with the energy format already placed in them. There were those who did their own, and that was fun and people liked to do it. Sometimes this was "interesting" if they didn't program them just right — you might have run out of cooking energy in the middle of preparing dinner for guests!

In their original state, crystals have an energy of their own, but not in a way that is especially useful for the purposes they were meant for. They might have a combination, or dual, energy where the energy in them can be both accelerated and diminished and they can work in many ways. People are doing that now, as you know.

Over the eons there have been many, many planets with physical bodies on them. They don't always use the Adam Kadmon model of two arms, two legs and a head. The Adam Kadmon pattern is a very common and popular model because it's very successful; it works well. But there are many, many planets that have many models. To get things in proper perspective, you must see that creation is much greater, much larger than you have any idea. In your local universe there are many thousands of planets that have life on them and many that do not. There are untold, unlimited numbers of universes — and that's just the physical part of the cosmos that you see. Many have interacted with humanity. Certainly there have been periods when you did not acknowledge the interaction, or find it appropriate to do so — and now is such a time — but it's still there and always has been. We sometimes try to isolate ourselves, but we can't really do it.

We have spoken of the two periods of mass ascension, and I compare these periods to a "harvesting." We again approach a harvesting time when those who are completing their lessons are to be "harvested." The Planetary Logos, Sanat Kumara, reaches certain plateaus in his cosmic evolution, and each time he reaches one of these it is a harvesting period. Humanity, as beings that live in his aura, partake of this harvesting. It is a joint evolutionary process working out on many levels — his more cosmic level, and the human level where the finalizing experience comes forth. It is a cycle of planting and harvesting on this planet, and this is how evolution takes place.

There is a six-thousand-year cycle, a twelve-thousand-year cycle and also a thirty-six-thousand-year cycle. Each time two or more cycles come together, that period is extremely important. That's why this one is so important. The actual "cutting of the wheat" will happen within a few years time, and that makes it very interesting on your Earth right now. This is the harvesting season, and there are many harvesters here to aid you. I am a harvester. The spiritual teachers come and we are the harvesters. If we see a little wheat that's almost ripe, we interact with it to help it to ripen in time. I would say generally it's a one-hundred-year period within the six-thousand-year cycle. It is a relatively short period of time, and its importance accelerates as you come closer to the end; then you see more and more effort by many of us. The end of the hundred years comes at about the turn of the century — around 1995 or after.

Will you ascend? Well, let us say that many of you will be very near that cut-off point. Some will and some won't; it's not an arbitrary thing. There will be a point of critical mass where we see that it's already engaged and will go forward rather automatically. The choice has been made and it's being followed through. When one cycle moves into another, it happens. Let's say that at the end of this 1995–2000 period some of you will ascend rather in mass, perhaps. Some will not, but they will follow shortly.

It has been said that at the time of the Earth upheaval, spaceships will remove some people from the Earth. In a way, this relates to the harvesting. It means that in the Earth's evolution, the vibration of the Earth is raised. After the New Age begins, those who haven't reached a certain point of critical mass, who have almost but not quite figured out how to graduate, will be taken away for a little while.

Now there has been a lot of speculation about why they are coming and if they are coming and whether we can avoid it. It is a probable event, very probable in my opinion. It is a part of the evolution of your planet and your planetary logos. In my opinion, it is coming forth. I have stated that your planetary logos, Sanat Kumara, really functions as you do. Both function in a particular, familiar mode of operation. You go forward and you live in a certain way. Perhaps you would like to break that pattern, but you find that the familiar is the way that you evolve. Sanat Kumara moves in that way. If he breaks out of this familiar pattern and the axis shift doesn't take place, then we won't have it. But it looks to me to be highly probable. His cosmic evolution is going to continue in this mode of operation for a while. The shift of the axis resettles the energies. If you keep with an ingrained pattern, you will reach your goal. If you break that pattern, then another route may be taken. Probably most of you will keep to your ingrained patterns.

There is a point at which you can evaluate how soon a pattern will be broken. In my opinion, Sanat Kumara is walking a familiar path and is using a framework that he has used and will continue to use for a while. There has to be a cleansing — there will have to be sweeping changes in light of the evolutionary process for the planet and the Planetary Logos. That is why I don't think it probable that it will be avoided. Some will ascend before the planetary shift. There will be those not yet at the point of ascension who will be moved temporarily and brought back after the planet has stabilized somewhat. There will be those who can't adjust, whose physical structures can't live in the new frequencies, who will leave the physical structure. But you are all spiritual beings, so you will go on. You can get another physical structure, you know. It's really very easy.

Atlantis Rising

W ELCOME, MY FRIENDS. THIS WEEKEND WE WILL BE CHOOSING CERTAIN stimuli to bring together into your perception more of the strengths that you once had and used in Atlantis. Those strengths are arising all around you now to form an energy link that will invoke around your planet a stimulus making the energy grid system more complete, more realized. We will begin with a short meditation.

Atlantis Activation

Within you a seed was planted long ago, and this seed grew up as your Atlantean experience. It has literally stretched within you into every cell, every part of you. I want you to go deeply now into your physical structure and caress, through your heart energy, this seed, this growth that you cultivated long ago. Sense that now. Look deep, my friends; it calls to you. The strengths are there in each cell, and we say to that seed, wake up! Wake up now! We invite those strengths that have been sleeping to come into the heart in a way that will energize the heart and allow it to expand and magnetize to you a clearer understanding of the Earth and of others.

And so the call goes out: Wake up! Wake up, little ones, wake up! Allow that call, allow it now. It stretches deeper, from this first level to a second level you haven't reached before, which is now awakening. Search your physical structure. Look at the cells and know what they are holding there. Wake them up! Wake them up! The call has gone forth to wake up the cells. Allow that now and notice the sense of radiance, of warmth within the cells. They are excited to be awakened; they have slept for a long time and now you are stretching, stretching, stretching, allowing this awakening. Say to each part of you, "Yes, it's time! Yes, wake up! Yes, wake up now!" There is a brief satisfaction with this. The heart is allowing it, the emotions are excited about it, the mental body can realize how important it is, and the physical body is allowing this stretch, this awakening, this sense of completion that is coming in with this energy. We say, Atlantis, arise! We say, Atlantis, come forth! We say, Atlantis, welcome! Stretch into it now. As the brilliance of that experience is awakened again, your body begins to reflect that. Allow the Angelic Hierarchy to help energize and help blend all of your responses. Note it working on the brain area. The archangels Raphael, Gabriel, Uriel, Sandalphon, Metatron and many more are working now with you. They are helping to activate what you are willing to activate. Allow it, trust it. Give the angels this active energy and let them connect it within your physical structure, within your emotional structure, within your mental structure and certainly within the spiritual, the souls energy, as it seeks out within the cells any points of strength from the Atlantean era and says, "Yes! Come forth! Come forth now!"

Energize it! Allow it! Let it awaken you. Get excited about it! Bring it forth! If you feel like moving, do it. Move and allow! Activate now. Take a deep breath and bring out this material that is there, which has been stored there in the cells. Activate it, welcome it, say to it, "Yes! Awaken! Awaken!" Take a deep breath, breathing in and out. Get it moving – actively, shake the arms, shake the legs, move the neck, move the head, move the back, allow it. Shaking it, moving it, allowing this energy to become active. And although we are calling this a meditation, it is a very active one, a movement, a flow, allowing the cells to move, to receive, to accept, to awaken. Yes! The joy of it! "Good! At last we are free; we want to express; at last we come forth now."

The soul level is using this energy now and allowing it to be active in your life. Awaken! Awaken! Awaken! And as you do, there is an energy change in the heart area, a sending forth of a radiance that perhaps you weren't able to send before, then a sending back by the universe of that active radiance. Yes, an allowingness of a sense of connection, a sense of gratitude for being able to receive in this manner. Let that settle in deeply – each in your own way, allow that now. And we say as a group, "Yes, we are ready. We are ready to understand again. We are ready to explore deeply the Atlantean concept. We are emotionally open to it. We sense the strengths of it. We allow it to begin to be who we are now."

Now I would like you to visualize the grid system of Earth. It looks simply like lines of energy that are intersecting diagonally, horizontally, vertically, energy that comes together, energy lines that come together all over your Earth. Now, about one-third of the energy needed to fuel this New Age is still tied up in Atlantis. I'd like you, through your energy structure, to sense a connection that will feed that energy from Atlantis into the energy grid system around Earth. Sense yourself as a part of that grid system and be willing to go back to that energy grid that was there in the Atlantean era and superimpose it on the present one. As you do that, something interesting happens. A galactic counterpart comes forth from the Galactic Core and the energy is sandwiched between the galactic, which represents the future, and the Atlantean, which represents a specific within the past. And what it does is spark, it ignites the grid system and it grows and grows and grows in its strength and intensity. Note the flow of the energy around the Earth, note the parts of it where it ignites, where it sparks, where it moves, sparking here and sparking there. Keep bringing it through your body into the grid system and note the correspondence coming from the Galactic Core. There is an expansion and an igniting. And, my friends, look! Your body is getting that too, from the past and from what we will call the future. It sparks within your physical body and there is a flow and the Earth is getting that all over. Look at it through various countries, igniting here and igniting in Germany, igniting in France, South Africa, Brazil, Tibet, India, Portugal and Vene-zuela. It is igniting all over your planet, and everywhere the spark sparks and ignites the grid system, bringing in the potential from the past and from the future and locking it into the eternal now. Sense that expansion and be willing to accept it.

❦ Use some deep breaths here because we are going to continue to expand this. Receive it with the inbreath and send it forth with the exhalation. Do it in your own timing, bringing it in and processing and expanding it out; thus you receive from Atlantis and you receive from the Galactic Core. You bring it into your now experience and you become an igniter for the integrative process for yourself, for the Earth, for the galactic level, for the universal level and literally for the Source Itself. Breathe it in, my friends, ignite it and send it forth. Breathe it in, ignite it and send it forth. Your body becomes vitalized here perhaps as never before. Allow that energy to flow through you. It's flowing through the chakra system and into the Earth, but it's also flowing directly into all of the pores, into every part of your body. Why? Because you've woken them up. You've said yes! to that energy from the Atlantean era. Sense that moving. It's going to be a wonderful creative base from which to energize your future, your New Age. And the means to do it are within your physical structure, your energy structure, your emotional structure, your mental structure and certainly within the soul level, within the spiritual perspective now, coming together, igniting and sending forth the flame of transformation around your Earth. Coming together through you, igniting, and again that flame of transformation moves around the Earth. Allow it to move. You breathe it in, you send it forth; you breathe it in, you send it forth.

❦ Note the responses of the kingdoms of the Earth – the mineral kingdom, the plant kingdom, the animal kingdom, the human kingdom and the kingdom of souls. Note the responses. Through you there can again be an ignition, an integration that ignites the transformational process around the Earth. So as you breathe it in, you expand it and breathe it out and ignite the integration of the kingdoms around your planet. Please relax now, rest a moment and become aware of this room again.

Atlantis was a time of innovation on your Earth. I have taught that the history of Earth is much older than sometimes thought, and one reason is that your Earth has been set very solidly in the third dimension — "This is the past, this is where Earth was." The more solid it is, the slower time is. As you move toward the fourth dimension, your time is in a sense speeding up, and thus your past took longer than your future will take. The stream of time has changed. If you look at the stream as you experienced it, these things happened millions and millions of year ago. If you look at it as you experience time after the Harmonic Convergence, it wasn't so long ago.

At the time of Atlantis several things happened. There was an awakening for humanity. If you went back to about 10,000 years into the Atlantean era, which was rather early, you would find that the colors and the way you tasted and smelled were different. The reds, violets, greens and blues were not nearly so vivid; most of you couldn't see pink at all. During the Atlantean era you developed your sense of color more and more, your sense of hearing — there were great research centers on hearing. This was the turnaround period when you learned to use your physical senses in a very special way. Much more of the light spectrum became available for you to use. Why? Well, it was just a part of the development of the planet. With the Harmonic Convergence, the color spectrum is again opening and there are more reds and violets that are much more vivid. The luminous part of the spectrum is becoming much more visible.

For you in Atlantis, this was wonderful. Suddenly there was an opening of the colors, of your hearing. It was a whole new ball game, a new way of existing on the physical level. Sometimes your beliefs brought you a way of looking at it from the past, so you didn't see the new opportunities. Many of you were artists during the 3000 years this change was taking place. You would start to paint and you would suddenly discover you could do things you hadn't been able to do before.

Return now to that time and visualize that experience of painting. You can pull from, let's say, the Galactic Core levels of association with these colors that you haven't seen on the physical level. That's what it means to spiral it: to bring it into contact with the ever-escalating levels of awareness that you can now plug into through that experience. Allow it to change, to flow, to grow; don't limit it. This is a nice technique. What does color represent? Colors are aspects of the whole, arrant they? Color is the electrical awakening of the souls energy; the souls response is seen through color. And the more you allow yourself to be that painter that we call the Creator, the more you will awaken those aspects and blend them within yourself. It doesn't even matter what you get. It's the movement, the flow, the awakening of a sense of change through this association with color.

You had a particular temple there for about a thousand years and you were all trained within that temple. It helped you learn about color. Some of you demonstrated it on a canvas, some of you worked with fabric, and some of you worked with what we call a hologram, a room where the colors were projected and you moved them around and learned to create intricate patterns of light with the color itself. It was fun, but more than that it was an integrative exercise — you had to learn to make the colors flow in balance. You all had that in your Atlantean bag of tricks. Well, that's a joke, but the point is that you now have these things that you've already learned to use. I'm not saying you don't already use them, but the goal is to be very conscious of how to bring the ancient skills and strengths that you had together into that nowness. That says to the Galactic Core, where you've placed your strengths, "Now they can come on in — look, were using them."

I want to talk about the Galactic Core a moment. I consider you to be a divine spark, an individualized part of the Source that has come forth as a stream of light. You haven't really come out of anything; you're still in it. A better definition would probably be that it is within the Source and it spirals, it's activated, it's growing from its intensification of understanding. At a certain point in this stream of creative energy you reach what we call a soul. This soul has responsibility for the energy on the physical level. Now, it's difficult for you on the physical level to really recognize what that Source level of you is. The physical level is so magnified that it seems you're tunneled in to a certain experience. This doesn't mean you are, but it seems that you are. So to really recognize what this Source level is is rather difficult.

There is a place called the Galactic Core where you've stored the strengths, stepped down the energy so it's more understandable on the physical level. As you invoke the strengths of the soul and integrate them on the physical plane you can begin to access the galactic perspective, where you have stored these Source-level strengths. As we uncover the strengths that you used in Atlantis, this will automatically invoke from the Galactic Core your expression of those Source-level strengths that have been activated in you. That's why this is important. The main point is to ignite an integrative process within you and to bring in those very cosmic strengths that the Atlantean experience opened for you but you forgot a little. You went into another body and you didn't recognize those strengths, so they went to sleep.

A good example is your ability to heal. In Atlantis if a body was brought into the temple soon enough — within a 24- to 36-hour period — you could say, "Get up and walk," and the body would do that if it was willing. You all had skills in association with divine law. You could regrow limbs — there were tanks where people floated and the limbs were regrown and the bones healed. You had skills as a healer in Atlantis, much more than you know. Why haven't you remembered? Well, certain activities took place in Atlantis, certain deep and difficult experiences, because of a basic fear that you all have about being unlimited. Isn't that interesting? You do — not consciously, of course, but subconsciously it's as if the Creator pointed and said, "You're unlimited!" And you said, "Who? Me?" It's a point of view of awe. We see the Source Itself, we see the Creator, and we don't understand that that's who we are. We've begun, but there's a gap in the process; we don't see that it's a step-by-step process. So the basic issue that all of you are resolving is your relationship with unlimitedness, which is your relationship with Source, and your security to build that Plan, or take what the Source is expressing and allow it to be built completely through you one step at a time. These are the basic issues that all of you are working at.

But you are very creative in how you can hide your potential from yourself. We can find a great deal of that in Atlantis. Every time you got to the point where you could use it, you would perhaps manage to die, and then when you came back in the next life you didn't remember it. Sometimes they would try to bring you back into a temple where you could remember it but you would decide to do something else. Each time you had an opportunity to really get in touch with your unlimitedness, you would only take it so far before there was a type of denial that said, "No, I can't use that yet because I'm not ready."

Well, in my opinion you're ready now. The readiness came in with the Harmonic Convergence, and it's time now. Through this Atlantean experience, by superimposing those new beginnings (Atlantis was such a wonderful time for the physical senses) and expanding that, we can do all sorts of things with it.

There was a great teacher in Atlantis named Thoth. You know him by many names — he was also in Egypt. Many of you have very close ties with him. Some of your greatest teachers took their initiations in Atlantis. They recognized their potential more completely, so in the Atlantean era they were about where you are now. And that's important because it shows how important this time is for you. The one called the lord Maitreya began to express his unlimitedness in the middle of the Atlantean era. Many of you were with him in this temple. There was a sense of sharing that you are only now beginning to get in touch with.

Part of the facility was underneath the sea. Now, we talk about Atlantis rising, but Atlantis was a worldwide civilization, so it isn't a particular geographical location we are talking about. But in that time you did live in the area that is now called Atlantis. In my opinion, the sinking of Atlantis was invoked three different times, and many of you through a group experience explored underwater where Atlantis would eventually be. Did you cause it to sink? Of course not — there was a series of events that did that. But there was a temple you had all built under the sea, and you often went under there with the lord Maitreya.

A Day in Atlantis

Our day begins, and you know it is going to be a day that you spend in the temple underneath the sea. And so you've been all night in a very special location. You've been praying and meditating. Your body is being prepared in a certain way so that you can, as you enter this temple, have the oxygen you need in your body to enter the water. You won't need a breathing device – you will know how to get oxygen from the water and from an enriching of the oxygen within your body. That has been going on all night and you have awakened.

You go into a very special room together. You can feel that the atmosphere is very charged – you couldn't really breathe outside anymore because your body has been changed. This atmosphere is very liquid in a sense, although it is still without water. You can feel the excitement. First there is a light enhancement. Feel that coming into this room. It awakens the electrical particles within the cells. Then you are given a garment; it is a silvery color and fits you very closely. You are given a helmet and put it on – there is nothing covering your nose.

Now you enter a type of a boat and you are being lowered right into the sea. Our destination is about three hundred feet under the sea. Look around you – the sea is very clear. There are beautiful fish, the foliage is beautiful – a beautiful environment. As you reach the bottom, a flexible corridor is attached to the boat and you go through this corridor and come into this wonderful undersea temple. The atmosphere is heavy – it now has water in it – but you can breathe and your suits are comfortable so you leave them on. There is a large room, and your teacher, the lord Maitreya, is there for you. There is a special chair that molds itself to your body. It is hooked up to an electrical device that stimulates a higher level – we will call it the Galactic Core – and it goes through a group process. Now relax and allow what is coming in to be there. Sense now the lord Maitreyas energy coming through this channel.

> All right, my friends, here we are in our underground experience, which is really a symbol of what is now possible for you. I cherish each one of you. Let us sense that connection into the group process, into the ability to breathe beyond certain limitations. Note how easily you can breathe what you hadn't thought you could breathe before. Note that the cells of the body, the organs, the brain and the skin are all awakening to a group perception, to a unity of trust, of coming together. The group is invoking certain visions, certain ways of viewing existence. The group will now prepare to do what it has done in the past – a deep Earth revitalization, Earth shifting. Let's all do it together. I will be here for a moment and then Vywamus will be coming back.

> There is now a doorway opening within the Earth – and it is not necessarily just the physical Earth. The Earth and its potential opens and there is a sparking that you can now

help Earth with. Hold on to your chair as this energy transforms, as it moves, as it is vitalized, as it is coming through you into the center of the group. You can work with it as you did in Atlantis. Use it to awaken others and to awaken you. There is a sense of revitalization as if you've been dunked in the energy and the Earth too is dunked in this energy that revitalizes. It is coming through this opening through the Earth. Allow it to move, allow it to spiral; it is very gentle and it helps the heart. You can trust it. It's a joyous experience and you're grateful for it, you feel that this is your role this revitalization of the Earth and you go deeply into it. You are connected into the group process so that through you the whole group dynamic becomes that tool that is so important now. Dear ones, we are together and I feel so privileged to be with you. Do you know how much love I have for you? And I know you love the Earth as much as I do. So let us again revitalize it. Thank you.

All right, this is Vywamus again. We are now viewing this room, which is beginning to rotate. Put a color, whatever color you wish, in the third-eye area as the room rotates, moving and moving, that the energies may through your physical body become more complex and physically solid. Sense that movement, that flow; it's on the physical level and it's rotating more and more rapidly, more and more rapidly. Remember to keep that color in the third-eye area, not especially focusing on the movement. Just focus in the third-eye area and allow that movement as it spins, as it moves, as it is more and more vitalizing, as it goes deeper and deeper and deeper into the Earth.

Now, my friends, sense from this deep temple, this deep room, an invocation going out all over the Earth. And although we are looking at this as you had the experience before, the temple is still there it's still there. Sense the connection into the nowness and allow that to be a stabilizing factor here on the Earth. Now gently you are unstrapped from your chair and you stand up and go back through the tunnel into the boat and you come back up to the surface without any trouble breathing. You are being taken into a particular room where you are very quiet for a few minutes while the oxygen level is returned to normal in your body and you can go about your activities.

Atlantis provided a rich variety of experiences. If you can think of it, you probably did it in Atlantis, for it was a long period of time and you did many, many things. There was one time early in Atlantis when another race came to the Earth. Humanity considered them to be gods. They were quite advanced scientifically and knew a lot of things. There were two factions among this group of people – one which cared enough to try to help humanity and one which was power-hungry. In fact, the reason these people came was that their planet was being destroyed by their inability to get together enough to create a clear world. On their spaceship they brought what they had created.

Now, some of these "gods" joined together with Earth beings and, for a reason I'm not going to go into, a pollution came about. The children who were born were sometimes half human and half animal, or perhaps just a portion animal and mostly human. The chimpanzee and the cat families accepted the pollution better than others. There were temples in Atlantis to try to straighten these pollutions out. Certainly the beings that cared about humanity tried to help. The power-hungry ones did not – in fact, they built temples where things didn't get better, they got worse. They created out of these mixed beings a robotlike creature to serve them.

So you had these two factions, but because the light always wins out, the negative faction was driven from your planet. However, this period in Atlantis did occur in which things were very difficult. All of you served in temples where people had accepted a body which was neither human nor animal but a combination of the two.

What kinds of beliefs would bring this about? One is the fact that the Earth can seem like a separate place. It has, for some of you, a connotation of less-than; it's seen as less than divine, separate and perhaps a little dark. But the belief most responsible for that event was a sense of confusion about structure, about a structure that could be supportive of your creative process. A few of you have had lives in this type of body, but I would prefer to approach it from the healing point of view. Many of you were healers, some of you surgeons. To give you an example of what occurred, there might have been fifty operations on one of these beings to return them to the fully human state. And think of this, my friends: 95% of those that were healed this way would revert right back the night before they were to leave the hospital. Now, what kind of beliefs do you think you would get as a healer in a case like that? You would lose hope.

Now, not all lost hope, but certainly you had to be very, very balanced to heal under the circumstances. These were generally rather small research facilities and were there for a period of five hundred years or so. What brought you out of this was the development of the regenerating waters. It seems if you put the creatures in the waters before they could regress, it would hold, and about 50% of them could be saved. You didn't think about healing them all the way in the water. However, what you did was wonderful and it began to bring the healers out of it. Not only that, there weren't nearly as many being born – they mostly went on for about three or four generations, and a few into the fifth and sixth. As you began to figure all this out, some who were healers regained hope in the healing process. But that's a very deep thing, this hopelessness within the healing process.

We could divide Atlantis into three main periods: early Atlantis, middle

Atlantis — the part where your abilities were used most fully — and the ending period in which there were difficulties with power. An important event occurred just before you entered the middle-Atlantean period, and I'm going to address this issue because it *seems* to prevent you from accessing the fullest use of the abilities you had in the wonderful middle-Atlantean period.

This period was very similar to your Earth now. It was a very sophisticated period; many of you had your own airplanes, and many of you were businesspeople who also had spiritual aspirations — the business community was really quite extensively developed. You had many, many, many connections to other civilizations, and on a street in a typical middle-Atlantean community you might see people from Sirius or the Pleiades — not all the time, but it wasn't unusual to meet one or two a week. It didn't shock you if they didn't have a familiar body type or were wearing a breathing device — if you saw someone who looked like an upright alligator walking around with another way of breathing, it wasn't too shocking. Often, of course, they would be riding around in some sort of vehicle. This is an example of what we term "interesting," but I guess the term you use is "weird." You are now entering again this full-flowered, full-blooming use of your potentiality but again you are blocked.

The people from another civilization dressed in rather simple brown robes and were very "spiritual" — you really admired them. They were very quiet people — you could feel their good nature, their wonderful responses to life. Soon you began to say, "You are our teachers." Now, keep in mind that they didn't say to you, "We are your teachers." You put an expectation on them, which is why were talking about it today.

Now, they had a way of evolving themselves that is entirely different from your way. It is what I call a cocoon experience. They went into a cocoon and stayed for several months and when they emerged they *were* what you admired about them. You could feel their spiritual radiance and greater freedom, and they did this periodically as they evolved. Humanity really pressured them; they said, "We want this experience." And these very gentle people said, "This is our experience — were not sure it will work for you." But if you ask for something long enough and persistently enough, you will get what you ask for (that's what the universe tells you).

So one day these people announced that whoever wanted to could begin at the next period — first a six-month training period and then they would be in the cocoon for an average of nine months (interesting, isn't it?), after which, if it worked for humanity (and they emphasized those words), they would see what happened. Well, the first thing all of you said was, "Where do we sign up?" There was a great response and that is what invoked our present contact into the Atlantean era.

So for six months you were trained to live inside the pods. Some of your claustrophobia comes from this experience. It looked like a pod; it was round and brown, rather like a nutshell. It had a support system so you could stay in the physical; your metabolic rate was slowed down drastically, to just barely enough to sustain your body. And then, because they had learned how to do it, a tremendously powerful electrical current was connected into this pod. It's like saying to a drug addict, "Here is what you need; you can have it whenever you want it, just pull on it." Perhaps this isn't a perfect analogy in that this was not negative. But the use of it became an addiction, though it was not meant to be addictive.

After you were trained you were placed in the pod and told that your consciousness was connected to this electrical potential and whenever you felt yourself drifting you were to pull on it a little and bring yourself back into alignment. You would recognize it — there was a burst, a surge of energy that came through and it was very pleasurable. It would be rather like an injection of a powerful drug that would stimulate that feeling of connection in the brain. In my opinion that is what addicts are looking for — that powerful brain connection they are not able to get for themselves.

So what started out as a good idea became a very difficult experience. You would pull on this all you wanted, and the more you did it, the more stimulated your brains became and the better you felt. What was it doing to the rest of you? Well, your bodies were getting burned. Your bodies were not able to sustain that and pretty soon there was just a shrunken physical body and a huge brain that had begun to grow. The brain circuitry grew and the body shrank. You burned yourselves out and nobody made it through the experience. Many of you lived in the pods a month or two but you never did last the nine-month period until the pod would open automatically.

The system didn't work because you didn't have the same central nervous system that these beings did. They were wired differently; they were not human beings. You couldn't use their devices in a way that worked for you. Now, you might have if there hadn't been a deep addictive pattern that said, "Something out there is going to give me the stimulus I need to connect in here." You used that electrical current to do something for you that you needed to learn to do for yourself.

While you were in the pod it was certainly fascinating. Many of you remember this very well because you traveled to galaxies, to universes, to experiences that you have never yet been able to reconnect with. You perhaps were jumping ahead. Instead of going from point A to point B, you were going from point A to point J in one leap. Your physical body couldn't keep up with this and your emotional body wasn't ready for it. You hit the wall again as far as unlimitedness was concerned. You couldn't take your physical body with you and you couldn't sustain the journey at that level.

But in my opinion, if we were to put one of those pods right here in this room, I think you could do it now. Why? Because there has been an opening on Earth that connects you into your potential. Earth has evolved;

you have evolved — right now to about point D, which is totally different from point J. I think you could sustain it. But would you do it? Probably not — there are built into your system deep memories of how difficult this was and how it burned out the circuitry. Through affirmations we can go into this experience in an inner way and begin to use it as the next step from A to B.

This area was very important for all of you, and these beings wept when no one survived it. In the first place they had wonderfully open hearts and they really didn't want you to do it. They felt as if you were their children. They loved you so much and, despite your eagerness and your desire to evolve faster than you were ready for, they knew what it entailed and they could see that this was an experience that would have to be unraveled one step at a time. You have been working on this — let us say that the movie *Cocoon* was a very positive way to begin to view that area. What came out of those pods? Light came out of them — not death. But it has to be supported on the physical level, and that wasn't shown very clearly. Humanity is working its way through that one.

Here are two affirmations for working with that cocoon:

❦ As I am surrounded by the electrical potential, there is not an expectation which will burn out my physical vehicle.

❦ As I surround myself with this electrical potential, it does not invoke an addictive pattern that becomes self-destructive, now.

I'd like to take you to another Atlantean experience. This one I will also call a pod effect, but this pod was a particular spiritual center, a personal place of refuge. You often went into it and meditated — each one of you had one. These meditation centers were there for four thousand years, and you experienced them at different times. This particular experience was early on, but it was so powerful that, even if you were there later, you were affected by it — the energy of it permeated future experiences.

You were in your small meditative space — some of you were kneeling, some sitting or lying in your little pad. And there was what we will call a cosmic mistake. These things happen. It was kind of a "whoops!" and this reality slid into another Earth reality, another probable Earth. It was like a cosmic hiccup. What was expressed in the area where those meditators sat was obscured by the other probable Earth. That's a little hard to explain unless you look at it as parallel streams of energy — the little hiccup created an overlapping of energy right in that area and erased this particular probability. It didn't kill you — you survived on the physical level — but it took you into the other reality. It took you into the middle of a war, and you were right in between the armies as they were marching toward you.

Remember, you were meditating and this was a very profound spiritual experience. Your pad and everything was right there in the middle, and no one was more surprised than the two armies. They had electrical bars throwing bolts of lightning at each other, and you got quite a few electrical burns on various parts of your body. It was a difficult experience, and your physical bodies didn't survive that. Then the universe hiccupped again and your energy pads and your bodies were back in the original experience. Imagine what happened when you didn't show up and humanity went to see why, only to find you all burned and parts of you disintegrated. It was an interesting experience interwoven with this electrical-bolt-throwing.

They didn't use these meditation areas again, but the energy centers were preserved. Instead of decaying they became almost a wonder of the Earth, so even though people consciously forgot about the difficulty of the experience, here was the physical environment that somehow didn't decay. It was perfectly preserved and they wanted to go in and find out why. In a sense, the energy was still being affected by what had been — I believe by this electrical surging still tied up in this area — so it began to get a reputation as a place of great evil where you were drained of energy. You had opposing electrical surges coming into your body — you tried to put up barriers (this was in a subconscious creative process), but it still occurred and it was quite difficult.

Eventually the story was lost in antiquity, but still the buildings were perfectly preserved — for ten to fifteen thousand years, then suddenly they vanished and it was as if they had never been. Some of you were there when they vanished. What does it mean to have something that had stood through many, many, many circumstances — almost considered a miracle, although not a positive one — suddenly be gone? Where do you think it went? Well, the energy probably was just recycled into the spiritual. But from a physical point of view and a subconscious point of view there seemed to be a scattering, and that's what I'd like you to look at — the scattering of the essence as it left the physical level.

The feeling of scattering that many have comes from the vanishing. And the vanishing comes from believing you can't hold on to something, but more basically, from not believing that you can use that focus or that particular opportunity to take the next step in integrating your unlimitedness. There is a fear of accepting the unlimitedness that is always trying to come to you through an integration of your strengths or through an integrative process by way of a focus that you've chosen from your creativity. In other words, when the booth vanished and scattered, if you had gone into that booth and you felt that it was right for you to do so, you creatively, subconsciously already understood that it was going to vanish, so you said, "I will do this because this is the type of patterning I have." The action comes from the belief, not the other way around, because the belief is much deeper. It is part of the basic premise from which you began the activity at the Source level. You entered the booth because you knew it was going to vanish, and thus you created that to fulfill the prophecy.

This also shows you the power of your creativity. When you accept that power, you can change and you don't have to be regulated by any unclear choice or belief that isn't serving you well. Why? Because it limits. Why? Because it scatters. It doesn't allow the integrative process to be there. As you become more conscious of what you've created you can make clearer choices — especially in how to integrate, when you allow something to be a part of your life and use it in connection with a greater sense of purpose and fulfillment.

Let's say that you're an artist and you also like to dance and play the guitar and you enjoy working with computers. Integration means doing all of these in your life and enjoying all of them. Perhaps you can create a certain career where you can use all of them. And it doesn't imply being scattered if it fulfills a fuller purpose of bringing together through your strengths the flow of the soul. Beliefs are always triggered by an emotion, and we could say that in this area of vanishing, the belief that holds it all in is one of hopelessness of ever getting it together in the fullest sense. Humanity hasn't yet fully grasped the unlimited means of expression that it really has at a very basic level. That's why it's helpful to go into these areas and take a look at them and say, "Wait a minute! I don't think this is the way the system is supposed to work. That limited me — it didn't give me the full flow that I am looking for."

The reason for bringing up the subject of Atlantis is to take an area that was either very strong and you used it well, or wasn't quite clear and we want to clear it out and integrate it in your life so you can use it consistently. Isn't that what you want, my friends? To not start something and have it shoot off somewhere, vanish and be unusable. "Why is the universe doing this to me?" you would ask. Well, maybe it isn't — maybe you're doing it, and the good news is, maybe you can change it.

You are mature spiritual beings — you wouldn't be here if you were not. So when you can see the overall spiritual concept, this begins to put things in place for you emotionally. The spiritual concept of a flow is the one you want to begin to use as your support system — once you have seen that you can be supported by a spiral, that's it, my friends! Then you will be a fully developed cocreator. Will it happen in the next five minutes? Probably not, but it can happen whenever you get that realization: "My support system is the spiral, the evolutionary process itself, brought to me by the Creator — that's what I am supported by, and it can't go away; it's concrete, it's solid." Physical existence isn't solid — that's what's solid: your evolving support system. But usually what gets in the way are the expectations: "My support system should be there because that's where I am now." But by the time you think about it you're over here and the support system is over here and if you're looking for it over there, it isn't there anymore. It's changed. So the change and your ability to accept it emotionally is the most important thing for you. You might change through surrender, recognizing that surrender comes in steps. You might say, "I am willing now to look at it a little differently." What have you got to lose? Nothing but your resistance.

It is very important to acknowledge the support systems that you have. It's much more difficult to feel unsupported than it is to feel supported. Isn't that interesting? So if you let go of just a little bit of resistance, then what is real comes in rather strongly. Meditations can be helpful in allowing the divine support system to be active in your life.

You are in the middle of an intense period of integration, and because of this you're going to get some "Aha! I get it!" realizations and suddenly a whole area will slide in. That's wonderful because you might have been exploring that area for ten lifetimes — twenty lifetimes, forty lifetimes — and suddenly to see how that fits into your life is marvelous! Let's say that you've got twenty-five blocks that are six feet tall and you're trying to build a structure with them. How do you get them to float into position? Well, you can't just yank them, you can't pull on them. You have to enter the relationship with the block until you understand what it is composed of; then it floats into position. When all of these areas fit together, that is a very important point for you.

Some of you have reserved a place for yourself in Source, like a chair you were sitting on before you were individualized and you said, "I will leave that there so I can go back to it." It's really a structural part of yourself and it can be as high as 50% or 60% of who you are. It's held on to through the emotional responses of needing to go back to something, to be sure that you are not pushed out of something so that you couldn't get back. Emotionally that can be very draining because there is a wholeness, and if you have a structure that is 65% complete but there is a piece here and a piece there missing, then what you've got is something that can't hold energy and isn't supportive of you. Those pieces are what you've left in the Source and haven't brought with you into manifestation. Most of you have a certain percentage that you've left, and you might not be aware of it. So the integrative process isn't just one block, it's a piece of this and a piece of that. If you are willing to risk emotionally communicating about how you feel and have the courage to stand up and communicate in situations where what you're getting back is a conflict or something that isn't integrated, then if you communicate you can keep drawing out that potential, that percentage we talked about, bringing it into manifestation until you've got more of yourself. But your emotions have to allow that. It seems to be, for some of you, a desperate grasp — this is the last part of the resistance from that Source level. So by beginning to draw it out, by knowing it's all right, by allowing that emotion to become part of the manifested state, you are freeing yourself at last. Being conscious of something allows an opening, a resolution.

There was a time in Atlantis when you were building a village. There was a wonderful pyramid-shaped mound of earth in the center of the village. Some wanted to get rid of it, but some said, "No, it's beautiful. How about if we hollow a part of it out and make a temple of it?" And this was done. It had some of the most wonderful vibrations in it and you loved to go in and meditate — there was room for quite a few to do that. One day, though, when many of you were in it, it collapsed. It hadn't been structurally designed to withstand an earthquake, and as the earth shook, it fell down. Many were killed and those who remained felt rather responsible.

There are episodes in life that trigger emotional responses that begin the burying of many emotions, which now you have to deal with. Emotions when they are buried get hard, get very crystallized. That doesn't mean you don't recognize some emotions — of course you do. And it certainly doesn't mean you don't have good emotions — of course you do. But still there are these buried, crystallized emotions that one does not acknowledge. You might even have some illusions about having them or say, "Well, there isn't anything there — I can't feel it and it's not important." The subconscious process does this; it deliberately does not face it. Why? Because it's painful, it's difficult. Because it brings up certain connections that one would rather not look at. Perhaps the process itself forces you to look at it — if you bury enough emotions, they begin to pressurize you. The pressure grows and grows — one thing that is very direct from that is high blood-pressure on the physical level. Or your emotions might explode at something very small, either at someone else or at yourself. This might then be buried again because one does not always want to look at it — it's such a painful process.

If you recognize this in yourself, it's time to make a very specific effort in emotional processing. Remember, 95% of you is clear — it's only 5% that isn't. It's rather like a gas; it spreads until it pressurizes both the physical body and the psyche. So it's time to take it out, look at it and release it. You don't have to put the energy into those old patterns anymore. They're simply something that has been misunderstood, misaligned, and you can now accept a clearer point of view. It is often not nearly as difficult to face them as it is to not face them. But one must come to a certain point where one acknowledges them and begins to process them. You can do this in any way you choose — get someone who can help you to flow them out so that you don't have them all stored within you. You can then look at your emotional needs more clearly. Put another way, what you've done is bury the needs, and you can't bury the needs — you have to *balance* the needs. You're ripe — a beautiful ripe fruit. You're ready for the stabilizing effect of emotional processing, pulling that out, releasing it, knowing it isn't yours — you don't need to keep it.

I would like to talk a little bit about what happened at the end of Atlantis. Near the end of Atlantis there was a certain plot — we could call it a power that sought more power for the sake of power. This was beyond the Earth, not from the spiritual level but from other civilizations that were considered higher. I don't consider them that, but the Atlanteans did. A group of beings came into the Atlantean scene and entered the temples there; many of you were members of the temples at that time. It was a very powerful experience — you were building many beautiful ways of healing and helping people. But suddenly the process didn't work as well and you couldn't figure it out – you couldn't pinpoint what was going wrong. Where you'd had harmony, suddenly there was disharmony. There were those who were arguing and criticizing, there was disruption and strikes – you had never had those before in the history of Atlantis. People stopped showing up for work.

Gradually some of you got together and began to figure out that within each temple there was a disruptive focus. Many times it was four or five individuals who were going around stirring up trouble with those who worked in the temple. Not only that, they also became a part of the guiding force of each temple and were moving it into what they wanted rather than what the temple had been created for. Over time this got worse and worse. You saw that this resistance was so entrenched and so difficult that you were fighting for your temple lives. But you couldn't always identify them. You would get rid of a few, then others would spring up. Some of it was so nebulous you couldn't get a handle on it.

Eventually most of you were forced out of the temples. You literally and politically were forced out and you saw your beautiful temples misused by these beings that wanted power. It got to the point that some of the temples were used to create robotic figures to do the will of someone else. What is the will for? How does one use it clearly? It is like a focus, and if you wish to serve humanity, how do you focus it? From the heart, but you also surrender. How does that work? It fits everything together, doesn't it? You choose to surrender to the soul, and the will allows that. If this is the level of the soul, then the will connects to that through a surrender process; then the soul can direct you. The will is important but you don't all use it clearly yet. At this point most of you are aware of the way you want to be guided and you are guided that way. But it's as if right now the will aspect is kind of flapping around because it doesn't know exactly what to do. If it's not through a surrender process, then it connects all right, but it shuts down the system. If it is used through a surrender process, then it connects to the soul level, which is connected to all of the group souls that are connected to many other levels, so you are using your will to connect into another level that is flowing more clearly – and that happens through surrender. But there has been much misunderstanding about the will as well as confusion between the will and the dynamic energy, and between surrender and allowing someone to walk all over you.

It is important to see how this worked in Atlantis, because you had focused your wills into serving humanity. You thought you had surrendered to something clearer, but it was a group process that wasn't clearer. You had surrendered to a group process in the temples and you were being guided by that, but somehow it wasn't working. Your collective will had shut down. The important thing to remember is that you had a misunderstanding about the will, and certainly a misunderstanding about power, for you were forced out of your jobs. But the most difficult thing was to see what the power structure did to humanity. They really began to control them. I think it would have been worldwide, much worse than it was, if that structure hadn't collapsed – the sinking of Atlantis and the destruction of the civilization. A convoluted structure cannot last because it isn't a divine structure – it may last for a while, but usually not for too long.

Power, then, that is directed through the choice area we'll call the will – your personal point of power, a choice you are making to use the will clearly. The Source gave it to you. And you say to the Source, "You have given me something – can I give it back?" What do you think happens? Jackpot! You have your personal key that opens everything to you. It's necessary to see that you do have that and you were given it for that purpose. But again, an important point to remember is that surrender is an eternal process. There are levels of surrender; you might say to a group, "I'm going to surrender this much and no more, because it isn't safe. I don't really trust the group yet." It's all connected with the amount of trust one has in the group process. Each time you make a choice (and it really doesn't matter what choice you make) as you connect into it with your will, if you allow it to be heart surrender, then there is an expansion. But there is also a basic fear of being unlimited, so when it starts to expand, a part of you that you've buried and don't recognize shuts it down and the rest of you says, "Look what happened – I can't trust that." So the heart wants to open it, and the buried fears keep shutting it down again. So it opens and opens and opens through more trust.

The misuse of power is the key that all of you are probably looking for here. The universe stores a misuse of power. This is what you call karma. It takes a picture of a misuse of power, and this picture must be transmuted. The misuse of power can come in several ways. If you have a friend who abuses a child and you turn your back on that, is that a misuse of power? In my opinion it is. It doesn't mean you have to force someone to do something, but there is an attitude here, in turning ones back on something, that is a misuse of power. All of you have that to deal with. It's the area of responsibility: "What am I responsible for and what am I not responsible for?" Although you have your personal responsibility, and that other person abusing the child has his personal responsibility, it meets in the overall responsibility of creating the Earth. That's where communication must come in regarding the misuse of power.

Now I'd like to discuss the life one of you had, but it's one that all of you may relate to. You were once a handmaiden, a servant to a family but in a rather honorable position, not considered less-than. The family was very wealthy and had a certain prestige, and you became a member of that family. You also cared for the children when they were born and you mostly enjoyed caring for the first two of them. The third one was a little retarded so you had to spend more time with that child; you had to explain in graphic, physical ways until the child understood. That worked for the first four years and then the child reached a mental barrier, although there was physical growth. The mental and emotional bodies slowed down and it was difficult to help the child understand. But the child loved to play with a certain type of kite. He got a lot out of running and running and watching the kite fly and feeling the breeze, and the kite was very beautiful. So as he got older he couldn't understand mentally and emotionally much of what was going on around him; he remained about four years old in that sense. The flying of the kite seemed to free him, and you encouraged him.

When he was perhaps 19 you were still with him because he needed someone, but he was physically quite strong from the running and you didn't always go with him. You would send a sack lunch along and tell him carefully what areas were safe for him to go into. But one day he didn't come back. His family searched for him and finally found him in the bottom of an animal trap. He couldn't get out of it and he was all curled up crying and felt very alone. When he saw you he tried desperately to climb up to you, but he couldn't understand when you told him to wait for ropes to be thrown to him, and he fell back and broke his neck. This was very, very difficult for you.

There was a burial ceremony in which the body was burned. (In my opinion that is the clearest way to dispose of the body, because it doesn't leave any residue to pollute your Earth. Much of the pollution in your soil comes from diseased bodies that have been buried.) During the ceremony you were standing there and a little bit of the essence was still in the body and you watched it leave. You knew it was to go and join the other part that had left the body, but instead it ran to you. It felt a little uncomfortable because it wasn't integrated into who you were, and you kept telling it, "I love you, but go and do what you are meant to do – don't stay in me." However, you couldn't shake it off and it became an aspect that was rather hard to integrate because it chose to still be itself and you couldn't blend it into yourself because it wasn't meant to be part of you on the physical level – although of course you were all a part of the same thing spiritually. But this aspect, through its fear patterns, entered you, who had raised it, rather than going back to the spiritual level. You had to deal with that for the rest of that life. It became a festering point within you and started a growth process that got out of control. Something similar to what you would call cancer developed in your physical body.

I am suggesting, then, that diseases such as cancer come from a core that you can't assimilate into yourself. It isn't always an aspect of someone else, but it's something that you don't seem to have any control over – it's something out of control. Then it takes a third thing to spark that – the desire for spiritual growth. Generally in the case of cancer there is a tremendous surge of energy, of life force, of power from the soul level. It might be only an instantaneous surge, but that's enough to start that growth that then seems to get out of control. Cancer is often something that is seeded in a past life and becomes activated — some even have it two or three times. What is done with it in the physical body depends upon the person and their beliefs, where they are and how they choose to use the opportunity that is given. An important area to look at is, when someone makes a choice that separates them, and that choice seems to create an aspect in you, then there doesn't seem to be any way to continue the integration or to allow that to be part of who you are. That's not really true but it *seems* to be, and that's what cancer is all about. It's part of the confusion — it's like a lump that doesn't seem able to be integrated into the greater perspective that you are trying to allow now. If that festers long enough — and it's usually the buried emotions that create that festering — then it pushes into an area, like a little pinpoint, and sets it into motion when it isn't supposed to be in motion. Then this moves and attracts other pinpoints that move, and this snowballs and they begin to join and enlarge. This is the important part: If someone who has set all this in motion has a shock, then that may be the beginning of the disease. The shock creates a crystallization. The universe then takes a picture and begins a process that cannot move beyond the crystallization. The shock itself holds in the disease.

If there is no disease when that shock happens, still there is a great deal of creative confusion. Someone might become almost suicidal because there is so much confusion in their life. The outer mirroring shows what is happening on the inside, and they begin to get mirrored to them all sorts of illogical, difficult experiences; they may be beings who have chosen to close their heart partially and thus have no direction. I am talking about this not because you are going to get cancer, but because you have been to these distant points and resolved some of the issues for yourself, at least partly, and you may begin to attract people that have these deep areas. If you see that in them, then what you have to do first is resolve the shock. Nothing can heal without that. If you can't get to the issue yourself, then someone on our level can help you look at it, because were going to have to remove the cause of why the shock is there. It is probably so deep that it goes clear to the Source level. We've got to look at that. People are in a state of shock when they are showing symptoms of hopelessness or are manifesting a life-threatening illness. We could also mention AIDS and diseases of crystallization such as MS — these too are diseases of shock, a shock so deep that people think they can't move. Often when they start to get well, they will regress because they do not believe they can get well. It is a case of shock. And even if you can't find the cause yourself and there still doesn't seem to be a resolution there after contacting us, you can hold out hope to them. You can embody that hope yourself and you can communicate with them in a deep emotional way from the heart, showing that you care. And that, my friends, is very worthwhile.

We haven't talked much about crystals. They were certainly your friends in Atlantis, and also probably one of the most interesting learning tools that you had. There were times, of course, when they powered your whole civilization – they were a support system for Atlantis. This was particularly true during the middle period of Atlantis. When in the latter days the crystals were broken up, some of you were deeply affected. Many of you had been in charge of certain crystals and felt a deep responsibility for them. When they were destroyed, you carried that sense of failed responsibility, not only for the crystals but also for the support system, into succeeding lives.

Now, when the crystals were broken up, was that your responsibility? No, it wasn't, but emotionally you may still feel that it was, and that's important. You'd love to go back and put those crystals together again. Well, roll the film back and see the pieces fly together again. You can do that; you can heal it that way. And think about it: The crystals create their own reality too, and some of the pieces are still around – they are very beautiful. But I am serious about advising you to go back and change some of those lives so that they come out differently. Will this actually change the past? Yes and no – everything changes when you change your perception of it. It might not change for other people, but it can change for you. So heal that perception – yes, you were a part of that period when the crystals were broken up, but you were no more responsible than anyone else, and you can go back now and release it. You have to forgive yourself; you have to forgive the universe; you have to forgive the crystals; you have to forgive the people that were there. Forgiveness, my friends – the heart has to heal it.

Atlantis: a land of opportunity where rich (and I don't mean monetarily) lives were experienced. You name it, you probably learned it in Atlantis. You had periods of war, periods of peace, periods when you explored scientifically, and periods in which the senses developed. The body itself became more flexible. There was a time on the Earth when you couldn't move as flexibly as you can now. There have been some changes in the physical structure since Atlantis: There are more vertebrae, and they are more flexible; there are more layers of skin; the blood vessels have developed; the characteristics of the nails and eyelashes and eyebrows have changed. Many physical things became functional or changed in the Atlantean era.

I would say that another really important thing to look at is the number of earthquakes – hardly a year went by when there weren't major quakes. Many of your fears about this are not so much from what has occurred in California (although you see it in that mirror), but from what occurred in Atlantis. There were times when whole villages were buried completely; there were times when everything you loved and knew about went down – great catastrophic earthquakes. Sanat Kumara came and ensouled the planet in the pre-Lemurian time, and as the soul aspect locked in more completely, electrical changes were made. By Atlantean times that level was assimilated, so we don't see as much electrical activity. The climate changed a great deal – early in Atlantis there was an axis tilt that caused a big change.

One thing we haven't looked at is marketing. Your country's approach to marketing, which is genius, really, though many people see it negatively — and it certainly can be overdone — began in Atlantis also. Advertising was used extensively. No, you didn't have billboards and television, but there were publications and posters that were advertising vehicles and little crystal devices that showed you advertising. This was perhaps the birth of your American civilization, its commercial side that is prevalent now. It seemed good then and it is good now. Yes, it can be overdone, but I think it's coming into balance — you'll find the next few years balancing that out. But I would look at Atlantis as the birthplace from which your present Earth has been created and the stepping stone to the New Age that you are now creating.

The temples were wonderfully spiritual places. We have talked about them as places of healing, but they were also places of great celebrations. There were twelve of these a year, and sometimes twice that, depending on the calendar year and other things. There were many holidays, but perhaps the most important ones were celebrated close to what is now July. At those times there were great ceremonies. You had candles, similar to those you have now, and as has been done in ancient times and also lately, there were ceremonies with thousands of people going up certain mountains where there were sacred fires. All of you remember these wonderful experiences. You remember being a part of something greater. You remember the teachers that were there. You remember the great beginning that was made in your association with ones you later became very familiar with as teachers and friends.

I would like to do a meditation. Some of you might not follow me all the way through this, and that's all right. Follow if you can, and if you drift off, the good news is that your subconscious is using it as a symbol and will benefit from it.

☙ *We come together to a village in Atlantis. See yourself entering this village. Notice what you are wearing. Everyone is wearing a loose and flowing garment — see what colors yours is. And notice that this is a celebration; notice the simplicity of the dwellings around us and come into this celebration. Now on a mountaintop nearby you hear a deep gonnnng! And another one: gonnnng! And another one: gonnnng! Suddenly from somewhere far above you, voices begin to sing and now you know it's time to light your candle and move up the mountain with everyone else, and you look forward to it. You take your place in line and each candle lights the one in back of it — your candle is lit and you turn around and light the one in back of you and soon there is a whole column of light. As you march up the mountain now you raise your voices in song — a column of light moving up the mountain.*

☙ *Sense that. It is evening and the air is cool and clear, and the light from the stars is visible. All is joyous — a celebration of light. That is exactly what it is called, and you have experienced it many times in Atlantis and you know* that everyone in your country is celebrating it too. You know that thousands are going up the mountains and you attune to them in the joyous movement that you make together. Notice it. You are together – it is the camaraderie that is important – and you are singing your songs of gratitude and your songs of caring and you are joyous in your celebration of moving up the mountain. It is not difficult – some places are steep, but you help each other. The little ones are lifted over those spots and they go running off carrying their candle. More and more – the older people are helped up, the younger people gratefully and eagerly help others, and the men lift the little children and carry them. A little one is being lifted up onto the shoulders, still holding his candle, holding it there and proud to be able to do so.

❧ Now finally the summit of the mountain is approached. Feel the gentle breeze that is blowing – it is cool but not cold. There are now hundreds of you gathering at the top of the mountain. Look around – as far as you can see, all of the mountains have lights on top of them. Hundreds of people are gathered on top of every mountain. And all over the voices echo – they sing of joy, they sing together in celebration of being a part of this ceremony. You all hear within your head the voice of a wonderful being who is spiritual, not on the physical level, and he says to you, "Come forth in your understanding. Lift up your voices together. Let us celebrate together. We are together. Let us celebrate creation together. We worship the process. We give thanks to the process. We are a part of the process."

❧ He says many things – each of you hears him a little bit differently. But what you do hear is the celebration. Lift up your voices in joyous celebration. Look around, look at the light. The light responds as light and it is as if all these lights are moving together. They become a spiral and the light spirals through you and you feel its movement, moving as light, spiraling as light. Now, as you keep this focus, we are going to bring in the teacher Lenduce, who will lead you in what is called a light-triggering session to aid you. But remember, your feet are firmly on the Earth, and yet it is the heights of the Earth and it is in connection with others – the group process and the lighting-up process where your creativity is focused.

❧ "All right, good! Well, how exciting as we see you move as light, flow as light, expand as light. The light expands, the light flows, you move as light, triggering the light, expanding the light, flowing as light. The light! The light! Expanding the light, moving as light, flowing as light. Yes, we are together, and yes, as Vywamus said, you are on the physical level, but you are also flowing as light, moving as light, triggering the light, expanding the light.

❧ "Expand! Expand! Expand! Expanding the light, moving as light, flowing as light. The light! The light! Moving as light, expanding as light. Expand! Expand! Expand! Move as light, flow as light, triggering the light. The light expands within you. How exciting! Yes! How wonderful to expand as light, move as light, triggering the light, expanding the light, flowing as light, flowing as light. Light! Light! Light! The expansion is light, the movement is light, the flow is light. Expand! Expand! Expand! Yes, as light, as light, triggering the light, expanding the light. The light! The light! The dance is light. The creativity is light. The movement is light. The interaction is light. The light that expands, the light that moves, the light that flows, expanding the light, moving as light, triggering the light.

❦ "Allow yourself to flow now. Move and flow as light, expanding as light, moving as light, flowing as light. The movement is light, the flow is light, the movement is light, the flow is light, creating the light, expanding the light, the movement is light, the flow is light, expanding the light, expanding the light, expanding the light, dancing as light. Yes! Dancing as light, the movement is light, the movement, the flow, the dance of the light, the expansion of light, the triggering of light, the movement is light. The light! The light! The light! The light! The movement as light, the flow as light, the expansion as light. The light! The light! The light! Triggering the light, expanding the light. Each moment that you live expands the light, flows the light. Each moment that you understand more expands the light. Flow as light. Expand! Expand! Expand, triggering the light, moving as light, flowing as light. Expand! Expand! Expand! The light, the flow of the light, the movement as light, expanding the light, flowing as light, moving as light. Expand! Expand! Expand!

❦ "The flow of the light, moving as light, dancing as light. The light! The light! The light! The expansion of light, the movement, the flow. The light! The light, the flow of the light, the expansion as light, the flooooow! The floooooow! The light! The light! The light! The movement as light, the expansion as light. The light! The light! The expansion as light. The light! The light! The flow as light. The light, triggering the light, triggering the light, triggering the light, triggering the light, triggering the light, flowing as light, moving as light. The light! The light! The light! Flowing as light. Expand! Expand! Expand! Expand the light! Expand the light, move as light, flow as light. Expand! Expand! Expand as light, move as light. Expand! Expand! Expand! Move the light, flow the light. Expand! Expand! Expand! Move the light, flow as light, allow it to expand you, allow it to expand you. Flow the light, flow the light, move as light, move as light, move as light, triggering the light, triggering the light, triggering the light. Move as light! Flow as light, as light. The light! The flow! The light! The flow! The light! The flow! The light! The flow! Expanding the light, the light, the light, the light! Triggering the light, the light, the light! Expanding, expanding, expanding the light! The light! The light! The flow of the light. The expansion is light, the flow of light, the expansion is light, the flow of the light, the expansion of light, the movement is light, triggering the light. The expansion as light, as light, as light, as light, as light, as light.

❦ "Now you see before you a wholeness of light. You enter it and the expansion becomes even more comprehensive because you are activating those parts that Vywamus told you about. How about gathering them up now and putting them into the part of you that is active and expanding them as light, moving them as light. Take that percentage and put it into the active part and expand it as light, move it as light, flow it as light. Allow it to express as light, moving as light, activated as light, flowing as light, moving as light. A trail of light! Expand! Expand! Expand! Expand! Move it as light, flow it as light. Expand! Expand! Expand! Allow it to move, allow it to flow. Expand! Expand! Expand! Allow it to expand. More expansion, more flow! Allow it to flow, flow it as light, triggering the light, expanding as light, moving as light, flowing as light. Allow it to expand! Expand! Expand! Allow it to flow, triggering the light, expanding the light, moving as light, flowing as light. The light! The light! The light! The flow of the light! The light! The light, expanding as light, moving as light, flowing as light. The light! The light! The light! The light! The light! Flowing as light, expanding as light, moving as light. The light! The light! The light! Expanding as light, moving as light, flowing as light. The light! The light! The light! Flowing as light, expanding as light, moving as light. The light! The light! The light! Flowing as light, expanding as light, moving as light. The light! The light! The light! Expanding as light, moving as light, flowing as light. The light! The light! The light! The rhythm of the light! The rhythm of the light! Expanding as light, flowing as light. The light! Expand! Expand! Expand! Expand! Expand! The light! Triggering the light, moving as light, flowing as light. Expand! Expand! Expand! The light! The light! The light! The light! The light! The light!

❦ "And thus you recognize the eternal rhythm of the light, the expansion as light, the flow as light, always triggering a new level of light, a new expansion within the light. Dear ones, this is the flow, this is the rhythm, this is the process.

❦ "Vywamus has asked me to wish you a good evening. Thank you, my friends."

❖ F O U R ❖

The Atlantean-Egyptian Influence

W HAT WE WANT TO DO NOW IS HELP YOU RELEASE AND HELP THE EARTH release a level of resistance that came from a particular event in the past.

Most all of you were present in Egypt, as you know, at a time when the society, the government and the structure itself found the movement of spiritual growth to be a threat. The spiritual growth movement came to Egypt directly from Atlantis. Many of you know that the teacher Thoth was one of the spiritual teachers instrumental in starting a new and more advanced view of spiritual evolution in Egypt.

We could call many of the Egyptians of that time younger souls. Let's say they were happy in their playpen. They felt comfortable, they felt that life was pretty good in that nice little area called Egypt. Then all of a sudden, the noisy Atlanteans arrived. To say that these newcomers were sophisticated is probably an understatement. They had many, many, many practices that the children of Egypt did not understand.

You, the Atlanteans, came and brought to Egypt a whole new level of being. It was tremendously more intense, and the young Egyptians said, "I don't know what this is all about. I don't understand it. Sometimes I think you are all a little bit crazy. I don't understand the practices and I don't even like them. What do you mean, you are taking over our area? Why are you here? What do you mean, Atlantis blew up?" Many, many questions were asked.

The point is that there was difficulty in assimilating the Atlanteans into the new land that was called Egypt. This went on for several generations. Your lives were longer then, and most of you were there for the equivalent of several of your present lives.

I want to tell you about a time before the Great Pyramid was built. It was still in the planning stage. To escape persecution by the Egyptians, you went into the inner Earth.

At that time there had been a change in this inner Earth. The new race that was coming and is now here was not there yet. The race that helped you was one that was just about ready to leave. After it left, the inner Earth was not occupied, so some of you went in there and occupied it for a while. You continued to live in the inner Earth for three hundred years because the government of the civilization in Egypt at the time you came from Atlantis didn't want you. They wanted you gone, and they tried to get rid of you. This didn't come about at first; it took several generations. They made it so difficult for you that you had to leave the surface for three hundred years. What you found there were some very, very powerful tools, tools for transformation (this race was a little ahead of you). And you were ahead, generally speaking, of many parts of the Earth at that time. You found tools that were indeed very cosmic. But if you give a child a toy — something that is very powerful — and they don't know how to use it, it can be very interesting. So there were these powerful transformational tools, and some of you burned yourselves a little.

What I am saying is that you had to learn to use these tools. You became rather leery of them, because some of them seemed to work in an almost opposite way from the tools you were used to. Now, wasn't there help? Yes, of course. But you had to recognize it, because it was the type of help that you have now through the channeling process. You had to learn to use it.

Sometimes one of you would say one thing and another would say something else, and then all of you had to figure out together the best way to use these tools. And to say that the cocreator process didn't always agree is an understatement. You know how it is now . . . .

You are all learning, in a group focus, to utilize the opportunities that are here as well as you can. It's like "We'll try this because we all agree, or at least the majority agrees, that this area is our next step — this is what we want to be open to in an organizational sense."

Sometimes you would get together and there would be a tool (a crystal). You would wonder what it was for, and your discussion would go rather like this: "Should we touch it?"

"I'm not sure we should. Look what happened when we touched that one. Let's think about it."

"What are you getting that it is for? I'm getting that it is for the dynamic energy."

"I'm not. I'm getting that it helps stabilize; it's not a dynamic tool."

After a few of these discussions, you had to decide how you were going to use that tool. Some of you were braver than others — or more rash than others. Some of you would get tired of all of the discussions and just go ahead and try them and see what happened. One morning they found one of you sitting on one of these crystals — you were all radiant, but they were not sure you would survive. You told them how it worked. That was helpful, though maybe not for your body. So you did gradually sort it out.

So what you, the Atlanteans, actually did after the destruction of Atlantis was transfer your consciousness. You took the plug out of Atlantis and plugged it into Egypt, and then the Earth supplied what you needed when you needed it. You were not aggressive. But the people in Egypt thought you were dangerous. They didn't understand your ways, they didn't understand who you were. They had heard about Atlantis, and instead of accepting you at the level where you were (you were willing to coexist, to go into the cocreating process on a whole new level), they thought you were going to use them as slaves. Do you remember seeing movies of thousands of slaves building the pyramids? Well, that's someone's memory of a possibility that did not really exist. Instead, it was the fear pattern of the younger souls who lived in the area of Egypt.

You had a lot of help at that time. Some great spiritual teachers took on physical form. We came from the other realms — the Galactic Core, the Pleiades and some of the other areas — and we came to you in Egypt. We began to make some things possible that perhaps would not have been possible for a while. Why? Because you had invoked that help through the abilities that were coming to you in this intense experience in the inner Earth. Most of you who had this life experience used your abilities then in a more cohesive and emphatically more dynamic way than in any other life you've ever had on the Earth, up until this one and its possibilities. So, through the tools which were developed, many things have happened.

All of you had to learn to use these resources on a level that perhaps you didn't even know you had. It stretched you a great deal physically, as well: You were all an inch taller when you died, so it really did stretch you physically, spiritually and creatively.

Affirmations

I now want to give you now some affirmations to work on to clear this area. I ask that you slide the following words (rather like a fortune-cookie strip) into an electrical blue lake. See it merging into the lake. Then see a golden light shining on the lake; as you do, the words are absorbed into the lake. They are integrated into it. Then from the lake there is an effect: it is a clearing. The whole area is clearer. It is like a splash into every cell of your physical body, like a washing from a clearer prospective of the cells. As this occurs, allow yourself to begin to form a spiral of electrical blue energy, starting at your feet and flowing around your physical body until it passes up and over your head.

Let these go beyond the mental body — you don't have to "understand" the affirmations.

You may want to hold on to crystals while doing these affirmations, one in each hand, or one you hold on to with both hands. Every time you do one of these affirmations the crystals realign the polarities. They rebalance your physical body. The crystals are a focus to help you do that. They also remind your emotional body that you are supported in the process.

❧ *I allow the stimulation of my creativity without invoking an unknown stress that seeks to distort the process, now.*

❧ *I know the cocreator level will not enclose me within a limited space where my unknown potential is too difficult to effect without "burning," now.*

❧ *In my spiritual questing, I am not coming to a point where the unknown will hold me in a manner that will be difficult to release, and I will be able to utilize that unknown space, now.*

❧ *I know that as I accept this new, powerful place which is flowing, I will not be caught in the unknown which seeks to burn me, now.*

Let's now talk about reversing the aging process — going back to the age you want to be. That can be done now. You know, as you move into the fourth-dimensional operation, you might as well do it while putting in affirmations. Decide what age you would like to be, and each time you do the affirmation process through the spiral, take a moment, take an assessment of the light within the whole structure of your body. See if you have any areas that are not as bright as the others, and brighten those areas of the body. All you have to do is shake it — the movement will help integrate the energy, or the light. Then rinse or flood your physical with iridescent pink color. The electrical properties of the iridescent pink bring a web of light, a light webbing that can rinse out the cells.

❧ *I am opening to this new level, knowing that the cocreator process supports me, and I it, without an unknown which burns or seeks to destroy me, now.*

Let's say there is still some resistance to that age after using the pink light webbing. This simply means that there is another type of pattern there that is perhaps quite heavy. If so, go to another age, a few years younger or older, and see if you still have that resistance, until you can deal with the specifics of that age. Don't stop clearing just because the resistance comes up; look instead for alternate ages. Perhaps there was a point that was so important that you emphasized it over and over again. It might not be negative — it might be that the age is important simply because it is a symbol of using your creativity on another level and there were some fear patterns of using it on that level. The age itself is incidental; it relates to an opening for your creativity that you didn't feel ready to step into on the physical level. This is what you are trying to release now, at this age when something happened to you. Each time you reach a certain age, it is a symbol of what has happened to you throughout your past-life experiences at that age. It is also a universal symbol of what has happened to the Earth, in the sense of numerology. Look for the clues.

❦ *This inner link which I now explore is not an enclosed area which I must remain in because of fears of destruction from going outside of it, now.*

❦ *As my consciousness goes to a new level within this group experience, I will not find, because of my association with this group, a limitation or restriction in the inner connection, now. (This would be a misinterpretation of the group energy; it isn't true at all, but some conclusions were formed from that event.)*

❦ *As we discover this new opening together, there will not be a backlash that seeks to wipe out the electrical responses/integrative process, now.*

You might notice what is happening to your crystals through all of this. They have changed, I can tell you. You've energized them differently because you've moved beyond the space you were in. The crystals are different too because they're embodying your energy as well as their own.

This process we just went through, we can call the creative process of releasing some of the burdens from the past. And looking at the scenario, the story I gave you, we will now process a little more consciously.

I want to bring up a point here. All of you are seeking to use your heart. It's the very center of your creativity, to be very trusting and allowing and very heart-centered. But because of these deep experiences, there is around that heart a wall and a shell. What actually happens is, you go into these affirmations and begin to release in those very deep levels, especially those areas that are tied up with your power; you begin to crack open and step out of that shell that you've encased your heart in. It's not that there isn't a spiritual part of you that understands. There is, and there is a physical part of you that understands and a mental part of you that understands. But the emotional part has woven that, because of the beliefs that are tied up with the situation.

In regard to your power, in regard to your unlimitedness, all of this is seeking to have you express in an unlimited manner. The only way you can express in this manner is through the center within the heart. That's the only way unlimitedness works, so every time you go deeply into the heart and release resistances against it, you open a little more of that barrier that you've put around yourself to protect yourself from your unlimitedness out of a basic disbelief that you can use it.

If you have not yet acknowledged that there is some resistance in the heart area, if you haven't seen what I am talking about, I'm not telling you that it has to be there. I'm not telling you that it is even yours — you've accepted something that isn't yours, in a divine sense. When you approach it, you might try to run away from it, because creatively, you don't know you can handle it. You don't understand that there is a divine structure, which I represent here in this class, and which is helping to guide you to take a look at that unlimitedness without stirring up some of the old experiences that happened before. The old patterns try to wipe it out, they try to take your consciousness away, telling you not to look at it because it's too difficult.

There's too much convolution. There's no way to focus it at all. See, that's what's going on.

The good news is, you keep releasing these very deep resistances, but it requires going very deep. If the subject is not too deep, then it is just an interesting subject, you can concentrate on it very well. But for each of you it pushes some button in your subconscious mind that says, "I don't want to look at that. When I looked at that before, things happened to me that were not good." And what that does is push the button of unworthiness that all of you have. Why? Because you are not able to instantly use your unlimitedness. This is not what you are supposed to do! But it is what many of you *think* you are supposed to do.

Do you see the difference? You say to yourself, "Through my individualization, I am supposed to have gotten it by now." But *that's not true*. It's your perception that's a little off, or not focused completely through the clearing out of the deep resistive patterns, which you can do by having someone like me bring you the overall area, and then having the group vehicle structure helping you. Then we can take a look at it. And even if you don't get it completely, you will have taken the next step to clear it out. Then, the next time it will be a little easier. Do you see that? Just by doing these affirmations and releasing these old patterns, you begin a process and it is important to follow and see what is going on.

If your conceptual mind can't follow all of it, that's not terrible; at least your creativity followed it. Your subconscious mind followed it. And, that's the breakthrough we were looking for.

You have to have that breakthrough first before you can process something through the rest of your body. You may have a belief that says, "When I get here, I can't go any further. This is as far as I can go." Now, you can think conceptually and you can try to make realizations, but your realizations arrant going to take you any further than right here, because you have set up the barrier that says, "That's as far as I can go."

That is why there are many techniques used in both group intensives and personal intensives. These help you break through and recognize that connection, the divine link, on a very personal level as well as the universal level. You wouldn't be here at all if you didn't think you were connected to the Creator. You wouldn't be here at all if you didn't want to be aware of your own potential. But at the same time you wouldn't be here in physical existence if you did not still accept some sort of limitation in regard to spiritual growth. That's the wall or barrier we are talking about. It has to be opened subconsciously before it can be processed consciously. So it is the focus for the subconscious that I often represent.

Now, if we get into processing that way, many times your mental bodies haven't a clue. For some of you that is not very comfortable. The mental body could say, "What do you mean, I don't understand that mentally? I didn't get that, which means it didn't do anything." I beg to differ with you!

It did something probably *very* important. It allowed you to use the strengths of your creativity and move forward in a way that will make everything that follows possible.

Now, that's the use of the dynamic energy that I bring you. The dynamic energy is a creative opening, a creative function, that isn't necessarily followed by all of the parts of you at once. But you can explore it and integrate within it later. It can be done all at once, but on the physical level it's probably going to take you more than five minutes to process what we have opened creatively.

That's my focus — bringing you these openings that you can then process on the physical level in order to manifest the souls purposes as clearly as you want. You can step into them, and you will sometimes bang your physical, spiritual, mental and emotional heads on these barriers. Were working with them now. That's the release that you felt — even if you couldn't tell what was released, that's what you felt. That's my contribution or gift to you. What you have done here is rearrange all the input to your physical structure. You could say that the endocrine system said, "But the hormones always flowed this way and now they are not flowing this way anymore." It's as if the parathyroid is doing much more than it did before and it's taking some of the burden or the responsibility off of the thyroid. It is also opening the thymus to a new level of contribution. Some of you have a change in the liver area. So there is a shifting within the physical structure, within the endocrine system itself, and it has to be gotten used to. These things really shift a lot of the physical responses, and through your body's movement you begin to get used to that.

If you could really go back to that body you had at age 25, you wouldn't know what to do with it. It would be a tool of the third dimension. Your consciousness has been prepared to live now in the finer and finer fourth dimension. This doesn't mean that you couldn't go back, but it wouldn't be the vehicle that you've chosen to be in now. So each day it will be important to get some movement and allow those physical responses.

So these particular body juices are flowing differently, as are the electrical responses. That's why it is a good idea to do some energy work on the physical body. There are many healers you could go to, but it is important that you assist one another with this energy flow. It will be important to just "get it moving" and keep it moving.

This area is a very deep one for all of you. When I told you about a life where you were the most powerful you've ever been on the Earth, we got into your power issues — and I don't mean misuse of power, but the unlimited use of yourself as a powerful divine being. Without a clear sense of your power, you have had a tendency to blame physical existence and your body: "I am limited because I am here on the physical; somehow it is the fault of the physical plane that I am limited. I wouldn't be here if it wasn't some sort of a limitation. Why am I here?"

There are several types of concentric patterns that are coming in. We've opened you, but there is more to deal with. The good news is, you can integrate this by getting someone to work on your body and so on, and then we'll take the next step. This has been taken into consideration, and the angels will be helping you with your heart connection. But you do have to go through the levels of it, the levels of releasing, perhaps the levels of blaming parts of yourself or parts of the universe until you can shift the blame to a less vulnerable part of your consciousness — shift it into allowingness, shift it into trust, shift it into the opening of your next step. Does that make sense to you? I hope that helps you a little.

All sorts of things do come up when we work with you. There is a power area for all of you. By "power" I mean divine power, the use of yourself in quite an unlimited manner. You all have quite a bit to do in the area of accepting your unlimitedness. We've talked about it in regard to the dynamic energy; we've talked about it in many ways. It has to do with accepting that you can really step out there, right in the center of this field of unlimitedness, and be a full-fledged, equal participating member of it. There are deep fears in most of you about doing that: "Maybe I won't be able to keep up. Maybe I won't know what to do. Maybe my responsibilities haven't been plugged into that plan." Well, it's not that you think that — your mental body doesn't think that. But there is something called an emotional response that tries to connect, and then the old patterns of behavior hold you back.

The basic one is at that point of Sourceness. The point of individuality is locked in. It wasn't locked in as a limitation. It was locked in as a focus, something you could focus on in order to discover your full Sourceness coming through the cocreator level. You're stepping into a greater acceptance of that. You could say you're stepping into *your full power*. What does that mean to you? It means something different to each of you.

Let's say that in the Atlantean experience you felt very impacted: you saw a temple you were very much a part of destroyed by those who took over the power. They said, "Come and be a part of our power," and you couldn't because you felt it was a negative use of power. You saw those who accepted it and you saw what happened to them and what happened to your beloved temple and to Atlantis. So, interwoven with the process come these beliefs about the use of power. When I take you into that situation, all of the power issues come up, along with everything in regard to power.

You do need to process what we have stimulated. I've taken you into a powerful place to look at it.

✧ F I V E ✧

Keys to Evolution

WHAT IS EVOLUTION? EVOLUTION IS GROWTH, A CONTINUOUS EXPANSION of learning based on what you have learned before. Consciousness, realization and understanding of who you really are would basically describe it. Evolution is a process that Source, the Creator, has chosen in order to clearly recognize opportunities presented as the process evolves. Evolution is a constant, with us all the time, whether it seems so or not.

I consider physical existence to be a big mirror showing you what you haven't yet understood. It also helps you realize that there are some things you do understand. Sometimes you get deeply involved with transformation and you begin to think there is only negative resolution. Life is really trying to mirror your abilities and your unlimited access to those abilities. The growth factor is built into the process.

Flexibility and adaptability allow another point of view to be mirrored to you so you can learn and understand. A particular environment is formed from the choices you have made, some of which you have enjoyed and some of which you haven't. You learn to be adaptable and stretch with those choices.

A new beginning or a fresh opportunity requires a lot of communication. One has to stretch and adapt to new opportunities and perspectives. I think there is an expectation people have about change, but expectations simply get in the way of some obvious changes. I am not talking about just wanting something to come out all right; that optimistic point of view is very helpful. However, when you expect, in a particularly rigid way, to go down a certain avenue, that gets in the way. It is like fabric that stretches, moves, adapts and flows. In that new beginning it's mirroring all of the things needing to be cleared, understood or assimilated to allow the new beginning in a way you all would wish.

So think of physical existence as a big mirror. Individually and in groups, you are getting mirroring of what needs to be done and understood by the point of consciousness being mirrored. That allows you to use this new beginning well. These are what I would call *keys* to the evolutionary process. What is mirroring bringing to you? It is bringing "synchronicities," or physical activity that reflects your spiritual learning. For many, this is the key to expansiveness you sought as an individual. Again I say, you arrant an individual; you are someone using the individual process. You are a Source aspect, one who is learning, growing, adapting and realizing for Source and Creator.

Synchronicities are meaningful coincidences. Let's say you go out to start your car, and the battery is dead. That's interesting. You have an appointment — how are you going to get to work? Well, you find another car and go on or perhaps you have your battery fixed. What is that telling you? First, there is a lot of electrical disturbance on your planet at this time. This is another symbol or symptom of a "gearing-up" process for a new beginning. The atmosphere of your Earth is more charged than it has ever been. There is intense electrical flow coming in.

If you have not learned to work with crystals, I would encourage you to do so. They can help you to distribute energy more evenly and less forcefully. Working with the large generators can be almost like riding a rocket. The crystal will bring focusing ability to you. Use your own knowingness and get a crystal that talks to you. Find something that will help you focus electrical energy at this time. Also, help one another.

The electrical energy is for using in communication between cities or a particular spiritual center called the Galactic Core. You can look at the Galactic Core as a physical location — and it is. Perhaps more important, it is the center within the heart that each of you has been trying to open. There is an electrical key that opens it. Perhaps this is the moment in time when many of you are going to discover, through this electrical key, what it means to open the heart in the fullest sense.

It is really tremendously exciting for a spiritual teacher to see the time approaching when you will be more aware of yourselves than ever before. Perhaps it is indicative of the fact that this raising consciousness, which is flowing electrically, is almost automatic.

This doesn't mean you won't have emotional traumas and quarrels. It means you will now be conscious, more objective about what is going on in your life, and more allowing of the process. The keys are there. The minute you feel a little stuck in a situation or don't know what to do about it, another key is mirrored to you showing you how to understand it. Because of the movement and the rapid change present, those of you who are willing to really look at synchronicities, who are willing to flow with change and clear the subconscious thought that change is destructive, can be helped by this key.

You can understand through your subconscious mind why and how you create your reality. Each time you have had a physical body and it left the planet, returning to the elements, you looked at it as a destruction. If somebody died, perhaps a loved one, you lost them, and that was a destruction. Or if you lost a job, that seemed to be a destruction. Whatever it was, built within the subconscious mind or your belief structure, change seemed to be a destruction.

Mentally, you know better. Conceptually you can see it is not true, but the emotional body says it is. Thus you get into a polarity split. You have one foot over here saying it is all right to change, and the emotional body over here saying, "Wait a minute, I am not quite sure. Every time I get into change, it doesn't work out or something happens and I don't feel comfortable over here. This is unfamiliar and I don't know if I am ready to step into that now." Reconciling a polarity split requires a willingness to trust the process. This is an important key to your evolution. Recognize that the rapid movement and rapid flow present on the Earth can be trusted. The Earth is a divine being that said to you, "I'm glad you are here." When you came, Mother Earth welcomed you.

As we look at the multiple streams of consciousness your soul brought to the Earth, you should feel quite at home. Some of you said, "I'm through, I have had it, I want to go. I want to be on the spiritual level only." Well, you couldn't find a better mirror than the Earth. She is a very clear mirror. You know the different degrees of mirrors; some of them you can see in without distortion, and some you can't. The Earth probably has one of the clearest mirrors of any of the planets that have centered in the third dimension as solidly as your Earth has been centered.

Now it is moving into the fourth dimension, which is a very clear mirror, and I think this is something to be grateful about. On the planet where I had a few incarnations (it lies across your local universe), if something came to me and I wanted to learn from it, I always had to take into consideration the distortion of the planet itself. It was always more difficult to see clearly what was really coming in. If you had come up to me and said, "I would like to be a part of the group effort you are building and I want to serve with you," I would have had to say, "Well, the planet is distorting that a little. I'll have to move back a little and take a look at it." Generally, what I would find was that the timing was off, and you were really telling me you wanted to work in about six months rather than right when you said it. It was usually a time distortion we got into. That is not happening on this planet; it doesn't happen and it has never happened. Perhaps some gratitude is in order for the Earth's clarity in this regard.

When you get up tomorrow, you might look at the synchronicities that come. Pay attention to even the smallest ones. At the end of your day, take time to go into a state of meditation and really look at what your day has been. Then look at it through the conceptual area. Do this for a month.

Write down some realizations or points of contact you have made through looking at the mirroring process.

The angelic kingdom is stepping up its contact as the Earth becomes more fourth-dimensional. The angelic kingdom can come into closer contact with you. I know that if you asked in a meditation, Gabriel, and particularly Raphael, or perhaps Michael or certainly Ariel would come. Ask one of the archangels to show you an enlargement of a particular synchronicity.

Again, look at the example of a dead battery in a car. This can be the result of an electrical disruption or interruption, or it can be a belief attached to the electrical process of destruction. Remember, interruption, disruption and destruction are very prevalent in the electrical area. The soul level, your higher-self level, is very electrical, and most of you are blending the personality of the soul level. Once in a while that ego-centered personality has a bit of resistance.

An electrical disruption, interruption or destruction can be a resistance against the complete energy of the soul coming in to run your vehicle and be the directive that runs your life. Pay attention to the electrical areas in your life; they are going to tell you a lot. If you find one, write affirmations. Then see the subconscious mind as a lake. It can be any color you want. There is a slide going into this lake, and you just slide the affirmations down it. After the affirmation has slid in, see a golden light shining on the lake and see the lake respond. When you see energy coming up out of the lake from the golden energy sliding in, see it go into your physical structure at the cellular level. Work with the affirmations on a daily basis. Invoke what you really want to occur. Allow it to go directly into the subconscious mind, and every time you do, it will make a difference.

The golden light is an integrator in the process you have set into motion by putting the affirmation into the lake. When you use that affirmation, what comes out of the lake and what you bring into the cellular level is clearer. If your battery won't start, you say,

> ❦ *I resolve the electrical disturbances by accepting a clearer electrical perspective, now. (The nowness is important because it brings in a focus allowing you to use affirmation at this particular point in your evolution.)*

If you use affirmations twice a day during the next month, it will make a difference. It may bring up whatever opposition you have to being perfectly clear in that area. Every time you use an affirmation, it brings up whatever it says. For example, if you try to convince somebody of something and they say, "but . . . but . . . ," these are their objections to what you are trying to convince them of. Still, it is time to be clearer electrically, and the electrical area is a very important key right now.

The evolutionary process is electrical in nature, and the heart is the center of the process. It is electrical and it has a radiant field. I look at you and I see interruptions in that radiant field. I am telling you, as you open up, you allow the heart to radiate more fully. Perhaps it is not as consistent as we would like, but affirmations will help.

Now we get into an interesting area called trust. If you get a chance in the next month, by yourself or with one or two others, go off into nature. It could be a park in the city, where you can be in contact with nature and trees. Really get in touch with the process on the Earth and say to the Creator, the Creative Process, the Source, God or whatever you believe in, "I trust your process; I'm willing to do that. Even if it sometimes seems intense, I trust the process and I am willing to surrender to it." Then feel how you can actually surrender one more time or on one more level. Surrender is an ongoing process. It is a giving up, a letting go and allowing the process to work. It is not an inactive state; it is very active. The process of surrender plugs you into the process differently than you ever saw it before.

Sometimes you feel pressured: You have to do this or that and you feel it is your responsibility. "I must do that, I need to do this, it has got to get done, I must do this." That's called pressure. As you begin to commune with your beautiful planet, surrender and say to the planet, "You're the divine environment upon which I am focused. You're a divine being, and I am going to use you (the Earth) as a symbol of the divine. I am going to surrender to you all of my pressures. I'm going to let go of them. I am just going to say, I release them."

Now what happens? First of all, if you don't get into a guilt trip, you feel better. If you truly do surrender the pressures, if you let go, it really feels good. You know these responsibilities were pressing so heavily — now give that to the process.

What does that mean? Does that mean you sit and contemplate the navel for the rest of your life? No! It opens you up so that the universe can bring you the solutions you have been looking for. It is the key to the evolutionary process. I've said it many times: You can't evolve by yourself, because you arrant an individual. You are a part of the process, and you have to open up to the cocreator level or the whole process in order to evolve in an unlimited manner.

As an example, say you wanted to be president of a multimillion-dollar corporation and you have worked for it all of your life. You know you can't do that by yourself. You may have certain ideas, and maybe you are very creative, but the implementation of a creative idea always goes through a divine structure. It always goes through a process that, in the fullest sense, involves the cocreator level. Humanity is a representative of the cocreator level. I am telling you, on the human level, you are living life as cocreators. Perhaps that doesn't always flow reciprocally in the way you would like it to flow — not yet. (We emphasize the word "yet.") But it is clearer, it is better. Since the Harmonic Convergence, governments are talking, and communication is much more prevalent. Of course, there is more to do, but it is moving — the communication is moving — and that is what creates evolution. In the area of communication, a key, the most important key, is a surrender to the process.

What is the process? Well, we have talked about it as consciousness. What makes up consciousness? Every one of you do, on every level – including the minerals and the plants. Have you ever asked your plant if it wanted to move? It is kind of fun to do that. Once you have communicated fully with every level, a sense of cooperation with that level comes in. It really supports the effort you are making in your life.

Let's say you are married or in a polarity relationship and you decide to change jobs. You know this will affect your partner. Ultimately you are going to make your own decision, but it is very nice to talk it over with your partner so he or she feels part of that decision that is also going to affect him or her. In important decisions made by you, daily, even hourly, there is a need to communicate with the process, with others, or with the Earth itself, to invoke their cooperation.

Or suppose you are going someplace and you don't quite have time to get there. You try to clear the traffic lane so there won't be blocks in the way. Now, what you are asking for is cooperation and communication. That is exactly what I am talking about. These communication links with humanity, the angelic kingdom and the overall Earth consciousness are very necessary in order to have a life that flows well.

How many of you have thought about asking to enter the mass consciousness in a very comprehensive manner? I can hear some saying, "I am trying to get *away* from the mass consciousness, not enter it." The mass consciousness is the storage system of everything learned – if we get comprehensive enough, it is the storage system of everything learned on every level. All of the data ever experienced is stored by the Source within the mass consciousness. There is the human level, the spiritual level, and a column of light that connects every level together. So there isn't only negative connotation about the mass consciousness. It is positive for 99% of you; only 1% of you are trying not to be affected by it. A good example of the 1% that affects humanity quite comprehensively is the fear that channeling is astral-oriented. The negative fear that most people are affected by is a bleed-through from the mass consciousness. One thing we are trying to do is to educate people, to teach people to channel so that they make a spiritual link – and that is not negative. The fears are from the mass consciousness.

Each time you show someone that they need not be fearful of something, you educate them. What they are frightened of is fear itself. Once they get over it, the mass consciousness is clearer in that area. Finally you reach a point of critical mass where, for most people, or at least those who have evolved to a certain point, a fear stored in the subconscious is no longer prevalent enough to pick up on it.

There is a particular technique with which you can symbolically access strengths stored within the mass consciousness as keys to the evolutionary process. This can be quite interesting and important. We are talking about the Akasha, where the records are stored. In connection with the Earth, there are seven levels of the Akasha. On the first through fourth levels there is quite a bit of distortion and difficulty reading clearly the future of probable events. In a time sequence, the Akasha contains as much of the future of your planet as it does the past. It doesn't store just the past; it stores all of the sequencing in connection with a physical planet.

If within the year there were ten different jobs you might get, there would be ten lines of consciousness in the Akasha, moving toward those ten different jobs. So if you asked me what job you will be doing in the year 2000, I would look and see from the seventh level, the clearest. I could look at how much energy you are currently putting into the jobs and evaluate, as of now, which job it looks like you will be moving into. Because you have free will and choices, we would probably take a look again in a few years, a few months or a few days. We have to keep reevaluating the amount of energy flowing into these future events, since some are not certain yet.

The future is as much a part of the history of your planet as the past is. But you arrant exploring it on this particular physical planet except through your choices and the keys you activate to lead you. I am talking about creative energy coming through the subconscious mind, as well as the conscious choices you make. It is important to build a bridge between the two so the subconscious doesn't say, "We never did that before – that is destructive." When this happens, your subconscious is refusing to explore a choice that your conscious mind is trying to explore and you end up with a split. So building that bridge, looking at what the subconscious contains, is the key.

There are alternate realities that are exploring everything else you arrant exploring now. There is nothing the Source has thought of that It isn't exploring from a conscious point of view. So there are parallel universes, parallel Earth's and alternate realities putting up everything you don't energize. Nothing is wasted; everything is explored. If you see an opportunity and say, "I wish I'd done that," or you meet somebody and you don't go on with it, you might be very comforted to know that, on another reality, you did go on with it, you did explore it.

You are an aspect of the Source, and it is just a question of what focus you are occupying at the moment as part of the totality energized by the Source. Please note the careful wording! You see, the Source is simply the Whole and It has energized Itself and said, "I want to explore everything and understand everything" about a particular topic.

This cosmic day is exploring courage and it is toning everything through that title, that theme. Look at it as a circle ten feet in diameter. You know how large a pencil dot makes on paper; one of those dots represents this Earth focus. If you put dots into that circle until it is all filled up, it would still be only about one tenth of one percent of what the totality of your consciousness is exploring at this time. All of those other focuses you, in your totality, are exploring. The Source Itself, of course, is virtually unlimited. The goal is to reach a point of realization. Through that, everything fits together. If your realization is profound enough, all of those other facets or points also get it.

You are creating a point of contact for all consciousness that has been directed through the point of origin the Source has given you. Your personal sourceness is evolving and growing as a part of, an aspect of, overall Sourceness. You have a director termed the monadic level. These are the points of contact making up the Source, or aspect of Source, and your unique strengths, skills and abilities are much appreciated, so unique and so exciting.

Djwhal Khul is so appreciative of every one of you — we all are. We see that you are learning, and how you are learning. It is so interesting and unique. Djwhal Khul fully appreciates all of your strengths and abilities. You create in such a unique manner; this is a reflection of the Source, the Creator Itself, that is so appreciative of all of you and constantly brings you all of these keys, these mirrors and ideas, so you can evolve.

I promised you a way to work with the mass consciousness, or the Akasha. Let's go to a cave that once existed in Atlantis. Some of it is still there — it is connected into a vast reservoir of crystals which exists in the Arkansas area, where many crystals are being mined. They will never be able to reach some of the crystals because they're so deeply buried in the Earth. Come with me now into this cavern. As we enter it, we are surrounded by amethyst crystals. We will reconstruct the cave as it was in Atlantis, except that it didn't have just amethyst — it had the clear quartz, diamonds, rubies and emeralds. Beautiful crystals were all around the walls and some on the floor of the cave.

Akasha Crystal Meditation

❧ Now find a place where you can sit down. As you do, the angelic kingdom will place on your head a crystal that connects you with the Akasha. Feel that. You might feel it on the crown chakra and on the eighth chakra, which is the soul star. Feel it coming in. There is an energy, a vibration, a sense of connection. Now connect down through the third eye, the throat chakra, the heart chakra, the solar plexus, the polarity, the base or root chakra and then down into the Earth.

❧ The energy of the crystal is literally coming through the angelic kingdom all around you. It is surrounding you in the room and within your chakra system. It is stimulating the pineal, the pituitary, the parathyroid and the thyroid, the thymus and the rest of the glands. Feel the physical body, as much as you can, vibrating within this crystal. It is as if you are in a crystal booth that becomes even smaller. You are encased in this beautiful crystal.

❧ It begins to vibrate. You can hear the vibration and the sound. Ask the angelic kingdom to begin to translate the sounds for you. You begin to realize that this sound can be translated into words. First become familiar with the *sound:* Establish a good contact with the crystal and allow it to surround your whole physical body until you can literally hear it. Be patient as you allow that sound to be heard. When you can hear it as loud as something humming, it is the Akasha, the movement, the beat, the literal life force that is stored there. Ask and write down what you are given.

❦ Sense now the crystal room. Let it vibrate, hear it – hear the vibration. Take it into the chakra system – the seventh and the eighth and all the rest of the chakras. Feel and hear it. Spend a moment with it. It becomes a living crystal within which your physical body sits. Hear it.

If you had trouble seeing it, just see that the crystal has different sides. You can start the sound moving so that it will reverberate from one to the other. It is like being in a new environment you haven't been in before. Perhaps you don't notice what is natural to that environment until some of the newness wears off. It might take a little while, so you might want to direct it a little more specifically.

For example, let us say you want to be a little clearer in the area of relationship, whether it is with a physical partner or just understanding the other polarity of yourself – both are important. You might ask for sounding particularly into that area of the mass consciousness that will help you – not necessarily into just your consciousness, but into whatever the mass consciousness really understands about the area you are trying to learn about. Trust the process and turn it over to the process so it can mirror to you what is important. Even if you don't hear anything, it can awaken a sound within your own life that will mirror to you. You might not get it in the crystal room, but when you come back out you might get it. It becomes an event, something coming into your life. If you can hear it now, write down this important information and perhaps it won't need to come into your life.

Once you have set this up and sent it out to the universe, you are going to get something – there is never a void. If it doesn't come in one way, it will come in another. If you have an area you are working on, you might ask for the next step in helping you understand or whatever you wish to gain. You can direct it that way.

I want to emphasize that it doesn't always come in as sound or information. You see, when you hear the sound you are really becoming a part of the universes response to your invocation, or whatever you are asking for. That really sets up a sense of unity. It is like a vibratory "aha" process. You make contact through your conscious desire to understand. You ask the question, the sound comes back in response to the question, and it simply has to be translated into an understanding or into an event in your life which will help your understanding. Even if it doesn't translate into words, it translates into a point of contact that will bring you into a clearer conscious understanding of yourself and the universe, in one way or another. So it works, my friends.

This is a nice way of serving the Earth. How about sending one up to help with peace, integration, clearer communication, heart-centered approach by humanity, or anything else you find important? One thing you could do is shoot the whole capsule you are in, out into space and see where it takes you.

The information we are getting is a key to what you have creatively been looking for, life after life after life. All of you have looked at the stars and said, "I don't know what I am looking for, but I am looking. I am really yearning for something." You were wishing creatively to have an opening. I feel this is the time you have been yearning for. It is this time you have yearned for, this time in which you can fulfill your purpose and be the unlimited being you have been seeking.

It is not so much the doing, for you are active this cosmic day. It is the beingness that we are addressing here, the access to unlimitedness. If you are sitting in your chair and you are not moving, if you are absolutely secure within your divine beingness, movement is so rapid that you would still seem to be sitting in the chair. The movement is flowing beyond your ability to perceive it. A fully developed cocreator does what you don't know how to do yet. A cocreator sets in motion, and the movement continues eternally. This is consciousness moving, but the cocreator has made his effort once, and he doesn't need to keep moving it because the effort is renewed automatically. The cocreator is sitting in the chair and moving, but if you saw him or her or it sitting in the chair, you wouldn't recognize the movement because it would be so integrated. It is like a great musician when he or she plays: It looks very easy. That is because it is so integrated. The process of integration means you have balanced all aspects and they no longer fight with each other. All parts of you need to be balanced. They need to be a part of the team. They need to be a part of the effort to recognize what your goals and purposes are here on Earth.

✧ S I X ✧

Earth's New Structures

WELL, GOOD EVENING, MY FRIENDS, AND WELCOME. ISN'T IT FUN TO BE able to communicate with one another and with us — those of us that have joined you at this interesting period in your Earth's history? Do you find it interesting? I would think so. Have you been watching your news and listening to what is happening on your Earth? Well, were going to get into that a little bit — maybe not into the specifics of it, but into the reasons that lie behind it. To help you understand, let us say where the Earth is going and how you can assist it to go there.

Now, communication is essential on the journey. We could say that your awareness level determines your communication. In other words, if you decide you want to take a train ride and you get on the train, you have the opportunity to communicate with the others who are riding that particular train, and you also have an opportunity to look around at the environment and see what is there, see the changes and see where you're going. What happens if you're very tired during the journey? You may decide to sleep or rest or pull back into your own awareness without doing any communication. Is there anything wrong with that? No, of course not. But if you do that, you miss an opportunity to communicate. It's time, my friends, to look around and see what is going on on your Earth, to communicate with each other about the global events that are occurring and take an interest in them. Many of you have gotten kind of turned off about doing that because perhaps the news always seems to you to be rather negative: "This is going on and this has collapsed and who cares anyway? That's clear across the world from me." But your world is getting smaller and smaller, and your neighbors now are the Chinese and the Russians and the Indians and the South Americans and the South Africans and the Dutch and the South Sea Islanders and the Australians. These are your next-door neighbors.

Last year there was an event called the Harmonic Convergence. We've talked about it so much because it was one of the two or three most important events ever to happen on your Earth. It occurred last summer, and in one sense you all kind of shook your heads and picked yourselves up afterward. You might not even have known that that was what you were doing. You looked around your lives and you said, "Well, I'm not quite sure who I am. I've been told there has been a big change," but some of you didn't see any change. Or more commonly, you said, "Old structures are changing; old structures are falling apart, and I don't know where I'm going, because what I had and the way that I related to it is no longer there." If I had to give you a percentage, I would say that about 80% of humanity experienced that.

Well, when a change this vast takes place — when you literally move into what we could call a new planet — it takes a period of time to get acquainted with it, and it takes a while to see what is there for you. Equate it to moving into a new house and getting acquainted with that house; you look at the storage system that you have and decide how you wish to utilize the space that is there. This past year, then, has been spent in an analysis of the releasing of what has been, in a psychological as well as an emotional sense. And now it is time to see how you would like to live your life.

Now, you might not get up every morning and say, "I wonder how I'll live my life from now on." Probably not. But in one sense your consciousness has been seeking to fit into the Earth's new format that was born a year ago. It's changed; it's different; it is not the same.

At the end of July of this year, 1988, you will begin to see the results of having gone to that new level of understanding called the Harmonic Convergence. And if you have been watching your newspapers, if you have been listening to the radio, watching the TV, you *have* seen the evidence of what I told you. There are peace negotiations going on, there are communications going on between people in a way that has never been present in what you call your modern civilization — not in the last few thousand years, anyway. It has changed. Humanity has matured and has grown.

Now, are all of your problems solved magically? No, probably not. But there has been an opening created to this new level of awareness, my friends, and the key to keeping it working is communication. If you get an opportunity to talk to someone, don't try to convert them — that's not my point — but communicate with them in a meaningful manner. You might talk about the Earth and what's going on in their lives, or share with them something they wish to talk about. But communication *now* is the key to allowing the emergence of what you would like to see on the Earth within the next ten or twelve years.

Sitting right here we have a couple of young men who are in school. Communication is extremely important for both of you at this time, and for all of those who are in some sort of an educational program. In school you need to ask questions. Now, if your teachers could hear me they would probably say, "Oh, good grief! Encourage them to ask more questions? They ask enough already!" What I'm telling you, my friends, is that asking questions *now* will produce answers in a way that it never has before. The answers might not come from the person you ask them of, but when you ask a question you are really opening yourself to the universe, saying, "I am ready to hear the answer in some way or another." So ask questions – you in your formal educational programs in school, and all the rest of you in your Earth school situation. Ask them – it really doesn't matter if you're 2 or 102 years old. Ask questions, because you will then help open the Earth to its new level. It's already open, but it isn't quite sure or confident in how to use this new level of awareness that is now there for all of you to explore.

An example might be the questions that you used to ask when you were a little child. Perhaps no one knew the answers, and your mother might have said, "Don't ask me that now, I'm busy. You always ask too many questions." But why is up *up*; and why is down *down*? Why are there two kinds of human beings, men and women? That would be an interesting one to ask. Well, I'm being a little facetious here, but those questions that you have thought you were "too old" to ask, ask them now. Open up and allow the universe to respond to those questions.

Now, I'm going to get a little bit esoteric by telling you that there has been a corresponding opening on the spiritual levels that has allowed the Earth to enter this more advanced format of living. The Earth's consciousness with its aggregate flow has reached this new level, too, as have each of you, and there is a corresponding cosmic event that occurred (as above, so below). There are levels of cycles, and this is the end of a 2000-year cycle and of a 6000-year cycle. It is the end of a 12,000-year cycle, a 24,000-year cycle and a 36,000-year cycle, and on up until we get to a cycle that is six million years in length. That's the most important and the most profound one, and it has to do with a galactic level of awareness. Some of you have heard me talk about the galactic level and some of you have not, but you know nothing is separate. You're all part of a larger level of consciousness. You're all part of a descending group experience, so for most of you now the *ultimate* group is the galactic level. There are other levels, but this is the one that is beginning to affect you in a way that you and the Earth have never been affected before.

I told you to ask questions, and here is one you've given me: Could the 2000-year cycle be the beginning? Yes, the year 2000 is the beginning. We are already in that beginning, or energizing it. We are close enough that it is the new beginning. Such a cycle has brought to the Earth every 2000 years a very important teacher. The Christ is the one who has been the teacher for the past 2000 years. But what I am saying is that there are other cycles that have various meanings, too, and they are all ending right now – or beginning a new level, whichever way you wish to look at it.

So this six-million-year cycle is a very important one to the galactic level.

It's the one that relates most closely to the galactic level, just as your 2000-year cycle relates the most closely to the Earth. Six million years ago, then, the galactic level reached an important point, just as you reached an important level 2000 years ago. And you might say the creativity level literally became ten times greater. This has now happened to you on the Earth again. With the Harmonic Convergence and this new level, your own creative potential is now ten times greater.

If you were a baseball player and you wanted to hit a home run, you'd now have ten times the chance of hitting a home run. Isn't that exciting? Well, I'm not sure that you all want to be baseball players, but I am sure you want to connect with your creativity potential, which is why I used the example. You now can go full-circle, or send out the message dealing with opening your creativity and have the universe respond. Then the message comes back to you, which is perhaps what a home run is, isn't it? So that has multiplied tenfold. Since the galactic level reached this stage about six million years ago now, you as a reflection are reaching it. The two levels are connected by this ten-times expansion. You could say the galactic ones know the system and they are now helping you on the Earth to respond to it. What I mean by "the system" is the system of expansion, of drawing to a ten times greater level of expansion. That's why it is important to ask questions: In one sense you get ten times more energy working for you when you ask a question, and if you get an answer — no matter what the answer is, whether it satisfies you or it's only a partial answer — then you have ten times more energy coming back to you from which to formulate a clearer understanding. So it almost doesn't matter what the answer is, or how much of an answer you get. It's the coming back that opens you, or completes you, or gives you that "home run" that is important. Can you see that? Remember, it's a completion mechanism that you've now got going for you — not only on the physical level, but on the galactic level.

Now, if we go back to our ball game, let's say you hit your home run and you're really rather surprised: Your batting average is not that high, or hasn't been, but all of a sudden you begin to hit home runs and your coach tells you, "Well, I can see that the ones I've been consulting with have given me enough pointers that I was able to help *you*, and I that's why you're making the home runs." Could you accept that? It probably depends on how much ego you have. If you have a lot of ego, you might want to say, "Oh, I don't think so; I did that all by myself. I made that home run, and no one helped me to do it." If, however, you can get the ego out of the way and take a look at the system, you will see that coming from the galactic level are the structural methods, the means, because the communication is easier. It too has gone to a ten times greater level, remember. So the ways to create and to complete your creation are stronger than they've ever been on the Earth.

I find it very interesting to have every age group represented here. All of you remember times during your life, no matter your age, when you tried to start something and it just fizzled out. Perhaps it was a diet – many of you relate to that – or perhaps it was a relationship or a creative idea of another sort that was never completed. The energy just didn't seem to be there for you, did it? You started out with enthusiasm and with the desire to do this thing. For some of you it may have been in the educational area. The energy for a creative effort just seems to fade out sometimes.

Now, do you understand that the system I'm referring to is the Cosmic Plan? There is a plan behind all of this that isn't something accidental. There is a consciousness behind the divine effort and your lives that has put together a nice plan for all of us. We can rely upon that. Anyway, the system, or the Plan, is now more responsive. Why? Because of the way that you are using the system. It's not that the system has changed, but that you have changed in your relationship to it. It is giving you advice, which means that you are hearing it for the first time – not especially consciously, but perhaps subconsciously, or creatively. I think that is probably the most important thing I've said to you. How many of you have thought that your subconscious was the "bad guy?" Have you ever thought that somehow, when you wanted something, your subconscious didn't allow you to have it? How do you feel, then, about the fact that your subconscious is being educated directly, or having ten times the direct input from this higher level of understanding that we are calling the galactic level? And that is just at the beginning point.

Let us say that you decided to go to a university, and let's say it is Yale or Harvard or Princeton – one of the traditional ones that is quite well established. And you have grown up on a farm, let us say, and you go into one of these large universities. Well, for a while the system can seem a little confusing, can it not? You don't understand it, or how to use it. Perhaps it seems more formal than how you're used to living. Perhaps you don't have as much freedom (or seeming freedom) as you had before. You have to use a different guidance system, and you have to change your understanding about what freedom means. Now, if you are going to this university, you have understood something: that in order to be free creatively, you must have greater understanding and greater knowledge than you had before. Therefore you are willing to give up the freedom you had, living on a farm, and go to a university so that you will have the formal training that you have chosen. Therefore you change in how you use life – you agree to take instructions, to communicate with others. In other words, you've completely changed the way you live your life, haven't you?

But for a while it may seem a little disorienting. In fact, they have a process called orientation, don't they? It helps new students to understand the new system. Such an orientation to the new system is really what you need, but – imagine this – you are going to have to orient yourself. Why don't I come to Earth to help you? Because it is not part of my job to do that. As I just said, doing it yourself is going to teach you something that we feel is important. You know some teachers feel more strongly than others; and there are "plans" and there are others who will be coming and you will meet some of them. Yes, you will meet some of them later in your life, but I have decided not to do that. It's not just an arbitrary choice, it's how best to utilize who and what I am to help the Earth. So it does not fit into the Plan as I see it and view it. That's why not.

Each one of you needs to understand the way to use the system and to access through it what you really want in your life. Now, depending on where you are and who you are, that will vary, but you would not be here at all if you were not somewhat interested. Some of you are very interested in finding out why you are here at all and trying to utilize the purposes of the soul level on the Earth. It's not going to be easy to find out. In fact, for many of you the amount of information you get may be a little overwhelming. Going into it a little more esoterically, as the Earth approaches the fourth dimension it is going to flow rather rapidly, and you're going to be able to get in touch with the means to fulfill the purposes for which the soul came. Opportunities are going to come in, and they will come in rapidly. To avoid overwhelm, then, you must see that you arrant on the planet Earth *as it was*. You don't have to worry about conditions as they were. They are not that way any longer. What you need to do is to understand the new system and how to use it, and be willing to be courageous enough to try it out. As the old saying goes, "Try it — you'll like it." Because it will flow more for you once you get the hang of how to use it.

Let's see if I can give you an example. Let's say you now have an opportunity. Someone says to you, "If you will move to New York City, I will give you a job there which will pay $50,000 a year. You have the qualifications. Not only that, but you can form groups if you want to for that spiritual thing that you do. I want you, and if you want time off I'll be glad for you to have it." So the universe is saying you are valuable, you're an asset, there's a place for you, you are going to have the abundance to which you are entitled, and this is how to do it. Well, you look at that and say, "New York City! I'm not sure I'm ready for New York City; it's such a big city, and all those people on that island. I don't know if I want to live in New York City." If I were you (and this is just my advice, my friends), and I got such an opportunity, no matter what my age was — with the exception of you two young men; I think your parents might have something to say about it — I'd say yes. Why? Because once you get into the stream, into the flow, once you've opened it up, then you can make choices to adjust what you don't want about that life, and it will come very easily. Probably such persons in New York City, after they'd been there a year or two, would have the opportunity to go with the same system, or company, that was paying them, to another physical area that they liked better. Or they might choose to leave that job and go into something else that was perhaps esoteric, and was equally abundant. What I'm telling you is, certainly you should evaluate the opportunities that come to you, but don't say they arrant workable just because they haven't worked in the past. *Now is the most important time to stop evaluating opportunities by what has been true in the past.*

For some of you this would be rather easy. If you have Aries charac-teristics in you, well, you'd probably do it rather easily! If you have mostly Taurus or perhaps Virgo, or perhaps some other zodiacal signs in combination and they say, "But . . . but . . . I don't know," then it might not be as easy. But talk to that part of you, because you all have a part of you that is enough like Aries or is open enough to begin to view life as full of opportunity.

This next year will catch you up, you might say, on all of the opportunities that perhaps you had earned — meaning that you were clear enough in your creativity to have them appear to you, but you weren't able to allow yourself to use them. Note the wording: "to allow yourself to *use* them." Therefore this is catch-up time. It's almost like having a fairy godmother. Don't misunderstand me — I'm not saying that your life is suddenly going to be a utopia. It can be if you believe that is possible, but the point is that the opportunities are going to be there for you when you recognize them and don't use the standards of the past to evaluate them.

You may say to me, "Well, if I don't know the system and I'm not to use the standards of the past, what standards am I going to use?" There is something called an intuition, and there is something called your higher mental body, and there is something called communication between the two of them. In addition, you can assist each other. Let us say you should think over by yourself the pros and cons; write it all down; talk it over with your spouse if one is involved; and then talk it over with some other impartial person whom you trust and ask them to help you evaluate it. But tell them, "I don't want to look at what I've done as a 'block' or a negative response from the past. You can use the strengths that you've gained from the past — all of your abilities, all your understanding; no one can take that away from you — so you have that as part of the system to help you evaluate such responses. The Earth is clearer, but for a while you're going to be trying to get to know the system.

Let's say you decide that you don't want to go to New York. Is that terrible? No, it isn't terrible. Just wait for the universe to send you another opportunity, but don't shut down. Keep communicating. Waiting, in this sense, is not inactive; on the contrary, it is a very active occupation. It is the looking at opportunities and recognizing them and knowing that you're not here inactively. Spiritual teachers tell you that all you have to do is *be*, and that's true. In the beingness that's all you have to do. But you signed a contract with God — the Source, the Creator — that said, "I'm going to be active this cosmic day. I'm going to express actively the divine part that I have been given."

It's time to be active. Even if you are currently retired, as some of you are, that doesn't mean there isn't activity — conscious activity — in the sense that I'm talking about it. The opportunities probably won't be in the business world; they may come to you from other realms, such as from the galactic headquarters, who in your meditation might say, "How about doing this for the Earth, and how about doing that for the Earth? And are you going on that trip? Well, when you go on that trip that you're calling a vacation, how about doing this for us?" So this is still a very active state.

This year if it works out financially — it will if you're not too blocked — and you get to go on a trip, ask, "What can I do on this trip to assist the Earth?" Some of you might go to a crystal store and buy some very small crystals and bury them in the Earth sometime when you're traveling. You could put a tiny crystal in someone's yard — they won't mind, will they? You don't have to tell them. Or put it in a flower — the flower will love it — in the country, yes, or the seashore, and later if it washes into the sea there's nothing wrong with that. Or throw it into the ocean or put it into a lake, or leave it in someone's apartment. Say, "I want to give you this little crystal."

Crystals are a focus of this new structural change that has occurred on your Earth. The structure of your Earth has changed, and crystals are a part of that new structure. You're going to help move it around a little, and that's what your Earth needs now: the movement around all of you and all the rest of its parts through communication so that it can understand all of them.

Perhaps if you're traveling, take some flower seeds from your area to the new area. Ask, "If these flowers will grow in your area, will you plant them?" Try to mix up your Earth a little communicatively. It's kind of fun. The crystals are very small and the flower seeds are not very large either. In this way, as you walk on the Earth you are literally leaving an essence or a trail of who you are. So if you go to an area, it's important to walk. Walk in the neighborhood. Say, "Do you mind if I go for a walk? Why don't you come with me?" And even if that person doesn't walk much, it will be kind of fun to walk and talk to them at the same time. But communication in as many forms as you can think of is important in this new Earth. The sooner that is done — the more you begin to blend it and mix the consciousness from other points of view — the better.

Now we are going to talk about the kingdoms of your Earth and how they are responding to this new level of awareness. The plant kingdom really does need your help. I've said to "hug trees." You know that's not hard to do. Share your life with trees — the big, mature trees. In one sense this is more difficult for them than for any other part of your Earth. We could say it is because of their longevity — they've been around here a long time, and remember, they have their *roots* in the old way of doing things, although the trees and all the plant kingdom are the most advanced kingdom on the Earth. (You thought you were, didn't you?) Think about the trees; many of them have taken quite a scarring in the pollution, quite a bit of flack in regard to your Earth and the conditions on it, so please be supportive of these trees — particularly the mature ones, although there's nothing wrong with hugging a young tree either — and really be supportive of the forests and the changes that are coming in. The mature forests on your planet are dying, as you may have heard. Now, that's not absolutely terrible; it simply indicates a comprehensive change — those forests are graduating into something else. Their consciousness is going to appear on your Earth in a different form.

The trees need your support. As they change, as they transmute, you might set up programs to help people be aware of what can be done to help them. Hospice helps humans who have terminal ailments, so how about the trees? Some of them are not going to recover from their ailment, if you will, on the physical level. They are transmuting their consciousness to something greater, just like a human being who is leaving the physical plane, but they need and can use some support. You can access that through the angelic kingdom, so those of you who are meditating every day, get in touch with the angelic kingdom and offer to be helpful in supporting the transition of the trees. That's going to be important, for in the next few years, and if they get a lot of support, some of them may decide not to leave the physical plane after all — and that's kind of nice.

If you go to the redwood forests, spend some time with your redwoods. They are rather like dinosaurs walking around on the Earth; they are that old and that much a part of your past. The fact that they are here at all is really rather miraculous. But on the other hand they are also part of your future, perhaps a bridge to it. They are in a unique category among the trees on your Earth. It's rather like having someone like Abraham Lincoln still walking on your Earth and knowing that the strengths he represents are as much a part of your future as they were of your past. Abraham Lincoln indeed reminds me of a redwood tree, and vice versa.

You will begin to note new species of plants, grass, and various types of foliage coming in. I would say it is probably a little soon, but in a year or two the scientists will begin to see that here are some species they've never recognized before, and this is going to be rather fun. (You can tell them I told you so — I knew about it before they did.) And what also occurred at the Harmonic Convergence — some of you have heard me say this — is that there will be new elements becoming a part of physical existence. There are now more elements than there have ever been on the Earth.

You could say that some of the elements are combining to create new elements, but some are simply new elements that have never been a part of physical existence. The Earth has in one sense risen to a new level, so part of existence that was "doing its own thing" and had nothing to do with the Earth finds itself associated with the Earth. Thus you are going to see responses from this new level, particularly in the mineral and plant kingdoms. Certainly you will see them in yourselves also — your physical structure will take in these elements that you've never had before. It's going to reframe the metabolic system. The glandular system is going to need your support for a while. Some of you have recognized that perhaps the thyroid, the pituitary, the thymus in association with the heart gland, the adrenal gland, and any of the other glands within the system will need this support. You might be aware of them if you've never been aware of them before, because they are becoming something different – they're growing, they're adapting to new physical conditions on the Earth.

The changing conditions on the Earth and the way physical existence is becoming enlarged as far as the basic elements are concerned are part of what seems to be an out-of-balance state. There are going to be other illnesses discovered. In my opinion, there will soon be another one becoming seemingly rampant on the Earth. Now, this is *not* a negative thing; I think you will all find solutions to it. It is simply a new level of awareness on the Earth and learning to deal with it, learning to function communicatively in a clearer manner within the conditions you've created on the Earth. We could say AIDS certainly has to do with communication.

The drought conditions are not due to a natural disaster but to a change that has come about through the Harmonic Convergence. The Earth's energies have gone to a new level . In one sense you're close to what we might call "fire," or the spiritual part of the electrical-magnetic scale that is heating up your planet. But the heating-up isn't complete either, because there are parts of the planet that are cold also. So what all these changes are really doing is rearranging your weather patterns.

As your Earth approaches the fourth dimension, it has used certain energy formations that come forth as weather patterns in a certain way. Those old energy formations don't work anymore because the structure is gone; it has disappeared. You are now building a new weather system from the beginning, and certain areas on your planet that have been hot and dry are going to become cold and damp. There are going to be profound changes. Vancouver is very close to the ocean, and in my opinion it is becoming a desert – it's becoming much warmer. In many, many areas you can see that your country is primarily becoming warmer. In the winter there are going to be pockets of quite severe storms and cold, but I feel that the conditions will be so unsettled for only a few years, and then the changes will sort of settle in, as far as your weather is concerned, and you will be able to rely on certain conditions again. They are not ever going to be what they were, because that old format is gone, it's not there – whether we talk about weather patterns or opportunities or anything else. It's just not there, and that's what your weather people are beginning to realize in their scientific discoveries. It's very difficult to predict the weather now, and it's confusing to be a weather person.

It is not uncommon to have unusual body changes and ailments, such as a fluctuating thyroid condition. The changes here on the Earth are not the only cause – a person has his own personal input to that – but let us say that the changes here on the Earth and the input of these elements is compounding all problems of that sort. They just make it worse; but when you get the problem solved it will be that much clearer. So we can look at it both ways.

What is predicted for Phoenix? Unfortunately, I think it is going to be somewhat hotter – a few degrees. I don't know that your weather is going to see as drastic a change, but it will be hotter. You've seen the trend, and I think for a while, as long as the greenhouse effect is still there, it will continue.

There is some dimensional switching going on – it's rather like the dimensional trains are switching around on the track. What I think will happen is, that will stabilize, but I don't see it going back to being any cooler, especially in a large area like this. I think your weather will simply be warmer, maybe even drier (if that's possible). I am not predicting that California will fall off, you know, so the old prediction that Phoenix will eventually be a seacoast is not my view.

Sedona will partake of this also – not quite as much, because it is at a higher elevation, but I would say the change to warmer applies pretty much for most of Arizona. I see it becoming cooler in parts of Colorado, Utah, into New Mexico, and certainly into parts of California – at least the eastern part but not so much on the coast, which I think is becoming drier. I think about a 70-mile-wide strip of the West Coast, from the tropical zone up north into Canada, is becoming much drier, and as it becomes drier it will also become warmer, which will change the Gulf Stream and so on. It won't attract the Gulf Stream, which is a part of the moisture content of the air in the way it has before, so if you have the drier conditions, then it changes the currents of air around your planet, and that is occurring.

Generally you won't have as much snow. In South America and other parts of your Southern Hemisphere, you are going to have some of the moisture that you may perhaps need. But some of your forests are not going to be there very long. You are cutting them down just as fast as you can, and that will create some loss of moisture. Perhaps you are going to have to replant some of the forests, and this is why your association with the trees and being supportive of them is so important. I would like to see that, because this universe is going to respond rapidly when certain groups begin to work with trees. I like to call these groups "green people." They will begin to open up to the new level of awareness among the trees.

There's no question that you're losing some of the bird species. One interesting one that's trying to be born now is a large, very aware bird, almost the size of a hawk. It hasn't quite come forth yet, but it grows well in some other galaxies and were trying to seed it into the Earth right now. I think you will hear about it within the next five years. It would be fun to have some new birds, and I think they will really be coming.

Now are you ready for this? The snake population is going to increase.

Think about how many of them like dry conditions. They are your friends, arrant they? I think you will see that if they increase, certain small animals will also increase, so there's going to be a changing relationship with the kingdoms, and they need your support.

Certain areas of the world have assumed certain roles on the Earth. Germany has agreed to be a reflector and a receptor from the Galactic Center in a way that no other country has. You in the United States have an important role also. It isn't quite as glamorous, maybe – it doesn't sound as important – but it is; it is perhaps even more important. It is an integration of what is really starting, and if you can, see that you in the esoteric community have been at it for a while, and some of you have matured in your understanding of conditions that are beyond the physical. What we are asking each of you to do, then, is some *integration of what the various races represent and what the various kingdoms represent* so that the peaceful Earth that you are seeking can come forth.

Now, did you ever want to be a virtuoso of some kind, maybe play the violin or be an opera star? Perhaps when you were a child you wanted to do something very, very well. Someone who concentrates that much on a particular activity usually gets a little bit out of balance. They put so much energy into one activity that they neglect some other aspects. Now, I'm generalizing – you can probably point out to me someone who isn't this way – but many times they are a little bit out of balance. I notice that and I wonder why those of you who know that change can be made through creative effort don't get together and become a counterpoint for these points of genius who really give your planet so much. I suggest that those of you who think a lot say to yourself and to the mass consciousness of your planet, "I have this strength: I can think." Because some of you say, "I think too much," and you use it in such a way that perhaps you're trying to think less. Well, say to yourself, "I'm going to use that strength now to help another who is perhaps so involved in a creative effort that he's turned that off a little. I'm going to be like a teeter-totter – he/she is on one end doing such beautiful things for the Earth, so I will be on the other end to help balance that." It really would do a lot of good.

Even if we look beyond sequential time and see that this was much truer in the past, if you agree spiritually to be such a counterpoint, you can help change the past! The past is not fixed – you can help change it now. Do you admire an old musician who you know had a difficult life? Then say to him in the eternal now, "I am going to help balance you out, I'm going to be there for you; I will help balance you spiritually and mentally – those are two of my strengths," and see yourself doing it. It might be one of the great painters, some of whom had psychological difficulties. You can partake of their endeavor, and if you are willing to do this, you are again going to open the door to your own creativity. Imagine that: you're going to get a benefit yourself! Because if you have balanced others, then they are going to help balance you, and the strengths they have can be used by you. You might suddenly find yourself playing the violin, suddenly drawing and painting, or suddenly, perhaps, a ballerina going up on your toes.

The way to obtain what you want out of life is by supporting others in a point-and-counterpoint relationship, and it doesn't have to be a person who is here in physical existence right now. You can do it from what you understand about your history on the planet. You have had very powerful lives in Egypt. All of you have been priests and priestesses in Egypt. And if you will learn to access those strengths that you had as a divine power within the temple in Egypt, you will be able to bring that power into your life now. It is extremely important.

Let's say you had a life in Egypt where about ten thousand people came through and you helped them. You died right after that and didn't really get time to receive any benefit. Sure, you benefited from their coming, and you learned. But in one sense you gave a lot more than you got, and you haven't collected on that one yet. It's not that you're going to get anything physical, although it could be if you wanted it. But creatively, all of you have opened and helped others to such an extent that you have not yet collected on those old debts karmically. You talk about karma as a negative thing, but it's simply a balancing, and the scale can move both ways. You need to accept creatively what you have opened to, and this is the year that the universe is going to bring that to you — *if* you allow it, my friends. You are ready, my friends: humanity is ready now to respond to the call. What is the call? The call of a more creative, cooperative, peaceful, integrated, flowing, fun, joyous, loving Earth!

Questions and Answers

Are the crystals already flowing fourth-dimensionally?

They are approaching the fourth dimension. You could say that the Earth is standing in the doorway of the fourth dimension. I'd like to give it a little push, and that's why I suggested that you move things around on the planet. You can't hold on to a rigid pattern if you keep moving it, can you? That's what I'd like to see.

What does the Hierarchy think about the necessity of voting? Suppose you really don't feel pleased about any of the candidates. Is it wrong to say "Well, I just don't want to do it anymore because it's not the way it should be going?"

Well, you live within the system, and in my opinion you owe it to yourself to find out about your candidates to the point of making a decision about which ones you wish to support. That's my advice. You live in the system; I think you should partake of it.

Vywamus, I'm probably the only one who doesn't understand the Harmonic Convergence. You mentioned a "lifting up." Do you mean the Earth literally rose physically?

Well, in one sense I do, because it's entering a different dimensional structure. But it's a redefinition energywise of what the Earth is. It's different enough that it's as if you move to another planet. It's like moving to another place to live when you graduate from school. The Earth completed learning in a certain way, graduated from that experience, and now has gone to a new space in consciousness to live — yes, physically. I am currently in the process of writing about dimensions because I think they are such an important thing for you all to understand. A dimension is a structure, an energy structure, and your Earth is learning to focus multidimensionally. But to simplify it we have said it is moving from the third to the fourth dimension. The fourth dimension is a more flowing way of living. That's its keyword: *flow*. The keyword for the third dimension is *magnification*. It magnifies the creative process so that you can look at it and learn from it, but as you learn from it, then it's time to flow it, to allow yourself to live at that clearer level.

When will we be in the fourth dimension?

Whenever you take that step through the doorway. In one sense you are already exploring it, because the fourth dimension is simply a part of several dimensions that you use all the time. But what I'm talking about is the *awareness* of how to use that particular energy format in a way that the majority of human beings will use it.

So it depends on when everyone gets to that point?

Soon! That's the year 2000. I would say much sooner than that.

Was the 2000-year cycle the love aspect, or courage?

Love is the quality that was anchored on the Earth through the Christ energy, yes.

Since this is the end of a 2000-year cycle, will we have another avatar?

Yes, the lord Kuthumi is already in training for that. You have an avatar every two thousand years.

Will he be accepted this time?

Not entirely. He doesn't expect to be. It will depend upon how ready you are to be peaceful, let us say.

I've been expecting people to be different, nicer, because of all the changes, and it sort of shocks me when I meet someone who is cold and nasty.

All right. There's definitely a polarity pull here. Everyone is being affected by the breaking down of old structures. For those who don't understand it, it is very threatening, and the emotional responses are due to a lack of understanding of what is occurring in ones life. There definitely is a polarity split. If you don't see beyond the immediate circumstances in your lives to the larger picture, then it can seem threatening to you emotionally. If you can see that all this is just the old breaking down, and that change is what is occurring, then it can help you be more balanced in your life.

Will these new conditions enable beings lower on the astral to communicate with the human race as well as the Hierarchy?

Well, what it is doing is raising their vibrations. At the time of the Harmonic Convergence, the negative being that was really the main focus on your planet lost a lot of his territory, you could say. And there really is a point of consciousness, you know, that responds everywhere, so there was such a being – there still is. But the communication was going on anyway. It has now changed, though, because it is lighter – there is not as much energy in it as before. The planets energy has gone up, and everything that resided on this planet has become lighter. Do you see that? So it's knowing. Some people have made a choice.

I've said this over and over and I'll say it again: In order to be negative you have to keep choosing *not* to associate with the positive; and you have to keep choosing it over and over and over and over and over again. You see? It's not just from one misunderstood choice, or one choice at all; you have to keep choosing it over and over and over. And you can begin to reverse the process at any time. That's the way the system goes. So, in my opinion, this being that had chosen and chosen and chosen to be separate is now choosing not to be. It is becoming lighter, and that seems important.

Will those doing healing treatments of any natural kind be hampered and not allowed to do them?

In certain areas of the world, perhaps. I think the heaviest part of that was over, though, with the Harmonic Convergence. Now, there may still be times when that is true in certain areas. I really think that some of that is on the way out. The clearer you are in your consciousness with "those in charge," the clearer you understand your relationship with humanity, because many of you have beliefs in there that say, "Humanity doesn't let me do my thing without trying to control me." The sooner you can change those beliefs, the sooner your Earth will be as you want it to be. You can tell if you're clear in the area by seeing how clear your emotional body is. If something makes you angry, if you get involved in it personally, then you have something stored in the subconscious mind that you need to clear out.

A Place of Peace

❦ *I ask you now to close your eyes. Tonight let's visualize going into a New Age temple. This is a beautiful, peaceful place. In my opinion, many of them will be gold. Let us go up the steps now; they are white marble. We enter a very peaceful place – we go into a place rather like a vestibule and we hear soft music playing. We continue to walk within the temple. There are beautiful stained-glass widows, the marble is cool under your feet, and it feels very peaceful. In fact, peace is what you recognize. Peace. Spiritual peace. You feel comfortable; you feel so good; you feel loving, you feel trusting. And within the temple you will find your own place where you wish to be. Go there now. Sit there and allow the peace of this wonderful space to fill you. Literally you know that this peace is here on the Earth and you are partaking of it. You feel the divine power from this peace. You allow it to come into you now. You feel the peace. It fills you, sustaining you, and as you have a need, you know that this is what is being filled now on the Earth: a peaceful place where you may experience serenity, joy, and as you look around, the coming together of those who truly believe in peace. Thank you, my friends.*

❖ S E V E N ❖

The Plan for the Earth

I LIKE TO THINK OF THE EARTH AS A TWINKLE IN THE CREATOR'S EYE. AND IT seems to me that as this Earth was conceived, it was conceived very lightly, with great joy, with great appreciation. That sense of lightness hasn't always been seen on the Earth. But the plan is certainly one of light, one of understanding, one of a complete, integrative sense of humor. Perhaps you can see that sometimes. Once in a while, if you get to a point where everything seems kind of stuck and you begin to laugh, then things become not so stuck and things become not so serious. I think what happens is, you really hook into that plan, the plan for the Earth. Thus, laughter has been a great remedy here.

It seems to me that this rather small planet is more directly connected with laughter and a sense of humor than any other planet in this galaxy. I think that is important for you to know.

Now, as you meet some of what you call your extraterrestrial friends, you will find that some of them don't have the same sense of humor that some of you have had. You directly access that sense of humor more than most. It's not that they don't "get it;" it's that they respond differently to getting it. Perhaps it is important to recognize that; it can be very helpful when you finally allow yourself to have all of these visitors and to recognize them.

So that is the beginning – a twinkle in the Creators eye that became your planet. Now, whenever a planet is born, it has a group that says, "All right now, the Creator has conceived this. It's our role to find what to do with it." If you can understand that there is a Cocreator Council that has divided up responsibilities on what to do with it (eleven different ways plus you), then you begin to glimpse that there is a process that takes over and begins to develop the ideas the chairman of the board or the overall point of view has given birth to.

Certainly, your Earth was not the only planet that was born. There was a whole physical birth that took place at the beginning of this cosmic day. Your Earth was a part of that overall plan.

But let us say that you are putting forth a marketing idea (which in a sense is what a cosmic day is, my friends). You must develop it. You must decide how each market area fits into the overall scheme of things, the overall plan, and you must see the strengths that are in that area.

Now, you might ask, how could everyone see the strengths when it had not started yet? Well, those who guide such new beginnings are not in sequential time, and they can sense the overall development already. Perhaps they don't have the specifics of how it will develop. It's rather like being able to attune to a city such as Phoenix: you can see the city, but around it there are pathways that come into the city that are eternally being constructed. You are not sure which will become six-lane highways and which will remain rather narrow roads. Those are the choices that the people who develop the city will make while they live here.

So the ones who set up the plan for the Earth could see the ultimate, overall development. They could see certain phases and certain high points, but they could also see many, many choices leading to the various points of development on the planet.

That might help answer your question, "How can you tell us that in the eternal now you can see the outcome, but you can't tell what our choices will be?" You see, choices are how you get to what we can already see, and thus what will be there. You choose *how* to. You've already chosen to be a part of the plan. That plan is structurally designed and set up.

Your choices lie in how you approach it and how you use your creativity within it. That's rather important because changes affect your choices rather rapidly. For example, suppose we see, coming into Sun City, a tiny little road and only a small amount of people and not much activity there. Then suddenly there are 10,000 people focusing into that area. The road has to be widened and the cars and trucks come. Then those 10,000 bring another 70,000, and they attract 10,000 more. What has happened is that one little potential has expanded beyond what, in the overall scheme of things, we could recognize.

Now, that is not bad: that is the plan. The plan is flexible enough to take all of the alternatives and present them as a concept. Then you and your creativity get to use that in any way you choose, both individually and within groups. The groups then learn to communicate enough to invoke the part of the plan's development that you choose to develop. This happens not only consciously; a lot of it is on the subconscious or the creative basis.

So the plan is moving, is evolving along with your choices here on the Earth. And some of those choices have surprised us, there is no question about that. You could say that of the overall probabilities for the Earth, you would not be where you are at all if we had guessed a little better ("guessed" is a very good word). If we had been able to connect a little better with the Hierarchy, I think your development would have been a little different. So we don't always guide you as well as we would have liked to, based on seeing what occurs. We have our moments of saying, "Oh my goodness. Did we do our job very well?" It's like everything else on every level: We are not infallible; we are learning, truly, in our own right.

I have mentioned several times that in about the year 1900 a tremendous choice was made, and you have seen what followed from that. This climaxed in about the year 1943, with the Second World War, the advent of Hitler, and many other things. Certainly, the First World War was a part of it. It almost took you into a storage area (you can't really go outside the Divine plan) that really would not have served you very well.

We watched that with great interest, but also with great concern. Our resources were strained to the utmost. You might not think that spiritual resources can be strained. I don't mean that it was so difficult that we couldn't handle it. I don't mean we reacted emotionally; it is not an emotional strain. But think about this (it is quite important): We were using what had been set up to guide you (our full resources) and then tapping into all of those other levels with as much of our own creativity as we could. And it *still* didn't seem to be enough.

We didn't know what would occur. We had released the planet to its own choices, but within those choices we were allowed to be as supportive as humanity would allow. So we began to call on a great being. And this being was Adonis.

We began to call upon him and he made a tremendous difference because his main feature, or his central theme, is the heart. As far as I am concerned, he is the *heart center of your universe.* Your Earth would have been entirely different if your Second World War had ended differently and you had allowed more of certain restrictions and limitations than you already did. You had already seen some of those restrictions and limitations manifest on your Earth. Those are now releasing. It has taken this long to release those that were set up — particularly in the European area, although there are many in this country also that must be lifted. It will be your turn to lift them now, and this is probably the timing for it.

The point is, with Adonis help, these restrictions and limitations can now be released. This is what we call a spiritual war. It is not necessarily a physical war, although a part of it manifested on the physical level. It is the allowingness (this is an interesting term to use in connection with war) of the heart which simply overlights those who have chosen not to be a part of the plan in a way that dissolves some of what they would like to do and some of the power they would like to incorporate within their being.

It takes a great deal of light to do that, a great deal of awareness. Let us say that you were one of those beings who got caught up in a power play and you were getting more and more into having your own power. You didn't care who you hurt. You just didn't care.

Certainly you can recognize examples of this in the Second World War. All sides had some of this. There were certain people who got caught up in that, no matter where we look. But you were still kind of borderline: you were open to being brought back into a more heart-centered focus. At that time, what we had to do was convince such beings to come back, in order to keep your plan on schedule, to keep you from going into what I've called the storage room.

How could we do that? There had to be a flooding of love onto your planet. Certainly you might ask, couldn't the Christ do that? He *was* doing that. We were doing that — I was called upon from where I was. We were all doing that. All of us who would ultimately be involved with your planet — all of us — were flooding your planet with love. But it didn't seem to be enough. The necessary response was not there.

There had to be a kind of lifting of your planet, before it was ready, in order for it to accept that love. This was done. Then, probably the hardest part for all of us was to let go of that. After we had in a sense forced that love on the planet, we had to release it.

It was like having a child who has hurt himself, and has done it over and over again. You know that the child doesn't need to hurt himself, but you also know you've said that over and over again. You gather the child into your arms and you heal him. Then you know you must release the child to hurt himself again, if he chooses to. You've given him all of the love that he can accept, all that his environment can accept, because that is all he is currently open to. Then you must let go.

Let me tell you this: The plan is very interesting. It teaches those of us who guide a particular planet a great deal. It teaches us, on a cosmic level, to let go. It teaches us that there is a guideline.

It's rather like this: There is a library. We would call that library all of the potentials that the plan opens for you on the Earth. Humanity has ten or twelve volumes open. We, in an energy sense, have to read those volumes and say, "All right, they're invoking this, they're invoking this, and this." Now we must follow that direction. We are not free to do what we think would be helpful or go outside the plan. Why? Well, overall, the plan knows a lot more than we do. So even if we can't see it, we must follow the guidelines that are in the book. We've got to go by the book.

This is very difficult sometimes, such as when we feel that what you've done is take twelve volumes and combine them rather indiscriminately. It's like, why would you put celery in a cake? Or whipped cream on spinach? The point is, sometimes the combination of choices is kind of far-out. That far-out connotation stretches all of us.

The good news is, the plan does know better than we do. When you put them together in an interesting combination, were ultimately going to get something very good. It's just that every one of us has to keep energizing what you've chosen and keep integrating those choices. That is what the plan is, also. We, your spiritual friends, are the ones who help build the connections between those twelve volumes in my example. Then you can come into them in a way that will be more helpful.

In other words, in 1943, because of the choices that you had made, we built a bridge to the Harmonic Convergence. It was set up, and all you had to do then was keep moving along that spiritual bridge. Certainly there were choices that you all made at that time. We could, because it was close enough, see where it was leading. We could tell at that time when your Harmonic Convergence would occur. Until then, we hadn't locked it into any particular time frame.

So timing is interesting. There are so many choices. It's similar to your economic situation now: the timing is the most difficult thing for all of us to tell. It has so many options in it. It's easier for me, Vywamus, to see the inner choice that will work out than to see the outer event and how it will affect the inner. Of course, I do look at it and I do integrate it and come up with my guesstimates about your economic situation.

Of course, the economy of one particular nation will be affected by the economies of every other nation. It will also be affected by the approach of the specific teachers that we are talking about.

Understand that the plan is administered on the local level, but it is also administered on the solar level (which we haven't talked about very much lately) and also on the galactic level, and the universal level. There are also several levels within each of these levels. Then, within the full Cocreator Council there are several levels.

You might find that sometimes an Earth is going along quite well, and then the chairman of the board sends down a message. Now, the chairman of the board feels that a change needs to be made, because from his elevated or more conscious perspective he has seen a possibility that really has been invoked, though it isn't seen on the local level. It isn't yet grasped. This sends us scrambling sometimes, I can tell you that. The chairman says, "We must do this . . . ." "We must do *what*? Are you kidding! What does he mean by that?"

We have many conferences over this, my friends — conferences on what is to be done now in regard to your planet. So we are following direction, spiritually. I'm not saying that this isn't a spiritual direction. We enjoy it. We love it. We don't fight it. But conceptually, it stretches us. That's good — that's part of what the plan is. It is a conceptual stretch for *everyone who exists in it*. Not only a conceptual stretch, but an emotional stretch, a physical stretch, a mental (logical) stretch. Certainly a logical stretch — some of this doesn't seem a bit logical, but somehow it fits together. We think, Well we had to look at logic from another level, and it *does* fit together. Imagine that.

So the plan is miniaturized, of course, and each one of you receives your own part in it. That complete miniaturization of the plan affects you in many ways. It gives you your own option of directly using the clearest level you can reach. If you have the ability to reach the Cocreator Council (not many of us do yet) and you can reach it very clearly, your potentials within the plan are absolutely unlimited. The plan will absolutely direct you in the easiest and clearest and best way to do it.

If you have a few hang-ups that get in the way of making that clearest connection, then you rely on another level, the highest level you can, to connect you. Whether or not you consciously recognize that level does not even matter really, at this point. What we do on the local level is to recognize it and take direction from that higher part of you, the soul, the monadic level, from the choices you have made.

In other words, we of the hierarchic level are the ones who can see the connections that everyone has made and how clear you are in them, and we are guided by that. We don't arbitrarily choose for you; we see what you have chosen for yourselves, then we help you to evolve through those choices.

Let me explain something to you. You will find that I, Vywamus, can be rather stern, perhaps, and rather direct. I may go into the core and hold someone there in spite of their emotional squirming. Why am I doing that? Because they have asked me to do that, on another level. I am not doing it from my own choice. In regard to you, I don't do that.

I am directed by the plan and your connection into the plan, what you in your miniaturization have chosen for yourself within the plan. Then someone else might come to me, and we might not go very deeply into their material. You probably have seen that also. That too is not only because of their fears or their emotions, but it may be that they are being prepared in a whole different way.

And although perhaps they seek to connect with me to do what the Foundation is doing, that might not be the deepest way they are ultimately going to learn. In point of fact, they may be connecting into a tremendously deep program on the galactic level, and if they were to get deeply caught up in the Earth transformational process, it would interfere.

So they might be left with some of their material, over a period of these lives, and you won't see that they are making a lot of progress. That's why I tell you that you can't really tell where someone is in consciousness. In order to do that, you'd have to see the whole plan and what they've chosen within the plan and how that fits together.

We will be talking more about that at a later time. We'll talk about job opportunities within the plan — what it is that you've *chosen*. Now, some of you are thinking about two or three choices, going back and forth on it. You might decide that this would be a good time to go into those choices that have been made previously and look at them so you can see that you are really ready to make the next choice. This will also help you to make that next choice by opening you to the career possibilities that are there for you.

Now, if you work for a large corporation (and we do, my friends) the chairman of that corporation looks at the resources and says, "This one would work well here. This one should perhaps go into this career." That is a focus that spreads out, and there are many, many possibilities within that main focus. That is important to recognize. But we cannot escape, and we need not try to escape, the categorization given to us by the Source. This is the ultimate stretching of the resources that all of you have.

The way you will become unlimited is by going into, rather than resisting, that career choice that is waiting for you. An example would be healing. What does healing mean? It means so many things, doesn't it? You see the infinite choices that are there within the overall goal of "healer."

It might mean healing a planet. It might mean healing a solar system. It might mean being there with your light energy that radiates to points of resistance and releases them. It might be hands-on healing, working specifically to integrate the various cells of a physical body into a clearer alignment within the plan.

There are those of you who specialize in healing who go to a point of irritation on this planet and heal it. When the plan is going to a new level on the Earth, they are in there lifting it. There are times when you feel very tired because you've lifted a whole planet. You are the ones who help lock in that new level. Certainly, it doesn't have to be a burden. In the physical level it can seem to be a burden, until you finally get it.

There are those of you who work individually — that is, with individuals — and help heal them emotionally. There are those of you who are conceptual enough to help people integrate their whole four-body system.

There are those of you who help others link with the soul, and that is your specialty. You help others connect with that soul level, and thus the monadic level, the spiritual link, the spiritual connection.

There are those of you who help open up the potentials of others, by saying, "Yes, you can take that new step, that next step. Look at that — see what you have done?" There are those of you who mirror other peoples potentials to them.

There are those of you who are going into the planetary logos field — you have been chosen for that position. That is an overall guidance for a planet. When you read the Sanat Kumara book you will understand what that means.

There are those of you who will do what the Christ did for a planet: go in and anchor a particular heart quality, and not in a sacrificial manner, but in a manner of service. "This is my job, this what I do to help the plan."

There are those of you who are supportive of the angelic kingdom. Thus, you may be going on to a higher educational opportunity. This has been called the path to Sirius; many of you have heard of that. It means several things. It means going on to a more cosmic university to be trained to assist the angelic kingdom. Some of you may be going to teach there.

There are those of you who will ultimately no longer be here on the physical level. You will be here on the inner level supporting those who are here physically. There are those of you who are "exiters," who help others exit and enter various levels of consciousness, some of which you call death, but I don't exactly mean that, either.

There are those who facilitate the walk-in state. There are those who facilitate the dimensional switches that people go through. There are those of you who are planning to be at the cocreator level of responsibility – many of you are, and eventually all of you will do it. Perhaps some of you will use it as a career opportunity that you will do over and over and over and over again.

That's that full Cocreator Council responsibility – being one of eleven streams of beingness at a very, very cosmic level that guides a whole cosmic day. They might call upon you and say, "Well, are you going to do it today?" And you will have done it almost every day, and you will say "Of course," because that is your career opportunity. That's the one the Source Itself has chosen for you.

There are those of you who set up, with the angelic kingdom, prototypes for cosmic days. All of you have done that. We call them the scientists of existence – those miniaturizations of cosmic days that lead to a cosmic day. When an idea is conceived by the Creator, it is then prototyped to see how it will work – not that it wouldn't work; we know the Creators ideas will work. It's just a question of whether we can interpret it clearly enough so that it will work – "we" being those parts of Creator that are actively engaged in using our abilities to allow it to work. It will work, one way or another. We just have to decide on the best way to work.

So when an idea is conceived, there may be anywhere from twelve to one hundred different prototypes set up, and some of you as scientists will be guiding those prototypes to see the outcome. This is not done individually; it's done within a group focus. But some of you will be guiding those prototypes to see which will be used. Even after a cosmic day is fully automated (fully set in motion, in the fullest sense), if it is pulled back, it isn't simply thrown away. These prototypes are again miniaturized and allowed to finish.

So, as you can see, there is a process here: the miniaturization and then the full use of the cosmic day. Some of you are engaged in the important activity of allowing the system to fit into whatever choices have been made by the overall guiding council; this is your ultimate goal. It can be likened to a computer expert, a systems analyst, allowing the systems to interrelate with each other in a way that has been chosen. I think it's important to recognize how much choices affect all of these systems.

For example, you were all part of a cosmic day that was one of my favorites – I simply loved it. But it only lasted about the equivalent of ten minutes and then was pulled back. I often attune to that. It really is distracting for some of us when something we really enjoy is not utilized by the group. I think you can all recognize that.

This is one of my favorite subjects and I really enjoy it. The prognosis for your planet and its unfoldment along the lines that we see is very good. There is less and less energy (and this is very new) going to a complete, destructive economic collapse. It seems to me that just in the past two weeks or even more, the chance of a complete collapse has reduced to about a 60% chance. And it is dropping all of the time.

I think one thing we have to recognize is the effect that these cosmic beings are having. In my opinion, humanity is accepting them more easily and learning from them much more quickly than I, certainly, could have predicted. I think it is wonderful that there is so much more acceptance of them.

All this doesn't mean that you arrant going to have to change your economic system; certainly that is necessary. But it seems to me that it may be easier than previously expected. You might say to me someday, "This is terrible. How could you say it was easy?" Well, I'm telling you that it could be easier than I thought it might be — it *could* be.

These things are sticky. I would be the first one to admit that I can't always tell. If you see all of the predictions that are made all over the world by many, many beings, you will see how often it is not *exactly* the way they perceive it. But if you look at it logically — which I like to do — the fact is, your system must be released, must be let go in order to bring in the alternative systems that are clearer and freer.

❖ E I G H T ❖

The Group Service Vehicle

How can we stabilize the group effort?

SOME OF YOU WHO ARE WITHIN A GROUP KNOW THAT THIS CAN BE A constant effort. To definite what being stable means, we could perhaps say, "having a constant and invariable focus of the purpose of the vehicle." Thus a stable group effort would include the ability to maintain a focus — although it actually contains much more. Stability becomes necessary when an organization begins to get larger.

Isn't that true also with an airplane? I think so. A small plane, of course, needs to be just as stable as a large one even though it may contain only a few people. Now, if you have a larger airplane that holds many people, if it is unstable, you have affected a lot more people and the imbalance will be more noticeable. The Earth, at this time in its particular evolution, needs all the stability it can get. The more points of light we have from stable service vehicles, the further we can go to reach the goal and the sooner we will reach the New Age.

Have you ever thought of your group service effort as the stability factor for creating the New Age? It's true, it really is.

What responsibilities do I have as a member of the service vehicle?

That's a rather vast one, isn't it? Do you think that each person within the group has unique, sometimes overlapping responsibilities? In order to see what responsibilities each person has within a group vehicle, perhaps the best way to reference that is to look at what responsibilities the group vehicle has. Then you cut it up in little pieces so that all of the responsibilities of the group vehicle are met.

Now, what are the Tibetan Foundation's responsibilities as a service vehicle on the Earth at this time? I would say that a major thrust of the

Foundation is to help people understand that there is such a thing as evolution. Many don't know that. For those who have been thinking about evolution a while, that seems almost impossible. But I assure you that it is not. There are many who believe that existence simply is and that nothing happens — you just exist. So perhaps part of the Foundation's training is to show them what evolution is.

There are many other purposes: to aid the Earth; to prepare people for the New Age; to fulfill the Cosmic Plan and so on. Your awareness of self as an individual and how you fit into the service vehicle, seeing your responsibilities and your place within it, will aid the whole group to open channels, to evolve group consciousness — to be an example as a group.

So we could say, then, that the Foundation has some responsibilities. Have you invoked the service vehicle? It's an opportunity, is it not? Do you look at it that way?

How do my purposes fit into the overall purposes of the service vehicle?

Well, I would say that the Foundation is rather a "blanket:" or "umbrella" of purposes and about anything one wants to do in the area of service can have some part within the Foundation if the group feels it will be helpful in its overall goal. There are many, many things that can be added. Again, it will depend upon the group consciousness itself which areas are added. You can make the Foundation as broad an application of service as the group consciousness feels is balanced. (Right back to balance again!)

It seems to me that at the present time on the Earth you should perhaps list four or five main purposes. Then every time you think about adding something, see if it fits into one of these main categories. If it does, then it probably should be added. If it does, then say to the group consciousness, "Do we want to stretch the Foundation in this area? How much of our present resources of people and energy can we place into this area?" It takes some planning, some organization.

I don't know anything that is more organized than the Source. It really has put it all together. If you've ever looked at nature, you know that everything has its place and does it well. It's beautifully organized. You won't ever find an elephant that doesn't have a trunk, that sort of thing. (Can you imagine an elephant without one?) It's organized that way.

Let's say, for an example here, that you've always wanted to do some writing. Do you think the Foundation could use you? Then what are your responsibilities? How about making known the area in which you would like to work? Probably the Creator is not going to knock on your door directly and say, "Will you do it?" But if you say, "I want to do it," then He will welcome the effort with open arms. That's seeing the responsibilities of service as an active role.

You might sit down and look at your strengths. Djwhal Khul, I know, through Kathlyn and Janet and many others, keeps asking people what their strengths are. If you will look and see what they are, then these strengths can be used in purposeful service. As you evolve you might find a new one you didn't notice before. You might consider having some brainstorming sessions in which you evaluate each others strengths. It's sometimes easy to see strengths that others have not allowed themselves to see.

How can I view my service most productively to aid the Source, the Earth, humanity, self?

First of all, see self as Source-level material. Sometimes we don't think about it that way. You really are Source-level divinity. Your perception has to match what you are, and I know you are all working on it. Productivity begins as you seek to activate the invocation of service from the Source. This is extremely important within the Divine Plan. Does the direct invocation bring forth everything that is required, or is more than invocation necessary?

An invocation is extremely important. I think that is why religions have used the rosary and prayers. They recognized they work; they found out by utilizing them. You must evaluate, as you learn your creative process, how clear you are on that invoking process. That is also a part of it.

Let's say that the Source has a beautiful cake. It's lovely — pink frosting with some white, a beautiful cake — and It said to everyone, "You may have this cake as soon as you can invoke it clearly." So you begin to invoke it. (The cake is a goal — it's not meant to be an actuality.) The prayers go forth and you begin to invoke your particular brand of cake. You get up the next morning and look around. There isn't any cake there. Well, you start praying again and you pray and pray, and the next day it's still not there. But you think you can almost see it; it looks like it's just about coming. The next day when you get up, you can smell it a little. It seems like it has been baking, you see, and you're smelling a little of the fragrance and you're getting hungry. It seems very good. Then, the next day when you get up, you can just about touch it. It's almost there. The following day you have it for breakfast.

What am I saying? That the invocation works gradually; as you keep invoking, it works. But you must know how you're doing on the creating process. At each specific point you need to evaluate what has been cooking in your invocation, what ingredients you have selected, how they are blending and if something must be done to bring forth those ingredients in a clearer, more easily defined manner.

Now, let's say that the Source had said this cake was available, but when you began invoking it, you got a little confused and thought the cake had something different in it. Let's say you got it mixed up with cherry pie. So when you invoke without clearly defining what you are seeking to bring forth, you might get a cake that has cherries in it, or a pie that has cake in it, you see. You might get a mixture, because it will come forth the way you invoke it.

A clear understanding is needed of what you are invoking — the specific ingredients of the invocation process. It doesn't mean you can't have the cake. Let's say you know that it has flour, sugar, milk, eggs, baking powder, perhaps vanilla. You might also decide what size you want. (If it is an immense cake when you get it, then you better invite someone over to help you eat it!)

Viewing your service most productively means understanding how you personally are doing in your creating. For you here it is seeing how your specific efforts fit into the goals of the service vehicle, and then bringing those forth in a combination of invoking and clearing.

What steps should we begin now to reach the goal of a widespread thrust to increase humanity's awareness of this important time on Earth?

We can make plans for developing and using our resources, and frame in some goals. Begin a gradual process of invoking your goal and becoming clearer about it. Then bring in communication — reach out and show that the Foundation is here, allowing others to choose whether or not to participate.

Try to develop the resources to meet the needs of humanity — that's it exactly, isn't it? Try to have personnel, in a practical manner, that choose to aid the Foundation on a daily basis, or people who can give some time to meet the needs of humanity. That's probably an ongoing process.

Well, tonight I think we are establishing four or five major goals and seeing how other points fit into these major goals. Next we see how your individual goals fit into those goals and how you can then fulfill this four- or five-part major synthesis. That will help you, because I don't think you've always seen it clearly. But recognize this factor called evolution. Every time you begin to understand a goal, does it keep moving a little? Your goal should include the factor called evolution, so that it is not quite so disconcerting when it moves, because you've already foreseen that it's going to.

We are really talking about an invocation of light, which means an invocation of the Source-level experience, for the Earth. Certainly, love and caring, allowing and sharing and all of these things are part of that invocation process.

What specifics should the service vehicle take into account as it attempts to serve in a balanced manner?

At this time within the Foundation one of the major ones is communication. As you get larger and more spread out into different areas of the country, then comes communication, and it is an ongoing process. Into that communication area also build an evolutionary factor. You might consider how that can be done. Let's see what other specifics were going to add, because we need to put evolution in all of them.

Planning and organization: Take into account the people themselves and their point of evolution, their strengths and the areas that they enjoy, the amount of time that they have to aid the group effort — that sort of thing.

Learn to evaluate (I didn't say judge) the ones who work with you. Notice if there is an area that someone working with you avoids. (Janet doesn't mind if I give this example: She doesn't like mechanical things, so if you see her not doing mechanical things, this is an area she is working on.) That's a point of evaluation within that persons evolution. You learn by observing – not judging, but observing – the way that each person serves within the service vehicle. Thus you learn the strengths that may be utilized in service.

Some are good at creative ideas. You utilize that strength as a resource of the Foundation. You pay attention to others and begin to see beyond self in a way that will allow you to evaluate how their strengths may be used within the service vehicle. You begin to blend your perception of what the vehicle is into a blending and understanding of the whole purpose. That's a good learning experience for everyone.

The group consciousness and its rules and standards should be set by the group consciousness itself or those who selected or placed in position to speak for the group. If you are able to see a strength in someone, when you see a need within the group you can tell those who seek to fill that need that there is someone who can do it. The group consciousness, it seems to me, is just that – a group. We put at the top of our list coming together and communicating. The group need is to serve others, and those who have the abilities within that group to fulfill those needs also serve and evolve self. That is an important part of group service.

It is important to look at your other resources when you're taking into account your attempts to serve in a balanced manner – your physical and spiritual resources. It is important to evaluate the area of the country or the world where you will try to reach and communicate with people. It seems to me that an invocation comes into a service vehicle from specific sections of the world. Do you see that as light, you are there and you are being invoked by humanity? That doesn't mean that you shouldn't take an active role, but going into an area where you have not yet been invoked is premature.

How do you know when you've been invoked? The spiritual plane will know who has invoked the Foundation. I hope you'll ask us (the spiritual teachers), because if you go prematurely, it takes energy. Although energy at the Source level is unlimited, within the Foundation it has not yet been invoked in that manner.

In creating a cohesive/blended service vehicle what are the basic factors that allow integration?

Allowingness. Total cooperation. Communication. A sharing attitude. Willing workers. Recognizing its divinity. A clear focus. Being an example. Dedication. Unconditional love. Joy. Unconditional service. Commitment.

How can I realize that I am the Source not responding as one who takes from the service group, but one who augments, participates in and supports it?

Have you ever thought about the Sources point of view? Yes, clearing self in order to recognize it. The tools of the Foundation are very helpful. You might seek within the realization process how to realize that Source-level support that you are. I thought that I would mention it to see how you would respond, because I think we rarely look at it from the Sources point of view.

We are attempting to get in touch with the subconscious mind, because realizing self as the Source level Itself is what each of you wants to do. The subconscious mind and what it has experienced in the past does have an effect. If you can see that, then by looking at this you can see what you are really creating within the group effort and within self. Then, having seen that area as not completely clear, you'll have an indication of what to work on.

How does it all fit together – the many pieces, the many levels? What can I do to integrate my understanding of the group service vehicle?

One of the most important answers is to recognize that the group is a workshop in Source-level living that will stretch to the basic level of the Oneness. How many levels are we working on? Would you agree that it is a multilevel approach? When you integrate your understanding, what does that mean? You have to see what the concept is first and then fit it all together. The Source level is the concept within which we are seeking to fit it all together. And what is it we are fitting all together? The particular vehicle you are building.

Now, how do you integrate understanding within that group vehicle? Communication, yes, that's extremely important. What is communication? An interactive factor.

We need to take the word "integration" and apply it to this interactive factor, or communication. If you add the factor of evolution to communication and integration, to understanding self at the Source level, that certainly is the goal. Then this realization of self at the Source level will become more and more a part of what you can integrate into your understanding. But you also allow others to communicate their current understanding within self. That's important, isn't it? We all evolve. We all realize more and more completely, but by allowingness the communication within a group vehicle becomes what was meant to be: the learning experience of the Source, because the Source communicates Its learning.

The path of evolution *is* the plan. We communicate our own particular understanding of that plan within a service vehicle. Communication of the plan has not so much to do with self. I would say that in communication or any other area, stretching is important, and because service is the vehicles purpose, the stretch must be as elastic as possible. What does that say to you? As you seek to communicate it is important to try to anticipate the next part of the plan. How do you see do that? Well, one way is to *be* that

Source-being who can see the plan. Is that possible? I think so, because the plan is here, reflected onto the Earth, isn't it? The plan is working out at both the Source level and the Earth's level, and we have our place within it. If we stretch self, we can get in touch with the evolution of that plan. What is that process? Intuition; invocation; trying to see the whole picture – can you see that perhaps it is not just one thing? You are probably not going to see all of it. You will gradually see more and more – that is adding the factor of evolution into it. The Earth experience is the Cosmic Plan reflected into physical existence; there is only one plan.

Evolution is the goal, and your realizations are the means of evolution. Communication must contain the cosmic stretch called evolution, and we've said that seeking to get in touch with it at the cosmic level (Source level) through several processes is necessary – the conceptual area, intuitive, certainly the logical processes, and you might add to this by viewing the group service effort and what is happening within it.

On the physical level you have a workshop that is called the group service vehicle. You seek to view through communication and stretch toward understanding the more cosmic workshop level, then view what is being created. It is similar to what I said about baking your cake. You see through what is being created and what is actually coming forth.

We've said we have to view the group and communicate, taking into account the factor of evolution. How does that stretch you? Let's be very practical: You have here a very small office. Let's say you've got ten people working in it one day. Everybody's walking all around everybody else, the phones are ringing, the machines are going and there are people coming in and out to see what the Foundation is all about. The landlord comes over and he wants to have a little talk with someone and then there are several interruptions happening during the day. What is being created?

Can you see as the energy of the group vehicle becoming busier and busier and busier? There is an increase of the pace of the Foundation. The energy is there. Each one of you is a specific point of energy. It is about learning to take these various points of energy within the physical framework of the Foundation and have them work together very harmoniously. It isn't always easy, is it?

How do you do it? Well, you take practical as well as cosmic steps. You work within the framework here at this group vehicle. You do what you've now done. You get more space. That helps, doesn't it? It gives you a little more moving room. That way each person who comes in can be more separate so you can handle it a little easier.

When the framework of your Foundation stretches in Denver, in Santa Fe, in Phoenix, then that framework allows much more to be done in the service area, doesn't it? It promotes growth. That's practical and important. All of you are light, and you are the Source – there is no question of it. Right now you are on the physical level, working as light. This is an important point to be made: the physical is not any less desirable. In my opinion, right now it is very important (and perhaps the Creator has spotlighted it just a little) to understand that physical creation in the service area reflects the Cosmic Plan, reflects the purposes of the whole cosmos.

I am looking at the Foundation and its expansion and the purposeful extension of it on the physical level. As you invoke and clear to create it, it is going to allow the Cosmic Plan on the Earth to extend. That is a worthwhile goal, my friends.

Eventually there will be a number of centers that are not too large. Why do you think that might be important? Because increasing the number of areas rather than being limited to one specific spot gives us the opportunity to keep expanding. You can contact more people personally. That's my point here; the more we can do that, the better off the people, and that's our goal.

When those on the Earth plane have a personal interaction through a channel with one of us in a place where they can go and feel comfortable with a group of 20 to 40, they have then a means of getting in touch more personally with self. This does not negate the large outreach to new people, which will come forth within the Foundation. In fact, eventually these audiences will be very large. But the small group is important, where people get to know each other and where communication can be personally received and they can feel personally involved.

Now, if you take several small groups and place them in a larger one, you have the means to communicate in more than one way, don't you? This is using the way that the Creator works. If you have a goal of reaching maybe ten people, that may be just what is needed in a particular area. Ten people here, ten people there; I would encourage these small group focuses. Now, you may also want to integrate into the larger group focus. We are looking at individuals and then small groups that can then be integrated in an ever greater manner. It is at this level that the consciousness can be rapidly integrated to the New Age level.

Here is a note from Alazaro on solving problems — her "dunking it in the Source formula!" I promised her I'd tell you. Let's say that you've seen a problem area — too many people; or something that you see not moving as you would like, whatever it is. Alazaro says, "Please see it as a sheet. Write one of your false beliefs on it (whatever it is), then dunk it up and down in the light, in the Source. This will take the reaction out of it and there will be a greater clarity in that area. It is rather an instant specific for feeling better." It truly does work.

The group service vehicle is to me exactly what each of you has been searching for. If you now objectify your view of it to include the Sources view and see that there is no difference, then we have a specific, practical means to have the Cosmic Plan work out within this physical planet we call Earth. I congratulate each one of you on your participation. Thank you.

✦ P A R T S E V E N ✦

TOOLS OF TRANSFORMATION

Vywamus, 1985-1990

❖ O N E ❖

Potentialities of the Soul

W E ARE GOING TO SPEAK CONCEPTUALLY. WE ARE GOING TO TALK ABOUT gearing in to the potentialities of the soul. The soul is that part of self that made an agreement with the Earth. It said, "Yes, I see this beautiful little planet and I will come. I will bring a share of the light to this planet and I will aid that planet to become what it can recognize it is."

Your soul perhaps wasn't sure about becoming physical, but when it was pointed out to you, when you saw the whole picture, *most* of you wanted the desirability of becoming physical. So you came dancing into physical existence. Now, some of you had been physical beings before and some of you had not. Those of you who recognized the familiar pattern of physical existence said, "Well, good. Here we are again and it's a new role perhaps but the play is the same one." Thus you began to experience physical existence. The goal was to see all of your potential, all of what you really are, through a physical focus that lit up that potential. It really did!

The light comes forth proportionately into physical existence, and when it is complete and integrated by everyone who has come to the planet, then the full potential of each being who makes up that light can be seen. By coming together, by integrating into that physical experience, each has earned the opportunity to evolve on the planet. I say that it truly is a privilege — it *is* a privilege to be on the physical plane. Do you know how many beings are waiting in line for a physical body? You might not have considered it, but the line is quite long and grows daily. I am now beginning to be identified as a teacher on the Earth, and I get requests: "Can't you get me in? I really want to go." I really do get these requests.

Why this planet? you might say. Your Earth is placed very solidly into the third dimension. It is literally a pillar of light within the third dimension, and it is much more "solid" than some of the other planets. It agreed to be a stability factor for this dimension. Now, when you are evolving and growing spiritually on every level, you look for such stable opportunities, and this is why so many beings are seeking to come to Earth. Not only that, but the Earth is at what we could call a very critical point in her evolution. The cosmos has literally turned a spotlight on the Earth and is looking at it. I don't mean the cosmos is giving unbalanced or undue importance to Earth, but in the dance of existence, the dance of creation, there is now a focus that emphasizes both the Earth and the third dimension. When you view the third dimension you see Earth as one of those pillars of light. There are, in this quadrant of your galaxy, about five hundred columns of light that are used as stabilizers, so you get a sense of what your Earth truly is.

Your souls, which bring the light, could be called the vehicles, the means by which the light is transmitted to the Earth. Have you ever thought of yourself as a vehicle that brings light to this planet? It's fun to think about that; these things are fun. It's fun to dance and be joyful, fun to think too, fun to conceptually view the Plan, and that's what we really are doing — looking at the manifested Plan as it works on the Earth. The means to evolve the Earth is the soul level. Each one of your souls, then, is a key. You are all keys in this Plan, the evolution of the Earth.

How do you get in touch with all of the potentials here? Perhaps of foremost importance is recognizing that it is done one step at a time. One step at a time you get in touch with that potential. Do you *have* to? No, but for most of you one step at a time is appropriate. Why? Because the *journey* that we are undergoing is the purpose of existence. You wouldn't want to miss it, would you? If you went from point A to point Z without doing it one step at a time, you might miss something at point E, F or G. In fact you *would* miss the excitement, the interaction; you would miss many things that are valuable to you as budding cocreators. Did you hear that — "budding cocreators"? You are already cocreators, but you have to recognize it again, one step at a time. That is important.

Eventually the Source is going to say to you, "Create for me something — just something small, like a universe." You will begin to understand what existence is and how to put it all together — to take your creativity as a cocreator and balance it and ignite it. Through that ignition will come forth a response of the Whole which creates whatever you can envision as a cocreator. Because you approach the creating process in an absolutely balanced manner, what you create is absolutely balanced also. The ignition process, then, is an important one. As you practice your cocreator skills as a soul on the physical level, it is important to consider ignition. [See Part 7, Chapter 8, "Increasing the Igniting Process through Polarity."]

A cocreator is one who unifies the creative process, who uses it in absolute freedom — divine freedom, purposeful freedom. Many of you have wondered about being free. Some of you have felt forced to come into physical existence or to live in a certain way. How can you be free to unify yourself within the soul level, to educate, to clear each aspect of self so that it understands, so that it knows, so that it shares, so that it becomes a full divine partner? I tell you, this is exciting! It is exciting to define yourself as a cocreator who is learning more and more to accept *all* aspects of self.

I have noticed that the male and female energies are important for all of you. Thus in every way that we can think of we will be emphasizing the male and the female streams because it's an idea whose time has come. Your Earth is a little ahead of schedule in its evolution. It has moved in a way that surprised us, which is wonderful! Your planet suddenly took a rather giant leap forward. Your Mother Earth said to herself, "I can do it, I can do it!" You know the story of the little train — "I think I can, I think I can!" We are attempting to show the Earth and all of you, through the polarity area, how you can continually bridge the gap from "I think I can" to "I knew I could — I did, I did, I did." That is what working in the polarity area can do for you, because it is the area of receiving energy. You gather it all up and begin to understand conceptually, emotionally, physically and certainly spiritually, because you must synthesize it through the four bodies. Each particular stream of energy — for instance the female stream — must understand spiritually. It must conceptually see, it must emotionally understand, and certainly the physical format must be recognized as able to move you forward in the manner you want, and to receive also. Then in the dynamic flow of energy you must spiritually understand what this means, and I wish to talk about that a little.

For many of you the dynamic flow of energy represents your relationship with Sourceness Itself, with evolution, with the Source as It evolves. For many of you, then, clearing and understanding what you really believe about your relationship to Sourceness is important. Now, with your divine intent, the *desire* is to become one and to serve — the *desire* to participate. Divine desire is another term for it, but with your divine intent you love the Source, you love God. You do. But perhaps there are a few beliefs getting in the way of your understanding.

Let us say, then, that at that beginning point (of course it wasn't a true beginning, but this is a change that many of you call a beginning point) when you were individualized, the Source looked at you and said, "Let's look at our relationship in a slightly different format. How about being my partner?" Well! The Source showed you, spiritually, conceptually, emotionally, and in a very practical way which we could call physical (though it wasn't at that point), what it would mean to be a partner of the Source.

Now, at this point all of us are working (I include myself and all of us on the spiritual realm) to understand what that contract was and what it makes possible. We looked at that magnificent gift and we said, "Wonderful — I think. I'm not sure how I will use it. I want to use it. I desire to use it comprehensively. Am I going to be able to fulfill my part in the plan?" Some of you wanted to do so much that you said, "Well, maybe I won't look

at that right now; I'll just begin. I know it will work out. I know it will."
But already deeply buried within self was a qualification of the full view of
self as a creator. Now there are a handful – I can literally count them on
my spiritual hands – who did not do that. Some went directly to the
cocreator level. Isn't that interesting? Is that a better way to do it? Not from
my point of view. They are forever specialists within the plan. They haven't
seen the glory of the plan in an experiential manner, so perhaps they are not
used as widely as all of you. Those you might be envying are wishing they
could experience all you experience.

So you can see, from that wonderful beginning with your Source self,
in a step-by-step manner, the building of the plan. Each one of you begins
again what the Source began long ago when *Its* Source knocked at Its door
and said, "How would you like to be my divine partner?" It is a spiral that
moves forward eternally and with great assurance. Eventually, dear ones,
you as full-fledged creators will say to all your little sparks, "How would you
like to be my divine partner?" Do you see the pattern, then, of existence –
the increasing self-awareness of all of the hearth, the unfoldment of the
Whole until, through an igniting process of truly cosmic proportions, it all
begins again?

Sources are unlimited, unrestricted. There are as many levels of
sourceness as you can conceive of, and more. At that level it is a little bit
staggering to think about, but I have studied it. The Source and Its
unfoldment has been one of my specialties, and I say to you, the magnificent,
glorious sweep of the Plan is one that each of you would probably like to
join me in studying. It shows you how everything works, how everything
fits together – truly, the way existence is created.

As you unfold and understand yourself as a soul, you begin to set up
more and more lines of communication with the cocreator level. Many begin
with the soul-merge process, the cocreator level – the monadic level, it is
called, because cocreating is the job and the monad is the being who performs
that job. The monad, then, gets very excited as the soul enters the physical
realm in a very comprehensive manner. It says, "Look – we are moving
forward now!" and it makes itself more and more available to the soul. Just
as the soul notices when its personalities are evolving, or becoming, or
lighting up, so the monadic level notices when the souls are integrating, are
becoming, are radiating forth and invoking a contact. Perhaps you have
gotten up in the morning and said hello to your monad; if you have, it's
appropriate! First of all, sense yourself as a soul when you do that. Stretch
into as much love, allowingness and balance as you can conceive at the
moment, and you begin to just barely glimpse this monadic level. That's
important, because the monad *is* self as it enters what I have termed cocreator
university. The cocreator level is far more than a one-description job. It has
many levels, and you learn it just as you would to become a doctor or a priest
or anything else. You go to a university and you study, literally, to become

a cocreator. All of you are now in the physical equivalent of that cocreator university. That's why we're helping you to understand who you are through the light of the soul. You as a soul are daily involved in discovering yourself as the soul vehicle which can unite more and more with that monadic level.

As I've been talking here, there has been some shifting of energy. Have you felt it? What is happening here? You are taking that good exuberant energy and you're studying it conceptually, so it is energizing the conceptual, spiritual, emotional and physical. We are taking the energy we've generated and we're aligning it into a pattern that you can use in your understanding. Is it not appropriate in your cocreator university to approach learning in many ways and then to see what it is you are doing overall? I think it is.

As more and more light comes into the soul level, you begin to form what is called the crystalline body of light, which is simply the ideal energy format that the Creator gave you to utilize on the physical level so that you could respond to your cocreator ability. It is perhaps, for most of you, not the complete use of your cocreator ability, but the next few steps in the discovery process of it.

As you seek to understand yourself as a soul, there will be a layering process, or what I've termed a gearing process, in which these aspects of the soul begin to click in, or fit together. As an aspect is understood more clearly, that light-correspondent, the crystalline body of light, joins the light within the physical structure that you have *allowed* to be present. For those of you who have merged with the soul, have anchored the full light of the soul (or as much of it as you can recognize at the moment), it builds up the crystalline body of light in a rather awesome manner.

Let's say you turn on one headlight in your car and you think, Well, that doesn't seem balanced; I need the other headlight. So you search deeply into self until the other headlight is turned on. Then you say, "The headlights are on; what do I do next? It would be important to turn on the motor, wouldn't it?" You turn on, or begin to work, each part of the automobile. In the same manner you turn on, or light up, or recognize *consciously* in the crystalline body those parts that are available for use as a physical vehicle of light in your discovery process, in your interaction with the Whole and with others who are doing the same thing. Now, if several of you get together, and one of you says, "You know, that other headlight isn't very bright, and I notice that your horn doesn't work . . ." it's helpful feedback from an objective point of view. You can help each other — and many times from the spiritual level we can help you — to light up that structure more and more once the soul-merge has taken place, to hold that light-correspondent. That is why we are advocating the soul-merge, the third initiation.

Over and over you have heard spiritual teachers say, "You are light, you are love, you are joy." And you try to remain in contact with that, don't you? You try, but before working with soul, perhaps you didn't light up that quality enough to remain aware of it. Thus, as you build piece-by-piece, or unit-by-unit, in your understanding of light and how to use it, you can hold that quality, and it becomes permanent on the physical level. As you touch into the light that you are, the Earth moves in its more permanent understanding of light. That's what happened recently, and it's why the Earth is eight or nine years ahead of itself in its evolution.

You can all become promoters of light and help others to see why it is important to keep searching deeply within self, why it is important to understand the availability of a light structure on the physical level, and the very practical means of your evolution.

Earth, of course, has both polarities, but the receptive energies are perhaps greater than the dynamic ones because of a dedication you might say she made. I feel that later this will become a little more closely balanced; it is working that way. These are the components that make up her creativity. She is seeking balance just as you are. She is as balanced as the aggregate consciousness of all of you allow her to be.

You are seeking through the use of the two polarity areas; this is an image that you are wearing. You are seeking to use what is real, and both qualities of your energy — the receptive and the dynamic — are real. You can wear any sort of a garment you want on any level, can't you? This is simply the garment you are wearing. But more importantly, you are wearing more and more that body of light. You see, you really are light that has become physical. Light contains both qualities, and its interaction creates more light; that is the way light is created. An astrologer might feel that the influence of the planet Mars could fill in some of the dynamic energy. That might be effective, but not in the fullest sense. There are ways of looking at this on many, many levels, but each person — as well as the planet — is seeking to discover within self the use of both qualities of energy.

You are seeking, and change goes on all the time. Now, if you are looking for a particular point where you can recognize the change, that's an individual matter. Each time you remove a pattern you open a door, and you do have to recognize that a door is open. You do have to go *through* the door with that dynamic energy, and then *receive* what is within the door. Pattern removal is, you might say, a partner to the realization process. You need to take out the blocks so you can make realizations. Realizations, when you can unite them, go from the monadic level to the physical level and move your evolution to that point. But you must become conscious of or make a realization of that point in order to utilize it.

When you remove a block, the removal doesn't quite light up the crystalline body, but let's say it prepares it for the lighting-up process. Some of you, when you work in the realization process, come to a point we might call critical mass. You may have noticed this. You take out patterns in an area, and you take out more patterns and more patterns, but sometimes the area's still there, isn't it? This obviously would indicate a major area in your evolution that needs some realization. So you make small realizations — you see one component and say, "Well, I don't need that one," then you get rid of another one, and another one, until finally it comes to a point of critical mass where the realizations are integrated enough so that your reality, or your evolution, or your truth, or your perception, or your light, can accept that point more clearly.

✧ T W O ✧

Realization Techniques

1. THE REALIZATION PROCESS, AS BEGUN THROUGH MENTAL analysis, is the synthesizing and blending of specifics or components relating to one area in your life, and arriving at that point of awareness where you can see the whole picture concerning the point of view from which you have been operating.

2. What components should be put together? Well, perhaps in your life you are seeking to understand a relationship in which you are a participant. Now, that relationship, if it is a one-on-one relationship, contains two specific focuses: yours and your relationship partner's. But it contains, beyond that, another focus – the blended perspective. So the realization process in this case contains three components, and to really understand it you must see the relationship from these three points of view. To realize the whole you must energize it from each of these focuses and experience it, or at least become objectively a part of it.

How do you do that in a one-on-one relationship? There is a focus we call "love," and you experience it upon whatever level is available to you. It is part of the realization process to use that love focus. You can view each of these points through a love lens, because when you look at something with love you can see more clearly and it flows better for you. Love is a lubricant for existence.

So if you view yourself with love and see your particular point within the relationship, then view the other person with love and see what point he or she is occupying, you have two points of view to blend. Then the most interesting part: View the whole that has been created by this pairing, the joint consciousness that you have built together, called a relationship. If you view this joint consciousness without love, you may see separation, but relationship partners are not opposites, are they? They are part of the same thing. The love lens helps us to see how it all flows together, how they both contribute to this joint consciousness.

Now, let's say that when we view this relationship we see a familiar pattern that each partner is working on – for instance, neatness. What if every day you have to walk over your partner's clothes or hang up his or her dirty towels? If you view this with love, perhaps you pick them up joyfully and forgive. If not, then you have an opportunity to assess what both of you are working on right now. You realize that your partner, who is struggling to realize his or her own divinity, perhaps has a few focuses not yet integrated into that clear perception, and that perhaps you do also.

If you are faced with these dirty clothes, does that mean that you are not clear in this area? It might be an important symbol, a synchronicity for you. Possible conclusions that could be drawn about your programming from this symbolism are: (a) You feel that you are unable to clean up your act because of others' resistance; (b) You are stuck holding on to things that are not useful in their present condition; (c) You feel compelled to accept another's clogged or disorderly view of existence; or (d) You are afraid of having a clear road to your goals.

In approaching the realization process concerning a certain area of your life, you use your awareness to see the components that you bring into this area through your beliefs. They may or may not be reflected into the physical; some may be on the emotional or the mental level. Certainly your relationships with everything in that area will show you what is involved. If some components are not obvious, you could ask a spiritual teacher through your channel or others.

Allow yourself to view each component comprehensively, knowing that each specific has an integral part within the whole concept that is being viewed. I would like to encourage you to keep looking at a specific, once you have found it, going within it further and further, then to keep expanding within it (ask yourself why you pulled it in, etc.). Thus if the obvious specific is the dirty clothes, by going deeply within, you see what they symbolize. Also, as you synthesize your points of view in the relationship, through love you understand what you are both working on and how, perhaps, you can work together on it.

Now, someone has suggested that we discuss physical existence under this area of realization. All right, what are we attempting to realize about physical existence while we are here? Its free-flowingness, its compatibility with the whole, or its appropriateness? What is real for you in this area? If one has a limited perception of the whole, then the physical plane itself seems to contain everything. It seems to contain a concreteness beyond which nothing else exists. A limited perception of the whole is the reflection that does not see the connection into self of divinity, does not see that the physical mirrors divinity. How do you clarify that mirror? If you look into your

REALIZATION TECHNIQUES

1. Approaching the realization process: How does it become evident what components should be put together now?

2. Allowing self to view specifics, comprehensively knowing that each specific has an integral part within the whole concept that is being viewed.

3. Seeing the whole through a specific:
   a. emotional response
   b. conceptual response
   c. integrated response
   d. buried response
   e. noninvolvement (that becomes a response)

4. Using a trigger as a key to stimulating the complete view of a conceptual area in order to bridge the gapped point.

5. Penetrating the illusion as the focus into a specific area is encompassingly entered.

6. Reaching deeply through the "lighted up" process into self's stimulated and presently experienced point of evolution and touching the connection called a realization.

7. Alternative means of realizations:
   a. physical stimulation through the physical experience that activates the accessibility of the contact point
   b. visual techniques that can be used symbolically
   c. conceptual stretching that enlarges the target area
   d. light enhancement that invokes light availability and its encompassing corresponding
   e. energy techniques that activate and enhance awareness enhancement
   f. interaction with others; communication
   g. heart chakra exercise

8. Viewing the ideal and allowing it to invoke the realization
   a. color
   b. music
   c. physical interaction with the various Earth kingdoms
   d. hierarchic interaction that creates availability

9. Perceiving the blending process that brings forth the realization; also other techniques that activate all the specifics.

10. Achieving the goal of realization that ultimately results in the soul-merged state.
    a. techniques
    b. light enhancement
    c. heart chakra exercise
    d. invocation
    e. service lens that creates the realized state

mirror and become aware of all four of the kingdoms – human, animal, vegetable and mineral – developing here in physical existence, and then become aware also of the fifth kingdom – the kingdom of souls, the Hierarchy, those who help humanity – then you have the true five-pointed focus of evolving consciousness on the physical plane. Seeing this whole view of consciousness and getting in touch with it allows that clarity to come forth in your mirror.

It is necessary to look beyond self's perception, beyond the species' perception – beyond, truly, any limitation. Clarity comes forth when you are able to do so. Even if you have things that you are perceiving as a limitation within self, when you can see the whole, you go beyond them. It is a matter of self-integration into whatever is there so that the whole is self. *It is not negating self from the focus that you have always been,* because what you have is strong, is beautiful, is divine. It is simply expressing that self through everything else. So it is the refocusing that allows the mirror to be clear about what truly is the whole.

The viewpoint of the spiritual teachers is through every focus. They can see through every focus; they can appreciate through each person's focus and each kingdom's focus. The blending, then, of your perception into every focus is the major realization for each of you.

Another component that appears often in humanity's view is separation. This is an erroneous perception of incompleteness of the universe. If you look at only one component, it appears intellectually that it is not complete – a separation seems to be there. How then can you reframe beyond it? In the experiential mode you can for a while experience beyond it. You can do it for a little while as you delve deeper into that causal area and reframe beyond it. With your will, see yourself beyond the barrier of separation, achieving a connection with divinity. You can do that by referencing a positive or inspiring *experience* that you had sometime in the past and bringing that connected feeling into the present; or you can use other ways such as meditation or invocation. The divine connection becomes attracted by your divine intent.

Pain and suffering are other interesting misconceptions of humanity. For many, pain and suffering seem automatic. Have you noticed that? They seem to be focuses that are very easily referenced. The ability to focus into the divine approach, which contains no pain and suffering, comes from using the will method of refocusing beyond it, as mentioned above. It will also require for some of humanity the releasing of patterns about it. But the realization is that you can put together a life on the physical plane that is free of pain and suffering. This realization has to come first in the sense of being able to allow it. You need to be able to conceive of a life without pain and suffering and go ahead and activate that which you have realized.

We have stated before that when these old patterns that you have removed begin to take shape again due to habit patterns of the body or mind, you can deenergize them by consciously pulling your energy back from them. You have already removed the patterns, so there is no emotional compulsion there.

All right, what are we attempting to realize about physical existence, then? It is the same as any other spiritual level. It has no separation, no limitations. How is this concept realized? It is realized by using it in service, by *being* this concept, free of limitation, free of separation. Using realizations that you have made helps you to explore those realizations completely, to really reinforce them, to keep them realized so that you don't lose them. In physical existence it is necessary to explore completely all the specific restrictions and limitations that you have discovered within your belief system.

3. a. How can you see the whole through a specific? How can you locate an unclear area? An emotional response such as pain, fear, loss, overwhelm or anger indicates that an unclear area has been referenced through a specific experience. Now, you need to look at what was happening or what you were considering mentally just before this emotion was triggered. Follow that deeper and locate the false belief that lies behind this emotional trigger that has stimulated this unclear or programmed area.

b. Sometimes you may find that instead of a specific, you have located a whole area that is not clear — for instance, physical existence.

c. You may also have an integrated response which is a combination of the conceptual and the specific.

d. A buried response would be indicated by a hidden or barrier effect. A point of nonconfrontation with this area or concept indicates a buried response.

e. Noninvolvement is similar to a buried response: You notice an area that you compulsively feel you should have nothing to do with.

To give you an example of this whole area, let us discuss purposes. If you are seeking to understand your purpose/goal area, you need to be able to conceptualize or see the whole picture of that goal clearly. If you do not see it clearly, it is because you have stirred up one or a combination of the above responses. For example, you may have a past experience or series of experiences of failure to meet this particular goal. Trying to conceptualize this goal will bring forth the emotion attached to this past experience. This may also stir up noninvolvement, nonconfrontation or a buried response. In fact, there is usually a cyclic pattern of responses that you will go through as you seek to understand and clear in this area.

4. A trigger could be defined as something specific that occurs which stimulates an unclear or programmed area within self. It can be any of the following:

a. an emotion

b. an idea

c. a concept, which then fits into a larger area

d. a view of the whole that you hadn't considered before

e. a stimulus brought to you by a friend

f. an interaction from another dimension (perhaps brought to you by another aspect of self)

e. a triggering from the Source level of the views you have of self on every other level.

5. To penetrate the illusion as the focus into a specific area is encompassingly entered, one must realize the nature of illusion. Illusion is experienced when one has not clearly seen the full role of self as an active creator on the physical plane. If one accepts his or her self-creativeness, this very acceptance penetrates any possible illusion because it states clearly, "I have created, therefore I can change, I can create more clearly, I can create more encompassingly, I can understand more completely."

6. By reaching deeply into your presently experienced point of evolution through a process of lighting up this area, you can stimulate a realization.

What has been termed "light" is the creative process as it interacts and creates. To utilize a specific that we can call "light" or "realized life force," the interaction of the planes of experience is consciously synthesized. One must see the interaction through the four planes: the spiritual interaction with the mental direction and the emotional trigger interacting on the physical level. See how that literally explodes into a potent creative force that is a realization, the realized point.

Creativity, then, is light that interactively, through its interplay of specific joining points on the various planes, allows an exact point or focus to be reached from all possible points that have been considered and blended.

7. a. Physical stimulation through a physical experience can directly access a contact point that is the realization itself.

b. There are many visual techniques that may be used symbolically. Certainly one is the cabalistic approach. By actually using one particular aspect of self — one particular focus — that you energize, and interacting with it (even personifying it), you may find that many interesting realizations come forth about your handling of this area.

You can reference the subconscious mind symbolically. This is how our false belief system started. You can also look at the logical self, the Source level of self or the soul level of self. By interacting with each of these aspects, you can recognize limitations that you have put upon self in these areas and remove them.

Certainly various colors can aid realizations. Ask someone you are working with why they chose that particular color they are wearing today. Find out how they feel about that color. If it's red, did they feel that they needed energy or that it gave them more strength? Look deeply at what the energy of that color symbolizes. Keep making a point of contact about the color and going more deeply into it for a realization.

If you wish to have another, choose a color they are not wearing, and say, "I am throwing you a ball. What color is it?" That will stimulate the visual feeling area and allow something to be recognized.

c. Conceptual stretching sometimes enlarges the target area. Certainly one interesting way to approach it is by seeking to view an area from the Source level. Do you ever cook soup and say, "I wonder how the Source or Creator would view this soup?" That is a trivial example, but when you have worked with a programmed area and gone as far as you can on the mental, you might then seek to see this area from the Creator's point of view. This will get you beyond the previous concept and, whether it is one little step or one giant step, you can see the framework a little better than you could before.

Each time you stretch yourself conceptually into a point of view you have not used before, it allows you to look at more specifics in your physical existence. And if you keep looking at these specifics, putting them together, synthesizing them, you will go beyond a particular point of limitation that you formerly accepted in your physical existence. Keep seeing the possibilities beyond your present concepts and you can literally stretch into a larger perspective – and that stretching will become automatic.

d. It is important to enhance your light by invoking light availability and its encompassing, corresponding awareness. The more light you can conceive of as available to you on the physical level, the more your awareness increases. Your surroundings are "lit up," and you can "see" more clearly. See yourself as a body totally composed of light and hold that for a time in your meditation.

e. Djwhal Khul has given interesting energy techniques that activate and enhance your body. In these you use your imagination with energy, smelling it, walking in it, feeling it, being one particular kind of energy. You could have a play in which each of you were using only one component of energy (first ray, second ray, etc.) and see what comes forth from that.

What does energy work do? Is there a difference between imagination and what you consider to be real? When you imagine something, it doesn't mean that you choose to be permanently associated with it, but it is a real experience while you are using that particular energy focus. You can use it to allow yourself to view beyond what you have viewed before concerning energy usage. Each individual has a different reality that, in a basic sense, has no impact upon anyone else's reality. In a basic sense there is only your perception and your connection to divinity.

Try perceiving your physical body as only energy and notice how it operates. Be more aware of the energy centers (the chakras) that affect your physical body.

8. Viewing the ideal can invoke a realization. This is an interesting exercise in creativity. It should be realized that it works similarly to an affirmation and will activate the entire area being viewed. In clearly visualizing the ideal that you wish to bring forth, incorporating some of the following images in your visualization might be useful.

a. Incorporate color into it. If you are visualizing the ideal relationship, put in the color that represents this ideal for you.

b. See interaction in your ideal picture; produce it in the form of a drama in your visualization.

c. Use sound. In this case you would not be channeling it but producing a sound pattern of your own through your intuitive processes.

As you thus view and activate the ideal, you will stimulate any patterns in that area and you can remove them. Realizations should also be made about limitations that you have placed upon receiving this ideal in your life.

9. This is a continuation of the above – the blending process that brings forth the realization after you have stimulated it with a visualization.

The visualization that references an ideal will activate all of the specifics in an area, and in the active state they will become more obvious and can be utilized in a logical perceptive manner to enter the whole.

Thus when you view a specific reaction such as anger, look at the exact specific you were considering when that emotion was evoked. Perhaps you will find that you feel betrayed when you seek this ideal, or that someone has used you. Notice that the perception may lead to a feeling of sadness or loss. One focus into an area will lead to an adjacent point and continue on to another. The ability to synthesize comes through conscious awareness of the blending process as a means to achieve realization.

See objectively how you are using your emotional energy – how you feel – and this will actively connect you into that unclear area that you have stimulated, so that you can realize your erroneous perceptions there.

10. There are techniques that can help you achieve the goal of realization resulting in the soul-merged state.

Begin to evaluate nonjudgmentally to see exactly where in awareness each person you meet is, and become that person's point of view as much as you can. By doing that consistently, daily, with everyone you meet, you allow that soul-merge state to come forth. Self is the oneness, and this is more than an intellectual exercise, because self literally becomes that oneness from every point of view. When someone you know then makes a major breakthrough in awareness, appreciate what that person has learned and use it as a key to your own potentiality as the Source.

Perceiving oneself through the service lens leads to a quick recognition of unclear areas. Allow yourself to look at 100% service and see what is keeping you from that goal. Many areas of unclarity can be recognized in that way. See also areas in which you feel you are reluctant or unable to serve, and see how your beliefs about self have affected this area.

✧ T H R E E ✧

Understanding Light

I WOULD LIKE TO *LIGHTEN UP* YOUR UNDERSTANDING OF LIGHT TO HELP YOU know what light is and how to use it consciously. What if I asked you, what is your understanding of light? Would you include in your answer the following, as one student has done? "There are many levels of light. Everything is light acting on some frequency. The light we seek enhances our understanding of all reality. It is the light of knowingness. Friction produces the visible portion of light. Everyone produces an expression of light."

These are good comments. Why then is it important that we talk about this subject? Because in order to use it we need to understand that we already have it. Yes, the goal is to use everything that you have in a conscious manner, in a way that furthers your evolution, to see everything clearly and then integrate it. We are talking about integration of your understanding through the use of light. We will look at this from many perspectives.

When you begin to talk, something literally happens. What happens when one begins to communicate through words? An energy exchange takes place which you can express peacefully or aggressively in many ways.

Did you ever think of your weather patterns as having a synchronicity with your communication? If you haven't thought of it before, let's consider it now. Let us say that in Colorado there is a snowstorm or a severe windstorm, an energy that has begun to flow strongly and to intensify. As that occurs, it begins to communicate through this intensification of energy. If it were not snowing there, the communication from that area would not be so intense.

So what does the snow say to other areas? What communication is being sent to your planet by a snowstorm? Temperature, cold, moisture, difficult transportation, danger, beauty – there is a whole experiential mode within a sudden snowstorm. When a truly severe snowstorm is happening, the media concentrate on the subject exclusively. They describe all the ways it is impacting the community; they become totally involved with the snowstorm.

The Creator knows what It is doing: This is an exercise in communication. It is literally a light exercise. You know that no two snowfalls are identical. Each snowflake is inputting into that situation a particular message, and each being experiencing that situation is receiving that message. The message will be received differently by each person or animal. A kitten with no prior experience of snow that jumps off a window sill and disappears into a snow bank is more than surprised; it must react to get itself back on track in some way. Each time one becomes involved in an intensity situation, full communication becomes the means to understand what situation has been created, and from that comes the understanding to create light.

How does that work? Well, there must be cooperation in the area in getting roads cleared, bridges checked, people rescued; all must be geared up to handle something that appears out of, or beyond, control — something somehow fated. I have used this scenario because with your understanding and growth and your ability to create, you set up situations that you can't, at the moment, change. It is suddenly there. You can learn from it — you can see how to avoid setting it up again — but at the moment of intensity, through communication, something is coming in to you. It is through communication that it comes in one way or another.

Let's create another example. You have a job, and you go to work in the morning and the boss comes out frowning and he says, "You're fired!" He turns around, goes into his office and slams the door. You can't believe this is happening. You want to know why, but when you knock at the door he refuses to allow you in or to discuss it. Through the door he says, "Go! You know what you did — just leave!"

Well, you haven't a clue — you don't know what you are supposed to have done. It takes communication to figure out a particular situation and what to do with it. That communication will help you "lighten up" your life so that the particular learning experience can be processed. We have to have enough "light on the subject." It is light itself that gives progress to our learning. With light on the subject we can figure out how to learn from that scenario. Once you get through that slammed door and can sit down with the boss and talk it out, then you can straighten out the misunderstanding and probably keep your job.

So it takes an effort to overcome what seems like a gap in order to understand and use light. Now, you are using it all the time, but one needs to use it in its fullest sense, use its full potential. One needs to come to an understanding that light can be used comprehensively as a tool. It is between the unconscious and conscious uses of light as a comprehensive tool that you often have a gap in understanding and creative practice.

You all have abilities that you haven't accessed. You all want to be a little more loving, to be a little more loved, to be able to use your creativity more fully; you all want that. The seeming gap comes from your inability to access light, your inability to use light as a tool, to shine that light on what your abilities really are until you recognize them fully and claim them. Under the light you rejoice at seeing them clearly, and you can then incorporate them within you and use them. Unless you use light to illuminate your abilities and recognize them and thus create a magnetic effect, you don't draw them to you.

Perhaps this seems too esoteric, so let's take it down to the Earth plane. There is a schoolroom with about twenty children – it's a first-grade class. In a sense this is where you are yourselves. For those of you who are about ready to graduate from physical existence, cosmically speaking, this is where you are. Many Earth people are at a preschool level, but you are in the first-grade cosmically speaking. Why? Because you've recognized, you've "lit up" enough of your abilities that that door has opened and you have entered first grade.

All right, along with the twenty children there is one instructor in this classroom – no, let's use the word "facilitator" rather than "instructor" or "teacher." This facilitator sits there all day, but if you don't ask a question you're not going to access what it is possible to experience through this contact with your facilitator. This facilitator is a point of light, truly, and you must project using your energy; you must communicate with this particular point. When you do, a window opens, and light comes forth, and you sit in the light because you opened to this facilitator. It takes your ability to see that you must invoke something, that you must realize you have something available that can bring forth the point of contact with the light and allow that light to be used by you.

So, we have our twenty children. Some of them are quite precocious. One of them sings, "Ya, ya, ya, ya, ya! I can do this and you can't!" Well, you've only just come to the first grade and you haven't learned that yet. You begin to cry, but then you look at that other child and you think, I can do that if he can – I know I can. At first you were hurt, but you picked yourself up and knew that you truly could do it. As you say to yourself, "I know I can," that energy of conviction goes forth to the facilitator and opens up a point, and back to you comes the light.

The response comes back to you because you said it with conviction: "Yes, I'm going to project to that point and make the effort and do it!" What I want to put forth to you is the sense of how it works. Have you ever felt an opening, felt open? If you think back you'll remember that feeling. What happened was an energy projection from you, which brought back a response from the facilitating process, which is light. What comes back is a clarity of understanding and absolute assurance that yes, you could do it. It may be something in your physical activities or something in your inner activity. We call this a realization, don't we?

There is a place in the cosmos that we've talked about as "Galactic Headquarters." (What you call it doesn't matter.) It is a place where those who have a knowingness, those who have assumed a particular point of responsibility, follow what happens in this quarter of the galaxy. They are beings who hold a point of consciousness, a caring — they truly care what happens to you. They are great administrators of the Creator's Plan for this part of your galaxy.

Let's suppose that you become very skillful in invoking and receiving. You have become skillful in saying, "Look, look, I can do it! I'm doing it!" It goes forth from you more and more. Don't you suppose these beings notice? I tell you, yes! You begin to create, through the interaction, more and more light, more and more light, and that light lights up the galaxy. I assure you, we can see that energy.

How do we notice you? We notice you by the amount of energy you are putting into allowing yourself to enter a clearer relationship with your creativity. This is what we are talking about — this energy exchange that literally impacts that facilitative core. If I sound excited it's because I am! It's such a wonderful thing to see.

You know, at a carnival, there's this structure where you take a big hammer, and if you hit hard enough, something runs up a gauge and rings a gong. Well, when you hit the facilitator, the cosmos goes "Boing!" Don't laugh — I'm telling you the cosmos does respond. You are hitting that core of creativity and allowing, to the degree you can accept, the resultant factor, which is more light coming back to you.

Your light becomes greater because the energy has now become a part of what you recognize on the physical plane. It is like having a three-way light bulb that is turned up higher and higher by the number of times you hit a button. You access that core of creativity and the light intensifies. Each one of you has chosen to keep accessing more and more of that core.

What do you think happens to the heart center during this process? I think that many of you are working on the heart center as never before. The heart center is responding as never before, and I'm very pleased. But let's talk about the mechanics of it. It seems to me that in light we are looking at the mechanics of creation itself, of how it works, of how the Creator has set up the evolutionary process. Light is the evolutionary process in action as it comes forth through communication. The resultant factor, light, creates something so you can see the creative process, and then you can get more light. It is a self-perpetuating process. Light begets more light. Sounds biblical, doesn't it? That's exactly what was being talked about in your Bible. It was used in regard to the birth of physical beings, but each one of those beings was light. Light begetting light . . . the sequence is eternal. We are talking about evolution. This is how it all takes place and evolves.

I often talk about the Source as a circle. Within that circle every point is a point of consciousness, a point of light. If you could see this circle of points of light, you would see It as a pulsing, a motion, a rhythm that is never static. But because It is so immense, so light, It (so to speak) spins off other Source-dimensional focuses of Its own. In this way more sources are being created.

I feel humanity has found it most difficult to conceive of light, and there is a great need for humanity to come to this understanding. It is Source-related, and when you can understand light completely, you will understand Source, the Creator, completely.

You aren't there yet? Well, be patient with yourself. We are going to take it on many levels. We are going to talk about light on the physical level, but it is important to keep stretching your understanding of it because it really isn't physical at all. You get the effects of light on the physical plane, but the nature of light is not physical. Generally speaking, humanity seeks proof of Source. It seems to me that light is proof that there is something greater, that something exists beyond the human level. When science truly understands that light is not physical, they will have moved their understanding beyond the physical. Not all, but many of them still talk in terms of a series of molecules and atoms and haven't considered fully the overriding principle that guides the evolutionary process. The overriding principle could be referred to as light, though in the fullest sense there is beyond it a consciousness that guides it. In the manifested state it is light that is the evolving principle of creation. In minds that use the word "light" to denote incandescence, an absence of darkness, it takes an effort to see "light" versus "Light" through sameness and difference.

All right, let's create a new scenario. If we have a man and his wife stand back-to-back with their hands touching firmly behind them, what have we here? We have a male/female polarity. We have points of contact through which they are aware of each other's physical warmth. There is the pulsing movement of their blood, but there is another pulsing movement. If you were observing and your third eye was open, you would see a light being manifested. Beyond the fact of male/female vibration in the polarity level, what is it that makes it light up? There is an energy exchange that is the basic unit of creativity. We have the receptive and dynamic energies that flow and spark, but it is the movement itself that creates the stability. In other words, they come together and their light components together create a stable unit. This movement itself creates light. But we are not speaking of movement for movement's sake alone. If you want to get a fire going, you twirl a stick against a block of wood until its movement produces a spark that ignites your dry leaves or twigs. The movement represents an outreach that will result in a return. Movement persisted in will eventually spark the creative process fully, and we get the "boing" effect.

The man and woman are each feeling a pulsing and a flow and sensing symbols such as a rose in the heart center and a rainbow connecting the crown chakra and heart. They are picking up this energy from their etheric, but what they are looking at is the creative process in action between the polarities. There is more light, more energy, more flow.

I would ask you to try this touching action with another if possible. The experience will bring realization closer. It is important to be sensitive to how light is created. Every time you take a step, light is created, but it is most important to see this happen in relatedness with others.

Note as you stand back to back, hands touching, all that you see or feel or sense. Do you pick up color? Is something occurring in the third-eye area? There is a gathering process going on there – sense it. This third-eye area is the storage vehicle for your light potential. As you allow yourself to bring in that light through this rhythm, this energy interaction, this communication, you have the means launching light through the third eye, into that facilitator we have spoken about.

All of you have wanted techniques, have wanted to know how you can create more clearly. This is such a technique. Learn through the rhythm of your life, your everyday living. Learn through the rhythm of your daily activities that there is a gathering process into that interpretive part of you, the third-eye area, that can then be the facilitator for lighting up the creative process, for involving and summoning it, because it has a reserve energy that's being gathered, put together through your daily activity. The only difference between you and those who have graduated from physical existence is that they have learned to use certain means, or tools, of light projection. The following is such a tool for you to practice.

Stand, and imagine that eight or ten feet in front of you is a screen, perhaps electric blue in color. Take the energy that's been gathered up, that you've sensed coming into the third-eye area, and beam it from the third eye onto this energy screen. What occurs will be different for each person. Project for as long as you like, and when you stop, see what comes back to you. Some will see it, some will hear it, depending on individual development. If you think you're not getting anything, then imagine – make it a fun game. So, again, a beam of light goes from the third-eye area where it has gathered, because of the motion of your life, onto a screen that you visualize, know or imagine. It is an energy screen – a creative screen. It is a means of projecting your light out from you to another location.

You have tried it, so let's review what some of you have experienced. These are personal reactions, not reactions everyone will have, but they are helpful as examples of the possibilities.

"It seemed to affect the throat area and salivary glands."

In this case the response went into the physical rather than being focused in the etheric. This can happen if one really believes the response must be run through the physical first. The etheric, of course, is a part of the physical, but you may want to start at a physical sensation. Addressing it as a point of light energy may help bypass most physical reaction. What we seek here is to learn how to work with light, how to use it as a projectile. You might start by putting an electric blue light completely through the chakra system, from the crown chakra to the base chakra, anchoring it gently. Then project your light. Now you are using it as a light probe rather than seeking a physical focus. You desire a projection on the screen of what you have gathered and a response back from that onto the screen afterwards.

There were red and blue lights, a "sparking" in the heart area, a pulsing light from the third eye, and a tingling at the back of my head.

Very good, you did very well and had no problem areas.

First the third eye tingled, then there was warmth in the heart. When I began projection to the screen there was an explosion of white light and a hint of pictures that I couldn't quite identify.

They were creative images, but there wasn't enough focusing to make them clear. That really is our next step.

The projection went well. It seemed as though white light went right through the screen. There didn't seem to be much coming back. What there was, was indeterminate and seemed to need more energy to return.

Our next step will help. There wasn't enough energy coming back, but practice and also imagine grabbing on to what is coming and pulling it in. You experienced the gap we talked about. Now, this is not some far-out metaphysical exercise. It is the means to create a contact with your higher abilities. It has a lot of divine power when you use it correctly.

There was a ribbon of blue through the chakras that turned to lavender. It was off to the left, not running centrally through the body, but was brought back to center. Then there was a white cross, but not a vertical cross, and it popped up into the third eye. Projected on the screen it was blue and very uniform. When it came back it curled up into a ball and came right back.

It was projected as structure, at first incomplete, but it was the beginning of a structure that will allow the manifested state and then come back as a whole. Very odd.

In the first exercise we stood with our heads touching and we both got a sharp pain. When I visualized the screen I projected words on it, affirmations, and then the energy came back as though it were a wave that washed over me.

You took things beyond this first step. You were intense about it and it is powerful. Neither of you should do this exercise again right away. Wait until your head is better. This is powerful indeed; it is creating a contact with that integrated center, the inner seeing. The third eye is the inner seeing, your physical eyes are the outer seeing. When you begin to use this third-eye center it integrates the seeing process and becomes so powerful it really is surrounding the creative process, the creative process on the physical level and the creative process on the inner level. Through the third eye you contact both points of view. It is the integrative center for your creative abilities. That is why anything that is projected from that point is such a powerful tool.

When I projected blue light on the screen, it spread out over the whole screen and then came back to one point.

You tend to create from one point. When you were being offered the ability to understand that you can create from many points, you immediately brought it back to one point but you stretched beyond at first, so that was good.

Why do I feel rather "spacy" after doing this exercise? What do I do to clear it?

Well, stand and walk. As you put each foot down, feel that there is a rod from your foot that projects ten feet into the Earth. This grounds you and connects you firmly with the Earth. You are not used to working with light techniques. For a while they can pull you up. Say to yourself that you can use these techniques as practical exercises of activity on the Earth. Use physical movement.

Color – I saw beautiful blue/white that turned to peach and then yellow gold. When I concentrated on the third eye and projected from there I didn't see anything, but a very strong power came back. It seemed to lift me off the ground.

It lightened you, my friend. That is exactly the effect I wanted you all to see – the ability you have to use what seems paranormal but is not. These higher abilities are called paranormal because they are so powerful in lightening you. You were getting back the effect that is light.

Can one do this exercise either with someone else or alone?

Yes, however I suggest if you do it alone that you keep moving a little as you do it. Walk or sway, or just lift your feet in place. It will keep you from getting spacy or light-headed physically. Sense a gathering process through the movement, whether a physical or creative movement. That gathering is symbolic of gathering all of your resources together, integrating all of your abilities, so you can project from the third-eye center, which is the mechanism for such a projection. It is your creative flow. We are using the tools of creation as a symbol to show you that you can do something beyond what your intellect calls "normal."

When I projected my screen it dissolved and a kind of golden form appeared. It was indistinct and I tried to make it more distinct. It turned into a creature that was half human and half bird and reminded me of the Devil in the tarot card deck, and I tried to get that back.

So you invoked your own personal devil? I think not. It was literally an Egyptian symbol that you used well in Egypt, and not a devil. The gold showed that. Gold is a very integrative color and you therefore did create a symbol of power that you used in Egypt with a touch of fear because in the way you used it, it had a lot of power. You can go back and use the screen to help clear something about that symbol, or you can tell your creator self that you don't want to use the screen in that way.

Now, as you contact your screen, there is an energy from the third eye that flows into the screen. Flowing back to you is an energy exchange that enters the etheric level and then enters the physical level and it lightens you. But also it goes to the third-eye area and generates a progression of the integration that you had originally. So your ability to use this process will keep increasing. You train your spiritual muscles, so to speak, to be used in connection with your physical life. These light techniques can be the means to become more than human — to be that level of creativity you are all seeking.

Thank you all for sharing your experiences.

You acknowledge you have contacted your screen, you project gathered energy and it flows back into the third-eye area and the next level of energy is ready to go forth. You project it forth, and this time you look for form. Some of you found form the first time but were not able to hold it or identify it.

Let us say you are looking for abundance — money, perhaps, but you want creative abundance, the flow that is true abundance. You are looking for that, you want to be of service through that and you can project light into that area. Now, this exercise can be used with great purpose. You establish a screen, and this screen is the point where you can manifest and see full abundance. You can project your light to create it in an energy form, and it will take shape right there in front of you on the screen. It takes first that point of contact and then the building of your resources in the inner eye until as you contact it you get an energy imagery that comes back to you. It may take time and practice, but it will work — you will create something that comes back to you. The abundance of the Creator is there. Remember the facilitator? Be open to projecting your gift enough that it keeps coming back. Each time you allow yourself to receive again, it builds up in the third eye the next level of the use of this area, for it is self-perpetuating. If you do this with persistence and you visualize an energy pattern that flows with whatever your subconscious recognizes as full abundance, there will be a response.

If you like, you can project from your third eye a visual picture of whatever for you represents full abundance. You can imagine on the screen some pattern, some flow that embodies that for which you desire the abundance. If you want to work with people in a way that will abundantly facilitate in others the use of their potential, you project onto the screen, through your third eye, an energy picture that will allow that. You can allow your subconscious to create the energy pattern or you can decide to project a picture on the screen. You can see people coming to you and see them leaving with a light of new awareness around them. This will allow your subconscious to see what you project in a way that is more representative than an abstract energy projection. Whichever way the projection is done, be sure it is complete. Look carefully to be sure the pattern is complete as an energy representation or as a visual picture. If you are visualizing a person but you have only part of the figure appearing, notice and fill in what is hazy or missing. The third eye is like a muscle, in a way, and as with any muscle it needs persistent training. It will therefore help if you do it every day.

Let us say you want to know what the weather will be tomorrow. Instead of turning on the television, try turning on your third eye, projecting into the weather movements for your area and seeing for yourself. Go through the screen and see. If you are going to a city that is strange to you, before you get there project a light through your third eye and look at the city through that light. When you get there you can see how close you came. It is a good way to give needed exercise to your third eye. Should you use a crystal on your third-eye area? Well, it could magnify it, but it would be like a crutch, and you have the ability to develop clarity without a crystal. The inner crystal that is already there will do the same thing, so in this instance the answer is no.

For those who feel uplifted above the Earth and have been instructed to ground themselves, there is this to be considered: You have chosen to come here to Earth, yet some of you keep trying to pull away before you are really ready to leave. You have full creativity on other levels, so the goal is to bring it here. When you begin to be in touch with your higher selves, you feel a pull, particularly if now you're here and you aren't too thrilled with your choice. So ground yourself and accomplish your earthly goal — then you can leave if you wish.

We are going to go now into the subject of light development on planet Earth. The light spirals completely around your planet every day. Within this 24-hour spiral there are other spirals. There are centers of the spiraling process and there are points in the spiraling process; you could say there are about seven major spiraling points within the whirl. There is one spiral centered over Austria, another over Greenland, another over northern China, another over Brasilia, another over Mexico City. You might look at Mexico City and try to see the center of the spiral through your third eye, as astronomers can see them in the heavens. However you see these spirals, the light is moving, with a centering point where it begins and then it moves upward.

There is another centering in Australia. You have the beginning of a spiral in Kentucky. There is a teacher, Atlanto, who has lit up that area for you. These spirals move, but they are really not directional. Some of you will see them moving clockwise, some counterclockwise, but the important fact to recognize is that this energy is rather like a galactic shifting process. All is motion, all is light! There is this swirl of energy that moves and interacts. None of these spirals act by themselves; they all move in sync with other spirals of energy. The seven I have noted are very large spirals within which are much smaller spirals of light, and we can say that one tends to be electric, one magnetic, one rather dense and one lighter. Each one has its purpose and function. There is a movement and a sorting-out process of light — it has components. We look at you — you are divine human beings. Each one of you also has important light components. The components in light fit together in particular ways. There is always movement in the light. In looking at your planet we see that certain portions respond to the light more than other portions.

China, with its ancient origin in its light, became stuck in its movement for a while. It has opened to the light in a remarkable way since the Harmonic Convergence. Tibet, the ancient center of light through your Planetary Logos, has literally been vandalized and raped due to certain effects that humanity has created on the planet; only recently has the light begun to filter back into that area. There are certain areas of Europe that are just now beginning once more to integrate the light. Your country is responding well now to the light, but for a while there was not the use of light in your world. As light moved along the spiral it came to a loop that had been torn and had to be mended to allow light to function in an evolutionary sense in certain areas. This was noticeable over Austria more than over Germany.

There is a process that the angelic kingdom facilitates that allows the spiral to be complete. Humanity has torn it down through activity and pollution, truly forms of rape, but since the Harmonic Convergence some of these things have changed and shifted.

Importantly, and cosmically speaking, there is coming your planet a light projection that really has never been present before. I feel it will enter through the Kenya area of Africa in the next year. It will be an important facilitator for integrating the spirals of light — the seven developing points of evolution over the planet Earth.

We want to give you who are beginning to take your first steps as cocreators the right training so you can use your abilities wisely. You must use them without abusing either yourself or the planet. That is what's happened in the polluting area: you haven't used your cocreator tools well. The Black Forest is being destroyed, but if you could go there and project light through your third eye you could heal the Black Forest. That is the key. The third eye uses the light to project into the trees that cannot now receive light through the sunlight as needed. Your planet needs healing, and you can give it healing.

What I have given you here is but one of hundreds of light techniques that can, and will, be used eventually on your planet. The term "light techniques" will become a household word, and then Earth will be a Garden of Eden again.

Did you know that was how the Earth was created? At the galactic level a being with enough consciousness to do it projected the image of the Earth into the place where it is. It was imaged through that creative process that the third eye represents, and this whole quadrant of the galaxy was placed in position by those who know how to do it.

Where did these vortexes, these points, begin? Well, the points were seeded in the beginning by the ones who represented the Creator and who brought forth the physical planet. But they were activated by those living on the planet — your energy interaction. Remember — how was life created? By communication. So as humanity lived and communicated, these energy vortices began to be activated. They were seeded, yes, but seeds must be nurtured to grow, so you had to give them your own understanding of what light is and your own ability to communicate. The difference between light vortices and energy vortices is that you on the Earth plane can more easily activate the energy vortices — and you do. The light is a tool that is consciously projected by those of a level of consciousness that allows them to creatively see, to visualize, its use. The energy vortices about which you know do more or less have a specific focus — for instance, the one in Kentucky has a future, a potential and a very specific function in the New Age.

The light vortexes, when their complete spectrum has been activated, are electromagnetic. Some of them have not reached that point and will be either more electric or more magnetic for a time. If they were complete, your planet would have ascended.

The exercise I have given you needs to be used with discrimination. If you are developing a lot of power, you can overdo it. If you experience painful or disturbing reactions, back off a little and go back to the blueprint with it.

✦ F O U R ✦

Understanding the Dynamic Energy

W ELL, GOOD EVENING, MY FRIENDS. HOW MANY OF YOU TOOK THE TIME
to feel the energy this evening? It is a soft, getting-ready-for-some-
thing energy, and that "something" is the beginning of a new level of
understanding that the Earth is beginning to embody now.

Our subject is the dynamic energy. Those of you who are working with
metaphysical concepts understand this as the male energy, and perhaps you
are looking within yourself at the polarity area, but we are going to look at
it just a little differently tonight to try to help you see it as a part of a process,
part of an overall plan. Although you might not always recognize it, would
it be fair to say that sometimes in your lives you get a little bit caught up in
the busy-ness of life and you don't perhaps see what's happening all over?
You wouldn't be entirely human if you did not experience your lives rather
completely, sometimes at the expense of looking at the overall picture.

But you are ready to graduate to that. In fact, that *is* the next point that
is ready to manifest now: Although you live your lives in a very positive way,
an ever-expanding way, you will start to be as concerned (not in a negative
way, but in a very positive way) about the lives of those in China and those
in Europe, those everywhere else, because you will know that you are all
together and what someone does in China will affect you in your life. You
could say that if your nose itches, someone in China may scratch it. Well,
that's a joke, but you're getting that close, truly, to the point where an instant
association from one side of the planet affects the other side of the planet,
creatively speaking. There is a much greater coming together with the
creative effort.

Now, it's a wonderful time to be here on the Earth, and one that you've
chosen very carefully — you've all chosen it. The aspect that you call the soul
— that wonderful spiritual part of you that knows and responds and doesn't

have any sort of resistance, that really understands and is joyous – is literally jumping up and down inside of you. Have you noticed? There is a lot of activity, and we could say it is the dynamic expression of the soul as it seeks to help you express the joy and appreciation you have for being here on Earth. And you might consider that to be a little person moving and dancing right now, and it's kind of fun to look at it that way.

So there is an acceleration on the Earth. Some of you experience it as life in the fast lane, and this can be, in the business sense, for example, quite intense, with life seeming to require a lot of you, and the more you do, the more comes in, and there are many, many decisions to be made – a *lot* is required of you. Why? Well, perhaps you're not listening to that little person that's jumping up and down inside of you and saying, "I'm the one who has the answers! I'm the one who, when you get in touch with me, will make life that joyous and wonderful experience that you're looking for." In the dynamic energy area, you might be jumping one way in your life and the soul is trying to jump in another or is trying to show you the easy way to jump. Certainly you have seen pictures of kangaroos – what do you notice about a kangaroo as it jumps? Does it seem difficult? No, it seems effortless – although there is some effort being made, it's a part of the process and it just expands and moves and there isn't any difficulty in that jumping – it's a part of the process. Now, I'm not thinking of you as kangaroos – that's not my intent here – but there is a process, a flowing process, that we call the dynamic energy, and it is available to you through this soul aspect.

Now I am going to give you some far-out concepts. I want to tell you why this time is so special for many of you. Does this apply to everyone? No. It applies to several thousand of you on this planet who have reached a certain point in your evolution. It is perhaps safe to say that your planet now contains spiritual beings that have experienced a great deal and are ready for a certain summary process. There are others that are not ready for a summary – they are what we can call high-school people. And there are those that are grade-school souls. This doesn't mean they are any less than; they are as divine, they are potentially as integrated as everyone, but they have had less experience. So there are all levels of experience in the souls present on the Earth. But for many of you something important has happened and several things have to come together to allow that event, or that process, to occur.

First of all, there is a maturity within the planet, and to take that up a level, there is a maturity within creation itself. Now, those of you who have heard me before know I like to talk about cosmic days. It's like a day in your personal life, but this is a day in the life of the Creator and all of Its parts, so it's very, very cosmic. To give you an idea of the length of a cosmic day, most of it's not in sequential time because it's experienced on the spiritual level, but this particular cosmic day is scheduled to be 4.3 billion of your Earth years, and we are about 3/45 (three forty-fifths) of the way through it, and that's what's important. There is the beginning of a summary process of this day, and we have reached that cosmically.

Since the Harmonic Convergence, there is a maturing, or a process, beginning also on your Earth – a summary process. So your planet is mature enough to allow what I am now going to tell you. Also, on the individual soul level, the soul has to have reached a certain point of maturity, and many of you have reached that.

Now, I'm very excited about what I am going to tell you, and we haven't talked about it before. Many of you have heard about walk-ins, and you've heard about them from one perspective only. When a soul occupying a physical body is in distress and perhaps very deeply disturbed emotionally, it may have the opportunity to leave that body, and another soul enters that is willing to take over what that first soul was trying to resolve. Now, this does not happen often, comparatively, but it does happen. But what I am going to describe is something else. It is a little different and it is a more cosmic event because it talks about the overall Plan and how each part – you – can aid that Plan.

Many of you are what I call cosmic walk-ins. And within the past eighteen or twenty months and continuing into next year, a very experienced cosmic level is looking for souls that are mature in this rather mature setting of your Earth, and they are going to be the guiding light perspective of this soul that has built this vehicle that you call your body. This is very important because it represents a dynamic content that has never been here on the Earth before, a process of integration that is indeed cosmic. To give you an example, there are many, many, many, many, many (get it?) many, many, many levels and alternate realities being integrated right now here in your life.

Now, what is an alternate reality? Let's say you are 21 and you have thought for a long time about marrying someone, and you almost marry them but you decide not to. There is a part of you that did marry them, and there is a fork in the road where this alternate reality has a life in which you are married to this individual and you experience a certain life flow because of that. In this reality you didn't marry them and your life takes a different turn. Now, do you think that in that marriage there was perhaps learning? Yes. Do you think that perhaps there was greater understanding gained? Yes. And if you multiply this by an almost limitless number of perspectives, you begin to see why I am so excited about this time here on the Earth. This more cosmic perspective that is willing to now guide you here on the Earth through the soul aspect that is surrounding you as your auric field, as energy, life force, as understanding, joy, love, allowingness, trust, enthusiasm and gratitude is now available to bring together all of those alternate realities, to bring together many levels on the spiritual plane that are seeking to be integrated.

What does that mean? "Sounds all right, Vywamus, but what are you telling us?" I can hear the wheels turning now: "That's so conceptual; bring it down, bring it down." Well, let me see what I can do about that. Let's say that you are one of the ones I am talking about. Let's say that tomorrow you have an important decision to make: you have an opportunity to present in your job a paper that will make a difference in your career, that will give you an opportunity to use some of the skills you have been trying to use for a long time but seemed blocked. You haven't gotten the opportunities that you looked for in your job. You can call upon this more cosmic aspect and, my friends, you will be surprised at what comes forth, for you now have a tremendous invoking power that you haven't explored yet. I would say to be a little careful what you ask for, because now, really, as never before, when you dynamically connect with what you want, you are going to get it. So you want to be very sure that you use your heart in order to invoke it, that you see clearly what it is you want.

Well, I don't mean to frighten you, and I know I'm not, but you have a power connection open now that you haven't ever had before. Because of that, in my work with you I'm going to look very deeply into the power issues that are involved and we will be clearing that out. All of you — all of you — have misapplied power. You might not have done it consciously — you haven't said to someone, "I'm going to murder you because I don't like the way you look" — but perhaps you have turned your back on someone who needed help, and the misuse of power came in another way.

Now, was it your responsibility to help that person? Maybe not. But it wasn't your responsibility to turn your back on them, either. You see, these things are important to resolve now because in the subconscious mind there are stored, within the emotions, some certain guilts. Let's say that you turn around and someone is asking for help. He has a difficult situation — he's fallen down and broken his leg — and you don't help him. If he broke a leg, do you think you caused it? No, not at all. But perhaps within you is stored now, in the subconscious mind, some guilt. "Look at that: he's suffering and I didn't help him." What we have is an emotion that isn't resolved within your relationship with others, and this emotion gets inside and festers and builds up some levels of guilt that are hidden too.

What we're talking about here is this power that is coming in from a very cosmic level, and you want to apply it as clearly as possible — I know you do — and you want it all to come through the heart. You want to say to the Creator (or whatever name you want to use — God, the spiritual level), "I'm open, I'm open — utilize me for the Plan, let me help. I want to help and I want to have a good life, too." Those go together very, very well; there is no opposition at all. But sometimes you send a mixed message to yourself; it is to yourself and then to the universe. And the universe gets a little confused. It says, "You're telling me one thing over here and then you've got some guilt hidden there . . . . What is it you want me to do for you?" Now what happens? In the past, pretty much nothing would happen. There would be some feeling of stuckness and you couldn't see anything manifested. Well, my friends, those days are over. And that's what's important to know about now. What is occurring now is that the spiritual power is building within you in such a way that you're going to manifest in spite of those blocks, in spite of anything that might stand in the way. And no one is more surprised than you are. It's so interesting to see that: "I did that? I got that? How did I do that? I don't know, but there it is."

That brings up another issue. Many of you really want to be unlimited, don't you? Hmmm? Do you know that's one of the biggest issues you all have? You really do want to be unlimited, but there is a part of you that is afraid that perhaps you can't be, perhaps you can't do it well enough, and so on. Now, let's say that in spite of all your resistances you manifest something wonderful, perhaps a relationship that you didn't know you could have — there it is, full-blown. "I've got it, there it is, how did I get that? Well, look at that!" Now, it would be really nice if you could keep it, if that's what you want, but there is perhaps a little part of you — and this is what needs to be resolved now — that says, "I don't know how I did it in the first place. In the second place I'm not sure I'm worthy of it, so it might go away and I might not be able to keep it."

I'm not saying that you think these things consciously, my friends, but there is a process within you that needs, now, that needs to grasp and hold on to something so that these blocks do not wipe out what the dynamic energy within you is bringing in. Because the manifestation of it now is not going to be difficult. I repeat: It's not going to be difficult. But holding on to it and then expanding and integrating what you have manifested is the next step. That's what we are all here to figure out how to do.

One of the things I would like to get into very deeply is the Atlantean issues. I find that very important. We look at old patterns that have come up through Atlantis and we look at the strengths that are there from Atlantis and then we begin to balance them through meditations and affirmations, decrystallizing the subconscious mind. Then, my friends, you need time to smell the roses — an integrative period where you reflect on what you've cleared and allow the dynamic energy to gather up again and manifest the next step for you.

It is necessary to see exactly how many levels are being resolved here. There is a Planetary Logos, and this being is just like you — no difference, except he's a little more conscious than you are; not a great deal, in a cosmic sense, just a little. And he has understood how to take a concept — and that concept was a reflection of the Creator — and apply the energy of all of you, of all of you who have ever been on this planet, and build a framework in which all of you live and of which I, Vywamus, am now a part also: I have interwoven my energy completely around your planet. This being gave birth to this concept through his heart, through a training program not different from what many of you will undergo. You know what happens when you go to school and are ready to graduate — you start to look at career opportunities, don't you? And some offers begin to come in. There is a place called the Galactic Core. It is the headquarters for many of you, as far as your next step is concerned, and it is administering much of your activity now. Many of you are in line for Planetary Logos or Galactic Logos or Universal Logos. Does that sound far out? Well, it's far out, all right, but not so far ahead as you may think. It's perhaps necessary now to know what your next step is.

For some of you it is the use of yourself as an avatar such as the Christ was. Is that so far out? It isn't, because each career choice will bring you a very special training. You will need to be very clear in order to fulfill your task, and your training has begun. It began with this cosmic input, and you will find that teachers such as I, in working with you, are slanting our work — we are focusing it in a certain direction, looking at what your next step will be. It's like in your senior year of college, when you need special courses and special understanding in order to open up that career opportunity.

For example, let us say that your soul has chosen to do what your Christ has done for the Earth and what many other avatars have done — they have brought to the Earth a particular heart quality. The Christ brought unconditional love; through his energy he literally permeated the Earth with unconditional love. Did the Earth accept it all? No. It accepted all it could, but there has never been an avatar on Earth who was accepted more than 20%. Did that upset the avatar? Not at all. He knew that the planet accepted as much as it could. And many of you have chosen as a career path to provide this service for another planet.

So let us say that you have made that choice. Teachers such as I, Vywamus, are going to make absolutely sure that you are clear in the heart area. Anything that gets in the way of allowingness, anything that gets in the way of trust, we are going to help you with — not only we, but the whole universe — because if you agree to assume a certain responsibility, the universe says, "Oh, so that's what you're going to do, is it? Well, here's what you need to do to get there." Now, this is not negative. But it is intense, and perhaps what you see in your life or what you've seen with some of your friends, where things don't look fair, you wonder what's going on and why that life (it might be your own) is so intense.

A good example, my friends (and believe me, I'm not advocating it), is someone with cancer. They are going through a very special cleansing process. AIDS, or one of these other diseases that seems to take you to what seems like a point of ending, is in fact bringing things together so that some new birth can take place, and most of the time, not all of the time but most of the time, it takes you from one physical structure to another.

Again, I'm not advocating this, but the person who contracts one of these diseases has reached a point in his evolution that is extremely important for him, and through a misinterpretation in the body and in the subconscious mind, this intensity is experienced in the physical structure. A good example is cancer. With cancer the cells themselves won't accept the light and they begin to misinterpret the signals of the soul. The energy gets out of control and then there is the traveling of the cells, perhaps through the lymph system, all over the body, and many times there is then a confusion within the physical structure, so the organs don't function correctly, and death ensues. Remember, I don't advocate this, but there is something being resolved through this that can't be accomplished any other way: namely the allowingness of the soul to have a new physical structure level to express with.

Or more importantly, it may be that there is one very important stage that all of you have reached — and I want you to pay close attention to this. You're finished with the Earth, and you're mature enough to graduate except for probably one, or perhaps two, major areas. Now, that's interesting. And you may say, "But I look at my life and I don't feel like that." But it's true: If we get down to basics, it's all tied up in one or two areas, and sometimes a soul, through an illness, can wipe out a major area like this and in the next life be much freer than they otherwise would have been. Again, there are other ways of doing it, and it seems to me that you are all learning those other ways. But if you can't, then the dynamic energy, not applied clearly but coming in anyway, will wipe out the old slate, polish it a little on the inner level and give you a brand-new opportunity.

The process of ascension is the resultant effect of being polished by the dynamic energy over and over again until it shines so clearly that everywhere you look, through these eyes, what you see is light. At the time of ascension, everything is light: You look at flowers and they're light; you look at a table and it is light. There is light everywhere. What has been physical for you turns to light. And, my friends, you are all close, and the dynamic energy is going to keep giving you a new opportunity to look at that now. Because of the cosmic walk-in situation, it's almost as if every day you have a new life. It is that comprehensive; it is that much change; each day a brand-new opportunity. That is what the souls are so excited about. Get up every morning and say, "Today I have a brand-new opportunity and I'm going to use it as wisely and in as heart-centered a way as I can. I'm going to trust." Plug into this new, fresh start where there is enough energy, an unlimited amount of life force and energy, coming from this spiritual level.

This is a complete shift taking you from an individual process into a more group-oriented one. This group that I am talking about is very cosmic, and your soul — this soul that is very mature now — has recognized that on its file-card index are all of the specialists that it is now willing to use to have a more unlimited expression, a more creative expression. Have you always wanted to be a dancer? Try it! Your soul knows how to dance. It can say to some of the greatest dancers that have ever been, "Help us!" — and that will begin to flow through you now. It might not all come in five minutes, but it will be at least ten times freer, ten times more powerful. Many of you have wanted to dance, or play an instrument or write poetry, but said to yourself, "I can't do that." I would say to you, put the dynamic energy into what you think is unknown and try it, because you have those capabilities on a very cosmic level. And it's not just you – on tap you have the resources of this whole galactic level. This is one planet in one solar system, and the galaxy contains billions of planets. Let's say that your soul and its experts have experienced only in this quadrant of the galaxy; that's still a billion planets, more or less. Do you think those resources might be valuable? And can you actually access all the strengths there? Yes, you can, because there is a coordinator in the twelfth chakra that is coordinating that effort; it is literally coordinating efforts in your life as you are living it, in your life as you want to live it, in your life as you *can* live it.

Now, the question that is asked of me more than any other is, "What are my purposes? Why am I here?" The first thing I answer is that there isn't just one purpose – not ever – because one thing you are all trying to understand is that there isn't just one way to do anything; there are always at least six ways to do everything. There isn't just one truth; there is the developing understanding of a clear way of being that works for you and is your truth. So if one way doesn't seem to work, you can do it another way. That, my friends, is an important piece of information for some of you because you are looking for the place where you can say, "That's my purpose, and when I reach that place I get to stay there and everything is going to be just fine." Well, guess what? That's not the way it is. The way it is, is that you will gather up your understanding of your strengths. If you haven't done so, sit down with your soul and your mental body and list your strengths. Some of you feel a little shy about that; it seems like an ego exercise. But I'm not talking about strengths that are just yours; you're renting them. They were entrusted to you by the Creator – they are the Creator's strengths manifesting through you. List them: What is it that you do well? You will begin to see that those things are what you can use in your life and you will use them one way, then grasp another strength and add that to the creative framework that you've built, and keep adding strengths until you reach the point that we call the fully developed cocreator level where, because you no longer need to be physical, things really come together in a very cosmic manner. I am not saying the physical is limited, but it has a specific purpose, and that is why you are here.

Now, our subject is the dynamic energy, and believe me, that is what I am talking about. I would like to give you a definition of the dynamic energy: a dynamic principle which is you. It is you in manifestation. This doesn't mean that there isn't a point of beingness behind this dynamic principle; the beingness has *created* the dynamic principle. You are a part of that desire nature of the Source to explore and discover, and this dynamic principle is always working through you. Mentally, it's what gives you curiosity; spiritually, it's what gives you that thrust to help another as your heart expands and the impulse to share with someone you know an experience you've had. Now, that person may or may not relate to what you've said, but many times it gives them a glimpse in their own life of something they're looking for. Even if it doesn't, it's the dynamic principle at work; the dynamic principle is used for communication.

We have defined the dynamic energy mostly through the polarities: the receptive is like a little cup that gathers up and integrates, and the dynamic energy thrusts into that. Because they come together and join their energies, there is an expansion, a new birth – on the physical level a child is created. But there is a creative endeavor that is expanded so that process is at work all the time. The Creator, at a certain point in Its evolution, said (and this is the cosmic day we are talking about), "I want to explore everything; I want to learn; I want to grow; I want to understand everything." And potentially It does understand everything, but It also wants to expand. The Creator is expanding Itself – always there is a spiraling, an unfolding, a discovery process at the highest level. And It set up a system, and that system thrusts what has been integrated into a new level so that It can explore that new level and learn from it.

This is the dynamic principle at work. There are times when you feel that things are simply integrating, that you just need to be quiet. That's a time when you are probably putting things together, getting ready for the next dynamic connection that opens you up to new possibilities. Some of you are rather impatient – you would like to get to that particular level that you're looking for *right now*, so the integration period isn't nurtured as well as it might be. When the desire for integration comes, try to indulge yourself.

Now, you may say to me, "I am so busy. I haven't time to go off by myself and integrate for a while." But let's say you have an evening. Now one interesting thing happens: time is not as it was. It's shifted, it's expanded, or it has changed its adamancy. You don't have just twenty-four hours divided into minutes and seconds the way you did before; it can be shorter or it can be longer. One thing you can do to help yourself is say, "I have an evening and I want to use it fully; I would rather have two weeks." In this way you can expand that evening to a full two weeks; you can accomplish as much integration in one evening as you would in two full weeks.

Now, how do you do that? Building a concept of energy, say to yourself, "All right. This is an energy format; it's this big, and it's violet because I like violet; it's transformational as well as integrative; and I'll put in some gold because gold is integrative, too." Then lay that over your evening and say, "This one is as full as I need. Maybe I don't even need two weeks, but this is what I need now." Bring it in, or be creative and think of another way to do it, but actually take charge of your time now. Use the dynamic energy to change your relationship with time. You are ready to do that. I'm sure you've had an experience in the past year when, knowing how long it took you to go a certain place, suddenly you were there and you feel you couldn't possibly have gotten there as fast as you did. These things are happening, and what do they mean? They mean you've telescoped time. We're in the fourth dimension – this isn't a third-dimension Earth anymore. You've brought the foundation that you've built from the third dimension into the fourth and now you're learning to use it. The fourth dimension is a flow – just as you can turn on a faucet slowly, turn it on more rapidly, or really let it pour out, so you can adjust the process by recognizing that you have those creative powers and letting them flow through you. It's an interesting concept.

Going back to your integration, spend your evening – you might plan it a little – and ask the higher self, that specific within your higher self that you call the soul, what you need at this time. Do you need to walk in the woods? Do you need to be by the water? Do you just need to be quiet in your room? What do you need? Then make the arrangements for that particular integrative period and allow it to happen – and trust the process. You might later think that nothing happened, that you didn't feel anything. But integration doesn't work the same as the dynamic energy.

Many of you have interesting beliefs about the dynamic energy; you like to see things happen, so you like to have it working so you can tell something has occurred. But with integration there is a sense of wholeness, a sense of unity, a sense of satisfaction and a sense of connection. That is what you are looking for in these quiet times. For some of you it may take the form of a meditation. It can be a moving meditation – I really like them because they allow you to begin to see that there is movement within integration. There is, of course. The receptive energy has, as part of it, a dynamic content, and the dynamic energy has, as part of it, a receptive content. In other words, in a meditation there is movement, and that movement is the dynamic part of the meditation. You might not notice the movement if you are being very quiet, but it has a dynamic content in it – you don't get one without the other.

Once you've integrated and you get up the next day, you're all excited: this is a new beginning. You erase the old day and connect very cosmically, and then I say to you, "Get ready!" because whatever the next step is for you, it is going to come in. And again you might say, "But Vywamus, I did that and I didn't see anything." Do it the next day and do it the next day; most of you won't have to do it more than three times. But you may be looking for something and not see what has occurred. You might not be looking in the right area. In other words, many of you don't know what the next step is for you. Let's say that what you want is a relationship, and what you get is a new job. Well, maybe in the new job you'll meet someone. So you have to look beyond the immediacy of the event to see the plan that the universe is really bringing to you.

I think it might also be important to work with some specific affirmations. I have given a system in which you simply slide the affirmations into a lake [see page ix] that represents the subconscious mind, and you can try that if you wish. There's a more elaborate process, but that's the main part of it. I give all sorts of affirmations. Sometimes we use the negative part and then the positive part with it. The reason is, if you say to yourself, "I am unlimited," the subconscious takes a look at that and says, "Well, I can see here and here and here where you weren't unlimited." So if we direct what might be called a negative statement very specifically to those areas, it can delete that part so you *are* more unlimited.

But in a direct affirmation, how about saying every morning, upon getting up (put it on your bathroom mirror):

❦ *I surrender to the purposes of my soul.*

There is nothing more powerful at this time. No matter what you want out of life, the soul wants the best life for you, the best life you can have — the one that is the best connected, the one that is the most fulfilling, the one that uses your abilities most completely. The soul wants that for you.

And you, my friends, are capable of bringing that into manifestation right now.

✧ F I V E ✧

Tools of Transformation

L ET'S START WITH THE SOURCE. I'VE STUDIED IT OVER THE EONS AND ENJOYED
seeing how this Creator, the Oneness, this being that we call All,
evolves, becomes, tunes in. I will discuss that for a moment.

Let's say we are calling one particular point a beginning. It is not a
complete beginning, but a new level, a new point of view. The Source, the
Oneness, has been considering, has been evaluating, has been reflecting and
has at that point begun to activate a new beginning. We call this new
beginning a cosmic day. On this cosmic day the Source considered, "What
will I learn? What will I now enjoy and experience?" In a sense the Source
begins to compose, as in a piece of music or a poem. Some of you take part
in one cosmic poem and some in another, but all of you are taking part in
this particular one. You have been activated – you have been sounded forth.

Now, if you look at a piece of music when you are playing it, there is a
combination of notes that are always present within this particular music.
But you aren't touching all of those notes at once, are you? So some are
being actively contacted. The others are a reflection of that active state, or
what we could call an inactive point within the activity of being sounded
forth on a particular cosmic day. From this particular concept everything
else flows. There is a rhythm, a flow, a vibration that contains an active
point and an inactive one. Neither one is better than the other – they
complete each other. Again, a cosmic day in an overall sense is an active
period which is followed by a cosmic night. The Source, the Oneness,
experiences actively during the cosmic day and reflects, plans and synthesizes
during the cosmic night.

Each of you truly is a reflection, is a part of the Source. We can begin
to see then that your activity also contains active periods and inactive periods.
We have already stated that in this song, in this tone, in this cosmic day that

the Source has created, you will have periods in which you go forth with great joy and periods when you reflect upon what you have learned.

One such active period is what we call physical existence. You approach it for the learning, as the Source Itself does. You come forth to learn and to understand. Now, the vibration of physical existence seems to be happy for some, and thus there is a tendency not to see beyond it. It seems to be all that exists. Now it is necessary to again see beyond physical existence. This, my friend, is transformation.

Transformation on the physical level is the process of framing in beyond that which we have called "self." Each of you perceives the Whole, the Oneness, through a perception called self, but now each of you is in the process again of perceiving self as the Source Itself. This means that you, my friend, will in one sense step aside and reference existence from every point of view. That is what transformation truly is.

Let us look at an example. Have you noticed the popularity of marathon races? What is the true purpose of this? It is to have an experience. The whole thing is to have an experience that we are calling a marathon race. There are many beings who will take part in this race. Sometimes it seems that every point in the race is filled with beings, and that is why I am using this example. The race, then, contains perceptivity at every point, so the Whole is getting that experience. So to truly appreciate, one must see from every point of view.

Now, in the race there are those who are seeking to win. There are some who are not — they are just seeking the experience, taking part in this event. And it isn't especially important to them whether they are first or twenty-fifth or one-hundredth. But there are some who want to be first. Sometimes as we seek to transmute self, the active mode gets to be referenced a little compulsively. There are those who become equally compulsive in the inactive mode. Why is it that beings in a race want to be first? I'll tell you why. If you make that first contact point, that thrust (remember we said that the event contained *being*, or a perspective of the Source at every point) at first — or what you might call the territory on the physical level — there is a connection, a total connection that is made for an instant with the totality of existence.

Now remember, we said that is the goal on the physical level: to connect with the totality again. There are those who are seeking it through an action, and being first in an event plugs you in for a moment but only for a moment, because the Whole considers from every point of view. There is a stimulus zone as that takes place, and the one that is first says, "Yes, I have made that contact and it is wonderful. I have achieved."

In one sense that achievement is an illusion because they are looking for something outside of self. They are looking through their achievement for that which they already have within self — the ability to connect with their divinity, their perspective that can allow them to see every other perspective.

In one sense your Western world has been in the active mode. Can you see that? It is all about achieving, and again, I am not saying achievement is wrong, but anything can become compulsive, and anything that is compulsive must be balanced. In the Eastern approach they have contacted the inactive. They've looked and found very much there but they have not used the other half, the active, the completion of the transformation. Some may have completed the active state, and so the inactive is for them completing what has been done. For many of you, when you were in an Eastern life, you completed that and now you are putting the two halves together — the completion process that transmutes.

In your seeking to understand self, to transmute the concept beyond self's needs, wants and desires, you have a living workshop here to employ. Every day, when you reach that new day, are you looking at those you are coming in contact with and seeing what their needs are, and putting aside your own? As you do this more and more you begin to become that point of view that is the Oneness. This is why, when the spiritual teachers make contact with you, they can appreciate and enjoy the uniqueness of each of you and your perception. They do not judge it — they see it as a point of view of the Source that is uniquely unfolding, a unique perspective of the Oneness. This is truly important.

How is it then that we get "out of self"? For many it is through service. It is a part of the transformation. In order to see the Whole you have to see the Plan, and the Cosmic Plan is the Whole. That's all there is to it: the Cosmic Plan, its concept and its experience — and each of you is taking part in it.

Does that negate a personal life on the Earth? Of course not! The Source is learning from your unique point of view. As child, who is not that little spiritually, begins for the Source in this new physical structure. In one sense the slate is wiped clean, but of course, there is within him the creativity of what he has experienced in the past. But this new opportunity will show, for the Source, something It has not considered before — a new way of perceiving. The Earth then is synthesizing and blending all of the perspectives, all of what has been, and reaching a new cosmic level that it will appreciate in a new way. The Earth has nurtured you here for eons, and this consciousness too is transmuting through the interaction with the kingdoms of the Earth. So when we talk about going beyond self, it is important to look at all kingdoms.

Consider the plant kingdom. What has it been doing for eons? It has been perceiving existence for the Source. Then humanity creates pollution, and what happens to this kingdom? It continues to perceive and it continues to aid the planet — in fact, it serves to absorb and deflect some of that pollution which has been created by the human kingdom. It gathers it up within itself, and this is part of the transformational process. The plant kingdom is literally taking on some of the responsibility for this very important point on the Earth. By attuning to a great tree in a metropolitan area and appreciating its service, you are acknowledging its efforts. Have you ever done that — gone to talk to the trees? You know they're very happy to be acknowledged — they truly do enjoy it. The blades of grass — how many of you have thought of them as you walked on them? They don't especially mind — they're used to it — but how would you like it if someone walked on you? Well, the point is, acknowledge that service to the Whole is coming forth. It really is important.

We've learned to appreciate the part of the plant kingdom we call the flowers. Do you know how evolved they are? They are glorious spiritual beings. Their beauty is almost beyond compare. This particular planet has a very evolved kingdom of flowers as beautiful divine focuses. A rose is very rare in the cosmos. Look at them — see the varieties that you have, appreciate them. See the violet-colored roses and remember that the Violet Ray is a symbol of transformation. Go deeply within it.

Consider the animal kingdom. Do you know the glory you have on this Earth in the bird species? There have been periods when there were incredible numbers present. It is important to acknowledge the transformation process of the Earth by acknowledging the evolution of the various species of the animal kingdom. The animal kingdom has group consciousness, you might say, so if a deer senses a forest fire, all of the animals sense it and they flee. That says something important — that they also, through this group connection, are sensing the transformational process on the Earth, perhaps more than many human beings do. The animals are ready, the flowers are ready, the mineral kingdom is ready. Are you ready? They don't necessarily require an attunement to trauma — they require an attunement to change and to becomingness. One must let go a little of the perspective of what has been, both on an individual basis and a worldwide basis. The Earth will transmute — there's no question about it — and the means to do it will come from each of your actions.

In the broadest sense each of you is a tool for transformation. That is what it's all about. You came forth in this particular lifetime excited about it. The soul level of self says, "Yes, we've worked for eons here on the Earth." Here it is, this spiritual focus that has entered sequential time on Earth. To what is the transformation leading? To an awareness of the Whole. That is so important — an awareness of the Whole. Your tools of transformation are as many ways as you can creatively envision, imagine or get together to help you see the Whole as self, but not from a self focus. And that's the difference: The Christ said, "You are love." Appreciate it, view existence as love. Love is not a single being. You share it with all everywhere — it is a part of the Whole. All of these attributes that you are seeking to cultivate are means of connecting with the Whole.

I'd like you to do something for me right now. Concentrate for a moment on nature. See it unfolding. View it as in those glorious violet-colored roses. It is opening, and as it opens you become aware that everything is a violet rose. Each of you bears an attribute that allows this unfolding to take place. Stretch, unfold through your attunement to the rose of transformation. Can you feel it? Can you literally see this room as a rose? Can you get in touch with that? It's beyond self, and yet it is self. Be the beauty that is there, be love and appreciation.

Now, what are we doing here? We are using a tool of transformation. We are saying that there is a time to talk about conceptual material, there is a time to delve deeply into understanding of what transformation is, and there is also a time to experience it. There is a time to work with symbols. One symbol that will lead you forth is the cross. It has been called the cross of matter — the entrance to what is termed spiritual energy (the energy of the spiritual plane) as it interacts with the energy of the physical plane. The center point is the point of contact.

This point of contact where you balance and get in touch with all of the energy there, is also part of the transformational process. If you perceive self as that contact point and see self expanding in all directions — a circle that is ever-expanding — you begin in another experiential life to view as the Whole. These things are important — all of them.

Another good tool is color. Many of you work well with color — the spectrum of the Whole. Don't limit it to the seven colors of the rainbow; get in touch with all of the possibilities of color. Look at the colors and get beyond self perspective — look at the Whole and view self. How does the Creator, the Whole, view? This is an interesting tool that will lead you forth in the transformational process.

There are those who are focused on the points within self that are still being worked on or being cleared, and they don't see the bright areas. Do you think the Source does that? Do you think when the Source views you, It looks only at those areas you are working to clear? Perhaps the Source looks at your self rather completely, appreciating the learning experience that is going on. The Source uses Its perception of you as a divine being in order to view you.

Djwhal Khul has defined the monadic level as the individual perspective of self at Source level. When I talk about the sounding-forth process and your unique tone, your unique vibration within the Whole, Djwhal has called this your unique perspective as the Whole at the monadic level. This does not mean that you are any less spiritual at any other point. We could also equate it to the perception of the Whole as It journeys forth in a unique perspective to fulfill Its responsibilities on a specific cosmic day. On another cosmic day it might not be sounded forth.

Consider the relationship of the Christ consciousness to the soul. A soul is a specific of the totality; the monadic level is a specific. Each of you as the Whole, a reflection of the Source, is like a circle with 360 perspectives. We are calling one the monadic level, another the soul level, and another the physical level. At a specific point in the evolution of a physical planet, there is another specific called the Christ consciousness. It is a specific of the Whole that is utilized to aid the transformation process. It is usually focused by a being with the spiritual "know-how" to do so. The lord Maitreya, as the Christ, has done that for the Earth.

This means that in each involvement with a physical planet, this specific is, you could say, embodied by a being (although it is a spiritual embodiment rather than a physical) as a focus of that particular transformational quality that is called the Christ consciousness. It comes forth to the physical level to anchor a point that will lead to the transformation of each specific being that comes forth on that level. The Christ also brought forth a specific we call love, but more than that, he was utilized as an archetype for what all of you are also doing. At each point in existence, whether it is physical or not, there is an archetype. Each of you belongs to the archetype we call the Adam Kadmon – the heavenly archetype that comes forth on the physical level. But there are other specific archetypes utilized as evolution, or the unfoldment of potentiality, takes place.

We have spoken of cosmic days. There have been about one million of them. The present cosmic day was truly not a beginning, although each one begins a whole new level. As for the number of monads, they are as unlimited as the Source Itself. Now, if you get in touch with the fact that this cosmic day has 4.3 billion sequential years, you begin to look at the vastness of existence. (Not every cosmic day is the same number of years; they don't follow sequential time, really, but to help you understand I place it in a sequential connotation.) So the vastness is unlimited, the potential of it is unlimited. Thus, if you can see that you *are* the Source, that says something about each of you: it says that each of you is unlimited.

Let us go a little deeper here. Part of the transformational process is the acceptance of that truly unlimited quality of self. It must be accepted – there is no limitation, there is no restriction. Every time there seems to be, it has to be reframed, reunderstood and reevaluated, because restriction truly is not a part of your divine being. Most of you are understanding that more and more clearly, and realizing and accepting it. What does the word "accepting" mean to you? It's different from perceiving mentally or intellectually. It's accepting self as Source-level material. It's looking and saying, "Yes, I think I Am." That is not an egotistical statement, it is a divine statement.

Let us talk about the ego. It is truly a part of the personality – the center of it. The ego has a purpose, and it is no accident that each of you has one. As you begin in a physical existence there is a need for something to center on. The ego provides you with an individual perspective from which to reference self and keep building your strength. At the point of transformation, it is necessary to reframe beyond this strongly built-up individual. Now, you don't throw out the baby with the bathwater – the ego is a part of self, a strength – but what you do is reeducate it, knowing it is a part of something much greater, and use its strength for the Whole. If once in a while it seems to be strongly entrenched, well, that is simply a part of the learning experience and part of what you are doing as you evolve on the Earth.

Accepting self from every point of view is important. If someone brings to you an interesting learning experience, take a deep look within and see its meaning, because when these things come up, they indicate an interaction with the Source. It is that strength that is used as a lens for viewing existence as service to the Cosmic Plan. It is the key. That strength that you *are* aids the Whole, which you reference as self. That's the great key to transformation: referencing self as the Whole. But it goes beyond that. Perceiving the Whole from a reference that you call self means being able to see self as one of the beautiful divine beings that are on the physical, appreciating them, looking and saying, "Oh, how interesting! Look how uniquely they are created!" Look at your divine strengths and appreciate the unique creativity from every point of view.

Perfection is what you are. Your divine beingness is already perfect. Your expansion into your potentiality can be considered perfection, but it is not one particular point that we reference as forever being perfect, because you are ever becoming, continuing to expand.

The conceptual area is seeing the whole picture, continuing to learn more and more to see it. But you begin through experience, experiencing the Whole through interaction with others, really beginning to see that other point of view. When someone comes to you, say to self, "I am standing here, and there you are, and I'm experiencing now from this other perspective, from your perspective." That pulls you out of that one-pointed focus that we call self. Nothing is wrong with self, but as you begin to see the Whole you can use the experiences of daily living to show you the concepts of the Whole. So the conceptual area is viewing the whole framework around which either existence or any one particular area is built. But of course, the quality of *evolution* into perfection must be built into it.

✧ S I X ✧

Soul Integration

TONIGHT WE ARE TALKING ABOUT INTEGRATION, NOT ONLY ON THE SOUL level but on any level. When you begin to integrate anything, you take many specifics and place them into a container, or an energy format. You begin the process of aligning them to a state that allows the use of all of them as one composite to fully come forth. We will state this in many ways.

When you enter soul territory, your purpose is to understand yourself so well that you will know who and what you are at soul level. You begin, as you travel toward or pass the point of soul-merge, to be aware of self as a multiplicity of abilities. Each of you as a creator has many abilities in every area. On the physical level, what you are trying to do is integrate all of those abilities into a usable package that can be explored extensively by the creative processing that we call the Plan. The Plan is for Sourceness to discover, to learn, to gain understanding, to move forward in Its unlocking of prob- abilities and to bring forth a balanced use of these abilities.

Let us say that you are seeking to integrate in your understanding all of who and what you are at this particular point in your evolution. You are seeking to see love come clearly. You are seeking to see the alignment of your will with the will of the Creator. You are seeking to see how to utilize the will aspect and the love area for the Sourceness. You seek to understand service and how to be of service to Sourceness. All of these and many other aspects are seeking to come along in a balanced manner, integrating all of them into a usable product of Sourceness on a physical level. Integration is bringing forth a product of Sourceness that can be used physically (if we are speaking of integration on the physical level) to serve, to unfold potential on every level.

As you begin to consider what integration is, know that you are tuning in to that basic level of Sourceness and seeking to bring forth specific components that may be digested physically and then brought forth and used in service to the Plan. It is more than that – it is the use of self on the physical level that is self-satisfying; it is loving, allowing; it is breadth and scope of what Sourceness is. Stirring up the ingredients that are being integrated allows a balanced use of the ingredients to create a specific vehicle for experiencing. That is the purpose of integration: It allows you to use the product of integration as a vehicle within which to go forth.

All of you are integrating all the time. You might not have thought so, but you are. There is a process called active integration and a process that could be called nonactive integration. All of you are working with the nonactive state all of the time. Much of this is within the subconscious processing. It involves pulling specific beliefs, or perhaps misunderstandings, from the subconscious that are available as they come to the surface. Have you noticed that as you seek, searching for a way to do it, you see life mirroring it to you? Then you say to yourself, "Oh, perhaps I need to clear this area. I can see life is bringing back to me something I don't want." This is an area of nonclarity, but you can't quite figure out what to do about what you see in the mirroring process. You get a clue here and one here and another here.

Let's say that you are married and you have a son, and this son is the "apple of your eye." You love him and are very proud of him. Suddenly you notice something: Your son is becoming a little belligerent toward you sometimes. He's not as respectful as he was – in other words, he's a teenager. Because you see that this is mirroring something to you, look to see what you are learning from the process. You see some anger, some belligerence; your son is not relating to you as he did when he was a child. To put it all together is difficult, so you are integrating all of these components in a rather subconscious manner. As you observe and consciously recognize what the mirroring process is bringing to you, there surfaces a whole conglomerate view of the area. Suddenly there is a crisis in your relationship with your son that brings the situation to a head. Perhaps the son runs away from home, perhaps there is a confrontation, and then what happens? Well, you see what the problem is and you understand more clearly. Now, I'm not saying a confrontation must happen, or that it is the ideal approach. If you can come to understanding without a crisis, that's fine.

Now, if you go into this area before this subconscious integration has taken place, that is when you get into confusion. Because you pick up in some of the area and see only some of the components, you may miss some that have not yet been integrated. This is one reason why, in experiencing an intensive, we say the second day is more digestible. The second day you feel that things are coming together. This is because during the night, on the inner planes, I lead you through the subconscious processing that is going on. Yes, I do work with you at night; we put all of these components together, and you bring back what? Well, it is then possible for the conscious mind to begin to recognize and to bring out all that has been stirred up and is now available. Now it can come forth nicely organized and integrated.

The next state of integrating is the active one. After the conscious mind receives the "lump," the conglomeration, it says, "Look at that! Here's all this from the subconscious, but what does *it* know? It's not logical, and it's put all this together, and just look what it has created. That's not what I want." Life has mirrored the past that you don't want to create in this manner. So the subconscious has to be reeducated. The conscious mind begins to sort it all out consciously and begins to file the information and assemble it into the pattern you want to have it in.

In the example given, you might see that communication with your son has been perceived by him as something you were too busy to realize was needed. Perhaps he felt you did not listen or respond to his need for freedom as a teenager. Whatever it is, you begin to see from what has come forth why this area has not been assimilated or integrated.

Now, what does this mean, "as you come forth as a soul"? Many say, "I am a soul, so what do you mean by 'come forth' as a soul?" We are talking about allowing the soul's abilities to literally be anchored within the physical structure. The energy formula, the light, all that the soul *is*, becomes anchored physically on the Earth. Why? So the Earth will be benefited. That is a part of your soul's mission: You anchor its light component on the Earth and allow the Earth to learn from it.

When you turn on a flashlight, what is the first thing you notice as you look? That it needs to be focused. To get a clear focus, the light component has to fit into a proper sequencing or fit in a manner that allows you to make practical use of the light. So integration after the soul-merge entails focusing all of the light aspects of the soul so that they can be the means of seeing more clearly on the physical level as you integrate.

There is nothing — absolutely nothing — that is more enthusiastic than the soul. It comes forth on the physical level, finally, after wanting to do so for a long time in the sequential sense, or in the eternal now, working hard to bring it forth. And it says, "Good!" and it has all these soul experiences coming though as the soul tries out all manner of new and interesting facets of physical living. Sometimes the person feels confusion, but it doesn't have to be confusing. In that case fine-tuning is what is needed.

It is necessary for a personality that becomes integrated into the soul level to let go. But as you let go, you become receptive. Letting go does not mean becoming nothing. It means allowing self, as a component of the soul, to be very active. You get a chance to look at everything and then input your perception into the other aspects of the soul that seek to be integrated. So now we have another component that can seem confusing. To use again the flashlight as our symbol, you seemed at first to be *holding* the flashlight. Then the light came forth and anchored the soul, and now suddenly you *are* the flashlight. You don't have control of the flashlight, but you have the complete allowingness to be an integral part of the flashlight. It is a difference in perspective.

So as the soul begins to come forth, it draws from physical existence many learning opportunities for the self and for the Earth. In addition to drawing forth these opportunities, there has been a different point of view brought forth through self. We call this going from the personality level to the soul level. You view from a different point, and that can seem confusing. It is in fact the best way by which to clear up the means to integrate the soul. At first it doesn't seem possible to do everything, to be everything – and yet to allow everything.

When you were in school, you moved up each year to a new level. Each new level brought an acceleration of learning and more responsibility, and the teacher expected a great deal from you. But you are both student and teacher. As the soul begins to integrate on the physical level, each specific lesson is fine-tuned by the soul, and will be there forever. It will clearly be a part of your life and a strength and a tool to aid self and the Earth. Each specific lesson can be seen clearly at soul level; that is a strength. The lesson can't be postponed anymore, for the soul shows clearly all the components, telling you to look at it now and integrate it all now. The soul level, as it comes forth on the physical plane, is learning, is serving, is joyously going forth. It presents the opportunity to use whatever needs to be used to learn and understand. It is exciting, and it is the way it was meant to be.

If you, as a personality that has merged with soul, feel things are moving too fast for comfort, then I suggest you relax. Don't do anything for a while. Disconnect for a time; do it consciously. The learning won't stop, but you'll get a chance to catch your breath a little. You have switched from active integration to a more inactive integration. It is appropriate at the beginning state to do this rather than to be overwhelmed. Take a deep breath, knowing the process is what you want – you are seeking it. But decide to take a moment of rest.

Souls seek to use sequential time. When children come to the physical plane they are interested in toys; likewise, your soul has a new toy called sequential time. It wants to try it out, and it is literally bringing forth the learning through sequential time. It is taking pictures of the learning process and learning through the use of sequential time.

The soul that has been focused in the eternal now understands the eternal now completely. It comes then to the Earth plane and sequential time. It starts to do something and it says, "Good." Then it stops and looks at what the learning situation is. Let's say you are on a walk and the soul sees a flower. Well, it hasn't before seen it up close on the physical plane. The body is ready to go on walking, but the soul wants to see the flower. Click – it takes a picture, and that flower becomes a part of the soul-level memory bank. Do you see what it's doing? It's building in your memory the soul-level memories that it can use.

Why doesn't it have soul-level memories through the memories of the physical structure? It does, but these are more clear, because all the energy of the soul is now anchored in the physical, enhancing the ability to see the flower as it *truly* is. You have a more powerful lens now, through the soul-merge, with which to view physical existence. The soul wants to look at absolutely everything. It takes pictures of the physical level to store, then it learns from it, it looks at it and eventually has acquired so much understanding of the subject that, were it a skill such as ice-skating, you could become a professional skater in a rather short time — if you wanted to, of course. The soul can do this in absolutely every area. It knows no restriction, no limitation. The purpose of the soul is to do this as it comes to the physical level, and nothing is too small, too minute to consider. This might be confusing, since in your past memory track, which is still active, a flower is just a flower, a muffin is just a muffin. The soul might look at all the elements involved in the ingredients of a muffin, and when you reach for a second one, it could consider the calories and decide one is enough.

The soul begins to direct your life in ways that, at first, are subtle. You have an impulse, and then you decide that you really don't want to do that. You want to — no, you don't want to — confusing, isn't it? Or something comes out of your mouth, and you say, "I'm going to do what?"

So we are talking about allowing self, as a soul, to gain the use of the structure of your physical vehicle for service. If you have any questions in the area of understanding what service is, the soul will be happy to inform you. It will clarify it for you in every way, and it is perhaps one of the most important areas the soul will clarify for you. It will happen almost automatically.

I think it might be helpful to bring in the analogy of children — children as a point of new beginning, the creative processes that are just awakening your creativity as it now goes forth as a soul. Many of you have misconceptions about new beginnings, about the child within self, its owner and his appreciation of what it means to be a child, and the joy that is available from that childlike state. If you can get in touch with that child, it can teach you. This is the soul in its wonder, in its love and its appreciation of what physical existence offers for your instruction. Have you ever found yourself bending down to watch an ant? Have you ever found new interest and appreciation while watching a nature program on TV? This is the soul learning on the physical level. You find yourself studying a rock and seeing how it fits into its surroundings, and how an area symbolized by that rock can be integrated into a subject about which understanding is desired. So it begins the active integrating process. This is an important statement: that life begins, more than ever before, to be symbolically engaged, thus lessening, negating any sense of separation of the planes.

You who live near the red-rock formations of Arizona might, upon looking at that red rock, find your soul being reminded of a specific cosmic learning experience it had. It might use that cosmic experience and translate it to a physical level that can help it in the integrating process. Never forget, you *are* the soul integrating on the physical level. The personality is *not* in control, and though you might not yet have responded consciously to this format, it is because you haven't known *how* to look for it or at it, you haven't seen all of the components. You've seen one here and another there. What do you get when you put the components together? The "robe of many colors" — and you are wearing that as a soul. You need to see it, to get it in focus, to get it finely tuned, to see how it all fits together.

So integrating is, first of all, allowing yourself to recognize that you are not as you were. It has reality to some of you, but to others it doesn't seem real. Look in the mirror and see yourself in a rainbow garment, and know that you are seeing the soul. Then, right at that point, let go! You relax; then you are open to absorb. The subconscious, in one sense, takes over at that point and it's all right here. You need times when you're not trying so hard. It is good to get away for a while if you can. If you must stay where you are, you can nevertheless relax. The subconscious is wonderful. You sometimes think of it as the bad guy, but it is a wonderful mechanism that creates. Let it create the integration you need. Let it do its work. Let it bring you that which can then be assimilated by your conscious mind. As you do this, you might start to relate to this part of self more completely, because you will begin to merge the two together, working toward the ultimate integration.

After you've begun to find that relaxing can be fun, then ask your subconscious, "How are you doing?" If you get back a lot of love and a sense that it's going along very nicely, good — you can keep right on relaxing. If you get back agitation, well, you might want to see why. Most of you, I believe, will see that this is beginning to come into balance and you will feel good about it. It's only when you push too hard, when you feel you have to be doing something, or that all of this can't be absorbed at once after all, that you get into trouble. Then you are uptight about it. Remember, the soul has no trouble doing everything at once; that is its strength. You will find it amazing to watch it do many things at once while enjoying and appreciating each. This is one way you can see the progress you are making in allowing *self* to be the *soul*.

Simultaneously you begin to notice that certain things are coming in, and you tell yourself, "All right, no big deal; I'll just keep flowing with it. Integration is taking place." If someone comes to you wanting help and wants the solution in ten minutes, well, the soul has it right now. Pressure from the need to function in sequential time doesn't exist for the soul. The soul looks at the ideal and sees the solution, and you will allow it to come forth. If you stop and relax, you get yourself out of the need to control the situation, or be anxious or overwhelmed about it. What you are doing is breaking the old pattern. You stop and focus the conscious mind on the subconscious process and allow yourself to perceive the integration taking place within self. You disconnect a pattern that comes from the past, when as a personality it was difficult to handle more than one thing at a time. If you have a reactive pattern within self, then by breaking through it and saying, "I'm not responding that way anymore," you consciously redirect your energy.

When you need to make a decision, relax. Some of you, as you serve, need to make immediate decisions. Relax, take a few seconds, and then make the decision if it truly needs to be done immediately. That moment of relaxation allows you to bring forth all the components of soul. It allows the integrated usage you have allowed so far to come forth into being. When you get uptight, you shut off this integrated response; expectations of how and when and what's appropriate get in the way. Sometimes you seem to ride a crest of energy and then find yourself in a trough. When the low point comes next time, view the soul. View its energy and thrust deeply into it, or perhaps feel you are floating on it. Relax into it and see what comes forth. It is tension that you are creating that causes this up-and-down swing. You can try too hard. Relax and allow the soul.

You are no longer only the personality expressing. You are the soul now, and things are never going to be the same as they were before soul integration began. You now have a different formatting; it's not meant to be framed as it was before. Perhaps you still have many of the same components, but you have rearranged them and added many more. Your responses to living are going to be different — they are going to be better. The soul is joyous in its knowing of what life can be on the physical plane. The difficult part of all this is to awaken to self truly as soul.

When many things seem to need action on your part at once, and you'd like to ignore all but one action and shelve the rest for later, there is an old pattern seeking to say that you can do only one thing at a time. Allow all the aspects to come in, and relax into the acceptance of them. It may take a while before you handle them cumulatively, but that's all right. It's important to relax into the lesson each time and say, "Good. I accept all of this; I can see each part is important. I'll keep that focus and also get on with it all, and do it at once." A digestive process will take place subconsciously because you haven't put up a barrier — you have accepted it, and it will become a part of what you are working on in a multiple-focus way. Don't limit self — the soul cannot be limited. Acceptance: that's what you are working on — the acceptance aspects of the soul as they begin to come forth more and more. They seek to become a complete focus that you can use all of the time.

Some of you tell me that at times you feel a real need to just sleep. The cause can be many things. It can be seen as a nonconfrontation with the life process. But in the integrating process, it might signal the need to integrate at the subconscious level rather than the conscious level, or in the passive rather than the active state. It might allow you to relax into an integration that, were it to be worked upon actively, you could not yet integrate, having not yet learned how to do it.

In a soul-merge class, there might be several students working together. In this case, the composite energy becomes a part of each member. A specific combination of energies is used in order to perceive self as a soul. A vehicle is built, composed of several different energy formulas. It becomes an integrated energy similar to what we might call an oversoul. That oversoul has become permanent and is literally a part of who and what you are; it is a soul that mothers you and helps you. You can call upon that energy. As you individually go forth, you have that mothering energy supporting you. You can go through the soul-merge without this oversoul energy, but because part of what you are learning is that you are the Whole, that you are Sourceness, you don't get in touch with that realization without intermediary steps. A group of six souls coming together in this way is an intermediate step toward understanding yourself as All That Is. If you feel you have a weakness in some area, then what you are talking about is the personality. The soul has no weaknesses. What you don't have yet in the case of weakness is the integrative use of that soul level. Because of the oversoul created by the group, you have its nurturance to call upon. The members of such a group are chosen carefully so that in combination, since each one is particularly strong in one area, all the strengths are there. Therefore each member can use the integration of the oversoul to help activate his or her usage of all of the aspects in an integrated way.

Being in a group is helpful to some people, but for some, group work might not be appropriate. There are many usages, and there is no average. Some might use the monadic level. The spiritual component might direct you. All of you can call upon the Source, and I assure you that the deeper you penetrate the Source, the more excited the soul will get about plucking from It all the needed learning material.

We have spoken often of the way the mental body, the analytical focus, rather takes over for some of you. Now, this can be a block to integration, so you will have to relax that analytical approach. How about establishing a love focus and putting the analytical into it? Submerge it in love! Do it with your divine intent. Tell yourself that you dedicate this very good analytical process to immersion in love so that it may be more relaxed and come forth in a more integrated manner.

Integration of the personality-self with the soul is a new way of approaching the learning process. The habitual processes are going to protest: "This isn't the way we've been doing that!" If there seems to be confusion, you can relax into your evolution. It's possible to try too hard, and it really is an automatic process. That spiral that you are is going to go forward, so relax into it and enjoy it. Perfection is what you already are. As you move forward in integration, into service, you are gaining in the use of your potentials. Perfection was given to you when the Source distributed among all Its sparks Its own divinity. You don't know the amount of potential you have. You don't realize it. The means to understand it are gained through a step-by-step process. It is an unlocking of the usage of what was given to you as a divine being. The idea of striving for perfection is rather destructive because one never meets one's expectations. If one has just learned to crawl and feels like a failure because one is not an Olympic runner, the sense of failure is a negative input. By learning to unlock the potentialities one step at a time, one learns to deal with them gradually as they come. Even when the process quickens, it is still meant that each step should be integrated into useful availability. Even after soul-merge, it will be a while – typically at least a year – before the wide *use* of the integrated abilities. Before that, you gradually glimpse what might be clear after a year. When traveling toward a town, you can see it and know you're seeing a town from quite a distance, but when you have entered the town you move among all its details knowledgeably and can utilize all that you see.

When I speak of relaxing I am really suggesting you relax your *expectations* of what will come in at you at soul level. The soul is going to keep creating on the physical level, but as a personality you've had expectations that you had to control or make come into being. The soul is going to keep on moving into its learning, into its service, and you can flow with it. You need not have the sense of anxiety and responsibility that the personality so often expressed.

Imagine you are standing on a spiral and it's moving. If you are balanced and relaxed, you can enjoy the view. If you are entirely caught up in the need to establish or maintain your balance, you don't have a chance to see the view. You can't fall off, because the spiral is what you are, but you might not enjoy the process of spiraling forth.

There are times, even when you are making progress, when you feel you've lost the key to something. It is the key to completing the soul-merge. Sometimes it's merely perceived as having been dropped, and sometimes the key *has* been dropped. Take a look at the circumstances going on at the times you feel you have dropped the key. See what's happening, for there will be clues there to help you find and use the key again.

Now, let me address channeling the soul. What will you experience? Well, it will vary, but you might think about the soul as energy. If this finer energy comes through your channel, or you become aware of it, perhaps it's been there all the time and you haven't looked – haven't been aware of it.

If you allow that awareness to come forth now as the soul, what will you experience? In an energy sense, you will experience perfect balance, perfect perceptiveness of physical existence. That soul of yours understands the physical plane and Alazaro's free-flow completely. While you are channeling the soul, bringing it in, perceiving it, this energy will harmonize and balance self.

You might allow it to be an energy experience. Have you ever had a day when everything flows very well? You are functioning then at soul level. Now, you might have noticed the difference when you are not doing this. Well, what you should do, of course, is bring the soul back and reharmonize your day. That's easy for a spiritual teacher to say, isn't it? You can become aware of the soul through a toning meditation. You can reference soul through love. Allow love to flood self. Become love!

Using a soul name would be a way of creating a specific opportunity to interact with it, to put your attention on it. But through what other ways can you know that it has responded? If one feels a desire to dance, then the soul level creates the harmonious need to express rhythm through the body. Be aware through the senses? Yes. What does a soul smell like? Perhaps a beautiful rose, whatever symbolizes divinity within self. In your past experiencing many of you have had lives in which, during a very spiritual experience, you became aware of a flower. It might be a rose or a lily.

Do you think anyone has ever *felt* the soul? Would there be a surrounding energy that feels very balanced, very harmonious, so that you could put that energy out right here and literally walk on it? Yes! The soul doesn't have a specific shape. Why couldn't you flow with energy and then experience it? Well, we're trying to tell you there's not just one way. There isn't a right and a wrong way. It will be your own unique interpretation of the soul level.

✦ SEVEN ✦

Activity As the Key Ingredient
in Soul Integration

SOMETIMES IT SEEMS AS IF YOU'RE VERY ACTIVE, DOESN'T IT? SOMETIMES you're running around, but is that true activity? No. Running around, or spinning your wheels, as some of you say, sometimes seems like lost motion or wasted effort. Perhaps you're always learning, and from it comes forth some sort of resolution. But what is it? It isn't truly activity in the most divine sense. It seems to some of you to be "chaos" or "motion" or "physical energy," if it's on the physical plane, or "resistance." Well, sometimes it can be resistance that keeps you moving so that you won't have to get in touch with *true* activity. I don't mean that you are consciously doing that; you are simply trying to get in touch with your own evolution through all this running around.

Activity is *interaction that has a purposeful direction.* Activity is the Divine Presence as It learns, as It becomes, as It creates. This is the Source Itself in a manifested sense as It has come forth to discover and learn. That is what activity is. It is not the running around that is sometimes focused on the physical plane as activity.

Now, what is *directed* activity? A focus upon accomplishing something at work? All right. Daily, then, you direct your life toward the fulfillment of a job goal, let us say. That is directed activity; at least it is in the ideal, isn't it? Other examples would include working on ourselves purposefully to become of service to humanity; interaction with other people; interaction with various aspects of ourselves; or interaction with other levels. What is another example of interaction? Channeling is interaction with various levels; teaching is interaction with people; working with animals is interaction. All of these interactions *direct* activity, and that direction leads to what?

Accomplishment, achieving a goal one has set for oneself. It completes something – a level of learning or a level of understanding – and what does that do? It directs or begins to direct another level of activity. You need direction on levels, because if I say to you, "You are all cocreators," you recognize that, but perhaps the full use of that ability comes forth level by level, step by step. What happens if you set a tremendous goal for yourself? Let us say your goal is to walk on water. If I said you all could do it, you would perhaps believe me, but if I said you should see that as a goal, then what? You'd need some sort of direction on how to get to it. You'd need a step-by-step how-to-do-it kit on how to achieve that or any other goal. So activity, as it is directed in a step-by-step manner, accomplishes the goal.

Now, the title of this chat we are having is "Activity As the Key to Soul Integration." What does that mean? Soul integration is allowing that real identity level of self to come forth in a synthesized manner, right in your physical life, to direct your life. Some of you understand that very well and some of you are just beginning to understand it. The *directed* activity that each of you is engaged in daily is the key to accomplishing that integration of the soul. Before you can use anything, it must be integrated, synthesized, blended and put together into a usable format. So we will talk about how-to-do-it-time in the area of using the soul.

An activity, then, is the stirring together, the blending together, of all of the aspects of the soul into a viable format that is an integrator for your life and for your interaction with others. Does this sound rather esoteric? Well, what I'm saying is that all of you are looking for a key, a method, a way to have the type of life that allows development of all your resources, all your abilities. Some of you are running around looking for it in many ways – not physically, but running around in consciousness.

One of the clearing methods used in this area is pattern removal. It must seem to some of you that you have taken out a million patterns, with millions more waiting in the wings. Well, sometimes we give you these patterns to give you something to do. Have you ever thought of that? This doesn't mean they aren't valid, or that it doesn't help you to remove them, but all of you are trying to *do* something. In the doingness of soul integration, or the integration of self, we direct the activity by giving you these patterns. It gives you a direction, a sense of purpose, that keeps you from just scattering your efforts.

As you purposefully seek to put together the life you really want and to aid the Earth at this time to integrate its various possibilities, to have the type of Earth that you really want, how do we direct that activity? Sometimes I give you patterns for the Earth, but how else? What do you think spiritual teachers are doing? What sort of interaction with you and the Earth is helping to direct the evolution of the Earth? What sort of directing process is going on at this time? Anchoring the light, helping you to change your own consciousness, unifying scattered energies? Yes, but how?

There are at this time many, many signs on your planet of the purposeful direction of those of us on the spiritual plane as we seek to guide you and to direct this evolution. For example, let us say that members of a metaphysical group meet some Fundamentalist Christians. Do they have anything in common? They have dedication. They are reaching out in their own ways toward truth, and spiritual teachers answer any invocation that goes out from any group — yes, of course we do. But how are we using all your strengths to stir up evolution and direct the process? It is activity, *directed* activity, that will get us to the goal of a united Earth.

Successful blending of groups is achieved by giving them the focus of a common denominator. For instance, a management seminar would have greater acceptance than would a seminar designated as being spiritual or political. It's not that one avoids saying that one is spiritual — that's not the point at all. But you take key ingredients from both and show them what they have in common. You help them to focus on the strengths they share rather than on their differences. We do this perhaps rather subtly, but it is a part of our subject because it is activating key ingredients, thereby activating individuals who have strengths in these areas.

So we have two groups, and we activate by planting a seed in one member of one group, and that person will approach a member of the other group with a thought that will begin a blending of energies. It is the blending of energies that will allow them to find out what they have in common instead of their differences. Focusing on a particular strength or area that both recognize as important can lead to shared activity. Perhaps patriotism can be a shared strength. There may be different ideas about what should be done within a country, but everyone wants a strong country in which all may live the good life. Your own country began, did it not, through the blending of many differences of opinion to create a strong union that could then establish a new beginning, a new understanding and a new activity upon the Earth?

In keeping with this, you have the Pope coming to the United States and many people meeting and greeting him and making arrangements for his visit, and they belong to many religions. I want to bring out the religions because I see a blending of them, an openness now. The Pope and other religious leaders might not be focused specifically on that blending, but they are the instruments of it; they are the activity focus or the means to allow it to take place — they stir it all up, don't they? The Pope goes forth to various areas, he talks to many people, and, speaking esoterically, what is his purpose? Why is he here? He anchors light and is a visible, tangible focus of faith. He's a unifying factor because he brings attention to the religious aspects of life that can inspire a deeper searching within people of all faiths to activate spiritual meaning in their lives. So you can be inspired by others who don't believe just as you do! Isn't that interesting? The Pope can become a catalyst who causes one to examine, to question, to become introspective; he causes directed activity (whether he realizes it or not) toward integration.

All right, if the Pope were standing here, what would you ask him? Why can't women be priests? Well, I think he would tell you there is a directive that doesn't allow it, a particular structure that he's holding because he was directed to hold it. I think that is important, because what I am seeing in many religions and spiritual groups is that once a specific dictate has been accepted, then there is difficulty in letting go of it, in seeing that it is not engraved in stone, in seeing that a structure is simply a format for *supporting* activity but it is not the goal itself. Structure *must* evolve, it must grow in order to keep pace with evolution on your planet. A direction that is given must be loose enough and flow well enough that it can include all possibilities — and all possibilities include the integration of your planet, integration that is the bringing together of all perspectives into a joint, unified activity that will allow the Earth to reflect true peace, true unity such as has never really existed on the Earth before. Once or twice the Earth began to approach the unified level, but it quickly turned away again. You must see that once you obtain a unified level of peace or integration, you can allow that activity to remain. Evolution does not take away what has been, *if* what has been is already unified. That is important.

Think about your own lives or the lives of friends or relatives. Sometimes you feel as though you've really "got your act together." Everything is flowing well, the activity in your life is flowing nicely, and then something happens and the flow is gone and life seems to fall apart. So ideally you want to keep it all together and see that the activity, when it is directed, doesn't fall off. What happens when someone loses it? The loss of direction is often nonclarity, confusion that has you going through that revolving-door syndrome in which you reiterate the same activity over and over again rather than going beyond it.

Let's say there are twenty-five or thirty religions in your world (there are a great many more, but that is enough for our example). And say the goal is to allow a synthesis of these religions, these philosophies — not in the sense that they all believe the same thing, but that a directed activity comes forth on your Earth that can allow peaceful, harmonious flow to Earth living and to the place where you live it. You want it all to flow harmoniously. Let us say that we on the spiritual level are helping all twenty-five or thirty religions (and we are) to see the positive qualities of all of the others. On the inner planes we are having classes on this, and all of you are attending them, so perhaps the subject seems familiar.

Now, perhaps an event happens on your Earth that doesn't *seem* to have anything to do with this process, and yet it does. Let's say you just had a national election. How does this fit into the integrating process? Does it fit and does it affect the directed activity as you seek to integrate that activity into a specific goal? Focusing many minds upon a common goal or intent can be helpful, but an event that is shattering can be divisive, particularly if it is some sort of military action that may be violently opposed. It can lead you back into a patterned response to the area of integration, rather than the new way that will lead to true world peace as it can be maintained. You could say it takes you back to pre-Lemuria, to those patterns of "We must defend because we will be attacked."

On the other hand, when you see a united effort, such as feeding the starving in Africa (imperfect, certainly, but the situation is better than it has been for a long time), what does that do? It creates an idea. It allows the integrative process an ideal on which to focus. This gives you a good example of what can be done. Are we saying then that activity as expressed physically within every level – self, the community, the country, the world – then affects your evolution and the directed activity (as we've used it here) toward the New Age that you are seeking, or world peace? Yes, it does. In fact, we are delighted with the activity on your Earth, because there is less controversy – well, less than was seen or forecast. So you are doing much better than was anticipated.

You could say the spiritual teachers have an energy blueprint and we put it on the Earth and see which activity has which energy – its kind, its degree, its amount, its direction, and how balanced it is. From this we make these forecasts to see how you get from point A in your evolution to point C, through, of course, point B. You are doing much better than you perhaps had any thought of doing when you came into this life. Most of you set up a projection for your life through this blueprinting, forecasting system that the spiritual teachers gave to your soul level. You looked at what was probably going to come forth on the Earth and you set up the flow of your life with this guidance system. Astrology is another way of saying that you can forecast, through what *you* have allowed to come through self and the Earth also. Of course, it doesn't always work out as forecast. Why? Well, I'm going into something called the will-and-choice area.

What is the will? Determination to do a thing? A thrusting force? Acting on what you perceive? The will means to become active, whether you are a divine Source, a human being, an Earth or anything else. Now, we are talking here about will without differentiating between various levels of will. Personal will makes an effort, it gets things started, but it has not the full scope and understanding of the whole picture because it comes from a particular focus rather than a whole perspective. The divine will is all-encompassing. In the area of polarity the dynamic energy is the igniting process of your creativity. So what is the difference between male polarity, or dynamic energy, and the will?

Personal will is more a way of forcing, and dynamic energy is a more balancing type of energy. The Source certainly uses the will at a divine level to activate, so how does that fit into the male polarity area? Let me state it this way. The divine will brings forth the framework within which the polarities can interact. Certainly the dynamic energy-flow is established by the connecting part that we call the divine will. This is important because most of you have used the will aspect *instead* of the dynamic energy or the male polarity, and in a directed activity one sometimes tries to *force* a goal, which doesn't work. Why can't you force a goal? Because it is not in the pattern of the divine will. What does the will, used on the level where it is forced, set up for you? Obviously you are going in a direction you want to go rather than the direction divine will has set. Is that not activity that is scattered? You *can* accomplish a goal by forcing it, but in the divine sense, the fullest sense, after you have forced it, there is what might be called a boomerang effect. It might not boomerang on the goal, but it will boomerang on your balance or your use of energy.

What we have said is basically "Thy will be done, not mine." What happens when you seek to use your own will? At that moment you separate from the divine structure that the soul level of self has made available to you. You are wandering around outside it, or so it seems. "Thy will be done, not mine" is not when everything stops; it's when, in fact, everything starts.

A true surrender is not a lack of activity; it is an alignment, an allowingness. And then what happens? You enter into your potential, that main flow, and it can be entered only through the activity of surrender. True activity, then, through the surrender process, allows an open-door policy to begin to manifest in your life. What does open-door policy mean? Opportunity.

In your life on the physical plane you meet opportunities, and sometimes they come about in a rather subtle manner. A friend might say to you, "Would you like to go have a cup of coffee and talk a little?" So you go and talk. Is that an opportunity? It can be. That friend might just happen to mention something that is important to you, or you might facilitate something for him or her that is very important. So the opportunities are not only your own; they are opportunities through which you can aid others. If you had said to your friend that you were tired and didn't want to go, you might or might not have closed the door on an opportunity. Does that mean that you should never say no? Of course not. Whatever your choice was, it is never fatal, not something that keeps you following the path of refusal forever. You can always make another choice. You are making a choice every moment, and you do not just surrender once; you surrender at every moment, at every choice you make.

Now, sometimes your soul, through your willingness to be actively a part of the Earth and be aware of many things, can get messages through to you that you can later use in your evolution. But if you are not aware that you are choosing interaction with others and choosing opportunity (or at least allowing the possibility for an opportunity to come in), then sometimes you lose that direction for a while. Some of you have experienced this in the soul integration. The direction seems to be flowing well, seems to be integrating well, and then all of a sudden there doesn't seem to be any flow or integration. What happened? Again you've lost your direction somehow. So pause and think about the kinds of choices you've made lately. Again surrender the will to the highest good: the Source Itself. See what happens. You will find your life regaining purpose, and there is motion and integration and activity in the divine senses. Purposeful direction comes through the surrender process.

Sometimes one is reluctant to enter the area of realizations, but the realizations are the key to making growth. Where there is reluctance, you get a lot of patterns, and working with the patterns can break up the energy that is blocking the area. When the energy is broken up, and you do choose, little by little, the surrendering process, it begins to direct that energy beyond some of the blocks that may still be there. You can see that in the Catholic Church there have been many who have chosen to become nuns, surrendering any participation in the stream of worldly matters. They remain very active, but the directed activity comes from their surrendering process. They are often teachers or nurses and are involved through the directed activity of the Church as an entity as they surrender to it. Sometimes having an earthly, physical focus outside of self can substitute until you are able to direct it through your own growing understanding of how to do it within self. A group energy can begin to direct the transformational process when you take part in it and agree to serve it.

Patterns are a means of easing into the release of blocks. They literally break up the energy. If you have an energy barrier, a mass of energy, use of the patterns can help you ease into the block of energy without creating unnecessary resistance. Then you can break it up and go beyond it. Service and the realization process are as important, if not more important, than pattern removal. We sometimes reference past-life experiences to help you see that you have made the same spiritually nonproductive choices over and over. Then make you realize you want to make better choices this time.

What occurs in the realization process? You see how you created that blocked area. You see how creative you were as you put together the exact components of that block. You see that if you put it together with your creativity, then you can choose to take it apart and go beyond it. It is as though you were writing a play: You can read over what you've written, and if you don't like the way it comes out, you can rewrite it. You can give the characters lines such that they interact more lovingly with one another or in a way that allows each to learn from the other.

For many of you there is a holding on to your own needs because it seems that if you don't have those needs met, you won't *be* anything — there just won't be anything left. There is a loss factor that you get caught up in. Suppose you were given a complete, divine package by the Creator, and He said, "Here it is — a gift. Here is your divine beingness. I give it to you, no strings attached. You can have it now." Then getting to use it as completely as the Source Itself uses *Its* divine package is what you are trying to do. But there is a gap between the two perspectives of using your full divine gifts completely and seeing how the Source uses full divinity. This explains the appearance of loss. There appears to be a loss of your complete use of your abilities. You have not yet seen how to use them as fully and effectively as the Source uses Its abilities. Many react to this divine gift by saying, "Who, me? I'm not quite sure I'm ready to use that divine package comprehensively and fully." Again we face the surrender process. We face the need to surrender fully and we say, "Yes, I'll bring it forth now. I am willing to choose an alignment into that process of using my divine package." (If it doesn't happen completely in five minutes, then you maintain the focus and use whatever time you need.) You can go back again to the past-life scenarios and see some sort of limitation there and, in your new attention to surrender, choose never to accept that limitation again. When you let them all go, then we greet you as a full-fledged cocreator!

Many people are now beginning to approach the point of perceiving that there *is* a Divine Plan. It is a point of balance, of maturity in the ego-personality, of integration, and the soul can come closer, even though not completely anchored in the physical structure. The mental-body development and its interaction with the emotional body and its structure through the physical must have reached a certain point of integration, and also the acceptance of the spiritual body must have reached a certain point. It would be difficult for someone to accept or know what full surrender is without having balanced about 50% of the four-body area. This 50% is at the soul-merger territory, so to speak. You have anchored the light of the soul into the cellular level of self, and balance is the result. Anchoring the soul begins the directed active state. For most of you it takes the soul-merge, the energy level of the soul aligned into the cellular level of self, to begin the alignment of the will to the divine level. The energy body of the soul is much greater than the energy body of the personality level, so it perceives in a correspondingly greater manner, and you find you retain more of what you learn. I used 50%. Naturally the percentage will vary, but you can see that if you've balanced by about 50% the use of the four bodies, then you begin to glimpse what home and the completed cocreator state truly is. Home is the fully surrendered use of the choice, the will area, to the Plan.

Now, the emotional body is the one that might feel some loss as surrender begins to occur. It might feel insecurity or a sense that something is being destroyed as the mental body begins to nudge it. The mental body has begun to see the possibilities, and the physical body, which has been clearing, wants to *do* something as this directed activity begins to take on a format. The emotional body needs to be comforted and supported, and you can do that in your overall consciousness because the other aspects of self will help with it. You could personify each of the bodies and see your cast of characters surrounding the emotional body with caring and support. The spiritual body in particular can say, "We're here for you, and I, the spiritual body, am eternally your source of support." When the choice of surrender is foremost in your mind — that is when you can see that the whole will respond to it and you can know that you are working from a one-pointed focus within the whole. You will not lose that one-pointed focus when you transcend it; it will always be there for you. But as you are seeking to transcend it, you might feel a need to prove it, so to speak. As you begin the surrender process and you see that humanity benefits, that your life benefits, that you are getting results because it's working, that will speed it up. Perhaps seeing that it's "proved" to us, and works, is a personal area, but the Source *gave* us personal perspective. It's all right to have it as long as you recognize that it will continue to include every other perspective also. In other words, there is no need to feel guilt simply because you still have a personal will and personal perspective; instead you will recognize more and more that using it in alignment with the Plan accomplishes a great deal more and is truly a more practical, clear and natural way to operate.

How can you help someone who has not quite reached that 50% balance in the four-body area to move into some experience of surrender? Well, when you say to someone "surrender to the divine will," the words don't have meaning for them unless they have already glimpsed what it's all about. You might use a personal experience to explain it: a person who has chosen to have children and to take on the role of parenthood will understand something of what it means to surrender. A teacher who has chosen teaching because of dedication to the good of the students could offer a glimpse of surrender. There is truly nothing quite like the surrender one enters into for the Divine Plan, but if you can somehow bring even a glimpse down into the Earth level, it may provide a seed that will quicken, either immediately or later, at a point where evolvement allows it. No attempt to offer an opportunity for enlightenment is really lost. In a future life, that truth that was mirrored to one through a physical being lifetimes ago may be realized. You have all worked with spiritual teachers in past lives, and what they planted in you then, you are now activating — it is now growing.

A question has been asked concerning the grid system of energy surrounding the Earth and whether one can tap into it and use it as an energy source — say in machinery. This is not a part of tonight's subject matter, but the answer is yes. In fact, you and mankind do tap into it. The directing of the energy relationship with the grid system is necessary. When you are tapping into it on a random basis, you are not using the *direction* as an opportunity. You might intensify a problem area instead of using it as a stabilizing influence. There is a very dynamic energy running through this particular area of Earth [Arizona]. It is really a combination of energies, but we will speak of it singularly. It has in it the potential for allowing old patterns to be dropped. If you are having a difficult day and your emotions are stirred up and you tap into this part of the grid system, it can intensify whatever you are caught up in. If, however, you tap into it at an angle that relates it without expressing it as a square (as in astrology), and if the angle of interaction is helpful to you, then it can help stabilize your life. You could say that the grid system of the Earth is the energy structure of the Earth. All of you have a component energy structure within self, and the Earth's energy structure can be used to help balance and stabilize you.

If you want to use the grid system to run an airplane, then you have to study the grid system. You have to understand what kind of energy is available, where the plane is going, how to make sure of a constant supply, and how to combine the types of aggregate energy that run through the grid system where you are (they are not the same all over the Earth). The grid system literally is a webbing. It is not, however, the same as the twelve-energy pattern-flow that Djwhal Khul gave you. It is interlocking energy — literally the life force that encircles your planet.

Let's say you want to drill an oil well. You go where you think is will be easy to tap into oil. You have to know what particular energy you need and know what energy that area contains and what purpose you will use that energy for. On the other side of the Earth, there might be some other type of energy required for this combination of energies you need, so you would tap into it in a rather intricate way. There might be five different areas you would need to tap into. Then you would need to maintain an opening into that flow so it won't shut down on you. As you can see, it means you must understand a great deal more about energy than you do. We plan to have energy-synthesis classes to help you understand energy and perhaps understand the grid system. You cannot speak of the grid as high or low — it is all a part of the etheric web of your Earth. The grid system can be tapped into for any level of use. You are, through the physical planet, tapping into the cosmic energy, which is literally unlimited. Your Earth is a much greater receiver than any of you are individually. Your Earth's use might not be totally unlimited, but I can't imagine humanity using it up.

There is a correlation between the energy systems — the meridians, the acupuncture points of the body, the grid system of the planet, and the cosmos. An you can tap into the flow on every level and use the higher chakras and higher rays to purify, cleanse, activate, stretch, align and sensitize. The higher rays are there to sensitize the energy flows, that you may recognize the abilities that lie within them.

Meditation to Sensitize to the Energy Flows

❦ Become as balanced as you can and take some deep breaths. Do not cross your legs.

❦ Now begin to sense an energy. It is coming in through your head, through the crown chakra. I am not going to talk about the chakras. Don't do anything about it, just sense the energy there.

❦ What is the energy doing? It fills the head. Is it seeking a direction? Is it moving in a random manner? Try to sense this energy.

🐞 Now it is in the ear area. What is happening to the ears? They are being sensitized to this higher possibility; the energy is there. Listen now to the energy within the ear area. Now that energy comes into the eyes. Seeing takes place in many ways, but right now sense the energy only in the eye area. It is as if the eyes are eager for this energy; they receive it; they sense it. The energy is present and the eyes are receiving it now. In the third-eye area there is much energy.

🐞 Begin to sort that out. Send some to the left, some to the right, some to the top of the head and some directly down to the rest of the body. Send a little to the ears, to the mouth, to the cheeks, to the tongue – energy all through the head. Now it has been sorted out, it has been directed. Now sense this energy as having a purpose.

🐞 It has come together in its purpose and now it's moving into the neck area. Sense the energy in the neck. The throat might feel full of energy. Note it. Feel it. If there is some pressure, then send the energy beyond the throat, down into the body or up into the head; it doesn't matter, for it isn't directional here. But sense the flow of the energy in the neck area. It is flowing now. The head has directed it and the throat and neck begin to experience that flow.

🐞 Now it is entering the heart area, the upper chest, the shoulders, the upper arms. Sense that energy. Sense it. If a sense of pressure develops, send the energy beyond it, and if you need to, take a deep breath here and don't let the pressure build up, but sense that a lot of energy has been activated within self.

🐞 Now the energy moves to the solar-plexus area, the stomach area, through the small intestines. Sense that energy. It is there; it is very active within you now. Again, do not let pressure build up; allow that energy to flow. Now it flows into the lower intestine and the sexual area, and then to the base-chakra area. Sense that energy that's there, and if the pressure begins to build up, flow it down to the legs. Flow the energy; the hips are feeling a lot of energy and now the upper legs respond to this energy, this active state that is coming into self now.

🐞 Now the lower arms and hands are feeling energy, and the lower legs, all of the extremities are feeling this energy.

🐞 Sense the energy throughout the whole body. It is a very active state within self – a lot of energy. You are sensitized to the entrance of energy by noticing it within the body and directing the flow of it – a purposeful direction throughout the physical structure.

🐞 Now let's use this energy. You are all active, and now I will direct it for your Earth. See a beautiful stream of blue energy coming forth from self. See it in any way you wish – through the third eye, through the crown chakra, through the heart, through the other chakras, through them all if you wish. Send it now to the Earth and see the Earth literally surrounded by this blue *light. Light up the Earth now, flow the energy to the Earth. The Earth is benefiting from the active state within self now. All together now, energize the Earth. The blue energy goes forth and it encompasses the Earth. It flows and it begins to lighten the Earth; the Earth becomes lighter and lighter. More and more blue. It raises the Earth now.*

❦ *That flow through self to the Earth – you have used self as a transmitter of energy through your active state to aid the Earth. The Earth literally sings with energy as it rises. It goes up, up, up now. Feel it, know it, see it, sense it. The Earth is getting lighter through your efforts now. Flow with it as it goes up, up, up. Sense it.*

❦ *Now through the heart center send the pink stream, the love stream, and surround the Earth with the love aspect. The love aspect goes forth now. As it goes forth through all of you, through the active state that you have recognized, through your active recognition that you will surrender now to the creative process, you will allow through this surrendering an alignment process into the Earth and its divine becomingness. Sense then the evolution of the Earth; get in touch with it and celebrate it. You have surrendered to it and recognize that it is working now.*

❦ *Gradually now begin to come back, but know that the Earth continues to utilize the energy of you all, the transmitters that you all are in its evolution. Each one of you has, through surrender, through divine intent, through love, aided the whole, and of course self, at the same time.*

I thank you, dear ones, and good evening.

✧ E I G H T ✧

Increasing the Igniting Process
through Polarity

Vywamus through Lillian Harben

POLARITY CONSISTS OF TWO STREAMS, AT LEAST IN THE PRESENT COSMIC DAY.
In other cosmic days it's been more than two; many people remember
the triangular days when there were three polarities. But in this cosmic day
there's a balance of two polarities, the male and female.

How do you see your polarity? You can see what you believe about your
polarity from what you mirror into your life. If you're female you'll probably
mirror in your male partner what you believe about the male polarity. If
you're a male, you'll probably mirror in your female partner what you believe
about the female polarity. If you want to look at what you believe about your
own polarity, often your female friends will reflect that to you.

You can look at your polarity in your body. The right part of the body
represents the male polarity and the left part the female — especially the arms
and legs. You can notice whether it's the right side or the left side that's
bothering you and you can trace it back to something in the area of that
polarity. The best balance of polarity is when the two are creating together.
The way the creative process works with the polarities is that the female is
receptive and the male is dynamic. The female gathers all of the information
together and puts it in a nice little egg and then the male fertilizes it. On
the other planes the male ignites it; he makes it happen. So the female puts
it together and the male makes it happen. That doesn't mean that if you are
without a female partner or a male partner, half of your ability to create is
gone. This all occurs within the male and female polarities, and if you
balance them within, then you'll be able to be creative and dynamic at the
same time in the same process.

There are very few people who can really use the dynamic male polarity. There's a lot of confusion about it. The male polarity has a little bit of the female, and the female polarity has a little bit of the male in it. It isn't black and white. When you are looking at the mirroring of your partner, it's probably only 75% to 90% accurate. Though the subconscious does a beautiful job of hooking in all of these relationships to fit your particular needs, still it's very difficult to hook in absolutely everything. To find somebody with everything that you believe about the male polarity is rather difficult, so what usually happens is that your relationship partner has most of the qualities, but some of them you won't recognize as being within yourself, so it really doesn't have any relationship to what you believe about the female and the male polarities. If you've had several emotional-relationship partners, it's interesting to look and see the repeating pattern in those partners. Do they never support you emotionally? Do they always look at their needs first, or are they dependable? Are they responsible? Look at all of these things repeating in your male or female polarity partners and you'll see what your belief is.

So when you come to the point at which you understand somewhat what your beliefs are about, then it is helpful to personify the male and the female polarities and have them talk to each other. Have your male polarity talk to your female polarity and see what he thinks — what he'd like to see changed about her, why they can't work together, if they aren't together (and 98% aren't; we've seen just a few balanced polarities in all of the time we've been working). Then talk to the female and see what she sees as missing in the male polarity and why they can't work together. Now, in a marriage or an emotional relationship, if you're a female and the relationship is with a male, you will tend to use more of your female polarity in relating to that partner; the partner will tend to use more of his male polarity in relating to you. Someone who is really balanced polaritywise can easily do that: they can have a good relationship if their polarity is very balanced, because if they have a relationship with someone of the opposite sex, they will tend to accentuate their own polarity. In the case of homosexuals, it has been my experience that they mirror the polarity of the part they play in relationship. You can still see the mirroring effect in a homosexual relationship, but you have to look at it in a different way.

You will often find that the male polarity will feel about the female what she's projecting herself. The male polarity might say, "I don't feel that any of her creativity is worth igniting at this point — none of it looks very good to me." The female will say, "My creativity isn't really worth igniting." So you see, you've got this false belief that extends over both of your polarities and they're picking it up in their own way. That's usually the case if you can find how they go together and you can find the overall belief that's causing both of them to react in that way.

I'd like to go back to that perfectly balanced situation in which the female is creating and the male is igniting. In other words she plans what needs to be done, gathers all of the information, has it all in a nice little package, and then the male comes along and makes it happen. If you want to design a picnic table, the female might decide how she wants it to look and make a sketch, then he does the work. If you're having a party, she gets everything ready and has everything all laid out, and he comes in and pours the drinks and goes around shaking everybody's hand and igniting the party. So it's working together like that. They both understand what their role is and they both are willing to do it. Neither of them feels put upon because they both have roles within themselves. Of course, this doesn't mean that a single person can't throw a good party!

But at this particular time 98% are not balanced, and that is because there's so much in the mass consciousness having to do with polarity. There are all kinds of misunderstandings about male and female polarity that we inherit. For example, a lot of people use the *will* as a substitute for the dynamic male energy. They say, "Gee, I can't seem to get this going, so I'm just going to *do it!*" They are bringing through the intent to manifest, but it's a forcing. There's definitely a directional aspect to the dynamic flow on all levels. It knows where it's going and it knows what it's going to do, and nothing stands in its way. You've probably met people who have such a dynamic flow that when they want to do something they just prepare and it happens, and there aren't any pros and cons or plans B, C and D. To me it's the cosmic fire that comes through there. The cosmic fire is the electrical part of the undifferentiated white light. It's the same as the kundalini force, which is dynamic energy. It's based on the life force. The undifferentiated white light can be separated into the rays plus the cosmic fire. The force of the kundalini is directed. If it's undirected, there's a problem, because it's always trying for a direction. If you feel like it's undirected, then it's on its way there but it's getting blocked; it's being resisted at all of these points and it keeps moving in some direction to where you can let it through. That's why kundalini can be a problem if you don't have a clear channel. It just as often comes in from the top as from the base chakra. It is a natural thing flowing through the transformational process we use. You notice before the soul-merge that there's a lot of work done on the etheric body. We do a lot of work checking that our spinal flow is clear. The teachers have brought in a lot of different things checking on that. They make sure before the soul-merge class that that's pretty clear.

The Indians and all of the ancient peoples have recognized this cosmic fire, but sometimes yogic exercises will bring up the kundalini unnaturally. This can open the lower chakras and start them up but sometimes all the upper chakras stay blocked. We unblock the higher chakras right away so that as it comes up it doesn't have anything stopping it.

What is the role of the dynamic force in your daily life? Well, creation itself — it is a part of the creative process, and that's why it's so important to study and understand and be able to use it. The creative process itself will balance your spiritual development and enable you to move toward the ascension. The dynamic force is regulated by a perfect balance in the polarities. This dynamic process lets you move forward with the impetus needed to move to the next levels, to open the higher chakras. It takes quite a bit of energy to go past that crown chakra, open into the higher chakras and make ready for the body of light. This dynamic force is actually the electrical properties, and when you are clear and bring it through, it is the total energy of the creative process. The dynamic energy comes through and manifests whatever has been invoked in creation on the spiritual plane by the Creator and the cocreators. On the lower planes, whatever you are invoking will be made manifest through the creative process, utilizing the dynamic energy.

Have you ever had something that you desired to create be created very easily — maybe with just a thought, and the next day there it was? And have you had other things that you thought about and invoked but nothing whatsoever happened? The difference is that in the first one you did not block the dynamic energy; you used your invocative energy and it automatically started triggering the dynamic force. It was triggered by thoughts and emotion and desire, and those create an opening for it to come in, but if you put up a resistance, then as it comes in, it doesn't go any further. For instance, if you believe that you want something but are really unworthy of it, then it stops there. So if you keep invoking it, the dynamic energy blasts a hole through the resistance, but that can also be uncomfortable. If you keep invoking something that you have a strong resistance to, and you invoke it with a lot of energy, pulling in a lot of heavy emotion while invoking it, then you can blast through that but it will come to pass in a chaotic energy format. You need to be very clear and calm and in a loving state of mind as you create, or else the energy will become chaotic because you are creating through a chaotic type of thinking. That will create something that you probably don't want.

So before you get ready to create something, it would be wise to get in a very calm frame of mind and center yourself in a meditative state. Then open the third eye and the crown chakra and invoke from there. Always invoke from the highest chakra that you have open. When you feel you've opened your eighth chakra comfortably, then invoke from that chakra, because the higher the chakra, the more rapid and dynamic the results.

In order to know which chakra you're invoking from, center yourself and your consciousness at that point. If you are working from the third eye, center your consciousness there and see yourself as being in the third eye. The crown chakra you might see as the thousand-petaled lotus; in the eighth chakra you'd see yourself above the crown chakra in an even more encompassing energy. Some people would see it as green-violet, because that's the way they reference it. It would be ideal for all of you to keep a calm, loving outlook and realize that you're creating all of the time and to remember that you want to create something that everybody wants and needs.

Perhaps you've noticed that the world today seems to consist of many unmarried people. Marriages don't seem to last, and a lot of people are choosing careers instead of getting married – even the young people. You question the purpose in this and whether everybody needs to get back to the married state in order to balance. As we have said before, there's a great deal of misunderstanding about male and female polarities, and up until recently it hasn't been talked about much. Everybody thought it wasn't good to bring everything out into the open. It's very good that there's now much more of a feeling of unlimitedness in our society, which is showing up in the number of people choosing to be single or just having relationships but not making a permanent commitment because they want to pursue their own growth. There are certain advantages for society in having made this changeover, because now it's allowing this examination of what polarity is and what marriage is and what commitment to the other sex is. And it comes to the point where you're asking, "What is this two-screened system?" It is the basis of creation. So it's not a bad thing – it's an okay thing. It will be useful because people will keep studying it as long as they go into and out of relationships. They will eventually look at repeating patterns. Perhaps they can see what their beliefs about polarity are when they can see a situation repeat itself. It begins to impress upon you if you marry four alcoholic husbands! Then you begin to say, "Wait a minute! I think I have a problem here." There's nothing like repetition to make you look at something, and that's the advantage of changes: You get the chance to look at something you've never looked at before.

There might be one partner who is into metaphysics and one who is not. The first one might begin to drift or pull away from the partner who is not and go toward people who are in metaphysics and form new relationships. Often they believe that the male polarity is not capable of spiritual qualities or that it can't understand the spiritual principles. If they remove that false belief, sometimes there is an opening there. In many cases there is an opportunity in relationships for allowingness. Once you have totally cleared, your own male and female polarities – and often your partner – will dramatically change. Your partner may make a surprising transformation, because he or she no longer has the hook that he or she came in with that you have to play this game. Once you drop the hook, then they may play the game but not with you, or they may not have to play the game anymore.

What do we mean by "totally clearing the polarity area"? We have repeated that you're not going to be completely clear until you can manifest the cocreator level. Actually, the complete clearing would be the cocreator level, and I don't expect that tomorrow. But as you move toward that clearness, it's most noticeable in the creative process. When you aren't creating any more of the emergencies on the male or female side, then you will notice your creativity has become more balanced. As you notice that you are creating in a clear, comfortable, unforced way, then you know that you've reached toward that clarity and you've moved along toward ascension.

Sometimes you can notice that you need to look at the polarity area. One of our group had a sudden feeling down her left side and across her heart as she got out of her car today. Now, that is the receptive side symbolizing the gathering process: "I'm going to gather it, I'm going to use it, so that I can make some sense out of it and create from it." So she had gathered this particular sound vibration that she picked up from music in the car, and it suddenly stimulated experiences she had had that were very traumatic. You can always look at what side is reacting, and it will tell you something about what your problem is and what area you're working on. That reaction tells her about her female polarity. It tells her that she is very aware and very receptive but also that there's some programming there which says, "As I feel that particular vibration I know I'm connecting with something that is frightening." So there is the fear, the tingling, the resistance that she felt. (The music she was listening to was "Heaven and Hell," and she hadn't gotten past the Hell part. It is a particularly stimulating piece of music. Those vibrations are definitely tuned in to the lower aspects, so I don't advise playing it.)

When someone has a heart problem it is felt on the left side, and if someone has a liver problem it's going to be on the right side. Does that mean that heart attacks are a receptive problem and hepatitis is a male problem? Not necessarily. I think you can tell more about the polarities from the limbs. For the organs it would be more accurate to go by the chakra area. If the organ is just a little to the right or left of center, it does not particularly associate with the polarity. But if you can't move your right arm or if your knee doesn't move, then you're in the polarity area.

Someone might say to you, "I have great pain in my heart and also in my arm, and I can hardly breathe." If they don't know anything about metaphysics you shouldn't say, "Well, how is your left polarity and your receptivity?" That of course isn't practical. But if they're metaphysically inclined, it is something to look at, because at every point we have a choice. There's a choice whether or not to accept a physical disability, so depending on how advanced you are in the metaphysical area or in your own growth or in your own knowingness, it is often worth looking at — unless it's something that's too much of an emergency to take the time to look at.

Suppose you have a recurring injury — in the right leg for instance. The right leg usually indicates that there's a resistance to moving forward, a resistance to taking the thrusting action to move forward dynamically. It's something that's important to look at.

What about the balance of the polarities in the monadic level? In the monadic area the polarities are quite well balanced, which is necessary at the monadic level because creating at that level is much more serious. You're given this playpen, as Djwhal Khul calls it, here on Earth where you can create without causing too much trouble, but in the monadic area you don't want to create in an unbalanced way.

You might wonder why your body has things like an appendix which it doesn't need. Is that someone's mistake on the monadic level? The blueprint of the Adam Kadmon, your particular type of body, was very carefully designed for the energies that were prevalent at the time the model was started. Since then several modifications have occurred naturally or, let's say, selectively. The appendix did have a useful function at one time. Some people don't find the tonsils necessary, but they have had and still have a creative function. So nothing redundant was really put in the body, but we have made them redundant through our development. I think you'll find that as we approach the New Age, the body will change a great deal because the higher energies will make a lot of the digestive process unnecessary. It will allow much more rapid healing because the body's resistance to healing will be lightened. Of course, the DNA itself will change a lot, becoming more fourth-dimensional, so to speak, so that you will be able to stop aging and even reverse the aging process, which you have already started to work on.

There will be some changes in the reproductive process that will make it quite a bit less burdensome on the female. It will become possible to use the creative process outside of the body and to allow fertilization outside of the body. The digestive system will not be used quite as much and the male and female genital systems will not be used quite as much. The respiratory system will come into play more as far as breathing is concerned. You'll find many "breatharians" who can bring in through the breath the energy they need to sustain the body, and that's why the digestive system won't be as necessary.

How can you use the male polarity right now? How can we tell the difference between the will and the male polarity? You never feel pressured when you use the male polarity. There's a comfortable and direct flow, and you just feel that it's happening without any resistance. You can visualize yourself at the point of the crown chakra and know that you're there and there's no resistance to your male polarities. Just allow this to happen. This would be practiced to allow that triangle of the male and female polarities to come to a perfect balance and see that flow coming together, totally blended, totally moving through your body. That will provide the visualization to the subconscious and beyond it. It may of course stir things up a little because of the resistance, but the more you can visualize it, the more you can accept it and look at causes.

We may need to clarify the use of the divine will versus human will. The will area is a little different from the dynamic flow in the male polarity. The will area is what you'd call the first ray, so it is a little different from the dynamic energy of cosmic fire. When the first-ray energy is aligned with the divine energy, it flows very smoothly. If you've always had a lot of will that can be aligned into service, you can make yourself do things, but what you're trying to do is to use the male polarity, and that might be what you haven't yet caught on to. Instead of trying to use the will you can use visualization in accomplishing something because you want to get it up to where it's in the spiritual plane – beyond the polarity level to the monadic level – where you know that the polarities are balanced. You establish yourself in that point and wait until you feel that flow and then begin to work. You have to experience the point where it's already balanced. Of course, that is more of your potential – you aren't going to stay there today, but you will one of these days. It's just like the situation before the soul-merge, where people reach for the soul and could enjoy the feeling, but then they'd keep slipping away from it.

I've been asked what you can do on a day-to-day basis when you're interacting with people and you see that they're unbalanced or that you're unbalanced when you're with them. Well, you can look at your job and see how you might advance the female polarity in that job. If you're interacting with a male, you might want to see if you can do the female gathering process to the point that it would aid a male in doing the igniting process. Sometimes in your culture women use the male polarity in work more than the female polarity. You can see which one needs to be used in your job and use it. That's comfortable for your work, but when you need to balance within, it means balancing the two roles and allowing each to do their own job. With a relationship partner you want to have the sex that fits your body, but in a job you need to take the role of the male polarity because that is what that job needs.

The important thing is to be aware of what you are doing, which role you are taking, and what you're trying to do, and not to mix them at any time. At any given point you're either *gathering* or you're *igniting*, but you're not gathering and igniting at the same time. In a lot of offices there might be a boss and a secretary. The secretary gets all of the reports and information ready and then she gives it to her boss. He takes it and goes out and sells this material and manifests it in the physical. This is acting out the female/male polarities as you have them in the body. There's no reason why he couldn't just sit there and gather all the information and then go over to his other polarity and go out and sell it – if he were perfectly balanced within and had a lot of time. You can do both jobs yourself, but you should know when you are moving from one to the other; if he started to go out to sell and noticed that he didn't have the right information, went back and gathered some more information, then went back again to locate the person he's trying to sell to – you can see how confusing that would get. You need to be sure that everything is gathered for the ignition. The ignition is like lightning: You don't keep calling it back in!

Vywamus through Janet McClure

Igniting means "to experience the flow." The goal is to keep pace with the cosmic day itself. In other words, there is an ideal role model, the Creator in Its interaction, and we seek to build the interaction that can dynamically follow the evolution of the Sourceness. Each time you seek to create through the will alone you are attempting to encompass a structure, a flow, but what you're really doing is shutting down or closing off the flow. You box it in, you enclose it. As the will enters, it literally locks the creative process. Now, it might lock it into a level of a creative effort, but it can't flow beyond that because it's locked into one particular level by the will. It is necessary to take the will and connect it at the divine-will level and open that flow so that it can reference that ideal, the Creator's dynamic flow. In other words, you can use that dynamic flow of the Source Itself through yourself. But the only way you can enter it is to relax and allow. You might say you allow the structure of the flow to become identified as that cosmic flow instead of the personal flow, which is more limited. It must flow so that it can become all-encompassing.

You're surrendering to the creative process itself, which contains that dynamic portion of it. Without that surrender process you don't get the dynamic portion. You get a limited portion that you can ignite in a sense through the personal will aspect, but it's more limited. It does allow creation, but only a limited perception of it. The goal is to encompass every point of view. Have you thought about that? Eventually you're going to be that Source that can view from every point of view. To ignite that major effort does not take forcing; it takes letting go. The more you try holding on, the less dynamic it is. It becomes more and more limited, or more and more *set* in the structures you are familiar with or that you've used in the past. You don't get into the full potential in your sequential time.

As you learn to flow in sequential time it's for a learning process. You really take a look at the learning process, and each moment you learn and you let go of what has been, and then you can go to the next level and energize it and learn from it. The soul takes a picture of that and learns from it. It is a letting go of what has been through a sequential time. The igniting process can also be used in that manner, learned through in that manner. Each moment the soul can learn. In this area of igniting, the soul is still learning. It's not an expert in this area yet, but it's much more comfortable with it than with the personality level. It can learn by taking a look at your igniting process. In fact, this is what is happening with each of you. The soul becomes more and more involved in your life as it begins to guide your life. It is perhaps not satisfied with using the will, which limits you, and it is learning the thing that will work for you on the physical level.

Because the soul hasn't been involved very much on the physical plane as it comes in now, it sees this and it says, "It'll never work. It just won't work. We might as well get rid of that approach because it isn't going to work." Then what happens? The soul begins to look at it and says, "Now, let me see. I want to look at that." It will pull, and mirroring to you will be an event. And the soul says, "Oh my goodness. I don't think that that was what we wanted to create. That didn't work. Look at that." You might bring in a patterned response in this area of the polarities as the soul is digging around in it trying to learn about it. And that's what all of you are seeing in one way or another. It might not mirror to you on the physical plane, but for some of you it will. And within all of you there is a certain amount of this. It may be simply in the thought process, in the holding-on process rather than the letting-go process.

Now, for some of you there are deep fears in the igniting process, and that's why I've begun to talk about this Heaven and Hell connotation. You always wanted to know what Hell was. Well, I propose to tell you my perception of it. At the Source level there is the energy that is part of the cosmic day, and that is what we might call directing energy, evolving energy — energy that all of you are learning to use as you learn to create. This is what has been termed "Heaven": directed energy.

"Hell" is perhaps the energy that is not yet directed. Let's say that this tape here is the cosmic day. The paper, which is the field around it, is the area that is seeded. It is an energy area that contains all kinds of energy, particularly the dynamic energy. It is the area that the Source will flow into as It evolves. It has not yet been entered by Sourceness. It is not yet directed. It is undirected energy, but energy that is very vibrant, very dynamic.

If you enter that — and most of you have accidentally — then this energy, because it is not yet directed, surrounds you. It knows innately that each of you is a creator or a potential one. It comes to you for direction. Now, because you have not yet completely integrated your creative understanding at the cocreator level, when it comes and looks for direction from you, you don't know how to give it direction. So what you get is chaos. This is "Hell." You have entered the undirected chaotic energy that you are not capable of giving full direction, and the result is called "burning in an eternal fire." It doesn't mean that you will burn there eternally, but those beliefs are there. When you entered it "accidentally," you were pulled out of it by Sourceness or by the directed energy of those who embody it. From that, beliefs were formed about dynamic energy and what happens if you ignite the creativity: "Will it again involve me in this chaotic energy that I don't know how to direct?" It's part of the subconscious — what I call illogical logic. It puts apples and oranges together and gets nice pears. It simply uses what it has within it and comes forth with a perception that you're stuck with until you can realize beyond it. So the key ingredient to learning to use your dynamic qualities is to resolve your relationship with this chaotic energy.

Now, it has a hook in it, and that hook is the self-worth area. The hook is, "Well, if I get this I probably deserved it. I probably am caught up in it because I didn't do something right." That's another part of that illogical logic. It doesn't go with anything, but the subconscious puts it together that way.

You are all seeking to be secure in your creative process. You're seeking to bridge the gap in your perception and understanding of how to use your creativity just as the Source is using Its creativity. There is a gap between the Source's usage and your usage of the same energy. When you fall into the gap, that is chaotic energy. Most of you are seeking to bridge the gap with the dynamic energy. You fall into the gap and you say, "Uh-oh. My self-worth has put me here and I don't have enough energy because I've lost it trying to get out." Most of you are coming along well in your understanding of this. You're beginning to see that that bridge is primarily trust. Secondly, we're going to really get into love. What is love? It's easy enough to say, but what is love? What does it mean to love? How does this love structure, which we've all said is the Whole, work?

In your own channels you will begin to receive information on love. When you put together all of the information that all of you see, then we're going to have a structure of encompassing love that helps you bridge the gap to that dynamic, creative level all of you are seeking. Yes, it is rather the "abyss." You know, that was kind of a revelation to me, and I think it is going to make the difference: the love area is going to bridge the gap for you!

So a lot of you are afraid of the igniting because the igniting is what threw you into the pit. In that pit there isn't any energy. You haven't bridged to the energy of the Source. It's also a separation, and many of you have had patterns regarding separation from the Source Itself. So why did the igniting throw you into the pit? It simply is a misinterpretation of that event of entering this energy that had not yet been directed. There is a lot of the dynamic quality of energy there, but no one except the cocreators had used it in a directed sense. No one knows how to do that because it is not just a matter of using it — it is a matter of making the integrative process a part of it.

Let's go back to the polarity issue. You remember the female stream that gathers and integrates and the male that directs. Without the interaction there's not a clear, balanced perception of the way creation exists. In order to utilize this dynamic flow, one must have a clear interaction between the two flows. You're always going to have to look at both sides. If you're looking at the receptive energies, then look at the male or dynamic energies too. "It takes two to tango," as the old saying goes. The causal area as I have stated is basically in the receptive energy. There's going to be a bouncing or an effect from one to the other.

Now, have you noticed that when you experience something, most of you form beliefs about it? This falling in the gap was an all-encompassing experience. Think about Heaven and Hell. How often do you hear those words? It's very much a part of your mass consciousness now. So what is Hell? It's not being able to integrate your life, isn't it? When you get very scattered, isn't that Hell?

Meditation

❧ See yourself and your twin polarity. If you are a woman see yourself as the woman that you know as the physical body but see a man there also. If you are a man see your male physical body but see a woman there also. This twin focus allows it to be a loving one. Place a stream of pink energy in your heart chakra and flow it to your polarity partner. Feel the love flowing from you and to you. Sense this flow. Now raise this personal view of the polarity area to the cosmos itself. Sense it and now become a center of that flow. You send forth love and you receive it from every point of view. This is a polarity focus. It is necessary and it flows. It allows and it flows. It releases and it flows. It is dynamic and it flows. It relaxes and it flows. It expands and it flows. It allows and it flows. There is a flow there from the heart center that is a polarity. Sense that flow, the reciprocal flow of All That Is as the heart centeredness is emphasized here. Structure the flow through the love area. It flows now. It becomes greater and it flows now. It is ignited and it flows now. The structure enlarges and it flows now. Greater and greater and it flows now. More and more and it flows now. You accept love and you send it forth. The polarity of existence. The flow. Sense within self a resolution coming from the love area. A resolution. A learning. A completion. And again send out love and feel it flow back to you. What have you built? A support system through the love area. The polarity and allowingness of that polarity interaction is love. Accept the dynamic flow of love energy. It is self and your creative interaction with All That Is.

❧ Come back gently, knowing that love is an igniter when it flows reciprocally. What it ignites, dear ones, is you and your creativity. Thank you.

✧ N I N E ✧

The Integrative Process of Your Electrical Structure

Y OUR MERIDIAN SYSTEM CONSISTS OF A FLOW OF TINY IMPULSES WHICH stream from the great brain center, although you have other centers within the body that also send out these impulses. We could call the heart an even greater center, potentially, than the brain. But none of you as yet are able to use the heart center as dynamically or as completely as you will within the next step in your development.

Your heart, which centers the flow in many, many ways within your physical body, is already being used comprehensively. It is a main integrative point within your body, but its greatness electrically is just beginning to be expressed.

Your electrical system is awareness, or consciousness in motion. Its movement is excitable, it is magnetic, it is radiant. It delves through its expression into every part of your body, creating the means to use that vehicle as an instrument that houses your awareness.

Each electrical impulse flowing from the brain stimulates the cellular level and the systems that create a life process within your physical body. The developing centers are changing from the specific third-dimensional vibratory rate that was your base electrically to a more subtle, a finer and perhaps a more intense vibratory rate. Some of that may seem in opposition, and your bodies think so, too.

Right now on Earth there is a great deal of sorting out of all the electrical possibilities within your body. You might not realize that all of your organs vibrate at a slightly different rate, so the overall vibratory rate of your body is a composite of many different vibrations held together by an integrative process within the centers. You have many subcenters of integration – in your shoulders, in your hips, at the bottom of your feet and many other places. But it seems to me that the heart and brain are being especially stressed by this time of change occurring within your physical structure.

Each vibration is a beat, which is the life force in action. It beats to the tune of your consciousness in that particular area. One of the most important processes you are going through physically is balancing the vibratory rate of the right and left side of the body — the polarity. For some of you there is an irregularity in the beat of one side that confuses the other and creates an electrical response which cannot create a harmonious integrative process. If you have insomnia and patterns of anxiety, part of the physical reason is an inharmonious vibratory compatibility factor between the halves of your physical body.

Your electrical system is the perfect integrator. Its pulsing is both radiant and receptive. It is the Source's consciousness in movement. As you look at what you have manifested in your physical body, it shows you exactly what needs to be done in order to have that harmonious and free-flowing vehicle mirror a clear understanding of your piece of Sourceness.

Symbolism

The Body Representations

Toes	Specific focus within foundation
Feet	Foundation
Ankles	Flexibility within new effort
Calf	Substance of forward movement
Knees	Full movement that bends to divine will
Upper Leg	Support of forward movement
Hips	How movement fits into main part of manifested purpose
Trunk of Body	Structural support system
Left Side of Body	Receptivity
Right Side of Body	Dynamic flow
Middle Back	Heart radiance
Lower Back	Support
Neck	Connector into manifestation
Head	Divine thinking; concepts and putting together concepts
Teeth	Specifics within the thinking process
Hair	Thoughts
Shoulders	Structural support
Upper Arm	Cocreator level
Elbow	Flexibility
Lower Arm	Support for grasping process

Wrist	Mobility
Hand	Grasping life, potential
Fingers	Focus
Fingernail	Growing focus

The Internal Body Representations

Brain	Administrative center
Pineal Gland	Contact point with soul and monad
Pituitary Gland	Blending/integrative focus
Thyroid Gland	Regulatory organ, a control factor; reflects whether control is in balance
Parathyroid Gland	Focus to "grasp" soul energy
Heart	Radiant center
Thymus	Regulates higher abilities of the heart to receive and share from the heart's point of view
Breasts	Nurturing focus
Lungs	Physical expander of life-force area
Liver	Integrator into cocreator process
Gall Bladder	Sorting out the process, discernment
Stomach	Digestive tool that breaks up emotional resistance
Spleen	Puts things together that are clearer through physical expression
Kidneys	Releasing process for old emotional patterns of behavior
Adrenals	Key to balancing endocrine system, regulate clear use of soul level
Ureter	Connects your personal releasing to that of mass consciousness
Bladder	Brings in another universal focus as a stabilizer
Small Intestine	Bridge between soul and monad
Large Intestine	Bridge between soul and the Earth
Bowels	(lower intestine) Bridge to Earth
Uterus	Receptive expander
Vagina	Receptive flow connector
Ovaries	Divine possibilities storage system
Gonads	Connection to genetic expansion
Testicles	Dynamic storage
Skin	Main releasing organ
Connective Tissue	Active use of the plan
Blood Vessels	Purity
Bones	Acceptance of divine structure/the plan

Functions of the Chakras

Soul Star (8th)	Needs to accept divine equality
Crown (7th)	Accesses potential
Third Eye (6th)	Motivates integration
Throat (5th)	Motivates part in the plan
Heart (4th)	Center of progress; home base
Solar Plexus (3rd)	Motivates the heart
Polarity (2nd)	Movement
Base (1st)	Foundation

✦ T E N ✦

Magnetism

I T IS DELIGHTFUL TO SEE ALL OF YOUR SHINING FACES, TO SEE YOUR AURAS. I'D like to say that I think all of you polish your auras just for me. They are so bright and shining, and you come together in the brightness. It attracts all of the angelic kingdom, so let us begin by attuning to the energy in the room and see how many more of you there are besides those with physical bodies. You could say this is a class that is being taught in many kingdoms. You have some plants here, and some beings that are called little people, some beings who are close to the Earth.

I want to give you some conceptual understanding of magnetism, but also some experiential understanding of it. We keep feeding the conceptual into your understanding so you will know what is happening on the Earth and why things are occurring as they are. Does the Earth seem a different place from a few years ago? It's simply not as it was, is it? You might call it instant effects from causes. They just come up and slap you right in the face. What has created that? Well, it's called magnetism. What does the word itself say? From a physical standpoint, it is a force that attracts to it whatever it can. In the case of humanity, we are attracting to us and the Earth that which we need for the evolutionary process.

By clearing, understanding ourselves and releasing patterns and misperceptions within self, magnetism attracts opportunities to you. It is a mechanism that is mutually attractive. I have defined light as "the interactive factor of vibration" — as two types of energy come together, they create light. The mechanism that attracts and brings them together is called magnetism. It is that mutually attractive force that creates an interaction from which light comes forth. It is very important to see what is happening within each of you now. The soul level of self, the spiritual component, is your real identity. It is that part of self which understands beyond what you understand. It has a growing perception of who and what you are and why you are here; it is that part of self which is united with other souls to create what we have called the Plan. That is what the soul is. And it is *attracting* everything it needs to create a clearer understanding within the physical structure and within your consciousness here on the Earth — a way to share or do its part in the Plan. The soul, then, is the magnetic factor within self, and that is why life on the Earth is becoming very interesting.

Have you noticed this year that the energy of Earth is going up and down, up and down? Some of your emotional and energy bodies are sailing up and then sailing down. Your physical bodies might be saying, "I don't know where I am. Everything is sailing up and down and I can't quite see who and what I am!"

Now, the spiritual body is really hanging in there, saying, "I'll guide all this. All you have to do is flow with it. We're going to *attract* all of what is needed to understand what is happening." The spiritual body is attracting all of what needs to be understood in order to create more and more what is called a new age, or a clearer way of interacting on your Earth.

Magnetism, then, is the cosmic equivalent of that energy that you've had, used and become familiar with, over and over, for perhaps 2000 physical lives. Suddenly it has a more cosmic quality — a lightening factor as well as a "lightning" factor. Both are present. This is the dynamic quality of cosmic energy.

So life has become very stimulating. Have you ever sat on a bolt of lightning? That would give you an idea. Some of you are sitting on it right now! It's called the soul. How does it feel to sit on a bolt of lightning? Shocking? Interesting! The shock syndrome is present within you. Some of you are feeling a little overwhelmed by what's going on, and what happens when you feel overwhelmed? *You shut down.* How many of you have felt occasionally that you have been shut down? It's because you're sitting on these bolts of lightning but not being able to utilize all of what that energy is invoking to you: many, many opportunities or chances to communicate or to become more visible in what you're doing. The heart center is the key for handling all of what is coming to you. As your heart opens and you become more aware of self as a love-centered being, it opens you instead of shutting you down.

The goal of course is to be open, to connect — and the heart is the key to connecting. So all of this fits together. Imagine that! The Creator in His resourcefulness has given us a tool called magnetism and then given us the way to use it. The do-it-yourself kit of creatorship, you could call it.

❦ *I'd like to have all of you close your eyes while we stimulate or send into the room a lot of energy. See if you can get in touch with that. If a lot of energy means a red color to you, then see red coming in and stimulating you. Sense that, and if you can't feel the energy, then know it's there. If gold means a lot of energy to you, bring in a golden light. If white means a complete spectrum of energy, bring in the white. Make a choice, and sense that energy coming into self now. As it does, center within the heart. Place a ball of energy within the heart. Now sense an openness, an opening of this ball of energy. You might see it as unfolding, rather as a flower would. Open this ball of energy, open it, open it now! It is more open. Now the flower is there, coming from above, and the energy within the heart is opening to it. Sense that opening. You open more, and more, and more. You are opening now within the heart. It is a very balancing experience. The energy comes in from above, and the heart receives it. It opens to it. Structurally you become very open and allowing of the energy to come through to self. Just sit quietly now, but remember: Open! Open! Open to this energy!*

In your very busy lives, you don't have to sit with your eyes shut and envision energy coming into self, but as life becomes very active, as opportunities come in, this is the energy that is being received. Many times it comes in through interaction and communication with others. The energy comes in, and you sense it and say, "Enough! I've really had enough for now. I need to close off a little." Instead of doing that, open up your heart and allow that energy to be used through the heart center.

Now, this energy has a great deal of electrical-magnetic content. And what in the world does that mean? We could get very scientific, but let's not. Let's keep it so that we can understand it. Well, we started with that bolt of lightning. What happens when a bolt of lightning comes forth?

It's a high-voltage reaction that goes from the Earth to the sky.

What happens to the whole environment in which the lightning is active?

It creates a chemical reaction in the surrounding atmosphere.

Yes, there is a response in the environment. It contains something that you see, hear and can feel. How many of you can *feel* lightning? That's the very active state of magnetic energy. You can sense it, see it, hear it; you can experience it totally through the senses. That's what you're dealing with here on the Earth now.

Have you ever been in New York City? What sort of environment is there? Hustle, bustle, active, dirty. Do you think there is a lot of that energy there? The air crackles with it, doesn't it? Perhaps it's dirty because it's so electric in nature; think about it. It is attracting particles that need to be cleansed, cleared. It is literally the means to cleanse and clear everything, and it's there because it's been invoked.

Why do we mention New York City? Well, there is an intensity about those who live there. They practically run over each other, trying to get to wherever they are going, so they can hurry on to somewhere else. That hurry-hurry-hurry syndrome is invoked through this electrical response, this crackling in the air. A clearing is created by that energy. It can bring a sense of anxiety because it speeds up everything, including evolution. In the fullest sense, it is directed, but you have to be able to attune and see that direction. It is not directed at or through any one individual, but into a much larger framework, a much larger environment. The way people behave is their response to an environment that crackles.

It's very interesting to enter an area after an electrical storm. You notice that it's cleared out, fresh — it's like a new beginning. It is peaceful, there is harmony — openness is the word I want. It's open to life — yes, life! The electrical energy has stimulated that openness. That's what it is doing for all of you, and that's what the Earth is invoking. Thus there is, at the level of those who planned the Earth, a stimulation, and the means to stimulate it is this electrical magnetic energy. It is stimulating the whole Earth, and all of you are responding, accepting a "piece of the action" through your soul. The amount of response you can make to it is in direct proportion to the degree to which you recognize your soul in physical existence. It truly is interesting.

You can sense the power of this electrical-magnetic energy. It is powerful, and learning to handle it is important. It is literally what is stimulating you now on the Earth — a tool of great magnitude. When you encounter all this energy and shut down and can't use it all right away, it becomes a congealed mass deep within the cellular level of self. You could say the nucleus of self gets stirred up and it becomes difficult to identify those areas within the nucleus — within the core — that are your strengths. It gets stirred up, and some of you pick up patterns from the mass consciousness that say, "When we break up the nucleus, we have a nuclear explosion, we have an explosion that is difficult to live beyond. It irritates, it doesn't allow that nucleus to be utilized in a whole manner." What all of you are trying to do is to see yourselves holistically, are you not? You want to see all of your strengths, all parts of self, and to utilize them in a clear manner. But perhaps there are blocks in the subconscious that say, "When I work with this nucleus, when I direct a powerful energy at this nucleus, it's going to explode." On a personal level, this makes the energy body rather scattered, for it does scatter all the energy within self. You do have some tendency to scatter the electrical-magnetic energy as you work with it. It is a reversal effect: Instead of being cohesive and whole so that it can be used, it scatters and can't be used. It isn't serving you well. You might want to remove that false belief. Remove the pattern so you can look at the core, the nucleus, and find it is a directed energy that identifies strengths and allows unity to be present within the nucleus. That's the goal.

Let us say you're a small boy with a kite, and the kite is hit by lightning. What happens? It might come right through you to ground that energy. Some of you have had that happen without ill effects remaining in your belief structure. You said, "Oh, well," and you came back into another physical body and started all over. But some of you have received it as a trauma. Now, you could say that Source — the whole Plan — is literally beaming energy down to the Earth. It is simply reflective energy from the evolutionary process as a whole, which is reaching, as astrology would say, a critical degree. It speeds up the interaction, and thus your planet is literally at a point of such intensity that all of us on the spiritual planes have joined you. We know a good thing when we see it! We know that some of this comes before the resolution that expands the whole. And so we want to be a part of it. Certainly we are here to help you, but we're also here to take part in this dynamic expansion of everything that has a connection with your planet. Some of you think of this planet as a dark one without a lot of light. We don't see it that way. We look at it as a planet that is coming into its own and really understanding existence perhaps more completely than ever before. It is getting in touch with the dynamic part of itself. It really is!

I'd like to demonstrate something now by having one of you stand back-to-back with Janet. Does it seem to form a duality? Now turn face-to-face — this allows a magnetic flow that was not there in the back-to-back position. This symbolizes the two halves of self — facing, accepting and creating, or not creating, not accepting, and turning away from the magnetic flow. You receive part of the energy but without identifying. It goes into an area of other unidentified energies which you haven't learned how to use.

You can begin to change this by *facing* an opportunity, a person, a situation, through a heart-centered response. Open your heart to the magnetic attraction and it comes to you. The heart is a "valve" that responds to electrical-magnetic energy if you allow it to do so — if you take out the resistance.

Let us say someone comes to you for help, but is not interested in channeling. You can say that you experience similarly and that you understand. This starts the communication flowing, and as you begin to sense what this person needs and a way to help him, the heart opens — and that energy flows in a dynamic way between the two of you. The heart literally responds and you can sense it. The heart is not separate from the head — they are utilized together, and you don't turn off the head just because you open the heart. The head *is* an important tool that God gave you. You have all of the tools to help make a difference for this person.

❦ *Let us stand up and stretch. Really stretch. Now, as you stretch, try to sense energy coming from the ceiling. It flows all the way down you. Sense it going through your feet and into the ground. You are connecting — a conductor of electrical-magnetic energy. Feel the connection that comes from the Source and flows all the way down through you. Thank you. That charged you up.*

When you're awake at night and can't sleep, sometimes you're too energized to sleep. You're not integrating your energy. Can you turn everything off? You can start blending it, bringing it into alignment. It becomes quieter as it begins to blend. You can do it this way: Put the four bodies to bed — take the spiritual body and tuck it into bed, then your mental body, tuck it in next, then your emotional body, and the physical body. Now all four of you are tucked in to go to sleep. It is easy. Sometimes the mental body takes a little persuasion. You can open the heart center, which permeates the four-body system: That communicating link — that openness — will integrate and allow you to go to sleep. That's a good technique.

Attuning to Source in a meditative state can be very helpful in connecting to that unified space; that's what the Source is — a unified space. You can have it anywhere. It is this unified space that all of you are seeking. You approach that, or begin to bring it into self more and more, through the heart-centered connection.

Each individual in the class has been assigned a color corresponding to a specific ray. Each one of you is looking for all of the pieces of who and what you are. The gold helps you to do that. Through these colors you can tone your awareness of the electrical-magnetic energy. I suggest that for a period of at least two weeks, all of you wear these colors I've given you. You might like them so well that you wear them forever; but you don't have to wear them. The inner visualization is much more important.

When you perceive harmony in everything, as we do on the spiritual planes, then that's what you will see from these opportunities. That can come about gradually through allowingness and trust in the heart area. By going through the heart center and opening, the opportunities are softened, you might say. What's going on is the sorting-out process from this electrical-magnetic energy. It's going to peak in about July 1987. It really is beginning to approach that point, and from that peaking effect I think the Earth will have softened a little in its relationship with this electrical-magnetic energy. I think you'll see the difference after that. It's not going to hit you in the head, probably, but if you have eyes to see, you will see it. Nature is integrative and organizational; it softens the perception or it causes the perception to go through the heart. And the heart understands in a way that softens how you deal with a situation. It can soften the opportunity too. When you use a balancing mechanism within self first, then you have something to land on, to step on. It's the four-body idea again, and the physical *is* the opportunity under that spiritual umbrella.

Accepting a situation is always important. It doesn't mean you can't change it if it's something you don't want, but first you have to accept it. Why? Because first you have to accept that you've created it. Then you look at it; you decide if that's really what you wanted to create. Did you create this because you wanted it or because you believed it was what you had to create? If you have created what you wanted, then perhaps you congratulate yourself a little and say, "Good, I can see that," and you allow yourself that little pat on the back. "Good, that's a productive creating. I'm doing well, look at that." And then you connect with the heart to see what the next step is for you and to see perhaps how you can share it. At this point service comes in — seeing how you can share that joy and that expansiveness that you're experiencing.

Meditation

❦ *I'd like you to establish a point of security, a nice stable position. Move your feet around until you feel very stabilized. Get into the chair so you're comfortable. Feel very secure, very balanced. You might take a deep breath or two and release it so that you feel very balanced indeed. Now coming in, above the crown chakra, a couple of inches above the top of your head, is an energy. And this energy is white. It is all-encompassing. Every color is within it, and it runs now through the heart, the solar plexus, the polarity, the base chakra, and now it flows out to the Earth. The white light that is dynamic – sense that flow. It becomes a lightning flash. Sense it now. Open to it. It flows down on the crown, third eye, throat, heart, solar plexus, polarity and base chakras. Again it flows down into the Earth in a return flow. It flows now, the dynamic energy flows now. Be very stable within it, be open to it. And now focus on the heart. Within it grows a pink rose. Open that heart center. Sense the opening there. It becomes more and more open. Open! Open! Open! Open! And the flow is still coming down into self, and the heart is still opening, opening, opening! And the flow is coming down into self. And now the flow becomes blue. It becomes blue. And it becomes green. And it becomes yellow. And it becomes orange. And it becomes indigo. And it becomes gold – and it becomes violet. It becomes luminous with all of these colors. Sense that and the heart opens, opens, opens and expands, expands, expands.*

❦ *There is a heart-centered approach to all of this energy, as it flows in, flows in. Accept the flow, the flow, the flow. It flows in and the heart expands. It expands and the rhythm of existence becomes clearer as the heart expands, expands, expands. And the energy becomes a dance, a dance. It softens, softens, softens, softens – a flow that is soft. The rhythm flows, it flows, it flows, it flows, it expands. Open, open, open, open, open, open! Expand, expand, expand. The rhythm of the flow and the electrical nature of the flow are being emphasized now. Sense that rhythm, that flow, that flow that expands, the flow that expands. A rhythm. A flow that expands. The flow that expands, a rhythm, a flow that expands. A flow that expands.*

❦ *Now pay attention to the Earth, and sense her, her rhythm and her flow, a flow that expands, and see it expand, and see it expanding all over the Earth. And see the heart center of the Earth expanding. It softens, it softens, it softens. It flows, it flows, it flows. It expands and expands and expands. Then take it up into the cosmos – the whole cosmos is flowing and expanding. The electrical energy is flowing and the heart center is expanding. Sense that expansive nature which is the heart, the heart that expands in all of the cosmos: a flow, a flow, a flow, expand, expand, expand. And it softens,*

softens, softens, softens, balances, balances, integrates, softens, softens, radiates, radiates, radiates, becomes brilliant, brilliant, brilliant. Sense that brilliance all over; the brilliance softens, softens, softens – brilliance, brilliance, brilliance.

❦ This is light that has been created through the flow, through the expansion, through softness, through the beauty, through the openness. Expand, expand. This is evolution. This is the whole in its expansive process. This is self, but it is a unit within the whole. This is the process as it works out through self.

❦ Sense that rhythm, that flow, and allow self now to integrate. Harmony and balance come forth, and the heart – the rhythm of the heart – is very even and balanced, harmonized by the expansive nature that has been triggered.

❦ Let's be quiet a moment or two. Recognize that this is the electrical; it is the quality of existence that vibrates in the cosmos, and you are attuned to that cosmic vibration now.

✧ E L E V E N ✧

Competition

A T A PARTICULAR POINT IN YOUR PLANET'S HISTORY – 1000 YEARS OR SO before the alien consciousness experience – you were visited by two beings who had shut their hearts. Proportionally, just a very small part of existence lives without the heart. They represent the part of the Source Itself that hasn't integrated yet.

There was a sense of power and competition. Some of you can feel that deep area of competition, which is never really addressed. For a while, perhaps 100 years of that 1000, these two beings warred to become dictator of your planet Earth. There were some of you on each side. You liked each other, but there was something that you were connected to that didn't like the other. So when you would try to work with each other there would be something opposing it, something very subtle. There would be something like a shock when you would try to make your creativity come together – an abrupt pause in the ability to flow it together. That pause was your connection with one of these beings. Literally, it was their interaction through all of you.

You were in two camps. There was an arbitrary claiming by these two beings: "You're mine, you're mine, you're mine. You don't belong to me, you belong to the other one." It wasn't so much that they gave some of you away; they *pushed* you away. Some of you were pushed away by both of them and some of you were claimed by both of them. It was quite an interesting time.

This stimulated all sorts of competition. Competition was there openly in everything that was done, and this perhaps didn't serve humanity very well. It was in *everything*: "My service is more important than yours" or "I don't relate to what you are doing, so go away." It was that shoving away. If you got shoved away by most of humanity, it could be quite isolating and alienating. Perhaps you can see a pattern of behavior there.

At a critical period, the odds became even. Someone would say, "Our dress is very pretty." Someone else would say, "Well, don't you like mine?" "Yes, it is equally pretty." So in seeking a level of equality, there was even some sense that competition had to be stimulated in order to get into equality. Have you seen that pattern of behavior? "I have to go through a period of competition in order to see equality." This isn't true.

Basic equality is there — it does not have to go through the competition area. This pattern of behavior says it does, because from the closed-heart basis, everything is competition. It says, "I need this power." Why? "This is the only thing that gives me a sense of being." In the fullest sense it's what we all are looking for, but most of us use the heart which means — running it through the system or the Plan or the Creator's understanding of power. When you turn that off, what do you get? You get chaos. The only way it seems you can organize chaos, in cases of the closed heart, is through competition. "The only way I can put my universe in order is if I take it from you. Then I'll have it." It doesn't work that way, does it?

If you can draw beautiful pictures, and I say, "I want that ability" and I try to grasp it, what happens? There is no way I can get your ability to draw by taking your ability. This is a power struggle. Some of the power struggles have been that silly. They are a desperate grasping to hold on to creativity. You couldn't possibly get what you are struggling over. By making a choice not to use the heart, the door has been shut.

I have often told you that it is more difficult to shut the heart than any of you know. It is very hard to do that. The Source Itself keeps trying to open it up. There is so much love and trust and allowingness there for you. It is magnetic, it's very difficult not to respond to. And it takes a great deal of creativity to close it completely. That's an important statement. It means that those who have closed their hearts don't use their power well. They're very powerful, but they haven't integrated it properly. Closing the heart is a very interesting way to get powerful, isn't it?

So these magnetic beings created two very powerful points of view. Many of you felt like you were the ball in the middle of a very strenuous baseball game. You had no more control, you were out of control. How did that blend? What do you think that did to your beliefs about integration? Did it make you think it doesn't work? Exactly. That is the reason I am giving that to you as we work on integration.

What eventually happened is, they both left, and one of their confederates came in and took over. So the two faded out and the third was created. This third being was an expert at grasping that creativity that is working within someone else and taking it away from them. He ruled the planet for almost 500 years.

What was the spiritual government doing? They were helping as much as they could, but allowing the choices that had been made here on the Earth.

There were slave races at this time. There were genetic changes and many types of encoding and implants. To help what? This being was capable of functioning with a physical body or without and was trying to ensure his rule of the Earth. For a while it looked as if your planet had become possessed by this being. It seemed that he would rule it for a long time.

At that point the Plan was able to help you, and it did. There was a being of great light who we will call a fully developed cocreator, one who had never come in contact with the Earth and never really actually did. It is very difficult for a fully developed cocreator to come to the physical plane because it seems so small. It would be like you trying to step on a one-quarter-inch square. How do you put a huge being on just a tiny spot without squashing that tiny spot?

So what he did was this. He said, "The Earth is clear enough that it's invoking my help. I can't step on that planet, so what we'll have to do is create a new one." So, this Earth got erased. He said, "Okay. Now, here is your new Earth. I'm creating it, it is larger, it is wiping out all of this. We're giving you a new opportunity, and eventually you will have to look at it." It was a time similar to the Harmonic Convergence, only much earlier, where the energy became so different that you had a brand-new planet.

Remember, within this brand-new planet you had this very sticky and heavy pattern of behavior — the dictator, and all that that represents: the heavy use of power, the heavy, underlying competition for that power.

You were about ready to deal with this and forgive it. Then there was another incident wherein another being tried to come. You were clear enough that you didn't allow it, but it stimulated the old pattern. That was really the last straw, and it brought in that first drop of alien consciousness.

It can't come here physically, so it comes here in its energy format through the use of its creativity. It is united here, and there isn't anything that we can do about it. Then comes the process of getting beyond that, which you did. Then comes the feeling that you are going to pull in hopelessness. I'm not trying to tell you that you haven't made good progress on this. You have.

There is a process of hopelessness as we go around in this pattern. It doesn't seem to resolve, or something comes in just when we think we're beyond it. It is not hopeless; it is the emotional body's belief that it is caught in this trenchlike effect (the vacuum effect).

The key to understanding the dynamic energy is to understand the receptive energy. It is the other half of the process. If you see this pattern of receptivity — yours and the Earth's — as a vacuum or trench with all of this heavy stuff coming in, then there is no way to resolve that. That is one point of view that all of you are seeking to resolve.

In order to resolve the use of the dynamic energy, we must clear the receptive energy. This gets very hard and crystallized. In a sense, you may protect the deepest part because the belief says, "When I open up to my receptivity, what pours in is all of this negative material." That keeps you from opening as much as you would like, and it's why we have to break through this one in order to get to the next step. This is getting to be a very powerful time, and it is stirring up these old patterns about competition and hopelessness and so forth. I hope you can see how important that is.

Affirmation Process

Visualize not only the system, but say to your soul and your monadic level, "All right, now, there is going to be a triangle of us — me here on the physical level; the fully developed soul level; and the fully developed monad — a triangle of energy. As you energize those three points, you begin to spin them, creating a spiral. Ask the three points of view to put these into the lake, and stir the lake, as though you were using a food blender. You will have the strengths of all of the levels blending and breaking up any resistances to putting that into the creative form.

Add this process to your affirmational work for a while. See how clear the lake is. See if you have lumps in it. If so, you might strain out the lumps and press them between your hands and squash them. In any way you can, get rid of the lumps, see your lake clear, and get it smooth again from input that might shock you.

There is a pulling back from the integrative process with some of you now. As you get deeper into the affirmations that are really important for you, they can become shocking and not really blend into the subconscious in a way that can move it, can motivate it. You are getting some of that shock, it is a symbol of the process integrating.

Affirmations to Clear the Dynamic Energy through the Clearing of the Receptive Energy

Remember to use all three points of self (self, soul and monad) to do these affirmations.

- 🐦 My receptivity is not a trench into which heavily energized power convolution pours, now.
- 🐦 There is not an inaccessible level creating a hopeless disintegration within the flow of my creativity, now.
- 🐦 There is not an absence of contact keeping me from blending together all perspectives to expand my receptivity, now.
- 🐦 I am not hopelessly surrounded by this alienation. I can allow the integration from all points of view, now.
- 🐦 Alienation is not my name. I am not cut off by any splitting off of the process through a trench that seems to dump eternally on me, now.
- 🐦 I can access this clearer level, and when I do, there is not a shock or alienation proving to me it cannot integrate, now.
- 🐦 As the creator process manifests through me electrically, I do not have a mishmash which has no direction because of any betrayal in the process, now.

- ❦ I am not wandering, eternally unable to integrate because the process is unintegratable, now.
- ❦ My strengths do not get stuck in an overall process that is too convoluted to use my strengths clearly, now.
- ❦ I am not victimized through communication with the process as I blend into it and distinguish the strengths within myself, now.
- ❦ The overall picture is supported by the process. There is not a breaking down of the process entangling, distorting or destroying my purpose area, now.
- ❦ As I see the beauty of the existence flowing through me, there is not a degenerative process that will suddenly capsize my clear contact, taking away what I need, now.
- ❦ As I strengthen my resolve and my purpose area, there is not a splitting off emotionally, expressing the acceptance of what cosmically cannot work, now.
- ❦ I recognize that my responsibility level is not impacted, destroyed or lost through a trenchlike effect which I must avoid, now.
- ❦ The sorting out of levels is not a painful experience as it heads into the desired link, the desired bridging process, now.

✧ T W E L V E ✧

The Receptivity Area — What It Is and How to Use It

OUR SUBJECT IS RECEPTIVITY. MANY OF YOU USE THAT TO "BOUNCE" IN AND out of the physical. Isn't that an interesting statement? Well, perhaps that's a "teaser"; we will see how that fits into our subject a little later.

Receptivity is really very important. What is it that we are all trying to receive? Perhaps understanding, love or the many abilities to create in as joyous and unlimited a manner as possible. There are many, many things that we are seeking to receive. If we were to go around this group and ask, there would be many different good responses, but probably you would say they are not truly the main goal of your life, for as a divine being you are seeking to aid others and to extend them a helping hand.

How does receptivity fit into this? Well, can you really help anyone else until you've received, until you've helped yourself? You've heard that statement many times before. We have to get into the basic nature of receiving to see how to help others to receive. We have to see the whole picture.

You were born as a divine being. Does that mean that there was a time when you were not a divine being? No, of course not, but there was a time when you began to experience as an individual. We are speaking of that as a "cosmic birth time." Let's equate it to the birth of a physical baby. We'll say this is a girl child, because after all, you men have lived other lives as women, just as you women have been in male incarnations. You who are males in this life have enjoyed being female, because in the receptive or female role you may have seen life as more of a gift than you do in the male role.

All right, we have our baby, and she's in her crib, wearing a pretty pink dress with lace. She's pretty and she's newly born, and when you see a newborn it's a special thing, is it not? What is so special about them? Well, for one thing they're very open. What do I mean by that? They're very receptive. They have needs that they want met. When they are hungry they cry; when they are comfortable they have ways to let you know about that. Their needs are met; they receive from those caring for them. They make their need known and someone comes and meets the need.

Let's progress our child to age three or four. At some point she discovers that there are other children around who have needs that they want filled. Our child finds that the needs of those other children seem to interfere with her needs. She is an only child, but one time a cousin comes to visit. The cousin sees a toy that is very special to our little girl; it's the toy that she takes to bed with her. The cousin wants it, and someone gives it to this other child and tells our little girl she can't have it — that she has a visitor and she must let the visitor have the toy. What happens? She learns about others, and she learns that receptivity flows both ways, and there has to be an adjustment through allowingness. All of these are part of the heart or the love area; through allowingness, receptivity is adjusted.

We will say that our little girl is mature enough to allow the cousin to have the toy. What does she get? Well, the mothers or fathers may reward her with a lovely smile and a compliment and say, "Look how good she is! She's allowing her favorite toy to be enjoyed by her cousin." What happens, however, if she screams and yells instead of allowing? Eventually she gets the toy back in the name of "peace." Then what? Well, then she is told, "You're a bad little girl! You didn't share." Thus the idea of force is introduced.

This is important; think about this. What happens to our little girl's beliefs in regard to receiving here? If she has shared her toys, allowed her heart to share, and trusted that she'll get the toy back, then she is rewarded and perhaps her heart opens more fully. The receptivity area is continually reinforced and opened and there is a reciprocal flow of energy, a reinforcement of opening further in receiving. But if she has not shared her toy, bringing in that force situation in which the toy is given back but she is reprimanded, then there is a closing off of the receptivity area.

My point is that when you began to be an individual, your experiences feed into the receptivity area. Through each experience, through each lifetime, you build up a relationship with receptivity. You build it step by step. It's really rather complicated; it gets to be a push/pull or there are different points of view within you about receptivity. You want to receive *and* you truly want to share — you do — but there are contrary and unresolved beliefs about the results of sharing that perhaps close off that receptivity area. You really are the beliefs built up through a series of many, many experiences of just how you receive.

I'd like to suggest something to you. Although you really do create your life from the beliefs that are stored within the subconscious mind, there is an "overriding" technique, a way to wipe out the receptivity blocks that you have. You can allow yourself to be very open to receiving. Does that sound like something you'd be interested in hearing more about? I hope so, because my main thought tonight concerns that.

I talk to you about many things, and you might say that I am a spiritual psychiatrist. That's what I am, and I like to help people discover who they really are. I like to help you go deeply into why you haven't seen who you really are. I like to find that beautiful, centered, loving space that all of you know is there. You find it at times for about five minutes and then something comes in and you've lost contact again. Does it sound worthwhile to find that centered, loving space and function from it all of the time? Isn't that the goal that we are looking for? It really is. Let's see how together we can discover that space and consider some techniques to help hold on to it.

If you are learning to ride a bicycle and your goal is to ride in the Olympics, you want to be very professional. Perhaps your older brother is an Olympic rider, so as soon as you can get on a bicycle you start. First it's a small bike and then a bigger one and finally a full-size one, and you practice and find you can ride for long periods of time. Then you're riding with your brother on one of the hundred-mile trails that professionals train on. You go up and down and this way and that way; you train yourself until you're very good indeed, and your brother says, "You're pretty good now; I think you'll be in the Olympics someday." He is very pleased about it, and that reinforces what your goal is. You are happy.

One day there is an accident, and your brother who has been getting ready for the Olympics is hurt. There is a pulled ligament which is not going to heal in time for the Olympic tryouts. He has been your idol. You've looked up to him and emulated him and you're very sorry that this accident has prevented him from his chance to ride in the Olympics.

Your brother says to you, "You mustn't let this deter you. This was just an accident; my leg will heal and in four years I'll try again. In ten or twelve years you'll be ready to try out. Don't let this stop you." But you see, right then within your subconscious mind a seed is sown. You may not be aware, but that seed says that even if you get very close to your goal an accident can stop you. "Look at what happened to your brother."

So let's progress time and say that as time went by your brother changed. This happens to people — they change goals or perhaps they progress in the way they understand life. Your brother has changed and in four years doesn't even want to try out for the Olympics. But you keep your goal and you become good enough to try out for the Olympics. You need, however, to recognize that the little seed that was sown years ago is still there. You can't get the memory of the accident out of your mind. It comes up a lot and you keep wondering if you'll have an accident. Because this seed is buried in the subconscious, you might not see what is happening. When you think of the accident you immediately push the idea away as being "negative," something you don't want to look at.

I am not saying it's helpful to dwell on it, but as you approach your goal, that seed situation becomes a little barrier, a little fence. It helps if you know it's there and why it's there – and of course it can be dumped. Sometimes you just need to know that, because you are extremely mature as a spiritual being, you've already encountered just about everything. Believe me, my friends, on the Earth and in the spiritual planes, you've done and been and had opportunities to do just about everything. I tell you, this is true with virtually everyone attending here tonight.

It is interesting and can be helpful to be told of experiences in past lifetimes. But perhaps the most interesting thing is to see that you accumulate wisdom; you accumulate knowledge through your receptive process. You keep receiving, and what you are receiving is, let us say, the Plan, or the divine experience as you partake within this creation that our Creator has set up for us. Certainly the goal of receiving is nothing personal. There is nothing personal in it at all. Did you ever think of that? Does that deflate the ego balloon?

The receptive mode means allowing Source, the divine, God, to receive. You really are an aspect of the Source, of the Creator, that experiences and receives. So if you look at it that way, it is not so important to see that little fence, that little obstacle in the path. God, really, has nothing to do with your ego. It has to do with your receptive ability of the God within you – that divine being that lives right in your physical structure and is so beautiful, so divine. When you look in a mirror you may not see it, for the ego has such a limited viewpoint. Its viewpoint is not Godlike. It has a strength – it has one perception in which it's very strong, and we don't throw it away. But we teach it that there is a much greater point of view to be received, and that point of view is God, the divine. What will ego understand? It understands the main theme of *this* life that you've built; that's a perspective of the divine, and that's what you've received in this lifetime. That is good! Don't chastise the ego – just educate it. I've said it many times: Don't throw out the beautiful baby with the bathwater. Wash the baby, the ego, which is the center of the personality and part of that divinity of self. Keep it open and receptive enough to be sensitive to the plan of wholeness within it. The leaping over the barrier is what allows the action of opening to your potential, allows the quantum leap from personality to God on the Earth plane.

Now, in the example we were using, you are approaching the Olympics – the pinnacle of your Earth experience. All of you are at that level; you wouldn't be attuned to this lesson if you weren't. You are very mature as spiritual beings. You get to "ride in the Olympics," or the fast movement of the Earth at this time. But your receptivity area must keep up with the current pace of the Earth. There are others riding in the Olympics also;

everyone who recognizes the Earth's evolution at this time is an Olympic team member. You are all in it together. I mean by that that this receptivity area is open to development, to growth, to sharing and to understanding in a way it has never been open before. On August 15, 1987, your Earth became more open, more receptive to many things. You can look around in your daily life and wonder why certain things haven't changed. But instead of looking at those separate things, see the overall picture. Look at the peace overtures that have been made. Look at certain things that are communicated in a different manner. In order to use this increased openness, this more receptive nature, one must understand receptivity. That's what our whole goal is in this lesson.

So now you are this child, and you are ready to try out for the Olympics. Will you be selected for the team? You will if you have confidence that you can receive that level of proficiency and then validate that confidence. Does that sound too simple? Shall I say it again?

It will work for you if you validate it. The definition of the word *validate* is "to prove true or correct, to give substance to, to confirm." It will be so for you if you are able to receive at this level of proficiency that we are calling the Olympics. Your Earth right now *is* the Olympics. Although you might have to step over a subconscious barrier, you can do so by validating the proficiency that you have gained to be an Olympic star. Is there anything wrong with seeing yourself as "tops" at playing a Stradivarius or being a professional ski-jumper or a Pulitzer Prize journalist? No, of course there isn't! You've all experienced those things or their equivalents; you've had lives where you were very, very good in some area. As you seek to attain any goal, the level of proficiency of whatever kind you have attained in the past can help you. Your being is aware of past maturity and competency, and that gives you confidence that you can equal Godlike maturity again by validating it.

If you are approaching a high level of proficiency and you really want to reinforce that you are able to function at that level, how can you validate or confirm it? Let's say that you want to be secure as you enter the Olympic trials; you want a way to validate your proficiency before the trials so that you will feel very secure as you begin the trials. How can you do that? By a test run? Yes. By evaluating the ability of other contestants? Ah, but you are not really competing with anyone else. The only one you are competing with is yourself, my friends. You are the only one you have to convince; once your self is convinced, that's it! Isn't that interesting?

All right, how do you get confidence? Visualization is a good suggestion; it is an affirmation to visualize yourself performing perfectly. What else? Well, it certainly helps to keep a positive frame of mind, but if there is a barrier deep in the subconscious, it may keep trying to surface. If it's there you don't try to ignore it or push it away; you convince it that it isn't operative. How can you convince it? You receive! What do you receive? You receive the validation that you are looking for. How? You are a divine being and you are connected with something. With what are you connected? With the Source. Do you think that is where you can find the validation you need? You do! Good! Then you can ask, through your divine connection, for this validation that will allow you to have the security you need to use that level of proficiency that you are just approaching. What about that subconscious barrier that may (or may not) be in the way? Sometimes you don't recognize that there is a deeply buried resistance as you approach a goal. If there is no such barrier, it doesn't hurt to ask the Creator so that you may receive the validation anyway, does it?

Some of you in the metaphysical community have beliefs about this from your past background and you don't enjoy it like I do. But I want to tell you this. I like to get down on my knees, my friends. I like to talk to the Creator this way. I've been known to surrender and say to the Source, "I am within the plan, I surrender to the plan." Then I leap up and say, "I know this is a very active state, so may I please receive validation for the next thing I am to do?" Surrender is not something that lets you just sit on a chair and say, "Well, I've surrendered. Now bring it to me." That's not the goal. The goal is to validate each step of your receiving in the plan as it comes through you, to really contact that — to step over the barrier, to use whatever technique is divinely responsive to opening that next step, to be receptive to the stimulation of the plan.

Remember, I said that each one of you is an aspect of Source, although you think of yourself as an individual. In some sense that is an illusion. You are Sourceness; that is what you are. This Sourceness is growing, it's becoming, it's learning. It is learning to create from a physical point of view, and the ability to express that in an open, receptive mode through the surrender process is what I am speaking about tonight.

Receptivity, then, is a part of the heart center. The heart is what creates the plan. Without your heart, nothing happens; there may be a sense of a lot of activity, but nothing really happens. Have you ever noticed that? If you try to leave out love — the heart center — there are really no connections made. There is no real understanding if you leave out the heart.

The receptivity is that area of specific spontaneity that the Source, in Its loving focus, uses to activate your heart center. Its spontaneity may connect in with the heart center of each and every one of you. Receptivity is the bounty of the love aspect, the heart aspect of Sourceness, or the Source in Its sensitivity to Its creative heart.

Each one of you is the Source. When you communicate, Source is talking to Itself. When you love, you are Source appreciating Its various aspects. When you walk, Source is in movement. The Source is receiving Its creative process in all of Its aspects and building the plan. Receptivity, then, assures sensitivity to the creative plan and understanding of how to use it to communicate the next step within the plan.

Let's go back again to our child. There she is in all her beauty – and I tell you, this child is an avatar, a beautiful spiritual being who will shed light and love and laughter and joy upon your planet. Who is this little avatar? You! She is each one of you. Look at you in your beauty, in your imagery, in your openness, in your sensitivity, in your allowingness, in your trust. Woven into this are experiences that have not yet let you validate all that I've just said. I have that opinion and I will keep it, and I invite you to share it with me. In order to understand it one must have sensitivity, receptivity and empathy.

Suppose you have a piece of fabric – of velvet, with a soft pile. You can feel the beautiful, soft sensation of this fabric. The pile results from threads cut off at a certain level. Let us say that each of you is one of those threads. The Source is caressing the fabric. The Source is nurturing your individual points of view. You also can learn, through your sensitivity, to appreciate the fabric that each individual thread has created. You appreciate each other's contribution to the whole. The fabric is there and you can use your senses, and that's important because your physical senses are symbolic of divine senses. You can literally hear the Source speaking. Have you ever listened to what a group of people were saying to each other? Listen beyond the words and voices to what the Source is communicating to Itself. Why? Because that's what you're all looking for – the way to see and appreciate the rhythm of Sourceness. To receive clearly one must literally sense the flow and the rhythm.

Let's say that you have a relationship partner. The two of you are talking. Both of you are tired, so although you're talking, you're not really listening to each other. Are you really communicating? What happens to the communication? The vibrations in the ideas and emotions go out into the ethers and are scattered but stay around. That's brought us to an area I wanted to address. To receive a message, the four-body system must hear it all at once. The receptivity is at its fullest when the emotional, mental, spiritual and physical bodies all hear the message. Only then do you truly get what is being communicated.

So you are tired and your physical body has "had it" for today. Your emotional body isn't working too well and your mental body thinks that, since all the other bodies are shut down, it might as well go to sleep. Then there is talking. Your spiritual body may be ready to listen, but it looks at the rest of the bodies and sees that its message can't reach through to the physical, so it cuts off the message. As has been stated, the communication goes out into the ethers where it may be stored in the spiritual body and brought into the other bodies when they are all receptive. So remember: To validate your next major Olympic run, the message has to get through on all four levels.

What can you do to bring in this four-body receptivity? Well, you could have the spiritual body call a "committee meeting." It can point out that there definitely is a problem and that, together with some inner communication, the outer communication will clear and be received. Probably the clearest way for many of you would be to get the spiritual and the mental communicating. The mental will communicate to the emotional, which in turn can reach the physical. Another way to do it is to have the spiritual go directly into the physical, alerting the emotional and mental to become receptive. The two teams, so to speak, will then communicate with each other. The communication seeking to be heard may be from the Source level, or from a friend, a mate or an *opportunity*. Yes, an opportunity can communicate.

Many of you have already created the ability to validate that next step, but perhaps you have not integrated the four-body system enough to allow an opportunity to be heard. It takes the alignment of all four bodies, not just one. If opportunity knocks and the physical body by itself answers the door, it may take a look, not recognize the opportunity, and slam the door in its face. If it's the emotional body that answers, it may say, "Oh my, I can't handle that!" and bang goes the door. The mental body may open the door and stand there analyzing, and by the time it's finished analyzing, the opportunity has gone. And the spiritual body can't seem to get down to the physical. If they'd all go together they could welcome that opportunity. When the spiritual, inner communication comes through, it allows the opportunity, the receptivity, which makes validation of the next step possible.

What is receptivity? It is having a balanced perspective, being sensitive to the whole communication, being able to validate, in a step-by-step manner, your evolution *for* the Plan, your evolution *as* the Plan . . . your evolutionary process.

Do you find it difficult to know when you are in a state of openness in the heart area? Well, you are in that state when you offer to help someone; you are in touch with it in a very practical manner. It is something you use in your daily activity — it's your caringness, your sharing with others, the contribution you make to society. Can you see that it's there all the time? Your awareness as a being on the spiritual level, though you are focused on the Earth, is what you all seek to validate. You want to know that there is something you are doing on the spiritual plane as well as on the physical. You can see through your senses that you move your arm, but there is a correspondence on the spiritual level that moves also. Visualize physical existence as a point within the circle of the whole. When you make a movement, the spiritual area makes a much larger movement. You are literally responding for the whole picture, so how can it not be there when you are moving? The point is that you are a connection whenever you move. The whole is connected to the point, ensuring movement on every level. We must have the ability to see that there is structure — that in life there is a Plan. In the morning say to yourself, "All right, today my day is going to be a part of the Plan." You get up, get dressed, eat breakfast and meditate, and you have a sense that you are connected into this Plan. You see that there is a specific concept that you can look at and from it see that although this day is *one* day, there are other days, and they flow together.

If you can't quite contact something this day, there is a space within this concept as a whole where you *can* make that contact. Each time you contact something, that is validating a part of the structure. Everything you do is part of this structure; you are gradually extending as you move within it. You build the structure one step at a time, but the conceptual blueprint, the Plan, is already there. You are simply validating that Plan that the Creator has already given you. You are activating it. When part of the structure is solid enough to hold you, you take another constructive step and make it equally firm. As you do this you see that the whole Plan was divinely constructed and you need only "make it so."

You want hints? How about watching the synchronicities of your life? You're being given what you need; you just haven't noticed. Suppose you are in the flow of your activity for the day, walking down the street, and a woman dashes out in front of you screaming "Fire!" The ensuing arrival of fire engines and all the noise has blocked your flow. Why were you caught in an emergency? What part of yourself does this woman represent as she runs out calling "Fire"? Why has this stopped your flow? Look at the synchronicities of your life when they get your attention. They will tell you how to integrate.

This is a bit off our topic, but I'll touch on it. Some of you know of the five higher chakras, but some of you don't. The eighth is the seat of the soul, and has to do with healing also. The higher chakras are your higher abilities and the energy that the abilities represent. Each has a specific function and a specific color that corresponds to one of the higher rays. The ninth chakra has to do with the body of light. The tenth chakra literally anchors the body of light into the physical structure and balances the relationship area. The eleventh chakra bridges to the integrative state you are looking for, and the twelfth chakra is the ability to integrate completely. Obviously this is not the whole picture.

You are creators, and it is important to know your tools. This Earth is your creative focus, or the structure that's been given to you. As you begin to validate, integrate, what is being mirrored to you by the synchronicities of your life (when you can accept and learn from a particular aspect) is that you've built something usable onto the structure. When the structure is completed, that is your "passport" for leaving the Earth. Most of you seem to want to do that, but when you get "there" you'll probably want to come back as a teacher. (That's how it usually works.) You have to accept Earth before you can leave it! You weren't sent here as punishment! There are people on the spiritual plane who are in line, wanting an opportunity to come to Earth. There are angels who are in awe of those on the physical plane; they know it is a privilege to be here. Those of you who are here are very mature. You've learned a great deal; at some point you must accept and appreciate Earth living. The emotional body often has a lot to do with this. Some of you have wandered from one part of the Earth to another, never finding just the right place to stay because you were really seeking the divine within. There was, in this, a great deal of confusion and loneliness coming from your being unable to validate from within. You've heard that over and over and over, and one of these days you're going to say, "I do not suffer." And you won't. At first it seems just a statement you can't realize, but you will. The emotional body is involved here. Wherever you live, whatever your relationships, if subconsciously there is a feeling of not belonging, not being truly a part of humanity, then the emotional body has to decide that it's going to be happy wherever it is. "I do not suffer!" It is interesting that when you are on the verge — just about to validate, just about to step over a barrier — that is when you put up the greatest resistance to it. You try to hold on to the familiar at that moment of feeling rather lost before you step over into the validation of truth have sought, leaving an old illusion behind.

I have said there must be an alignment of the four-body system. If there is a weakness in alignment — say between the mental and emotional bodies — then a stimulation must be applied, but in just the right area. When we are working with the energies of the Earth, for instance, we might apply stimulation in Alaska to have a response in Afghanistan, or in China to have a response in Brazil.

Meditation by Lenduce

❧ *This is Lenduce, and I invite you now to see a golden light. This golden light comes over self. Bring it over all of your body; see the four-body system as gold light. Stretch that golden light, expand it in every direction. Send it deep into the Earth. Expand it horizontally over the Earth and expand it to the Source level directionally in this example:*

❧ *The golden light goes everywhere, more and more, more and more, and as you get that moving you recognize that each of your golden lights is blending, blending. It blends and expands and expands. As each light contacts another, there is an igniting process of the light.*

❧ *The light ignites, the light expands, and there is a triggering of the light process. Now, through this golden light expansion I would like to use this triggering process. Remember that a trigger is a contact point — literally an expansion that is very rapid. View this through the following.*

❧ *The golden light expands, and as it contacts, it triggers. It triggers more light. The contact is made, the light expands – contact – light expands – light – trigger the light – move the light – flow the light. The contact is made as you continue to expand the golden light. The light expands – contact the light – the light ignites – trigger the light – expand the light!*

❧ *This is communication: your light expanding, moving into others. Expand the light – contact – trigger the light – expand the light – communicate as* light – flow the light – expand the light – trigger the light – the golden light – expand – expand – expand! Trigger the light – expand the golden light – the flow of the golden light that is expanding now. This is an eternal process; it continues to expand; you communicate with others.

❦ The golden light expands. It triggers more light. Contact light – expand the light – spiral the light – expand! The light is contacted, the light is triggered. Trigger the light – the light – the light – light – light! Flow the light – expand the light – the golden light that keeps expanding.

❦ This is the integrative state of All That Is through communication, through the contact with others it keeps expanding. It keeps flowing, it keeps growing. You are balanced, integrated within this golden light, and your bodies are the golden light as you integrate with others. There is an expansion; there is a triggering – flow as light – expand as light.

❦ There is a magnificent sense of expression. There is a movement, a divine flow, dear ones, to the heart – the heart. Become aware of the light flowing from the heart – from the heart and into the heart – and into the heart as a reciprocal flow.

✧ T H I R T E E N ✧

The Power Area — A Sorting-out Process

TONIGHT WE ARE GOING TO TALK ABOUT POWER. I'D LIKE ALL OF YOU TO sense, coming into this room, a lot of energy. We are bringing it in liberally tonight. This is divine power; it is, of course, life force. It is the life force that you utilize to help create the plan — the Cosmic Plan — that beautiful unfoldment that is there for all of us to participate in. It is there, but you need to plug into it, so power is your plugging into that plan. It is your being able to allow it to work through you, allow it to energize you.

Did you ever walk around feeling, as you say, "spacy"? You are rather "out of it." You don't feel very connected with the Earth or with much of anything; you are just floating. You don't know where you are but you're not where you'd like to be. What has happened then? You're not connecting into the power. The connection has become out of alignment, and that power that can be yours is not presently available. Where did it go? What is happening?

Energizing the Past

What usually occurs is that instead of energizing the present, the eternal present, you are energizing a past. You are emotionally stuck, caught in, considering, worrying about, or moving in a past that you are re-energizing instead of energizing the present opportunity. Something comes along when you are caught up in this. Perhaps a friend says, "You're kind of out of it — is there something I can do?" Many of you are doing energy work on each other, and the energizing from one to another does a great deal to help bring you quickly back into the present with its opportunity. Your life force, your power, is realigned in the energizing work done with another. When someone is helping another to bring energy into the present, usually that person will be able to access and hold on to that energy, though not always permanently.

You can bring yourself back into the present by realizing what it was that triggered the past and its emotions. This is what we call "making contact with a realization point." You have heard me talk about realization. You remember? A light bulb flashes on and you say, "Oh yes, that's how that works." You may have heard something ten thousand times, but flash! you got it this time. What happened when the light bulb went on? There was a flood of life force or power that came through you. That integrates you; it takes you out of this past-tracking and puts you all together in the present.

The only difference between you and what I call a fully realized cocreator is that their consciousness does not wander or turn away from the state of eternal integration with the now. It stays right there, though of course for them, "right there" is almost everywhere. Their integrated consciousness expands to include much more than we are yet able to do. It doesn't wander; it doesn't miss the mark of connecting fully. Its power is not dissipated into what has been. That's why they have gone beyond the sequential time in which you live. Your consciousness hasn't learned to integrate into a focus and hold that focus eternally. Truly that is the only difference.

Many of you seek to learn to meditate, or have learned to meditate. Well, I think there are at least two thousand ways to do it. How about the method that says you must quiet your mind? You try to do that, and just because you want to do it, suddenly the mind is very, very busy. All these thoughts are scurrying about and you're telling yourself you shouldn't be thinking, you shouldn't be thinking, you shouldn't be thinking. This is dissipating the consciousness and it sets up a resistance pattern. The way to quiet your mind is to allow it to extend through a conscious focus, a divine power focus, into All That Is — not all that was, or will be, but All That Is.

As I said, there are many ways to meditate, and each of you will find the one that works best for you. Perhaps in past lives you have used a method that has become easy and familiar. The method does not matter particularly. It is the connection that results from the method used.

The goal is to have the four-body system, particularly the mental body, so aligned into this full grid system of your power that it can flow in any direction and remain connected, remain integrated, remain in contact with what is now. It takes practice, but as you are able to do this you will become able to bring this back from the meditative state and use it all of the time.

You know that there is a grid system of energies upon the Earth. They are the energy lines of the Earth's magnetic field. That also is a good meditation. It's a great connector. See yourself walking the grid lines of the Earth. You can walk the lines the way an acrobat does. What you are doing is validating for yourself and for your four bodies, particularly your physical and emotional bodies, that there is a tracking system and you are a part of it. It gives you a sense of direction physically and emotionally.

Meditation, particularly using visualization, really helps your four-body system. Moving the physical body in meditation is important also. So you can use a walking, a running or a balancing on an electromagnetic power-grid meditation. I'm perfectly serious! If you are walking where you can do it without startling people, hold your arms out like wings on a plane. If there are people around, feel how it would be to do it. As you are walking along you are plugged into an electrical system of inpouring energy that fills you. So your workday has been hectic! You are tired and in need of energy. Think of this as you walk home or walk to and from the bus or down the mall.

Sensing Ley Lines

It is good to know what ley lines run through your area. Here in Vancouver, British Columbia, there is an area of which I am very fond. Janet has to space her appointments with time in between, so today she went for a walk — she likes to shop. She went by a street just before Robson Street, called Harrow Street. Right along Harrow Street, about two blocks toward a bank at the intersection of Dave and Butte, there is an important energy grid system. If you check it out you may notice the area of your third eye being activated there. It goes clear down into the center of the Earth. What happened there was that early, very early — thousands of years ago on your planet — there was a spiritual teacher who lived right there. He had a small dwelling there that he energized. He was a very integrated being and knew how to plug in directly to the Earth. What he did is interesting. He made his own plug, so to speak, and left it there for you. In other words, there is a very direct access to the Earth's energy in that area.

Would you like to have a "plug" in your house or apartment? Well, putting it in and having it work would depend on how integrated you are and how you allow it to work. The more integrated you are, the better it will work. The way to do it is this: See the place in your house or apartment where you want your grid system and plug to be. Lay out the crossing lines (like the strings in a racket) and begin to walk the lines. Walk the lines both ways until, when you enter that room, you can know those lines and feel the energy along them. You'll have to work on it, but when you get to the point that on entering the room you see the grid system and feel the room as energized, then you'll know it is ready.

At a time when you are free to use an uninterrupted twenty minutes to an hour, sit down in the middle of the grid system. Sit there until you can feel that grid system becoming like an energy spiral. It spirals either clockwise or counterclockwise around the whole room. It is not concerned with sequential time, for it is in the eternal now. That is what we want to energize here. So sit in that until the spiral is so strong that you can identify with it; it becomes a part of you. You can sense that spiral particularly in the third eye area. You may not see it; you may only feel it. Or perhaps the physical body will feel it or you may know it with the spiritual body. There is no one way; you will find your own way. Sense the activity in the third eye and plug the energy in at that point. If you have done it correctly there should be a flood of energy that comes clear through your physical structure, and what I call a "bouncing," that is, a bouncing of energy that unites you — literally — to what I call the cocreator perspective.

Your Power Connection

The goal of course is to stay there. But sometimes you get a glimpse of something that fades, then you see it again and hold it a little longer, and each time the connection lasts longer until there will come a time when you can hold it. This bounce is so profound, my friends, that you won't have to wonder; you will know because it bounces you into this powerful integrated space that speaks to you. When you experience it you will be sensitive to everything in the room, including the presence of the angelic kingdom, the activities of any devas, the elements that speak to you, the Planetary Logos (Sanat Kumara) and his activity. You will be sensitive to the universe through this integrated point that you have created. It is indeed worth experiencing. It gives you a little glimpse of the only thing you are fated to experience, the only thing that must happen — you must reach your cocreator level. It is your destiny. Power is what allows you to glimpse it and move toward it.

You may think we want to talk about personal power and the assuming of it, and I do, but I want to approach the power area in several ways. When you use the power grid and the bouncing to the level of your own power as a cocreator, several things happen. Life becomes joyous, it becomes harmonious, it becomes self-satisfying in the sense that you are fulfilling your purposes in the Plan. It is the self-realized state.

Some of you have resistance to assuming that full power. Why? Well, there can be many reasons. Some of you get confused about power and what it means to be powerful. It does not mean a person who is a world leader, has a leadership role, and is politically powerful. It could, but sometimes such a person is a figurehead and has very little power. Power is really in the life-force area. Power is an indication of how integrated and how plugged in to the Divine Plan you are.

The Divine Plan is life force in action, and the only way life force knows how to act is to act within the plan. There is only the plan. The plan can absorb anything it is sent; it can use it. It doesn't use it the way you put it in perhaps, but it can use it. The plan is a divine one; it is flexible, it is a growing, evolving plan; it is a tremendously unlimited plan. The plan allows for change. Many of you don't realize what that says. Is it already written? Has it already been completely planned? No! It has been outlined; it has been suggested; it has room to unfold.

For some of you there has been a psychological problem about the fact that the plan is ever being revised and rewritten. Most of you know that we speak of a cosmic day. This particular one is 4.3 billion Earth years. It is a conceptual framing-in of a theme to be explored, so to speak. For this cosmic day the theme is courage. This day is about three-quarters over. So let's say that preparation is taking place for the next cosmic day. Is it all lined out, cut and dried so that one just goes in and experiences what has been planned? No, not at all! I have been very interested because it's been on the drawing board about ten different ways, none of which were acceptable. Perhaps that doesn't fit your idea of perfection, so you need to think about what perfection means to you, and what is occurring now within the plan. The plan is open-ended. It is expansive; it is developing something that has never been done before, and therefore it is experimental. The Creator is ever inventive, ever innovative, ever curious. The cocreator council that administers the plan for this Creative Beingness is ever open to change.

Let's say that one morning, cosmically, you get up and say to yourself, "Good, I'm going to be a part of this cosmic day. I'm going to have an assignment; I'm going to have a very interesting day and I'm really looking forward to it." You report for work, and guess what? The day has been reframed, and they say "Sorry about that, but this day isn't going to go off the way we thought and you're not going to be a part of this day. You can go to sleep again and be a supportive link until it's your turn to waken and be active."

What do you think would happen to you emotionally? Well, it would depend upon where you were in the evolutionary process, wouldn't it? If you are mature enough you see that you have a role and that if you don't perform in one way, then your power will be used in another way. You will see that it is as important to be supportive of a cosmic day as it is to be active within it. But (and I do it too) we find it hard to accept because we enjoy the active state and being a part of it. Truly, only about ten percent of all creation is active at any one time. Ninety percent is being supportive and being a power base, a power reserve, until change begins to create what you could call a magnetic flow that draws you once again into active participation.

The Plan is not a hodgepodge; I didn't mean to indicate that. What I meant to indicate was that it is very flexible and flows in whatever direction is the most expansive and creative direction for the exploration of the subject being explored.

Courage, the Theme of This Cosmic Day

As I said, the subject of this day is courage. At the beginning of this cosmic day, the concept of courage was energized. We've been exploring what that means ever since. We've been learning about it; we've been expressing it; we've been supporting and energizing courage. I love this cosmic day. I think it has been especially glorious. I say "has been" because as we come to the final quarter of it, we really are beginning to prepare for the next cosmic day. But I have enjoyed this one and I know that you have, too. We have found a particular use for the archangel Michael during this cosmic day. Such a glorious being! The archangels, the angelic hosts, have played such an important role in this cosmic day.

The power, again, is the Source in Its expression, in Its manifested state, in the use of the divine state. Beingness is without activity, but the expression of It is very powerful. Thus, as we learn about courage we begin to see beyond the activity of it, into the state of beingness that courage represents. You get to that point only in about the last quarter of a cosmic day. Only in the last quarter do you begin to explore the state of being that is associated with the theme of the day.

Many of you will find courage, and perhaps the need to explore it — not in a negative sense, but the courage to say, "This is who I am; this is what I believe in; this is the divine that I am aware of now." It takes courage sometimes to do that. Do you remember when you were a child, and all of the children were doing something which you didn't feel was appropriate and you didn't want to do it? It took courage to say, "That's not for me!" I think one thing that is going to help the drug scene is in this area.

Keep this in mind, my friends: these things are not abstract. Sometimes I'm told that I am abstract, but I tell you I am not a bit abstract. I am one of the most practical and down-to-Earth teachers that you have on this Earth, but I stretch you conceptually as we talk about it. The most practical advice I can offer is: learn about what's going on "up there," because it is mirroring "down here" into the events that you call your everyday life. The power that is up there! Think about it! (The words could be "inner" and "outer," but I think "up there" and "down here" are expressive.) The power that is up there, then, is being reflected down here. That is more powerful than what you are doing on the Earth plane. If I went to a teacher with a question, that question would be (and no one has asked me this question), "What's going on up there that I need to be aware of that will help me live my life here?" You see? The mirroring of that level, the power, the life force that is being generated there, is coming through here, and that is what creates the physical experience. It's not the other way around.

Now, I recognize that when you're in a physical structure and you're surrounded by humanity, it's easy to think that that's your level of reality (and in a sense it is). But your reality is not, is never, complete there. You know that. So the power comes from there, my friend.

For those who have the courage, I have another exercise that you can do; it's a very interesting one. I would ask you to try it when you really want to be open, when you really want to accept change, because it will change you. You can ask through the archangel Michael, because it is his territory. Plug in, literally, to this courage theme on this cosmic day. Doing that will take you to the center of the activity level of this cosmic day. My friends, if you ask for that, if you say, "I want my energy to come through this theme that is coming through this cosmic day," it is going to do many things. First of all, whatever areas you have in regard to courage will become apparent to you. If, for example, you were very courageous as a soldier, and you saw many of your friends killed and your civilization destroyed and were perhaps taken into slavery (many of you were, in Rome) and as a slave were put into the arena and made to use your courage to kill a fellow slave, then that might come up for you, along with the need to deal with that. Or (this is a good one to look at) suppose you need courage to face your own unlimitedness, your own power. This may come up for you.

If only you could see yourselves as I see you, as I enjoy viewing you! If you could see the power that flows through you! If you could see how powerful you all are, then perhaps you would have a clearer perception of how to accept it. You are such powerful beings! Where is that power centered? It is centered in the heart area. There is no power without the heart area. The heart area is the core through which all power flows.

Some people seem powerful without any heart, but is that true power, does it last? No. The only way power can last is if it is built through the heart area. It is the center of the Plan: the heart, the unconditional love, the allowingness, the trust, the cosmic glue, the connector, trust that allows that power to be integrated. When someone storms up to you and orders you to do something, does that approach make you want to do it? No, though if there was enough fear in you, you might do it. You wouldn't do it because that person had convinced you that you and he/she were together in it; it would be because the approach was made in a way that pushed you away into a fear of what might happen to you if you didn't do it. The power area, when used properly, is literally a force that ignites the connection, that draws into you the power from others, from the whole Plan. It energizes that grid system we were talking about. But it must be sent out from the heart.

I have told many of you that you really aren't individuals. You really know that. You are a perspective of divine beingness that is going through an individualization process in order to understand who you are. The way that the power comes back to you in the fullest sense is when you let go of that concept of being an individual. When you say, "This power I am running through this structure is the Creator's, and has nothing to do with me in the personal sense. I am a mechanism for the Creator." That does not mean that you do not have a perspective of your own — of course you do. You have a unique and very powerful perspective; you are a unique "baby cocreator" that is going through the cocreator process. Your perspective is respected by the Source and by all the other cocreators and by all of humanity, but it is not an individual.

Using the very term "individual" puts up a wall, a barrier, a cutting off of your power. It puts up a wall that says, "I'm so individual that I can do it all myself." I've said it before many times and will keep saying it: You don't have to do it all yourself; you have each other. You have that cocreator level that can empower you. Yes, you have to accept it, but you don't have to do it all yourself. You do have to accept self-responsibility – that's not the same thing. You have to do that all by yourself. So many of you have been burdened with this. I don't throw stones at people of various religions, but I'll tell you one thing, my friends: there are branches of some of your religions that teach that they alone must save the whole world. My goodness, what a burden! Their faces are long, very sad; they have to save everyone. They have to do it. Well, you don't have to assume other people's burdens, or other people's power. There is a plan, and that plan is fully cognizant of what needs to be done. In fact, it's one step ahead of you all the time. It's there! Whenever you're needing energy or needing the power, it's right there for you. It is! All you need to do is open the door and allow it to come in. There is always an answer.

You know, if sometimes you're feeling tired or alienated, and you look but there doesn't seem to be anyone or anything there for you, all you need do is call upon the angelic kingdom. Just call on Michael or Gabriel or Raphael or any of your spiritual teachers. For an immediate connection, call upon the angelic kingdom, for they are the connectors. The archangels are particularly powerful beings; ask and you shall receive! You are, remember, a baby cocreator.

I've seen this work so well. I remember seeing a channel (another channel in another area) who said, "Oh, I'm so tired. Michael, help me!" Her doorbell rang and a friend said, "I thought you might be tired; I'm here to work on you." It took about two minutes for her to receive help. The friend, of course, was already on the way. You can allow the plan to work to bring you that power; it will come in through other people.

Haven't you had a friend say to you, "I've brought you something" or "Here's a book I think you'll enjoy"? If someone gives you a book, don't put it away to get to later. Look at it right then, even though you may not be able to read it all at that time. Open the book, let it fall open, and read what's there right then. The power is trying to come in; there is something there the power is bringing you. The creative process is knocking at your door; you're being empowered by the plan. You really can't miss. How many of you are there on the Earth – five, six billion? That's a lot of power on this planet. Is that not powerful? You are all utilized by the plan, hopefully in a conscious manner, but even if it isn't conscious you are nevertheless used.

Perhaps you ride a bus to work. You sit by someone. They may need just a "Good morning" from you. It's not the words you say, it's the energy that is a part of them; they need that energy. You are giving them the stimulus of a cocreator shove that helps them open to the power that the plan can bring through them. If you touch another – and I mean communicatively, not necessarily physically, but emotionally, mentally, certainly spiritually – it creates a link that this plan can flow on in a way it couldn't flow before.

If you keep dropping water on a rock, eventually there will be a depression worn upon it. Every time you create an opening for others, it allows the power to touch and touch and touch again. The power of that touch creates an effect. The power of the plan will work upon you and others in a positive way because it is who you are.

Power Plugs into the Plan

We are looking at power in a slightly different way perhaps, but that's good because it stretches your understanding of what it is. Again, it is a plug into the plan. That's true; you have to plug into it spiritually, mentally, emotionally, and physically. If your emotional body isn't plugged in and your mental body is wandering and isn't plugged in, then the spiritual and physical which are plugged in don't have the cooperation of the other two. But something interesting happens. For one thing, you energize the Earth a lot more when your emotional-mental structures are not as plugged in. Isn't that interesting? We'll use the symbol of the cross — one vertical and one horizontal line. If your mental and emotional bodies are on the horizontal focus but off-center, and your spiritual and physical lie on the vertical line, then the energies are not balanced and the heart cannot become the integrated center. So the power passes through you and the Earth gets it. The Earth can always use the energy, but perhaps that's not the goal.

You can energize the Earth in another way, and you do. When your four bodies are working in alignment and the heart center opens well, then the radiating effect surrounds rather than penetrates the Earth with your power. You actually do that as your heart energy becomes that radiant core surrounding the Earth. The Earth would rather have that more electromagnetic energy. The power we've talked about, in an energy sense, is very electrical and magnetic. It has opening abilities.

The way you empower the Earth matters. The more conscious you are, the more the power becomes a magnetic core. It is an integrated empowerment and it surrounds the Earth rather than penetrates it. In this way it is less impactful and more heart-centered; you are consciously empowering the environment.

If you sit at a certain location, will that location be empowered? The answer is that it will depend upon how you have empowered it. Some of you concentrate your empowerment in a specific location where you are and feel that when you leave that place the empowerment will no longer be active there. Some power will remain. The more consciously you empower it, the more you leave a vortex of energy there. I gave you the exercise that will build a spiral, a vortex of energy, and if you create that power at your location it will be permanent. You know of the places on the Earth where an energy vortex has remained for centuries. They were built powerfully and are still powerful, and in fact their power evolves. If the power is placed there in a way that, in contrast to a spiral, is flat or static or straight, it doesn't last. It needs the upward curve of the spiral to create an electromagnetic effect.

If you want to find the opening to the Earth in Vancouver that I mentioned earlier, you won't have any trouble finding it, because it's the whole block. In fact, the effect extends, in all four directions, halfway into the surrounding blocks. It is very powerful; you will sense it. Some of you may not like the energy there at first. If you don't, figure out why. For some of you, getting in touch with something so integrated is very interesting. Remember, I said some people have a residual resistance to integrating or opening or entering the self-realized state because on another level they aren't sure they can handle it. Well, of course you can, but emotionally you may not recognize it or even believe in it yet.

Have you ever known a child who felt very close to his father and admired him tremendously and saw him as invincible? The two spend a lot of time together. One day something comes up that the father can't handle, and the child realizes his father is not invincible. This is shocking, a disappointment, but the child gets over it. Yet the energy in the relationship changes because the child realizes the father isn't going to be able to solve everything for him. Some of you cling to a dependency relationship to the Source, the Father, as One who will take care of everything for you. When you see your own unlimited potential, it changes the relationship with the creative force, the Father, and you begin to view that relationship differently. Until you reach that point, you may go into an energy area that is attempting to put you in contact with your power by being a very energized area where you plug into a lot of power that triggers some resistance because you don't yet truly trust your own unlimitedness.

The Third Ray

A question has been asked about the third ray. It is called the ray of concrete intelligence, and we identify yellow with it. Others use different colors for it, but I like yellow for the third ray because it is the lighting-up screen by which you view your life. I like this area of Vancouver. The third ray here is going to light up your understanding of yourself and your life. It has a penetrative and precise focus. That's why it's called the ray of concrete intelligence. There are many ways of interpreting the ray system. Djwhal Khul has given extensive information on it, but this is my interpretation of the third ray. It's a specific lightening process that illumines the creativity so you may use it more clearly. Since the Harmonic Convergence there have been many changes of responsibility levels among the Hierarchy. Many changes are taking place right now, so I don't want to get into naming the master of the yellow ray.

One of you reports feeling something "funny." Well, what you feel is the energy of the soul. It is much more electric than it has been. There is a penetration into the cellular, or atomic structure. I have spoken of the particles that are coming in, and the soul has been sprinkling them upon you liberally. How much can you receive? I'd say you are capable of taking in an unlimited amount, one step at a time.

You ask about emotion, but are you asking about the overall consciousness of the planet – the mass consciousness – or are you asking about the emotional body of the planet? The mass consciousness is the overall consciousness of the planet, but, differentiating that from the emotional body of the planet, you have a direct link with that as well. All the other kingdoms have links too, including the hierarchic level, so humanity is only one of the factors that have to be taken into consideration in the emotional responses of the Earth. Because of the evolution of Sanat Kumara, the Planetary Logos, and his increasing maturity, the emotional body of your planet is ahead of the human level of emotion at this time. This hasn't always been the case, but as the maturing planet faces its deepest issues, it, in turn, focuses for you the same opportunity.

The Harmonic Convergence caused tremendous change – tremendous! The environment is much more stable since the Harmonic Convergence. There is more needed in the human response to this clearer environment, of course. You know how volatile the age thirteen is in the life of a child? Well, that's where the planet was in, say, 1982, 1983 and 1984. Think about it. That is about the level of the planet's emotional maturity, and since the Convergence there has been real growth. It's about age eighteen now, and that is an interesting age, too. There is more maturity at eighteen than at thirteen, but it is an important age, isn't it? In my opinion, by the year 2000 the emotional level of the planet will equate to age twenty-one or twenty-two. That is magnificent! Responses coming in from the level of the Planetary Logos, the Solar Logos, the planetary beings, the Galactic Circle – all these beings are inputting to your Earth in a way that has never happened before. The Earth has matured enough emotionally to recognize this input and use it. These are giant steps and possibilities and openings that have occurred here on Earth. If you're feeling the changes around you, well, they are here and it is good. There is a goal, and it is to become aware of all these beings on other levels and recognize them as partners. You may draw upon their strengths and they may draw upon yours, equalizing the process. You are no longer the dependent child; this cooperative partnership brings you to the maturity you are seeking through an integrative process that empowers you.

How can you think of the word "power" without affecting the personality ego? This is what I was addressing when I said that you, in truth, are not an individual. You are a Source-level perspective that is being empowered by the plan. You are a unique perspective, but the power has nothing to do with your persona. You are a Source-level vehicle that is being used by this empowerment. You can use the words "divine power," or "heart-centered power." For many among humanity, being clearer (in the subconscious sense) in understanding power is going to be necessary in the next four or five years in clearing out what power does to you. I've talked through many channels about what you might call the defend-and-attack mode. "I have to defend myself because someone is bound to attack me." It is the power that we associate with attack that must be reframed, reunderstood, rethought to mean that this empowerment is allowing me to unfold potentiality as a part of the plan. I am speaking to those who are conscious enough to know that power is going to have to be explored in many, many ways subconsciously. You see, whatever a person is holding that isn't clear will come up now; it's time to look at that. It will come up either in their lives or in the evaluation of their process in something like a personal intensive, where we lead them through the creative process.

Now you ask about the Pluto energy, and it could be a probing, a transformational influence. Some people subconsciously fear the negative effect of Pluto, the dark side. If I see you have brushed against that (sometimes it comes close to those who are power hungry), I will tell you and work with you on that. You are all children of light. You are not evil beings, yet you have to be aware that there are those who have chosen a separate path. There are those who are not running their power through the heart area. They are using power in a way that perhaps compensates for not understanding about love. Remember, the plan can absorb everything, and the negative doesn't have to affect you when you know and you believe that it doesn't.

✦ PART EIGHT ✦

YOU IN THE NEW AGE

Vywamus, 1986-1990

✧ O N E ✧

You in the New Age

WE ARE GOING TO TALK ABOUT *YOU* – EACH ONE OF YOU – THE PART OF you that understands, the part of you that yearns perhaps, the part of you that accepts and the pwart of you that realizes that *now* is a beginning. It is a beginning that is indeed cosmic, a beginning that is perhaps an opening to what you can be within you that has never been possible before – an open, new beginning. That, my friends, is what is here now on the Earth, and you participate in it, each one of you. You *are* that new beginning, and although you've heard these words before, I think you will now hear them in a whole new way. Perhaps we could say your heart will hear them. The sound of what I've just said reverberates through the heart opening and begins to speak to you. It says, "Yes, finally I'm beginning to glimpse what I am capable of sharing with this Earth – what *I* am sharing with Earth. Because of what I am capable of sharing, the Earth returns the favor and shares it with me."

There is a crystal chamber that I want to tell you about. This crystal chamber has lain deeply asleep since Atlantis. We will call this chamber a "she" that is awakening. She is waking up, and I think you are going to hear from her shortly. The reverberations of her energy are going to echo so loudly that humanity will go to her physical location and open her, and some of the secrets that have been hidden there since Atlantean times will again come forth. Are these New Age opportunities? Well, perhaps, but maybe it's more a going back to the Atlantean opportunities, opportunities that lie asleep in that crystal chamber, and a looking ahead to see what lies ahead in your New Age. Within that crystal chamber are what we could call some crystalline cylinders that will give you the exact blueprint of your New Age. So if you have the type of viewing device the Atlanteans had, they can show you visually what the year 2100 or thereabouts will probably look like on your Earth. I would say that from 2100 to 2300, the type of architectural drawings or images that are buried there will be constructed by you. Why? Because it's there already — it's been seeded into your Earth, and these deeply buried capsules that I have called crystalline contain the process of seeding into your Earth. The mineral kingdom, which represents that basic foundation of physicality, already has within it the seeds that are now sprouting onto your new Earth. Actually the sprouting has taken place already and needs only to be tended — watered, you might say. With what? Again, within the heart chamber lies the means to further growth.

How do you access that? Well, you're doing it already, but the accessing of it goes deeply beyond your individuality. It goes deeply into the seeds of what your Earth is becoming. As we discuss you in the New Age, we will also discuss the next few years on your Earth. I will attempt to show you what I see in the area of growth upon your Earth. We can, so to speak, also plug each of you in, but let's go to the larger picture for a while. Let's see the cosmic reflection of you by through looking at your Earth and what it is becoming.

All right. Up on a screen flashes the crystal chamber. In the center of it is a giant crystal which could be used as a crystal ball. The Atlanteans used the crystal to visualize and to see within, but they also used it as an energy generator and a connector into the energies of the Earth. As you look about the crystal chamber you will see amethysts and sapphires and rubies and diamonds and all the many types of quartz crystals. All of these are feeding into this crystal ball; all of them are creating, from their particular point of view, a connection into this energy with which we can use a projection process to see what is coming.

Let us move into the year 1988. As we do so we hear what sounds almost like a drum roll — a basic energy that is going to keep reverberating. Like the pounding of a great bass drum, the sound pours forth and we sense an energy surge coming out upon the Earth. What does that mean? It means that there is an energy emerging with a particular rhythm that has not been experienced on your Earth before. It was previewed by those who lived in the Atlantean era. They could see it, and they recognized it was to come. They expected it to come sooner than it has, but I would say it is coming at an appropriate moment for your Earth. So by the means of this drum, you enter into your New Age. It symbolizes not only a great deal more energy but also your ability to get in touch with a harmonious rhythm of existence here on the planet that you've never been able to touch into before. I have told you many times through many channels that there is a rhythm, there is a flow. This rhythmic flowing allows you to keep flowing, first one way and then another, and remain flexible, not rigid, within the life process. Let's say you keep rolling with life, rolling with life, and having appreciation and a measure of joy. If you have some expectation of life, and you hold yourself within those expectations, there is a flexibility that allows that ideal flow.

Perhaps someone doesn't meet your expectations in a relationship. You are capable of saying, "Oh well, let *me* do the adjusting. I will move with the flow, and because I allow myself to be that adjustment, then I will stay in the rhythm. It doesn't matter where I am in the rhythmic flow; I can be the one who adjusts in such a way as to keep myself in the flow." Thus it is the heart center and its allowingness that guides you so that you remain within the rhythm. You do not say, "All right, I expect the other person to make the adjustment in the relationship; that person must meet my expectations; I'm staying right here until they do." *You* flow, and *you* allow.

In January of 1988 we see the mass consciousness of your Earth understanding this possibility for perhaps the first time. We see in the area of communication an environment that will be more flexible so that each one of you can be more flexible also. You will see this reflecting within your nation's communications at a higher level. See that! Feel that! Stretch self, because you function all the way on both levels. Not only can you understand the Earth and be flexible on the Earth; you can understand cosmically, and this allows that communication level to be responsive and allows you to be responsive yourself. Open to it — open yourself. No matter how open you feel you have been, and are, you can always be even more open both to the Earth and to the cosmic level.

Those of you who have been coming to "points of realization" in your efforts toward development know that this means opening something and looking at it. Sometimes the process is similar to wanting to buy a house and then working to buy it. You finally buy the house, move in and furnish it, and it's only after all the elements are put together and you are there for a while that you find yourself saying, "This is really a great house! Look at it — it's attractive and comfortable. I really like it. I have something here I can really relate to!" So by July 15, 1988, many of you are going to realize what the Harmonic Convergence truly was, and you're going to be able to use it. In a sense, the mass consciousness of your planet will recognize that also. I'm generalizing, of course; there are those who would not understand the Harmonic Convergence if you talked about it for hours. But there are many who do, and will, because there is an opening and the seeds have been planted.

The little seedlings are doing well. Have you looked around? Have you looked at your planet and seen how much seeding has been done? There is an understanding of why you're here; there is a sense of the continuity of life; the mass consciousness is no longer closed into the idea that death ends everything. Life after death is accepted now more than ever. This might be a digression, but many of the people who are passing over into the spirit planes are making the transition more easily. They might be surprised at what they find, but they soon want to become a part of the activity and service available to them. Some of your students have volunteered to work with those who are passing in order to assist their transition. The important change is that those new arrivals in spirit are saying, "What can I do to help? I see the Plan, I want to help." They don't say, "Who's going to help me?" They say more and more, "What can I do to help?" This is important. By July 15 both those on the inner planes and you on the outer planes are going to see what can be done to help.

So from July 15 there will be an acceleration of consciousness. But what about on the physical? Well, during the summer months I think you will find something very interesting. In the first place, when people take vacations one of two things happen: Either they get into such frantic activity that they have to go back to their jobs to rest, or they go somewhere and rest and reflect. (Some balance the two, of course.) In a period of reflection you begin to listen to that inner voice. It might be that you have never heard any inner voice before. Something says to you, "Hello! Hello!" and you say, "Wait a minute! I must have eaten too much or I've been seeing too many movies. This is strange. I don't understand." But as you begin to validate that inner voice, others begin to sense that there is something going on within you; and then there is a reply. All of you here have that inner voice and recognize it, but others hear that voice of yours, too. They might not say, "I hear it — you've got a little voice talking to you, and that voice is talking to me too, and I'm going to answer it." But they might sense that something about you is different, that you're so much brighter than before, more loving, that the door to your heart is more open. They might say, "Why don't we spend some time together? I'd like to talk to you." What is happening there? Well, certainly that's a nice acknowledgment for you, but it's because of that communication link that is opening on your planet. The inner planes are really talking to the outer planes. The inner plane is simply that inner point of view; it is an intercommunicative link. Right now, and particularly after July 15, that interplane communicative link is going to be especially open, especially communicative, and that's important. It truly is.

So a realization made by each of you says, "I understand what harmonic communication means." It opens up a communicative link that allows the inner plane to communicate possibilities to the outer plane.

What is the spiritual goal in all this? The spiritual goal is to have the inner and the outer so communicative, so interactive, that there isn't any difference. If you look within or without there is no difference — it is the same thing, because the communication is flowing in all directions. In a very real sense that relates right here on Earth to your everyday, mundane activities.

If I look at one of you — and I want to communicate with *all* that you are now — all that awareness on the inner and outer planes will communicate through yourself, and to me and also to physical existence. This is a very practical linkage system for bringing what is needed to manifest your New Age on Earth. Am I saying that this will suddenly appear on July 15? Well, it could, but there are always points where an opening is more nearly complete. You can allow yourself to be, in your awareness, a point of great openness because you recognize now that this linkage is coming. You see, the goal is for all of you to be very strongly conscious of opportunity — opportunity to cooperate, opportunity to communicate, opportunity to utilize your potential, opportunity to integrate into that potential.

The Source, God, has said to you, "You know, *you* have this opportunity. You are as I Am." And that opportunity, that beingness, must be used in a very practical way on the physical plane. You are all very busy interpreting that and doing it right now. Each time an opportunity comes up, you have to decide how to interpret it and how to use it now — whether you *want* to use it, and then *how* to use it. I would suggest that between now and July 15 you start practicing. Use the opportunity to practice! The next time you are in a suitable situation, turn to the person next to you and talk to him or her. As you talk with the person, see what you notice about that person that isn't physical — something you *know* is there and is a strength. Do this often so that as you interact with people in your day-to-day life, you look beyond the physical. As you look at your neighbor, as you look into the eyes, you might see a joy level there. You might sense it has been buried but is now beginning to bubble forth. It is obvious and potentially unlimited. You see it and enjoy it so much that you begin to embrace that joy, hoping that you might also be that joyful reflection of the Source. That's an opportunity that life has validated, and as you validate it, it becomes more real for you, the Earth and everyone else to interact with. It is a very practical tool for recognizing possibilities and opportunities. You have all danced with joy many times in many lifetimes, and although life might not always seem joyful, it is basically an experience that leads to the joy of true communion with the Source.

This opening that is coming about July 15, 1988, will literally be the beginning of the *use* of your New Age. A rapid period of building will take place, and I think you will see it in many physical areas, particularly in hammer-and-nails building construction. People will build new homes, new summer places or survival shelters, or will repair, refurbish or add on to physical structures. I would say you will see a resurgence of architecture, with experiments in new types of architecture. There will be experiments in ways that are Atlantean, or indeed intergalactic in nature. There are those here on your Earth who are facilitating the redevelopment of crystal power. I met with one the other day. It was a friend I knew on the spiritual plane who is really quite an expert on the use of crystals. He had really enlightened me in that area. He has shown me a structure, from the perspective of the galaxy level. I asked him if he was bringing that technology to the Earth. He said it was part of why he was here, and I agreed that the Earth is ready for it.

So through seeding into the mass consciousness and the universal mind level, an awakening, a breakthrough into the knowledge of the electrical nature of energy and how to use it will come forth. There will be the direct infusion through beings such as my friend who will come in and talk (in a rather hidden manner) to experts in this area. They will be talking not only to experts but to some not considered experts who truly are – sleeping experts, you might say. You will also see the seeding of some of your scientists, who are waking up in a metaphysical sense. They are going to discover, to progress – one here, one there – to an understanding of a scientific principle. You are also going to find that some channels are "just happening" to bring in some advanced scientific principles that scientists have come across that made them say, "Where did this come from?"

There are many ways that knowledge of and use of this new energy are being brought so that you can utilize it to build the foundation of your New Age. This will be happening from about July 1988 to the year 2000 or possibly 2005. Whenever there is a foundation you will find a lot of new ideas. It's a very exciting time to live on the Earth! There will be so much that is new, and at about the time you understand something, somebody will bring in something that will make it obsolete. "That's old-fashioned; this is the new." This can be exciting, but it doesn't mean one lets go of old principles; of course not. You're building a solid spiritual foundation on your Earth, a foundation of knowledge of how to use the changing, escalating views of consciousness in a way that has never been possible on the Earth.

Take for instance electricity. You are going to get plugged in to the Atlantean understanding of electricity – you are really going to understand it, and there will be a lot of publicity because very ancient material has been uncovered that really works. At about that time someone will come up with an even more advanced way of using the energy, and that in turn will be superseded as you move beyond in constantly changing awareness of how to use electrical energy. Why? Because the electrical-magnetic energy is the motivator, the force, that is now present on the Earth and is evolving the mass consciousness. It is that structure that is being built on the Earth. Thus each one of you in your own understanding is going to get a chance to break through, to really understand the concept of electrical-magnetic energy and work with it in a very encompassing manner.

You will find that we who enjoy interacting with you on the physical plane are going to stretch you electrically. We are going to talk about light probes; we are going to talk about how to connect in electrically. You are electric in nature, and the more completely you can be connected in your understanding of this, the more you are going to understand yourself and the cosmos and how to connect and ignite. These are terms of which you might have some understanding, but by the year 2005 these are going to be in the everyday language. Everyone will be talking about igniting and electrical flow – not just your scientists, but everyone.

Here is a chair – an ordinary chair. In the year 2005 a chair will be an electrical system, not a solid structure such as this. As you sit in this electrical structure that is supported in nature, you can make it go up or down or turn back; if you want to turn over you can press a switch and it will flip your body over, or this way or that way. If you want to watch TV — which will probably be a complete room, not flat but three-dimensional — you can set your electrical structure wherever you like, and light beams will play in any color. You can have a light show. The structure you live in won't be solid mass unless you make it so for privacy. You have the means to construct anything with energy. Do you want a house in one particular shape? You make it that way, and when you're tired of that shape, you press a button and the electrical energy will rearrange itself to a new shape. You will be able to use this to project to wherever you want on Earth (or Mars) for a weekend, or to go to a Council meeting. This is *not* teleportation; it is the use of electrical structure in a way that allows you to be supported in it. Many of you will be able to use teleportation also. So it is the use of electrical energy in a way that supports or projects or moves you. You will have as complete an understanding of what electric energy really is as there has ever been on the Earth. You are now at only a preschool understanding of how to use electrical energy. It's always been rather a mystery to your scientists — they don't understand it very well — but this is a frontier for that understanding, and this year is a time of breakthrough in that area. You might not know about it for a while, for how many of you are in touch with the physicists in the advanced scientific research centers? However, you are probably doing some of the same work, although the scientists don't know that. All of you, including the metaphysical centers, are going to be at that frontier, breaking through in the understanding of the use of electrical-magnetic energy. That takes us back into the use of color, crystals, and all those tools that allow you to understand this more completely.

What is the purpose? Well, everything grows electrically, and the purpose is to understand the electrical nature of the Source Itself, because It is the projection of consciousness, you might say. That is how consciousness moves, the "embodiment" by which consciousness moves. It moves through an electrical sparking system. It manifests and comes forth. The rhythm is established electrically, and your understanding will allow you to see the basic rhythm of existence more clearly.

We, your spiritual teachers, those of us you call the space commands, are accelerating our program. There are in the acceleration process a number of plateaus and points of acceleration that are important. The Ashtar Command and some of the other commands have asked me to give you some of these dates.

The first very important date comes on March 23, 1988. It is a point where the space commands would like a communicative link into as many of you as possible. Certainly those of you who are interested in channeling anybody at all — the Hierarchy, your soul, the Creator, God — will get in touch with it on that date. I would suggest a meeting of as many channels as possible gathered in an open-ended meeting, beginning when you choose and ending when we get through. We are making a date with you for that day. This information can be validated through channels in other areas. The contact is being sponsored by the space commands, but the entire Hierarchy will take part. March 23, 1988, can be called Phase One.

Phase Two happens to coincide with the July 15 date. At the time of Phase One you will get further information about what we would appreciate having done in Phase Two. Phase Two will involve, let us say, a surge of recruiting channels for the space command. Further information will come in regard to that.

Phase Three seeds an integrative process spearheaded by a particular being who has not yet appeared on your planet but will do so and will be channeled. The channeling will probably not begin until about 1989. We are seeing an acceleration of those who are joining together on the spiritual plane and asking to be linked communicatively to the physical plane. There is an upsurge and broadening of this. Interestingly enough, in Kenya there is a very important link to this great being who will come in 1989. Kenya is an important area.

Phase Four you can't even imagine yet, and Phase Five is even farther out! There are five phases that have already been laid out for planet Earth at the galactic level of participation. That's what we are really talking about — the outline of what we, your galactic friends, can do to aid the planet Earth: we can make it aware of its ability to communicate galactically with other members of the team. It *is* a team!

For those of you to whom this sounds far out, I think your growing awareness of what this really means will come in the next year or so. If you hear the term "galactic" often enough it begins to seem real to you; you can *allow* yourself to entertain the concept.

Let's go back to our crystal ball. Its energy format is right here. One thing that I think is going to make it extremely easy to recognize is the amount of change appearing in the kingdoms. This has already begun; some species of the animals and plants are transmuting. Humanity has thought it doesn't want to lose some of these species — they call them endangered species. It isn't easy for you to tell what is appropriate and inappropriate when a species starts to die out. I suggest you ask your souls about this. Sometimes when you try to hold a species on the planet you are not doing it a favor because it is transmuting into something greater, but sometimes it is important to be supportive of a species that is not quite finished. It will be important to have guidance at this time about whether or not to try to help a specific bird survive, or whether you should surround it with love and assure it of support as it moves into another and greater format. The plant and vegetable kingdoms will be undergoing this same thing. There are going to be periods when humanity just can't get some vegetable to grow because it's through with the Earth. On the other hand, some small vegetable you've never noticed much before or a brand-new one will come sprouting up on the Earth. You can ask these new ones if they've come from somewhere else in the galaxy — you can attune to them, I assure you! There are going to be some puzzled scientists, especially the ones who think of the physical plane as static in regard to life forms. The kingdoms are changing, there's no doubt about it! There will be new types of grasses and grains and vegetables and flowers.

The color spectrum is increasing, and people are now going to see colors they didn't know existed because they hadn't been able to register that particular part of the color spectrum. This will be especially noticeable in the blues and greens and in violet, as well as some others. You're going to look at yellow in a different way. Have you noticed the increased use of sparkle and shine in clothing? That will continue, but I would say the use of it is going to change a little. Those using chemical formulas to create color are going to get a particular color quite unexpectedly. It will appear "accidentally," but then will be available for reproduction. It's just been born on your Earth and is part of the birth process of your New Age.

Sounds? Yes, you're going to be able to hear what dogs and cats have always heard beyond your ability to hear. They will also hear sounds new to them. The cat family has long had a greater range of sounds available to it; they are tuned-in animals. There will be some new cat forms, new birds, new insects and some new creatures rather like rabbits. I have told you of a creature "friend" I had that was rather like half rabbit and half cat. I'd like to see him on your Earth. Maybe I'll see if I can seed that form on Earth. There is a rabbit characteristic you'd just as soon not have? Well, that's interesting. As your awareness increases, all of you can seed into your physical experience exactly what you want to experience. I could seed into my cat-rabbit what I would like it to contain as long as it didn't interfere with any ethical point of view, or with what your mass consciousness has created. But as far as I can see you haven't said, "No cross between a rabbit and a cat!"

Think about your own physical structure. It contains light, but as you validate that, you *are* light, and this is going to change your physical structure. There will be (you'll all love this!) a tendency to weigh less. It won't be all that much — I'd say about a 2% loss at first, to become 5% in time, at a rate of perhaps 1% per year.

We spoke of color and the fact that new chemical processes would come out with new colors. The physical eye will have to evolve enough to register that new color. These things happen at the same time. When the consciousnesses of humanity and of the planet evolve, then everything happens at the same time. The physical structure grows into the ability to see whatever is being "born," and through chemical interaction, guidelines are established that support this — usually through the endocrine system. You could say that as evolution takes place, the key to all sorts of change — whether it be in channeling or increasing your understanding — is the activity and interactions of the various glands and hormone secretions. Your endocrine system can be equated to an orchestra. One particular instrument responds to the invocation of the others – the sounds, the vibrations, the stimuli. Thus as evolution takes place, the endocrine system stimulates the change. It facilitates it through the bloodstream by placing the hormones within the bloodstream, then it invokes a response in a particular part of the body. The body vibrates to a new possibility.

The eye is a good example. With its change comes the ability to integrate the seeing process, which all of you are opening. The third eye is opening. What facilitates that? It literally is the pituitary and pineal glands. The thymus gland, which has not been very active since you were young, experiences a sort of rebirth. In a rather complicated way it comes alive as you wake up. As you begin to recognize that you are growing and evolving spiritually, the thymus gland begins to be stimulated by the light of the soul. As it wakes, it begins to stimulate the interplay of the various glands. It is very close to the heart center, and the opening of your love center is the stimulus that allows you to see you are growing spiritually. I won't go into each particular gland, but the point now is that these glands change on the physical level. Your physical vehicle changes in the New Age.

Your mass consciousness is also a vehicle – a group vehicle – and you are all components of the mass consciousness of the planet. Each of you is like a new drop of hormone from the awakening thymus gland in the heart center of the Earth. Each one of you is stimulating mass consciousness to be aware of who it is on the physical plane. Drop by drop you stimulate and the mass consciousness grows.

The end of 1988 will be a new beginning, of course, as 1989 comes in. One thing that I think is going to be very interesting in 1989 will be the different use of the angelic kingdom in physical existence. The angelic kingdom has never really been involved with the third dimension. You don't often walk down a street and see an angel in a physical body coming along, do you? They might come in their lightbodies, but you don't see them manifest very often in the physical. I'm not saying that you're going to, but as the Earth energy gets lighter and lighter (and I think 1989 will be the beginning), the angelic kingdom will become substantially more visible to humanity than ever before. Think about what the angels are like. There are untold numbers of angels, and they will begin to use the physical plane more and more. As far as the Earth is concerned, what would you say is the most important thing that will happen as a result? They will bring in more light. There will be more of a love connection with everyone, and more joy. There will be a greater awareness of the validity of the angelic kingdom. This kingdom is literally a linkage system. Since the angels express the will of the Creator perfectly, a closer alignment with the Source will be realized as they come closer to the physical. It takes a willingness to move closer to the Source and to allow the Source to move closer, which in return brings another response of willingness, so there is a circular movement of response. Angels only occasionally become part of the human family; it is not part of the Plan, but occasionally there is some crossing over.

From where does one draw the energy to create an electrically magnetic chair?

The beginning of that will be an understanding of how to use crystals as a focus. Within the universe there is an unlimited supply of energy, so it is really a matter of focusing it and bringing it into your reality. You become aware of it all around you; you focus and tap into it. Crystals help you to do that, and they are the beginning of the tapping-in process. It takes you beyond your present understanding of electricity. You won't need to plug a line into a source somebody has generated. In fact, your own heart is the only generator you need electrically.

Is it true, as some scientists have said in their lectures, that it is dangerous to bring crystals into your home because they have picked up harmful radiations and they amplify those energies?

It is true that there have been times on the Earth when that has occurred with certain crystals. It is generally not true, but if one has personally come into that sort of situation, one might have the point of view that all crystals are like that. If a scientist has in his past experienced such a trauma with a crystal, then his past will affect how he looks at things. Whenever you look at something about which you have a fear pattern, the fear is very real, and you don't see beyond the fear into what else is true for that situation. Although a crystal might harbor some inappropriate radiation, it might also contain some very, very cosmic radiations that many times practically negate the less positive ones. So you won't be affected adversely. You have to look at the larger picture as far as energy is concerned to really understand it. That's going to be very helpful for those who have suffered radiation bursts, because one does not need to have a reaction to an atomic explosion – there is a way to negate that undesirable effect, and that way is already there! See the larger picture and how to use what *else* is there! That will be an important breakthrough in scientific circles. Your scientists have the ability to expand and see how what they have zeroed in on fits into the larger picture. (They can't yet measure that with instruments!)

Are the unfiltered radiations from the Sun helping in the transmuting process on Earth?

Yes, of course they are; they can be viewed as harmful or helpful. A lot of it depends on the belief structure. One needs, within the physical structure, to have the "filter of the soul" coming in. Light is really the vehicle that carries all of the energy components, no matter what part of the spectrum or whether you view it as "good" or "bad." One needs to learn to see this, and it is beginning to be seen.

What is the spiritual significance of 1988?

The year 1988 is a realized point that allows the reality of the creative energy of each being to be used on the Earth. By that I mean that abilities will begin to manifest that you never knew you had. You will begin to use communication in a manner you never before manifested. You will begin to use communication in a manner you never before knew you could. Each being on the Earth has a unique point of consciousness that, by the end of 1988, will be manifesting in a completely new way. There will therefore be an enlargement in the communicative vehicle of the Earth.

The year 1987 was quite surprising on every level. We had known for thousands and millions of years — or *always*, in terms of the eternal now — that the Harmonic Convergence was coming, but we didn't know some of the choices that humanity would make in the use of this important event. The level of consciousness rose to an unpredicted high. It moved rapidly and, in fact, after August 17, kept moving up and up and up. We looked at it and were really amazed! That's partly responsible for what happened next: It went up and prepared to settle in. However, there wasn't an energy structure built yet to support it, so it backed down to about where we had expected it to end up. We think the settling-in process is about complete. As that settles in, what then happens electrically is a full connection to what that means. The power surges forward from about December 21, as I see it. So the settling in of what is basically the possibility of your New Age is what occurred in 1987. There is not yet a full realization of what that means, but the settling in and empowerment, the energizing of it, took place. Though you might not be aware yet of the fullest realization of the Harmonic Convergence, still it stretched each of you to whatever degree you could handle, and has made progress much easier.

What will happen in Australia on February 13, 1987? It has been said something will take place then.

Well, there is a series of events taking place. The one in Australia in February could be said, esoterically speaking, to be the brightening of an energy point that will literally be a beacon invoking energy from the cosmic level. There will be other beacons at other points on your Earth. The Kenya area will have an important one on June 19. There will be one about April 15 in Australia which I will not speak about at this time, for several reasons. These are, you might say, adjustments of the energy that was plugged in in 1987. There are actually several ways of looking at that February event in Australia. Looking at it in a rather comprehensive way, it is a part of the realization process of the empowerment of the Earth's energy field, now at a new level.

Tell us about the meetings scheduled by people in the Los Angeles area. Are they being planned as a gathering of a large number of channels as requested by the space commands?

It's part of the cooperation of various levels of awareness, and really the space commanders are dealing with rather small numbers of people. The command wants to deal with a much larger number of people because they represent a point of view that is saying, "Come into your own — *now!*" It is an augmentation of your spiritual government. The hierarchic level has brought in this increased energy through the many beings who have come to reinforce the Hierarchy. As the spiritual government's awareness of the opportunity to aid the Earth right now grew, the Hierarchy brought in their friends to participate in the administration of aid for your planet for a particularly important period. We are having a gathering here in this part of the galaxy, but it is not especially just for you. It is to brighten this part of the galaxy — no, it's more than that — it is to brighten this particular point of the Source Itself. It is to increase the awareness from this perspective of the Source. All the available tools in the cosmos are being used to do the job, and we hope that on every level there will be full participation. It is the turning on of the mass consciousness rather than of a limited number of individuals (although we can work *through* individuals). But it is more the mass consciousness we are trying to reach.

Negative ETs and the Secret Government

THERE HAVE BEEN ALIENS IN CONNECTION WITH YOUR PLANET THROUGH-
out its history. You have always had beings come, and all they had to
do was know how to get here. I would say 95% of the ones that have come
to your planet have been very compatible with you — they have been very
spiritually oriented, and most of them have been your teachers and your
guides. The interactions have been good and helpful, although not always
known by the public.

Of the incompatible 5%, though, some of them have been scientists that
really had no understanding of the emotional body. In fact, many of them
had very little understanding of physical structure or the human scene,
though they did do some experiments and so forth. This too has happened
throughout the history of your planet. At the present time, this material is
being brought to you by various individuals, and there is some basis of truth
in what is given. It is not understood completely from one human being's
point of view. Individuals see it only through the type of material that they
have been able to read and understand, and from their own experiences.
This does distort things somewhat.

*Yes. The higher levels of the CIA and some of the higher levels of these beings
do know the plan.*

Well, they know some of it. They don't know all of it. What we are
looking at is a use of power on your Earth, and, of course, the Trilateral
Commission (it doesn't matter what you call it) is a power group on your
planet that controls the Earth. What is now going to change is that control.
As some of this material comes out, it will speed up the process of breaking
down some of these systems. That certainly is helpful.

But the available material doesn't tell everything. What is missing is that the involvement is not just American; there really aren't any national boundaries. The primary individual presenting this material came across much material in his official duties. Being a very ethical and a very spiritual man, he was at first aware of them, but he thought that the governments would do something about the situation as he saw it. Later he became quite sure that nothing would be done, so he is now bringing the material to the attention of the public. Now, in my opinion, this is probably the first of several exposés not only from American naval officers, but from different countries and different individuals who have seen some of the hidden workings of your planet.

Now, of course I am not advocating the things that have happened here — it certainly was not my choice — but I am telling you that many things have gone on besides this. This is only one aspect of a much larger picture. I do want to say that these particular beings, the ones who have done the mutilating, are not as widespread as the material indicates. There are only a few of them. Certainly they have some weapons, but some of that has been exaggerated also. What is interesting to note is the permission given by what I will call the Trilateral Commission in regard to the abducting of humans and to the mutilating process. This is really a part of the evolution of the planet, and it has happened before. There have been at least seven or eight times when such an event has occurred. Humanity was always able to solve it, usually with some help from us, for the plan moves, it evolves, it isn't stopped by something such as this.

These negative beings have said that they created the planet. Well, that is not true. They did not. They are not known, this particular race, for telling the truth. It is a difference in culture. They try to follow where they think they want to go and then they tell whatever fits into it. So I don't know that I would say that they lie, but let's say they certainly have an interesting basis for ethics.

They have not developed an ability to sustain an effort on any planet. They've had experiences on other planets, but I wouldn't call any of them their home base. They have literally gone from planet to planet, trying to find a way to sustain themselves. I think the reason is interesting: They are not of this universe. They are from another universe. Their life force is literally from another universe, and they've never been successfully converted to this universe. The fact that they can exist as well as they do is a surprise to me. I wouldn't think they could at all. But I have found some of you who are from other universes and are here. I am always surprised that the life force from one universe can be partially used, enough that you can continue your lives. They don't integrate very well, just as these beings have found that they aren't able to exist very well without depending upon a source of life force that is beyond their own ability to create within this universe.

As you all know, there is a higher plan, and you hold your Earth as custodians. The planet isn't yours; it is yours to develop and yours to grow and to use. There are those who set up and maintain some sort of safety zone around your planet. And you will probably say to me, "But what about all of this abduction? How could all of this have happened?" Well, it isn't as widespread as it is purported to be. There is some of this, but there is also within your human race, murder, rape, many, many things that you do to each other. In my opinion it is just about the same thing. The reason I think there is so much more fear about it is they don't know these aliens, and thus it seems so "alien," so unknown. But it is a part of the learning to live together beyond all of the things that you do to one another. I don't see much difference. I see it as part of a straightening out of the power structure.

Now, if we talk about aliens, we can talk about the beautiful spiritual people who live at the center of your Earth. And no one is frightened of them. You see, I can tell you about certain areas of your mountains where there are colonies of aliens that live there because they look just like you; they have been accepted as part of your Earth. But they don't come from the Earth, and they don't intend to stay here. What they intend to do is to help you with some of the problems you have — not only the alien situation, but the atmosphere, and the coming economic crisis. So you have 90% more "positive" aliens than you have "negative" aliens.

Is it true that there are three or four thousand?

Well, I don't think there are that many, but maybe close to three thousand. But if you look at your planet, that is not very many, is it?

They look like humans?

No. They do not look like humans at all.

I read in a channeled book that the negative pole exists only on this planet, and so the belief that anything negative comes from outer space is an illusion.

Well, you know I think that is an oversimplification of your Earth's position. I think it is rather an ego statement to say that your Earth is doing something that no other planet can ever do. Although your planet is unique, there are other planets that have a similar role of helping to resolve polarity issues. I would say that every planet that sits as solidly within the third dimension as your planet has (and there are a number of them in this galaxy) has played the same role. You could say it is that heavy vibration that helps to overcome this polarity splitting.

Let us put it another way. The denser the vibration, the greater the magnification of the issues, and the more it is able to resolve them through your clearer understanding of the splitting of the polarity, or what you call a negative/positive effect. Because that is all it is. I agree that there really isn't anything negative, but there appears to be because the issues split it so far apart. The basic issue is the heart versus the non-heart state. That is what I define as a negative/positive, and you can look at it in many ways. There is a far-reaching plan here. There are thousands of planets approaching the third dimension that your planet has been in. There are not many that are heavier than that, but there are a few.

So it is always interesting to sort things out spiritually. It is necessary to see that the plan never ever uses just one resource. That is why many of you in your soul work go from planet to planet to get a slightly different slant on the thing you are working on. You as a divine being have been working on the polarity issues within physical existence, and most of you have been on other planets. Are you working on them just on the Earth? Of course not. You are working on them wherever you are. Do you see that? The denser the planet, the more it magnifies. The Earth has been (though it is no longer) one of the densest.

Is it true that the inability to resolve this came from Orion, through Maldek, through Atlantis, and that we've been working on this all through the galaxy?

There is a certain very heavy karma, if you will, or an inability to resolve, that is coming through that, yes. I agree with that. But it is oversimplifying to say that the Earth is the only planet. That is what I am taking issue with here.

Makeup of the Secret Government

What is the secret government? Can you explain something about it? On Canadian television I saw something about a secret army that started after the Second World War and was involved in the Kennedy assassination and Irangate and all of this.

It is a part of this whole thing we are talking about. It isn't only American, of course.

This secret army is the same as the secret government?

Well, it is a part of it. What you are discussing is the enforcement part of the secret government, but only a portion of it. I think it is probably important to recognize that all governments are affected. They might not all have an army that is physically controlled by this — not all of them do — but they all have to report to the secret government. Many of your governments are puppets of this secret government. They are chosen by the secret government. It is the power structure. About 95 individuals hold the power and the financial resources to control your planet.

Where are they? Are they sitting together?

Sometimes. But they don't live in the same locality. They meet sometimes, and some of where they meet is in the material. They've had these secret meeting places. But they have a correspondence in several planets that helps them also. It is really a multileveled system. There are several planets that have power on your Earth; they are not black or dark or white — they are gray. Some of them are clearer than others. Some of them want to help the Earth and some of them are just in it for the power. It is kind of a mess! It is quite a mixture.

The secret government is not negative?

Well, it certainly isn't for the best interests of your Earth. Sometimes it is simply confused. There are negative aspects of it. In my opinion there are some aspects that may have started out as positive but then got hooked on power hang-ups.

But it is more positive at the moment?

No, not especially. I would say it is old, it is done, it is finished, it is time to release it. It is a tight structure that may have begun in some cases to help the planet. There were those who thought in this instance that good things would come from the landing of the aliens and the exchange of information and so forth. But then in the unclear use of the power, it became convoluted; and once a system is set up, until the spiritual areas opens, the system tends to be self-perpetuating so that the control issues become very entrenched; on the physical level it generally takes rather a large change, a great breaking down of the system. This is why I feel so strongly that the Plan will oversee the breaking down of the economic structure all over the Earth to make these necessary changes.

Do the CIA and this power structure control the drugs and use that money to fund the underground bases and the secret government?

Yes, they do. It is true.

Is it also part of getting a criminal element set up to get people on drugs and then unemployed, and then take away welfare and guns so they can then take over the government?

Somewhat. I think that is a little exaggerated. But certainly the money was funded as stated. Great funds were drawn into war preparation. The countries – not just the United States, but Russia and others – said they were preparing to defend themselves against war. What they were really doing was building space stations on your moon, and certainly on Mars. Both of these are rather well known as having stations. They are there. To refute them is to put your head in a paper bag and say, "I don't want to look at that." That is quite well known.

Are they still functional at this time?

Yes, they are still functional.

Now, another thing I want to comment on here is that this didn't start in 1947. That is when it was noticed that these beings had been coming to the Earth. They didn't tell you that for a long time. These beings have been visiting the Earth for at least 500 years, some of them. It reached a crisis point when they arrived in greater numbers. That is when they really got noticed.

But the solution lies in the willingness to change on this planet. Old systems of handling things that have gotten so entrenched must be broken down and gotten rid of. They must be allowed to break. They must be broken down. Then – and only then – some of these things can change.

Could it be that Kennedy was shot because he was going to tell the public about the CIA and the drug money?

Yes. Your President Kennedy was a great being and really a very spiritual being who came to your planet to help. I wouldn't call him an avatar, but I would call him someone who cared enough as a soul to make a great difference — a very spiritual being. And other countries have had these spiritual beings who have come to help and then something has occurred.

What about Bush? Bush is part of this, and he was running our country.

Well, that part I don't agree with. I don't think he was involved in the way people have said he was. Many people were associated with this who didn't really know what it was all about. And there are some who haven't been named who were more heavily involved with it. This material, although good and timely, is not complete. I won't give you more.

Okay, but what do we do now? Those guys are underground in the Four Corners area, tearing up the Indian reservations. They think they are holding the planet hostage. What do we physically do right now?

You make the government aware — those who are not aware — because as you know, most of your government doesn't know anything about this.

The presidents don't know anything about this?

That would be like saying that people in wars don't know what is going on in them. Some of them turned their backs on it and didn't look. This is true with some of the presidents and some of the leaders of other countries. They didn't look, they didn't want to know. So I would say that the first step would be to open this up on a planetary level to all of the governments, to really have leaders with courage say, "My goodness, this is a mess, but here it is. We are into it, so now what do we do together?" There need to be meetings open to anyone, in which your leaders will allow openness and allow the press. That isn't always positive — sometimes the press is into sensationalism — so that too has to be handled. But there is the need to have the people know and to have the governments know, and then to make choice.

Now, can you not see that you on this planet have a great deal of creative and divine power? If you can get your act together, you are going to solve it. There are those who are here now just waiting for the opportunity to help you invoke what you need to solve this problem. But you must do it together. Can you not see that this is one way that may force you to get your act together?

So it is a positive thing?

Well, from that point of view. I don't advocate forcing anything at any time, but I will tell you, that is the way this planet has evolved. Situations have been created that you must solve, because the whole planet is in danger if you don't. You will solve them, because you have great creativity when you do put it all together.

But it looks, at the moment, that the negative group of extraterrestrials at the Four Corners area have a weapon.

That is overrated. Overrated. Overrated.

But the government believes it, so they might as well have one.

But the government is overrating that weapon. I will tell you that.

The Hierarchy wouldn't let them use it, would they?

The Hierarchy would not interfere at this point.

What about the space command?

They might. Some of them might help you.

What do they look like? The material I have says the Sirians look similar to us, but their bellybuttons are in different places. Now, the Zetas look completely different, but the Zetas aren't the bad guys. The actual negative beings, in my understanding (and I may be totally wrong), look similar to us. Like the men in black. Sort of humanoid.

Yes, exactly. The ones that are giving you the trouble, when you look at them, they are not like you. You may see them as resembling you, but their true appearance is not like you.

Are they physical?

Yes, they are physical.

How do they look to you? I've not seen one. The stuff we've got says they could pass for humans – unless you get their clothes off.

Well, that is what I am telling you. They do not look like you in their structure and in their internal organs and in the way they have evolved. They do not, because they are from a different universe. Now, they do pass, I agree with that. But there is an essence, an emanation, from them that is very different from this universe, and anyone passing, anyone who is rather sensitive, would recognize them.

So they are not from Sirius?

Yes. But as I said to you earlier . . .

Ah, that was a stop-over!

Yes, exactly.

Can I take a shot at that one? It is only their physical bodies that resemble us. To the extent that you can see any of their other bodies, there is no question. You can see their souls in their eyes. If you can use your inner knowledge and look past the structure, then the differences are obvious.

Well, their physical bodies are not similar, either — they come from another universe.

They put up a hologram and it looks like the mountain, doesn't it?

Yes, some of them have done that, but you are generalizing. They have done different things. Some of them have gone deeper into the Earth. But I think the ones you are talking about are just barely within the Earth. As a group, they are not very well united. They don't agree among themselves very well. That is important to know, as it will make them easier to deal with.

They say Teller is underground frantically working on something that he thinks will exterminate them. Is that true?

I believe so. I think there is more than that. I think some of your German scientists are cooperating and helping — those who are aware of this, and of course most of them are not.

But Russia and the United States are total allies in this. The defense aspect is just a front.

Yes, but can you not see that that is true on all of your planet? Do you not understand that there are plays within plays within plays, and that is what this is? It is a play that has said, "We will set up a structure in which we will need a great number of arms, so we will fund all of these arms and then use the money differently." In order to have that, you had to create the Cold War. That makes sense. Because the Cold War went on for so long in spite of everything that was done. How could that have happened? Well, it couldn't, really. It was an artificial thing that was created and held in place through the power structure.

America and Russia at the moment, at least as seen in Europe, have come very much together.

They will allow humanity to see that they are friends and cooperating more, because they have built that into the power plan. I think it is important to look at that too. Because, in a sense, they are feeling the pressure by those that are wanting to get this material out. So they are softening, creating diversions and so forth, to give "disinformation" — they throw up smoke screens so that you can't really follow what they are doing.

Like Majestic-12 instead of MJ-12.

Many, many things. The point is, your planet isn't going to allow that anymore. This is the interesting part of it. Because through evolution you've entered the fourth dimension, and that really is going to make a difference. That is part of the solution here.

The Role of MJ-12

I have heard that the twelve men who constitute the MJ-12 — are actually trying to protect the mind of humanity. Is that true — that they really believe that humanity itself would not be able to withstand this?

Yes. That is what I meant when I said earlier that the motives for some of this were very positive. They didn't think humanity could stand this type of information. I think your governments and your power structures have always underestimated humanity. They've always thought humanity couldn't stand anything, and in my opinion, this is one way that you are rather unique. Certainly there are other planets that are as able to withstand, you have great courage, great adaptability and a great deal of heart on this planet. I want you to know that. You are very able to handle it. In my opinion, you can handle anything that you've created. Why? Because you've created it. And you can handle it. You can deal with it. I think that is the most important thing to get out to humanity. There is nothing that has been created on this planet that humanity, with its spiritual knowingness and its greater and greater soul infusion, if you will, can't deal with. I think that knowing that can help.

People have to realize, though, that even in your metaphysical community there are many who don't know that they create their own lives. So coming at them is this event. It is a mirror, but they don't always know that. If they recognize that they've created it, then they can change it.

What about these twelve men right now? Have they gone into a place where they are only interested in the power?

They are holding a thought form or a crystallized state. I would say that half of them really believe that what they are doing is still for the good of humanity. I think the others we could call sleepwalkers. They are still doing it because it is there and it is all they know. It has been there, and that seemed to be their role.

Are they being used by the 95, then?

Yes. Many, many people are being used by the 95.

And they separate us with doubt because they don't want us to be friends with another country [the group Vywamus was talking to was composed of citizens from half a dozen countries]. On a soul level, they don't want us to have allegiance to the planet.

And I think that is key — to gather in groups, to have great groups of people from all over the planet coming in. Great power. We will do some spiritual things, and perhaps even create a tape that can be given to people. We can do that, and I tell you, these spiritual things, if you believe in them and use them, will help. There are some practical things to do.

Who are these 95 people? Are they politicians?

They are often families in which power has been passed down. Often they have much money. The families have cousins and aunts and uncles who live all over the world and often have great arms factories. Some have had the steel factories, and some are certainly into the stock market, the great banking conglomerates and the great holding companies. These people are from all over the world, particularly from the developed nations. Not so many are from your third-world countries.

I don't care to state names, but there are still, within those 95 families particularly, some great souls that come in and try to administer the wealth in a much more positive manner. The unfortunate thing is that perhaps that doesn't always continue within a family. So the next generation may not have that type of approach. But some of them have really had good intentions and have tried to administer what they have inherited and to help many, many people with it. So that needs to be looked at too. I think both sides of the picture need to be seen and then what to do about it through communication and not through fear. I would encourage these people who are presenting it to do so in a way that isn't so shocking. It frightens people. All the fright accomplishes is the closing down of avenues of communication rather than their opening.

How Humanity Can Help

I think one some of your great healers could be sent to them. These beings don't even know they are wearing energy from another universe — their racial memories do not contain this. If the healers would move that energy into the format of this universe, that would be the first step. These people are desperate; this is part of the problem. They don't know what to do. They feel like they are going to be annihilated. They are grasping at humanity; they are saying, "Help, help, help!" A positive action would be to help them help themselves. In other words, change their energy. Work with it. It would take volunteers. Your governments and your control experts would have to allow this, but it certainly would be a positive step.

Would it entail working on their etheric body? Which body would you work on?

To begin with, the etheric body. They would have to allow that.

But they are so negative.

But their soul isn't. You can ask their soul for permission.

Yes. They are desperate, and desperation often allows things that are not otherwise allowed. You see that? Now, that is a very positive thing. So you might tell the people that part of the problem is that they don't fit in here. They need help to have their life force accept this space, this universe. I think anyone can understand that. Through something that they didn't mean to do, they never put on the garment of this universe.

Now, it takes someone who heals at the Galactic Core level at least to see that. It will take your very best healers on the Earth. A very pure, open, clear channel can also bring one of us through. Of course, that is the same thing, isn't it? This could be figured out. I am sure you would have plenty of volunteers. I certainly would be willing, in whatever form, with whatever channel, to make that available. I guarantee that. I am willing to be a part of that. All of us would do that, if permission were given by these beings. Without that, of course, we cannot do this.

Could people like us help? I don't know any great healers.

Well, they will be there, believe me, if humanity is willing to do this. It will take a heart opening from humanity. The fear, the terror, must be released. They must be approached through the heart. If humanity will do that, you will be able to invoke the healers and they will come. It is not something that you have to think of mentally. It is something that will spiritually unfold and will be invoked through the heart action.

So people like us can't do anything?

Yes, there is something you can do. We will create some meditations and we will talk specifically about what you can do, because if you want to help these beings, they need to be healed. Now, you have healers here — you sometimes call them psychics, but really they are not — who can see inside the physical body. If certain changes could be made in these beings' physical structures, then they could live. Not only that, but also the desperation would fall away, and they would probably be willing to go somewhere else. Why? Because they could live somewhere else then. They do not understand this clearly. Talk to their soul levels. One thing that happened to them is that they cut off their soul level. But the good news is that they can't be here on the Earth now because of the level the Earth has gone to. So there are aspects of their souls trying to get in. You can help with that. Then they will be more open to the process. That is something specific that can be done. They have to accept it — that is what you can't do.

It's like the hundredth-monkey concept.

Yes, they are already picking some of that up. It is confusing them.

Yes, that is what Zoosh says — they are starting to have good dreams.

That's right, and they don't understand it. Let us say you get a group of five thousand together. They don't have to be *together* physically, but they have to be together at some time so that their soul levels really join together. You just set that up with a large group here and other groups in other areas. You set it up so that the time comes together. Then we can give you some techniques to do this.

Great! I have a personal technique. I had to go back and open my heart to those beings that terrorized me and I started to see the correspondence with these negative extraterrestrials. Because they are the past of us.

Well, many of you have had experiences where you've had some difficult experiences with aliens. There is no question of that. There is nobody in here who hasn't had one, to some degree (some of them maybe more intense than others). So you resolve issues yourself through this. The mirror is there — you must forgive now. It is time to go beyond that, to forgive and allow clearer interaction with these people. That is what you can do. I wish I could say that was all there was to it, but economic changes also need to happen. And they will happen.

Do these beings have lungs? Can they be above the ground?

Oh, yes. Yes.

Why do they have to go underground?

Well, they are hiding.

Part of it is that they think they cannot survive in the third dimension.

Yes, but they would find a place to hide behind certain holograms and illusions that they have created. Sometimes they will put in a new mountain in a mountain range. If you went there, you would just feel a force field that you couldn't enter. It would be another mountain that seems to be just part of the terrain. They've used camouflage in various ways.

If you came in contact with this, you would sense a strangeness. You might even smell something; some of you would, if your senses were quite acute, since their process is different. It is a chlorophyll process.

They are chlorophyll-based?

No, there are some that are truly chlorophyll-based; these others have tried to use that process because they've been desperate. They have been trying to survive and they've experimented on different systems, and their essence has, if you smell it, something of the chlorophyll, like the plants and so forth. But you might not notice anything. Again, it would depend upon how sensitive you are.

How serious are these 95 families and MJ-12 about protecting this information? Are the people who are bringing out this information in danger, or is there a loosening up now such that they want this information out?

No, there is some danger, there really is. But perhaps in the spiritual work we can make a difference. We can loosen that up, because mostly it is stuck. But there is some danger as far as the physical level is concerned.

I've heard about an experiment on Mars.

Mars did have a full-blown civilization that didn't exactly fail but rather was finished in a sense. Mars was really almost "used up," though not in the fullest sense. What has been established there is the beginning, in my opinion, of more life on Mars. There is a colony there now. It hasn't been established in the most positive way because people have been taken from their homes and placed there, and have been forced to work there.

So that whole slave labor thing is true? About people being taken . . .

Yes. Some of it isn't as bad as that. Again, we are going to have to look at that. But I am telling you that there have been those who were forced to leave their homes and go and help with these colonies.

Where did they come from, these people who were taken?

From the Earth. From various people who have disappeared on your Earth. They took them there.

Who took them there?

The people who established the colonies.

Who are they? The secret government?

Yes. Representatives of them, is probably a better answer to that. It isn't that those 95 families did it themselves, but through their finances and through their power they directed it to be done.

Interplanetary Travel in History

How did they get there?

By spacecraft. There are spacecraft now on your planet. There are spacecraft that can go from one planet to another, although you haven't been told that. You had space craft as early as the 19th century. I don't think that was known.

I've never heard that! I thought it was the 1940s.

That effort was abandoned and a second effort was made later, in the 1940s, after the Second World War. There was an earlier one that was then abandoned and buried so completely that nobody much knows about it.

Was it true that the first attempt to go to the Moon was faked?

Certainly it wasn't as presented. It wasn't as presented because you had been to the Moon many, many, many times. Do you remember Jules Verne? Well, about that time.

Why would they say we went when we didn't?

Well, because of the fear patterns about telling humanity. It is for the same reason that they would not tell about aliens.

Because you don't float, there is gravity there?

Yes, there is gravity there. The whole thing was misrepresented. There is some gravity, though not as much as here, and there is some growth there. There are some plants and so forth in certain parts. There is a partial rotation, as this material gives; there is some area of growth and some atmosphere.

And on Mars, is there not a group of people who are living there that are not physical?

There is, and I've talked about them. There is another level, a whole civilization. But I was talking about the level that you are on. That is the one that is no longer there. They put the colony on it but they didn't stay. A decision was made that it wouldn't do what they thought it would do, so at that time they just abandoned it.

Where did they get the technology?

Well, from space beings.

Positive ones?

Yes.

And it just got lost? The whole memory got lost?

Well, yes, it did. It got lost, but purposefully lost.

Who? The power structure?

Yes. Your secret government buried that. You've been flying around for a long time now; thousands of years ago you did. So periodically you've learned how to do it, and then the power structure has buried that again, or sometimes a catastrophic event has occurred that was so difficult that you forgot. You've had two or three nuclear holocausts that have destroyed the civilization, and then there was the 500-year war, the pre-Lemuria thing.

How did they get to Mars?

They went into a spacecraft and flew to Mars. You have spacecraft that can do that.

Did they borrow the spacecraft from other beings?

They learned how to do it from other beings — from alien cultures and certain scientists who, once they got into that, were never allowed to go out again. All these things that have happened on your Earth have happened other places.

How much are Germany and Austria involved in this?

They are certainly well into the power structure. They have their wealthy members who have participated in your secret government, who are good standing members of the secret government.

Have we got these aliens as well in Germany?

The negative ones? Not right there, but close.

Can you be more specific?

Finland. There are more, but I don't want to tell you.

Did Hitler get in contact with these beings?

Certainly. There was a cooperation between the power structure, which then fell through. It was no longer cooperation. Hitler was supported earlier in the effort and then was no longer supported. They found him too dangerous.

My friends, these evenings are always interesting. The purpose, of course, is to aid the planet. I thank you. Good evening.

✧ T H R E E ✧

The Galactic Core

WHAT DO YOU THINK THE GALACTIC CORE IS? I'VE BEEN TALKING ABOUT it for a while. Many of you have been channeling from it. But what is it? It can be looked at as the center and the transmitting focus for the Divine Plan for this quadrant of the galaxy. It can be looked at as the spiritual center from which radiates the Sourceness that is appropriate in this part of the galaxy. It is refinement of Sourceness. It's responsibility. It is an aspect of Sourceness. So it really is a radiating and receiving center, both. It's really a transmuting center, and one that activates our own radiant cores. It activates consciousness.

Melchior is the head of this galactic quadrant. His subdepartment is spiritual, of course, but he is also the director of all of the levels, including the seventh level of the Galactic Core. There are others who are department heads, if you will, and are a part of that energy also.

If we look at that radiant core, it is the active part of the Cosmic Plan. Sometimes there is a reflective part, but this is the active part of the Cosmic Plan.

From that, what occurs? After you activate something from a radiant center, what occurs? What is the next step? You have to integrate it, certainly, on the spiritual level. What happens before or during the integration? Its purpose is to activate. Then what comes forth through that? It's a level of blueprinting that is on its way to becoming physical. It's a particular relay station of blueprinting or reenergizing the Divine Blueprint, activating it, sending it on to the next step.

What happens to consciousness as it is revitalized? It expands, and through that expansion it creates. It creates unconditionally. It is the spontaneity of the Plan itself. It is very cognizant of the Plan and its opportunity to manifest it unconditionally at that level. It allows every point within itself to create as seems appropriate at the time, but at that level it is unconditional. It isn't qualified by particular beliefs that stir up resistance from the physical level. There is very little qualification of it, because it is administered by ones who are quite clear. They have cleared out resistances. That's why it is important. It also stimulates all levels, and that stimulation comes from the direct input from the Galactic Center. Through the Galactic Core you have a level that is clearer than any of the more physical levels, and it is now supervising the activity and the development of the Earth.

Now, why would you think that's important? In an energy sense, it clarifies each level so that you can see you are a part of the whole. Such a direct access, which doesn't go through the less clear points of consciousness, is able to stimulate you more directly in your unlimitedness. It's just that simple. In other words, if you are going from the hierarchic level that is associated with your Earth, into physicality, less of your unlimited perspective gets realized. There have been fewer "ahas," cosmically speaking, so you don't get as stimulated with your unlimitedness — and that's what you miss, my friends. That's one of the most important things you miss on the physical level. On the spiritual level, you are stimulated more directly by the levels that are clearer. They come to the physical level through several levels of logic and hierarchic function. Now, I am not criticizing these physical levels. I'm just saying that the more directly connected you are with the Galactic Core, the better.

There is a wide assortment of things going on now. The galactic teachers are able now, because of the Earth's evolution, as well as your evolution and the evolution of the various kingdoms on the planet, to begin to directly access the Earth and create directly. They can create directly in connection with the Earth. Will they? Some will and some won't. There will be some galactic teachers here, and they will create directly on the Earth. Most of them will probably create a physical structure that they will come in, and it will be like an affirmation of what a physical structure really can be. That will be an affirmation of unlimitedness to you.

The point is that you are being stimulated now in different ways from ever before. This does not negate the process that you've used over the eons, which was set up for this planet. That is the support system called Sanat Kumara, and it is the environment within which you make your free choices and live. Now, I know all of your mental bodies are running around seeing how this all fits in. This is what I am trying to help you see.

When a physical planet reaches a certain point in its evolution, which this one is just beginning to stretch into, it attracts the interest of the group, which is the Sourceness Itself as we have differentiated It. Perhaps we could call it the cocreator council, which we've talked about in various ways. Some of you have heard me refer to it as the eleven plus one, which gives you the twelve. That is the director that has been chosen for this cosmic day.

So let's say at a particular point the collective chairmen of the board begin to be interested in this one "manufacturing plant" (Earth) that is producing very well and whose quota has gone to a wonderful new level. There is a sense of "We want to understand what is going on, and perhaps, because this has such great potential, we'll get more directly involved with it." Now, in order to help you do that, these beings utilize the clearest level possible to access this physical plane. And their direct connection at this time is through the Galactic Core. Perhaps briefly, before this planet is through with its lessons and its learning, there may be some stimulation from the universal level. In my opinion, when you all talk about being stimulated multi universally, you are really talking about something beyond the physical level. You will eventually be stimulated on the physical level multiuniversally, but here I am talking about a full spiritual center, one that is about as intense as many of you can see and take, at this point.

So this Galactic Core is beginning to prepare you to use your body of light on the physical level, if you choose to do that, and however you choose to do it. There is a broadening of the creative base and a bringing in of a more direct access than ever before. It's as if Sanat Kumara at a certain point in his evolution begins to pull in another teacher, another level, but also another consultant who helps the parts of him see what is needed. The Galactic Core contains these consultants, and *you* are the parts of him. You are the *cells* within his overall structure.

I think this is wonderful because, again, it is like going to a university that has guest speakers who talk about subjects that the local professors haven't gotten into yet. They are the clearest level of it that it is possible to contact on the physical plane, at least if you are on Earth. If you were on another planet (and you have been), you would recognize some of these beings, because you've known them before. They are not strangers to you, for you have always had a part of you that is a *direct link* with the Galactic Core.

Why? Let's look at the point in sequential time when your soul said, "I agree to be a part of this planet, Earth." You looked at the plan for that cosmic day, and there was an introduction course. You were trained to participate in this cosmic day, and that included certain functions as a soul. Then you helped create that — you helped create the planet. You helped create all of that with your energy. You locked the creative process into the Divine Plan that was to be developed that cosmic day.

So are you familiar with this planet? I would say you are. You helped to create it, and therefore your energies are literally a part of it and also part of the administrative headquarters from which you helped to plan it. So when you now, in your evolution on this planet, begin to invoke from that headquarters (the Galactic Core) from which you helped plan, you begin to say, "I think this is familiar. I've been here before, I know you. This energy is familiar." Of course it is — you helped create it, you helped it to unfold. Now, *that* is how that fits together. And it fits together that way because you chose for it to fit together that way.

You came into physicality for several reasons: to help create it and be a part of it, but also to learn those areas that aren't yet clear to you. That, of course, is an eternal journey, one that we look at very deeply in the personal intensives. We probe into that to see what the resistances are. You really are being stimulated in a lot of ways that you don't yet understand mentally, but there is so much going on spiritually that the unlocking of your mental understanding is perhaps the next step. Aren't you glad?

We would like to develop your association with the Galactic Core. I'd like you to see what that really means as it relates to manifesting the clarity of the soul on the physical level.

The archangels are a focus from Source Itself, so they are present everywhere at once. There is nothing local about the angels; the Earth hierarchy is the local government of your planet. But there are also the other levels of the Hierarchy — the solar level and the galactic quadrant level. Keep in mind that there is yet another overall galactic level. Up until this time, their communication with you has been through channels, through the stepping down of the energies. But there is now going to be some direct access. This is what is different — this is what is new. This is what is so powerful. They come with the permission of the system. They are sponsored by the system. They don't bypass it; they come in connection with it, bringing an extraordinarily clear perspective to the Earth and to all of you.

You don't yet understand what this clear level really means, so it filters down through the system. It goes through the belief structures that all of you have, through the belief structures of every country, of every continent, through all of the belief structures that have ever been on Earth throughout your past history. It goes into the belief structure of the *future* history of your planet, before you deal with it. It isn't very clear yet, but it is one of the *direct links*, and that's very good.

Some of these beings from the Galactic Core could begin to manifest themselves into physicality soon, possibly within the next few years, bringing their own bodies. But the overlighting (I prefer that expression to overshadowing) is starting already. I can't be more specific than that right now. Some of this is very delicate — especially this overlighting process. It's done to stimulate in a delicate way and it really emphasizes that.

How can all of this help manifest the clarity of the soul on the physical level? Could we say there are experts now, mirroring? There is an energy web, an etheric web around and within the planet Earth; this is the Divine Blueprint, the Plan for the Earth, the energy manifestation of it. There are infinite numbers of reflections that we've called little mirrors that interact with it.

In a space sense, there is a grid system that is being stimulated both within and without. There are points of light, like big cosmic mirrors, that have been placed in various parts. We'll call that the solar level — for us it's the Sun. These large mirrors of spirituality represent the inner resolutions you are making. Then there are some larger mirrors, representing the galactic stimulation. Now, that's not just still; it's moving. It surrounds the planet Earth as an extremely powerful vortex.

Now, five of the beings that are a part of this are beginning to approach Earth. What do you think happens? They act as five mirrors within that galactic approach that will be overlighting. What happens to this spiral or grid as they approach? Every part of that grid picks up a part of that energy and amplifies it at every point. The integration has to take place in every other level that is already energized. That's exactly why your lives seem so confusing right now — you are polishing and cleaning the mirrors as they approach.

The good news is, these mirrors are also stabilizers. You can visualize these as rods of power that hold and stabilize; there are five of them holding now at certain points of the Earth. They are in India, Germany, Brazil, Greenland and South Africa. That's very important information. It begins to explain to you what is occurring around your Earth.

I look for more rods soon, being put in to stimulate China — three into China itself. Then there will be one here in the United States. There will be nine or perhaps twelve over the next year. Because of that, there will be a constant reaffirming of your direct link with the Galactic Core and a repolishing, or redefinition, of these mirrors. Understanding this will help you to not be so confused. If you have a day when you are confused, it will be because of this tremendous polishing of all of these mirrors. You have had this twice already this year, and it will occur many more times. This will foster a redefinition of who you are as a person, as an individual within the plan, and also as a collective group called humanity. Now you can see why, just when you think you've almost got your purposes defined, this whole redefining of the Earth and all of its energies and what that means can occur. It shifts everything again.

Perhaps this begins to make a little sense if you think about it; it shows you what's going on now and why we've begun to talk about the Galactic Core. It's administering the evolution of your planet in a way that is much more direct than ever before. This doesn't interfere with the plan that's already been formed and the energy that's already here; it just keeps making it clearer and clearer and more powerful — more directly aware of its unlimitedness. And this gives you the chance to be more aware of your unlimitedness, which is why the subject of unlimitedness keeps coming up.

We have to begin to define what that means within the physical structure. What does it mean to be unlimited in a physical structure? Is that possible?

How? By maintaining the divine identity of that monadic level that you have when you come into the physical structure, and allowing the identity energy to radiate from within. As that radiation continues, the physical structure is not seen as a barrier to that expression.

This contact that is being made on the galactic level can be a stabilizer keeping you in touch with that unlimitedness. In other words, until you are able to do it for yourself — until the planet has gone to a new level — these are the rods of power.

We are saying that it is possible to live in your physical body in an unlimited manner. You are learning about your body of light. It can include the physical body. I have said to you many times that you can teleport. You could teleport today, right now, right this minute, if you really could accept that your body of light contains the physical level.

I would like to stimulate you and help you with that next step in your developing association with how to get around this planet without trains, planes, buses or cars. That step is important, because for some of you it is an indicator of the divine link that would prove to you that that link is there for you to use. If you could move from here to Turkey with your own body of light containing your physical, it would affirm your unlimitedness: "I'm not limited here! I can move, I can go anywhere on the physical level." You can move it, you can flow.

You will also begin to see auras, and some of you can already see them. That's not quite as much of an affirmation, but if you break through with your inner seeing too, then that is helpful, isn't it? Some of you are doing well. Some of you have just a tiny web of illusion about being cut off from this sight. Some of you are really moving into it, intermittently. Some of you are seeing quite well, but you need to turn up the color definition a little to see it more concretely. When you see the colors differentiate more and see the symbols that are coming to you, that is called the language of light.

The point is, you *are* ready to teleport and you *are* ready to understand the language of light and you *are* ready to precipitate on a wall whatever you want. You are ready, *now*, to do these things. I, Vywamus, would be the first one to tell you if you were not. I would not say it if I did not truly believe it. You are ready for these things! Perhaps, through these beings at the Galactic Core, you will gain a more real connection with it.

You can sense, then, when you step out (it takes courage the first few times) in your body of light, with your physical body in it too, that there is a connection that you can flow on. And because it is spiraling around the planet (it's stable, but it is moving within the spiral energy), it can take you anywhere you want. You are *not* just jumping off into deep space when you do this.

You have not only the Galactic Core connection; you also have the energy gridwork of the system. You could travel on the energy grids that are already there. But the most powerful way is to get in touch with these Galactic Core-level beings that have already set up their tracks within your atmosphere and within your planet.

❖ F O U R ❖

Restructuring the Cellular Level ✓

W E'RE GOING TO TALK FOR A WHILE CONCEPTUALLY TO HELP YOU
subconsciously (this is the housing for your creativity) to begin to
identify more precisely the new energy here that you can use in your life.
And I think that can be exciting and another step for each of you, because
I know that each one of you has certain goals, certain areas that you want to
understand more clearly. And the locking in of this new blueprint, this new
level on the Earth, can help you as you do it through yourself and your
creativity. Then, of course, it helps the Earth overall.

Quite often, several times in the history of your planet, the blueprint
(which existed for the exact energy structure that the Divine Plan has
produced) has been altered, has been changed. Why? Well, because of
evolution. There is a clearer understanding on the Earth, and although you
may look around the Earth and say to me, "Vywamus, I don't know, it
doesn't look that much clearer to me," I tell you it is. It is clearer. The fact
that communication is taking place on levels where it couldn't have even a
year ago indicates that something has occurred. What has occurred is literally
a new beginning for your interaction, for your Earth, for living your lives.
I've said several times that you're on another planet since the Harmonic
Convergence. It isn't even the same Earth. And it is even more important
to recognize the opportunities that are here now.

Now, let us go back a little and I'll tell you what occurred. There was
a . . . let's call it a test marketing. There was a change in the year 1900 when
this new blueprinting system was tested. Many of you were here, not
necessarily in this body (some of you in another one), but your creativity was
here in the year 1900. In that year there was what I might call a pregnant
pause in the energy of your planet. It was almost as if almost there was a
pause that led to what we might call hope. Hope that perhaps humanity

would avoid some of what did occur later on, some of the wars. And in 1900 the Hierarchy on your planet, in connection with other levels — certainly the solar level and certainly the Galactic Core level — said, "We'll try it out. We'll see when we put this new energy system in, how humanity does with it. So in the year 1900 it was laid in.

Now, the Cosmic Plan is open-ended; do you realize that? It really is experimental. Isn't that interesting? The Creator is learning new things all the time, so there isn't a fixed system that has a particular point that it wants to reach at a particular time, although we make projections and say that the probabilities are that by the year 2000, for example, certain things will have occurred. But there is experimentation, not in the negative sense. (Some of you have a little bit of programming in that area because you may have been on a spaceship where they tried to see what made you tick and it didn't feel very good.) The point is that this experimentation is saying to you, "Now, how much can you recognize of your own strengths, and how much can you recognize of your own unlimitedness?"

So the Divine Blueprint was laid in the year 1900. Now, I would have to talk to each one of you individually to tell you how you did with it, but the point is that you have memories of it. Right now in this room, the angelic kingdom is lighting in the energy as it was in the year 1900. I think it might be interesting for you to begin to feel that.

If you can, try to sense it in the head area and in the third-eye area. Sense it almost like a stream of sparks that make contact and become liquid, dripping through the physical structure. Some of you may be able to feel this, and some may simply feel a little bit of warmth, a little bit of movement in certain areas. We're laying in more and more of this right now so that you have a glimpse of the way it was done in the year 1900. Why? Because I want you to see the difference between what was laid in then and what is available now. The wattage is stronger now. There's more current in it now, but the revision of the Divine Blueprint began then.

Now, let us say that you begin a business, and you have certain ideas that you would like to create. You know how it is when you start by yourself; pretty soon you can't do everything yourself, so then you begin to hire people to assist you. Now, as you hire them you begin to turn over to them some responsibilities. (At least if you're wise you do, otherwise you're going to get buried in a lot of detail that you can't handle.) Pretty soon the creative idea that you began with begins to expand. Why? Because others add their creativity to it, and the original plan that you had probably becomes modified a little bit. The other people's input begins to create maybe in the same general area, "but why don't we try this and why don't we do that?" So if you're a wise businessman, you accept the creative ideas of others if they seem to fit in with what you're doing, and you expand and perhaps expand and expand.

You know, my friends, I was in business when I was on the physical level. I enjoyed business and I was good at it. Why? Because I allowed other people to add their creativity to mine, and we expanded a great deal because of that. The point is, we could look at the Divine Plan given to us by the Creator as an exercise that is similar to a business. We couldn't exactly say it's a business, although perhaps its business is transformation, is evolution. The Source gives all of us equal responsibility in this plan, and it begins to change and grow and be modified by the creative input that you and all of your friends bring it. That's why the plan is not fixed. That's why it isn't set in stone, you could say. It is open for change.

Change is one of the things that is perhaps most important for you to learn to handle. Well, you've heard it before: the only constant that exists is change. And perhaps this change right now is in terms of bringing in the Divine Blueprint that is a little different than it was. It's been modified, it's grown. It has a great deal of electrical content. The reason is that each of your personalities is allowing much more of your soul content to come through you than before. Thus this electrical energy has much more of home in your physical structure than perhaps in your last few lives. So in 1900 it was not as electrical, and some of you didn't pay much attention to it.

I would like to show you the difference. See how much you can get in touch with. We laid in the blueprint in 1900; the wattage of that same blueprint is going to be turned up right now. We're doing it now; I want you to feel the difference. It's being updated by 89 years – updated in the amount of progress or evolution that each one of you has made, and there is a lot of progress or evolution that you have all made since that time.

There is, then, a sorting-out process that is going on within you. Let's say that some of you have been standing under a tree and lightning struck that tree. Guess what? In the subconscious there may be some fear of this electrical energy: "You know, when I get a lot of that it shocks the physical and that's very difficult. It hurts and perhaps it destroys the structure." There may be memories of that.

I always try to bring people the areas of difficulty in a particular area. And so if it is all right with you, I'm going to give you three major categories. Believe me, it's interesting to note that in this whole audience there are only three categories of electrical areas. I would like to tell each one of you which category you fit into; I think that will be interesting for you. First, we have those who have stood under a tree and the electrical flow was there and perhaps they lost the structure. At least they were burned by it. The tree syndrome, we call it, the electrical syndrome.

Then long ago some of you (there is a group here together tonight, it is kind of interesting) were on another planet together as slaves, my friends; and if you didn't behave you were beaten with an electrical whip. So there are a number of you who have the electrical-whip syndrome related to this electrical energy.

Now, the third one is rather interesting. In Egypt, many of you (I think you know this) had very powerful lives with priests and priestesses. Some of you took initiations in Egypt, and in one period you were put in a kind of sarcophagus and it was plugged in with crystal and power – and sometimes the crystals shorted out. Now, if they did that too extensively, sometimes you got a nice shock out of it, but sometimes the physical structure didn't survive.

You all fit into categories. Now, why am I going into this? I feel that the most important thing you are dealing with is accepting this Divine Blueprint, which is extremely electrical in nature. These experiences have caused perhaps just a little resistance within all of you. What can you do about it? Well, I'm suggesting that, whatever category I give you, you go back and change that experience. Go back and take out the experience that occurred there.

One thing that I discovered, and I think it's important, is that you change it gradually. In other words, change it in steps. Take perhaps three sessions to change it. For example, if you were hit by lightning and you didn't survive, then perhaps you could survive it in the first step, although it still happened. In the second step, it may have struck nearby but if you were in the third step perhaps it didn't happen at all.

Why in steps? Because if you go back and you try to change it all at once, your subconscious doesn't recognize that it was the same experience. It says, "Well, that was interesting; I'm glad we didn't have that experience." It doesn't see the connection with what is stored there from the past life. So learn to make these changes, because you're in the process of sorting out whatever limits you.

The Electrical Nature of Soul

Do you know that each one of you is completely unlimited? You're learning you are, but perhaps you can't yet see it in yourself completely. We are looking at what I think is an important area: the bringing in of the electrical energy of the soul so that it may activate the Divine Blueprint evenly. That's very important, because what I'm seeing is that this has been laid in. Here is an example. If we look at an energy field as a grid system (and of course we're simplifying it) with lines running this way and lines running that way that fit in the crown chakra, then instead of its being evenly distributed, we've got holes in it, you see. It's accepting the energy only partially. I want to do several things tonight to help you to even out and accept more and more of this energy that literally comes through the eighth chakra, which is your soul star. It is the part of yourself that the soul has made available as a physical gate to bring the energy through the eighth chakra.

One tool we haven't mentioned yet that can be very helpful is the Earth (you know, that thing that you walk around on every day). The good news here is that the Earth has embodied a new level that all of you now are trying to reach. For thousands of years you were the leaders; the Earth was coming along well, but you were a little ahead of it. It's turned around now. The Earth's energy and its acceptance of its potential is a little bit ahead of yours. So if we begin to invoke the Earth's energy coming up and helping you balance the crown chakra from that direction, between the soul and the Earth, don't you think it will be better? I think so. I'm seeing bumps all over like you get when you have measles. Some of you look like that in this electrical assimilation. Some of it is assimilated in one place and not in another, particularly not in the solar plexus. How many of you can relate to that? Sometimes it feels all charged up there, doesn't it?

Because the main chakras do not have an even distribution of this Divine Blueprint, I thought that we would work specifically. This is research. I have not done this before; you are the first. We'll see how it works. That's important here because you are what I call a metaphysically sophisticated audience. You've heard many different things, haven't you? And it's interesting and it perhaps activates many things in you.

Now, let's see what we can do to settle it down a little, to allow it to assimilate through your spiritual body, your mental body, your emotional body, your etheric body and — perhaps most importantly — into and through your physical body.

You could look at a cell in many ways. Each one of you looking at a cell would see something different. You wouldn't see them exactly alike. But I want to give you the simile (they don't really look like this) of a cylinder. We will say each cell is a cylinder, and we want that cylinder to be absolutely clear and then allow the electrical flow to flow clearly through it. Now, some cells sit this way and some cells sit this way connecting with other cells. So we have the network of energy that flows through them, the electrical energy. It really becomes like a gridwork in your physical body.

Particularly important is the brain area. The pattern of the left hemisphere of your brain is not the same as the right hemisphere. You know that. And the vibration level is not the same. What unifies them is the soul. What allows them to speak to one another, to hear each other at their different vibrational rates, is the energy of the soul.

So you see, by learning to bring this more electrical energy into a blueprinting system that is more evenly distributed, you are going to begin to bridge the hemispheres of the brain so that your logical side talks to that part that you call creative and musical and so forth. So that your knowingness speaks to the logic and the conceptual area. So they can create together the type of life that you really want. That's our purpose here this evening. Do you think it might be fun to try it? Even if you don t, let's do it anyway and see what happens. Remember, life is full of new things. This is something new and I invite you to try it with me.

First I would like to go through the audience, giving you which type of electrical trauma you have: the tree, the whip or the crystal. And you will know which one to go back and work with. That can be helpful because, as I said, the goal is to assimilate the electrical energy well, and some of you are doing it better than others. All right. Now I invite you to do this in a meditation. So if you wish, close your eyes.

Contact Your Energy Grid System

❦ *Now, the crown chakra lies two or three inches above your head. Let's activate it as golden energy flowing in that electrical gridwork. Spend a moment or two just allowing a foundation to be established there. You don't have to visualize this. If you can see it, fine; if you can't see it, imagine it, then know it. If you can't know it, then sense it or feel it. It doesn't matter. Simply make contact with an energy grid system that is gold in color and flow the energy through it now. Flow it both ways. Follow it one line at a time, just follow it, even it out as much as you can until you can imagine a current of energy that is evenly flowing in this great system. Spend a moment with that. Do a little toning to help you with that. Just spend a little time getting in touch with it.*

❦ *All right, now envision or know or imagine the soul star, which for most of you is another five or six inches above your head. You have other higher chakras – the twelfth, the eleventh, the tenth, the ninth; the soul star is the eighth. Those chakras are also taking part in this process, but we are focusing now on the soul star. I invite you now to pour energy into the soul star. It will run through into the crown and begin to be distributed throughout the chakra system. I'd like the core to be electrically blue, but I invite you to keep monitoring the crown chakra. Pour it now, but see that it pours evenly; you don't want any holes in the crown chakra. If you get it centered so that the outside doesn't have enough energy, then pour it a little differently. Envision it pouring as evenly as possible through the crown chakra. Now please put that on automatic. When you get it evened out, then put it on automatic so that there is some, not a tremendous amount, but a constant pour from the soul star. It's going into the soul star and from there into the crown chakra. Know that it's dripping on down to the other system, but right now we're going to ask that a reflection of your crown chakra appear within the Earth.*

❦ *Follow that down now to the core of the Earth. You're going to invoke from the Earth the help that you need. There is an electrical energy format, a blueprint there that is going to reflect back to you like a mirror. Ask for that even if you can't see it. Imagine it. It is an energy reflection that is coming back and it is absolutely balanced. It is coming from the Earth, and now you've got that down in your feet. You're standing on it, your feet are actually 'in it, and now there's another level that's settling in and you're sitting right on it, so that you have two levels, one at your feet and one at the base chakra.*

❦ *Now I invite you to continue to pour through the soul star chakra, and as you do, a corridor of energy forms from each part of that chakra downward, connecting with its corresponding point on the base chakra; then down to its* corresponding point at the feet, where you have already connected into the Earth. There are fine lines of electrical blue energy dripping down and making the connection like those in caves – stalactites and stalagmites, which come together. The energy is dripping down and making these formations and it is like an energy column surrounding you. It is centered in your chakras but it radiates out and brings the streams of energy down into your physical structure.

❦ If you feel like moving a little, please do, because there may need to be some physical adjustment. You may need to move your back, you may need to rotate your stomach a little, your shoulders may need to be moved a little, or your arms or your legs. Adjust your physical structure now as you keep developing this energy. This is extremely important. Allow it now because the angels are helping you to bring in this new blueprint. The body hasn't used it this fully before, and it's coming now into the energy structures of your spiritual body, your mental body, your emotional body, the etheric level that surrounds the physical body, and then into the physical body itself. So there is an alignment process going on. Allow the angels to help you. We are there in great number. Some of the greatest healers that have been on your planet are here tonight to help you with this.

❦ Now I would invite you to begin a slow breathing technique in your own rhythm. Be conscious of your breath. Breathe in and hold it for a moment and then quietly breathe out. Become aware that you are learning to vibrate this energy in a more evenly distributed manner. Even if your imagination says this isn't real, or you say to your imagination that this isn't real, it is. So allow, just allow it to process within you. I want to hold you within this focus for a while. Make sure you monitor the energy so that it is still pouring through the soul star into the crown chakra.

❦ And you might note, now moving beyond the crown, what is going on in your third-eye chakra. I invite you to see it as a clear energy disk, a clear energy disk in the third-eye area. Even out the energy there. Let it be a process of these small columns of light that are this electrical blue energy. Keep straightening it out. If you need to, take in your spiritual hand the Violet Flame and clear out something. If you find some breaks or something that isn't complete, cleanse that now with your Violet Flame. Work on this.

❦ The next chakra will be the throat. I'm going to invite you to work at your own level. When you feel that the clear third-eye energy disk is now being penetrated by these columns of blue light that drip in the formation of the ideal Divine Blueprint in the crown chakra, then move on to the throat, seeing it as an energy disk that is transparent. Even out that energy.

❦ When you feel that is balanced, then move into the heart, doing the same thing very gently. When you've done that, move on to the solar plexus. Even it all out. Then the polarity chakra – and check again the base chakra.

❦ Now I want to give you some time to do that, and to help you I'm going to simply allow a little toning. The energy needs to be stabilized enough that *your subconscious, your creativity, really gets the idea. This is the ideal blueprinting. We will take it this far and afterwards we will proceed. So let me give you a little time.*

❦ *Keep working on your chakras. Keep cleansing them and connecting them into this blue energy. Keeping working with it, keep allowing yourself to sense now the connection between all of the chakras. See if you can feel it, one balancing out the other. You may feel it perhaps most strongly in the solar plexus area. If this is an area that sometimes seems stirred up for you, it's going to feel a lot of support in this process if you allow it, because it will sense the connection electrically. We are stimulating, then, an electrical flow that is organized into the Divine Blueprint and is unique for you but is a part of something greater on the Earth. So keep organizing it, keep working with it. Keep allowing that flow. Just be patient.*

❦ *One of the things that is important in this type of work is to stay with it for a few minutes, to really relax and allow the process. Many of you get a little impatient trying to hurry it. It is important just to allow it, relax into it.*

❦ *This, then, is the new blueprinting system that is available to you. Now the Earth is stabilizing your feet area and you may be feeling some energy there because your feet have never before been as connected in this way. See if you can sense a stability that wasn't there before. Take that to the base chakra. Be sure, absolutely sure, that you visualize or know or imagine that your base chakra is a clear energy disk. Many times when you have a headache, when there is so much energy in your head you don't know what to do with it, all you have to do is open your base chakra. So open it now. See it as a clear energy disk. The energy flows now all the way down and then it connects with the energy of the Earth that is flowing up. See where that comes together for you. For some of you, perhaps for most of you, as you develop it and reach a certain level of maturity in this use it will be at the heart. See if you can touch into that now at the heart level. All right. Now I would invite you to do the following.*

❦ *Create in the center of the heart area a vortex. I would like you to see a spiral; it doesn't matter whether it is clockwise or counterclockwise. Neither one is accurate because it is not in sequential time nor in space. Your physical heart isn't really in your spiritual heart. So it is simply an indicator for whichever direction of movement that you're imagining now. Let the energy of that ideal blueprint drip through you. Bring it up from the Earth, uniting it in the heart, and spin it, spin it, spin it. Do it gently, but spin it, spin it, spin it. And then allow it to radiate out. Allow it. This opens the heart in a way that, if you continue to do it, will make a great deal of difference in your life.*

❦ *Now, I like pink in association with the heart. See if you want pink there. If you want it electrical blue, that's fine. But see what color you chose to use there. Then spin it, spin it, allow the heart to radiate out. As it goes out now it tells the universe, "I've got my act together, I'm balanced here. Look,*

I'm using the ideal blueprint." And, believe me, the universe will notice and it will say to you, "Good. Here is mirroring of that balance." And you begin to receive from the universe balanced mirroring. Some of you aren't used to that. But it can come back to you, and what will come back are the types of activities, types of response from others that you want, the types of mirrorings that are very balanced. Someone may say to you, "How lovely you are." "I appreciate you so much." "Can I help you?" "Oh, thank you for what you are doing." "Here is an opportunity for you now." Does that sound good? All right.

Soul Is Partner of Earth

Gently, then, come back. But know that this process is something that, now that you've begun, is going to work. It is like starting a landslide; it will continue to progress. Now, what you might do when you go home is to monitor it just before you go to bed. See what's going on. And remember, if the chakras, your energy centers, are clear, are seen as transparent disks, it's going to help you. This motion, this sense of connection coming from both directions, is important because your soul is a partner of the Earth. So why not bring in that divine partnership and acknowledge it?

One thing that you can also do is to sense that the Earth is spiraling as a heart. That's kind of fun, isn't it? And as the Earth spirals as a heart, see what is awakened within you. See the feeling nature, what feelings come up from it for you. Some of you aren't very much in touch with your feelings. You have a tendency to bury them. It's not so bad to have feelings. They're not just negative, they can be very positive.

So the mirroring will come in several ways. It will come in spiritually as reflected to your spiritual body. It will come in mentally, it will come in emotionally, it will come in etherically. And I tell you it will come in physically. It can really make a difference. This kind of a process is probably one of the few short cuts available. (I think there are a number of you that like short cuts. I know I've heard that from you, you're in a hurry to go somewhere. I'm not quite sure where, because all there is is the process.) So by acknowledging your connection with the Earth and by really accepting it from an energy point of view for soul, you will create together the type of life that you're looking for. I think our energy approach can be very important in this regard.

Soulness, then, is simply the level of your true identity that is used to create your life purposefully on the Earth. Can you see that identifying it as energy and welcoming it begins to make changes within your physical structure too?

How do you feel? Can you tell that something is processing within you? I can tell. I invite you to view through your third eye the energies in the room now to see how they've shifted. It's good practice. The pattern is more regular, more orderly. Perhaps some of you can sense that. There is divine order. In a sense what we are doing is a synchronicity of really feeling in divine order. Can you see how important that is? All of your emotional bodies are trying to understand that, trying to understand divine order and feel connected within it and feel a part of the universe. As you do energy work it can be extremely important. There are about a million ways to do it, and so I'm sure that you will find those areas and those methods that will work for you for a time.

But let me tell you something: The methods and ways of processing need to be changed from time to time. Now, I'm not telling you to run from one person to another, but I am saying that a method should grow and evolve and become responsive to the changes on the Earth. That's why I, Vywamus, am changing some of the methods in the Foundation. They keep saying to me, "You know, we just get this and now you change." Well, it's kind of fun and they're very good about it, but it is a constant process. It's like riding an elevator. As the elevator goes up it gets lighter and lighter and more responsive to a new level of intensity of light energy. And so your elevator is perhaps three-quarters of the way up, meaning that you still have another quarter as far as the whole Earth association is concerned. Now, that is good news for many of you. Some of you are really anxious to get off the Earth. I've noticed that. And so sometimes you individually shoot up the other quarter, you might say. So if you are interested in doing that, exercises such as we are doing today and other energy exercises that you really relate to can be especially helpful now.

Time-Warp Changes

Some of you heard about the time warp and the changes that came in last week — and they really did. It's almost as if all of this came together, and you took a big, deep breath upon the Earth. You note the pause — that's where we are now. It is a pause before a new level of awareness becomes active. All of you are now seeking to understand that new level, but perhaps you haven't jumped in with both feet yet. Think about this week: For some of you there were delays; for others, certain expected activities or certain expected responses didn't come in; for some others there was kind of a scattered effect; and others created a tremendous amount of activity because you felt that you had to do a lot, seeing that not much was going on on the Earth. Isn't that interesting? So there are different responses to this week, and there is a gearing in of a new use of time that has never been here before. Many of you are going to be able to use time much differently. It already is available to you.

There will be more of these time warps. There will be a cosmic opportunity to begin to widen your perception of time and of space, to really see that the bridging process of these cosmic realizations (because that's what this is) has become available to you. We might say it is a bridging between sequential time and the eternal now. You all want to recognize the eternal nowness, right? But bridging it has seemed difficult – there seemed to be time and space, and you could only do one thing at a time, right? Wrong. You will be learning to do many things on many levels and focusing them here on the Earth. Just because our exercise bringing the energy in through the soul star was moving in one direction, doesn't mean it was really flowing in space. It wasn't actually doing that; it was an activation of that Divine Blueprint. That's what we were doing. And then we were feeling a response from the Earth; this is literally two approaches to activating that Divine Blueprint.

Now, the good news is that as you learn to function on this new level you're going to eventually be able to use at least four or five different approaches to a project all at the same time because there will not be the same sort of sequencing. Time stretches, expands, contracts. Space goes from here to there, but you merely need to go here and bring what is there to *you*.

You see, there will be a different use of time and space on the Earth. Is that a long way off? No. The indicator of it was this past week. The point is that *this is going to be happening on a regular basis*. It's not just a one-time occurrence. It is part of the evolution of your planet. This is the doorway of the focus into the fourth dimension, and you're now bringing what? You're bringing all you understand about the third dimension into the fourth dimension as a creative base from which to flow fourth-dimensionally.

This change is a bridge built so that you could bring the third dimension – which says, "This is the way it is: there's twenty-four hours in a day, twelve inches in a foot," those seeming absolutes – into a focus in the fourth dimension, which is much more fluid and flexible. But you do bring in the basis of the third dimension, all that you've learned about living, into the fourth dimension.

You brought that in, and the two of them came together at that point about a week ago. They touched each other, and as they did there was a sorting-out process about what *is* time and space. Now, if you've had something you've been trying to fit together, they may have bounced back and forth. But eventually if you keep fitting them together, they're going to get locked together. So for the next few years – it might be as little as one year, it might be as long as five, depending upon all of you – you will be doing this. There will be those times when the third and the fourth dimensions come together and you'll get an opportunity to begin to reassess the energy, how you used it, how you created before, into the nowness.

Now, I have a system – doesn't everybody? I have a system of teaching and I've done a book about dimensions. In it I divide the dimensions into nine pieces, like a pie. We could look at it in twelve or sixteen or twenty-four pieces, but my pie fit for me in nine pieces. I am attempting to tell you that you are literally multidimensional. We could say that the third dimension *was* your creative base, while the fourth dimension is your creative base now.

That's important in the blueprinting system, because this new blueprint is a more flexible, moveable one that flows more completely. The system you had before was rather dense and inflexible. This one has a fluidity and a movement that allows you to adjust.

I want to get into that a little, because I think that gives us an opportunity to have this crown chakra and all of these connections that we've built from it clean up cells in a very special way. If we had built this in the third dimension when the Earth was still in the third dimension, well, I could say what you have built here is much larger. Let's look at it as this wide, representing the area that fits over the crown — but what you are building is actually much larger. If we look at it as this size, then there are fine lines of that blue energy that drip down, forming a particular pattern centered in the heart, where other lines of energy come up and meet. They radiate out, having created a radiating center in the heart. Now the cells of your physical structure are within that radiating field. If we had built it when the Earth was still in the third dimension, it wouldn't have reached all the cells in your physical body. But now it does — not only reaching your physical body, but extending beyond that into the etheric body, into your emotional body's energy, and a little further out into your mental body's energy. Most of you are now reaching even beyond to your spiritual body's energy. So the complete energy and flow can be cleansed, but we're going to focus now into the physical body.

Your Organs Are Changing

One thing that is happening to each of you is that the whole endocrine system is readjusting. That means all of the glands — the major ones that you recognize: the pineal, the pituitary, the thyroid and the parathyroid, the thymus near the heart, your adrenal glands, sexual glands, the spleen, also perhaps the liver — all of these major organs are readjusting. We talked about your growing new ones. What we didn't talk about is that they are speaking to each other; because of you're entering the fourth dimension, there is now a communication between these organs. Your liver might say to your kidneys, "How you doing today? I've really come through something! I don't know what's going on out there, but there's a tremendous amount happening." And the kidneys may say, "I know, I've been eliminating and eliminating and eliminating." The point is that they are communicating in a way that would not have been possible in the third dimension. Now that there is a communicative change and flow, it affects your physical body too, and that's very important.

For one thing (we're going to get back to the physical body in a moment), it means that if something isn't working in your life, communication about it is going to help you in a way it wouldn't have before. Why? Because it is easier now to communicate. The Earth is supporting the communicative effort. Does that mean it will always be easy to say to someone, "I don't like what you're doing." No, it may not always be easy, but it may be important to do that – not in the sense of criticizing, but in the sense of recognizing that as a divine being you're connected to them through the heart, and you don't have to like their behavior. Probably what you're going to get back is that they don't like *your* behavior. So you begin to process, to communicate, to change the mirror, because that's mirroring something to you just as you are mirroring something to them. It is important to recognize that communication is not only important – it's *essential* now. There is no way to avoid it.

Some of you are going to get unhappy. Is your goal perhaps to be happy? I'm not sure that I identify with that, but I do think that some of you who are still in the mainstream of consciousness have the goal to be happy. But no one on the planet will be happy now without communicating. Berlin is an excellent example; the West wants to talk to the East, the East wants to talk to the West, and they *will not* be happy until that occurs. Another area where we're going to see that is China; look for these deep changes in China. It's going to boil up out of the need for communication, which is freedom. Communication is freedom, the freedom to communicate fully in a very basic avenue.

Meditation on Cells

Let's get back to your physical bodies. I would like to have you visualize again. If you look through a microscope or through your imagination, you might not see the cells. But for our purpose I would like you to imagine your cells, simply knowing you have a nearly endless number of them; they're always being re-created and there are, especially now, more and more being created and re-created, which means that some that would have died in the third dimension are doing so now.

Part of the problem that you're having with your physical body is that you have too many cells for a while. You have to let in more energy now; you already have the physical ingredients, because you're literally part of the Earth's expression. The cells are waiting for more energy so that they can be used more completely. I think that's important, because some of the illnesses that are present exist simply because there are ten people (if you are a cell you call them people) for every job. Isn't that interesting? It indicates you're already prepared. All you need to do is to let in the level of energy, let in that higher creativity. Put all the cells to work – that's what they're looking for. They're looking to do their job.

❦ *All right, let's visualize a cell as a cylinder. Let us say they are clear cylinders; visualize or imagine them that way. Now get the Violet Flame in your hand. First look at the cells in your head and say to yourself, "I want to see those that need to be cleansed." You may see some black flyspecks in them, or black points of nonclarity. Get the Violet Flame in your hand and begin now to cleanse those cells. Ask that the soul's energy, that beautiful energy that we* were working with, to come flowing in to replace that black material. Now, work with it and know that some of your crystal friends can be helpful in doing this – the black tourmaline, the obsidian and several others. I would say that calcite certainly helps cleanse the cells; it has many colors and types. There are other crystals that are important. Learn to work with these and they will help you. Hold them while you are doing this processing.

❦ Keep bringing into your awareness cells to be cleansed. Look at them, and when they are clear in your head area (there are a lot to work on there), then move on to the neck. Pay particular attention to the neck, because it is an important area. Cleanse the cells in the neck with the Violet Flame. Keep working with it. Ask that energy to flow on out of the system. Give it back to the Earth; the Earth can use that energy, and you can recycle it and get in more energy of your own. So let it move through the system, remembering now to keep the chakras open as clear, transparent disks. There are many techniques for working with chakras. We don't always use this one, but for allowing that flow it works well.

❦ When you've cleansed the throat, then move on to the upper part of your body, including the heart area, the arms, if you wish, and into the shoulders and the spinal area. Begin to cleanse those with the Violet Flame. Then begin to ask that light to come in from the soul. It gets lighter and lighter; every time you use this Violet Flame it gets lighter and lighter. Certainly it can help to go to a healer, but know this: Your soul is the greatest healer contact that you have. Allow it to light up the areas for you now that need to be cleansed, so that you might see those cells. Ask the soul to evenly energize them now.

❦ Let's go into the solar plexus, into your sexual area, down into the legs and the lower part of the back. Now ask this energy to cleanse the cells and work with them. Imagine it moving into the flame; ask that blue energy to flow and see the cells get lighter and lighter and lighter and lighter. Keep cleansing them. Keep moving that blue energy through them. Then give it to the Earth. Just let it flow out. Be sure that you see the bottoms of your feet as open and the chakras as transparent. Then just allow those cells to be cleansed, deeper and deeper and deeper.

❦ This is a technique that you can use to good advantage more than once. This one particularly should be used perhaps even daily for a while. Simply check your physical body and go through and cleanse the cells. I'm going to ask you to do this. I'm going to give you a moment or two to finish up. Although you may not have cleansed all of them, finish up and then we will move on. You will get those that are most important cleansed out now.

Mirroring from the Galactic Core

❦ As you are doing that the angelic kingdom is setting up what I would call a mirroring device on all sides of this room. This one's going to be permanent. I think you will enjoy having this mirroring device here, but it may intensify some of the programs that you have here. (That's good because they're *transformational, anyway.) So there is this energy-mirroring process from what I call the Galactic Core, the mirroring from the Galactic Core. I would like you to imagine a mirror that is reflecting light now, an intense light, a level that you've never accepted before. But it's now available and it's coming into the cells, all of the cells. You've cleansed them and the mirror is there from all sides, brighter and brighter. Allow that light to come in; it is lighting you up more and more. Simply relax and accept it.*

❧ *I suggest that you pay attention too to the breath, breathing deeply and then exhaling, breathing deeply and then exhaling. And as you do, you know that you are gathering that light up into the life-force area, your lung area. As you exhale, the remnants of the dark black material are going out. So you breathe in this light from the Galactic Core and then you exhale the old resistances. You breathe in the clearer energy of the fourth dimension and you exhale the resistance to it now. Breathe in this galactic light and exhale resistance to it. Again breathe it in so it energizes every cell; you can feel it tingling, and you exhale it now. You become a center of light. Bring it into the center, the light core. Bring it in – this is your role. Allow it in, allow it in. Breathe it in. Breathe it in. It comes in now; exhale the old resistances now. Good. Keep doing that, breathing light in and exhaling resistance out; breathing in and exhaling out. Now go back to your normal breathing.*

❧ *Search your physical body. Pay particular attention now to the glands. The pineal gland, in association with your crown chakra, is full of light. Let it respond and communicate now with the pituitary gland, which is associated with the third eye deep inside your head. Let that flow. Feel that connection.*

❧ *Then take it now, communicating to the throat, the thyroid, the parathyroid – particularly the parathyroid glands, which grasp that new soul level. They're literally singing with light. Feel it now. Allow this light to vibrate within you. It is available now. Allow it and feel that flow now going to the thymus. Feel the thymus being rejuvenated. It is no longer shrunken. It became less important for all of you as you grew up, but now it is being rejuvenated, being reborn through the light, through the light, accepting the light.*

❧ *Allowing the light, allowing the communication through the throat area and now into the thymus and now into the adrenal glands above your kidney area. Feel that the adrenals are really accepting the light, accepting the light, allowing the light. Accepting the light, allowing the light, communicating in the light. Allowing the light, accepting the light, communicating in the light. Allowing that flow, allowing that level of communication from all of the chakras. More and more communication from all of the chakras. More and more communication, more and more light is flowing.*

❧ *More and more – flowing, flowing, flowing down into the spleen and into the sexual glands. Feel that now, all of it flowing into the Earth. More and more light in the endocrine system. Feel it flowing now, more and more light lighting up these physical glands as well as the energy centers.*

❧ *And the cells now sing and vibrate with this Divine Blueprint. Yes, it is available. And yes, you have awakened it. And yes, you can continue to use it on this level. And yes, it is your gift from the Creator. Bring that into the heart, my friends.*

All right, gently begin to come back. I'll give you a moment or two and then we will ask if you have some questions. Come back slowly. You all look very bright. You've brightened yourself up.

The electrical resistances – the crystal, the tree and the whip – you said to change them now. Would you clarify that a little more?.

I would suggest that if you haven't done any regression for yourself and you don't know exactly how to approach it, ask a friend who does to help you for the first time. If you've regressed to other lives, then you go back into that experience. The important part is to *feel* it. Emotionally feel in contact with it, or as much as you can, to get beyond just the mental area into the emotions. And then begin to release it, feel that release by changing the effect that you have created there. That's the most important thing. You can do it by yourself, but if you haven't done it before, it might be fun to have a friend there who can assist you. It doesn't even matter whether you consider it to be "real." I find that it *is* real; it's something that you have created. As I look in the Akashic Records at your stream of consciousness, each one of you, I've told you what I see there. But the important thing is to release the charge that is there emotionally and begin to free yourself up to a clearer understanding of what the electrical energy really is – the soul. That level of intensity, that level of wattage.

Do it at least three different times. Do it until you can release it emotionally; you might have to do it more than three times. But if you get a good emotional release, then release each part one at a time. But don't beat yourself with a wet noodle if you don't get a good emotional release, because for some of you it is difficult to get into the emotions. Do the best you can with it, and you can learn to do it. It's a good technique. If you find an area that is blocked in your life, then begin to use it. I think it will help.

Would you say something about going into the new decade, into the 1990s.

Well, first of all it's going to be exciting. It's going to escalate quite rapidly, I think. By the year 2000 you're going to have a completely different approach to living on the Earth. It really is going to be an incredible decade of great change.

One of the most important areas of change is the Earth itself. Certainly I feel there will be some earthquake activity. Some of it will be quite extensive. I don't look for a 10 on your Richter scale, but I do think you will have some quakes. Why? Because that's the adjustment process of the Earth. The belief structures of the Earth and the mass consciousness create a point of irritation, which then creates a lot of difficulty here on the Earth. But I think eventually you're going to learn how to handle movement on the Earth. You see the synchronicity of that? So that you will build – and it's already started – more flexible structures that will just sway in the breeze of the earthquake. I think you will learn how to do that, I see that coming in in this decade more and more.

I see changes in government, letting go of the old patterns. I certainly see a different source of occupations. I think by the end of the decade channeling will be pretty much respected in all strata of your civilization. Maybe not everywhere, but it will be certainly more accepted, as will the New Age healing and alternative medicine. Certainly understanding how to feed the physical structure is changing. Your needs are changing and you don't need to eat the way you did before. More and more, the New Age nutritional programs are important. So these New Age occupations (some of you've been looking for your purpose for a while), I'm sure you fit into some of that.

The most important thing is *how to be a part of the group.* Many of you have been learning in that area. We do personal intensives in Phoenix and we always try to help people with their group programming, because the New Age is an age of group experiences.

Twelve Great Temples

One of the most exciting things (not in this decade, but I think not too long after that) is that some great spiritual beings will be coming here physically who will start some great temples. That's exciting for all of you. Great temples – in my opinion there will be twelve main temples. There are going to be lots of others, but twelve that are staffed, if you will, from a very cosmic level. And they will come here in physical bodies. So I am excited about that. Already some of you are preparing, it seems to me, to be a part of some of that. Your subconscious (which is in sequential time) really does understand that and is waiting for the opportunity to be a part of it, to connect in with those beings. You may not have worked with them before, but now in this decade you will be getting in touch with those beings. That's exciting, isn't it? So there are some glimpses.

There are new species of plants, there are new species of animals coming in. Some of the older ones are dying out, not because of something terrible but because they're transcending the structure that they have and moving into other new structures.

Are there any specifics of change for Sedona itself in the 1990s?

I think so. The vortexes that are here are integrating, or trying to integrate. I would say the most significant point would be when they are integrated. The energy here is very good. It's high energy, but I think eventually it's going to be even better, a great deal better when those centers come together. It doesn't mean that they won't be there individually. It's rather similar to you as a cocreator: Eventually you will know that you've been in an individualization process, but you won't relate to your own self as much as you relate to that wholeness. This energy will be similar to that. In other words, it will communicate more clearly with the other centers. I think that's what's important, because what you have now is one kind of an energy over here and another kind over here, and it can be a little disquieting. It's wonderful, but then when you move from one to the other they don't always fit together. But they are learning too. So I would look for growth, a great deal of growth for this area, more and more people drawn here. We're going to have to learn to build those wonderful crystal towers like they used to have, to stack them up. There are going to be a lot of people coming in here, and you're going to have an interesting time trying to figure out where to put them. But I think we'll solve that too. The New Age architects will figure that one out.

There will be the need to solve the problems about the water here in Arizona. I think one thing that will happen is that you will be able to tap what is just happening now on the Earth. There are certain water reserves that haven't really been available to the Earth. They've been in another form, you might say, and now they are really coming in. I think by the end of the decade you will have the water reserves that you need. And you must learn how to use water differently. These new energy particles are going to help with the pollution and so forth, eventually clearing that up.

I think we can look for — maybe not by the end of the decade, maybe a little longer than that — a clearing of your environment. It's almost like it goes back to, well, what you consider the Garden of Eden, that type of thing — a much more lush and clean atmosphere of Earth. That doesn't mean that there won't be learning and that there won't be areas that haven't perhaps "got" it yet. But more and more there will be a sense of how to flow the environment so it responds to what you really want; then you can create the type of life that you really want.

I see Sedona as a great metaphysical center and, perhaps more importantly, a training ground from which many, many, many of you will go forth and teach around the world, and yet draw in others from all over the Earth. You can be here and communicate with the Earth. I think it's important for you to recognize that you're almost a cosmic ambassador by living here. You really are. And it's not that you appear important — I don't mean that — but there is perhaps the heart-centered approach to visitors, saying, "Welcome. I'm glad you're here." You may not always be that, but perhaps you can learn to be, because people are really being drawn to this wonderful area, and as they come they will bring you their energy and then it becomes even better because they've been here.

What about the channeled information that we've had about the possibility of an earthquake that will contaminate the groundwater supplies here?

There may be some quaking, and I think there may be an adjustment in the water at that time. I don't know, I would give that only about a 48%

probability factor of coming about. I think there are enough changes. One thing that you all can do, as you work with bringing this energy of the soul, this more electrical energy, is to begin to reduce the probability of that happening. Because the flow, as I said (and we are talking about the group soul, humanity's soul), doesn't have to use trauma or difficulty. Although there may be quakes – I don't think they will stop – I think you will be able to simply use that as the movement within the flow. Do you see that? Quakes won't necessarily contaminate anything; it just becomes part of an overall changing pattern.

So the more of us that can learn to channel these energies, the less probability that will happen?

Yes, in my opinion that is true.

Is the Golden One you've talked about closer now?

Yes. Ask to channel that energy or feel it in the heart. That is one of the greatest beings you have been able contact here on this planet. It is a great being indeed, on the same level as Melchizedek.

Is the Ashtar Command's plan for Earth evacuation still valid?

Oh yes. Ashtar is one of the greatest administrators that ever lived. He has it all figured out.

Is evacuation still in the plan if major changes take place?

Yes, I think so. I used to say that it is almost an absolute, but I have revised it to about an 80% probability. If it occurs, it will be for a briefer period than what I saw before. I think you will adapt a little faster. But I am seeing that still.

Are we going to have a pole shift? Is that the 80% evacuation possibility?

Yes.

When?

I'm still giving the year 1994.

Recognizing Divine Equality

About having love in your aura – could you help explain how we can produce that?

Love in your aura? Well, through your emotional responses. Certainly through what we've been doing today. Awakening the energy so that whatever movement you have in your heart magnifies through that energy. Can you see that? Certainly there may be blocks in it in your association with others. It is necessary to begin to understand what I call divine quality, that everyone is associated with others. Now, they may not be using their abilities equally at this moment on the Earth, but the principle is that God doesn't have any favorites. You as a cocreator can sense that if you view life through the heart. You can remind yourself, as if you have a child who is being naughty and you say, "Well, I'll look at that child through my heart area and I will remember that child is a divine being, although I may spank him a little." The point is that if you connect in through your heart consciously, you begin to be conscious, and then it becomes automatic. You recognize others through that love center in a way that says yes, we are together. You see, the response is there when you validate it through the heart.

We could do and we have done many lectures on the heart itself. It is the absolute center of existence, the core from which you create. It is necessary to explore it and to keep expanding it. A good exercise is to see the heart as a mansion. You may have gone into ten or twelve rooms, but take yourself into the others and see what quality of the heart is there in each room. You might find a room that is full of trust. "Oh my, I could go in there and feel that trust." This recognition of it becomes something that you can use in your life. So I would say that working symbolically with yourself and recognizing divine quality are important. But you have to be a little patient with yourself, don't you? You say, "Oh well, tomorrow I'll do a little better than I did today."

I work for some people who seem to be very antagonistic to the term "New Age." I'm a minority there.

Well, you do have differences of opinion on your planet. We've noticed that. We've also noticed that the way to a self-realized state or to an ascended state isn't done in just one way. There are many, many paths. They all lead to the same place. Probably the most important thing is to recognize that you create your own life, and from that everything else follows.

An Integrator of Religions

Now, in this decade, I think that you may look for a being rather like Gorbachev to function in the religious area, to begin to open doors and integrate or make available integration in some of the religions. I think from that will come a different idea of the New Age, one in which there can be peaceful coexistence, even if there is a slightly different focus in the religion area.

Have you still a way to go in that? Yes. But the good news is, it's beginning already. And you may not see it because there is a visibility about people who are quite adamant about things. But in the quietness of those who don't speak up much, there is lot of change. Just because they are traditional or fundamentalist (I don't particularly like that term) and have accepted a certain type of religion doesn't mean that there is not a great acceptance or openness.

You can begin now to incorporate an understanding of the times. That's really all it takes. From whatever point of view you approach it, be open to the change, be fully communicative, accept responsibility for your own life, do not blame others. It doesn't matter from what path you view that; it can be within one of the traditional religions.

So I think the antagonism will drop away. It will be perhaps intensified for a while because everything that needs to be resolved comes up. That doesn't mean it's worse; I think it's better. But it will, it seems to me, come up for resolution. You're seeing more of it. There really isn't, but you're seeing it more; it's more visible.

I would say too that much of this comes from an emotional insecurity or imbalance; as you process your emotional bodies, you are going to make a difference in the emotional body of the mass consciousness. When you were in the mainstream of consciousness, you processed other people's emotions. Some of you still take that on somewhat. So perhaps 50% to 60% of your emotional imbalance came from those who you were around when you took that in.

So is it not logical that as the mass consciousness comes to contain less imbalance, then this will get better too? And when there's that greater emotional balance, then there won't be as much antagonism. It all fits together in the process of evolution.

❖ F I V E ❖

Manifesting the Clarity of the Soul on the Physical Level

I SN'T IT FUN TO BE COMMUNICATING ABOUT LIFE, ABOUT PURPOSES AND certainly about soul and where it is leading you? Some of you have the ability to discern that a particular focus – in this case, motivating the purposes of the soul and the higher inspiration – is there for you.

Our focus is the soul: what it means to be clear as a soul and use that in your life. Our focus is the manifestation on the physical level of the higher principles of life and the ability to use them physically.

We are going to reach a new level in talking about the dynamic energy. We are going to be using many dynamic-type meditations. We are going to see that the physical responses are stimulated dynamically. The stimulation of the physical body, so that it "gets" how to use the new level that everyone has now reached, is very important. It is wonderful to think and to understand, to feel and be responsive to this new level. It is here, and you have looked forward to this as souls during the whole history of the planet. So how do you use this time of soulness on the Earth? Our connection into the dynamic energy will make it a little more real than it has been.

We want you to stretch to new levels through the Earth connection. The Earth itself is a motivator that many of you can use. It can be the sustainer, the motivator, the integrator, the nurturer, and any way we look at it, we are going to talk about how the Earth itself is able to assist you, both individually and certainly in the collective consciousness of humanity and of literally all the kingdoms.

We want you to use the directives from the overall soul level and the mirrorings from all cosmic levels. Picture a globe (your Earth). Then picture an infinite number of mirrors, coming into that globe from every point of view, from literally all of space. Each mirror shows your potential on one of these levels coming into the Earth. All the potentials can now be integrated into life upon the planet.

Dropping old burdens of resistance is a natural part of every group or individual event. The goal is to get through another level of understanding that the resistance or burden that seemed to exist just for you, surrounding you, really wasn't yours at all. You've assumed that burden — now you can let it go.

Use the heart as a releasing mechanism and as a new core for your creativity. The heart energy is the central area of all existence. For some of you, when you activated it, events happened that were the opposite of what you wanted, or perhaps they didn't manifest in such a way that you could recognize them as something you had invoked through your heart. If you give someone your love and they respond from their point of view regarding love, there has to be an integration of the two views of love. That's called allowingness. That's called trust. There is yet another, greater level of love and we are all a part of it. Not everything has to manifest through one's own perception of love — there is a lot of integration going on in understanding what love is, beyond the way you have understood it before. Once you get that understanding, at least enough so that the heart doesn't open and close like a doorway — once that doorway stays open, that can be the new core for your creativity. It locks in the responses from the Earth, from all of creation.

Let's talk about the manifestation of your soul's purposes on the Earth. Can you see that your soul isn't very earthy? It draws on all of its cosmic potential in order to bring into manifestation what you want on the Earth. Our goal now is to try to open you to cosmic links or cosmic points that you couldn't open for yourself.

We want to talk about the physical body. What's going on in your physical body? What are the cells really doing? And what in the world is a cell? I want to give you my opinion of what the cells are, what the cellular level is, and address the responses being made now within your physical body that can affect how you live the next few years. It is going to be amazing to see how those who should be getting older (according to the belief structure of mass consciousness) simply won't do it.

We are going to transfer all of your potential into your physical structure. We will be assisted by every teacher available (because we all consider this a privilege) plus all of the angelic kingdom. We will be building the energy within you and within the room for this purpose. This room has just received a lot of new crystals. Some of them need to be integrated into the room. Although it is full of energy, it is not as full as it seems. There is an energy locking-in process going on.

Drinking a lot of water helps to wash out the resistances (or the crystallization) that you are getting rid of. I've been telling you for quite a while now to drink a lot of water. If you will go through a period of drinking twelve glasses of water a day, you will get to the point where the reservoir in each of your cells is filled. After that, you won't have to drink as much; all you will need to do is keep the reservoir full. It is as if you will flood the physical structure so that then you don't have to drink as much. This is one of the most beneficial things you can do right now.

Links Within the Whole – Directives for Soul

You perhaps know intellectually that there is a plan here. There is something directing the soul level. In other words, when your soul came here, it didn't just happen in. It didn't just say, "The Earth is a pretty planet – I'll just drop in and visit." (Although that is true, also: It is an extremely beautiful planet.) Your soul is part of a level or a wave of consciousness (rather like a wave that comes to the shore) that has added its potential, its creativity, to what we might call the group or the integrative process on your planet. It has awakened new levels of creativity on the Earth – including your own creativity – through the opportunity that was given to you.

One of the most magnificent things about the plan is that you can rely on the opportunity it has given you, and your learning will be quite full from that opportunity. You may have noticed that – the opportunity to stretch into the manifestation on the physical level of what you need to understand *right now*, at this moment in the life you have chosen for yourself on the Earth. The plan (the directives from another level) links you into what you need to understand now.

Let me tell you what happened last night. We of the Hierarchy who are associated with you all had a committee meeting. We looked around and we said, "Well, it's begun, but what can each of us do to (for instance) help the economic strain that may be coming? What can we do specifically, now?" Now, interestingly enough, the consciousnesses of many of you were not aware of your physical structures, because it was on the inner level where physical structures are not usually taken (they are sometimes, but not usually). At that point I noticed something. Each one of you who has a body began connecting into that body enough so that your bodies were stretching and moving in your beds where you were sleeping. Not everyone who was there was sleeping, because of your Earth time differences. Some were awake, but some part of them was connected into this meeting. Some were in their physical bodies because of the time of the day; there was movement. They moved and flexed their bodies, felt a new position.

The movement was the acknowledgment of this new level that is now here. I was very pleased by this. It shows that the movement was so locked into the physical level that it's going to accelerate more and more until some of you recognize that *that is the goal.* That movement is the goal. The movement of the physical body is symbolic of the movement of your consciousness in welcoming the new opportunities, the new level of being that you can use on the Earth right now. It is almost as if the directive is there so clearly that it is part of the clarity level of the soul. Some of you, most of you, can now take a clear level of direction from the soul, as never before. That is the *collective soul level* on your Earth, and it includes the individual soul.

The directives are becoming clearer, and your responses are much more automatic than ever before. This is wonderful — I don't think you know how wonderful it is. At the time of the Harmonic Convergence, this possibility existed because, for the first time on the Earth, the souls became the directors. During the ensuing period, as you may have recognized, there has been a lot of adjustment. Some of you call it confusion. Others recognize, "Well, I know I am to do something; I don't know what that is, but I know there is something. And I can see that things have changed. I'll keep looking, and somehow it will all come together."

That's the type of period we've been in for a while. Some of you have worn your resistance very well, but now you have finally taken it off. It is becoming obvious that it was not you at all. These limitations were not you. As we look at you we can see the glowing of the other potentials that are there to an even greater extent than the beautiful colors you now wear. Sometimes what you are wearing can become a limitation, even if the color is one of your potentials. You get so focused on it that you don't allow the integrative responses or the integrative abilities of the soul to *shine out*.

So even your strengths can become a limitation if you are known for that strength and you recognize only that strength and you don't bring in the other strengths that you also have. Should you take off that strength? In one sense you should, because it says that everything you are comes through that. In a sense, you must open the door to integrating other strengths also. A good example is the four-body system — you can all relate to them. One of those bodies is your strength. Have you always *thought* about life or *felt* life — is intuition your strength or is the physical body your strength?

If you've only worn one strength, then it interferes with the integration of the strengths you have from the other bodies. Most of you are in the process of adjusting that. You are not just holding on to the mental responses; you've become more open to the others. As far as the higher abilities are concerned (channeling, knowledge of past lives, healing, bringing forward abilities you had in other lives) and the integration of them, there is a directive that goes out to the physical level that says to you the Plan will do that for you. The Plan, the cocreator level, whatever you wish to call it, will do it, and then the mirroring will come onto the physical level.

I know every one of you has said to that directive level of the soul, "Stimulate me now and use me now." And, my friends, when you ask, you shall receive. That is what is going on in your Earth now.

There has been an allowingness. This shows the beginning of that dynamic heart center, the core center that is literally taking directions from the overall soul level and allowing your physical structure to have the stamina to be well. It allows you to have enthusiasm, to leap out of bed in the mornings, to not have to deal with things like jet lag, to not have to refer to things that are not yours any longer, things that don't even belong on the Earth.

I see coming up a lessening of illnesses on the Earth, in one sense. That is, I think you are going to drop a whole spectrum of diseases in the next decade. There will be some others coming in because there are still some levels of learning in that area, but there will not be as many as there were. As consciousness integrates on a new level, there seem to be many things separating out; they are not there anymore. These illnesses symbolize — or are a part of, or represent — the old emotional responses that are no longer going to be there.

One of those that will be leaving is cancer. I think we are getting to a point where cancer is responding to a new level of soul integration, which is why some people get cancer in the first place: There is a major opening, a directive coming from the soul into the physical, and the cells do not get integrated into that new level. Some of the cells get lost, out of control, and there is a lack of coordination, a lack of a coordinated response from that directive level.

One aspect of how to manifest the clarity of your soul on the physical level is to include the cells in your responses. In fact, they are the responses brought through the angelic perspective. Sometimes there is a cell or two that goes astray — it doesn't function within the divine blueprint of the soul. If you have a technique where you occasionally ask all of these little lost cells to come back in, then you will not develop any cancer. In other words, it is when they get lost, and lost for a length of time, that they say to themselves, "I must find my own way." They begin to use the dynamic growth energy without the growth directive of the higher blueprint, or the energy of the soul, and that's when you get in trouble with the physical level.

Meditation

🐚 *Close your eyes and visualize your cells. See them as little points of light. Connect those points of light into a flow of light, like a grid system. Ask your soul to give you an image or, in your imagination or your knowingness, a way of looking at that grid system. Put it on a screen, or do it within your own physical body. Look at those lights. There is a movement in those lights. They are within a flow.*

🐚 *There is an overall movement. It is like several rivers flowing and interacting with each other. Within each is an infinite number of points of light that represent the cells. Look within this light network and see if you have a few that have not incorporated into it. Invite them in, invite the little unincorporated lights into the flow of the divine blueprint. See the cells now entering the flow.*

❦ Be sure that, whichever way you visualize these, you look in all of the areas of the physical body. Start with the head and go through the whole body system. Pay special attention to the brain area. Look at it as organizing the electrical responses within the brain – connecting, connecting, connecting those responses and bringing those cells into that energy gridwork.

❦ Now clear the rest of the head, and the throat, and go into the heart area. Many women get breast cancer because they are trying to open the heart, and there is so much energy when you create an opening that those points of light are not integrated into the new opening that the heart has made. See yourself stepping through a door; this is a door to the next level of using your heart energy. Clean out the whole heart network, the grid system, the pulsing beat of all of creation. Clean it out, bring the cells into the light networking of the heart responses.

❦ As you get into the heart, you are going to see that there is a radiation that goes out to the universe. It does so from the soul direction, the divine blueprint within the heart area. Include the energy of the throat chakra – clean that up a little so that the divine blueprint of the throat area is there.

❦ Let's now do the rest of the body. Include the arms and the legs, the solar plexus, the polarity and the base chakra (both in the energy sense and the physical body sense) – clean those up. Don't negate those lost cells – they have their function. We are not getting rid of them; we are going to move them to the ideal of that divine flow, locking this light into the energy gridwork of the soul.

❦ Now I'd like you to visualize, or know, or imagine that directive level. It is passed down (for lack of a better term) from the Source Itself. It gets to the hierarchic level around the planet. Connect into that, and through that go to a new level of cleansing of the cells. It's as if you are locking in. You finally say "Yes." It is the surrender process: "I'll allow myself to be directed, now, by this hierarchic level which I know is a cosmic reflector of all other levels that exist." Cleanse that now, just for a moment . . . cleansing, bring them in. Press the button, as you would on a computer; this contacts every cell that has not yet been integrated within the whole body structure, including the crown and the third eye. Sort all of that out, bring it in and allow it to enter that directive level brought to you from the Hierarchy. Now say gently, "Come in, little one (meaning the cells), come in, come in, we love you. We have a place for you. Come in, little cells, we have a place for you, now."

❦ Thank you. Now let that settle in by taking a few minutes of relaxation or movement, whichever you prefer.

All right, my friends. I think you will find that this meditation needs to integrate for a while, and then it will probably settle down some. Your cells appreciate what you do. They want to be acknowledged. In a sense they want to be led, directed. You can make part of your weekly maintenance program an invitation to any of your cells that can't quite sense that energy gridwork to come into it. Really visualize that and have them feel that connection to the energy gridwork. It will help, not only with preventing illness but with the integration within your physical structure and, certainly, within your life responses.

Now, let us say that an opportunity is trying to come into you. It may be an opportunity to utilize your soul level in a much more cosmic way, whether we call it being part of a healing center or performing the function that you have chosen in a way that is so much fun that you begin to attract other aspects of yourself into it. In other words, if you have what you call a mundane job, you may learn that the next step is to attract additions to that position.

In a way it's not only the acceptance of the position, but an attracting of other aspects to that position that the soul brings. Many times it is not external. It may be internal – meaning that if you look at the position you are in, whether it is a formal employment or "working for the Hierarchy" at this time (many of you are, in the fullest sense), then it is an inner acceptance that is necessary. It is a subtle thing. Certainly you have all intellectually and spiritually accepted your role, perhaps in a very full sense. But the body responses, the emotional body, the mental body and then the acknowledgment of what you are doing and where you are – the creative base of that can always be broadened. Your acceptance of your creative base can always be broadened.

Let's say you are having a very good day. There is a lot of communication. People are calling and dropping in and you are making a lot of connections. Everything is just wonderful. You go to bed and you are full of love and hope. Life is wonderful. You get up the next day and everything is not so flowing. Perhaps you have slipped back to the level you were at two days before. It is not as expansive as the previous day. What has happened? There was an opening created that accounted for your open day, and during the next day there was an integration of that opening. The integration of what you're opened to must take place. It doesn't have to be difficult, but it does have to be integrated. Sometimes the feeling responses don't seem to be partaking of the use of that opening that you've just recognized.

When you feel thankful that the universe is bringing you the opportunity you created, that is your soul input. That inner response is working outward, and you can see a reflection coming back to you of that next level. Then it seems to turn off. One way to look at it is to think of the soul as not directing, but that would really not be true. Certainly the soul can fall off, but can it really fall off? When you get it to a particular point, can it really fall off? It is only 29% of the time that the soul falls off and the personality level tries to take over. The rest of it is simply the process of gearing up for that next level in the use of the soul. It is not that often anymore that you allow too little soul response. It could respond. There are several things that could be done to open that up again, to keep it consistently feeling that the present opportunity has not shut down, that it has just gone to another phase — whether we call it integration or "allowing yourself to process what is now beginning." It is a process of gearing up to that next level and the use of it. For most of you, it is not that often anymore that you do not allow that soul response.

If you have a group and they are creating a center, a temple, it goes through several phases. It goes through a planning phase. Part of what I want to talk about is that everyone who is here, if you choose, will be invited to be a part of these large temples that are coming on the Earth. It will be four or five years, at which time there are going to be immense, beautiful structures that each one of you can be a part of, so you can do some sort of healing — not necessarily hands-on healing (though it can include that), but in the fullest sense, healing, or soul-level living, on the Earth for the masses that are there. So the universe, or the directive level, is continuing to process you toward that. There is no way you can fall off of that. No way at all.

In your life now, if one day responds in one way, it is important to recognize that there are other days that will respond in other ways. Change is the key. You can no longer look for days to flow in only one way. What you can begin to do is sort it out, to look for the different types of days your soul is using. This really helps the emotional responses. The emotional body must recognize that on one day you get many opportunities, and on another you sort them out, and another day some of these opportunities come in and say, "Have you decided yet?" or "What are you going to do about that?" These are other levels of the good day, but they give you a chance to make some decisions the next day in regard to what you've integrated. On an integrative day, the physical body gets to partake.

Can you be in a state of rest and still perform that function that you've chosen in your life (whatever that may be)? Many of you think of rest as getting away from the agenda that you've chosen. But you're moving toward something, aren't you? You are moving into an eternal understanding of how to live in a completely balanced manner.

Can you perform your function and still be in a state of rest? Rest is a momentary pause that allows reflection as well as integration of experience so you can then expand. It is simply the process of allowing a change of focus, which magnifies and changes. It is the need to expand the use of your strengths. Rest is the point where divine beingness begins to expand or move or integrate or change the way we are looking at life, giving us a new way of connecting.

What I am trying to help you see is that there is no way to stay at any one point. Your soul has decided to be a part of a very active, changeable state on the Earth. Why not use that as a positive and integrative opportunity in your life? Each time life becomes different, take a moment to rest and hook in that new opportunity from the soul level, from a new perspective.

It's like taking the plug out of the wall and moving it to another receptacle. If you will consciously begin to do that, you will be clearer. You can begin to direct, in the energy sense, the resistances. You can start brushing them off. You can then get rid of what you don't have to process later. You can learn to do it with the pause or rest.

Do you need days and days of rest? I don't think so — not anymore. Certainly there are times to take a vacation. But is that exactly a rest? No. For many of you it is a connection with the Earth that helps you to respond to the Earth more clearly. It helps your physical body get a nice, fresh perspective. I think vacations are mostly for your body. Certainly the mind becomes clearer and the emotions become clearer, but there is so much opportunity now to learn from the Earth.

The dynamic content of the Earth is available to you now. If a day is not flowing the way you want it to, how about doing a visualization where you take the plug from one connection and plug it into the Earth and let the Earth process you differently? This will do some incredible things. It will process you on the next level of understanding the dynamic energy. That's the first thing it will do.

That pause between is where you say to yourself, "Now what would happen if I allowed the Earth's responses to help me go to a new level in the use of this day?" It doesn't mean it will take the day away — you've chosen that day and you may need that day. But by including the dynamic responses within yourself, not excluding them, you lock in the use of the dynamic energy, in conjunction with the receptive energy.

Some of you feel that if this is a very dynamic day, then the receptive nature needs a whole different day, a recuperative or integrative period. That's not necessarily true.

We are trying to show you how close you are to moving beyond sequential time, but in order to do so, you have to understand how the receptive and the dynamic energies come together and work at the same time. There doesn't need to be a period where you integrate, because you have had this tremendously active, dynamic time. It can really happen more and more at the same time. It is the body that is learning to accept that, and the emotions too. But as long as you *think* you need an integration day, you will need it. Instead, how about plugging into the Earth? At least be willing to let the Earth input into the way you look at the integrative process and the way you look at change.

Change, change, change. Again, what is change? It's another perspective; evolution; growth. All of those things can be taken within or projected without, simultaneously — just by moving the electrical plug from the place where you plugged it into the Earth. Interesting, isn't it?

We are helping you to adjust the physical structure to move beyond the sleep state and the need to rest the physical. As you train your physical responses (by saying, "I'm going to take that plug out now and move it") there can be that period that literally clears the physical body of any need to sleep or to rest. That's the *ideal*. You will get there because that is the direction in which all of you are moving as you allow your physical body to be the lightbody here on the Earth. The point of ascension comes when that is fully integrated, and that is the direction that you are moving in. You are learning to have your physical body be a part of what you already recognize is going on.

We've talked about lightbodies and we've talked about soul levels, but what we are really talking about is your allowingness of your physical body to be directed by the soul clearly, on the Earth, in your life, which then manifests your purposes. Many of you will be directed to go to various parts of the Earth because your energy is needed in a particular part of the Earth. Maybe just visiting there briefly will help a particular area.

All of you are a part of that greater soul level, the cocreator level, and you all fit in. The good news is, you don't have to do everything within your own physical body. The cocreator level and the rest of humanity and the other kingdoms and the Earth are all going to help you. This group vehicle, this crystal chamber, the paintings that are symbolic of a great cosmic heart center, and the chamber that represents Shamballa, are acknowledgments that you have stepped beyond the need to do everything by yourself. This is not the full use of your individuality – you are never going to lose that.

Your openness and your ability to accept change can open the process to the cocreator level, and the cocreator level will mirror to you all of what needs to be done. At the same time you keep creating new openings through your dynamic responses, through your allowingness of the dynamic responses. That is what some of you have closed down, a little. What has happened is, you and the Earth have gone to this new dynamic level. Some of you have said, "I have enough to handle, I don't need any more." But the process is not done that way. What is needed is the ability, the willingness to keep that movement going through what we call change – to be willing, every day, to move your plug and let the Earth process it. It is a wonderful plan when you allow it to motivate you. It is already organized. All you have to do is plug into it on another level. That doesn't mean that on the physical level there is no need for communication. That communication is already in response to a new level, but is *there already*.

My point is that some of you strive too hard to make something organized for your lives. Rest is simply allowing that change, that pause where you can change and validate the fact that there is already something there that can direct you. It is important that humanity accept that the Plan is already there. What you will be plugging into is the Plan as it already exists on other levels, and all you need do is plug into it. You've learned as much from this focus as you can learn; now shift it to (or plug it into) the next level. You are plugging into that integrative directive level that has assumed responsibility for the evolutionary process of the Earth, of which you are a part.

I do want to tell you what you do at times like this: You really give yourself permission. You may have some resistance in this new area, and your emotional body says, "Oh, I can't go into that; there are beliefs that are resistances, betrayal patterns or loss patterns or something it feels is traumatic." You give yourself permission through this spiritual opening to begin to explore, to literally connect into, the electrical circuitry of your Earth's Sanat Kumara connection beyond those resistances. Sometimes it takes away the resistances – a level or two – and it begins to help you integrate into that next level of understanding.

This is not necessarily done through your mental body. So if you are exploring that and cannot figure it out mentally, don't worry about it; it is not a mental exercise. It isn't even in the fullest sense a spiritual exercise, except inasmuch as they're all spiritual exercises. It is a creative subconscious process that allows you to touch into an opening that might otherwise not be explored. You might miss it because you hadn't gotten to it yet consciously. In fact, you can do this for yourself.

When you go to bed at night, you can say, "All right, I step through the golden door. I give my subconscious mind (or my creativity) permission to explore." But be very sure you know what you are doing. You are giving yourself permission to go through certain resistances and into a whole new way of living, of being, of understanding. It may take you into an area where, emotionally, you will need to feel some sort of support. That doesn't mean there is not some support; it means that through some activities that happened in the past, you've cut off from feeling that support. The emotions might not be able to say, "I am supported in that area." That doesn't mean *you* are not; but they may not recognize it. You may be setting yourself up for some intense learning. It doesn't mean it has to be difficult.

It seems to me that this is an easier way than avoiding those areas, creatively. That is what happens. Because of the fear patterns that are there, you have avoided this area, and then you get to a point where you can't live without entering that area. So it takes a tremendous surge at that time, because you've built up many, many, many levels of resistance. It takes a major event to break you through that. But if you learn to do this every day, or at least several times a week, you will drop those levels of resistance. You will begin to explore those areas, and then they can manifest in your life more easily. Does that make sense to you?

So you begin to use the *finer level* of the fourth dimension, while we are still, here on the Earth, at the denser level of the fourth dimension. So you begin to stretch yourself on the physical level to that finer level of the fourth dimension and you explore, with your creativity, areas that you haven't been able to glimpse yet. Let's give you an example.

Let's say you've decided you want to be an artist, a painter, and you are beginning to bring forth some drawings, but they don't quite speak to you yet. You haven't quite got it. One day you find a new type of acrylic paint that you've not used before. The colors are absolutely wonderful, but you are not sure how to use them yet. Well, in this type of meditation you could step through this golden door and say, "I'm ready to explore with this particular tool that I feel connected to. I feel it in my soul. I really want to paint these pictures. I'm really connected. I've found the tool, but I'm not sure how to use the tool yet." Then, by going through this golden door and giving yourself permission to explore, you will begin to be able to get it moving. You will get it creatively moving. It may be that you will find some lives in which you attempted to do this but perhaps were not accepted, or perhaps something else will come up. You can get glimpses of them and you can process the resistance, although it is also a way of getting rid of resistance. Once you've given yourself permission, some levels of resistances really do disappear automatically.

Now, that's cooperating with the subconscious, instead of saying to it, "You're the bad guy and I know you have all of these old patterns of behavior within you and I don't like them. It is cooperating with it, knowing that you are going to get rid of those old patterns of behavior, but in the meantime, not letting the old patterns of behavior keep you from exploring the next step for you, creatively. That sounds to me like a good idea.

❖ S I X ❖

Communication with Your Monad

GOOD EVENING, MY FRIENDS. I AM A SPIRITUAL TEACHER WHO IS CALLED Vywamus. You may wonder, well, what does that mean? It certainly is not an Earth name, is it? But it is a vibration, a sound that calls to me. If you have a friend and you say, "Hello, Lillian," that sound speaks to her. It is a combination of vibrations coming together, a sound that says, "This is a friend." So when you call me you will get who and what I am.

And you may wonder who I am. I am a being just as you are. I am a spiritual being in the stage of my growth pattern where I no longer incarnate on the physical level. But I did that, too, as you are doing now, and I enjoyed it. I didn't ever incarnate on the Earth, but on another planet far from where you are physically. But I remember it. I remember it well. And now I come to this planet at this particular time. I feel that because I have "been there" in physical existence, and because I can relate existence on more than one level, perhaps just a little bit clearer than you can at this point, I have some understanding that I hope to pass on to humanity. So I am not a physical being at all, but one who has joined a team, a group — your hierarchic government — to help the planet at this time. I am brought through a number of channels. I'm available and always recruiting for the Plan. Tonight we are going to talk about what Djwhal Khul has termed the monadic level of self and communicating with it.

You who are spiritual seekers are truly seeking to communicate with Sourceness. And this is your personal version of Sourceness. This is your connection at the very highest, or you could say, most basic level. It doesn't matter if you call it high or basic; we are talking about the same thing — your spiritual part that understands much that you are seeking to grasp on the physical plane. Now, the interesting part of all of that is it is learning about life through you, also. In fact, you recognize that you are not separate — all of you recognize that, don't you? You are absolutely connected into All That Is. And I've used this simile to help you understand your relationship with the monadic level. You could say that your monad, which is a being that has much activity of its own, is busily looking through a telescope at physical existence. And guess who it sees on the other end of that telescope? You.

As it views you in your activity, it learns from what you are doing. And you may not have thought of it that way — that such a great spiritual essence can learn from you on the physical level. But I say yes, this truly is one of the purposes of physical existence. Because the vibration is slowed down on the physical plane, it literally lights up the creative process so that the spiritual essence, the monadic level, can learn and grow from your understanding of what you create in your life on the physical level.

Now, because communication really flows both ways, in communicating with this level you can aid it in its learning and, of course, aid self in your learning. The communication, then, is very important. So to understand how to communicate, to recognize when you have connected into this level of self, is important. The outreaching essence of your monadic level is really the soul level. And all of you are familiar with this. This is the ideal that has been brought forth for physical existence interacting with the soul on the physical level. But we are really going to a finer level than the soul — that spiritual essence, that very basic component that all of us seek to recognize all of the time. Now, perhaps we do it one step at a time; that's important to recognize. I've had so many say to me, "I don't want to bother with a spiritual teacher as a mediator. I want to go right to the Source." And I say to you, good — why don't you do that? But in the meantime, if you can't quite reach that point yet, I extend to you my hand and my perception of what you'll find when you get there. So it is necessary to see that progress or spiritual awareness unfolds gradually, but you have a direct access route: your own monadic level.

I want to give you an idea of what that level is all about because if you're going to communicate with someone, it's kind of nice if you know what they look like or if you have some familiarity with their energy or if you understand them a little more clearly. It makes it a little more real, doesn't it? And it is reality on that level that we are seeking to convey because while all of you have connected with that level, you might not have realized it. I guess you could say you don't know what it is. And so you haven't seen that that connection has been made.

Several of you have been in the traditional religions in this lifetime, to the point that you did appreciate them a great deal for a while. And all of you will reference from a past life the following example. Let us say that in the Catholic Church in one lifetime or another, you were sitting on your knees — oh, the Catholics like knees, don't they? (I am not criticizing, just noticing.) Anyway, perhaps you were a nun or a priest or simply a devout person in the Church. And as you prayed, suddenly your soul seemed to be in the room, seemed to be full of light, and there was a rather transcendental experience. Now, you've heard of that, and I'd say that there is not one of you in this room who has not experienced it in this life or in another. What is that? That is connecting into your own Source level. It truly is.

Now, what happens and why is that important? Well, part of what you are planning to do here on the physical plane is serve as light for humanity. And all of you, as part of your purposes, have literally agreed to bring to the Earth a certain light quotient – a certain amount of light. You said, "Yes, I'll bring to the Earth this amount of light." But you have to be able to conceive of something to bring it into physical existence. So as in our example, as this experience of light came into self, you raised your ability to conceive of light. And gradually more and more light was allowed into the physical level. Thus, the more you can connect with this monadic or basic level of self, the sooner you can fulfill your contract with the Earth and, more importantly for some of you, the sooner you can leave. Some of you don't care, but others are anxious to get away; I've noticed that. You've felt that physical existence was something you wanted to leave. Well, you know what? I think that when you do – and all of you are close to that or you wouldn't be here – you will have fond memories of how you played on the Earth. Perhaps you will remember when you walked on the beach and you saw the beautiful ocean and it reminded you of what? It reminded you of the basic level of creation, because it is the basic level of creation manifested on the physical plane when you can recognize that. But this is gradually born within self, and as it is born you become aware of it step by step and it becomes apparent to you that you are functioning on the monadic level manifested physically. And when that dawns on you, guess what? Your assignments take you elsewhere and the physical level is perhaps no longer your playground. Perhaps you get to leave. We find that often to be true: Those who recognize and utilize a particular framework or understanding completely, get a new one. It's like graduating from high school – you go to college. And when you graduate from college, you go out into that workshop called Earth, don't you?

Right now all of you are in cosmic kindergarten. Perhaps some of you have graduated to the first grade. And when you get through with the Earth, then the specific level that you call the soul, which is now awakening, stretching a little within all of you, will bring forth more and more connection with that monadic level. But you can begin now, and it is fun to do so. You might recognize this level of awareness by the way it enlarges everything. Let us say that you are sitting in a chair, meditating, and all of a sudden awarenesses seem to pop out of the woodwork at you. Perhaps the input into your meditation seems to be flowing from every direction. You feel that absolute connection. How many of you have had this happen to you? What is happening? The monadic level has become aware of a part of itself that is physically focused and has identified a need, identified your connection, your plugging into the flow, you could say. It said, "Oh, good. We're going to flow all the way to the physical level." And then it did so — it brought forth some specifics for you to consider.

Sometimes this can be very interesting. Some of you would take a look at it and find it fun to analyze, wouldn't you? This point and this point and this point, and you would consider it extensively. And that's not inappropriate, you see? From all of that comes forth what? A resolution or an understanding that is integrated because you've looked at this and this and this as they came in. Thus your physical life is more integrated after such an experience. The light components from that monadic-level experience, after being dealt with and understood, are a specific integrator.

We've been talking a lot about integration and what to expect from it. The integration that comes from the monadic level can be interesting, exciting, illuminating, sometimes compassionate, sometimes mental, emotional or physical. What does that say? It is encompassing. It is an experience that you partake of. You are not viewing life on a screen; you are living it. It surrounds you. And that's fascinating because it shows you that this level, which is called "spiritual" and which many physical beings will put on a shelf and attempt to use only sometimes, is available all the time. It is who you are.

I really get excited about this subject because it is the area that perhaps I am most closely associated with now. So I see the possibilities for the Earth and for each of you as you begin to awaken to this basic level. Now, does that seem to be skipping over the soul? I don't think so, because the Earth in its evolution is seeking its own soul level. And so in its aggregate consciousness or in the consciousness that is integrated from all of what you are, it is responding to this highest, basic level of what and who it is also. And that is supportive of your efforts to reach this highest level. In an earlier period on the Earth, it would have been more difficult for each of you to reach this level. There were those who did, because they were persistent and they felt absolutely connected to it and there was no way that it didn't seem real to them. An example is the lord Maitreya, your Christ. He always knew he was the monad; there wasn't any question about it. He simply assumed that everyone else did too, and kept telling them about it, you see? So once we are convinced that this level is real, that is when the so-called miracle occurs.

Life appears to be miraculous to those who are in the mainstream of physical existence and viewing the monadic level because it doesn't yet seem real. When someone uses the principles that the monadic level understands, humanity sees that as miraculous. Walk on water? Why, goodness, look at that! That's a miracle! Well, not if you understand the principle, and not if you understand the universal flow that's there. The monadic level views existence at the cellular level, not as being solid. Janet had an experience like that, in which the monad looked through her eyes just one time, and everything had big holes in it. The monad knows that this solid state is an illusion, in one sense, that at its fine level of perception, each little point can see between what are considered solid molecules. So you get a penetrating look at existence at that level and how it fits together in a different way than in a physical orientation.

The monad has many gifts for you. Want to walk on water? Talk to your monad. Want to teleport? Want to do any of these things – use telepathy? How about the monadic connection as an asset, as a way to aid you in doing these things that are considered beyond the human level.

Do you just pick up a telephone and call a monad – dial it and say, "Hello, there. Here I am"? Well, almost. You might not do it on a physical telephone, but you can do it on a spiritual one. Those of you who have worked as channels know that as a beginning, particularly, it's a good idea to have some way of focusing. There is a way to focus your channel, a way to connect in. There is a symbolic way for each of you to connect into the monadic level. It doesn't have to be complicated. It could simply be a color, it could be a name, it could be a feeling; an encompassing feeling of love will bring it every time. You can literally say, "Here I am on the physical plane. Look down your telescope now and see me, and we will connect, we will function as one. We are one, you know." And the monad will say, "Of course. I knew it all the time. I didn't perceive a separation from my end of the telescope."

Perhaps the monadic level will respond best to a particular summons from the soul. So let's do it this way. Each of you, no matter where your point of evolution, becomes the soul. Now wear it in any way you wish, and just assume it's there. Bring it forth in a vibration and then sit with the soul. Activate the heart chakra until that heart center is so big that it seems to be the universe – in other words dear ones, until the love center becomes all-encompassing. Then that monadic level will enter and guide you. Now, if it takes you ten times, fifteen times, twenty times, twenty-five times, that's all right. It's a step-by-step progression to this level. If you are one who has the feeling that all must be accomplished in five minutes, I tell you that it might take six. But the point is, the more encompassing your invocation – because that's what we're talking about – the more willing you are to be that Source-level being, and the sooner it will appear.

Now, that's an interesting statement. Perhaps in order to be a Source-level being you have to know what one is. Have you thought about that? A Source-level being is one that can appreciate and know another's point of view as well as its own. In fact, one might be more concerned if there was a certain problem. And one's own point of view would then be set aside a little and one would go deeply to see if there was some way of helping. So at the Source level, there is an awareness of the group consciousness. And that group is much bigger than any that you've seen. It's called "all of the cosmos." But again, perhaps you step into it step by step. You start with a nice group, but then you begin to see the needs of the whole. Your heart center is your leader here. And there's no question about it. If you have not yet understood what the heart center is capable of doing, then this particular area needs full investigation — and you will love it. It is a wonderful journey. If you find that you're not able to use the heart center as much as you would like to, then explore the reasons, look deeply into the subconscious, look to see what might be blocking that. Get in touch more clearly with who you are and what has affected you, how you got that way, will allow you to use that heart center more and more completely. The heart center is an indicator.

Heart Center Visualization

❦ Now I'll share a specific symbolic exercise with you. See the heart center as a large rose. This rose has an unlimited number of petals. Examine each one of them. Feel it. Smell it. Hear it. Listen to your rose. But become familiar with it.

❦ Now see it begin to move forward, and there's a vine that comes forward into your horizon. And on that vine is an unlimited number of roses. They are all species, all kinds, all colors. And that vine goes forward in a never-ending manner from your heart center. And you see, it's there for you. It's going forth just before you do. And as you go forth, you send your heart ahead. You send it out and it is there, ever supporting the whole, but ever supporting you also.

As you send forth this symbolic gesture to the whole, that monadic level of self will come forth. The monadic level of self appreciates, truly, the love center and uses it as a homing device, if you will, into you and your evolution. Does that mean that you can't connect with your monad until you're absolutely open? Of course not; you can. But this is a progressive thing, and it is important for humanity to work on that heart center, really appreciate it.

You see, as evolution takes place, there are specifics that you can do to aid yourself and to aid the Earth. Right now on your Earth the heart chakra and its response, working with it and attuning to each other, is important. The Christ, in his work on the Earth, began what you might call an anchoring process of this love aspect. It literally was put encompassingly into the vibration of your planet. And since that time, it has sprouted, and all of you then can utilize what the Christ made easier to utilize. And then perhaps one day when you have reached your monadic level all of the time, the Source will knock at your door and say, "Will you go forth to a physical planet and anchor love within it? Will you serve in this manner now?" That is on the agenda already for several of you in this room. Because the Source Itself in Its Oneness utilizes all of Its personnel very well, plans for the unfoldment Itself. It is supportive of your evolution, utilizing all of the components. Did you ever see nature waste anything? The Source on the physical level never wastes anything; it utilizes every component in the most comprehensive manner. We don't always see that. If we have a little pet that we love very much, and it's run over, we feel a loss, don't we? But that little pet in its loving association with us has gained much for the animal kingdom, and you certainly have gained much from this association. And we can say that the Source Itself has gained from this communication that came forth, this loving communication.

Now, the monadic level is truly encompassing. All of you, of course, in your evolution began that way. And we talk about cosmic days — some of you have heard me, and some of you have not. A cosmic day has also been called the day of Brahma. It is a conceptual framework within which the Sourceness explores, discovers, learns. And although they are not within sequential time, except on the physical level, this particular cosmic day is 4.3 billion of your years, with a cosmic night of the same duration to follow. That is not to say that every day is the same, certainly not. And because I enjoy these sorts of things, in my estimation there have been about a million of these days. As far as I can see they are going on forever. This then gets you in touch with the comprehensive nature of the divine. All of you are great beings — much greater than any of you have been — so when we talk about interacting with the monadic level, we are talking about a cocreator who potentially has the ability to create universes, to create magnificent things for the Source level.

Your monad is not yet creating universes, but potentially it is. And it certainly will when its understanding of the components of how a universe fits together is complete, Would you like to create a universe if you didn't know what was in it? You know, I've seen a few of those. That's important to understand too: that the Source in Its exploration tries literally everything. Everything is interesting to It. And thus if you look at Mother Nature, sometimes it's rather interesting and even a little humorous, isn't it? I think a giraffe is absolutely fascinating. So there is an exploration in the state of matter of absolutely everything. And beyond matter there's an exploration of everything also.

Your monad, then, is a spiritual being with an energy formatting. It certainly doesn't have a physical skin and bones and so forth. But it has a vehicle, and that vehicle is a life force, a combination of energy that is unique unto itself. It is there from its evolution. It is the combination of energies there from its evolution. And on the physical level you reflect this combination of energy.

If you're going to create a universe, you put in a little of this and a dash of that and a lot of this kind of energy, because that's needed as a basis. You will know the combination to use in order to create whatever it is you want to create on the free-flowing level. Now, this will be, in the largest sense, your monadic-level responsibility, but perhaps in your physical life now you can instruct and help the monadic level. You can literally be a partner in this cocreatorship. Isn't that exciting? You know, sometimes humanity thinks, "I'm not too much. I can see that. I have this little skin that I walk around in. Once in a while I injure a particular part of self. And look at that great spiritual being that I am. I'm much greater there." Well, I don't think so: You are really equal on every level. But on the physical level you are working in one format, and on the spiritual level you are working in another. Both formats can be brought together on the physical plane. I think it would be delightful if there were only monadic-level beings in this room. Wouldn't that be something? And why not? It is possible. It would allow the Earth's evolution to spiral forward. If we had three monads here, the Earth would never be the same, I can assure you. A whole roomful — how magnificent! Well, I'm ever an optimist, but it is in your future. And you know all you have is the nowness, so why don't you just put it right here now?

Then, for most of you, again the monadic-level connection comes filtering through the soul. But as that soul level becomes absolutely real, becomes absolutely who you are, then the monad gets really excited, gets really interested and begins to input into your life in a very interesting way. And I wanted to discuss that a little. Relationships are an area that you have worked on — it may be a man-woman relationship or a parent-child relationship or a friend-friend relationship. Relationships are an important area that all of us are seeking to clear.

Well, the monadic level is also a relationship. And perhaps the monad starts dropping a few hints in this area. It may say, "Have you looked at this?" And suddenly life will mirror to you what to look at. It may be the possibility of a magnificence in a particular relationship. To begin with, it will stretch you to show you what is possible. This is what the monad can do for you. Perhaps if you have any blocks in the subconscious, you will do your own mirroring. You will mirror if there are any blocks. The monad will show you what's possible, will inspire you, will bring forth a possibility that you can then seek to maintain. Perhaps if you are at the age where relationships are important to you, you might meet a man who is absolutely everything you ever wanted, and he seems interested also. Or you may meet a spiritual teacher who brings to you all of what you are looking for. All of these things then become available, are shown to you as possible. Life becomes stretched. You begin to glimpse the magnificent scope of existence itself through your association with this level. Inspiration? Call up your monad. Love? Call up your monad.

Well, I really do get carried away, don't I? But the monad is your ideal on the physical level. The monad, that basic spiritual part of self, wishes to be in your shoes because it is who you are. It wishes to look out of your eyes because they are its eyes too. It wishes to relate to your friends on the physical level because they are your monad's friends too. It wishes to guide you in your life because, dear ones, that is who and what you are. It truly is.

✧ S E V E N ✧

Accessing the Cosmic Strengths

GOOD EVENING, MY FRIENDS. WELL, THERE REALLY IS A LOT OF COSMIC energy going around. Did you notice that? It is a little different from a case of measles, though. You'd like to catch a little more of it. You'd like to really recognize how to be, on the physical level, that cosmic being that you're probably are you are on other levels. But how do you reach out and grasp that part of you and bring it to the Earth? Wouldn't you say that many of you — the ones that aren't trying to get away from the Earth, at least — are going to do that? The goal is to really bring it here, not to go *there* — at least not right now, until you've fulfilled the time contract that you've set up for yourself.

So there is perhaps the necessity of seeing what is going on on the Earth. I know you've all noticed that there is a lot, isn't there? Everywhere on the Earth, those areas that you thought were stuck perhaps just a little aren't stuck anymore. Perhaps you can't quite see *what* they are becoming, but they certainly are becoming it anyway, aren't they? What has occurred, literally, is that through the mass consciousness a great invocation has gone up. It is wonderful to see that beginning to manifest. That invocation is for more creative freedom. We could look at that in many ways, and we will be talking about it. But it is that invocation into something greater that is now allowing these changes to take place on the Earth.

I thought tonight we would assist in this continuing invocative process, that we would invoke from all of you more creative freedom. But what does that mean? Freedom is not getting away from something, is it? It is really getting *into* something. It is getting into that cosmic part of yourself and of the whole, and then really being able to use that.

Invoking a Cosmic Correspondence

You know, I like this picture over here. I find it rather indicative of the Earth right now. This one with the blue, rather cosmic background feels to me as if it were depicting your Earth right now. Maybe you could see that it would be like taking one picture of the Earth in an instant of change. You know that that is only one view of it and that you could look at many other views also. But this is one point where the Earth has reached what we will call an "Aha!" "Good, I get it! Aha!" the Earth says. This is a picture of it: the invoking of a particular connection that I will translate for you, or a correspondence, we could say, to the Galactic Core. This term "Galactic Core" is going to be a household word around your Earth soon. You may ask, "Well, what about my neighbor that doesn't even understand metaphysics?"

Although the term Galactic Core might not be used, what that represents and what it means will soon be a household word. It means really getting into that cosmic correspondence of who you are and being able to unlock that potential, bring that through you and understand it on the Earth. There is the beginning now of the realization of this planet's potential and the maturing, let's say, responsibility for this whole planet of what that truly means. There is a broadening base, a broadening creative base that is locking in this Earth's potential in relationship with what I will call the whole galactic quadrant.

What that means is – if we had a nice globe of the Earth (that really speaks to me of the Earth) we could say that the Planetary Logos, Sanat Kumara, has built an energy field which has allowed Earth to come forth physically. If we would then envision a corresponding light that is not parallel but is coming in this way at a right angle to several places – five in number – to the Earth, approaching now are five great beings at the galactic level who are coming directly into the energy field that surrounds the Earth. This is doing much.

If I tell you that one is coming directly into South Africa, it gives you some idea of what the power of that energy is and what is occurring. There is another one in India. There are several other areas where they are coming directly from the Galactic Core – not bypassing the system of the Planetary Logos and the Solar Logos and so forth but, let's say, being the means to further stabilize it and, like a can opener, open it up to another level of response.

So there are these cosmic energies directly accessing a level that is clearer, a level that has more consciousness, and that are affirming to the Earth over and over again, "Now you are free. You are free. You do not have to be in slavery through your past." How do you like that choice of words? I think that is really what they are saying. You don't have to be affected by what has been.

Your Connection with the Galactic Core

As far as you are all concerned right now, you have the opportunity to connect into the basic area of the cosmos which is this Galactic Core. That is where your future job opportunities are coming out of, and because many of you are studying there nights, it is nothing that you are unfamiliar with. It is the base from which all of the signals really come that is still physical. Certainly we could take it to a universal level and say, "Yes, that is still physical." But that is a stretch. That isn't real for humanity yet. There are those of you who stretch up universally and once in a while, you could say, multiuniversally, and you bring forth a concept, look at it and say, "Wow, that is wonderful, but now what do I do with it?" It is rather like a hot potato. It hasn't perhaps been integrated into the system.

What I am telling you tonight is that the ideas and the creative abilities that are stored within the Galactic Core have at least five light paths that now approach the Earth and are being locked into it. For this reason the changes that you see are coming. These energies are an affirmation of unlimitedness. They keep saying to you as you try to create within your limited perspectives, "No, don't use that anymore. Use a clearer and more unlimited perspective."

One of my jobs is to probe the subconscious mind — we talk about its power over you. But I tell you, this galactic message is more powerful than that. It is the means to let go of that. Now, that is confusing some of you because you have used your subconscious as the basis from which to create your life over and over and over again. Isn't it the mechanism that you've set up for the process? Yes, of course. But it is not isolated; it is within something greater. Certainly we have said, "Isn't that the soul level?" That is true also. But again, the soul is not in the vacuum. What we are telling you is that there is a directed response, and we are calling this the Galactic Core, which says, "You are ready to use that clearer part of you *now* on the Earth."

Tonight what I would like to do is to prove that to your subconscious. How would you like that? This type of invocation is not a mental one, so if you would all take your heads off and put them over here! You have a very strong mental body. If you wish, you can analyze it all later. But what we are going to do is show the subconscious mind that it has this direct access and have it move a little within. In a sense we will take your subconscious mind (if you choose, because you certainly have that choice of whether or not to do this) into the room of the beginning of your conscious recognition of the great effect that the Galactic Core can have upon you. Now, there are many, many teachers there, many, many friends. You have a correspondence of yourself there. Some of you know that; you've heard this. You are certainly what I would call a sophisticated audience up here. You've heard it all — probably all of it in as many ways as it is possible to imagine.

Integrating Your Creativity

Let's think about it as your creativity and the many levels of your creativity. For you right here on the physical level, the Galactic Core is the place where your creativity can be integrated, put together so that you can very practically draw on that in your life. You may say to yourself tomorrow, "I just know I am supposed to write a book." There are many of you writing them, and you are writing them on all levels. You've all written one on the Galactic Core level! It is true. You have that ability, and those abilities are being used there. So if that is your goal, then how about tonight setting up a way to access the knowledge, understanding, the point of integration which that represents.

In my opinion, that is what most of you are seeking to access – "How does all this fit together? What do you mean that I have this ability and that ability? What, in a very practical sense, can I do with that? How can they fit together so I can use them? What if my old programming hits me in the face again? What do I do about that?" All of these are practical questions. The answers can come forth through this part of you that knows and understands, certainly through the soul (again I want to emphasize that), but it is sitting in the directorship of your own life if you allow it.

There is a word here that some of you have used many times and have sought to understand – "surrender." How many of you have heard of it? Maybe that one is so charged that we'll use another one not quite as charged. How about "release"? Is that a little more comfortable?

You must, in a sense, get up off the chair that you've been sitting in and move over to the other chair that says "Soul Directorship" from the Galactic Core. The good news is that it is a very comfortable chair. It has a lot of support built into it. There is a sense of direction that automatically comes with that. It comes with a lifetime guarantee.

The movement is up to you. You must, in your releasing, allow that movement. How do you do that? Well, you have something here I think you are all familiar with – the heart energy. Some of you are harder on yourselves than anyone else. You have, perhaps, felt at times that your Earth has become quite a bit bewildering. There is so much going on and there is a lot of intensity. Some of you here in Sedona have insulated yourselves from that, and some of you have put yourselves right in the mainstream of it.

There is a tremendous amount of intensity here if you allow that to reach you. That intensity can be that little bit of a kick that maybe you need right *here* to move over *here*. I thought we'd put it that way because there is a sense that there needs to be a momentum: "Yes, I'll make that effort. I'll allow it. I'll move beyond the directorship of the subconscious mind." That doesn't mean that you won't continue to utilize it. But it comes in in a whole different way because it is put in its correct or divine perspective in a way that you have never perhaps allowed it to be in your physical life. It becomes integrated.

Again, I tell you that that point of integration is at the Galactic Core.

You weren't really able to reach that before the Harmonic Convergence, and then only somewhat and once and a while. But you get the picture of someone jumping up and down, shouting, "There's the Galactic Core!" After they look, they are down again; then they try to jump up again: "There's the Galactic Core!" And then down again. It took the Harmonic Convergence to increase the vibratory rate of your planet to allow a consistent glimpse into that area.

Now, every one of you has taken advantage of the libraries and learning and storage that is available at the Galactic Core. If you've been doing something creative (and you all have — you are creating your lives), you may find that you suddenly have an idea or you have suddenly "gotten" it or you've decided to sleep on something and when you got up the next morning you knew how to access something. Chances are, on the inner level you were researching it and working with it within the Galactic Core's library and research facilities and workshops — and perhaps the clearing of your etheric structure, which was transferred when you woke up to the physical structure.

Using Crystals to Clear the Physical Structure

One thing that is occurring, and one thing that is important, is how much clearer your physical structures are now becoming — if you let them, of course. They all are becoming clearer. The mineral kingdom is especially helpful right now.

Fuchsite can be very helpful. It has a lifting ability to the cells. You simply take a little piece and rub it into the cells. What I noticed is that if there is, from the subconscious, some clinging to the old level of those cells in a particular area or what you would refer to as the third dimension, the fuchsite helps lift out the material that is being clung to there and reenergizes the particular area. It can be helpful.

Calcite is also very helpful. It seems to me that as you approach the ascension process, various forms of calcite can be helpful for the integrative process of the four-body system. I like the pink calcite, and the red and the orange. The orange helps clear out the mental body.

There is, then, a system right on your planet to help clear you out physically so that your etheric and physical responses can be integrated into this Galactic Core. You are a combination of many resources, aren't you, a combination of many aspects? Some of you know that your strength is perhaps your mental body; for others it is perhaps the emotional responses. For still others, it may be the intuitive responses. Perhaps your strength is your physical body. The goal is to integrate all of these.

In order to really get it into an integrated state, assistance needs to be made to help the part of you that is the least responsive to this new level. Some of you here, particularly in Sedona, have come to help integrate your physical body into this process. Many of your souls have drawn you into this area of high intensity. I am generalizing, for this isn't true with every one of you. But there is the need to integrate the physical on all levels, meaning the dense physical and the etheric levels into this new level of the Galactic Core. I would say that generally you are drawn at this period to this area, meaning that you are all close to finishing up your physical existences. Many of you are finishing up — not only on the Earth but on many, many, many other levels — everything that is still considered physical.

So there is a fitting together — I think that is what draws you at this time to areas such as Sedona. It can be confusing, because you are still physical enough to look at your lives and say, "What I really want is for my life to work." You don't see it completely, perhaps, as the cosmic summary that is really going on. You are putting together the final touches on a very cosmic book that all of you are writing, and you are getting ready to start writing another one — you know, it just keeps going on. But this one is really being completed at this particular time right here on the Earth. The next fifteen to twenty years are going to see many of you really awaken to that new level.

Now, does that mean that you leave the planet? Probably not, for most of you. You may say to me, "Oh, I thought I would get to *go!*" Well it isn't up to me, it is up to your souls. And you know, some of us can be quite persuasive to a soul. We do say to them, "You've been so helpful here on the Earth, how about renewing your contract perhaps for another hundred years or two?" That doesn't mean that you might stay in the physical body, but it means that your association with the Earth is so deep that a certain resolution will take place before your contract runs out.

Your Presence at Earth's Inception

When the Earth was born, you were all there: You took your energy into it because you knew that you would be associated with it. Remember, at that level you were not in sequential time. You looked at this planet and you helped give birth to it! A planet is always born through the cosmic heart of the Planetary Logos. So in a sense you are already a part of that energy. You were already awakening to your Earth association, so you had a party, a celebration. This is a birthing party. "I'll stay around until the Earth gets to a certain point that, in my soul's association with it, I have agreed to stay." But sometimes we write in a few more clauses, and some of that is happening now to each of you.

There is a process that one goes through. You take a look at that (again we have that lovely little word "surrender") and you take a look at the other career opportunities you are beginning to energize: "Do I really want to stay two hundred more years?" I am just using this as an example of the process that all of you go through all the time, because surrender is not a one-time activity. It is a constant process of aligning through your heart into the cosmic birthing that is always going on on every level! *You* are always a part of it, so we are always celebrating new births. Then you come back on the outer level. I wish I could explain this more fully to you, because I never felt cut off by physical existence, I really didn't. But some of you do, and there is a sense of "They are celebrating up there somehow; I got to be at that party, but now I wake up — and where is that celebration? I don't know where it went. It feels like it left me out."

Well, the goal is now to bring that celebration to the Earth. I'll bring the balloons, how is that? The point is to really recognize the joy, the enthusiasm, the loving associations that are possible. Many of you are doing very well with that: the relatedness of each of you to the others, the fact that you've developed within the same system, meaning that you are a part of a greater being called the Planetary Logos, Sanat Kumara. Sanat Kumara is a part of a greater being who is called the Solar Logos, Helios. And Helios is a part of a greater being that I am calling the Galactic Core; I can give you the name of one teacher because I want to energize that: Melchior. Is there a correspondence there to the Bible reference? Of course there is. And this great being is coming in contact with you in your physical lives now in a way that has never been possible before.

So what are you going to understand? Systems within systems within systems within systems, and how they fit together. If you are feeling a little confused, that is what is going on. You are learning now to see how everything fits together from the level of the Galactic Core down to the Earth and *from* the level of the Galactic Core up to what we call the ultimate Source (which isn't ultimate at all; it is simply a new beginning). There are many more levels within that.

The point is that you are perhaps not giving away your power — not surrendering your power — but accessing it, perhaps for the first time totally, through your association with this Galactic Core. I think that is important, because it gives you something to trust. "There is a point where all of my abilities and all of my potentials are being stored." Certainly we could say they are stored at the Source. We could say they are stored within your heart. We could say they are stored anywhere. But in connection with the Galactic Core there is now a direct accessing to them into your physical life — and what that means.

Think about what it means for your physical body. It means that the body of light that we talk about all the time can be the basis for running your life rather than one you use which says, "I die at a certain age because my body wears out." Or "I have a liver that doesn't function very well" or "I have a pancreas that isn't working well" or "My blood vessels clog up" or all of these things that occur. Or "I don't remember."

There is now literally a way to access that light connection within each cell that will keep this body eternally the age that you choose. It is important to tell yourselves the ideal age that you are aiming for. What would you like to have as the goal? What particular point in accessing (for many of you as many as two thousand lives, for others a thousand, fifteen hundred) and plucking from those sequential lives, where is that ideal point, that point where there was growth in the cells and they were enthusiastic about life — that point where you would like to rest, let's say float, in your physical lives? I don't mean sitting and doing nothing, but that the cells would not activate any sort of resistance to the process of directing your part of the Plan or a joint life or being able to contact the Galactic Core.

Let's stop intellectualizing for a little while and do one of our invocations. I would invite you, if you wish, to close your eyes.

Invoking Your Cocreator Association with the Galactic Core

❦ Imagine with your knowingness or visualize a golden light in the round shape of a planet. That will be the Galactic Core. It is moving and rotating; it certainly is radiating. It would not be inappropriate to see it as a cosmic heart also. So if you prefer, the heart. Focus or perhaps put the heart within the light, the ball, the golden energy.

❦ I'd like you to now see a path. You are standing before it. You can choose, if you wish, to step on that path. That path will lead you to a point where you may choose to enter this Galactic Core. Again, you have a choice. If you do not wish to do this, then simply relax until we finish.

❦ See yourself now moving along this path. Perhaps you are with others. You don't do these things by yourself, so how about taking the group with you? If that feels comfortable, you can place all of Sedona on this path also. See how that feels. If that feels comfortable, how about placing all of Arizona on that path? Again, you may stop whenever you wish. If that feels comfortable, how about all of the United States on this path also? It is just more and more comfortable. There is more and more creativity being built into the path, into the momentum.

❦ Now, if that is comfortable, how about all of North America? And then South America. And then all of the Earth. We are building up a momentum, a great momentum that is propelling you forward, propelling you forward until you come in contact with that Galactic Core. Now remember, you haven't done this by yourself. It is not an individual goal. This is a goal, an association with others, an association with your planet, a cocreator-level goal. Feel that now. The great being that is Melchior draws you in with his heart, draws you in with his heart now.

❦ Let us go into a very special room. We have come into the Galactic Core; you may even see it as a spaceship if you wish. That is not wrong, either. You come to a particular room, enter the room and sit on a particular chair. You know that this chair is your power. You have to give yourself permission now to sit on it. You know that is being mirrored all around; everyone else is sitting on their chair too, so it doesn't isolate you. There is a sense of connection.

❦ Now, before you is a wonderful device. If you wish, you can enter it. It will come to you. It says, "I am the heart of all of the universe. I am the heart center that is available to you through this Galactic Core. I am a being that you can now access. Melchior has made this available. I am giving you my name as Adonis." Invite this being, out of whose heart the whole radiates, into you within this Galactic Core.

☙ Sense now what is occurring within your own heart. There is a new beginning here, a loving association you can trust. This is not unfamiliar; this is what many of you have longed for. Many of you may feel that that is home, a heart connection which is so strong that it unifies, electrifies, harmonizes, integrates and makes available all of your strengths, all of your abilities that you have carefully stored at this Galactic Core.

☙ Now more and more power is flowing through you, because you are in contact with the heart. The beauty there, the trust, yes. Yes! The enthusiasm, the joy, coming to you from the greatest being who has ever been in contact with physical existence – Adonis. Yes. Let that soak in. Let it radiate through you. A great being, but more importantly what he mirrors to you is your own greatness in association with each other. Feel that. Your greatness is a part of something that is much greater. You call it the Source. It radiates. It mirrors. It expands and expands and expands and expands and expands until it fills literally the horizons of your galactic responses, mirroring from every point of view – mirroring, expanding and expanding. This is who you are. The next step for you: a galactic being, centered within your heart, a galactic being who cares enough to have come to the Earth and now turns over the directorship for your path to that part of you on that level.

☙ Each in your own way, now, if you wish, surrender to that power. Gently become aware again of this room. You may bring your chair with you from the cosmic, galactic link. Bring it with you. Certainly you will bring in with you the mirroring of Adonis. This has been permanently placed within your heart. Thank you.

All right, my friends. I'd like some of you to comment a little to me right now about what you felt or experienced, or perhaps didn't experience in the meditation.

I was aware that I would be hearing you, and I thought, "Come back and listen to what he is saying!" I don't know where I went. I was just gone.

I think you went where we asked you to go! Perhaps you didn't keep the door open to hear. I think it worked quite well for you. I liked what I saw as I attuned to you. I liked the link that you made, the connection, so I think it is very important for you. I think it will open up some possibilities subconsciously or creatively. I like that.

Adonis, the Teacher
I had talked quite a bit about a teacher, a beautiful being called Adonis. You have known him in many other perspectives. So now to again find his

energy in association with this physical experience seems to me to be important and exciting for you. I think you may discover, if you allow yourself to do so (and why not?) what that means gradually over time.

Has it something to do with Adonis when you say "Adonai"?

Well, in a sense. I think that is one reason why the name Adonis has been given. Because, of course, this being has about as many names as you can possibly conceive of. You may have known him by another name, although the name isn't that important except perhaps vibrationally. (I'm sure that from his point of view he would not have chosen it if it wasn't vibrationally important.) There is a very good link or hookup now with this great being.

Adonis has chosen to be a part of a Venus training facility which is currently, and has been over a period of many millennia, training planetary logoi. So he is responsible for training on the physical level, and that is why he is on the physical level. This is not a being who needs to be physical, but a being who has found the strengths of the physical plane to be very helpful in understanding one's role within the Plan.

I had been physically very uncomfortable and I had a great sense of being freed. I appreciate that.

Good! That's wonderful. So there is a sense of, rather than being held in the arms of discomfort, coming into contact with the being that I have called Adonis. What is going on now is more a sense of being at home within your process. Do you see that is one reason why I helped you to make this connection, this link?

That energy is so immense that there is room for all the changes you are going through to be very comfortably supported, because that energy doesn't have to keep expanding. It is so expansive already in its nature that it can support you as you keep expanding over and over again.

Because you've brought that up, I want to tell you that each day your understanding of who you are (this may not come through your mental body, by the way, although it begins to filter into that) may expand at least ten times. If you keep multiplying that by ten every day, then you can see why sometimes your physical body might not be comfortable with this. You could say that the physical body makes room for a certain level of creativity and arranges all the chairs in a certain way and puts in a certain number of chairs; but the next day that is already obsolete, and it needs ten times more chairs and perhaps a greater understanding of how to arrange them.

You keep multiplying this daily — and I mean *daily*. Then you can see the immense amount of potential that is being locked into the physical structures right now. See? So you are building new organs in the physical body. You are all re-creating on a higher vibrational level — your liver, heart, spleen, kidneys, the heart center, all of these things are expanding in a sense; I don't mean physically, but in a vibratory sense. You have to see that not all of them are expanding at the same rate. Maybe your spleen is just a little ahead of the liver, which is a little ahead of the kidneys. The kidneys say, "Come on, now, where are we going and what is happening?" There really is some physical discomfort in this process. It is a matter of integrating all of your physical responses into this constantly expanding psychological identity that you are beginning to invoke now.

It would be as though you finally got to the university and you thought you had a certain career path. In fact, you knew that you did. You wouldn't give this up. But when you started seeing all the classes that were connected with this path, you found it so expansive that in addition you would need to go to that, this, and this, and this, and this, and this. You are trying to adjust to what is now opening before you.

It doesn't mean that you are going to have to spend a lot of effort in understanding all of this, because that understanding is coming in from the galactic level. Do you see that? It is there for you, so it is simply plugging into it and accessing it. It is much less actively mental (some of you don't like to hear that) than it is a releasing and allowing the spiritual to educate the integrative responses within you. So there is a complete realignment of the four-body structure going on right now.

It might not be felt that way physically but in the psyche: "Why doesn't this quite fit anymore?" There is discomfort within you and within some others is because the roles have sometimes reversed or shifted, and you are not quite sure how to function. That is what is very important to know. I think this is going to go on for most of you for the next year or so. So get used to it. In fact, the sooner you get used to it, the sooner you surrender to that level. The more you use the four-body system to energize your association with the Galactic Core, the way your soul has seen fit, through its more cosmic perspective, the easier it will be for you. That is the reason for the meditations in connection with the Galactic Core, whether or not you recognize what's going on.

For some of you this is entirely different, because it doesn't really validate the mental body. In fact, it is better if the mental body is part of what is surrendering to this process for a little while. If you can, let go of that and say, "I am going to allow that spiritual part of me — and certainly the heart responses — to be the one that now helps me to open to this next level of my creativity."

Balancing Mental-Emotional with Spiritual-Physical

That doesn't mean that you won't be using the mental responses, but they are not directing this goal. This goal is spiritual. This goal is aligning that spiritual into the physical level. Again, looking at it from the cross, this is that vertical column of your spirituality coming into the physical level. Certainly the emotional and the mental responses, which the other part of the cross could represent, are there. You are balancing them.

This is that spiritual penetration which has gone now to the physical level perhaps as never before on your planet. So that rearranges it this way: The cross starts to spin. How many of you have felt a little dizzy lately? Confused, particularly in connection with the mental body? That is because it is spinning. You could take that cross and get it moving. The spinning is done purposefully by your soul to say, "If you don't recognize beyond that level, we'll spin you out where you will come in contact with where you can more easily be.

Sometime would you talk about what we can do to help our physical bodies be more comfortable, because a lot of strange things are happening?

Yes, they are, aren't they? Well, I think the association with the mineral kingdom can be very helpful. Because, your planet, starting on April 15, 1989, went to this vibratory level that is the entryway to that galactic area. In other words, what is happening within the physical body is like a blinking on and off of that new level. It is certainly there sometimes, but you are not able to hold on to it. The energy penetrates into it, but you could say that some of your past programming, some of the subconscious responses, keep turning it off.

That is one reason for making the connection to Adonis and through the Melchior logos in connection with the Galactic Center. Because that penetration, which is centered from the heart responses, can stabilize the physical body. It can help it relate to the level that is expanding. It includes the physical level, but that level is really expanding as far as your association with the Earth is concerned.

So, I would get a symbol, something that reminds you of something that is stable. Can you think of a symbol that reminds you of something that is stable?

A lotus?

All right. That is good. It is stable, but it is also expanding, isn't it? It is stable within that expansion. I think that would work well. You could visualize yourself sitting in the center of that. I still encourage you to see the beam, or see that symbol within the Galactic Core. See a beam connection on the physical level of whatever color light you want. I would not advise white light because white light keeps out everything. And you want to let in the positive, don't you? So I like gold light for that reason. Gold is a more integrative color than white.

One thing that I am trying to explain to people is that it is important to reassess all of the metaphysical cliches that you have heard over the years. It seems to me that you are going to have to look at everything on a new level, because that is where everything is: "I do it this way because that is the only way I know how and that is the only way that has ever worked" won't work anymore.

Physical exercise is extremely important. I am advising that for everyone

— moving on your Earth, either walking or jogging or running. Some movement — dancing to a type of music that you like certainly can be helpful. Using your physical structure, moving it around, is helpful because it is a synchronicity of being able to move out of what is not comfortable to you physically.

I think it is important to recognize that you are resolving, through your physical structure, all of the illnesses on the Earth that are not valid and thus they can go away. Now, it doesn't mean that you are going to get the illness, that particular virus or any of that, but that through your structure you are making the resolution that is going to help the Earth finally get rid of it. Measles keeps cropping up again. It keeps coming up unless people are vaccinated. Well, it doesn't need to be that way. You are evolving all of your physical structures now beyond the point where they need to energize those old illnesses.

That is part of what is going on in your physical bodies. I don't mean that you are going to get the measles. But I do mean that if you take an average of 150 to 200 particular diseases and put them into a physical structure, saying to that physical structure, "Your job is to dissolve this, to handle it so that your perspective is beyond the need to feel threatened by these," then the immune and endocrine systems are no longer involved with these. Thus the Earth is a little bit clearer in their use. Then you put it into billions of bodies on the Earth; you are breaching a new level of evolution for your planet as far as those illnesses are concerned.

Now, take what we might consider a polar opposite of that and say that coming in from the Galactic Core is a wonderfully clear and integrated energy. You say to the physical body, "Now, learn to handle that, because that is the level of support that you can now use." Then you can see what your body is going through. It is handling one to release and the other to absorb and integrate. There is a lot going on.

Your body needs a lot of support right now, so eat food that's as natural as possible. I would say eat *very little* red meat. You know, I don't advise that all the time because I think some of your bodies can handle it. But right now it is very intense for the physical body. If it were me, I would cut down on red meat.

I certainly would drink a lot of water. I am one who advises you to drink twelve glasses of water a day. But I want to qualify that and say this: If you will do that consistently for a few weeks, you will, in a sense, flood the cells. Then it will only take maybe six or seven glasses to keep it full. It is like flooding a reservoir; then it doesn't take as long to fill it up again. But you need that cell-flooding, which in a sense keeps it from absorbing from the past some of these illnesses.

Many of you are having so many changes electrically that when you say, "Aha! I get it!" your whole magnetic field is going to reverse. If you do that two or three times a week (and some of you are), can you see how intense it is for your physical responses to have your whole magnetic field reversed two or three times a week? That is intense, isn't it? It means that the electrical responses within the cells are being directed differently through each new opening, through each point of integration. The parathyroids in particular are adjusting, and this throat area may feel it. The third eye is adjusting. There may be some sense of change there. For some of you it may be pressure from the old level. For others, certainly the beginnings of clairvoyance or the further development of it. And then in the crown chakra area, there is a *tremendous* expansion now available through the crown chakra.

Some of you knew Ascentia when she was on the physical level, which she has now left. By working with her through a rather difficult process that she had going in her physical structure, we saw the crown chakra open up about fifty times more than it was before. Certainly there was a complete rearrangement of the light quality, but I don't think you recognize that when you see someone and suddenly you can sense that their light is so much stronger, their heart is so much more vibrant and radiant, what has occurred is a complete shift in their relationship with that crown chakra.

On the physical level it will then affect the whole endocrine system — the pineal and the pituitary, the parathyroid and the thyroid, the thymus and the adrenals, the spleen. All of the glands will then shift. They have to raise their vibrational rate to keep up with that.

This might not occur in an illness. It might simply be in your old transformational process that suddenly something shifts so much within you that you really get it more. "My goodness! I knew I was light, but now I *know* I am light! I can feel it! I can sense it! I can touch it! I can smell it! I can taste it!" That is when that tremendous expanse is made. All of you are either in the process of doing that now, or you are ready to do that now. That is what is going to be what I might call grasping that potential of yourself within the Galactic Core. That is exciting.

It does take looking deeply within you. It does take a willingness to face what you've created and resolve it. You have the developing heart, and certainly the connection with the soul, to sustain your effort. You are not doing that and not becoming vulnerable through it, although some of your beliefs may say, "I'm not quite sure what is going on, and I do feel a little vulnerable."

Releasing to the Soul

By placing yourself directly into this chair and really releasing to the soul, you are going to allow a more intense mirroring than perhaps has ever occurred to you on this planet. Are you ready for that? That mirroring can bring in your strengths, your potential. If we consider it this way (I'd like you to really understand that), again our globe and around it the energy field that is called the Planetary Logos, the energy field of your planet, then around that the energy field that we call the Solar Logos. All of these interrelate, of course; one isn't just sitting on the other. One is within another. Then the galactic energy surrounds that.

Each point is a point of consciousness, a mirror. As you open your responses, there are an unlimited number of these mirrorings that begin to come through to you. You could look at it as standing here with mirrors on every level, levels and layers of mirrors that are beginning to be energized by you. That is important because it is not negative; it is your strengths. For every mirror is going to show you something you do not understand, what is trying to get through is probably a hundred mirrors that are showing something you *do* understand and trying to remind you of it on the physical level. So it is tremendously more affirmative than it is negative. Does that make sense to you? That is the way you'll be comfortable in life and have it work well. Just accept the mirrors that are there.

One thing that gets in the way for some of you are levels of illusion. That is another term that is interesting. What is an illusion? It is something that seems to cut you off. It doesn't seem to connect you. So there is sometimes some fear or an emotion (perhaps anger, loss — it could be different emotions) that connects you into an illusion. Generally that illusion is from something that happened to you in the past.

Let us say that you were once a king — you were King George — and you sat on your throne and waited for your people to come, but they didn't. There wasn't anybody left. They were all dead. You were a king, then, without any subjects. It was a time of plague and all your subjects had died, but the plague didn't dare kill the king. Isn't that interesting? (At least, he didn't die of it!) But there you were, isolated by being the king. Now, that is important for you, George, because it says that as you try to get in touch with your kingship, you are going to touch into this isolation. Kind of an interesting one.

You also have built into your system certain resistances to accepting your kingship. As the mirrors try to powerfully touch you into them, sometimes you try to activate that a little. Now, what is the key to that? The key is still surrender, trust, allowingness and saying, "Anything that disconnects me isn't real." The affirmation of that will lead you gradually step by step into understanding what *is* real. You can interact with each other with love and you can have in your life, in the way you are creating it, a constant evolution of your understanding of how to live it in the way you want to live it. It is moving so rapidly that it may shift almost from day to day.

Today I want to be a fireman. Tomorrow I am going to be a policeman. In a cosmic sense. It is important to indulge your fantasy in this way. Let us say that today you want to be a fireman. Well, go into being a fireman, at least in your imagination, and imagine what that would be like, really taking your creativity into that. Then tomorrow you would probably be through with it. Do you understand what I am saying to you? Instead of denying those things that come up for you or saying, "Well, I haven't got time," at least explore it in your creativity. That is a part of this flow, the flow of your creativity. Explore it. That is a part of the fourth dimension. And you are going to get something out of it.

Now, if that is real enough to you, if you are a cosmic fireman, the universe is going to pick that up, and coming back to you through those mirrors will be more energy. You'll get an invitation: "Are you interested in joining our cosmic fire department?" Well, I assure you that it will work that way. Because your imagination can often be the key to picking up the next response that is awaiting you.

So I would encourage you in imagination. That is why Hollywood has been important for you. The *Star Wars* saga: Certainly the warring part is an old pattern, but think about the various things — the Force, the ability to move around a planet, the interaction of the various races together, the young man who gets what he dreams of and studies and learns and grows. In a sense, you experience that through him, don't you? That is why that was so popular.

Do that in your own imagination, whatever it is that you feel growing within you. Allow yourself to energize it first through your imagination, then turn it over to the universe, and if you get some energy into that on another level, it'll come back to you with a full-born opportunity.

Constant New Opportunities

You know, opportunities are interesting. There is never just one. There are always at least six ways to do everything. So the good news is that if you don't get it today, just let it cook a little and another opportunity will come in and bring it to you. There always are many, many paths to the cosmic goals that you have.

You know, part of the discomfort is trying to energize the old path or the old way of relating to what is coming in, when there is a part of you that knows better, that knows there is an easier a way in which you can participate with others at a new level of understanding.

Your most important lesson has to do with each other, understanding each other. You don't understand each other very well. I am not criticizing. I am telling you that, for example, this person has all of these cosmic abilities that she is just beginning to reach, so you are looking at her first through your aura and then through the Earth's aura and then through her own aura. Then perhaps she is very actively working with one teacher, so you get some of that teacher's aura. And perhaps at this moment she is reactivating an old Lemurian pattern or something in Atlantis, so you are getting some of that. So it is very difficult to evaluate each other.

The good news is, most of the time (unless you are in a teaching situation) you really don't have to. You can just enjoy and love each other. Notice as she reaches and brings in another new ability that you haven't seen her use before; perhaps you could tell her, "Look, I can see how much clearer you are in that area. Look at what you are doing now!" She might not have noticed. I think that is one thing you can do — help each other see yourselves as you grasp your new strengths.

This other person has lots of energy in the heart area — much more than I have ever seen before. That is a new level of heart energy that perhaps you don't get to see, but it is very active now. It is going to open up the cosmos for you — not that you haven't explored it rather fully. But perhaps now is the time to integrate within that new level of what I see here. It is a rosy pink energy and it certainly is going to be responsible for a new level of awareness of who you really are, because there is some illusion still about who you are.

"I'm an Earth being." Well, yes and no. Perhaps not as much as you are a galactic being now. You are not really just of this Earth anymore. Not at all. Is that all right? Some of you aren't quite sure, but perhaps one of these days you will be. Because that is not something that is far out; it is deep within. If is a shifting of your perspective into the core of your true reality, that which is the real you.

I just want to comment that Adonis' energy seems so very familiar. I became aware when I was in the energy – perhaps it was my mind getting active, saying, "Where are the goddesses? We are getting the name of this god, but where are the goddesses?"

Built into the process of his own receptivity. You could call it he, she or it. It is a complete energy. But the full answer to your question is that there is a dynamic shift going on in the heart area, and thus the name may seem male to assist in that dynamic shift. At other times you might get a female name, which emphasizes the receptive shift. It doesn't mean that one is separate from the other, but it is merely an emphasis.

Someone said 1990 was going to be the first level of initiation for the rest of the world. Is there a truth to that?

Certainly there are levels of spiritual maturity on the Earth. I have been addressing those of you who are taking responsibility for your lives, who are saying, "Yes, I am responsible for my life. Something out *there* didn't do it." Spiritual maturity is where you do accept responsibility for yourself. And about the time you understand it, then you give it over to your soul to take care of. One is a process within the other. Certainly you begin to manifest the summary of the process when you accept responsibility for the self.

So we are looking at those on the Earth who are not mature enough yet to see that. There are all levels of spiritual being on the Earth. There are some complete beginners — those who are just beginning physical existence, coming in rather recently — and those who are "spiritual teenagers."

This year has specific points of springboarding from one level to the next. You could call those initiations, but what is an initiation? It is, in my opinion, a look at what is coming up much beyond where you are, and then a locking into the new beginning of that as well as the release of what has been.

What the lecturer was saying was that the rest of the world, the people who haven't been consciously spiritual, are going to take the first step toward being spiritual.

Well, I look at it as being a constant process.

Everyone of course is subconsciously spiritual, but an awful lot more people are going to be jolted into making a decision as to where they want to go consciously. In other words, probably where a lot of us were twenty or thirty years ago.

I agree with that pretty much. I would say that everything has speeded up so much that if you are here at all, you have already agreed to be a part of the process. Or else you are phasing out where you will not be a part of the Earth anymore. But I would say that 90% of humanity that has already agreed is in the process about like this: the foot in the air and now we need are taking that step. There are some who have tried to stay here that I feel will not simply because they could not. They wanted to, but they *could* not. They weren't able to handle this energy. You are seeing some illnesses from that.

Now, will you be able to see it on the outer level? Maybe not; it could be, but I doubt it. Consider it within yourself; maybe it is more important for your own meditative time, for your own releasing, and for your own heart connection to say to a little one who might be taking that conscious step for the first time, "I'm going to be a bridge for you if I can."

All the potentials that you've ever sent out, all of the alternate realities, everything that could be possible, everything that you ever sent out to the universe, is going to receive from the universe itself (tonight it would be the Galactic Core) a way to respond to you in a manner that you can recognize and use through understanding the various aspects of yourself.

I think it may take you this year to build up a clearer mental understanding of what we've initiated tonight. I think that it isn't any different for the rest of humanity. It is simply that for some, levels of illusion are built into the process when they say, "I'm not responsible" or "I didn't create this" or "Somebody is doing this to me." Then there is some illusion that detracts or keeps out that potential that is trying to integrate through them. That is the difference.

That is what you can do for your friends if they try to tell you (and they are asking for your help, of course) that somebody is doing something to them. Then you can keep pointing out in as gentle a way as possible, although some of may find your mouths opening now and saying to people, "You *are* responsible for your life" in a way that you've never done before. Why? Because illusion, my friend, has to go. *Illusion has to go.* The souls are really invoking that. I think that is extremely important.

That cosmic mirror is saying, "Look clearly and see who you are. Stand up and see who you are." Have the courage to say, "I am much greater than

I know." You have the courage within you to say that. It isn't an ego statement; it is a statement of your power as a divine being, and it is a statement which allows a clearer link with others because it also says, "You are much greater than you know. I'm not just saying I am, but you are, too." As we acknowledge that, then we begin to embody that power that we've really looked for.

The point of this discussion has been to have you glimpse the other levels that are already working in connection with you on the Earth, and although you knew that, perhaps tonight has shown you that the mirrors are infinite in showing you how that is working. The good news is, *you can't miss.* You can't avoid it, because that is your divine destiny — to be in touch with these other levels. My friends, if the cosmos can't bring it to you one way, I assure you it will bring it to you another.

Experiencing the Energy Garden of Sanat Kumara

❦ *I'd like to take you, with the permission of Sanat Kumara, into his energy garden. This is a beautiful garden that Sanat Kumara built in honor of Venus. It was very like a garden that he often walked there. Right now it is an energy garden and it is within what we call Shamballa. Perhaps you will come with me there. I invite you to do so. The angelic kingdoms are helping you, and there is an angel now holding your hand and saying, "Come, I will make it possible for you to experience the beauty of this garden."*

❦ *It is being energized now. Let us enter it. There are energy flowers. We can see them as physical flowers blooming in great profusion. But perhaps the clearest to me within this garden is its feeling. Everything that is being invoked into the Earth is felt here. See if your feeling nature can sense the cosmic level of feelings which have been gathered here into this garden. We can image that as flowers of every conceivable size and variety, beautiful flowers and beautiful beings which are like birds, only they are members of the angelic kingdom. And beautiful music is penetrating everywhere.*

❦ *Walk, then, with Sanat Kumara in this garden. This is the being who has energized you in connection with the Earth. He is like a father or a mother to you. Sense the beauty of this place and your responses to him. He is pointing out to us some new cosmic varieties of flowers he has planted. Look at those! Aren't they exciting? I like that. It feels good to me. Within here is every potential, every part of you, every possibility, linking into your heart, deeply into the cells. All of it available to you now.*

❦ *Through the first meditation we energized a cosmic link. Through the present meditation we bring it closer to the Earth. But you see, we lock it now into a concept, an overall energy concept of Sanat Kumara that is fully integrated, fully responsive now. Sense the power of it, the sense of presence, and it moves through you now, linking you into your potential here on the Earth. Invoke it now, accept it now if you wish. Allow it now. Trust it now. If you wish, place your hand within the hand of this being who guides the Earth.*

🐦 *Remember who you are – a cosmic being, a team member for the Earth. He too is a member of the team and he is saying to you, "There is divine equality. Accept yours now." Look all around you. Standing all around you are the cosmic beings, the Commands, the Hierarchy-level teachers, the Galactic Core. You, my friends, have only to accept your divine equality with them. They have accepted you. You have only to accept them.*

🐦 *Sense that possibility growing, coming deeper and deeper into your physical body, locking it in now with the help of the angelic kingdom. Let it in! Let in your potential! Let it in now. Let it in! Awaken to that level. Feel it energizing your physical body. Let it in now! Awaken! This is who you are. That soul, radiant and alive, full of power, is for the Plan. Divine power – allow it in! Allow it more and more into the physical body. Allow it in now. Relax and allow it in. It is flooding in now from the garden, from your potential on all levels. Allow it in now. Deeper and deeper, connecting more and more, allow it in. Relax the physical structure. If you find something tighten in your neck or your head, relax it. Let your arms relax and your feet relax, and the trunk of your body. Relax the solar plexus. Let go! Relax and allow it to come in. More and more, allow it to come in. Relax! Relax! Relax! Yes. Gently saying, "Yes! I am ready now."*

✧ E I G H T ✧

A Multidimensional Opportunity
and How to Use It

WHAT IS A DIMENSION? A LEVEL OF CONSCIOUSNESS, AN OPPORTUNITY for experiencing? All right, then what is the difference between a dimension and a plane? We speak of the physical, astral, mental, emotional and spiritual planes, and we talk about multiple dimensions, so what is the difference between a dimension and a plane?

The planes are the aspects of consciousness that function dimensionally. We are going to talk about degrees of light opportunity and how to use all of your aspects in a multidimensional approach.

You are here on the physical plane, but you are also on the emotional, or astral, and there is a part of you that's on the mental and a part of you on the spiritual plane. Are you functioning on the same dimension on all of those planes? No, and therein lies our subject. You might think you are functioning only in the third dimension, but you are not. That is particularly true at this time. You are really learning to use the higher dimensions that contain more light, but you are relating it to the different planes according to your understanding of them. If you understand your mental body very well, you might be able to focus there in the fifth dimension. If your emotional body, your feeling nature, is the one you relate to, perhaps that's functioning in the sixth dimension or the fifth. The physical body will probably be in the third or fourth. The spiritual focus could be as high as the ninth dimension, depending upon your spiritual response at that particular point that we call sequential time.

This subject is an intricate one because it has many components and we put sequential time into this. We could say that in the eternal now everything is happening at once, so that all dimensions are being energized and all of your aspects, or bodies, are open to using them. At that point where you enter sequential time, or become physical, you are learning to sequentially recognize the strengths of each of the dimensions. Each particular dimension has its own characteristic, has its particular part of the whole. We will use a nine-dimensional focus tonight. If we wanted to stretch you, we could go to twelve, eighteen or even twenty-two dimensions, but we will use a nine-dimensional focus. Numbers are very interesting. You can look at the whole in many ways; you can take it apart and put it together with various numbers of parts. It is important to recognize that, because you encounter books and lectures using seven, or nine, or twelve, and you're going to wonder how the systems can fit one into another. One is looking at the same thing from a different perspective. One does not negate the other; each shows you something from a different point of view. Each of you is a different perspective of divine beingness. We can look at numbers or dimensions or planes differently.

The first two dimensions are, you might say, passages, or ways in which consciousness begins. They are not really the workshop for living that the third through ninth dimensions are. There never was a beginning or an end, but there is a place where beginning and ending meet, and there we have the first and second dimensions.

It is important to recognize that there always has been and always will be a divine being that is called the Source. Has there ever been a time when there wasn't a Source? No. Is there ever going to be? No, never. But there is a level of learning that can be completed. That level has a transition space, you might say, and the transition space where a greater level begins is in the first and second dimensions, where one is finishing and the other is beginning. Then the third dimension is where a probe begins to understand this new beginning, the probe being physical existence, you might say — the most solid, compact part of physical existence. It doesn't seem, when I say that, to have as much light. It has magnified the creative process so much that you are looking at it as you do in the higher dimensions. If you want descriptive words for the dimensions, the characteristic of the first is *completion*, the second is *new beginning* and the third is *magnification*.

You are here on the Earth in the third dimension, learning, living, loving, supporting, growing and evolving. The third dimension magnifies all of those opportunities. Let us say that the love area is one that you are currently magnifying. You want to see and understand love more clearly. As it begins to magnify you see what we will call light possibilities within it, because you get in touch with it and understand it more clearly. This is called light triggering — it triggers your understanding and opens a corridor that allows you to use the higher dimensions within the love area. Now, usually that would be an unlocking for the emotional body, the use of love on the fourth or fifth or even the sixth dimension — a higher-dimensional understanding of what love is.

Though this light triggering, as Lenduce calls it, usually the mental body begins to understand or conceptualize more clearly what love is. So it might open up to the fifth or sixth dimension through this love opportunity. Then, the spiritual body, which *is* the light corridor that comes through all dimensions, truly, is lit up, or you recognize or validate it, at the particular dimensional opening that the emotional and mental bodies have been triggered to. The awareness of these two bodies, in combination, has been the trigger to contact a dimensional focus. We are going to go through this conceptually first and then experientially.

So first the love area is triggered by receiving love in a way that you never received it before. From that you make a realization about what love is, and a corridor of energy is opened to the sixth-dimensional understanding.

I have been asked if the fourth dimension equates to the astral level. In particular areas it certainly does. The keyword for the fourth dimension is *flow*. It is the flow potentiality, and that is why many of you are now looking for the physical body's response toward dimensions. You want to use, at that level, the awareness of light at the cellular and atomic levels. The third dimension is being transcended now by the physical structure. You are working on that, and the Earth is working on that now too. The Earth is becoming lighter. That is what all of you lightworkers are doing here: you are raising the molecules of the Earth, the atomic particles of the Earth, to the fourth dimension, and now it will also be sprinkled with the fifth. The fifth dimension grasps and holds what the fourth dimension has "flowed." You could say the third dimension is very solid, the fourth dimension is the flow, and the fifth dimension is an energy *structure*. The fourth is more emotional and the fifth more mental, and ideally one can use both simultaneously in a third-dimensional focus.

We are going to use "structure" to denote something conceptual in nature that is divinely arranged and approaching, for the physical level, the ideal. I say "approaching" because the sixth dimension is the ideal dimensional flow available in physical existence. Usually in physical existence, unless you have reached a point of evolution such as the lord Maitreya, the Christ, has attained, the sixth dimension is about as far as your consciousness will reach before the higher dimensions and your ability to use them pull you up out of physical existence completely. If you can consciously and continually reference the seventh, eighth and ninth dimensions, you become such a balloon that you can't stay down. Your buoyancy keeps pulling you up out of physical existence. So we are talking about learning to use the fourth, fifth and sixth dimensions practically on your Earth and then to use the seventh, eighth and ninth toward ascension. Have some of you been looking toward that? A conceptual understanding of the higher-dimensional levels is the key. It is also important, however, to have an experiential sense of it. Part of what Lenduce has come to the planet to do is to give you an experiential sense of what it means to be a seventh- or eighth- or ninth-dimensional being. Light triggering, then, is being able, while in the physical structure, at least for a time, to reference that higher-dimensional level. This comes through an understanding of the four-body system and how to use them at that level.

In the sixth dimension on the inner planes, as well as on the outer, you are using the multidimensional experience. I have said that the sixth dimension is the *ideal* as far as physical existence is concerned, so it might seem very celestial or heavenly to someone still focused mainly in the third dimension. On the inner planes it corresponds also to what is termed *heaven*. You learn to swim on the inner planes in order to understand it on the outer planes. As you evolve into the higher dimensions, you move in and out of them and keep interacting until that particular level becomes real enough for you to use that as your base area. It is difficult to have all aspects of yourself developing at the same rate. If you are an emotionally focused being, then the emotions will perhaps transcend first, and thus you will begin to experience that celestial quality of life, have some transcendental experiences, and you will then learn to view life mentally there. This draws in the spiritual level and begins to evolve the physical to that level. There is no reason you can't take the physical body to those higher dimensions right here, now, on the Earth. Because of the nature of the inner planes, there is more flow present and there is an opportunity to interact and to pass through all of the dimensions when you visit there at night while your body sleeps. You get to practice a lot at night, and then in the daytime you get to see what you remembered, what you have learned and gained and integrated from inner-plane experience. Many of the classes on the inner planes work with helping you to understand dimensions and then to put them together. The angels, the archangels, the consciousnesses that guide the planet Earth, all have been included by the Source in a structure that easily penetrates all of the dimensions so they can function throughout as the Source does. Angelic beings do most of their work on the fourth, fifth and sixth dimensions.

The third dimension is no less desirable than any another. It has that magnification quality that is most important for learning about your creative ability. Light really can be studied under a microscope in the third dimension. The angelic beings easily navigate all dimensions, but they frequent the third dimension the least because the use of light is different in the third dimension. This is because of the way it is used, the way it is magnified — it has a probing quality. We use it in the belief-system work where we probe deeply into the subconscious mind. The higher dimensions, four through nine, actually reflect what has been probed on the third. This is the structure, the means of using what the Source created in the Cosmic Plan.

Between the sixth and the seventh dimensions there is a corridor, and many of you have not explored that corridor on the outer planes, though you have on the inner planes. You rather like to slide down it, because it has a quality of lightness, and you "land" on what we could equate to a cloud.

What is this cloud? It is the densest part of the next three dimensions that could equate to the formative area, but it is also where existence first has any form at all. There is a coming together in a way that none of the other dimensions has. You speak of us as masters — well, we are really students with a slightly greater understanding, and you all have your own qualities of mastery.

Let us say that you are a genius on the Earth. You are a Beethoven, a Mozart, a great painter — you have a genius quality. This genius area is where that universal mind, you might say, resides, where ideas reside that have come out of somewhere — you don't know where, but suddenly you can connect with them at that level. It brings together what in the eighth and ninth dimensions has a beginning point for matter, a holding area for the solid state, the reserve energy, as it is formulated in order to bring it into the sixth-dimensional "heavenly" state. Is this the ideal or heavenly or ultimate? Of course not; we don't sit about and play golden harps. It is not the ultimate; more lies beyond it. What lies beyond it? Purposefully constructing a plan. This is the constructing or networking area on a formative level.

Now we get into a finer dimension called the eighth. Cabalistically speaking, this is the area of *all potentialities*. Potentialities for absolutely everything to be structured reside here and feed into the next area, where they are picked up by very advanced beings and a few of humanity. You can learn to access this dimensional level. The eighth dimension, all potentiality, is very visual and full of color. It is literally a color laboratory. There is a designing mechanism that works to create increasingly new and more comprehensive use of what we might call the visual color spectrum. It is always increasing and growing. Once in a while new colors, newly designed, newly formed, such as the five higher rays, come into physical existence. It has what could be called research laboratories.

The ninth dimension is the *overall design*. It is, in a sense, the Source's beingness as it has evolved into its fullest potentiality. The beginning and the fullest have come full circle in a realized Source-state of completion. So you could say that the ultimate for each of you is to function at that level, but the level itself is growing and becoming. It is necessary to recognize that this structure grows with creation. When you have reached cocreatorship, you will be able to reference that level and function in all of the other levels also. This is the structure that you would "play upon" as a cocreator — it's fun. The cocreator would see the use of the whole structure, that state of beingness, and be able to use it very creatively. We'll call it a think tank for cocreators. The third dimension experiences the *use* of matter, and there is a reciprocal action, a two-way flow — one up, one down. It is spoken of as involution and evolution, but they are not sequential in the sense that one comes and then the other, except when it becomes physical. In the fullest use of the plan they are both happening at the same time, but there is a rhythm, a "dance of creation," flowing both ways.

Your physical body responds to the triggering of the other planes. As you learn to navigate in the higher dimensions, that response will equate to whatever is contained in the dimension you have touched. You who feel stuck in the physical body are stuck there because you haven't learned to navigate in anything beyond the third dimension. Your body will be less stuck when you can recognize emotionally, mentally and spiritually that you can function in the fourth dimension. You will get in touch with the flow, which will then trigger into the body and let the body move more easily, be more flexible — the blood, the molecules, the heartbeat, everything will flow more freely. The whole body will respond to a flow, and when you get to functioning on the fifth and sixth, you begin to idealize the physical structure. The aging process stops when you raise your body into the fifth and sixth dimensions. The body of light flows through all of the dimensions, but it is really recognized only on the fourth. The body of light is already there in the physical structure — you become aware, validate or turn it on and use it as you interact with the higher dimensions. You are accustomed to thinking in terms of vibratory frequency or rates, and of course the densest vibratory rate is at the third-dimensional level and rises through the fourth, fifth and so on; the finest is at the first, second and ninth.

At what level does form come into the dimensional picture? Well, at two different places; the highest level is the seventh. We have to define form as something different from the physical, which is the beginning of the idea of form, you could say. The fifth level would be the next reflection.

Can you assess how you feel now? Lighter? Why is that? Because we are communicating with each other, accessing the enhanced group energy, assimilating new material? All right, that's good. Dimensionally speaking, what has happened? Most of you are on the third dimension mentally, but because you assimilated new input, you have expanded into the fourth, or the flow-area dimension. The flow takes you with it if you allow it to. For a while at least, that fourth dimension will be open to you. What do you think could shut it off again? Most of you do shut it off. Why? Habit patterns? The struggle to understand? Well, what happens when you struggle to understand? You are so focused in the mental body that the flow is blocked. There is then a pattern in which the emotions trigger a sense of overwhelm and you begin to shut down.

The most important thing to learn at this time is to remain open. How do you remain open and get the physical body, the heart, the flow, the attitude of constant interest to work together? That is the goal, isn't it? The opening will occur, and will remain, when they work together. What level do you contact when you work with affirmations? You are trying to access the ideal, and so what level would that be? The sixth? Yes, exactly.

Now, suppose you simply say to yourself when you are getting information that is new to you, "I am going to stay open to this. I'm not going to accept or reject, and if I feel myself beginning to shut down I will quickly remind myself I am just receiving." Well, that is received if you are open to it. This works until you hit an idea where there is an emotional trigger, and then you begin to shut down. If you do, well, you can open up again and keep opening until the opening is permanent. That's the goal. We speak of love as being important, and it certainly is. Love is, literally, that ideal structure that you are trying to bring in.

We'll dramatize a bit here. I will ask one of you to be the mother and another to be the daughter. All right, your daughter has come home from school and she is experiencing a pain in her knee so bad that it's all she can think about. If there is obviously no serious medical problem requiring medical treatment, what can the mother do to help her daughter release the pain? A kiss, a cookie, a hug, some rest, and the daughter is feeling much better. What the child was looking for was mainly attention, loving support and literally an acknowledgment that the mother cares and is there for the child when needed. It's amazing how that basic assurance opens the child to healing energy.

In a dimensional sense, what happens when the child knows it can depend on the mother's support? The hurt had shut down everything, the child felt impacted, its attention literally magnified that third-dimensional learning experience. Now Mother can just magically fix everything with a kiss, a cookie and perhaps a promise to stay up later. Mothers know and use these things very well, but what sort of dimensional exchange was going on? What dimension was the mother acting within? The sixth dimension is the ideal, and Mother represents that. The little one then tries to gain access to that ideal through the mother. The kiss and the cookie represent a focus, a step toward an awareness of that level, and invoke the emotional body. The emotional body is realizing and recognizing that ideal through this interaction.

Has the mental body been used much in all this? Well, it noticed what the emotional body was receiving and it is attracted to and takes part in this sixth-dimensional experience. Thus there is a freer way of thinking, feeling and being. The mother reflects a certain opportunity for the child. You must remember that when the mental is searching for an ideal or an opening or an opportunity, it touches into the ideal level briefly, although it might not remain there. These touches are flashes, really only glimpses. When the child touched into the sixth-dimensional level it didn't stay there. The emotions went there and were nurtured and then came back to one of the levels of the third dimension. Through the desire reflection of the mother, the child flashed for an instant into the sixth dimension. So the nurturing area, the love area, is what lightens and accents the ideal, and that's what you are all looking for through love, that ideal level.

Let's try another scenario. We have one man and one woman (we are going to bring the polarities into this). The man and woman are dancing. They haven't danced together before, so they have to adjust to each other.

As they dance they begin to respond to each other, to spark a balanced energy into a rhythmic flow. They are using the dance area to enter the fourth dimension. As they begin to relate to each other in the movement of the dance, what happens dimensionally? What is the goal in the male-female relationship? To create a oneness, a blended wholeness, is it not? So as you dance creatively within your female-male energies, both of which are present within you, you begin to structure that wholeness, which allows you to reference the fifth dimension emotionally, mentally, physically and spiritually. You put this into the workshop of the third dimension so that you can magnify the process by seeing it come into you through others. In the third dimension you can observe and reorganize if needed. That is what the third dimension is for — so you can see if you have any bugs in the system. So you can play dimensionally by purposefully creating a play or situation, an interaction that you focus toward what the ideal represents.

Many of you want to change aspects of your physical body — you want to change its weight or its ability to move freely. Well, you can literally embody the ideal size or movement that you want by envisioning it as physical reality. You are a living affirmation, a moving affirmation. Act as if your ideal *is*. Granted, this could bring up opposing beliefs, but if you really want to let go of them, then begin to act out, to embody, your ideal. The physical body needs to understand that there is an ideal, and you need a visual picture of that. You see it, you feel it, you make it real for yourself, you accept that you already embody your ideal, and your physical structure will say, "Oh, that's how I look. All right, can do!"

Certainly there might be patterns to remove, and certainly you might need to go through the emotional significance of that, because maybe emotionally you haven't seen that ideal — maybe only the mental body has seen it. So you need to bring the four-body structure into acceptance of the ideal of what *is*. Once you begin to affirm that ideal, you really are going to move in that direction; there is no question about its effectiveness. The four-body acceptance is important spiritually, mentally, emotionally and physically — only then will you have results in weight, movement, aging or whatever. The key of course is the emotional body, for it is the one that needs to accept most clearly the ideal. It needs to become very familiar with that sixth-dimensional level.

Another scenario: You are passing along a street and you see a child sitting on some steps. You notice the child is crying, so you ask what the trouble is. The child says, "It hurts, it hurts all over." You can see that there is no need for medical treatment, so you put your arm around the child and you talk softly for a while about other hurts that have happened and gone away, and about things that are fun. You ask if the child has been to Disneyland; the child has, and begins to smile at the remembrance. You say, "Let's go across the street and play on the swings and have a good time."

That is using the interdimensional technique by finding an ideal and allowing it to stretch you. You might not, at that particular moment, be able to hold on to what that ideal is, but touching into it even briefly will lift you toward that ideal. In the experience with the child it was the emotional body that was affected, and that was the key. The emotional body needs to know there is an ideal to hang on to. The one who helped fill the need also felt better by embodying that ideal, and perhaps touched into a higher dimension also.

Everything comes down to your relationship with the Source as you develop your cocreator-level abilities. You are literally thinking about the Source and your relationship to It on all levels all the time. You might not consciously recognize it, but every time you are looking for that ideal, that ideal *is* that Source-level relationship. There are varying degrees of understanding about that relationship, and an affirmation of the ideal keeps affirming for you the clearest use of that relationship. You have a multidimensional way of looking at that Source-level relationship. Each instance of touching in to an ideal level, even if only for an instant, you could compare to dipping chocolates until the chocolate coating is even and ideal. This completion could equate to that cocreator level, which then brings a new beginning. That takes us to the first dimension again and opens up that second-dimensional door, which then begins a whole new level of experiencing on the cocreator level. It is an open-ended system that takes you through all levels. So I'm very sure that a cocreator experiences various dimensional qualities of his own learning and being and progressing.

Love is the structure of the ideal – the design, the glue, the flow, everything. The sixth is the ideal, and there's kind of an illusion about it because it is never enduring. It is ever-evolving, so in a sense you never reach it. To reach that ideal you get into fifth-dimensional experience and get a smattering of that ideal, but because it's evolving, by the time you've figured out it *is* the ideal, it's moved. You could say the sixth dimension is the workshop for the evolving of the ideal and you use it as a light-triggering means to process that ideal.

It is perhaps easier to touch into the sixth dimension through interaction with your own four-body system. Light will teach you, whether or not you interact with others, by suggesting to your physical body that it embody that ideal. The embodiment of the ideal is a wonderful trigger for learning. The subject, as I said, is an intricate one, but yes, you are dancing to the rhythm of a multidimensional opportunity all of the time. The rhythm is a combination of the conscious and the subconscious, and a great deal does happen on the subconscious level. The goal is to make it a cooperative event. The subconscious many times recognizes the ideal more easily than the conscious, because it is the creative part of self and it can respond to the ideal. If you are walking in a park and suddenly a ball comes and you catch it, is that a conscious response? Not really, but you didn't miss or drop it either; the subconscious caught that ball. One needs to harness the conscious to the subconscious rather than the other way around. Creativity is easier when the conscious can be used rather than the subconscious.

Light and Rhythm Meditation

❦ *Take some deep breaths, and as you become aware of self, focus deeply within, go into the third-eye area. Place your attention on the third eye. Relax. Just watch that area without looking for anything in particular. Just watch.*

❦ *Now you begin to sense a rhythm. You can literally see, or know, what rhythm. It is there, it has a beat, a beat, a beat, a rhythm, a beat. It begins to pulse, pulse, a rhythm, a beat, the rhythm, the beat, the pulse, pulse, pulse.*

❦ *Now from the third-eye area a beam of light, golden light, is projected into that rhythm, that pulse, that rhythm, that pulse, and you begin to follow that beam of light. It projects further and further into existence, and you still hear the rhythm, the pulse, and more and more golden light projects further and further until it takes in all of your city, your state, all of your section of the country, and now the whole of your country.*

❦ *The rhythm, the pulse; the light is getting brighter and brighter. It is expanding and now it includes all of North America. It expands, the light expands, the rhythm, the pulse expands until all of the Earth is alight and you still hear the pulse, the rhythm.*

❦ *Now, within this pulsing you see flashes of light. There are flashes here and there and you still feel the rhythm, but now there are other rhythms that interact with the basic rhythm. Thus there is a multidimension of rhythm. Sense that – the basic rhythm is still there, the basic rhythm, but here light and there light and then overall light that is still expanding. You expand within it. The light is expanding and there is a light there and a light here and it continues to expand until the galactic expansion is present. You still hear the basic rhythm, the basic pulse, with the light here and there, and it continues into the light with the basic rhythm, the rhythm and the light.*

✧ N I N E ✧

Cosmic Stretching

AT THIS PARTICULAR POINT, MOST OF YOU HAVE LIVED UPON THE EARTH FOR about two thousand lifetimes. How do you feel about that? Well, whether you believe in that number or not, I think all of you are sure that you have experienced life before this lifetime. One of you said to me, "I must have lived before; I couldn't have got myself this messed up in one lifetime." I say you couldn't have become as *bright* as you now are in one lifetime.

When you can open, relax and allow, your knowingness will show you what the next cosmic step is. This is a cosmic stretch, a commitment, or what is called faith. It is saying, "I now make a commitment to that divine part of self, the soul. I will allow it to guide me each day and I know that from the soul will come very practical and very cosmic results." These are not opposites but parts of the same thing. Each day you will understand more clearly. You will begin to see how the Earth is learning and growing. You will see the very positive events that are occurring on the Earth, no matter what the newscasters Earth choose to broadcast. Instead of picking up the "disasters," your antenna will pick up the signs of growth.

What are they? How about the searches for missing children, the movements to house and care for the homeless, the food and education sent to countries in distress? What about the heroic deeds of individuals? Are not all these a part of your caring, the caring of humanity? When you listen and pay attention, you see and hear. Is this not a part of the cosmic stretch? It is a signal to those who listen with cosmic ears.

Have you ever watched a kitten or a lamb or a fawn or a puppy? They have the energy and enthusiasm of the very young. Small children have it too, don't they? Each of you now is cosmically ready to be that young, eager consciousness that discovers, that cares, that shares and that unites upon the

Earth to create what is called the New Age. This New Age is simply a more united space on your Earth created by each step you take, each sense of cosmic understanding you allow, and by being willing to listen to your soul as it seeks to guide you.

I bring this up because I've seen that soul tap you on the shoulder and say, "You know, *you* could do that." And what do you do? Well, either you don't answer or you say, "No way! What do you mean! I could never do that, and even if I could, I'm not sure I want to." You have felt that little nudge, haven't you? The soul is eager for you to experience all manner of things as you choose to do so — not everything at once, of course, but the soul is enthusiastic about what you *could* do if you chose. If you decide to go ahead and try since the nudge is there, then you often find that, yes, you can, and you can even go farther into a more cosmic way of living.

Often other people do things so well, so beautifully, that you think you could never do it so well. Why not? How did they become so accomplished? They expected to be able to do it, they were committed to their idea and they tried and tried and practiced. But they added another element also—trust. Trust is a cosmic awakener, a connector, and it is important in your daily life. Getting up in the morning is an act of trust, a commitment to the Creator. You go to your job trusting yourself to meet the needs, the challenges, the relationships of your workday. This trust is unconscious and you are rarely aware of it, but when you consciously begin to use trust, you open possibilities. If you were faced with crossing a deep gap by going hand-over-hand along a rope secured on each side, you'd need trust, wouldn't you? You might just launch out in a reckless, suicidal, unconsidered rush of energy. But when a spiritual teacher seeks to connect you to a point of ability that you are seeking beyond your present level, you perceive a gap that must be crossed. The teacher asks you to trust the connection, even though you might not see it, and to move out and bridge that gap. A spiritual teacher doesn't ask more of you than you are capable of doing. You might see the gap without seeing the connection that we see, but perhaps you can trust that it is there. That is it — being willing to trust the connection into your more cosmic ability. You trust beyond what you can see you can do in an area that is physical, mental, emotional or spiritual. The physical area for some of you is where the abyss or gap is.

Now, suppose I gave you a choice: to go and buy some flowers or go on a picnic or read to a little blind boy or go into a closet and sit and do nothing but see what developed. Would any of you choose the closet? If you did, would you really do nothing? No, because you really are learning and growing all of the time. You can't really sit absolutely without experiencing. Actually you are stretching cosmically all of the time. You are also stretching to the emotional response of others and to the group emotion that we have developed. You are making mental evaluations and adding to or adjusting former perceptions spiritually. There is an attunement process, and this is the guiding system that will guide you in each bodily area. Even the physical body, through a spiritual knowingness, can say, "Yes, I can cross that abyss." If you believe and trust, you can do it. For this to happen, your spiritual knowingness and your belief structure about crossing the abyss would need to be in alignment. Your emotional body would perhaps need to be supportive of the physical body. From that four-body alignment you could make a leap into a more complete use of self as a divine being.

In the New Testament we have the story of Christ walking upon the water. Is this what you call a "big deal"? I don't see it that way, but I do see it as a cosmic indicator. It shows when your trust will allow you to accept a cosmic ability beyond a seeming limitation — it can be done. In itself it's not so important, but it shows that limitations generally accepted upon Earth to be there are not there.

I bring this up because you are beginning to approach the abilities like clairvoyance, telepathy, teleportation and other cosmic abilities that truly are available to you on the Earth. Teleportation is the moving of a body through knowing that the body is a manifestation of light and can be moved by a processing of light. The body is a physical structure, yes, but it is light incorporating various components of energy. It is truly an energy manifestation and can appear anywhere; it can be moved around from one space to another as light. Why? Because light is beyond space. When you can attune to it at the level where it exists, which is the spiritual plane, you simply shine the light in a different space, and its physical correspondence along with it. If any of you begin to do this, the reaction, especially from the press, is going to be interesting. Humanity will begin to see that there's been some cosmic stretching. Of course, you don't learn to do these things in order to prove something to humanity. Basically, you see that the Source, God, the Creator, the Whole, gave you unlimited abilities that you can learn to use right now, here on Earth. The Christ, the lord Maitreya, showed the way in this area, as others have also done. They showed it can be done right now on the physical plane; it can be stretched into. But you might see it as requiring one step at a time to reach this goal. Moving in a spiral, you will keep touching upon your learning experiences on the Earth, and whatever you need to learn as you move up the spiral will be mirrored to you. The cosmic stretch will keep you moving within your commitment to what you have to learn in order to grow and understand. Many of you have within you the wonderful motivation to help others — you really want to help humanity at this time and that is very important. As you move in the spiral, it will seem like a circle — you will seem to come around to where you started and it will appear you haven't accomplished a thing. You might give in to a sense of failure or a belief that the effort was wasted. However, the path spirals, and when you come around it's not the same place, but levels above your starting point.

The word "responsibility" has been much misunderstood on the Earth.

Responsibility is a structure by which you agree to evolve. It is also a spiral, and you cannot be "stuck" in a structure of responsibility, because it's always moving, always becoming. Some of you tend to see responsibility as a structure that encloses you. You haven't seen that it is flowing, it is evolving. You say, "I know I am responsible for my life and my growth, I know that I want to stretch into the cosmic abilities, and I know it isn't going to happen in five minutes. How can I see that all this really is occurring?" One way is to keep a journal. Write at least a few sentences each night so that when you go back a few weeks later and look at the record you can see what has been coming forth in your life and what area is being emphasized. You will begin to see repeating patterns of a particular flow and you will realize that the circling is really moving on a spiral.

Let's say you have a daughter who is one year old. You know what one-year-olds are like: they have a lot of energy. So one evening you write in your journal, "I had difficulty keeping up with my one-year-old. A year later you are still keeping your journal and you note that two-years-olds are even more active than one-year-olds, yet you record that now you are better able to keep up with her. By checking back to your former entry you can see that you have made progress in the use of your energy in that year. It takes allowingness to see that progress really is being made day-by-day. Astrology offers signposts by which you can get in touch with timing and energies, if you are interested.

So as you awaken your own sense of divine timing and begin to loosen the hold of "I should" or "I expect," then you will feel that cosmic stretch moving you quickly onward like a fast-moving train. You cannot turn off your evolution. You *are* stretching cosmically, and being *consciously* aware of it is what we are addressing here. You might look at your Earth one hundred years ago and note the changes in attitudes and how they are expressed.

Have you ever wondered what is in store for you, not just a week or a year ahead but a century ahead or two thousand years ahead? Well, I propose to stretch you beyond sequential time. I am preparing to discuss a goal, but beyond this one there is another and another — a truly cosmic stretch, a journey. A rubber band can be stretched until it holds several items together, but there is a limit beyond which it snaps and breaks. What is that snap — what does it represent? A release of energy? Yes, that is true. Where does the energy go when it is no longer a part of a containment? It leaves its space of containment and goes beyond it quite suddenly.

As you learn and grow, you might feel some morning as though you were that rubber band and it has snapped. You literally have a more cosmic understanding than you had the night before. What has happened? You might not realize how busy you are at night. Perhaps you were with spiritual teachers in a class or a group, and you experienced the "realization process." Then on the inner planes you were more quickly able to flow with the energy, the realization, and stretch your perception. When you wake up and remember a dream, the dream is symbolically telling you the process you underwent on the inner planes. You might not be able to see what the symbols mean, so it is important to find out. There are books that explain symbology, or your friends, or a channel might be able to help you. Always remember that the dream is talking about you, about various parts of self.

Suppose you dream of your son who has suddenly received a job promotion or a new job. You might look at that as the part of yourself that is growing up, the part that you have been nurturing, a step forward in your evolution. Your inner growth in understanding has promoted you in your evolution. Isn't it interesting to realize that you learn and grow on both the inner and outer planes? The learning experience is even more emphasized on the inner planes than on the outer planes. You have reached the point where you can begin to reference the continuity of consciousness. You can bring back from the inner planes the rubber-band effect of stretching and allow it to stretch you on the outer planes also.

When you do something you really enjoy, do you learn from it in a different way than from something you dislike? I think so; you put more of your energy into it and there is an opening within self. If you have reached a time in life where demands upon you are lessened — perhaps "retirement" — you can begin to access the learning of lifetimes that the busy-ness of earlier years kept you from touching upon.

When in the morning you plan the activities for the day, why not consciously decide to learn today something you didn't know yesterday? You know *Webster's Dictionary?* Very interesting; I enjoy it. As I pursued that book, I began to see how you can stretch your understanding and use of words by reading such a book. You can become more expressive. What does the word "comprehensive" mean to you? A gathering of information, understanding many areas, integrating knowledge? There are many ways to find meaning in a word — as many ways as there are people who use them. When you encounter a word or activity that is new to you, do you take the time to look at it and learn from it? As you move into the metaphysical community, there is a specific vocabulary to become acquainted with, but there are many common words that you find you are using in a rather limited way. You have been missing out on one way to stretch cosmically. Increasing one's understanding of words might seem a very simple thing, but I recommend that you take a particular word and ask yourself how else that word can be used: "What else can I understand from this one? What other word might express my intent better?" If one has only a hazy idea of the meaning of a word when one hears it, the consciousness tends to slide past it, seeking the more familiar words around it. You don't get the benefit of digesting the energy the word represents. The learning process (and age has nothing to do with it) comes to a point where your soul says, "It is time to go forth and examine words or experiences and intuitions and really find their full energy expression." It is because your soul has reached that point that you are here.

One of the best ways to stretch cosmically is to make a commitment. It need not be earth-shaking; in fact the best way is to make a commitment to yourself. It might be a commitment to achieve whatever you feel your body weight should be. How would you word that commitment? "I resolve to eat only the amount needed by the body to maintain its ideal structure." Such a commitment is toward a particular action that aids a part of self as a part of the cosmos. If you said you were going to lose ten pounds, or twenty pounds, you wouldn't get the same result as if you said, "I see the body's weight and I see that its structure would be ideal with less weight, so I am committed to creating that ideal." In this way you see commitment through motivation that will accomplish a cosmic understanding, a cosmic stretch. Anything you commit to can accomplish this cosmic stretch. We are talking about motivation as a step toward commitment, and we are talking about relationship. Do you think extending your relationship with your soul, and through soul to the Creator and all creation, would be a good motivation? Yes, it is your spiritual awareness of the contact into the creative energy, the Creator Itself, that is the motivator that brings you here tonight. It is the proportional importance that you put upon each motivation or relationship or commitment you make that will accomplish that cosmic stretch. If you are learning to ride a bicycle and you spend twelve hours a day riding, you are going to learn to do it rather well, aren't you? If you are motivating self and making commitments to yourself as a divine being, you are going to accomplish this cosmic stretch.

What could interfere with this accomplishment? Well, the misuse of expectation can do it. Of course you expect to have a relationship with the Creator — and you already have it — but if you look at self and self-development and expect a certain result within a given time and it doesn't work out that way, what happens? You *perceive* that as a failure. You feel you haven't lived up to something you made integral to your commitment. Well, the good news is that evolution takes place every moment of every day, and you are a part of it. A baby, when it is learning to walk, takes a lot of spills. But even though the spills hurt sometimes, the baby is trying again after a bit of comforting encouragement. Babies *know* they are going to walk and walk well. Again I say, those of you who are retired or semi-retired have a wonderful opportunity to learn to walk cosmically; you have the advantage of available time to practice the steps. "Allowingness" and "understanding" are key words in the learning process, which never ends.

Now, can you assess the growth of evolution in the last one hundred years? You can see the inventions and improvements in lighting, transportation and communication. Child labor has been abolished, slavery is no more, and there is less prejudice toward others' ethnic groups. Women have come into greater freedom and stature. Through travel and communication we are more aware of our common humanity. The exploration of spiritual values and the reality of other planes of beingness are opening up all these, and more.

You have questions about teleportation. The key to teleportation is to see self as light, knowing that light (because it is not woven into sequential time) can be anywhere and everywhere. Light that has become physical, as in a physical body, can literally be anywhere. So we will show you more and more that you *are* light, that there is nothing else but light within you, and we will be helping you remove any beliefs that say this is not so. You learn to see and to believe that all is light and understand the mechanics of it. You must focus the light and the direction of the light and visualize the stream of energy going exactly where you intend to move it. You move from one focus to another. If you can teleport and want to take someone with you who is consenting but unable to focus as light, you can do so; it is not impossible. There is no set program for developing such areas as astral projection, levitation, walking on water and teleportation. Individuals will differ to their desire and ease of manifesting these things. You astral-project now, but conscious astral projection might, for some of you, come before teleportation.

We want to help you establish some reality of the use of the higher energies. Sound is a help in this, and we are working with sound. You know the seven rays, but there are higher rays that have come into the Earth at this time to aid evolution and create a continuity into the New Age experience. You have five higher energy centers that correlate to these higher rays. Each one of these energy centers holds certain abilities, opportunities for learning and being, that are beyond anything to which you are accustomed. Getting acquainted with one of them and understanding its potential and how to use it is what we wish to help you do. This is going to lead to all these abilities that seem extraordinary but really are not. They simply are not yet recognized as part of physical life. Healing ability is generally considered extraordinary, but you are already beginning to run the energies through self to help others. Perhaps this is one of the first abilities to be awakened. One must be discerning about healing. People create their situations through free will — even physical conditions — and I personally am careful about giving healing unless I am asked for healing. People sometimes get angry about unsolicited healing prayers because they feel their free will is being taken from them, or the condition might stem from an entrenched belief system they are not ready or able to release.

The Northwest of the United States is a center for the New Age. But there is, everywhere, an integration of all religions going on at this time. It will take time and might not be visible at all times, but the Spiritual Hierarchy is helping to integrate the religions of the planet. When something new is proposed, it seems for a time that oppositions come up that cannot be reconciled, but they will be. What will help in this area is having trust in the ultimate evolutionary process.

Sequential time and other alternatives could be the subject of another whole lesson. It is necessary to realize that on the spiritual level there is no sequential time. However, let me paint a picture. You are standing on a height, overlooking a river, and you can see all points of the river at once. Because you can see the whole length of the river, you are observing not individual points, but the moving flow of its entirety. This is how we view all your activities. So the sequential activities of a hundred years ago and of the present are all part of the one flow. They are different focuses, different perspectives.

Alternatives, then, to sequential time can be called dimensions. There are basically nine dimensions. The third, fourth, fifth and sixth dimensions are more or less physical. The seventh, eight and ninth go beyond the physical plane. To go back to our flowing river, again we see a flow, but the flow could be divided, could have branches. At one point the flow divides and there forms a tributary. The dimensions are like these tributaries. You are seeking to see, as you evolve, that all of your abilities at Source level have a flow to them. You explore them, taking almost every available route along the way. Not all souls choose to come into the physical and into sequential time, but almost everyone uses this paradigm because it is a valuable tool by which to gauge evolution, to help you see the evolutionary process itself. Often a certain lifetime is for a specialization, a special focus, such as music or business, and it is explored deeply. Then, when you can see beyond sequential time, at soul level, they are blended. Each specific that has been a deep penetration through sequential time has allowed the development of an ability that is then integrated on a higher level. The thrust is made, through sequential time, into a deeper understanding that can be integrated on the higher level into a more complete understanding.

We are emphasizing integration because when you begin to understand the use of integration, it takes you out of the third dimension of sequential time and puts you into the use of it on the fourth dimension. You might say that 90% of what must be integrated on the third dimension must truly be integrated before you can move into and use the fourth dimension in an encompassing manner, flipping back and forth between the third and fourth. As you begin to integrate your understandings on the Earth, you pull up the use of your energy. You become lighter and you contact less and less that third dimension. But if you have not integrated your understanding, you become like a yo-yo. You might be moving well in the fourth dimension and you focus on that fact and think, "Oh, I'm doing it." Then you find you've plopped back into the third. This is because integration has not taken place in some area. Integration is truly the key for the use of that fourth dimension.

When you are in the fourth dimension, there is a flow in your life that isn't there in the third. It is less dense. You can see ahead to what is coming without being surprised, and it flows. You begin to reference time in a different manner. You can see what the soul is seeking to do. It does it, and it works. You feel secure within that flow. It is the level you are all seeking now.

We work in many ways to aid you toward understanding what integration is. We use patterns and classes and vary our means to fit your individual perception. We use every creative means we can devise, because integration is important.

The use of the will to evolve to the fourth dimension has not been understood clearly. Balancing the male and female polarities is an important factor. In order to create, the dynamic male energy must be activated, whether in a male or a female body. It is the male polarity that will ignite the next effort you are trying to make. This is not the will – if the will is used in lieu of the male polarity, you will get a problem. About 98% of humanity, including those who are in a male body, don't use the male polarity – the dynamic energy. This area is one we are going to keep working on.

It truly is difficult to know when one is being judgmental and when one is not. The word "judgment" has for many of you a negative connotation. I prefer to use the term "discernment." You see, you can use discernment about a situation or a person without necessarily stimulating a negative emotional response, even though you have come to a conclusion. You look at a person and see strengths and areas that need working on without judging the whole person and saying, "Oh, that person is terrible!" You don't get caught up in unbalanced emotion or make unwarranted assumptions.

Discernment leaves room for the balance of allowingness, love, trust and nurturing. With discernment you recognize that this person is a divine being with areas being worked upon. Because you too are a divine being, you also see the strengths and the accomplishments and arrive at a point of balancing the strengths and weaknesses without unclear judgments about only the "faults." When you perceive others in this way you leave open your opportunity to learn. By allowingness and nurturing, we learn and grow in our caring – to truly care because it is so much fun. And if the person asks you to help them, you get back a return flow.

We have here an ongoing learning situation for the Earth itself and all life forms upon it, so we look at how and where the energy is being put into this learning situation.

◇ T E N ◇

Overview of the 1990s

I T IS TRULY A WONDER TO BEHOLD WHAT IS OCCURRING ON YOUR PLANET. YOU are not yet seeing it as completely as I am. One of these days you will, when you allow yourself to awaken to that new level. So we might say that the keynote of the 1990s is *awakening*: an awakening to a conscious level that literally sees more clearly what it wants and then invokes or demands it, in the divine sense. The 1990s will demand freedom, the heart-centered response, and consideration for others.

Another word we could use in connection with the 1990s is *generosity*. What does that mean? It means being able to see for the good of all — beyond your own needs — and then function from that whole point of view. That doesn't mean your needs aren't met, but it does mean you can see the whole picture. More and more you are guided by that soul aspect. More and more your soul is choosing where you will be and how you will live.

The Earth is literally at a new rate. This creative dancing has begun. Let us herald it through the activity in the Soviet Union, Europe and China. You are not being told about, and you are not understanding yet, what is going on in China. So I thought I might review it a little for you so you might see it.

Freedom in China

First of all, there is a struggle between the present power structure and what the people are invoking. You all know that. The good news is that if you repress a people, you create a unified group. If you create a unified group, that group can literally invoke what it wants. What this group of humanity wants is freedom. In China, as with the eastern bloc nations, you've seen that freedom is coming further along. If you think about the vast numbers of people in China, you can see that there is an even larger invocation that is being made.

Underneath the surface in China there is a breaking up of the old power. Look at it as a line of energy. There are parts of that energy that are being broken up, so that the grid structure, the energy that has been holding and repressing the people, is no longer able to contain them. I would say that 60% of this has already taken place; there is still approximately 40% to go.

I am going to give you a prediction here. Remember what a prediction is: I look at lines of probability, how you are creating from different streams of consciousness coming together and then invoking a certain condition. We could give you other probabilities, but the following one looks very good to me — about 75%. There will be a being rather like the leader of the Soviet Union (in the sense that the world has invoked him or her) who will appear in the religious community to help you unify the religious philosophies. There is a very good possibility that this being will come from China. As that probability comes about, there will probably be someone working behind the scenes. In other words, it won't appear in your newspaper for a while. So the breaking up takes place by a unification that is much more religious than the political leaders will recognize. If so, they won't pay too much attention to it, because they don't give too much credence to religion over there. But it's going to sneak up on them. When it is rather firmly established, I think you will see a breaking up of the old. Will there then be a religious environment in China? Not entirely. There are still many young people who have not awakened to the fact that they are greater than what appears on the physical level. I do think the religious foundation will set the course that will allow the Chinese to get the freedom they are seeking.

When that occurs the Earth will never be the same again. Think about China and how many people there are in comparison with the rest of the world. While this occurs, many of you will be going to China to help. I think that in many ways China is the key for the integration of the various religious philosophies on your planet. This will come after this period that I have talked about.

Religions don't have to actually integrate or unite. What they have to do is allow each other's space through what we call heart energy, allow-ingness, or generosity. They can say, "I believe one way and you believe another, and that's all right. We can be together in the same space without trying to force each other off the Earth."

War

I do not believe you face a global war. I do think there will be some hot spots. I think that if you look over the history of your Earth, it is a little naive to think it will all go away in five minutes. But it is going. I told you several years ago that, through what I call grace, the Planetary Logos (Sanat Kumara) had literally promised you there would never be another global confrontation. You've had many of them. The history of your planet is much longer than you know. It has been practically destroyed by nuclear means several times. There have been many, many destructive earthquakes. There have been floods; you know about one, but there have been others. The planet is much, much older than you know. There has been a great deal of destruction. Why? Because that's what you believed had to occur.

We have talked in the past about patterns of behavior that are worldwide. One of the greatest ones you are now learning to overcome and it is breaking up: the pattern of behavior that says, "I must defend myself because someone is bound to attack me." It was very prevalent in what we call pre-Lemuria. Some of you are beginning to think, "Maybe I don't have to defend myself after all. Maybe an attack isn't coming." What a novel idea! No one ever thought of that before! That can really work. There doesn't have to be an attack that follows after I defend myself.

This realization is beginning to dawn on some groups. Maybe we can be free together from these old patterns of control and manipulation. What if we got rid of those who believe that way? Well, I don't agree with the means they are using; it seems a little violent to me. It's the beginning of sorting out beyond certain old patterns of behavior. The key, my friends, is China. I would follow that as closely as the media allows you to.

Another place that I think is extremely important is South America. You are certainly seeing some "interesting" activities in Central America. I don't have too much comment on what is being created there, except to tell you that I think this is only the first of a series of incidents that will show you that you must be more specific, that you must express more clearly what you want in this New Age. This event is one of confusion, of not really understanding the roles that each of you has, either as a country or as a person within a responsibly created New Age. This is the first of the hot spots to build up. The good news is that you learn from them.

My advice to you is to understand as thoroughly as you can both sides of what has happened in Panama. Look at it from the United States' point of view, from the Panamanian point of view, and then perhaps from the New Age point of view. This last one would help you to bridge those two seemingly diverse points of view. That is what you can do individually. Sometimes don't you feel as if you can't do anything, as if you don't know what you can do? What you can do is build a bridge. Your consciousness, through the energies and the love and appreciation of your soul, can build a bridge between the differences of opinion. This is what you can do specifically. How can you do it? You can see both sides as energy. You're going to get a lot of red and a lot of controversy in that energy. Then you can build a violet bridge. This represents to each of you unity and peace. The violet is a transformational color that unifies. It doesn't remain static; it allows that flow to keep moving and transforming. You can choose whatever color seems appropriate to you. If you use pink, put a lot of very vibrant energy in it. Use a luminous pink with a lot of light energy, or perhaps the pink-violet. Whatever color you choose will be appropriate.

There is a lot of anger in Panama. Basically, what is being processed in Panama is anger and betrayal. Of course, we could talk about the drug trafficking, but I am not going to get into that because there is so much behind the scenes that you are not seeing. It is like a charade, my friends: The power structures are not at all what they seem. The point is that as you learn to view behind the scenes you can say, "That's a play, that's not real." You see, you are learning on this planet to go beyond what is an illusion, what *seems* real, and find the divine reality that exists behind it. Each of you can help unite beyond the illusion. It will get better, I promise you that. I don't give promises without feeling that I can keep them.

One of the things I see as I view your country now is a sense of frustration. And there is a sense of being alienated, without really understanding. There is some distrust. There is some hope coming out of the processing of all of these emotions within you, within Central America, and within the world. Each country must now assess its role in the New Age, get over the illusion and the delusion of what has been. You are relating to each other not from what has been, but from what is now possible. Your United States, the Soviet Union, China, Panama, France, England, Italy — all of these countries must now assess who they are and what they are in relation to what is being born now on the Earth.

New Energies

We talked before about the Harmonic Convergence and moving at that point to a new Earth and about the fact that on April 15 or 16 of this year [1989] you switched on the use of that new energy. You are at that new point, and you as a country and as individuals must now clear out illusions or delusions concerning your part in this new Earth you are creating together. Each country now must assess and give up these old delusions, illusions, this old way of relating to power. As I've said, there will be the need to negotiate with those who hold the power on your planet. This is coming.

There will be less illusion, less delusion. What do I mean by that? Well, we get back to the old idea that you create your own life. How many times have we said it? How many times have you heard it? You will finally get it. You will say, "I created it; therefore I can change it. But I recognize that I don't do it by myself."

Thus we get to the next step of group living, really beginning in the next few years. How soon? Whenever you are ready, my friends. It's beginning now, but I would say that in 1992, 1993 and 1994 many of you will say, "Well, you know, it would be more appropriate to live with others who think like I do." I don't mean just metaphysical groups. I think there will be many scientific groups, particularly those that are working on research together. We haven't talked about that, but there are going to be some scientific breakthroughs, particularly in the areas of disease. I look for many research teams to actually go into the mountains, to the desert, or to a rather isolated area, and live together and research certain illnesses. Then you are going to see certain cures springing up all over your planet. Because they are grasping it from the universal consciousness, one will get it here, one will get it there. Then we'll put it all together and you will have a holistic cure for many of your diseases. That is coming in the 1990s. It is already beginning.

There are four research facilities looking at how to organize the cells of the human body so that they don't let in any sort of disease. They will recognize that disease is not possible. Why? Because the Divine Blueprint will be allowed to guide the cells as never before. This is, of course, more from the direction of the soul level. But the scientists are going to think that they discovered it. We'll let them have that little illusion. But that's not so far away. It's on its way; it's being developed now. We may even see it in 1990, possibly 1991 or 1992. We could call it cell manipulation or cell unity or the soul's ability to govern each detail of your physical life. That's truly exciting, because there is a Divine Blueprint that will do that, just as soon as you let it.

The disease called AIDS will certainly be solved rather soon. I'm not trying to discourage you, but I have said many times that there is another disease waiting in the wings. These diseases represent what you are learning. When you clear one, then there is another one to look at. The good news is that one of these days you are going to reject one before it gets here. You could tell it, "We don't have room for you on this planet. We aren't having diseases anymore." Won't that be fun? I'm not just making a joke. I think that's finally really coming. That's called evolution. You know, you are only one of the five thousand planets that run diseases now in this particular quadrant of the galaxy. Most of them have given up diseases. You can also.

Another exciting thing is the use of certain scientific tools. The use of laser beams in many ways is coming. Laser art is fascinating. I took a course in that. I studied laser painting and found it fascinating. We didn't have that on the physical planet I was on, so it was something new for me. I enjoyed it.

I think the scientific community is going to change, beginning in this coming year. There will be new careers made from the union of several careers. There could be a chiropractor who would also study some art forms and then some basic assimilation of crystalline energy and several other things, putting together a whole new type of career. Some of the careers that are already there are going to be augmented with others that seem rather New Age now but will come in finally to the mainstream. Part of your learning will be to assimilate and allow those, and to allow certain religious philosophies. Recognize that they are not evil or something that is going to take you from the path that you have selected. I know this will work because I can see it and it is very interesting as I look predictively.

There will be a new acceptance of things like astrology. I look for the reunion of astronomy and astrology in maybe three or four years. There will be times when certain ones who don't believe in astrology and who are rather closed to some of the New Age disciplines will have their health improved through them. In other words, it will be proven to them in a positive way that these disciplines can be helpful and are not "evil." Gradually, through the gathering into the mainstream of these occupations, the religious philosophies will come to feel less threatened by them. There is going to be some help in that regard from a being who is what you term a walk-in. (I don't agree with the terminology, but it is one that is popular.)

Art and Music

I think some of your souls might get just a little pushy here. If you suddenly have an urge to paint, I would encourage you to indulge your soul and do a little painting (that doesn't mean you have to be a Rembrandt). There is a new art form developing on the Earth. This is a group art form, a New Age form; it's never created by any one individual. You can do your part by allowing your soul the opportunity. If it wants to mess around with some oil paint and a canvas or charcoal or carve some wood, I would encourage you to allow it to do so.

Or perhaps it may be music. You may suddenly find you want to learn to play the violin or the piccolo or the cello or the piano or the harmonica. It will be rather persistent; if you ignore it, it won't go away. It just keeps trying to come in. Or it might even be dancing.

What you are doing now is learning to experience through all of your bodies. Each time you work with an area that your soul is attempting to put you into, you are making a bridge, and you can all get into the new art form from that process. I would encourage you to do that. This needs to be a part of the 1990s. Every one of you has already had some input from the soul in this regard, though you may not have let it come into your conscious mind. Some of you who are very busy probably shoved it out as fast as it came in. You said, "I don't need that; I don't have time." Open the door again, because — wonder of wonders — when your soul focuses on something, time is found for it. It also allows you to function at a new level. That level is more balanced; thus you get more done. Your life opens up in a very remarkable way. I promised the angels I'd say that, because the angels are the ones that are backing this new program and setting it up. You can now get in touch with them more consistently. Some of you are close to them already. Some of you know it and some of you don t. The point is, indulge them and your souls in the creative effort.

A New Teacher

There is a being that is going to be available in a way he has not been before. Some of you know that. We are currently writing a book through Janet on Sanat Kumara, the Planetary Logos. In it we have explained that there is a teacher stationed on Venus who has not been available. He has purposefully been behind the scenes, because his function is to train planetary logoi, and he does it well. He has set up a base in Venus (you could call it an out-of-the-way way station!) in a remote part of the galaxy so that he wouldn't be visible. It's like a research center. You have not heard of him before nor worked with him yet. Some of you are moving toward his training facility for training planetary logoi. The point is that he has decided to come forward to help the Earth at this particular point. I'm not going to give you a name (he asked me not to do that), because you are going to get different names. I don't think you will miss this contact once you recognize that it is in Venus. Attune to the energy of Venus and ask if it is appropriate to connect with this being. I think you will find it most helpful at this time.

He is a cosmic being with a cosmic heart. His area of strength is the heart. He can train consciousness to a level where, as a planetary logos, one can attune to everything that is going on, on every level at the same time. That has been his expertise: integration. Do some of you want to learn how to integrate a little more? I think that is on some of your agendas, to fit the ability and the function of your higher self, of your soul, into the format you've created on the physical level. This being can help you do so through recognition of what it really means to give unconditional love, to be open, to be allowing and trusting and yet be where you are within the process — how to balance through the heart so you don't get walked on, controlled or manipulated.

The Other Kingdoms

You need to integrate your understanding of the various kingdoms on the Earth. Your association with the mineral kingdom is important. Many of you have felt the need to use and relate to various crystals. Some of you have not, but it is important to understand crystals as your friends, whether or not you own any. (We might say that you "rent" them from the Earth.)

The wonderful plant kingdom has always been ahead of you in its evolution in the fullest sense and from every way we look at it. Thus it is guiding you now to a new level, where your association with plants becomes even more important. They are often the assimilative tool by which you integrate.

Thus the food area has become more important than ever before. Some of you have to let go of red meats. I think that's just as well for most of you. I am not opposed to red meat if some of you feel you want it sometimes. You will find that as time progresses, most of you will want it less and less, and eventually not at all. This may be true even with certain fish, certain fowl. It will be more and more back to the basics with grain, and this is not because of an emotional response to animals. I am talking about the assimilative ability of the plant kingdom, the vegetable kingdom. It has a special ability to assimilate, so that when you wisely use them in your body and learn how your body responds to them, then in a synchronistic sense your own assimilation benefits. Your life begins to integrate. You begin to get mirrorings of opportunities that fit into the areas to which you want to go. As you begin to sense how to integrate, the universe begins to send you the opportunities to do so. The plant kingdom can be helpful in this integrative process.

Your association with the animal kingdom is changing. They are much more than before – perhaps you've recognized that. They are more your partners now. I think you can understand that through the dolphins. You all feel very close to the dolphins, and you recognize that they are not inferior, but a divine equal – perhaps even a little wiser in certain ways, possessed of a particular unique viewpoint one can learn from. Certainly they represent a record storage system of your planet that can lead you into creativity. That's true for all of the animal kingdom. The 1990s will bring you to a new definition of your relationship to the animals on your planet. Some of them are leaving. My friends, don't try to hold them back, because they are evolving into something else. Embrace them and say, "See you on the inner planes." Then recognize that they are changing into something greater, as far as form is concerned.

There are great gatherings occurring in the animal kingdom, almost like conventions. This is an experience relating the inner and outer planes, meaning that some are traveling in their astral bodies and some in their physical bodies. You will begin to notice news of great gatherings of animals around your planet. This is like a consciousness convention, where they begin to communicate the changes that they understand. They have speakers. (I've been asked to go in June to Kenya for one of these. I will be there to assist these animals in their integration.) Perhaps the elephants talking to the rhinoceroses, with the response coming through certain large cranes and other beautiful birds. (The birds are really the leaders in all of this.) It is a beginning of what will be the New Age animal kingdom. Certain large birds and mammals will be leaving. Most of the animals are becoming smaller. I'm not saying all of them are leaving. One that is staying is to me a structural marvel: the giraffe. Every time I look at a giraffe, I wonder why it is. It's technically impossible to be a giraffe! Yet it is there right in front of your eyes. My friends, there are marvels in your animal kingdom that are beginning to be understood.

You will begin to see why you have an animal kingdom. Have you ever wondered? Why did God create the animals as part of the Earth? You will see that they are rather like children in their joyous, open response to life that some of you resist from your more sophisticated point of view. Sophistication is now being educated by the childlike qualities of these beautiful beings that are created by the Divine. So there is a melding, a blending, an integration of the animal kingdom.

Let's not leave out the human kingdom and what Djwhal Khul called the kingdom of souls. This doesn't mean the two can't come together. He defines the kingdom of souls as the hierarchic levels that are guiding the planet as well as those of you who are allowing the soul level to be your guidance in your physical structure.

Thus we see that all points of the consciousness spectrum of the Earth (which is circular, spiraling) are inputting to each other and creating your planetary evolution. No longer can you be alienated. It isn't possible to be alone anymore.

If you are on a high mountain you may think, "I am alone," but are you? Think about the fact that there has been civilization for millions of years on your planet. That consciousness is still there. It is evolving and changing in response to all other consciousness that exists everywhere, but it is there and it surrounds you. It just isn't possible to be alone. It is possible to recognize that you are a part of everything greater and to consciously allow the integration of all that you are part of to take place. You have to allow it; you have to direct it. You have to be willing to bring it in — to bridge the old patterns of behavior.

Economics

The 1990s are a time of 100% economic change. You have created a convoluted economic system here in this country. I think you would all agree with that. It is tied into the power structure on your Earth. We've talked about the fact that there are about 95 families (some of them passing from generation to generation) who control your Earth. It goes beyond the national governments, which are really an effect rather than the cause of this power structure. The old economic system needs to be let go in order to negotiate with the power structure for a freer economic system, a freer way of living upon your planet. The only question is how and when.

We would like to see a gradual letting go so that the new system can come in and take the place of the old one. This is the ideal. Instead of blowing everyone away and then trying to figure out a new system, it would be better if there could be some kind of negotiation. The one that's going out could then pass the one that's coming in and they could shake hands. This is the goal. This is what we are trying to create in all religious communities, in all metaphysical communities, and in people that really care about the Earth.

There is a need to let go of greed, for greed is the key factor here. You are all divinely supported. If you have x number of dollars in the bank, and in the next few years there aren't any banks, I say that if you put it in once, you can put it in again. You created the money there in the first place. I'm not telling you that you have to lose your money. I am telling you that what supports you in your creativity as a divine being is not money in the bank. Do you see the difference? There has to be a change in the old fear patterns that say, "If I let go of this system I will not be supported." You have to get beyond the greed of hanging on to what you have because you fear you won't be supported without it.

This means that you will have to look at the Earth and go to those who control it. What will probably happen is this: The changes I predict that begin with the economic system in this country will then escalate into the world from here. The negotiations will begin with those who really control your Earth. Some of you are going to be involved either directly or indirectly in those negotiations. It will probably be bargaining: "Will you take this if we give you that? What will it take to get you to let go of this?" As you begin to barter with them, something wonderful can happen. There can be an opening and a sharing where you all win, rather than one giving up something and then the other giving up something. You will probably start with what is familiar, the bartering system or negotiating. The point is that this is approaching, and some of you will be directly involved with it.

The first quarter of 1990 is where you might see the change. February 16 is a date to watch. We will see a strain then. Whether it will be obvious on the outside, I don't know. I do know that the system will respond to that date. There will be signs. What I am hoping is that through your meditations and through your more aware understanding of what's going on, we can build a bridge to the new system as the old system passes away, gradually, gently.

There may be a period during the year, if the whole system collapses suddenly, when you will need to have reserves. I have suggested financial reserves that will last about 90 days. This is my estimate for the time it could take to shift systems. Does this necessarily have to come about? I'm giving it only a 50/50 chance. This is my best estimate.

It looks to me as if a major shift will take place in 1990 — a 75% to 80% chance, very possibly in the first quarter. If it does not manifest physically in the first quarter, then I look for it in the fall. I don't know. It's like an energy grid system where the grid must be looser, more flexible, softer and more responsive to the new divine grid (or to a clearer, more flexible system on Earth). If there is a collapse, then you will need an adjustment time in this country for putting in place a system within which you can function. There will be some stopgap systems that can be set up, but you don't want to get locked into these. If these things begin to occur, invoke the Divine Blueprint for the Earth, no matter where you are — the expanded one. Do this and tell all of your friends to do this. Try to bring the ideal, evolving system in.

As the dollar does its thing, it will have an effect on the whole Earth. What propped it up in the past was Japan and sometimes Germany and some of the other European countries. This can't go on forever. It will be just as well to get it over with, like cleaning out the attic and throwing out what you don't need. Start from a clearer space economically. If you look at your country, it's living much beyond its means. There is a need to restructure the economic scene. I think we will see a domino effect that will go from country to country until you have a restructuring all over the world. It may take a year or two before you see the complete collapse in some of the stronger countries like Japan and Germany. You will see it much sooner in the Third World countries. It doesn't have to be a collapse. I've been giving this prediction for a while and I am now 25% more optimistic than I have ever been. You can do it much more easily than you know. Why? Because of the openings we see on the Earth. What you don't yet know about China has made me optimistic. It could be done in the 1990s. Whether or not it is, you will soon need to let go of this convoluted system. What it is going to do is change some things, like counting on Social Security or a pension fund to support you in retirement. The money doesn't support you; your creativity does.

From these changes will come certain communities. Everyone will bring their own strengths. You will go back to a more basic way of living on this planet. I think 95% of you will enjoy it much more than you have enjoyed the present way of living. You are neither betwixt nor between at this moment. There is an adjustment period needed. So another keynote for the 1990s is *adjustment period.*

I think you can see that the 1990s are developing as the nitty-gritty time of beginning to manifest the New Age through the economy from your ability to allow your soul to direct your life, and from your recognition that you are part of humanity. And, humanity is a part of you.

I had a vision last night. It had to do with a mass migration of people. Is that happening now or is that sometime in the future?

Some of it is beginning, but it is mostly in the near future, perhaps even as soon as five to ten years. There will be mass adjustments in China. But I think your vision is more in the future than now.

For many years I have focused my light on Russia. A few months ago I got the message to switch to Cuba. What do you think about that?

Well, Cuba has been a hot spot in the world, at least from the viewpoint of the United States. There are certain souls who will help cool that off. I think you are one of them. There is a need to let the people be freer. Much of it has started already. It has begun spreading. I think you are being asked to help physically and spiritually. In fact, you are already helping on the inner planes.

In the last few months I've had the desire to try to learn to speak Hawaiian. Can you tell me something about that?

There are some of you who will have a desire to learn unusual languages. Sanskrit is one; Hawaiian is another basic language that is not widely used. These are basic communicative tools. Once activated, they can create a communicative environment that will allow language to change in a more orderly way. So try it, at least a little. Just playing tapes of the language and attuning to it may be enough. This has to do with the evolution of the language process, which is one communication method on Earth.

I am feeding hundreds of birds every day, from house wrens to ducks. I wonder if I am doing them a service or a disservice?

Some of both. You are fostering some dependency. On the other hand, through your heart-centeredness, some of them are gaining a sense of confidence in their association with humanity. What needs to be done is to balance a little. Perhaps you need to talk to them on the inner planes. Tell them, "I am only going to allow you to come for a little while. Then you can be independent again." If you talk to the soul level, I think you can balance that out.

I have a great desire and affection for quartz crystals. I went to Mount Ivy and bought myself a crystal mine. I've been holding it for a long time, and I have a lot of crystals around me. I do not yet understand why I bought it and what I am to do with it.

Anything you want. You are a custodian. It's coming full circle from your Atlantean association with crystals. You were a powerful priest in Atlantis, one who in a particular ceremony awarded the crystals a particular type of initiation. Crystals remember; they have drawn you back. It is time to progress and decide how to fit that into your life. Because of the importance of crystals to humanity, you may wish to do something with them. Many that come out of the mines are ambassadors from the quartz kingdom coming to help the little ones. They consider you the little ones that they can help. They are very eager to come out. Some of you think it exploitative when crystals are taken from the Earth, but this is a misunderstanding of the mineral kingdom. You can't exploit a divine being that is your equal. They are invoking the connection with humanity and the integration of their kingdom with humans. That would be the reason your soul involved you with it. The old pattern of granting them an initiation is what connected you into it.

You must recognize that a crystal's function is to organize communication. That's why they are used in so many communicative devices. They actually organize bands of communication that don't overlap, and you can communicate through those bands. Let us say you bring a crystal out and it is an ambassador. Its consciousness has strings of energy that connect into a powerful creative crystalline structure. It has cousins, aunts and uncles that are literally all over the planet. You begin to build levels of energy structure over your planet by using the crystals in various ways over their clear, communicative bands. You are not as clear as a crystal. A crystal has the ability to define energy and organize it well. You are really doing the crystals a service by taking them to Russia and New Zealand and Peru. Moving them around helps build a tapestry of energy around your planet.

It's like weaving a network of energy that can invoke the Divine Blueprint of a higher level of consciousness around your planet. That doesn't mean you want all of the crystals out of the Earth. You'll bring out only those that are ready to come.

Are we not changing our minds to a crystalline form? Will this change our vibrations enough that we will be able to understand the ancient mysteries?

Yes, I would say so. As you hold them in various areas, as you rub them and work with them, you set up an energy gridwork that will raise Atlantis and open up the ancient mysteries. That's how it can take place. You are building the energy gridwork that allows that to occur. In the next five years, you can do that if you try hard enough.

Many of you lived during a time in Egypt when there was great persecution. So you entered the chambers underneath the great pyramids and lived there. You had guards at the entrances so no one could come in — of course, you couldn't go out, either. When you were able to leave, some of you left certain things there. You were afraid to bring these things out with you at first. Later you forgot they were there. One of these days, soon, those things are going to be brought out. You will have some "secrets" that I am looking forward to. These are powers that you had, ways of healing, ways of surviving in certain situations, and many more things.

Don't the crystals also create protection?

Yes, of course. There has to be enough integration on your planet to invoke that through the crystals.

Scientists have noticed the disappearance of frogs in certain areas. Where are they going?

There are two or three different answers to that one. Some of them are being consumed by other animals who have decided they are tasty, although they had never eaten frogs before. Some of the frog species are evolving into something else. And some are gathering in certain hidden areas and they will reappear later; it's almost like a group meditation. They go into caves or under or within the Earth. There is a group meditation process facilitated by a species soul level throughout the whole animal kingdom and all the way up to the Solar Logos, including the Planetary Logos level. There is a complete readjustment within the animal kingdom. You may see unexpected events such as this occurring, because they are all readjusting. There are many adjustments going on in the animal kingdom.

What is becoming of the cat kingdom?

Certain of the species will be leaving, but there are some new ones coming. The roles are switching in the cat kingdom. A cat is no longer just a cat. What would you say is the most obvious characteristic of a cat? Could we say free will? Independence? They are psychically aware, are they not? Because they are so aware on the psychic level, what they are aware of is frightening them just a little. It is both their evolution and all of this coming change. They can actually see it when some of their species leaves. They are able to see down the corridor of time. They remember the Egyptian days, for example, when some of their species were temple cats. That was also true in Tibetan and Mayan cultures. There were guard cats. The rest of the cats didn't like it; it was for them almost like having a dictator. I don't think the guard cats were dictators; I think it was the species' opinion of the role these cats played. They were never really understood. The point is, they fear that this is happening again. There are some cats that will approach the human kingdom again in a way they have not since Egypt. They are having to adjust to the change of some of them leaving and some of them approaching humanity again. They have fears in regard to this.

Is there anything we can do – for a household cat, for instance – to help it adjust?

You can visualize and invoke the soul level of that particular animal's energy format and bring that in. If the animal likes crystals, put one where it sleeps, particularly a blue crystal, one that has been coated with gold. These are very electric, and not all cats can tolerate them. These crystals bring in that higher energy of the soul. If the cat will allow that in its auric field, it is very helpful. If it is a very healthy cat, it probably will allow this.

As many as 40% of the domestic cats have a particular illness. Did you know that? There is a lot of cancer, a lot of growths within the cat kingdom. Some of them are not malignant. When you go in for a healing, take your cat with you. Work with the cats on your planet. Use crystals and healing techniques that all of you learn.

Put one hand on top of the cat's head and another under its chin. Just hold it there for a while. Put one hand on each hip area of the cat. Hold it there for a while. Put one hand on top of its head and the other on its paws for a while. Run some energy into its tail.

A cat's tail is very sensitive. They don't like it to be held, but you might try it for a few moments. Run some energy into it. The cat will be very surprised. It will seem to like being stroked backwards. It might not like it, but it can be good for the cat. It can bring in the energy of the Earth at the higher level and help the animal to accept it. The basic core of this is getting the cat family to accept this new level of energy on the Earth.

Connecting the cat kingdom to the present Earth will help them be free of the lot of their diseases. Some of these diseases are from the past. It's as if you pull in emotional responses through events that happened before, through your connection with the Earth as it was, not as it is now. Crystals can really help do that.

Are dogs going to be affected the same way cats are?

No. They aren't anything alike. They aren't on the same ray or the same system, but they are learning to energize divine equality. They've never really considered themselves animals, so they have to accept first what they are, and they're learning to do that. Eventually we are not going to have any dogs on your planet. That's not in the immediate future, but within 500 years. That energy will be pulled back for another cosmic day and will no longer manifest. There is a lot of heart energy there invoking the dog's acceptance of each level of creativity, which then allows it to expand that. It's like many of you having to accept who you are in order to expand. That is the greatest lesson for the dogs on your planet now.

I've seen the white tigers that perform in Las Vegas. They seem to be more people-oriented than the regular tigers. Would you comment on that?

Those particular tigers are. They have developed an affinity for working with humans through what they are doing. Perhaps they are ambassadors for their kingdom. You could say they are on their best behavior. You notice that some of these animals are not typical of their species. I would say that these are not.

We're going to see many changes this year, including those in the animal kingdom. I hope you've gained a sense of awe about the process that is going on. I have the utmost confidence in each of you. Allow yourselves to create a much freer Earth.

I thank you.

✦ PART NINE ✦

COCREATOR UNIVERSITY

Vywamus, 1989-1990

✧ O N E ✧

The Cosmic Walk-in

GOOD EVENING, MY FRIENDS, GOOD EVENING. WELL, IT IS A LOVELY EVENING. Did you all know this? The softness of the air . . . and there is a lifting of the air tonight. I like it. I think if you tried, you could all fly tonight. The air feels that supportive.

Well, it is a tremendously exciting time to be on the Earth. I think you're going to see that in a way that perhaps you haven't allowed yourself to before, because a tremendous opening has occurred, and I'd like to talk to you about that tonight. It is the time for every one of you in this room to acknowledge that a door has opened, a very cosmic door. I've called this a cosmic walk-in state.

Now, it has nothing to do with the way you've previously looked at walk-ins, because nothing has walked out. You still have the soul that has been guiding you, whether that is the original soul or a walk-in soul in the original sense. But it is there and it takes a little understanding and perhaps a little getting used to, to understand what I'm going to tell you. This is why I am so excited about all of you and the opportunities which exist here for you.

Maturing of the Cosmic Day

Let's start by recognizing that there is a plan, an overall plan, that these things don't happen just by accident. And this plan has a particular framework around it that we call the cosmic day; many of you have heard me talk about a theme on the cosmic level that is being explored. And there are many of these cosmic themes; we are currently within one that is about three-quarters of the way completed.

Now, the Earth is also maturing, she's growing up. Likewise you and your soul are maturing and growing up. A cosmic walk-in situation occurs when existence and the cosmic day format have reached a particular level of maturity, the physical planet (here it is the Earth) has reached a level of maturity, and you as an evolving soul have reached a particular level of maturity.

These things come together and an opening is created. And through that opening comes a perspective that has never incarnated before. That wasn't its job before! It's a specialist, so it has waited: it has been doing other things on another level, but it has waited for this particular time and this particular opening to come into your life. And it's true with everyone here – there are no exceptions. There are several thousand of you on the planet to which this has occurred or will occur. It is in the process of occurring on the Earth now, and it is so exciting to see this

Now, what does it really mean? Well, let's say that you've always wanted to use musical abilities, or let's say that lately you've been getting an inkling that you would like to study music. This perspective that is more cosmic will begin to access abilities that you didn't know you had. So it will stretch you into those abilities, one step at a time. Maybe you've all heard that a few times: one . . . step . . . at . . . a . . . time! Sound familiar?

This cosmic perspective is an integrator. It has the ability to integrate anything in your physical lives, to put it together, to help you understand levels, situations, to help you understand other perspectives, other people, other countries, and what's going on. In other words, it can help you understand everything in your lives in a way that you couldn't before because you didn't think you had or didn't know you had reference to that cosmic point of view.

Now you might say, "Why is it doing this? Why is it coming?" Well, that's its role. Its role is available to you as the physical format of what it is. You two came together. It's not that it is different from you, but it is perhaps an integrated focus that has yet to explore the Earth. It doesn't know anything about physical existence, and it is going to have to learn that.

Now it comes into your body. And it is a lot of energy; this is what it is on the physical level – an energy and an awareness level; consciousness that is manifesting and coming forth into your cells, into the meridians of your body, into the brain, into the skin, into the heart, the liver, the lungs, into your teeth. Get it? It's coming in all over. This has been energized for everyone in this room since the end of June 1989, and it's still going on for some of you. There's no one here who won't have it by July 1 of this year. Most of you have already received this opening.

You might say, "Well, is it a trauma like I've heard that walk-ins have? Is it something that is difficult, and then this comes in to soothe?" No, it isn't. In fact, you might be having a very calm, peaceful day, and it's as if a bird flies by and drops a seed. Now, do you notice that seed? Maybe not. But that seed is growing. That seed has been fertilized by the Earth's energy, and also by its growing awareness, to a point where now you can begin to sense (if you are willing to do so, and perhaps even if you aren't) the incoming possibilities. We talk about the New Age, we talk about the beautiful temples, we talk about many things that are coming, and you may have wondered, "How do we get from here to there? What is the Plan? How do we get from where we are now on the Earth to where we want to go?"

I tell you that these cosmic perspectives are the means to do so and that you have now, within you, this opening; it is very exciting to see it beginning. That's really what the Harmonic Convergence began.

But it needed a year or two in order for you to begin to prepare your physical bodies and begin to, let's say, get oriented into the new energy that came in at the time of the Harmonic Convergence. Have you ever traveled and experienced something called jet lag in your physical structure? You all were a little jet-laggy at the time of the Harmonic Convergence. You had traveled from one planet to another planet – a more energized Earth. And there needed to be a period of relaxation and recuperation. You may not have thought of it that way – your lives may have been very full – but with the stimulation by this very cosmic perspective that I'm calling the cosmic walk-in, I don't think any of you were ready for it a couple of years ago. You weren't then, but you are now, whether you know it or not.

Soul: The Regulator

There is a level, then, that's called the soul (you may have heard of it a time or two) and it is the regulator for all of this energy. I am saying to all of you that an affirmation – you have a choice here – that says, "I surrender to the purposes of my soul," spoken daily will be very helpful in this integrative process. It's as if you're busily putting on a new energy garment, and you may have your sleeves on but it is not over your head yet. For all of you there is a varying degree to which you have assimilated this new energy.

How many of you have noticed that there's a lot going on, energywise? Some of you have and some of you haven't. But it is this process of putting on the integrator itself. Think about it – it almost seems like an opposition, doesn't it? "You mean in order to integrate my life, I first have to put on a point that can integrate?" And my answer is yes.

In other words, this is such a fast-moving time and such a cosmic experience that we're gearing up for here on the Earth, that you needed to bring in a level of consciousness that has never functioned on a lower level. It has always functioned on a much higher level, and so in a sense it's stepping down. This will be very easy for it. You – in your physical perspective, that part of you that is on the Earth – are stepping up your energy to meet it so that you can be that soul on the Earth that does whatever is needed.

You can travel extensively without the jet lag, because the cosmic walk-in will affect your physical body. It's also very balanced emotionally. How many of you have noticed that perhaps the emotional is something you're working on? It takes awareness in order to bring change, doesn't it? Perhaps that's the most important part.

Are you ready for this one? Your energy in your awareness has been squared — the amount of energy, of life force and consciousness that you had before. It's proportionally a little different for each of you, but it has been literally squared. And you will begin to notice things like that. Even beyond what I said before, tremendous energy surges are coming up. It's as if they're getting ready for something. I think it's for what we are talking about tonight: the use of this level of energy, this cosmic point that has never been there before.

Part of the integration of this cosmic walk-in is an energy which really is galactic in proportion, centered at the Galactic Core. It administers many, many probable realities — alternate realities, whatever term you want to use. You know, if you've had an experience where you almost did something and then you made the decision not to do it, this part of you went on and did it anyway. Let us say you got married in the alternate reality and in this one you didn't. So there are those two expressions (and I'm simplifying it) that are now going to come together, are going to integrate. That's another way of saying that integration is taking place from this cosmic point of view.

Integrating Alternate Realities

For many of you there are as many as 300 to 400 different perspectives being integrated — that many alternate realities in physical existence and beyond it. Now, if that seems a little overwhelming, remember that the plan, the Creator, God, your soul (whichever words you care to use here) never requires more of you than you can do, or if so, It always brings you the means to do it. Just when you say, "My goodness, this is too much," here comes that cosmic point of view and it says, "Oh no, it isn't. It's very easy. Here I am, and you can rely on me."

Now, for some of you this might not seem real for a while, but I don't think there's ever been anything more real, my friends. This is how real it will be to you on the physical level: When you have something you don't think you can do, make that little extra effort and go ahead and do it — you'll be surprised how well it works out. Because there is a stretching ability that is there for you, that's being administered by this part that is on the cosmic level, the Galactic Core.

Beyond Individuality: Expanding toward the Whole

One question that I've been getting is, "Is this all me? Is this a cosmic part of me?" Yes and no — yes, of course it is, but it is also the next step beyond what I call your individuality. We talked about the Source giving you your individuality; you're then going to express it until you can realize yourself again as that whole. Do you recognize that? This is that step beyond individuality. This is that next step that you've been looking for. In other words, that cosmic perspective that I'm talking about now is an integrated one. It's kind of a group response.

If you have an operation, the specialist might not do the preliminary work. There may be nurses, someone who gives you the anesthesia, and others who perhaps open you up. But when it's needed, that specialist is there to perform the precise work which will help you to be whole! To be *whole* — that's what we're talking about here. So the plan is wonderful; it always brings you the next step. And this next step is to go beyond what you've considered to be yourself.

Many of you say, "I don't need anyone else." You've heard the metaphysical community say this many, many times — "I am responsible for myself; I don't need anyone else." Well, perhaps you don't need them to make your realizations, but you need them, because you are part of them and they are part of you. You need them because without them your heart is not complete. Without them *you* really are not complete. Many of you have learned this in the heart area. It is only when someone seems to feed into your programming a little that you try to pull back. Eventually that will be gone and you will not have that. But in the meantime there is a cosmic perspective that on that level is bringing in other opinions, other ways, other strains.

Some of you who didn't know you could sing are going to open your mouth and sing like a nightingale! You'll probably wonder, Where in the world did that come from? And in the movement of the body, some of you who have felt, Well, I couldn't do that, I couldn't *do* that, will be able to move your body in a way that you couldn't before. And it may change the body. It can, and I think it will. For some of you, your feet might grow a little longer. For others, it may recontour the body itself. There is a change on all levels. It's really, in a sense, joining a cosmic team and then focusing from that team level rather than from personality needs. It's looking at life from a higher perspective.

Now, I am not saying that if you really have a block in some area it will immediately fall away because of this new opening, but I tell you, it will be softer. It will be easier to surrender to the soul and allow the soul to help you with that area so that it isn't as blocked as before. It truly is exciting! I am going to write a book on this because I think it is that important.

Symphony of the Soul

Let me give you an analogy here. Let's say your soul has written a symphony — the Symphony of the Soul. It's hired an orchestra, 120 pieces, and they're going to play the Symphony of the Soul. They sit down and tune up their instruments, and then they start to play. If you listen you will hear themes repeating through various sections of the orchestra; it is a harmonious flow that moves in many ways. Now I'm going to energize this in two different ways. First of all, in this harmonious flow as the orchestra plays, it creates at this time on the Earth an opening in the third dimension, the foundation called the third dimension where the Earth was.

It had been nice and orderly, you could count on it — seconds, minutes, hours, days, weeks. You had it all figured out. It flowed very well. But now, as you enter the fourth dimension, that's not the way it is anymore. There is a cosmic input and then a surge that integrates that input in the time flow that you call the fourth dimension. There is a process of integration, and then it flows from that on the physical level. All levels participate in that orchestration that is being played by the soul on the physical level. It's no longer cut up in little segments.

You needed that cutting up in little segments for a while. Why? Because if it wasn't you would get rather scattered. It felt very good and you felt secure. It also defined things very well for you. You could see very well in the mirroring in physical existence and understand yourself from that nice, orderly little flow. Let's look at that a little bit.

Let's take the orchestra apart a little and look at the first violin player. He or she is playing certain notes or a certain combination of notes. And if we stop the action, stop that flow and notice the one note that the first violinist is playing — one out of 120 — we find your life. Remember, one note — we've stopped the action. One note — that's your life; that's where you are now in your life. You've learned to look forward and back. The first violin plays — and you've learned to regress, perhaps, and look at what's been, and you've learned to open up to what you want to come next. But you haven't explored beyond that. Remember, the soul is playing a symphony; the soul has a 120-piece orchestra playing. This perspective that comes in is going to *help you notice the other notes* that all of the other instruments are playing. Because this cosmic perspective is there to help you understand and integrate the strengths that have been gained from all of the other parts and all of the notes that have been played.

I'd like you to think about that and see the opening that has been created now. That is the gift that the Creator has given you to understand, so you can begin to say, "Well, I've always thought I was the first violin player, but here comes the tuba, here comes the bass drum, here comes the harp, here come many other perspectives that have grown strong in the way that they express. Now they're going to help me as a first violinist."

There is a flow from other expressions. These are called alternate realities. But what does that mean? It simply means that other strengths that have been explored by your soul in another way are now ripe — think about that. They've ripened in their own way, and now you get the benefit of that. They're ready for you to digest, to eat, to integrate, to literally play them, too, in your soulness. So it is the integration of a whole soul's perspective which now becomes available for you.

I've been thinking about this, trying to figure out how we can help all of you, because you might not notice that birdseed. Just a little plop, and there is that opening that you might not have noticed. And I decided that one thing we might do tonight is to use a little sound, a little mantra, and work with color in relation to it. What I'd like to do is to water that seed for all of you tonight.

You might not know why you came tonight. You may say, "I don't know why I'm here. I didn't know I was coming, but I suddenly found myself coming. I don't usually come; why in the world am I here?"

I'll tell you why you're here. I sent out an advertisement on the inner level about what I was going to do tonight, and your souls were attracted to this because for each of you there is an important point of integration that we want to water now. Now, let's do it together. I ask that you close your eyes now.

Flowing the Cosmic Walk-in Energy Through

🐦 About eight inches above your head I'd like you to energize a color, a circle. If you prefer, it can be a jewel that is many-faceted in its turning. Now, you may use violet, you may use gold, you may use electric blue, you may use pink. I want you to energize that as the soul in its twelfth chakra, which extends above the crown from six to eight to ten inches, for some of you twelve inches. Energize that and feel that energy begin to flow now from the twelfth to the eleventh, and from the eleventh to the tenth. It's dripping down from the tenth chakra to the ninth, and from the ninth to the eighth – to the soul star.

🐦 Now, here in the soul starw (which is a couple of inches above your head) I'd like you to just let it be energized. Let more and more energy come from that twelfth chakra; let it drip through the higher chakras above your head. Then it starts to flow through the system, through all the other chakras in your body. When it gets to the base chakra, let it flow down into the Earth.

🐦 But I want you to keep your awareness at the higher chakras through this color, and I want you to notice what happens as we energize the sound. Each will experience something in your own way. You may want to see the base chakra as a clear disk through which this energy can pour. So if you begin to get a lot of energy, be sure your root, or base, chakra is open. Let this go into the Earth. Let the Earth share it now.

🐦 Now I'm going to use an ancient language, and I will tell you what the words mean. (I wouldn't advise you to ever let someone give you a mantra in an unfamiliar language unless you trust them or unless you know what it means, because these are very powerful tools.) The one we are going to use means: "I bring down this possibility and I allow the divine power of it to anchor in my physical body." This literally invokes the full use of what I have called the cosmic walk-in. So we will energize that for a moment with this mantra, each in your own way, then let that flow into the Earth.

🐦 Gos-sno aho-o-o-ma! Gosna aho-o-o-ma! Gos-sno aho-o-o-ma! Gosna aho-o-o-ma! [Repeated for two minutes.] Now let that flow, let that flow through you. Let that flow and move. I'm going to tone a little through Janet; don't try to do it yourself. Pay attention to the flow. Just let it flow, let it move, let the energy flow now. [He tones a minute or two.] Let it flow, let that energy move, let it move through you now.

🍃 And now there is a soft mantra, continuing to work with it. Join me if you feel so inclined: Hassna ko-nay. Hassna ko-nay. Hassna ko-nay. (This means: "I open my heart; I allow this energy to flow through me.") Hassna ko-nay. Hassna ko-nay. Hassna ko-nay [many times]. All right.

🍃 Sit quietly, my friends, because the gift you are receiving is a cosmic gift indeed. As you recognize it and allow it to pour through you, it will create a strength of purpose, a strength of being aware, a strength in the support area, and a strength in the service area. All right, gently, then, come back.

Become aware that you can give a gift now to the Earth; it's almost as if in your base chakra, you could take a ball full of that energy and put it down into the Earth. I feel that some of you have that a little stuck — we're a little far-out tonight, maybe, but that's all right. Far-outness is at the Galactic Core, and that's a good place to be.

Energizing Your Next Step

For many of you the time has come to energize your next step after leaving the planet. That's part of what this cosmic walk-in state can do for you. It doesn't mean that you're going to go somewhere in five minutes, but it means you are already gaining certain resources. I would like to talk about that now.

At night you are studying — everyone here is. At the Galactic Core there is a specialists' school. It isn't for angels, especially — it doesn't discriminate against angels, but angels are doing other things. (I heard Raphael tell me just now that he's been there, so I stand corrected.) But you're going to school at night, and you have teachers at that level that you don't really know about yet here on the Earth.

We've given you the name of Melchior — and who is this? He is a being who is coordinating much activity at the galactic level. He is available to any of you who care to attune to him. There is another one that I wish to energize right now. He's not so much working with the Galactic Core as he is working on the universal level. I'd like to encourage many of you to attune to the being called Adonis.

Adonis is the same as the Greek — not the same type (what they say about that god is not so much true about this great being), but the energy has a certain similarity. This being is a great one that I might call the cosmic heart center or the universal heart center.

The heart plays an exceptionally important role in your lives now. Do you know that, in one sense, all of you at night are standing around stretching your heart open? Well, I'm not saying you're actually doing this, but there are cosmic heart massages that you're all having, massages on the inner level. You're working tremendously with the heart energy. Do you ever come back in the morning and really feel your energy right here, in the heart area? More and more of you are really waking up to that, remembering what's going on on the inner level.

Well, I think it's important to use the following technique, if you will. This is a very easy technique; some of you have used it, but if you haven't, try it. And if you have and you've forgotten it, then try it again.

Morning Exercise: Building Bridges

As you wake up in the morning, lie perfectly still. I know sometimes that "little room" is calling you — that's what wakes you up. But if you can, try to lie quietly before you move at all. See if you can get a feeling; many times it might be that heart center in the physical body, or it might be some emotion or thought. But try to go deeply into that. It will begin to bring back memories of the night and what you were doing, because that too can be stretched by this perspective that I've called the cosmic walk-in. It begins to bring to you continuity of consciousness, and you are all ready to build that bridge.

You know, you're building a bridge from the subconscious mind to the conscious mind. Most of you have built it rather well from the personality/ego level to the soul level. You don't throw that out; you put it up into something greater, and you're now building a bridge from the inner to the outer. All of these bridges that you are building are also another way of looking at that integrative process that I have been talking about. You're building a bridge between the emotional body and the mental body, between the spiritual and the physical — that's the cross we've talked about so much. Stirring in the heart area is the potential coming from that stimulation of balancing and integrating and building the bridge in the four-body process.

I want to explain the cosmic walk-in state even further. Let's say that we could put a physical size on your soul (that's kind of silly, but we'll try). And let's say your soul is eight or nine feet tall. Well, if we add this cosmic perspective to it, it's nine squared — that's how tall it is. And it's squared in its consciousness also. So it is a perspective that has a multiplying factor as well as an integrative factor. Can you see how important that is? It opens up for you any area that you're trying to understand more completely.

Getting a Cosmic Perspective

All of you are trying to understand the conceptual area better, into the higher mental area. Do you recognize that you want a greater understanding of the whole picture, that you want to see things more completely? If you don't know you want to, then I'm telling you you want to, how about that? Because it is the means to balance your lives and to be grateful for what you have, it really is. You know that exercise (many of you have tried it) of looking into the room and around the room to see if you could step into anyone else's shoes. If you could see the overall picture of a person's experience and how you fit in, then you'd go running back to your own shoes. You'd be grateful for having those shoes, for having this body that you're in, you see?

The overall picture helps us to open the heart, because we can see how fortunate we are and how wonderful it is to be a part of all of this. And perhaps gratitude and joy are partly what you're really searching for. Can you see that? When you're really grateful for every moment, you might say, "Oh, I sneezed. Isn't that wonderful?" or "Today I had a really good learning. Isn't that wonderful? Something came in and mirrored to me. I had an argument with someone — isn't that wonderful? Now I can see life more clearly from that perspective. I've been given a gift, the gift of the mirrors of physical existence. Beyond that are the gifts of the soul and its joy and its understanding. Now I have a new gift — and that's the gift that this cosmic perspective gives me. It's going to stretch me all over the map. How wonderful. And I'm grateful, now."

Am I putting words in your mouth? Well, perhaps a little. But can you see that when you approach life that way, when you can really be *grateful*, then it all fits together for you? That is the point of integration. It doesn't mean that you don't try to balance, but whatever you're doing, it works for you, because you are pleased with it no matter what it is. Isn't that interesting? Fall down and break your leg? "Oh, goody. I broke my leg." Well, maybe not quite, but the gratitude will lighten any effect that you have. It will! It will allow you to say, "Well, now, that was an important thing. I broke that leg in two — look at it." And it's going to hurt too, isn't that interesting?

If you can detach from that, if you can really view that leg and what it's going through with compassion but not get attached to it, then, my friend, you're well on your way to using that cosmic perspective. That's what I'm really talking about when I refer to this cosmic perspective. It's one that lets you be objective about life, still magnifying the heart but allowing you then to use every opportunity in your life to understand life more completely.

Contacting Alternate Realities

I was going to talk about Sedona a little and what's going on here, because it is from these alternate realities that the activity is so tremendous here.

The angelic kingdom and all the elementals are really several times more active in this area than they have ever been. How many of you have noticed? Good. The rest of you, pay attention, because there is a lot of centering of that activity here. You may ask, "What has that got to do with me and my life?" A lot — because, I tell you, there's a reason that you're here. And one reason is to physically be able to contact many of these alternate realities and bring the strengths of those experiences into this life. Maybe that is all that's left for you on this planet. You may be through with it except for that more cosmic integration. You know, many of you are very mature spiritually. You have one or two subconscious hooks that are very deeply hooked in, and you think you have to drag that all over the cosmos.

Part of what's going to happen, I think, in the next few years is that through your clear understanding, your more cosmic understanding, you're going to unhook that very carefully, and some of you are going to take off. Some of you aren't; some of you will stay here anyway, because the souls have many things to do now, but it will be from a point of integration. You'll know when things are integrated in your lives. How will it feel? Good? Life flows, doesn't it? It works! It's wonderful! If we can have that all the time, isn't that going to be wonderful? That's your goal.

That's when you are ready to do what is called ascension, my friends. That's what this is all about. That's why you have time and space — to get that point of integration. And when that is maintained just about all the time, then you are ready to go on with the spiritual lessons, or let's say lessons on another level (because, of course, all lessons are spiritual whether they are physical or not).

Asking for Help

The point is that you're looking for that balance. And the angelic kingdom is gearing up to help you. All you have to do is ask for the angels. They will help you in any way you ask. If you say, "Oh, I've got a headache," ask them to help you with it. "I need to lose weight." Ask the angels to help you with it. Do you ever think to do that? Want to take off ten pounds? Maybe they'll help you. I think they'll do that. I just got an answer: "Yes, we'll help."

Any particular angel?

Whichever ones will work with you. The angelic kingdom is very malleable. Whichever ones you need will be there for you. Gabriel just said, "Through what I am, for you, in this area." The point is that you can ask for help, and that's where you are, many of you. You've said, "I'm going to do this myself." And the universe said, "Good, but not necessarily by yourself." Right? That's where you are. So you can ask for help. Please do so.

One of the most wonderful energies, as I've said, is Adonis. Melchior is also, and certainly, some of the other teachers, any that you work with. But the Earth itself, in her beauty, is too, with all the names that you've ever known. Have you ever tried to say all of the names of the Earth that you know? See what happens. You're going to get an energy response. That's kind of fun to do. How many do you know? Let's see — Earth, Mother Earth . . . .

Terra . . . Virga . . . Gaia . . . .

All right. Good. When you call on the Earth by all of her names, you get a different perspective. You get help from a slightly different point of view, because she pays attention. "No one has called me that in a long time," she says. "I listen from that ear."

Why is that important? Because it begins to help you to approach things from different points of view as far as your own integration is concerned. Now, you may have an area, as we talked about: that hook. And you've been hooked to it so much that you're looking at it only from this point of view:

"There you are. You're a burden on me, and I have to carry you around. I'm just kind of failing you and you're always there."

As you begin to use this cosmic perspective, you can approach that. You can look around and call the Earth from this point and name, and then from another. "Help me look at this. I knew you as this name, so let's look at it from this point of view." And as you begin to do that, it gives you a really fresh way of approaching an area that you may have gotten into a rut working on. "I've worked on this so much, I'm tired of working on it. This has been a block of mine, and I can get rid of it."

Or perhaps there is an area you don't know you're working on. You only know that your life is not yet as unlimited as you would like it to be. Or you don't feel quite satisfied. One of the questions I get the most is, "What in the world are the purposes of my soul?" Whatever they are, you haven't yet focused on them enough to really see what they are.

Try this technique: Call upon the Earth. Now, if you're asking for the purposes of your soul on the Earth, don't you think the Earth has some knowledge of that? I think so. It's part of the Earth's plan, so ask the Earth to help you with it.

We're talking literally here about a divine being. We're talking about the energy put together by the Planetary Logos, Sanat Kumara. Now, where did Sanat Kumara get the energy to build this overall structure on the Earth? Have you ever thought about that? *From all of you!* It's *your* energy. From any soul that was ever coming to the Earth he took all that energy, put it together and then put that energy in his heart and gave birth to it. And that is the conceptual framework, the overall framework within which the Earth lives and all of you live.

It went through a process, but the point is that that process is very much a part of you, and you can use it. It is a resource of yours that I don't think many of you have called upon very much.

You might also learn to call upon his headquarters. There is a headquarters on this planet. Where is it? Well, it's on the etheric level. There's some of it in the Earth, and it's called Shamballa, or Amenti — you have different names. You could see how many names you could find in calling it. Some of you have done meditations there and some of you have not. And if you go into that energy, there is a strength, a resource of the whole plan for the Earth, that you can contact.

Think how exciting that is. You know, Sanat Kumara put together what he calls an energy garden. It is a garden that has energy flowers, if you will, wonderful, wonderful energy that you can contact in Shamballa. There's nothing more supportive. Perhaps you're looking for support. Perhaps, if your emotional body is saying, "Poor me. Poor me, I'm tired. I'm doing all of these things and I still don't know who I am. I've come to Sedona, and Sedona was going to tell me all of this, and I'm just not quite sure who I am yet." Well, there's a wonderful place in Shamballa, this energy garden, where you can feel the support of someone who cares and has always cared about you.

Many traditional religions (not so much now but in the past) reached to this level to worship God, Sanat Kumara. The Father *was* Sanat Kumara. Certainly he steps down the energy from a higher level; he has always done that. But there is a sense of the Father in this energy. This is wonderful because, as you know, basically all that exists is all of you plus the Creator. You are cocreators together with the Creator – that's All That Is. And as you figure out your relationship to the Creator, then you are what He is. That's all that exists. It's very simple, isn't it? Are you glad to know that it's really very easy?

What the journey is all about is figuring out "Who am I in relationship to the One that created me? And the gift that He/She/It gave me is *unlimited expression*. Why don't I express unlimitedly yet, and have I failed because I haven't? How do I get in touch with it?"

Do you recognize these questions? Well, they're going on on many levels within you, and this cosmic walk-in is one way to access them. Wouldn't it be interesting to introduce your cosmic walk-in to Sanat Kumara? Doesn't he know it? Of course he does, but how about, through your consciousness, bringing your cosmic walk-in perspective, marching up to Shamballa and saying, "Here I am. Here's a cosmic part of me I want to introduce to you. We are partners in the Plan."

You know, I never do anything without intent – the intent to help you. I am what is called a spiritual psychiatrist, so we go deeply into issues here. I do this on the inner level, too. So what are we energizing here? We're energizing what I call *divine equality*, your equality with the Planetary Logos. Because, my friends, there are at least ten of you in this room who are going to be one someday. It's not that far off; it will happen in this cosmic day. Many of you are going to grow up to be what Sanat Kumara is. And if not, then maybe your role is to be a galactic logos or maybe a universal logos. Whatever it is, you need to get used to the idea of divine equality, of really understanding that, as great as you think these beings are, you are just as great. You're not any better, but you're just as great.

So in these inner dialogues with divine equality, you begin to energize that within your subconscious mind. Now, I didn't say control; I didn't say manipulation – I said divine equality. So there is a balance that is needed here, a balance. How many of you can feel there's just a lot going on here in the third dimension?

Opening to the Cosmic Walk-in Energies

I'd like to show you something. Follow me, either with your knowingness or with your clairvoyant abilities, because in this room we've placed a particular energy that really illustrates energywise what I'm saying about the cosmic walk-ins.

🐾 We've placed a white energy against the ceiling. (Again, you're going to have to look at it through your third eye.) It has some white clouds and some pink clouds – the angels have salted it a little for me with clouds. Coming from that, then, is a flow of violet, and a flow of pink, and green and blue, and many of the colors of the rainbow. When they reach about here we will call that, in our "cosmic room," the physical level. And here, flowing over the floor of this room, is a lot of green, a very lovely green.

🐾 Now, if we were to look at it in the third dimension (we've set it up with a fourth-dimensional flow), we would see a precise rainbow, like a rainbow striping, and then a swirling. Then it comes into the physical level and kind of blends into that green, and you can't really tell there are other colors. You might get a glimpse of violet once in a while, or a glimpse of pink or a glimpse of blue, but it's really settled down pretty much to the green.

🐾 But in this new opening that we've called the cosmic walk-in, what we're seeing is almost like an energy trench. There is an opening here, the white color that comes together in what we call a trench – it's not a sharp division, but there is an energy flow that rolls down to this green. Through that is coming right now a pink. We put the trench all along the center of this room, and here are the banks of it in the white, all the way up and down. Coming in now is some violet and now some blue, and here comes some yellow, and here is the pink. The colors are really coming in. They're coming down, they're stimulating, they're igniting. The colors are coming into the green and here ignite, ignite, ignite, ignite, ignite, ignite, ignite! There is an ignition of this physical level, energywise, from the cosmic walk-in that is this energy opening from the very basic level. In this case it is the Galactic Core, the galactic perspective.

🐾 If you will look, my friends, with your third eye, you will see that this is one such entity trench. You'll have to stretch a little now, stretch with me; you're going to see one here and one here and one here and one here. There is an almost unlimited number of these trenches that have been added through what we call alternate realities, or the other perspectives or choices that you didn't make in this reality.

Looking at it as energy, the reason there is a lot going on here is because there is so much energy integration taking place, so much that is alive and moving. Life is more vibrant. Life is fuller. Life is expanding here on the physical level, and it is so exciting! Is anyone stuck? No way. No way at all.

Now, you might not see for a while with this third eye, but use your knowingness to really sense life swirling all around you, to sense these possibilities coming in and moving in a very, very, very cosmic manner. As we finish our evening we're going to do a meditation with that energy, and I think you will enjoy it. But now I would like to open it up to some questions.

Vywamus, last February 18 when you were here giving a lecture, you were giving dates and expectations on those dates. I wonder if you could clarify the October date when you foresaw a time of harvest.

All right. We have to go back a little to talk about it. We have to look at this whole year as a preparation for accepting a new level, for really using a new level that's opened. And if you talk about harvest, then you're getting close to recognizing and using the particular strengths or point of view that you've been trying to harvest or integrate. So I feel that by the fall some of you will have done that, and others will be doing it. It also gets into making room for those new perspectives.

Now, some of you have based your premise on an illusion. If so, you have to move that illusion over in order to make room for who you really are or whatever it is that's going to be harvested. In your October or the fall, it seems to me, you will be really working with that too — making *room* for the new level of understanding that has been working and energizing and building up.

You see, you may be able to ignore a little seed, my friends, but if it grows up to be a ten-foot-tall plant, then it's going to get your attention, isn't it? If you decide that that plant is who you are, then you've got to look at who you thought you were and perhaps release some of the misperception that was there. It's going to be a time of deep releasing in many, many ways.

Think about corn. What do you do when you take it out of its husk? In a sense you take it out of what it's been limited by. It may have been supported by it while it grew up, but now it's outgrown that. So harvesting has to do with that, too.

I understand it's a time when the dark brotherhood will be released upon the planet.

Well, there are many ways of looking at that, my friend. There are beings that have closed their hearts, and certainly they have created some sort of organization. I would say they've done it very effectively, because they don't integrate very well; that's part of not being open in the heart area. But certainly there is a process of assimilation going on upon the Earth now, and there are choices being made. And there are beings that are opposed to change, because it serves them very well to be powerful in the Earth as it has been or as it is now. So there is a resistance which sometimes comes up.

But if you can conceive of perhaps 100,000 (maybe this is stretching it a little — I'm always an optimist) cosmic walk-ins going like this [pretends to blow out a candle] to those dark beings — think about it.

It is a much stronger planet now than you know, and certainly there are going to be those who don't always agree with the Plan and who try to create, perhaps, their own plan. But this becomes less and less of a problem as time goes on, my friend; I think so.

If the cosmic walk-in draws in all the potentiality or all the different perspectives, how long will it take in sequential time?

I love that one. "As long as it takes" is the answer. It's much beyond this physical body's usage. You are starting a process that will end when you have evolved beyond the galactic level. And then you will be on another level. So we're really energizing, in first grade, what you will complete when you graduate from college.

Is this what you've been talking about occurring in me and causing a lot of physical exhaustion and tiredness?

Growing Your New Body

Yes, and there are several reasons. Perhaps beyond what I've told you tonight, there has been for two or three years a reenergizing of the Earth *body,* and of the physical body, too — you're growing a new spleen, new kidneys, a new heart; you're literally growing a whole new physical body. Perhaps one of the most important things you're doing is using some hormones that you've never before used in the physical body. Now, it would be nice if the whole body would grow at the same rate, but you know, your abilities don't grow at exactly the same rate, and your physical structure doesn't grow at exactly the same rate, either. So what happens is, you begin to energize the new hormones, and the immune system takes a look at that and says, "I don't know these! These are invaders!" It sends up signals (this is a simplification, of course) and the endocrine system looks at that and says, "I think we better have a talk with the immune system. I think we've got a problem here."

So all of this is trying to communicate within your physical body to allow the new level of hormones, of blood, of electrical flow, of the evolving tissue flow, of the evolving use of the brain. Even things like your hair are changing, you see. The energy centers here [the cheeks] are very important; the new ones at the bottoms of your feet are very important. So much change in the physical body. Now, basically we could say that there is a higher perspective that is causing that, and certainly up to this point it has been the fuller use of your own soul at this new level. But it's going to intensify now.

I think some of you in the past few months have been feeling the changes that are coming in, because you're building a stronger foundation for more and more of this energy. What will help is exercise.

It will help if you take two showers a day, in the morning and at night — and perhaps, before going in the shower, visualize yourself entering a phone booth and fill that up with violet flame, staying in for two or three minutes. In this way you bring even more residue up to the physical skin so you can wash that off.

Take very good care of your body, eating less stimulative foods. If you eat red meat, then eat less of it; let your body tell you — it may say to you, "I don't want any tonight." A lot of pure water helps wash this out. Swimming is very good, and also movement like walking – let's say gentle activity with the physical body, and getting enough rest, too.

All of you should take a couple of weeks at least to smell the roses this summer; it's kind of fun to do. When you feel a little bit tired, it means there's a lot of activity going on. You can also visualize the cells; I like to simplify the process and see each cell as a cup. Again, you can use whatever color of energy you wish; I like gold because for me gold is a very integrated color. You can visualize the energy coming into the cells; it comes in on the left, and the right is the polarity area. The problem for most of you is that maybe the left side, the receptor, fills up faster than the other side, the dynamic, and it starts kind of a chaotic churning in the cell itself.

Please don't misunderstand me. I'm not telling any of you that you have cancer. But when the cells start to fill up with this energy and it swirls and moves and doesn't have any sense of direction, they begin to misinterpret. When it creates a flow that is not energized by the divine blueprint of the soul, then it gets stuck. One cell comes over to another cell, and the first one blocks the second one, causing it to get stuck, and pretty soon you have a mass. There is a lump of energy there, and many, many, many, many cells have gotten confused because their polarity hasn't been energized enough to use the full integrated flow within what they are.

So you can visualize the energy (I would do it with just a sample cell), asking the cells to share with one another. If one cell doesn't have enough energy, another cell may have too much. See the energy filling up on both halves and spilling over, around, and see the cells washing with this higher energy. You can work with the cells yourself. Etheric work is certainly available, and perhaps a massage if you wish. But you can do a lot for yourself – stretching the body and moving it, and recognizing that it is going through a process that is every bit as intense as coming through the birth canal when you were born, many years ago. Your cells remember that birth process, and they remember that things grew after that, you see.

So you want that growth to be energized by the ideal blueprint of the soul. Ask the soul star to bring in the divine blueprint as it's meant to manifest through you physically. If you can't do that for yourself, then get some help from someone you trust. As you work with that and it becomes even, you want to see that the cells on the left side are energized with about the same amount of energy as the cells on the right are. That's part of what's going on.

You're changing, really, the use of the whole polarity system. And that's intense! A body has to really adjust in order to do that. So there's a lot going on. Keep working with it – you're doing fine. And rest, too.

A New Government on the Inner Levels

A couple of weeks ago a speaker talked about our Congress passing a law that would take away some of our basic freedoms – the writ of habeas corpus, the search warrant and right of due process. I'm pretty concerned about that. Can you give us any advice as to what we can do, or is consciousness going to change so fast that it's not relevant?

Yes, I think there will be more and more attempts like this. I think it's part of the decrystallization of the system. It doesn't have to be done like this, but this is the way that you've created it together. So it seems to me more and more that you need a whole new system, don't you? You can certainly write to your congressman, and you can try to get other bills introduced to change it back. But on the inner level, perhaps even more importantly, you can begin to create a whole new system. You can ask these cosmic walk-ins to bring their perspectives to the Earth as a government. You see, that's the goal. *That's* what will do it.

In the meantime, I think you're going to have to release the old system, to perhaps let it go. But why not try to communicate as clearly as you can with the leaders of your countries? Through that the new beginning will be seeded, too. Because through communication various levels speak to each other, right? And the leaders of your country (we've talked about this before) are not the leaders of your country. [Laughter.] They are not. But at least as you communicate with them, and if you get enough communication going into that level, it begins to seep through a little.

You might talk to the real leaders of the world on an inner level and begin to soften that up a little bit. If 10,000 of you could get together in a meditation and contact that level that is governing you — the power center of your Earth — I tell you, you could change it almost immediately!

Is there a day this year when we could focus on that?

That certainly is something to do. Begin to energize it in this window that is coming up the latter part of July. Anytime between the 27th and the 30th of May, visualize it, if you wish to do this, begin to see it. And then it will work; it will help no matter how many people are there. But if a group of 10,000 would specifically contact the beings that are called the Trilateral Commission, or the ones who have controlled the power structure of your Earth — if you would specifically invoke a contact from this cosmic walk-in level, it would be rather like a can opener. Can you visualize that — do you get it? I'll be interested to see what the can does when it is opened.

Certainly you would need to visualize rather specifically what you want to use in place of what you have now in order for the universe to understand. You see, this goes through the universe, and the universe has to have some specific directions. It can get most of it from the higher level, but you are on the physical level. Right now, because the cosmic walk-in situation is so new, it is still learning to use the physical level.

Much later — maybe it'll be a little bit into next year — I think it will come in more easily, the cosmic walk-in level directing the physical level. But right now it's just learning to do so. It's like walking into a physical structure the traditional way, where you have to learn to make the arms and the legs move, you understand. So this is making the divine power center move. Because that's what you want to change, and each of you as a soul has a divine power center. Where is it in your body?

The heart.

The heart/throat area, the whole corridor. This is the way you connect into that higher level. You must *choose* to do it; this is the center that chooses. It surrenders to something higher. It's what you were given — the gift of free will — given to you so you could give it back. So have something to give the Creator, to say thank you for. You can give it back. It's what you can do — giving back this power to that higher level that can then create the change that you want. Because it is the power change that you want on the Earth in order to attain the kind of Earth you want — and it's coming. It's coming, there's no question of that

What can I do to open up or accelerate the waking-up process?

Look deeply within your subconscious mind. Look at those blocks that you don't know you have but that someone such as I or someone else you trust can help you see. Look deep and have help with it. It's important for you to recognize that you can have help. You've taken the responsibility to know you can make these changes. But it's a little bit on dead center. That doesn't mean it isn't moving, but the analogy that I like to use is that, while you're all coming along, some of you are kicking and screaming just a little. So it is the emotional body that must be convinced that this new unlimitedness that the cosmic walk-in represents can work now. The emotions keep connecting you into something from the past.

Your big fame is something called pre-Lemuria. If you want to find out more about that, you can get material and read about it. We've given specific points to look at — trust is one, and several other things. [See Part Six, Chapter One.]

Is there one in particular I can call to help me with this?

Raphael. And Vywamus, if you wish — I'm available through a variety of ways. This is one of them. I will be glad to help you on the inner level. We have worked together a little, my friend, and you may call me directly, or through the channels that I work through. I am a specialist in the area of probing deeply and getting rid of those itty-bitty resistances nobody has anymore. Cosmically speaking, that's very true.

What would be your suggestion for working in this void space, this creative void where you cannot bring the past forward, where all the things you used to do aren't what you're going to be doing, but the next steps haven't come yet?

Well, sometimes you have a belief that says, "I have to do it all right now." You can't do it one step at a time. You really have to learn patience. I know you just love to hear that! But for you that's true: you need patience.

The way I like to look at it is this: Wherever you are now in your consciousness, whatever you are doing (even if you don't think you're doing anything), is the basis from which you can move forward. You don't throw that away. You begin to energize through your strengths. You could sit down – this is both a spiritual and a mental exercise – and list your strengths: What is it I do well? From where I am now, what can I attract to take the next step in my purposes or in my evolution (which are the same thing, of course)? As you do that, it begins a flow, and that flow will attract more and more all of the strengths – some you know you have.

So it is a process of allowingness, knowing that this will happen if you can trust it, and it will happen one step at a time. It wouldn't be appropriate for it to bring everything that you are capable of doing into your life now, and it's not going to. You know what would happen then? I call it a shock, too much for you, all of you. That's why it was set up this way; that's why the plan says to move into it one step at a time. You get used to one step, and you think that's it, and then all of a sudden the universe says, "No, here comes another one!"

So get a little bit used to where you are. That's part of what's going on. And then sit down and list your strengths; be willing to accept them. For some of you there may be some resistance in accepting them: "What do you mean, I'm unlimited? I can't see that I'm unlimited, but if I *am* unlimited, why am I not feeling unlimited? And if I am meant to be unlimited, why am I not unlimited now? I must have failed." So if you tried to use (and you do) your unlimitedness in the past, and you got a little confused in how to use it, that tries to come in again. So be as clear as possible in where you are now and what your strengths are.

I'm coming to the understanding about these electrical low-frequency waves that are being sent throughout this area, and I'm wondering if you might explain the difference between those and the energies of the vortexes, because a lot of people are blaming the vortex energies for these effects.

Well, it's quite easy to blame something outside yourself, isn't it? In the first place, I think more of the energy problem is coming in with what I just talked about. And it certainly can be projected to the outside. Let's say that your electrical system is not quite functioning the way it used to, and yet it hasn't quite caught up to the step where you're going. You might short-out many electrical devices; you might find your television doesn't work and your radio doesn't function well. That's not someone else's fault; it's something *you* are going through. So perhaps it's more important to get your own energy body straightened out than to blame something outside of yourself. That seems important.

Secondly, I don't see that there is a tremendous differential in the energy. Certainly there are higher energies coming from the portals and the levels of harvesting that the angels are doing in some of the vortexes. That's changing, by the way, and that may be part of what you're referring to that people are really getting in touch with.

We know through other channels that the government has built these electrical-low-frequency-wave transmitters to help control the population.

It has controlled the population — this is my opinion — at the level where they were *before*. It's not going to control them where they are *now* and where they are going. That's my opinion. So that's the difference. They are meant as a controlling device, but they didn't take evolution into account, and they didn't know about the cosmic walk-ins. The plan always has an answer. Now, if you really have within you a belief that says, "I am controlled by this sort of thing," then you may be. See, some people have that belief. They're working in the power area, which is very important for all of you.

My friend and I are experiencing a lot of static electricity. What can we do about it?

I'd work on the electrical flow within yourself. I would have you help each other with that in a hands-on type of work and in etheric work where you concentrate particularly on the brain area. Find some crystals that you trust, and particularly a generative crystal, a dynamic crystal — one that has a dynamic point. Working with the energies, first of all break up the energy in the brain area. Break it up and let it flow. It's as if you need to comb your energy field in the head, as well as in your hair. Some of the problems come from that matting down of the energy in the brain — you know, above the brain area in the crown chakra, in the pineal gland, in the pituitary. You can work to clear out the connection between the pineal and the pituitary.

For some of you, there are new hormones being used. They are being manufactured within your body by the pineal, and the pituitary is doing its best to receive them but not recognizing them exactly for what they are. This is an electrical readjustment, and you can work with the energy, particularly in the head, to clear the points back here. You can have those massaged.

Now, you might also work with a black stone — hematite, black tourmaline and obsidian in particular. I wouldn't want you to walk with them in your shoes, but if you're sitting down, put a piece or two in your shoe, beneath the arch of your foot, while the etheric work is being done on you as you are either lying down or sitting up. If you put them in your shoe, then they're not going to fall off; they'll stay in position. The dark stones, which gather energy, pull it out of the cells; they are going to take the spillover.

Static electricity is a spillover out of the ideal blueprint pattern of your soul, the energy flow. It's a spillover that you want to integrate into the cells, the spillover that isn't organized. I love working with calcite for the cells. There's orange calcite, green calcite, clear, pink, brown, yellow, gold, many kinds of calcite! It works in a very basic way with the cells. So allow the energy of the stones to help you clear out the cells, and as you do that, your electrical problems will disappear, I guarantee it.

This is the part of the process (it's not terrible), part of the emerging soul level that is structured on a much wider energy base than ever before. It's the difference between living in one room and having a 25-room mansion. It's about that great a difference. You have to completely energize and flow within that 25-room mansion, so there's a lot of adjustment to be made.

Isn't it good to steer away from thinking about the so-called evils that other people and governments are doing and put more energy into what's good and right?

Well, certainly. There are times, though, to look head on at something that is manifesting. You don't like to put your head in the sand like an ostrich. Things are there to look at, and you are responsible for what you create on the Earth. But to dwell on them doesn't do any good, either.

As far as the power structure on the Earth is concerned, you're coming to a point where you're going to have to face it, no question. I've said that as the old structure goes down the tubes, more or less, you're going to have to (and some of you will really be a part of this) negotiate with those who have held the power. That's facing it, but that's facing it in a positive way for a particular solution.

Vywamus's Chess Game at Harmonic Convergence

Now, there are those that are closed in the heart, there's no question of that. Let me tell you about something that was done at the time of Harmonic Convergence. This is concentrating on the problem area, but not perhaps in the way that makes it seem as if it's in control of you. At the time of the Harmonic Convergence I played chess with the one that you call the Devil, or Satan. What does that mean?

There is a being who occupies that space, that dark energy, and he was losing some of his territory at the time of the Harmonic Convergence. The whole planet was rising up. In my association with the Hierarchy, my role was to communicate with this point of view and to help it see that giving up this energy would be a very positive thing for it to do. That was my role. We took a group of 22 to the Caribbean and we worked with this energy.

So that's facing what was there — not dwelling on it as something that is controlling, but helping it to become lighter. It did become lighter through what we did.

What's the relationship between Sanat Kumara and the Earth Mother?

We could consider the Earth Mother to be the receptive quality or the female quality of the Earth itself, and the Earth itself to be the physical body of the being called Sanat Kumara.

In meditation I see him as a physical body – not the planet, but a physical body.

Yes, you can visualize that. But you are really looking at a being of consciousness that is able to manifest a perspective — its physical body is that large — as a whole planet. That is it, and the Earth Mother is that female or receptive part of it. You can get a visualization or a personification or a symbol of that, certainly you can. One has been given on the cover of the book, *The Story of Sanat Kumara* published by Light Technology Publishing — that is a personification of Sanat Kumara from a past-life experience. You too are probably viewing him as he was in a past life, and that's fine. He isn't like that anymore, you see, but you can view him that way because it's something you can relate to.

When you talk to the Earth, you are talking to Sanat Kumara, too — it's kind of nice to know that. Shall we do our meditation? I'll be leaving after that, so I want to thank you all.

Cosmic Heart Meditation

❦ *There is a cosmic space that has a tremendous love — I'd like you to feel that now. This love is shining into your heart. And there is a flow of energy coming from it, into you. It is not really outside; it is inside. And you can see it as filling up your heart now. (This is that energy we were talking about earlier in our discussion of the energy in this room.) Your heart is filling with this energy — you can feel it now. There is a love present — yes, a love — and with it is born a joy. Let that fill up your heart. Then, within that joy is an enthusiasm that just bubbles over; and perhaps a sense of humor is born there, too. You can feel it. And that is an energy — you might give it a color, a very exuberant color — an energy coming in from a cosmic point of view and flowing, spilling into your heart. It is there. Feel it now. Ha ha ha ha — and it laughs and it plays and it says, "My goodness, Vywamus, this isn't such a big deal. This cosmic walk-in, it's just . . . who I am."*

❦ *The I Am Presence then speaks, speaks, speaks to you now, through this heart. And it says, "Yes." And it has strength, and you can feel the power within you, and it motivates you. You become aware now of violet energy, and through your divine power, you send that now all over the Earth. The Violet Flame goes shining forth on the Earth, shining everywhere, radiating into every point of view. Get it into the corners, in the cracks, in the walls, in the lakes. This Violet Flame shines now. Let's put a little pink in that, representing the love aspect, the aspect of the heart. The power goes in and lights up the Earth, and the heart opens from it.*

❦ *Have you thought of the Earth as having a heart? Perhaps it does, in a way that contains all of your hearts. So open to that now. This energy, this pink energy, opens up the heart of the Earth, and you are within it and it is within you. And there is an expansion, and through that expansion again there is joy and enthusiasm. And look — the Earth shines! The spiritual sun, perhaps you can call it, is shining now on the Earth. So now we have gold, the violet and the gold, moving and swirling. And it has the pink in it, moving and swirling, swirling and moving — great vortexes of this energy. And now we put some blue in it, electrical blue, and we say to the Earth, "Wake up, wake up, wake up, wake up!"*

❧ The energy swirls and it moves, and you feel the enthusiasm within you. And yet there is a quiet place where you feel very balanced, and you listen to that voice within, and it says, "Yes, yes, yes" to this power moving across the land, to this divine opening. You listen, and it says, "Yes you can; yes you are; yes, yes to life." And whether it is in Moscow (look at Moscow, shining brightly there) or whether it is in Washington, D.C., (look at Washington shining brightly there), whether it is in Beijing (look at Beijing shining brightly there), whether it is in Poland or whether it is in Switzerland or South Africa, South America, Australia, Tibet – wherever it is, there is a shining now. Energize that.

❧ Energize that shining, that Violet Flame, that gold, that pink and, yes, that electrical blue. And now add another color – you select it. Add it and spread it all over the Earth. Allow it to permeate the Earth, and the Earth will respond. It is responding, and as it responds – guess what? You expand. You expand your understanding, you expand your acceptance, you expand the use of your divine power. You expand your stability, you expand, you say yes to life. You become even more unlimited. More and more unlimited, expressing now more and more of this cosmic point of view that says, "Yes, let's clean out the old illusions; let's clean it out now. Let's balance the emotions; let's clean them all out now." It says yes to life, saying yes to life more and more. It says yes to life; it says, "I am life. I am the Presence. I Am, I Am, I Am! now. And I invite you to get excited.

❧ This is the full use of your creativity, stretching you fully to serve the Earth – yes, dedicated to service of the Earth. It certainly brings you a good life. But it really isn't anything personal. It is the life of the Earth we are concerned about stretching now, stretching into that full New Age, that clear New Age. Visualize it now, shining all over the Earth, and see yourself communicating with others – hugs, if you will – communicating now, fully: "Yes, we are ready; we are ready now, and I am stepping into that I Am, I Am, I Am, now."

❧ Bring it back again to the cosmic heart center and see how that feels. And again the joy bubbles up, and it says yes. And you can feel the love and support of Sanat Kumara, of all of us, and certainly of your soul. You are supported, and you certainly are loved and cherished.

I thank you, my friends.

❖ T W O ❖

The Cosmic Family

THERE IS A SENSE RIGHT NOW OF A WONDERFUL NEW BEGINNING. HAVE YOU noticed? One way I would like to talk about it is to call you all a cosmic family. Now, are you the only members of the cosmic family? No, but you are good, card-carrying members of it – you all have a little printed ID that says "I belong." And because that's true, there is a sense of camaraderie beginning to permeate the Earth. It seems to me that every time I look at any of you, what I see in the heart area, pulsing, is a movement, a radiation, that I've never seen before. And I'm so excited.

Let me begin to energize – in a way that you might not have looked at before – life on the Earth. Now, to do that, I would like to go back just a little and go deeper into it, and I want to show you what is going on in your physical structures. I want you to look at the macrocosm and the microcosm and see that there is expansion even if sometimes it is difficult to allow.

Golden Particles – Electrical Tools

Right now on the Earth there are new particles that have never been here before – little physical building-block particles that are coming in. These are very radioactive and these are at the far end of the electrical spectrum, really becoming a part of physical existence for the first time, since the Harmonic Convergence.

What does that mean? It means that your soul, that higher aspect of yourself, has a new source of fuel. Let's say you have opened the Creator's toolbox on the physical level and you have begun to pull out tools that you never knew were there, and now you see them on the physical level. Let's say you've got this one, with its particular shape, and you're looking at it and looking at it and you haven't the faintest idea what to do with it, not even how to hold it. There is a sense of "This tool is here – I recognize it's a divine tool, and I want to use it, but my goodness, how do I use it?"

Now, if you once had a tool on another level, and it was similar to that, then there might be beliefs stored in the subconscious: "I tried to use that once before, but it didn't work out too well," or, "I tried to use it, but I wasn't able to understand how to use it."

So these tools, we could say, are fraught with symbolism for you, and your physical bodies (most of them) are having an interesting time with these particles. There is a worldwide flu epidemic that can be traced to these particles and your body's ability to accept them. For some of you, the metabolic system has all but shut down because these particles have literally gotten stuck in there and they're interfering with the digestive processes and with many things. You might find your weight fluctuating a lot or that there is not a good digestive process or that the things you have eaten before don't agree with you anymore. You might find that you have sudden cravings and you can't figure out where they came from. There's an interesting variety of experiences in the microcosm that are also going on in the macrocosm.

So your personal vehicle, or learning tool, or support system — your physical structure — is needing to be clearer electrically. So for many of you, the beliefs that you have stored in the subconscious in regard to the electrical area are coming up and hitting you in the face, or perhaps we should say, hitting you in the body, particularly in the metabolic system. Some of you have had some serious heart responses — not heart attacks per se, but more in the arrhythmia area. Certain disease is being emphasized — we're seeing more diabetes and hypoglycemia — from the inability to assimilate sugars and use them correctly. So the physical body itself is showing that these particles are clogging up the works. You don't know what to do with them.

Some have considered the particles to be invaders, and that is where the illness is coming from: "My body isn't familiar with this, so it sends out the team to push it away." There is an old rule, my friends, that says if you try to push something away, it comes right back. If you put energy into pushing it away, it comes right back. So the only way to really solve your relationship with anything is to accept it, to allow it to be a part of your understanding, to literally integrate it. And that's true with everything. But these particles are especially persistent — they are not going to go away. The goal is to allow them to flow through the system.

Now, even if you are not using your full clairvoyant abilities, ask your knowingness to give you a picture of this. There is a system, a flow, an electrical flow of your soul's energy on the Earth, and it is stimulated — it bursts at particular points that are dynamic. So the flow and then a burst, the flow and then a burst, and you could say that each one of these particles is what allows that burst; because they are so radioactive, they have a stimulating effect upon the flow of consciousness. Now, the Harmonic Convergence created the mechanics of how to use your Earth more clearly and at a higher level. We will say that the Harmonic Convergence helped you to set up like an escalator, but instead of riding, you've been walking up and down the escalator!

15 April 1989: Power On

Now, the time is coming when you're going to turn on this escalator; I see it as April 15. Isn't that exciting? It's finally happening – the initiation of the flow of the New Age on your Earth. Now, does that mean that everything will magically be solved in your lives? Probably not, but the movement will be there, the flow will be there – the ability to access the flow through your life in a way that perhaps you never have been able before because the format for the Earth, or the level of consciousness, or the environment, was not as dynamic as you yourself are.

Now, what does that mean? Well, all of you are the means that evolve the Earth, and of course the Earth reflects the overall consciousness of who you are. But there are various levels of consciousness on this planet, and while you're no greater than any other part of it, you do have a particular role. It's your turn to do something, you could say. And right now you are here – about 900,000 of you on the planet – as ignitors of this ignition process. There are others with other things to do, but about 900,000 of you are ignitors of the process. You are to embody these particles as clearly as you can, and then, through what you are, through what you become, that dynamic electrical flow will allow the system to benefit from it. That's the overall goal.

Ignition of the Escalator

Certainly individually you are learning to create in your own right, and there's a lot going on there. But there's a bigger picture that says you are all doing it together, you all have a role within this system. And perhaps the clearest way to ride that escalator is to share it in your understanding with everyone else, to see that you each have a particular role. And as you perform your roles together, there's literally an ignition through you that ignites everyone else. And it's that which is the escalator.

In the fullest sense it's not anything that you do; it's more how you respond to the system, to the process. There is a difference between saying, "I have to do it all for myself" and allowing yourself to benefit from the overall process that is already set up by a divine being who knew the best way to set up a process. I am forever amazed at the system – I think it's a remarkable one, how it all fits together and yours mirrors to me and mine mirrors to you and it works very well. So there is a system already working well, and all you have to do, truly, is be a part of it.

Many of you have said, "I'm not sure I can use this full system." This is psychologically what we might call the worthiness area. A few of you have worked on that one: "I'm not as worthy as everyone else," or "There's someone over here, look at what they're doing. That makes them more worthy than I am." Well, you've heard this might be ten million times –

and here's ten million and one. You're not worthy by virtue of anything you do, but you have been given an equal-opportunity contract by the Source Itself. Worthiness is attached not to what you do, but to what you are.

And what you are is a receptive mechanism for the process as well as this dynamic flow. Some of you recognize the polarity area here. Some of you recognize that we're really talking about the process — how it evolves. The most important point I'm seeking to make about these dynamic energies, these electrical particles, is that they're going to work within you rather automatically, as soon as you allow them to do so. The system is there already and they will motivate and move you as soon as you recognize that you can allow it. The system is in place; allowingness is the key. Allowingness, hope, trust, gratitude — recognize some of these. They are literally the means by which you create your life. We're talking about heart qualities.

Invoking from the Creative Opening that the Heart Generates

We're talking about structure — how things are set up on a divine level. The basic way you bring in energy is not bringing it down from somewhere; truly, it doesn't just magically appear. There's an opening — an acceptance, an allowingness (it's a heart quality) — that says, "Yes I'm ready. Yes, I want to serve. Yes," to anything that you're asking it creatively. It's the creative opening that the heart generates that allows that — whether it's called an electrical particle, the dynamic energy, the male polarity, the evolutionary process; these are all words for the same thing. It that allows you to, through that heart, create its energy — a radiant field that goes out to the universe and talks to the universe. It says, "I'm ready, I'm ready."

The universe says, "Good. Let's look specifically and see what you are ready for." It's in direct proportion to the amount that you send out. You say, "I have hope that I can connect into the process. I'm ready to walk in that flow. I am ready for her to stimulate me. I'm ready for him to stimulate me. I'm going to allow that." And as that message goes out, what comes back is just what you've invoked. However, it might not meet your expectations. It might not come back in the way you thought it would. Thus, if Alphie says to the universe, "I'm ready for a relationship," then the universe says, "All right, what kind of a relationship do you want? Let's look, let's see. Now, in that love that you sent forth, you qualified it a little: 'I want this and this and this, and I don't want this and this and this.'" Well, there's one particular person who embodies those qualities, but he doesn't send you back anything. "We'll take that under advisement; however, and we'll note what you've asked for."

Now, because Alphie is always learning and growing, the next time she sends out the message, it's even more specific. But now the universe has on file Alphie's card, and it looks and it looks and it says, "Before she asked for this, this and this. Now she's asking for something else — we'd better add that. But now, look, there isn't anyone — maybe on Alpha Centuri there might be someone, and if he's willing, he might come to Earth." (That's how some of the space beings got here, by the way — they were invoked.)

Thus you keep accumulating in your understanding what I will call charge, and it is literally an electrical effect that keeps building. You could compare it to a battery, and the universe stores it up for you. And at a particular point, when it's clear enough, almost like magic, suddenly it's there. Alphie will have knocking at her door her Prince Charming, who that says, "Here I am" — well, practically. When you become clear enough, the universe responds.

The Goal is to Pool Your Electrical Resources

The good news is that the universe is keeping track of everything you've ever wanted and everything you've ever worked on. There is an electrical system that is building, generating more and more energy until it gets to the point where it can respond. Now why is that important? Certainly you can have your Prince Charming; there's nothing wrong with that. But as perhaps you're beginning to understand, the goal is to pool your electrical resources. Let's say there are six of you who are willing to say, "All right, we're going to share this response that we are sending to the universe, and we're going to let it be six times greater so that it comes back not only with what we want individually but with what will assist the Earth to use a whole new level of creativity.

Now, what does that take? You've heard this term a lot too; it's called surrender. But what does it really mean to surrender? How many of you have wondered how to do it or why you would want to surrender? You get to the point where it becomes a goal. You might not be calling it surrender; some of you might say, "I'm going to let go of that — I'm not going to keep that around cluttering up my life." And what do you mean? You're not going to keep these half-formed electrical particles there upon your shelf. You're going to recycle them into something greater by putting them together with other people's perhaps half-formed electrical charges so you get an ignition that can serve you and the other people and the Earth and perhaps all of the other kingdoms well.

Can you see how important that is? It's using your resources fully, and we are talking now about an electrical resource. It's as if you have some flour and another has some butter and some sugar (well, not too much sugar), and somebody else has some apples — I like apples. And you put that all together and what do you get? As you share the ingredients that you're clear enough to have electrically, what you get is ignition, but it takes the strengths of each of you to make this ignition happen. This is the New Age, when humanity is using its strengths together and saying, "I'm willing to share it with you, and you can share your strengths with me." Whether we call it an electrical charge or an understanding, whether we call it a sharing of love or of allowingness or of trust, whatever we call it, when you share it together, it multiplies and it accelerates and it moves. My friends, that is your New Age — that is the flow that is beginning in April.

Network of Power

I call 1989 a bridge, my friends — a bridge into the New Age. There are many changes coming. Certainly economically. You have heard that before. I feel that they are beginning in this year. Now, what will happen? There are about 95 people on the Earth who run your Earth, in the power sense. And the Earth is clearer now. It's been controlled through the international banks and through the government by 95 powerful people and families. And this is not just Earth-related — these are beings that are on the Earth but they are connected into at least 35 other planets in other systems. So it's a network of power on a particular level.

Now that the Earth is moving, it's really going to break that power network — it's as if that network can no longer hold your planet, and it's going to break through it, energywise. You're going to lose some of the structure that you have economically. And in my opinion, it needs to change. Some banks won't survive the change. Some currencies won't survive the change. There are going to be countries that don't survive the change — probably small ones. But everything will change because there is a freeing up of the way the system is responding on the Earth. You have to let go, and letting go, or surrendering, means modifying the convoluted economic system that has been used on your Earth.

So I would say to do a little financial planning, just a little. Don't get frightened by it, but use your business sense to see how much you will need to provide on a 90-day cash basis. In other words, can you pay your rent, make your payments, eat and survive for at least 90 days without money coming in? For some of you, that's enough to do what? To take another look at the system within you and say, "Well, the old way of creating isn't working within the system. I think I'd better go to a new level of creating and use the system differently." Because the good news is, if you have created fairly clearly — and all of you have — even if the system goes economically, you can again, through an adjustment process, create clearly again. You've got your abilities, you've got your inner understanding — they can't take that away from you. That's the only thing you can take with you, you know, — that inner understanding, that learning, that perception of being able to create.

Now, I want you to look at the United States. I find that your country is wonderful, but perhaps there has been a fixation (in some people, anyway) on things, on possessions and so forth. Perhaps part of the clearing, part of the release of power, is to let go of things. You might think of power also as having to do with possessions, because things can possess you rather than you possessing them. So when we talk about a power release, we are not just talking about something that is with 95 people, but with all of the beliefs that you have about power, with all of your own struggles with power, and with all of the things that possess you. You will be given the opportunity during 1989 and 1990 to let go of those things that possess you.

You have to look at the system differently. Some of you will be involved in helping to change the system. Perhaps you can conceive of a large conference where these 95 people, who no longer have such absolute control – they're not quite sure what they have – know, through their chains of command, which goes into 35 planets, that they've been getting lots of flak lately because the system is no longer producing the monetary returns that they've promised to give. Keep in mind that these people are not individual entrepreneurs; they are more or less a group, and what holds them together is the desire for power, the desire for more money, the desire to control. The system, a new perspective, which is your New Age, is going to change that, so we're going to have negotiations with them. I'm going to be there, and I'm going to enjoy it. Perhaps now it's time for you to talk these beings that have been stuck in a pattern of controlled behavior out of it. Would you like to be on the negotiating committee?

I have a feeling they'll join – if they can't beat the system, they're going to join it.

Yes, that's right. They'll decide to let the system have a broader creative base and give away some of that power. It's not serving them well – they don't know why, but it's not making them happy. But it is of course a process that evolves those that are using the process, whether they want it to or not, because they've had so much control over it that now they get to use the system in a much freer manner. So that's why I said the system works. It's wonderful. I think we should give the Creator a hand.

So the system is going to really change. Will that be easy? It will depend upon where you are in consciousness, my friends. If you can be very allowing and absolutely trusting, and if your emotions don't get in the way and you can feel yourself supported, it will be a breeze.

Two-way Traffic

And there will be varying degrees of emotional and physical response to it. Now, the death rate is increasing because those who can't handle these electrical particles can't live here anymore. It's just that simple. Many of you are learning to handle them, and that's not a problem – it's a process, and you have chosen to stay, and you will evolve your understanding of how to use them. But there are those who absolutely can't – it's just too much. It's like jumping from the fifth grade to college, and they are not yet spiritually mature enough to graduate. They need the sixth grade, and the seventh and eighth grades. So many of them are going to another planet one in particular, although there are really more than one. So there's going to be a lot of what seems like loss.

On the other end of the scale, there are beings that haven't been able to come to the physical because there hasn't been enough energy here. They're coming in by the hundreds and thousands — that's wonderful. You're going to see some friends that you haven't seen for a long time. Why? Because they didn't want to take the time to live in the third dimension. But they're really here, and of course it is a multidimensional opportunity. The whole foundation of your Earth will be fourth-dimensional — this is what April 15 means. So those that can't use it will be leaving, and those that haven't been able to use anything else will be coming in.

So there is a lot of traffic, and some of you will be, and already are, traffic cops. We need help, and we've called for help. On the inner levels many of you are directing traffic — "You go this way, you go that way, and where you go I don't know but I'll find out." There is so much going on in the movement of your planet, it's a very busy time. How many of you have woken up lately and just been very tired — not in a psychological sense, but as if there's just been so much going on in the inner planes, you don't know whether you can stand more on the outer planes: "I need to rest here on the outer level." I think that's going to clear before too long. Give that another year and it will settle down. But now you're really directing traffic.

The System Is Positive — Let It Work

So there is a sense of connection into the process that stimulates you on the inner level, and when you wake up, then you're stimulated more by this change, particularly right now, this year. So be as balanced as possible, be as allowing as possible — yes, be creatively as excited as possible, because it's a wonderful time to be here. And be as supportive of each other as possible. If something doesn't work for you, find someone else with whom to share that "doesn't work" syndrome to see if they can help you. Or find an organization or teacher that you trust and get some help with it. Now. Right now.

Because the deeper you go, this year, into the understanding of who you are, the better — the easier it's going to be for you, and for the Earth. Remember, every time you clear a perspective, one of those control reins slides away without trauma. How do you like that? It's really true, and it's because the consciousness begins to deal with the system beyond the level of control that has seemed real. As you let go and you understand that control isn't necessary — you don't have to have it forever and there's not a tight rein on your creativity or your environmental structure — then the whole mass consciousness moves a little bit beyond that level of control that's been present for so long. That's what it means to turn on the fourth dimension — to allow it to flow, to let the system work.

It never was meant to be stuck, but in the third dimension, which is a magnification process, you looked at it and focused on it so much that it seemed stuck. You were so busy magnifying it that you blew it out of proportion. It's like having an emotion such as loss — some of you have experienced that a little, you've cried a few tears? And when you get in the middle of that, it becomes all-encompassing, you can't see anything else. It seems to say to you, "You're going to experience this loss forever, and all that exists is this loss." That's a magnification that blows it out of proportion. On the other hand, those of you who are very mental, you get into the analytical process and you do this: think, think, think, worry, worry, worry. Think, think, think, worry, worry, worry. And that's what I call a mental emotion, or anxiety. It goes around and around and around and you don't get anywhere with it.

So it seems to be a dead-end system, but it really isn't. And that's why hope is so important. What are we hoping for? We're knowing and realizing that the system is not destructive — we haven't lost an internal being yet. It's not destructive. It's not full of loss. It doesn't have to be full of pain. It doesn't alienate. It doesn't limit. It doesn't restrict. If it has seemed to, then these are self-imposed barriers. You know that, but perhaps you don't *know* it yet. You haven't said to yourself, "Aha, I have a tool, and I can see what I'm supposed to use that tool on — it's to, perhaps, fix me, so I'm more balanced."

Let's say that one day you are sitting there and either your emotions are bursting out all over or you're in this "think, think, think, worry, worry, worry" syndrome. Let's say you could apply a little cosmic salve to that. The cosmic family could be applied. Does that sound good? We could say that there is a way, a stimulating electrical way, whereby you can literally open an energy door clear to the core — let us say it to the Galactic Core. And you can allow that to soothe you, or to take you out of the loop that you're in, or to open what has seemed to be a dead-end system. It can be done through the heart area, and unless you have a serious physical heart condition, you can do this. If you have that condition, then don't do it. Either ask me further or find another system.

The Electrical Tune-up Button

But when something seems not to be working in your life, and it's the emotions that are stirred up, ask the process very specifically; in other words, go and ask for a tune-up electrically. You don't just say to the Source, "Help." That's all right too, but instead, "Help me in this way now. Use the tools that I recognize, that I already have." That helps you take responsibility for this change; it says, "I've already got them, but could you perhaps show me how to use them, or stimulate this heart area so that that radiance can move me out of this emotional pit or out of this worry, worry, think, think, think syndrome." Now, as that occurs (and I would do this in a state of meditation), you open something. It's called the heart. And you say, "All right. Now, perhaps I haven't yet learned to use this heart as much as I would really like to; I'm doing well on it, I'll pat myself on the back, but I want to take the next step. Could you stimulate that electrically?" Then visualize an electrical flow literally wrapping around the heart, penetrating the heart. See the heart in the center of an electrical spiral. How many watts would you like?

The most I can take.

What is the most you can take? Ask your knowingness. Each of you ask your knowingness.

What's the voltage? I'll just get 50,000.

All right, that's what I want you to ask your knowingness — "How much can I handle?" Ask your soul, your knowingness through your soul.

Now, the good news is, you have a button. You should not only ask your knowingness, but you should push the button to stimulate you with what you can handle. Push the button and say, "I don't want more than I can handle, more than is the next step for me." And then spend some time seeing the heart really in the center of this electrical effect.

The next thing would be to see, to embody some of the qualities, to feel them. In another words, allow this to work for two minutes — that's a good average — or tell it to work as long as it is helpful, but let's turn it off after two or three minutes. Then see how much you can feel. Have your emotional body make a connection into the heart, and begin. First, unconditional love. Go back to a time when you have felt unconditional love — many of you have had such a time, perhaps with a child when you first gave birth in one life or another (even if you're now in a male body, you've given birth to children before).

Does this blaze have to be in color?

Yes, that would be very good — electric blue, white, violet, gold or a rainbow of colors if you wish. I'm very fond of electric blue because it seems to me to contain electrical energy. And that can it shock the system, but not inappropriately. There are times when you wake up through a shock, and this is one of those times. You stimulate the heart, and it wakes up to a new level of activity. You don't want to electrocute yourself, and that's why the button says, "This is what is safe for me now. This is for me the next step." You see it wrapped in that electrical blue energy for that particular period that you have chosen, through your soul, and then you begin to embody the qualities. Now, you might want to prepare a list of heart qualities. There are four or five hundred of them; give me some examples.

Joy, unconditional love, trust, compassion.

Yes, good. Please use compassion, because in my opinion it will be the embodiment of the next avatar on your planet: the anchoring of compassion onto the Earth.

Humility?

Yes, good, be sure you add humility. My definition of humility is "divine equality" — understanding you are equal. You also want worthiness and a sense of security, but do perhaps four or five qualities that are the most important to you right then in that situation. Perhaps a sense of unlimitedness — that's certainly a heart quality. You can activate your heart more clearly through these particles because they are the tools that will be used by you in this electrifying process.

And remember, the process can be used by you in an accelerating manner now. And you can choose to ride — you don't have to walk up that escalator. I think that's wonderful, because then the particles are moving it, the particles are allowing that flow.

Does that have something to do with the silicon body? Is that like the soul-merge?

There is a light-merging going on right now, and it is sweeping away the unclear areas that haven't been seen as light. A particular level of light intensity is dawning. Whether we call that a silicon body or a soul-merge, it is a process that will allow you to wear it at one frequency and you to wear it at another, so what is being created is a frequency on the Earth that is whole. Your version of it is whole within what it is, but remember, it needs your light and your light and your light and your light and your light in order to be that fully igniting tool that opens up for you and for the Earth the New Age. It's exciting.

The atom when excited jumps into another orbit. Is that what this is doing?

Yes, you could put it that way. It becomes, let's say, a team member, because that other orbit has a clearer perspective; it is broader-based, more electrical in nature, wider-scoped, and able to use the system more clearly. It doesn't think of itself as isolated — it's going into the macrocosm.

It will jump into a larger or smaller orbit.

Well, but always more powerful. I'm not talking about physical size, I'm talking about creative size, or intensity. As I've said to many of you, and perhaps you don't like it, some of your bodies are going to weigh a little more in this New Age, but you will look thinner because you will be able to move your weight around and mold it any way you want to. But the body itself is now more compact, even if there is more light in it, because there is an electrical intensity level that is waking up the potential in a way that makes it seem more solid. So there is a sense of continuity built into the process through these electrical particles; no matter what direction they choose to go, larger or smaller, the process will use them at this creative level being awakened right now.

That's why we can know there is a system — because there is consistency within the level of understanding. Consider how someone can break through to the universal consciousness and bring forth an idea — Einstein pulled on the universal consciousness and brought something up. And in other areas of your solar system or even of your galaxy, that same idea was being used, not in the same way, but at the same level, creatively. That might mean that there is a planet out there in the galaxy that has a completely different system — it could be based on a completely different process than what your physical system is based on, but that level of creativity that Einstein pulled down will be stimulated and pulled down by someone in that system and used at that same level. It's like a spiral, you know, so the whole level is stimulated at that particular area of creativity.

Every one of you is an Einstein, and if someone you know is doing something that you admire, pull down your own version of it. That's why that is important. None of you has a monopoly on the system; you can all use it. In fact, when someone pulls down something that you admire, that action stimulates you, and it becomes easier for you to do so. So I would celebrate — "Look at what they're doing — now I can do it too. Look, look, we can all do it together." So instead of completion, you get stimulation, creativity, a fuller, freer use of the creative flow, and a wonderful Earth. Isn't that exciting?

Channelors and Channelers

My friends are coming here in large numbers — have you noticed? — and I wanted to talk about that. We call ourselves *channelors*, from all points of view. Some of us are beginners and some do not understand the Earth. It's not that they don't understand the process — they do, quite well. But they have perhaps never been on the Earth. So if they're working through a trance channel and the channel doesn't come back right away, they might drop the body, just let go of it, and the body just goes plop. So they learn, "Oh, look at that, I think I shouldn't have let go quite yet." And the channel might have wished that too. The point is, there are lots of newcomers here in the system, because galactically, you've become a training ground for channels. Now, that's good, and it's nice to know that, because you're going to see so many different versions of channeling. There's a lot of research being done here on Earth in how to use the channeling process more clearly, more extensively, more as a sense of completing rather than an isolating process. I don't know if you are aware of it, but some channels, after they have channeled for a long time, feel rather isolated, kind of angry — "I don't want to do this anymore! It's taking me out of something."

So be very supportive of the channeling process, try to appreciate it from all points of view and to help the channels see that they are part of something greater. Everyone is a channel, but I'm talking about a specific type of channeling where you are using words, music, dance, painting or writing without words as a triggering process into mass consciousness. So it needs to be stimulated in as many ways as possible. I've been asked to be part of a team that is looking at this, and so we that are the channelors are coming into it together. And then we're looking at it from putting into it certain levels of graduate students. Graduate students have some wonderful creative ideas. They look at the system in a refreshing way, and they certainly are giving us a lot to look at, and we are enjoying it. Sometimes perhaps they can gum up the works just a little (well, you didn't hear that from me). But we are training the channelors, and I think you are going to see at least 6000 new ones this year, and maybe more. That's good — just remember, these are spiritual perspectives given to you so that you can form your own perspective in line with everybody else's.

Now, isn't it wonderful to know that even if you get tired, even if you get discouraged, you're still moving? You can't be stuck. Can you have a perspective of stuckness? Yes, but you can't really be stuck. What is your response to that? Good. The system works.

I have a question about putting our talents together. How can we facilitate, how can we put together the talent that will aid each other best? First we need to create a talent, but how should we pick a talent?

Well, perhaps a brainstorming session. First, you have to decide who's going to do it together, and hopefully in these creative efforts there will be at least six — I think that with the six perspective, you get a much broader point of view that really works. It can be more unlimited after that, within the limits of your physical environment, but at least six. Now decide. This is where your mental bodies can get some good exercise, and your spiritual body can help too. What is the purpose of you coming together? Why are you forming this unit? Is it to live together, to be supported during this time? Is it to help each other, to be supportive of each other in the processes above? Is it to use the strengths in as many ways as possible? This might be the clearest way to go into this. You form units of at least six where you say, "I'm going to think of myself as a unit of six, and these others are five aspects of myself." If you can find five other people who are willing to do that, and be as unlimited as possible, then you've really got something very special.

You will have to be supportive of each other, even when someone is tired and says, "I've had it. This is not working and I've had it." Then what will it take? It will take five other points of view to convince him or her to hang in there for a while. Or set up a time frame — "We want to do this this year, we want to do this this month, we want to do this this week, let's set a time frame and then agree to make the effort for that long so that someone won't quit in five minutes and say this is too hard."

Then see what strengths will help this group to stay together. What do you need as a group? You need someone quite analytical and logical; someone whose knowingness is very, very good, or a combination of people with these qualities; and someone who functions very well on the physical level. You know, some of you could be called space cadets, meaning that you have spiritual strengths but you haven't allowed them to access the physical level, so you need someone who can help you access the physical level — in other words, if you get too conceptual, too far out, then they can say, "But what does that mean on the physical plane? How can we use that in a practical manner?" You need someone to earth-out the perspective. On the other hand, you don't want to get caught in the Earth's perspective, so you need someone who can say, "But let's look at that from the fuller perspective of the Source-level connection too." The intuitive areas need to be opened too. Then perhaps you need someone who is very heart-centered and will agree to function almost like a cosmic mother and say, "There, there, little one, it isn't working right now. Oh well, in five minutes it will work better." Someone nonjudgmental who will hear your problems, and who maybe can't do anything about them but is sympathetic. Perhaps all a person needs is a moment when someone will listen.

Each group will be different. Each purpose will be different. Each commitment level will be different, but there is a power in the group. Now, you all have these old patterns of behavior that say a group doesn't work. So perhaps one of the most important things you need to do is to clear out your subconscious in regard to groups, to really take out these old patterns of behavior that say, "You can't get anything done by committee – a committee never comes to a consensus." These beliefs have to go in order to allow yourself to be a part of this group. But the group is the physical symbol of that cocreator level, the full cocreator process, that you're all seeking to embody. That's the most important reason you're here – that's what brought you here – to understand the cocreator level.

When the Source individualized Itself, the Whole didn't split Itself apart so that It would become alienated; It individualized Itself so that It could see through every perspective. See and take in and learn and observe through an unlimited amount of energy or perspective so that as you begin to learn how to create again from that whole perspective, you go through what we call the cocreator level. You can't go from point A to point Z without going through the alphabet, and the alphabet is the cocreator level – alphabet soup. It shows you the process. Because one person will be clear in another area and can help you with that area. Allowingness, trust, and perhaps the commitment to make it work, are most important. And then if you hang in there, all you have to do is keep trying and it will get better.

Nonconfrontive Emotional Release/Clearing

I think I'm having some problems in assimilating this particle. I wonder if you would give me some suggestions on how to work with this.

At the point of your individualization, you accepted that there was a shattering of that whole perspective of Source through you. It wasn't that you meant to, it was that you came forth as an individual; you came through the birth canal, and there was a sense of shattering, a sense of "Instead of the whole pie, I only have one piece, and that piece is not nearly as good as the one I had before." That is what I mean by creative shattering.

The reason I put it in those terms is that it is electrical in nature. The Source said to you, "Here is a perspective that you are, that can grow electrically, that can grow creatively." But most of you said, "I want to go from point A to point Z right now. I'm not sure I understand that process — why bother with it? — we'll just go from the beginning to the end." Does that sound like you? You didn't want to take time to unfold the system, so you felt emotionally (this is the emotional body as well as the energy perspective) shattered. Not only that, but unworthy — "Look, it isn't working."

So here comes the means to evolve it, the electrical particles. It is stimulating literally all of the beliefs that you have in regard to your Source-level relationship. That is the most important belief that you have — "Who am I in relationship to the Source? Well, I know the Source loves me." Of course you do, and I love the Source. I know that I am nurtured by the Source, and I know I'm connected. But I also have another level of emotional beliefs, a system that isn't very clear — all of you have these emotional areas — loss fear, anger, frustration, betrayal, and whatever it is for you individually. They're all stored within your subconscious and within the physical system, and they become stimulated electrically.

What do you think happens when you stimulate levels that aren't moving physically? They're cooking, they are getting hard, they are crystallizing, because they aren't moving. You see, if they were moving and you stimulated them, they would just move more. But they aren't — they have gotten caught because you have been burying them and not validating them, so it's like a sandwich that keeps getting harder because you put layers on top of it and it gets very crystallized. When you stimulate that, it simply compounds the problem area.

These electrical particles coming in — are they the beginning of a process that makes us leave the soul behind and go on to the spirit?

Well, it depends on how you look at that.

Well, my background is Alice Bailey, and I had always heard that you eventually leave the soul . . . .

Yes, you do. My point of view is that the spirit or the consciousness is a stream of energy, and there are specifics within it — we've called one the monadic level and one the soul. But there are also levels, so you're really using the soul first of all; you merge with that, and as you step off the Earth, that is used like a shooting star . . . .

To the soul, to the spirit.

Yes, exactly. But it takes a while.

This is a beginning process?

Yes, that's right.

Mafu came to town recently and had a three-day event. In the event he brought forth an idea that we could bypass the programming of the soul and go straight to our Christ consciousness by using two tones. A friend and I, the day after the programs, had a simultaneous experience of having a thought — it was all polarized right in here — that created an ignition, and then it felt like an ascension of some kind or another. I was just wondering what it was all about.

It's valid. It's valid to do that, it really is. But the goal is to hold it so you can overcome your programming, and certainly the electrical particles will help you to flow beyond that. All of these tools are good, because they give you the impetus and the flow that you need, but the goal is to hold that point of consciousness. And perhaps if the emotions are so heavily layered in that they pull you out of it again, then it's good to process them so that you can hold it the next time.

You have all explored ascension. The point is to release the pressure within you so that you can hold it. There's a difference between the mystic path and the path of the metaphysician. In the mystic path, you make the spiritual contact and then you go straight up what's called the center pillar, and then hold it. The only thing is, if you get the least little bit out of balance, whoosh – down the pillar. Now, if you build it one step at a time, that is called the way of the side pillars, or the way of the metaphysician. You build it up a step at a time, and if you can't keep that contact in the center, there are side pillars to support you, so you have a good supportive base that you are raising up step by step.

I'm feeling a lot of the strong energies that you are talking about – some tiredness and other strong feelings – I'm responding to them as they occur. I'm also feeling a desire to have more of a focus, like a polestar, or something to go for, or a desire to do more inner work than I am doing.

We get sometimes a scattered effect. We're scattered by the very energy that we are trying to bring in, or our perspective is "I don't know what to do to bring it together, to really integrate it." So what is a symbol for you of integration?

Silence. Just a feeling of balance, perhaps?

Well, how about the Sun? Is it a point of integration for you?

I never thought of it that way.

How about a star? I think it would be helpful for you to have a symbol that represents integration and to place it within you and then let it radiate. And then it can be a very practical tool. I feel that you are really trying to see who you are from a soul perspective, as you've never seen yourself before. So to get in touch with that very specifically, after seeing this centered process, what you need to know is what your strengths are. What you choose to do with them is going to center you too. You need to sit down with yourself and be very honest and list your strengths.

Ashtar Command Increases Power of Crystals

The Earth has so much going for it now. Let me tell you this. In September 1988 the Ashtar Commands were given permission to increase the power of the crystals tenfold. And so they are ten times more powerful now. Now, that can be a tool that you can use – the mineral kingdom is more powerful. They also encoded a particular crystal strength within the rabbits, the snakes and the eagles. Isn't that an interesting combination? Think about what they mean to you symbolically, and that will say something – the part that multiplies well, the part that moves well and the part that flies well. How do you like that? Those particular symbols have been enhanced ten times on the Earth.

So your connection with the Earth is stronger, and you can use that. If you want a crystal as a focus, then choose one that says to you, "I can help you multiply your creativity." You'll have to talk to the crystal and see – I think you can find one. And I would suggest a clear quartz crystal – you worked with them a lot in Atlantis and you have strengths in using them. Start with that and you will be able to build from there. So look at your strengths, see what you want to create in your life – these are the focuses that will help you – and then look at the scattering. You need to look at it subconsciously, my friend.

When you said that there were a lot of souls coming in, I don't know exactly what forms. Are they all different forms?

That's very sharp of you. Some of them are coming into bodies and some of them are staying on the inner planes and being a balance (you call them guides sometimes) for the outer experience. Some of them are embodying other levels of consciousness as never before. This is a very interesting perspective, and I'm not sure that you've heard it before. Let's say that a soul that has never been here is focused in connection with the animal kingdom. It might act as a booster station for particular group souls in the animal kingdom. It might not incarnate physically on the planet except as that booster station. But it's still in the electrical system so these beings are in the electrical flow and, because they are very electrical, are boosting the whole system although they might not have a physical structure of their own. So they are working with the animal kingdom, the mineral kingdom, the plant kingdom and the human kingdom as boosters as never before, and also as your guides.

So channeling is one way too. How about blending with another soul and becoming part of that?

In what respect?

Well, I guess the term "walk-ins" is what I mean.

Oh yes, walk-ins too. There are so many ways to do it. There are many ways, but you might not have looked at that way I just told you – that's rather new.

Without imposing on cosmic secrets – whatever is comfortable – can you amplify a little why these 35 civilizations are working with these 95 power families? What's their payoff, what do they get out of it?

More power. More power.

The 35 extraterrestrial civilizations are really controlling the 95 families?

No, not exactly. There is a mutual beneficial power structure — "I'll rub your back and you rub mine." And it's valuable to someone who lives on a planet to have other options besides the planet they live on — other bank accounts, if you will, literally and figuratively. So they will, after reaching this certain point of power, contact other power structures that are equally powerful. It is people motivated by compulsions that are extremely deep and very powerful, so it is really more of a subconscious process than a conscious one. They would argue with that a great deal, saying, "We have control; this is nothing that is out of control." It seems to me that it is very out of control. But sometimes the more out of control it is, the bigger it gets — and that can include other physical planets.

Now, conversely, the more open the positive is — the more conscious you are — then the more you can contact other levels also. So why shouldn't it be in the reverse process? We don't talk about it much because that simply puts a focus on it, and we on the spiritual level are much clearer in the power area than you are, we understand these things more. We can't do it for you, though. Now, if we put a lot of energy into this focus, particularly on the spiritual plane, and we talk about it and we focus on it, it's going to get clearer. But what does that do? It pulls you into the use of that when you're not ready for it — you miss a step or two and that creates almost a vacuum in the universe — and that doesn't serve you well. That's why we are not allowed to interfere — because, although an area might become clearer, the whole process doesn't become clearer; it becomes less clear because you don't know how to use it. You have to be clearer, and we're very careful that we don't clear for you any more than you're ready to clear. Sometimes we help you and we're delighted when it is in line with your evolution so that it helps you rather than creates more difficulty.

Is this electrical particle bringing us into an etheric state?

It will ultimately. You are referring to the dense physical structure becoming less and less solid, though right now it seems more solid.

Will we be breathing ether, or still oxygen?

Eventually I think you might breathe ether, but not in the next few thousand years.

And in that etheric state, can negativity exist also?

Well, what do you mean by negativity?

I don't really think things are negative; I think it's a polarity that hasn't . . . .

Yes to what you are saying, except that your deepest, most profound areas you do not yet understand go to the core of where the energy is the finest — your Source-level relationship.

Is that in the etheric state?

Well, in the finest part of it, yes. The part that is just manifest — the point of light. You see, you are a being that is beyond any sort of manifestation in your beingness, but where it just becomes manifest is where the deepest psychological barriers are for you.

If you are in that etheric state, is it possible that you won't even know what is going on in some experiences on the Earth?

We're generalizing here, but if you were in that etheric state, and the Earth itself had moved into the etheric state also, you would be aware. Now, there are exceptions — we could call it the involutionary process, where as the Earth was being formed, many of you came to it in the etheric state as a prelude and to really be a part of helping to form it. So you were aware of the Earth and its formation while you were also aware of yourself in your very etheric body.

I have some intense jerking going on with some energy when it's coming through.

Where in your physical body do you experience this — in your third eye and in the neck?

It will throw my head back. Sometimes it will be like being pushed in the stomach, or it will knock the wind out of me; sometimes sounds come out.

And what are you doing when that happens? In a state of meditation?

No, just anytime.

But you're connecting in a certain way — do you recognize that?

It seems like everytime I close my eyes.

Now, you're making the connection but you're missing the connection, because you're trying to connect as you did before the Harmonic Convergence, and the connection has moved so you can't connect in that way. I would ask the soul to give you a new way of connecting, because you're trying to connect — the old Earth is no longer there, and you're being jerked into the new perspective of it. So you might get a healer to help you.

◈ T H R E E ◈

The Alien Consciousness

Early in the Earth's history, eons before Lemuria, your Earth was in a period one might call artistic. There were many artists painting beautiful pictures. There were great schools of art and dance and theater and music. In addition to its artistic endeavors, the civilization was also quite profound. Literature and philosophy were studied. You were close to the spiritual area, quite open to it. Many of the spiritual teachers would take a body form now and then, coming down and enjoying the beauty and the joy of Earth at that time.

Then a new level of awareness opened up within our Source; Source approached a new level. As it made this connection, it brought in a completely different point of view, a consciousness that understood from a different point of view. It attempted to integrate that point of view. This other point of view was, in my opinion, the greatest stretch Source had made. It seemed quite alien.

Now, this alien type of consciousness was not more advanced than the Source we know. It was simply an alternate expression of our Source. I have been attempting to give you a basic understanding of alternate realities, telling you that each time you make a decision one way there is an alternate part of you that experiences the choice you didn't make. That is also true with our Source. Its expression is complete, but it is ever gaining awarenesses and bringing in other points of view.

Our Source and Its learning is research-and-development-oriented, meaning the learning is open-ended as choices are made. As this alien point of view was being digested, we could say a little bit of it came to the physical level in a completely undigested form — it still had its alien point of view. It still did not communicate well with our Source and all of us.

As it approached the Earth, this alien consciousness lived by its own divine rules. It was not a negative expression — it was pure — but it was based upon a different assimilative process, a different way to integrate. Perhaps the most important thing to grasp here is its different system of integration.

Some of what I have just said is quite conceptual. I assure you, as we study this material and begin to explore it, you will truly begin to understand what it meant to humanity to be approached by this alien type of conscious-ness.

The first important point is that this alien consciousness definitely was not negative, but transcendental. It is difficult to comprehend from a physical point of view. We could say that it was not *meant* to interact with the physical level, but it *did*. Now, its assimilative process was to directly project consciousness to the level it was reaching (in this case the physical level) and then directly take the life force from the projections back into itself.

No free will or choices were given to those extensions. They had no direct life of their own. They were simply probes that allowed direct access and the gathering up of life force for the overall consciousness that existed.

As this consciousness approached the Earth, it assumed that its basic means of connecting would be as valid as it was at its point of origination. Humanity's connection with it was, from humanity's point of view, not understanding that there were differences in the very basic areas of life force and the use of consciousness. I will explain how this consciousness connected with humanity.

Keep in mind that although this is, in my opinion, one of the most difficult experiences humanity has ever had, it was not done from a negative point of view, from a conscious desire to hurt humanity. In fact, this consciousness loved its contact with humanity, appreciated the life force it received from humanity, and sent a great deal of love and appreciation. It was not reciprocated. Humanity feared, hated, and fought to be free from what seemed to it to be a completely destructive, negative contact.

Into this peaceful, artistic, joyful society, this consciousness came. It stretched what I will call an umbrella of itself over a particular geographic area of your planet, although it was long before countries existed in that region. That region included France, Spain, Portugal, and reached into the area of Germany, Switzerland, Austria, and a little bit of Italy. It was not, as you will see if you look at a map, a round or square area, but simply, from its point of view, a formation that allowed it (as it began to assimilate) to have the life-force resources on the physical level feed consciousness into itself.

As it made this contact, it literally erected a barrier or a wall. If you lived in the area over which the umbrella of consciousness stretched, you would no longer be able to go beyond certain points where this consciousness had put up barriers. It would be like a big tent, and you could no longer live outside of the tent. There were literally millions of humans within this large tent. Perhaps you were one of them.

If you were, the first thing you noticed was a darkening of the connection with the light. As a tent would come between you and the physical sun, so this consciousness seemed to cut you off from the normal connection you had with the spiritual, your higher self, your soul. Your light got kind of cobwebby or caught up in this consciousness because it was so different in its manifested form from the conscious system you were used to functioning in.

I am going to tell you about one person's experience, a young woman's, and then we will be more general later.

You awoke after the tent of consciousness had settled in and you found you had a headache. Your eyes had difficulty focusing, you noticed a little bit of a sore throat, and sometimes your heart pounded. Sometimes you simply felt tired. Your solar plexus felt stirred up, and there was a feeling of anxiety. The body itself was tired, more tired than usual, yet you did not know why.

You began your day in the normal manner, or tried to, but food tasted strange to you. It was even difficult to dress. In fact, your body didn't seem to be taking directions from your body-mind system very well. You had to think about moving your hand from your food to your mouth. You had to think about moving your arm to bring the food to your mouth.

The body didn't seem to respond automatically. Some of its functions seemed rather impaired, and when you tried to move too fast, your heart pounded. Fatigue created a cold-sweating process within yourself. You thought you were coming down with some sort of illness.

You were to play music, a type of concert, that evening, and you needed to rehearse. You forced yourself to leave your private area, going into another building not far from where you lived and meeting with others to rehearse for the concert. You quickly found out that everyone else felt what you felt, with variations. Some found their body trembling a lot. Some had lost the function of an arm or a leg and were dragging that part.

Since some were musicians who were to use an instrument, it was difficult to see how the concert could go on without certain key musicians. There was a lot of confusion that first morning. Then suddenly a voice broadcast throughout the area. Although it was not a physical voice, it was clear to each of you. It was not harsh or unkind, but simply a powerful transmission. It said, "You will not continue with your activities. These are not necessary. All that is necessary is that we are one." Then suddenly your desire to play music, your desire to communicate with each other, was gone. For a while you simply remained where you were; then each of you got up and moved back to your private headquarters.

You were instructed to remain there. Thus began the process of complete change from the type of life you had to what would be your new way of living. Suddenly all of the buildings, all of the structures you had, were gone. You knew there were no longer buildings, no longer parks, no longer forests, and yet when you looked you could no longer see one another. There was a cobwebby, foggy state like a twilight everywhere.

You could feel the connection with the voice. It told you what to do and you did it, not because you wanted or didn't want to, but because it was there. It was the only link you now had, the only point of connection for you. As I said earlier, even your own soul connection had been interfered with. It no longer spoke to you as part of your knowingness.

For a period of two or three weeks, life went on like this. You were given wonderful food. It appeared, and you were encouraged to eat all of it. Some of you noticed that you put on quite a bit of weight. That seemed all right. Then one morning (at least the voice told you it was morning; you couldn't tell any other way) you were told, "It is time for us to join together more closely." You soon found out that this was the most painful process you had ever been through. The consciousness bored into every cell, taking with it as it left most of your life force.

You were very open and relaxed at this first encounter, not realizing what would occur. About 95% of your life force was withdrawn from your body, leaving only 5% to run the body. Many died after that first contact, so the consciousness learned not to be greedy. Perhaps it was not greedy but simply did not know how much life force could be taken from a human body and still leave a functional structure and a point from which more life force could be gathered — for that, of course, was what this consciousness wanted.

In its system it had used probes. All of you became probes from which it could gather its life force or its consciousness quite directly. It wanted you to eat (and certain other things that we may get into later) to create more life force on the physical level. When the gathering of the life force into your structure reached a certain point, it was drained off through a joining process. The consciousness did not realize at first how painful this was for humanity.

Even after it did realize it, it didn't know what to do about the pain. It needed the life force; it was the means through which it lived. It didn't know another system — it had always used this system. It would be rather similar to asking a substance that is corrosive to a surface not to corrode it. Acid has always been acid, and it doesn't know how to change itself in order not to corrode what it is contacting.

For what was, cosmically, only a brief contact, this consciousness ruled a portion of your Earth. As it used up or killed off the humanity within its umbrella, its tentlike contact, it expanded and expanded and expanded until two-thirds of the Earth was within its sphere of contact.

It was 175 of your Earth years before the cosmic levels could untangle this unintentional contact and this drop (because that is what it was — a spilled drop) of that consciousness could be called to the basic level in order that an assimilative change could be made. Where this "acid" dropped on humanity there certainly was a corroding of fact which now needs to be transmuted.

I know how helpful working with this will be. I will be giving much material related to it. This is simply an introduction or a beginning. I would suggest working with this material in a similar manner to the pre-Lemurian material.

In giving you this information we are seeking to tell humanity what this consciousness was, but we will do it in stages until you get a clear picture of it.

During the initial period of contact with the alien consciousness, humanity was in such a state of shock that little was done to counteract or try to release or get away from the effects of the energy-drainage process. The first organized rebellion took place perhaps twenty years after the first contact. By this time a full 35% or 36% of the original contactees were dead. More of humanity had been recruited, however, through the spreading out of the consciousness on the Earth.

At about the center of the space where the Earth was affected lived a man who suffered tremendously, as everyone else did. Somehow he had the courage to try to organize a resistance. In my opinion, he had been able to save enough of his life force that his brain functioned more clearly than most. How did he do this? Well, perhaps within the intricacy of the brain lies the answer to that; I am not here to discuss that today. The point is, he had perhaps 10% to 12% of his life force left at the end of the draining process. Most of you, by the time everything settled in, had 6% or 7% left.

After the draining, you simply existed for perhaps two or three weeks. You were force-fed by the alien consciousness itself: It literally injected minute parts of the life force back into you — not much (probably one-fourth of 1% of what you had given up), but done in strategic locations of your physical body. It was helpful.

This alien consciousness found out that when it injected some life force directly back into the sexual area, its probe (which it, remember, considered you to be) began to revive and to again generate more life force on the physical level. So the sexual area activated first. Although it was not a joining together of two human beings, the sexual area was so active as a result of the injections that people were quite prone to very personal sexual releasing through many, many stimulations, some of which humanity still uses within self to release sexual pressure. There were other methods peculiar to the situation humanity was in then.

Gradually, through the gathering of this sexual energy, there was a flow of energy to the other chakras and a sense of being able to function; a renewal process began. For most, the draining took place every three to four months. Almost always, half this period, or the next two months after the draining, were very static or nonactive periods. During the third month you felt more normal, but in the fourth month there was the anxiety, the terror, the fear coming up from what you knew was again approaching.

This cyclic effect continued for most of you until, through what I will call an overeagerness, the consciousness drained so much of your personal energy that your body did not survive. Almost all of you died physically in this process. If you were involved with it, you died with it. There were a few who were still alive, but only a few of them are still on your Earth.

This experience involves so much fear, anxiety, pain, loss, destruction and betrayal that we must release it in stages, in levels. I know that once it has been released, humanity will be free of what has definitely prevented the trusting of *cosmic consciousness*. Can you see that there was an initial trust through linking to this alien consciousness? It seemed wonderful. It brought you love, it brought you the link, the connection. But it seemed to betray what you already knew or had experienced before this.

It was such an alien point of view that it blotted out or took away your memories of being clearly connected spiritually. It has definitely had a clouding effect upon humanity's ability to receive from the spiritual level.

We are all delighted to have this experience coming to "light" within the consciousness of humanity.

✧ F O U R ✧

Life Itself Supports You

WELCOME! GOOD EVENING, MY FRIENDS. WELL, I SEE HERE SOME FRIENDS who we've been working with on the inner level – and I say "we" because there are many who are together on the inner level. Then there are a few I haven't had the privilege of being with before, so in your cases I welcome you to our discussion.

I would like you first to feel the energies a little. This is a powerful time to be here on the Earth, isn't it? If you don't like the energy, wait five minutes. That's about the way it is – there is so much shifting and so much changing. I have spent the day rather focused here in the Sedona area. It was peaceful and yet hopeful; there was an awakening of the energies here – an awakening that I think will serve the whole area well.

There is an integration beginning to take place in this area; I think you might notice what I'm talking about within six months. And today was one of the first days when I noticed an effort at cooperation between the various aspects, the various neighborhood energies. There was a neighborhood gathering in which the energies conversed and some of the conversing became quite harmonious.

I love the title given me tonight; it's very interesting. Certainly it is clear how you here on the Earth are so connected to all the other levels. If we can give you a glimpse tonight of that connection in a way that you may not have noticed before, our evening together will have been well spent.

You all know you're connected; your mental body and your heart say, "We're connected to something greater, I know we are." But perhaps you never thought of it in quite the way I'm going to present it to you tonight. Perhaps together we can glimpse the next step in understanding how to be more open, how to be more into "it" on the physical level. And what is "it"? Well, it is life in the fullest sense. It is life as it flows, life as it magnifies, life as it enlarges, life as it supports, life as you can live it in the fullest sense, my friends. It seems to me that what is awakening is the fullness of life.

What do we mean by a New Age? Some have called it the Golden Age. I think we could call it anything we wanted to, but it's the realization that life exists here in a completely different way than it has ever existed here before. In other words, you don't live on the same planet. Now, your head knows that, but perhaps some of your patterns of behavior say, "I can't see that much change" or "I'm looking at my life and there's so much change I can't see anything else but change, and the change gets in the way of seeing what life can be." For some of you that is what is happening. There is a tremendous amount of change on the Earth.

The purpose of this period, in my opinion, is to get used to all the change, and to really recognize that the change is coming up so that you can see that change is the constant that exists — that change is literally what you can count on. It's always going to be there. If you have a circumstance in your life and you don't like it, then you can count on change to resolve it. If you have something that you do like, you can count on change to enlarge it, to make it even better, to enhance it and to help you understand yourself and that situation in a greater way. Isn't that nice! That's the plan.

You All Helped Plan Earth

There really is a plan. And who conceived the plan? Well, we always talk about the Creator doing that, but you all helped. Do you realize that you really got involved at a basic level and helped to bring this plan to the Earth? I don't think many of you know that. But when the Source said, "There's going to be an Earth," you all said, "Well, let's put in this and let's put in that, and we'll see about it — and I volunteer to come." The point is that you *did* help plan the Earth.

The concept of the Earth was really brought in through your energy, and if you have been here at all you might say, "I haven't been here since the beginning of the Earth." And many of you have not. But remember, where the Earth was planned, there is no time. Thus the concept of Earth in the nowness was something that you helped to create. Some of you said, "I think we should have elephants." The Creator said, "What's an elephant?" So you created an elephant. Yes, isn't that interesting? I don't know who did giraffes, but I'm going to find out because I'm very fond of them. This is really an original concept. Have you ever looked at a giraffe? He really is impossible, and yet there he is — a lovely animal. The flowers here are unique too. So I think some of you who were involved with the Earth have creative abilities that we don't see very often in the cosmos.

You might say, "But I've been on many planets." In fact, some of your metaphysical literature says that you're from a particular planet. In my belief system, and I think in most of yours, that really isn't true, because you are from Source — you are from everywhere. You aren't from one particular planet. What may have happened is that you spent quite a lot of time in a particular system — a Pleiadian system or an Orion system or some other universe system. But in the fullest sense now there is a focus here in regard to the Earth. Earth is the launching pad that you are looking for. I am emphasizing this because some of you are trying to leave. Some of you are saying, "I want to go here and I want to go there," while there are so many standing in line to come *here*, to the Earth.

You might be interested to know that we are doing some Earth tours this summer. And what I mean is that those beings who have either never been physical or haven't been physical for a long time are coming here on tours to see the Earth, and we are providing a vehicle. It looks rather like, spiritually speaking, kind of a box. We can gather up consciousness and put it in the box, and it would be rather like an undersea boat. Many people could come and see the underwater life here. So these beings that aren't physical can get in this little spiritual box and come and view the Earth.

Now, you might get in touch with that because it is quite a tour — it is quite popular right now. You might not think that spiritual beings would do such things, but they do, and you're kind of the "in" planet right now. One reason is the things that are occurring here — the joining of the East and West, the breakthroughs you are making in communication and consciousness, and the fact that you have been quite solid in the third dimension but are now rising to the doorway of the fourth dimension. The spiritual beings that come can be focused, but they can view the history of your planet and see the probabilities of the future. So they get a tour, you might say, of the progression of consciousness that has been taking place on your planet.

It is like part of a learning, an educational thing, and it gives us ideas about what to do next time — and perhaps, my friends, what *not* to do next time. There are things that perhaps you wouldn't want to repeat. There are certain animals that didn't work out; they just didn't survive. There are certain structures that would not be repeated. You had one that was about eight feet tall with an arm in the center of the back — and it kept falling over. The arms were little, only about this long from about the shoulders, plus one in the back. It was very thin and kept falling over. It would get down on its back and then have trouble getting up again. So some of these things that didn't work out will not be repeated.

Existence Is a Research Project

Now, why am I saying this? It is because *I don't want you to forget that all of existence is literally a research project.* Some of you think about experience on another level as being perfect. Perfection is not in the experience, generally; it is in the state of being. The Creator is perfect in Its being. You are perfect in your being. But the experience is a research-and-development project, you see. And it doesn't always turn out, even on the cosmic level, the way we think it might. This is very important, because you are looking for someone to help you achieve a level of perfection, an orderly structure. I have news for you: It is always going to evolve and become something greater. And you're going to perhaps throw out what doesn't work and say, "Well, that was a nice try in this area, but it just doesn't work."

And why is that important? Because your emotional bodies are looking for something that perhaps is not quite achievable. You can't find it in the doingness; you have to find it within you and within others in the beingness.

As you relate to each other, how many of you say, "Oh, they did that to me" or "Look what they're doing" or "Look what they're not doing"? You're looking at patterns of behavior — you aren't looking at the divine beingness within that person. They're using a certain pattern of behavior but that's not the real person. So the mirrors of existence (certainly all of you recognize that on a physical level everything is a mirror) are educational. Certainly they may show you patterns of behavior within yourself that at that moment you wish you hadn't seen — "That one again; look at that, it's coming in again." But it will also show you through the mirror the divine perfection that is within you, if you can see it, if you can look deeply enough.

Even God is Learning

As I look at this beautiful little one, what I see is her perfection. Yes, there are a few things she's learning, but in the fullest sense everything on every level is learning, including the Creator, including God. Many of you don't think of the Creator, or Source, or God, in those terms. You think about it as something that knows all and certainly has achieved everything. Now, the words "certainly achieved" and "doingness" are ever-progressive. That is the process of evolution. Beingness is something else; it is perfect, it is understanding, but it evolves, too. Beingness evolves through its expression, through its allowingness to be expressed through all of us.

One of the most important things that you are learning is humility. I say this often because, my friends, if I say something to you 10,000 times, still you might tell me on the 10,001st time, "I never heard that before; isn't that interesting?" And I say, "Yes, isn't it nice we discussed it?" Thus one thing you are seeking to understand is what I call humility, true humility. What does that mean? Well, there have been books written about it, about people who are very humble, who perhaps don't take for themselves, they don't know anything. That's not what I mean by true humility.

I mean someone who, when they see you, makes you feel that you have an equal partner there, that they are equal to you, and that you are equal to me — in other words, true equality. You're trying to see it in everything, everyone and everywhere — on every level. Even a child of four months is equal to you, though some of you think they know more. These young ones are really very, very aware. But the point is, the creative abilities are equal. The strengths are not expressed equally yet, but they will be, given time.

Let's think of the Source as a circle, and each one of us within It as a particular point. And you have a strength. What is *your* greatest strength? The good news is that underneath the patterns of behavior is that beautiful heart, and that's what I see. The point is that each of you has your strengths, even if sometimes you don't see them. We see them, and it is the combination of all of these strengths that we call the Creator.

You've heard this many times, but I'm going to say it again: Without you, creation would not be complete. It is true, absolutely true. Validate that, see that life itself loves you — because we could talk about the Creator, as It expresses, as life itself. It appreciates you. It's the nurturing that you're looking for. The expression of life is there for you, supportive of you, loving you, appreciating you. And it doesn't even matter what the circumstances are in your life; this love is never lost; it's there for you. When you can realize this, then you can say, "Aha, I get it! Life *itself* loves me. Life itself appreciates me and I appreciate it. Look how fortunate I am to be here. Look at what's been given to me. I am here. This is a gift." And do you see what that does? It makes a connection, and for some of you it is the connection that you are looking for.

Some of your emotions are stirred up, so I would say that support is one of the issues — or a feeling of not being supported, of being alienated or cut off. If you can feel the support, then anything is possible, and the means to be supported are there for you. I'd like you to close your eyes for just a moment, if you would.

"Life Itself Supports You" Meditation

❦ *You are alive. There is life force, and there is energy flowing in you and between you, among all of us, literally. I would like you to sense that. Let's make it a particular color: gold. And let's say that this gift is from the Creator, a gift of golden energy, and we are symbolizing this as life itself. It flows now; it flows in you and flows from you to others and then flows back again. Each time it does, it vitalizes you. Now let it go, my friends, to the cells – to each cell, which is a miniature universe. And let that universe receive this gold and let it wake up, wake up, wake up and say, "I am supported. I can feel this life force within me. It is life itself supporting me, life itself supporting me; life itself supports me." Say it with me, "Life itself supports me." Good. Yes.*

❦ *Now see what that does to your heart. I see in many of you an opening that says, "Can I really believe that? Can I really trust it?" And life says, "Try me, my friends. Try me and see."*

Monadic-Level Watching

Open your eyes again. Life is willing to prove it. Isn't that interesting! It will prove it to you if you allow it. When you realize, "Aha, life supports me," then two or three things happen. There is an opening, and those parts of you that are on a cosmic level say, "We got it, we got it! There is a connection made!" And the universe begins to respond. Several things happen. The monadic level (which in my definition is your contact with the Source) looks down with binoculars at what you're doing on the physical level and says, "I wonder how much I'm going to learn through this focus." Did you know that? You think about it the other way around, but some of Source could be a little bit on pins and needles. "Good, good. Look, look how well he (or she) is doing!" Very exciting. I think you can really feel that excitement now; I know I can.

So, looking through the binoculars, the realization is made – "Life is supporting me" – and the information goes back to the monad, which says, "Wonderful! Look at that. Life is supporting me." And in its immense understanding or immense power to understand, it begins to pull in the resources on a very wide scale. Now, if it dumped all those on the physical, you would go into a state of shock – literally, because it is such an immense power. But it filters through your soul. You've heard that a time or two. So the soul says, "Wait a minute. The physical structure at this time can hold so much life force and so much energy. We'll open it a little, step by step, but we won't burn it out like the other one. We won't burn it out; we'll regulate it a little."

Many of you have had a burnout because the monadic level has sent you too much energy. So perhaps you learn to go through the channels (familiar word); the channels in this case are the soul level and its various support teams. What does that mean? Well, it means the angels. And it means (I talked about it when I was here last, and I'm still excited about it) a cosmic walk-in. The cosmic walk-in is really a cosmic consultant beyond your own soul, beyond that part that your soul knows. There are other specialists that are now coming in to consult with your soul, and when you ask for help, it works. There is a whole team that goes to work. Or when you say, "Aha, I am supported by life itself," the team goes to work to create that, because you with the Creator have connected with it, and everything starts to happen. Isn't that exciting! It really is exciting that the cosmic walk-in process works that way. It does!

Now it will bring the next step, whatever that is. And if there is something that is in the way, then it will bring that through the mirrors to take a look at. Isn't that exciting? Sometimes it is, and sometimes you don't think it's too exciting. But that next step will appear in your life, and as I watch all of you, I notice that it comes in almost immediately now. That's the pickup in the pace – for many of you, within an hour. Now, that's pretty quick, isn't it? For some of you it comes within ten hours. If you're really into resisting, it might take a whole week, but that's not too bad. It's hard to release these next steps, but once you've seen that life is supporting you, you can allow it.

Remember that we talked earlier about change. Some have said, "I would like my life to go this way. This is the way I'm going. This is my path." Even if you don't know exactly what your path is, you'll still be this way. Because many of you ask me, "What is my purpose? What is my path?" You have at least a basic belief that says, "I'm going this way. This is the way." Notice the vision now. If you're tunneled into "I'm going this way, I'm going this way," the opportunities over here can't get your attention. They may say, "Yoohoo, yoohoo," but you're focused here on going the other way.

So perhaps you have to broaden your horizons and look around and see what opportunities may be there. They come in many ways. Perhaps an opportunity doesn't knock at your door and say, "I'm an opportunity." You may have to discover it. You will usually discover it through the circumstances that are already in your life, although you may meet someone who has a new suggestion or a new slant for looking at something. They may say to Alicia over here, "Alicia, why don't you set up a training center in Phoenix, because the things you are trained to do would be very beneficial for them." It might be that direct. Or it might simply be someone saying, "What is it you learned in Germany, Alicia? What have you been trained to do?" It may come in to get you thinking about it and wonder why that came up: "Why was that mirrored to me?"

My point is, when you are aware enough, when you are conscious enough to see what the mirror is bringing to you, then the opportunity and your creative base, the way you live your life, will expand. Because life is busy trying to bring you that support that you truly believe in. It says, "Yes, yes, yes. You're ready, you're ready! I have a live one, I have one that's ripe! Good, now we're ready to begin to support you."

Can you imagine the universe trying to support you but you being busy running away from the support because you don't believe in it? (I don't think it ever gets frustrated, but it might a little bit.) The point is that it's much harder to resist your progress than to accept it, although some of you have done quite well in resisting. As soon as you say, "Life supports me; why does it support me?" take it to the next step and say, "Because I've been supporting life." That's the next step: acknowledging what you've done.

You may look at your life and say, "I haven't done that much." You probably have done more for humanity in this life than you know, but let's look at the whole life you've lived on the Earth and the lives that you've lived other places. Let's take into consideration the whole spiritual experience. You've stored up what we could call brownie points all over the place. You've put them in storage there because you didn't know what to do with them. The universe didn't know how to bring the two of you together because you were so busy saying, "I'm not supported." You might not have said that, but you might not have consciously acknowledged that you *are* supported.

Your Emotional Body Connects You

Now, this is important because your emotional body is what connects you. It is the part of you that makes the connection, whether to other people or to the next step or to an important realization process that can lead to the next step.

When doing personal intensives, one of the most important things we do is process the emotional body and help it feel it is a part of your team. Many of you have taken those emotions and said, "Go away. You're in the way there. Go away; I can't stand all this pain." Or "I don't like this loss or this anger. I don't use emotions anymore." I can almost quote some of you. "I don't use emotions anymore because they get in the way. They are just not serving me well."

Well, what you do there is to set up a kind of rock. You put it right here in the solar plexus, making a little core there, and then you keep adding to it. I've seen one recently that had 36 layers of emotions buried in the solar plexus. What do you think happens to it? It gets very crystallized. It doesn't function very well. Those of you who work to process emotions with this crystallization know it is important to get that area softened up so it won't be so brittle, so it can flow better. As you let those emotions out, sometimes it's interesting, because the beliefs still say, "If I let them out, I'm in trouble."

So you have to begin to relate to the emotional body through this humility, or through this equal-partner type of approach. For most of you the important thing is to have your mental body acknowledge that the emotional body could be important; that's a major step for many of you. It seems as if the emotional body is in the way.

What about the people who have a lot of emotion that seems to be there all of the time? For one thing, acknowledge that it's a strength: "You know how to be emotional. You know how to use your emotions. Good for you. You have a strength." Next time I ask you what your strength is, you can say, "I know how to use my emotional body." You might not be using it as clearly as you would like yet, but the emotions are out and being used. You see, someone who doesn't know how to use the emotional body has to begin to dig and bring it up — and that's hard, my friends, if you've pushed it down for a long time.

What I mostly do with all of you in the work that we do together is to look at what we call polarity splits. What do I mean by that? I mean that when you try to take the next step and connect into it, something says the opposite. Generally, it has an emotional connotation — there is either a loss from the past or an anger from something in the past or a sense of frustration from the past, or some other emotion. It says, "I remember that pattern of behavior; that one didn't serve us well." So it says, "I'm not going that way; I'm pulling back this way."

When I talk about this, I think it is important to recognize that the part that tries to pull back in the emotional split is only about 5%. This means that 95% of you is well on the way, is willing to take that next step. It's only 5% that doesn't want to cooperate because there's so much fear from the past. This doesn't mean that the 5% can't get in your way. If you've got a gearing system that has one hundred gears, and five of them don't work, it's sometimes like the vehicle coming along with a flat tire — you can still move the vehicle but it goes a-thump, a-thump, a-thump. It's not energized as clearly as you would like. And that a-thump gets in the way sometimes.

Now the realization process: I've given you an example because I think it is so important — "Life supports me." Your realization may be, "*I am worthy as a divine being.*" Whatever it is, it begins to change that, it beings to resolve the fears, the angers, the resistance. You begin to see:

🐦 *That's from the past. I have that from the past. It has nothing to do with now or my present opportunities if I can see beyond that old pattern of behavior. Life is trying to bring me what I want, and I bring life the possibilities that I see in it. In return I give life my strengths. I give it my creativity; I am willing to be creative.*
These are good affirmations; you see that.
🐦 *I am willing to serve, and then I am served in return. I am supported. I am allowed to be as great as I believe I am.*

Isn't that an interesting thought: "I'm allowed to be as great as I believe I am." We don't get that out of proportion; we don't say that you are greater than other people. We say that you are a creative spark that has a unique point of view, one that no one else has. Only you have that. And Source has Its loving, allowing gift that has been given to you, and has asked you to use it. It didn't say, "I don't like to have you use it." Source didn't say, "I have a pattern of behavior that says you may not be able to use it." It didn't say, "Use it more later." It just gave you the gift and said, "Please experience, express, and I will enjoy it. I will be in contact with you as you express it."

What I see in 1990 is an opening on the Earth that will allow the fuller expression, I would say, of at least 50% more creativity in this year, if you are willing to do it. What do I mean by that? Let's say that you always wanted to be a ballerina. Why not? You know that is your goal, and you get on your toes, but it's just not comfortable. I know that you don't get on your toes right away. But let's say you just don't think you can ever get up on your toes. That's your belief structure. I say that this year you can get up on your toes. Why? Because you have the support system on several levels that says, "Let go of that which you thought was a barrier, and let's move beyond it."

Now, what does that take? Only one thing: *You have to ask.* That's it. It's that simple. When you come to a barrier, you must ask for help with it. Who do you ask? Well, how about your soul, to start with? Then if you want to place all your bets, you can ask the Creator, you can ask the angels, you can ask this cosmic part of you that is the cosmic walk-in that is helping. You can ask us, your teachers and your friends. You can ask each other. It doesn't matter how many times and how many ways you ask, but if you will ask, the barriers will begin to dissolve. That I am absolutely sure of. And

I don't say anything without thinking about it and really believing it. It's absolutely true, my friends.

Sometimes you don't know where your barriers are. Have you noticed that? Then once in a while you make an Aha! — a realization — and you think, "I didn't know that I had a block there, but it's been there all along." It's as if it is standing in the doorway. But if you find any area at all, anywhere that you're limited — absolutely anything anywhere — then that's a block, because you're meant to be completely unlimited in all ways. On the Earth? Yes, on the Earth!

The Earth is unlimited. You may say, "Well . . . ." But it is. It is an expression, though perhaps the energy format is not as widely scoped as at the Source level. I am not saying it is. But Earth is perhaps even more powerful in physical form, because it is more specific; it has a specificness physically, that it doesn't have spiritually. If you can see that, then you get a look at any area, anything where you are limited.

Why don't you all practice levitation, for example — or teleportation, or precipitation, or telepathy? You are meant to do these things. There is no one here in the room who hasn't used these abilities before. None of these things are new. Bill, you once knew how to teleport all over the planet. It was very easy. You did it very well. You appeared and disappeared, and people said, "Where's Bill?" They didn't know. The point is, these are not new abilities. Reba has floated around the cosmos many times, been to other universes and understood how to open many, many doors. She only has to remember, or perhaps trust, that this is there, and she will be able to use it now in this life.

One of the most important things that can happen is opening your third eye. Practice that.

   ❧ *A good exercise is to see or to imagine a blue light coming from the third eye. Project it, and look around someone's auric field. Look just around their body. Look at the electrical storage system. It is about that wide for some of you; sometimes it's this wide. It moves, of course – it's life force. Look at it and get in touch with its movement. Look and see if there are spaces in it, because you all have gaps in it. Smooth it, look at it, and try to see it. Then look beyond that at the auric field. Look at the emotional body, which is about this far from the physical body. Look at the mental body, which may be out this far. Look at the spiritual body, which may spread this far or this far, depending on how vitalized you are at the moment. If you are channeling, it may spread much, much further.*

Now, this life force is not just static. It moves. [Vywamus looks at someone in the front row.] For example, there is a beautiful yellow here that is moving, that is tumbling this way. And interacting with it is some green that is moving this way. There's a little silver that sparks, sparks, sparks, sparks, sparks. And she has a fountain of gold here in the head.

Learn to project through the third eye and in a sense disconnect the physical eyes a little, then use your knowingness to fill in the gaps. In other words, what you can't see, you know; and what you don't know, you try to see. You connect through the two processes: your third eye and your knowingness, which is perhaps for some of you more open than the third eye. Then pretty soon you're going to tell me what the auric field looks like.

And why is that important? Because your emotional bodies are looking for something that perhaps is not quite achievable. You can't find it in the doingness; you have to find it within yourself and within others in the beingness. When everyone can see everybody's auric field, are you going to have any surprises when you come here? Everybody will see where everybody else is. If someone has a power hang-up, you're going to see it as an angry, dull, pulsating red that irritates and is all over that auric field, that darkens it, that's like a possession. It's not pretty, my friends; you're going to see that. And you will probably have a place where these people can be put — not a jail, but a processing center where they can be helped to get over their power hang-ups.

You can also see where there are gaps in the etheric systems; these indicate that you've used up some of your storage system. This is when you get tired quickly and you don't recover soon because you don't have any reserves. You could have, and you will have, temples where people are assisted before they get so depleted. You will be able to see it.

The New Age Is Now

It is time for all of you to say, "Yes, this is the New Age. That time is here now." It's not later. It's not twenty years from now. It's now that we can begin to use these skills. I would like to see you have someone here — and it could be any of you, wherever you are from — having people come and telling them what their aura looks like, and then training others to do the same thing. Because as you do that, it's going to spread. You'll love this one.

One reason you're here in Sedona is that you have accepted some New Age responsibilities beyond what some others have accepted. That's not negative; be glad, rejoice. It means that you are aware enough that that responsibility is yours. The more you grow and the more you evolve, the greater your level of responsibility becomes. I tell you from experience, the more fun it gets, too, because you get to use your creativity in ever-more-expansive ways.

Perhaps as a summary of this half of our evening, I would like to say that *when you love life enough to recognize it loves you, then it responds and all of your blocks melt away as if by magic!*

I consider this cosmic walk-in that I mentioned to be perhaps the single most important thing that has ever happened on the Earth. It's that important. It's an opening beyond your personality.

For eons you have been working up to that. "I must recognize myself as the whole" — that's the goal, isn't it? You may not have known it before you got into metaphysics, but as you get deeper into metaphysics you find that out — "I'm going to eventually recognize myself as the whole." Well, the first major step is having a consultant that knows how to integrate, how to bring you past those barriers. And it is there for you. That cosmic walk-in/integrator is waiting for you to acknowledge it and to talk to it. Isn't that wonderful? It's on your team, you could say.

I'd like to draw these steps. We could say that here is the Earth, and then on another level (if we use it as levels or steps) is the Hierarchy, your local neighborhood government — we'll call it that — and the teachers you recognize: certainly St. Germain and Djwhal Khul and Lord Kuthumi, many of these beings that are doing a wonderful job in regulating and helping you have the planet that you like.

Above that — if you will, the next connection — is the solar level. You recognize Helios as your Solar Logos. Above that is the Galactic Core. Now, the galactic level is divided into four different sections, so we are talking about this quadrant of the Galactic Core. At the time of the Harmonic Convergence, the teachers that are on that level came in, as did a part of you that exists on that level.

Here's the Earth. See, it's a nice flow. From the top, you see the universal, the galactic, the solar and the local (I'm sure Djwhal Khul will want to be called local). The galactic level opened up at the time of the Harmonic Convergence. What is occurring now is that you are making brief contacts with the universal level.

The universal, then, is the level your cosmic walk-ins are coming from. They are trained at the universal level. This means that you are stretching your consciousness into a level that you have never been able to reach before from here, and having it come through the system, through each level, right into your life as a consultant to help you flow that life. See that. That's so exciting — to have a breakthrough that says,

> I may be focused here as an individual, but I can draw upon the resources of this whole level now that these experts in existence are making themselves available to me.

We could call that a team of beings, truly. They have not really been physical. Some of them were, eons and eons ago, but most of them are certainly no longer physical. Still they have expertise about the physical level through the universal perspective. I might say that some of us have to relearn about physical existence. I did.

Fourth-Dimensional Time

Time was interesting for me; I didn't remember time. I hadn't been on the physical level for a very long time, and I didn't remember how to sequence time. I was used to having it just be there, all in one nice lump.

It seemed simpler than having to remember the 24 hours in the day, because when I arrived you were in the third dimension and you had your seconds and minutes and hours and days. Now, the good news is, in the fourth dimension it doesn't work that way. Have you noticed? Have you ever of late gotten to a place much sooner than you thought you possibly could? Time is moving this way. It's a flow. You are no longer in the third dimension, or at least the possibility is there that you don't have to use it by sequencing time. *You're not locked into the third dimension* unless your old beliefs put you there and say, "Well, I have an hour before that appointment and all of these things to do." How about relaxing and saying, "I have these things to do and I have the time to do them, and then I have the appointment." See, it begins to reverse the use of time, so that you become the one that uses time, rather than time using you, as has happened to you a great deal in this third dimension.

The flow is there for you in the fourth dimension. These beings that are really locked into the flow couldn't reach you in the third dimension. It wasn't feasible to set up their use in the third dimension because they are able to help you flow what you need when you need it. They don't block it into minutes and seconds. It's kind of an exciting thing. But it is truly the most important point. Why is that? Again, I think the key is that it helps you stretch beyond what you thought was your individuality. Can you see how important that is? "I have resources now that I can use *beyond* my individuality."

In the Beginning . . .

The Source gave you a gift; it was your unlimitedness, your creativity. The Source then divided Itself up and said, "I want to do this because it's fun, because I'll enjoy it, because I get to share." These are the reasons for doing it. But as far as you were concerned, before you were individualized you were in the womb of Source, and you could stretch out and feel here — the feeling is the key here — and you could feel here and feel here. You were just floating; nothing was required of you, and it was nice and comfortable. And then Source said, "It's time to wake up. I've individualized you." And many of you said, "Who, me? No, I'm sleepy. I want to sleep this morning. I'm not ready to wake up."

Well, whether or not you were ready, it was time to wake up. Now, that's a fact. The first thing you experienced was a sense of individual movement, and because you hadn't experienced on an individual basis, it seemed to be taking you out of something. You didn't have the experience you had had before. You were now a being. There was a change, a comprehensive change.

And then we look at our circle [Oneness] and we see that it's been divided up. There were seemingly some barriers. In other words, "I stretch here and that's as far as my individuality goes. What do you mean, I'm just a piece here? Before, I could feel this whole thing. Now there's only my individuality. What does that mean?"

Many of you formed some beliefs about that: Did I do something wrong? Why am I here? Why am I limited? Why am I just a piece, if before I was the whole thing? You see, the emotional body gets caught up in the process and might not see the purpose of the process. For some of you that's very important.

Others said, "Oh well, there must be a purpose," and you began to look. And what you saw was literally the purpose. First of all, the Source said, "Look, look. Here's what you're going to grow up to be. Looks just like me, doesn't it?" And you said, "Good, good. When?" And the Source said, "When you're ready." But the next words you didn't necessarily hear. Those next words were, "I'll give you a process in which to do it. I'll give you what is called a cocreator plan." And you might have said, "Oh, there are others? There are others?" And the Source said, "Look around you. There are others. And this that I gave you is the whole plan."

Many of you said, "I want all of that now!" And again the voice said, "When you are ready, when you are ready." And you said, "But I'm ready now." And the Source said, "All right, then begin." And you started your journey.

The Eternal Journey to Wholeness

You see, you might not have understood at that point that it was an eternal journey. It seemed like just a step or two. You could say that your emotional body kept checking and said, "When will I be that which I have been promised? When will I be in the Wholeness again?" And then you began to ask, "When will I go back to that Wholeness, back to that Wholeness, back to that Wholeness?" Well, you never went out of it! But you didn't understand that this great gift was an eternal one that will keep stretching you. It will keep enlarging you.

Now, there is a time when you will recognize yourself as that Wholeness – the same as the Source Itself. What happens then? I don't know. I haven't gotten there, either. But what I am sure of is that that will not be the end. Because we know, my friends, that there are levels of Sourceness, and one thing that I help people to understand is that our Source is always merging into another level of Sourceness and enlarging Itself. And many of you have been bridges between the two levels. So we know that there is a process that is always enlarging and always becoming greater.

Now, some of you, when you didn't want to get up, said, "I want to go back to the womb. I want to go back and go to sleep again." Here's where you were, and you were going this way. [Vywamus draws.] Do you notice something wrong with that picture? The emotional body is not paying any attention over here, is it? When it understands what we've been talking about, it will be saying, "Life supports me." We're talking about your emotions turning around and noticing the support that is there for it in the eternal process, the process of life, of enlarging and understanding. So it is the emotions that have to be educated and taught.

I have a difficulty that I've heard many other people say they have: sticking with meditation and finding a meditation technique that works. Do you have any suggestions?

In the first place, I think there are about 8,000 different ways to meditate, so one is bound to work. In other words, do not force yourself to do one that's difficult; find one that's easy for you. How about a meditation where you walk in nature? You like that one? I think that would work for you. It can be as deep a meditation as sitting in the lotus position or whatever other meditation you do. There is one that is just right for you now. That doesn't mean that it can't change later. But I would not force something that's difficult. Do one that's easy — that's my advice.

When you say to walk in nature, do you mean literally to walk in nature, or to sit and imagine walking in nature?

No, I mean literally walking in nature — a moving meditation. Then what are you doing? Well, you're not thinking about your grocery list. You're thinking about the beauty of the Earth, you're getting into the responses of the Earth, you're digging deeply into the wonderful civilizations that have been here. You're saying to that cosmic walk-in, "Support me in this movement and allow me to understand as I move." I say, "move," and right now the movement is probably very important for balance. Anytime you're out of balance, move. You can dance. You don't have to go for a hike, but in this area it seems very appropriate to hike around.

Some of us have a misunderstanding in this individualization process — we think we're being punished, or it doesn't feel right, and our emotional bodies have closed down to the unlimitedness. Why didn't anybody tell us? Why didn't we hear it?

They did tell you. Tell *me* why you didn't hear it. I said earlier that if we tell you something long enough, eventually you do hear it. You're just now in the process of hearing it. Let's put it this way: On the spiritual level it's very difficult to get these things, to make these realizations. About the time you seek to do so, you float by them, in a sense, because something else has your attention.

In fact, that's what the physical level is for — to focus and enlarge the areas that you don't understand until you *do* get it. That is what it's for, and that is why it's such a privilege to be here — because there are many, many spiritual beings who either said, "I don't want to be on the physical level," or had circumstances such that they don't go to the physical level but have a harder time. This doesn't mean that there is emotional trauma on that level; there isn't. But it's a stuckness in the use of one's unlimitedness. And none of you will have that, because you've given yourself a gift: you've come to the physical level.

So when you ask, "Why hasn't it been done before?" maybe the timing is just right now to do it in your evolution. Why does the child walk? Well, they walk when they're ready.

It just seems that so much trauma could be avoided if that understanding were clear at the beginning.

But this is the process that is used to clear it. That's the purpose of the physical level. Can you see that?

I don't exactly understand walk-ins from the universal level. Are these our guides and higher selves?

No. I'm going to write a whole book on it. I know you don't all understand it. It's not the usual type of walk-in — nothing has walked out. Your soul has built a foundation here in your life, and what is coming in is an expert, a consultant who can help you to be more unlimited in your life. It comes from a level of consciousness that is clearer than you've ever been able to contact on the physical level.

Why is there so much excitement lately about extraterrestrials and so-called aliens?

Extraterrestrials

Well, they've always been here, but it may be more visible now. They've been here since the beginning of your Earth, and at times you've all been very excited about it.

Is this awareness increasing?

The means to communicate are increasing, so you all know that everyone else is excited, which excites you more. It says to you that there's progress being made. You know, we're making a connection, a link, and I find it very positive because about 95% of these beings are positive ones that are trying to help you.

There seems to be so much fear.

Well, there are the old patterns, and there are many of them. This is something that we look at deeply. They're all from the subconscious. For example, if as a small boy you were taken aboard a vehicle, and something probed you and looked at everything, causing pain in your body, you might have a few fears about it in this life. I want to add that it might not have been negative beings who did that. They might simply not have had the capacity to understand that that would hurt you.

I've been told that there are some wonderful things that are going to happen in Sedona within the next year or two. Can you give us some hint as to what they might be?

Changes in Sedona

I think there will be some facilities set up for healing that can use many of your abilities in a more organized way. Instead of somebody doing this here and somebody doing this here, I see the beginning of a more organized effort. There will definitely be some contacts (and there are already, but more visual contacts) from other planets. I think it's time for that. And Sedona is a very special area, energywise. I think one thing I have looked for for a long time that may begin to happen in this period is the coming together of all the vortexes' energies into one very large energy that is more integratable and more integrated. Now, what do you think would result from that?

More balanced energies.

Good, good. And more available for use. Sometimes when you try to use the energy from one vortex, another one wipes it out. Are you aware of that? They don't all energize you at the same rate, and it's very difficult to use them together. So if they get their act together, and I think they will, then it will be easier to use them here.

We could also call Sedona a dimensional door. I didn't say about the cosmic walk-ins that the reason you get so much cosmic help is that *you're going to be integrating dimensions and other realities into this life.* And I think you might see it especially here in Sedona. For example, if one part of you decides to get married, there's another part that doesn't get married, and that part that doesn't get married is living a life in another reality just as the part that got married is living a life here in this reality. The goal now is to integrate all of these probable realities.

If the energies of Sedona get as strong as I think they will, and more integrated, that's going to be a strength that will draw all of those alternate realities and various dimensional experiences together into one powerful focus that you can use in your life. Now, that's probably the most exciting thing. There are many ways of answering your question. I hope that helps.

With this growing spirituality that we can anchor here – and part of it is growing here – this community could well become exploited by development. I've seen more signs going up, saying "land for sale," and tourists coming in, and there may be some type of censorship related to the energies here to suppress and make it hard to make a living.

Well, you know there will be the need to communicate. And perhaps there will be the need for those of you who feel one way to make those beliefs that you have about your Earth really known – in other words, to work together to prevent that exploitation. I'm not negating what you, humanity, do to help get rid of, let's say, pollution and such things that are happening on your Earth. But I'm telling you that you're using a very small shovel. It's not that I don't encourage you to do it together; I do, mostly because it teaches you how to work together, to stand up for what you believe and to try to change things.

But there is a higher plan, and that higher plan is going to be what makes the difference in all of these major areas. One example is pollution. There are energy changes, shifts that will deal with that.

I don't understand the mechanics of all the vortexes integrating into one. Will it mean that we can go to Airport Vortex and feel the energy of all of them? Or would they all be alike?

It's a good question. It's like you in your individuality: You're always going to have the strength of your individuality, even when you recognize yourself as the Whole; you're still going to remember that point of individuality. Perhaps you will not reference it, but you could still go and feel the energy and it will be of a specific nature.

To help you understand that, let's say that one vortex is blue and one is green and one is yellow and one is red and one is violet. But there is an umbrella that is a rainbow of the full energy, too. So as you stand in one, you will benefit from all of them, but the specific nature of the one would be the emphasis of it.

How will the integration take place?

When the mass consciousness of humanity allows this equality to come in. This is a symbol of humanity being more allowing and coming together that way. So the energy responds to the consciousness on the planet. When you all recognize one another as equal partners – and this is what I think you are on the verge of doing, my friends – then it will take place. This is not something that is far in the future; I think it is coming in now. That's why I'm so excited. I am! So that's how the energy responds to the changing consciousness in your area and on your planet.

Many people who live here can't do anything but sleep. Is that a form of opposition to going along with it? What is it?

Well, it's an adjustment. I see a pattern where perhaps there's no sleep for a while, and then there's a lot of sleep, and then again not very much sleep. So it's changing relationship, first of all, with the inner dimensions, meaning that right now you're doing a lot of things on the inner level to build up for this integration that we're talking about. There are lots of things being done on the inner levels.

Like going to school?

Yes, and I would say particularly at the galactic level there is a lot going on. That part of you that will be in charge of you when you leave the Earth (meaning that's where your new job opportunities come from) is the Galactic Core. So you could say you're going through some training programs.

Also, there is an intensity on the Earth right now such that certain people are no longer going to stay. Some are leaving because they can't stay, and then there are the kindergartners who only came here for a little while anyway. They just came to look around and say, "Well, that's a nice Earth," and now they're leaving. So on the inner levels, you in particular are helping those kindergartners. In new ways your soul is helping you understand the possibilities that are here on the inner Earth and the outer Earth; and part of the integration is their blending together as never before. Think about the fourth dimension as not containing a time when you sleep just eight hours; you sleep twelve hours if you need to, or not at all if you don't need to.

I got out of bed at 6:30. At 7:30 I began to read the paper . . . and I woke up at 1:30 in the afternoon.

Sometimes it happens only once. That was an emergency, and we needed you. And that sometimes happens. You have volunteered for such emergencies.

I thought I was going crazy.

No, no.

As far as sleep goes, does it matter when in the day you do your sleeping?

It depends on the person. There are some people who want to go to sleep early in the evening, and then by early morning they're awake. And there are some who go to bed late and wake up early and then they take a nap. And then there are some who go to bed late and sleep late. It depends on the beliefs you have, which establish the biorhythms within your body.

There isn't one way to do it; it's just your choice in the moment. You can change that, but the biorhythms are not as easy to change as some things. Your body gets into a deep habit pattern. Most of you have had these same biorhythms for perhaps fifty, one hundred, two hundred lifetimes. It takes a major realization to change that.

Adjusting Earth's Vibrations

How about the solar eclipse that we had today? How is it going to affect humanity as a whole? They were celebrating it in Finland.

I look at it as very positive. I look at it as perhaps a blocking out of the old, and now we're celebrating the new. It's like wiping the blackboard clean. And the Sun really is the spiritual. You could say it's the physical manifestation of the spiritual, but keep in mind that the physical Sun really isn't hot anyway, because there's a spiritual Sun connected with it. So perhaps the vibrational rate of what you saw is now completely different after the eclipse than it was before. It varies quite a bit. It's like unplugging a plug through one of those eclipses, and now we plug it in over here because we can't do it with the old one shining quite as brightly. So it's simply an excuse system to adjust the vibrational rate on your planet, it really is. It's just the technique by which it takes place.

I think you're going to notice it. It's gentler and yet stronger — what does that say to you? That both polarities are being adjusted; perhaps that's the most important thing I've said all evening, because we were talking about polarity splits. This is helping; this shows that the mass consciousness has allowed that. Keep in mind that we, the spiritual beings and the local government, can't adjust these things, and the angels can't through our direction. We can't adjust it until the mass consciousness clears enough beliefs to allow that adjustment.

We're following very closely. The minute you make an Aha! we adjust the energy. The minute you realize something, we say, "Good, now we can adjust it again." So we're following it right up. And this is occurring more now than ever before.

The last time you were here, you mentioned August 1 and December 1 or 15 as major new energy points. Are they just more of the same, or are they specific kinds of energy?

Let's not take it out of the context I was talking about. This year, all during the year there are major adjustment processes being made in the energy. Look at it as a ship that's being raised by entering a series of locks. This year is that adjustment period. Economically, in the communication area, in the how-do-we-allow-ourselves-freedom area, the power area — everything is being adjusted this year, more than perhaps any year except one that came right after your planet began. Remember, this is a research-and-development project; they found out they had put you in the wrong place! So that was a major adjustment. And it was interesting, because two or three of you came and you couldn't find the planet, because it wasn't where you thought it should be. Everyone said, "Well, we're sorry about that. We put it somewhere else." Kind of fun, isn't it?

I have a kind of parallel situation with a friend who came from Montana. Both of us went to different places before coming to Sedona. She's taken a job, and I've been able to look at her in transition where I came from. I felt sad for her.

Well, that's a wonderful mirror, isn't it? That's becoming more aware of this. Life gives you all sorts of opportunities like that. Your children are your developing creativity. Your mother and father are your basic Source-level connection, receptively and dynamically. All of these are mirrors. Let's say you have a female friend. If you are a female, then that's an aspect of yourself. If you have a twin, you're always working with the identity area. So these are not accidents. These things happens and you can gain from them.

You know how I learn about your Earth. My hobby is to analyze the freeways in Los Angeles and to see the relationships of all the cars as they move. As they move around the system 24 hours a day, I learn more about the changing consciousness on your planet from that synchronicity than from anything else I've discovered. So as you're aware of the mirrors of synchronicity and what they are telling you, you become more conscious that life is not an accident. It fits together, all pieces of it. Life is as we said: it's a wholeness.

If we can go back and change some old past lives in order to affect some issues in this lifetime, would it make sense to go back as far as the coming out of Source to change core issues?

Oh, absolutely. Visualize yourself coming out and saying, "Oh wonderful, I'm being born! I have this wonderful opportunity and my emotions are very excited." Yes, absolutely. And then one of these days you'll convince yourself of that! What is it? It's a visualization and affirmations.

I would like to do a meditation now. I will be leaving after that, so I thank you much for this opportunity. I hope you enjoyed it; I certainly did.

Paint-the-Earth Meditation

☙ *Let us see together a violet ball. And this violet ball is the Earth's potential. Now let us bring that violet ball in and superimpose it over the Earth. See the Earth, a ball of whatever colors come to you – perhaps green and brown, or a beautiful white with the clouds or the blue of the sea, whatever seems appropriate to you.*

☙ *Bring this violet ball over the Earth. Now feel that coming through you, because you are there, too, on the Earth. And this violet ball comes into your physical structure. Now within the violet ball you see spirals. There is one main spiral around the Earth, and it is moving and spiraling. There is no right way – you can have it either clockwise or counterclockwise, because it isn't really in space; it's the process beyond space. But it comes in now, and you're moving it, and it's flowing, it's flowing. And it's also flowing within your body. Begin to see that spiral, that violet spiral, from your feet; and it spirals around your legs now, coming up around your hips and around your waist and your shoulders, and now up over your head. The beautiful violet spiral.*

☙ *And now let's sprinkle over the Earth, into these spirals, into this violet energy, beautiful gold. And it sparks, sparks, sparks! And it is igniting, igniting, igniting. The spirals move, and there is an igniting of the consciousness through these spirals. Sense that gold that is there now, really alive. This is life force, and it ignites here, and it ignites there. And it is raising the vibration even further as it spirals and moves.*

☙ *And now let's use some pink. Take a cosmic paintbrush and paint wherever you wish on your personal spiral – or on the spiral of the Earth, or on the Earth itself – a beautiful pink. Where does it need pink? In the heart, of course, the heart that cares, the hearts that supports, the heart of the life process itself as it supports you. Put the pink in. I think perhaps an electric blue is coming in there, too.*

☙ *Now bring the colors into the places, the rest of the colors. You may see orange, you may see yellow, green, blue, brown, silver. Bring them in now over the Earth. You may paint Africa green. You may paint the North American continent an electric blue. But paint the colors and see the spiral grow from that. All of the Earth. Australia needs to be painted right now. New Zealand, China, a lovely white expanse. Paint China your color. You choose, so that eventually through all of your choices it will be painted the whole rainbow.*

☙ *In fact, that's what we see now all around the Earth – the beauty of the rainbow. Coming into your spiral now is the beauty of the rainbow, and it moves and it spirals and it moves and it spirals, and it is raising the consciousness of the planet and of you.*

❦ *In your meditation now, look around and see that there are others there. You are not alone. All humanity is there within the spiral, and there is movement.*

❦ *Now sense that the animal kingdom is within the spirals. The animal kingdom needs your help right now – particularly the cats. Sense them moving into this spiral, benefiting from it. Paint them, if you will, a lovely electric blue – all of the cats, the wild cats, the lions, the tigers, the leopards, the house cats, the beautiful domestic cats, electric blue.*

❦ *Color the mineral kingdom as well. Now color your heart – it's the heart of all the kingdoms here. Finally, connect to life itself:* "Life supports me now because I support life."

✧ F I V E ✧

Cure for Disillusionment

S<small>OME OF YOU HAVE QUITE A BIT OF DISILLUSIONMENT. OVER AND OVER, IN</small> your desire to aid the Earth, to have a purposeful and meaningful life that you enjoy, you have fallen short of the goals you thought you should accomplish. It is important to recognize that if you did not receive a validation that the life you did lead was fine, was purposeful because it achieved the purpose of the soul right then, it was because that was what you needed. Perhaps more importantly, it was what the plan needed through you.

One reason I stress so much the need to get in sync with the plan is not that you are out of touch with it — you can't be. But once in a while there is something so deep in this area that we could consider you hopeless to ever achieve the purpose for which you have been created. That, of course, gets us into the conflict area that I have termed the Creator level and the cocreator level.

If you have been working with me for a while, you know how important I feel this area is. If you look at your life in a personal intensive or simply look at the synchronicities that come in, you will see that hopelessness, if you experience it, comes from your inability thus far to achieve on a Creator level something you are not yet ready to achieve or isn't in the purpose of the plan for you to achieve yet. So there is a sense of despair, of separation and of being used and, perhaps we could say, being pressured when your soul tries to function in the manner it is now.

Then what generally happens is, you get caught up emotionally in what you are not accomplishing, even though your life is expanding much better than you can see. Then, because the emotions get tighter and tighter, you draw energy away from the expansion that is there in what is going on in your life. You try to place to yourself elsewhere. By that I mean, you choose consciously to disassociate with a learning experience, but if you would just hang in there for a little while, you would achieve what the soul is seeking to achieve.

I'll give you one of the most important examples now that I see in anyone's life. Many of you have gotten involved with groups; you work with the group for a while and then suddenly you get frustrated and discouraged. You want to be validated in the group or you want to see that the group has some sort of a purposeful function. When you can't see that, you back out of the group, saying, "I am not going to be a part of this group anymore."

Well, I am not saying that is terrible, because certainly that is a choice. As you all know, I don't make your choices for you, but I give you this as food for thought. Perhaps you might consider it the next time a group experience seems impossible, hopeless, invalidating or exceptionally difficult. The group experience or group expression is what your New Age is all about. In fact, that is what the New Age is: groups of beings coming together and sharing responsibilities, sharing their strengths, united in a way which allows a purposeful, planned interaction with greater and greater numbers of humanity. It is the larger and larger numbers of humanity now ready to be processed to unite with the soul level that create the need for groups to process them.

This is the reason why many of you seek: to be a part of a group has set up some sort of a structure or a system to process very large groups of humanity. But in order to do that, the group has to have a structure that is stable enough, through those who have taken responsibility for it, to fulfill its function.

In other words, let us say that in a 25-member group, there is a difficulty encountered in a group meeting and ten people decide the group is hopeless so they leave. As you can see, that is a large percentage of that group's energy or, we could say (although we would have to generalize here), of its creativity. It could be that those who left didn't feel very creative in the group and that's one reason they left. But that doesn't mean they weren't creative in the group.

Your emotional body cannot always see how it is serving the plan; it is not yet aware enough to do so. As we talk about your emotional body, recognize that it is the part of you that is the least aware in 99.9% of all of you. There are some who are very able to use their emotions; they don't always use them the way they would like to, but they are very open emotionally. But even for this group of people, there is still not the awareness in the emotional that there is in the mental. The emotional body is not as aware as the rest of your bodies. Even your physical body is more aware than your emotional body.

Now, I am not negating the emotional body or saying that it isn't important. On the contrary, it is at this point perhaps the most important part of you in the area of getting your act together creatively and allowing yourself to be supported by the plan as it seeks to unfold.

There are many ways to do everything, and I have certainly emphasized that. I've said there are at least six ways to do everything, as a general average. But we could say that the plan for the Earth is moving in a certain way — there is an overall guidance system that allows it to grow. We could call that, right now on your Earth, the use of the group vehicle.

Now, a group, in my opinion, as far as humanity is concerned, would be two people or more. But we are talking here about a moderately sized group with perhaps 10 or 15 people at the core who are truly committed to that group (or would like to be), up to 300 or 400. Beyond that we get into the really large groups, and I am not really talking about them now; I think that's a little premature, so we will get to them a little later. But many of you in your learning have reached the point where, although you don't know it, you've learned about as much as you can as an individual. Isn't that interesting?

The next step is through the group vehicle. Recognizing that will be an incentive to stay with the group even if it seems difficult, because the group is bringing to the surface, in these difficult periods, exactly what you need to look at. Without that stimulation, and being by yourself, you might say you really feel stuck. Now, you might not agree with me on that one; you might say, "My creativity can only flow through me when I am really by myself. I can't get it all together in a group." For you that may be rather true because you have so much resistance to the group processing.

What I am saying is, look beyond that. All of you who have difficulties with groups also have the tremendous desire at this point to unfold your potential and to flow it on the Earth or at least to flow it enough so it is complete on the Earth and you can get on with something else. Some of you are very tired of the Earth; you've said, "I don't want to be here anymore, I want to go." You have sought, through your connection with the space beings and the UFOs and the various ways of contacting others (all of which, of course, are other groups), to say, "I'm tired of this experience. I would like to get on with my cosmic life somewhere else."

Well, the reason you are frustrated with the Earth experience is that over and over you have tried to unlock a sense of being more than you are now, and the main way to do that is through the group. But if you are resisting it, you are resisting the very thing that can help you achieve what you are looking for. So the group experience and how to use it is a key to your evolution. This is my whole point in this section.

Your creativity is unique. It is part of the whole, and without it the whole would not be complete. Perhaps that is difficult for you to conceive now. Some of you feel a little bit insecure and unworthy, and it's like saying to a drop of water, "Without you the ocean would be incomplete." And you look at the ocean and you look at yourself as that drop of water and you think, "I don't think I would be missed very much." But, my friend, you have no idea how much your creativity is treasured, how much it is valued, how much appreciation there is of you and your point of view. It is there at a very basic level from this great consciousness that we call the Source, the Creator, God, or whatever term you wish to use. It is there for you, as you are there for it. You might think about this: *You* are the support system for the Creator. Now, isn't that a statement! You might say, "But It's *my* support system." I would say, of course It is. But conversely, you are the individualized portion of the Source Itself. The Source in Its learning and growth and understanding gains a unique perspective through you. But you might have a unique perspective and you just look at it and you say, "Now what do I do with it?"

Your idea, your creativity, needs the skills and the creativity of others to allow your idea to manifest on the Earth. You may say to me, "But I have other ideas." Perhaps you want to paint a picture. "I can paint it without anyone else. I don't need other people's creativity to bring mine to the Earth." But you do. You know the old axiom: If a tree fell in the forest and no one was there to hear it, would it make a sound? To be more exact, would its effort affect the vibrational scale of existence? In my opinion, no. It needs the ears that hear it. It needs the interaction with others. If you paint a picture, certainly you don't need to have everyone tell you, "Oh, this is a wonderful picture," but eyes need to view your painting.

Now, there are some great artists who have painted things and torn them up or not let others see them. This is, in my opinion, an incomplete effort because it isn't shared with the cocreator level, with others, with humanity. Creativity, then, to be complete, to be completely acknowledged, to be completely expressed, must be shared.

That brings us back to the use of groups. There are all sorts of ways to be involved with groups. Suppose a person discovers a method for building a better automobile. First he conceives the idea, then he brings it to those who have the financial resources and the know-how to produce it on the physical level. That is sharing with a group, and it certainly will get you into areas that you need to clear. It has often been the case on your planet lately that better ideas have not been allowed to produce better automobiles. Why? Because certain power structures that were not used clearly prevented it.

If you invented something that didn't get completed, perhaps there was within you a resistance to allowing it to be produced clearly on the Earth through the group vehicle. There would be a resistance against taking away the power, money and resources present, if the idea of a car that didn't use gasoline were manifested. What about all of the oil refineries and the people who make money from gasoline? This would create within you a resistance to having your idea manifest on the Earth.

Now, don't misunderstand me. There would, of course, be many resistive points within our example. There would be a power hang-up within the mass consciousness — and there certainly is — to allowing this clearer vehicle to manifest.

There would be people who are not strong enough to stand up for a good idea because they fear they might lose their position, their means of security. So we can see that at many points where creativity seeks to go through a process of becoming physical, there is a stimulation through the cocreator level to look at that process, see what is not clear, and resolve it. That is what "Workshop Earth" is for – to literally take apart the creative process, often by stimulating what is not working, so that you can see a way to get it working.

If your car or your vehicle breaks down, you either look at it yourself to see what is wrong with it or you take it to another person who has the expertise to say you need a new battery, a new starter, a new transmission or whatever the problem is and help you do what needs to be done in order to get it running more smoothly.

Similarly, a manifested idea may work for a while and then need to be rethought or have all of its parts looked at again to see how it can continue to work. The cocreator level can assist you to manifest more clearly, whether it is an idea or a vehicle that worked for a while.

This is true because there are levels of clearing on the Earth, and the Cosmic Plan for the Earth understands the levels. It might say to you, "This is your role during this level of clearing, this level of discovery, this level of manifestation, this level of humanity's evolvement on the Earth." And you might say, "I don't like my role. I'm not being used in a way that I see I want to be used."

Now, in the first place, as we said earlier, what may be wrong with that statement is that, in attuning to your soul's purpose, you're always going through a basic level of commitment that says, "I am a creator and my goal is to be a fully manifested *Creator*." This is absolutely true, unshakable, irrevocable – no way can we challenge that – it's absolutely true. The only thing is that it is for later. That's not now. You may say, "Can't it be now if I can realize it?" And I would say, probably not! Because the whole Plan isn't ready for you at that level now. There is an unfolding process, and you have a role in the plan *now*, right now. A little later you'll have another role.

You will continue to change and grow beyond the point of view where you are now by allowing it, by sharing it with others and by allowing the mirrors within the group process to show you what to clear out now so that the role that is there for you now can be acknowledged, accepted and, perhaps we could even say, gratefully enjoyed.

Now, if you feel particularly stuck at the moment, you might want to throw this material in my face. (I don't have a face.) But I am seeking to point out that even if you feel stuck and caught, that is a very small part of your life. The other 95% of the life that you have right now is good and productive, and is serving the plan as it needs to be served.

Let's say that you attune to something that you will be doing 50,000 years from now in the plan – perhaps a special training program with the angelic kingdom that will unlock your understanding of color, of energy, of how to connect through color. (Such a program would be very, very, very good.) You may say to yourself subconsciously, I'm getting in touch with that. And as you do, you open a door consciously and the conscious mind says, "Good, we'll do that now." Two things happen: Immediately you are putting less energy into the role of the soul as it seeks to manifest through you now; and you are putting a kind of forced energy on the plan.

Now certainly I am not telling you that you can't connect with your purposes beyond where you are now. But your concentration on them should not take you out of your ability to accept your role now or your ability to see who you are now and that what you are doing is an important part of the plan. Then, through your attunement to what can be inspired by it now, you can say, "I will be looking forward to that; it's a part of me that I really want to explore and I'm really looking forward to it. But for now I will just recognize it is there and once in a while I might ask my soul if there is some sort of preparation I can make for that." If you put too much concentration on it, then it pulls you and your energy out of the plan now. And that makes the plan incomplete.

Now, if it is complete enough, you can pull almost 90% of your energy out of the plan now. You can't ever pull it all out; that isn't possible. But think about it: If 20,000 people on the Earth pulled 90% of their energy out of the plan now, it would set your Earth back about ten years in its evolution. If they did it in a way that opened others up for doing it (and that can happen – it's like a domino effect), we would see the result very early on your planet. There would be a complete change in the use of the plan, and the spiritual guidance system of your plan would have to look at so many alternatives and so many different ways of guiding the now completely changing plan that the guidance system would be all into alternatives rather than how to guide what is manifesting now. For those of you who know anything about management, this would be likened to management by crisis, rather than clear, supportive management, because you will have planned for the next step and seen how it can unfold.

This plan in its wisdom knows what you need. If you can surrender and accept that role, it will unfold for you a gradual acceptance of your abilities and your evolution, and at the same time it will help your emotional body understand support, because the plan will reflect back to you its gratitude for your serving as you are or, we might even say, just living as you are. Service is of course indicated many ways, but in our analogy, serving and living mean the same thing.

As you actively enter the transformational process, each of you seeks a goal. That goal (and it is a good one) is to express the creativity of your soul as fully as possible. Certainly might not say it that way, but you might say, "I want my life to work. I want to have good relationships. I want to have abundance. I want to have a job that I like." This is allowing your potential to manifest on the Earth. The good news is, the plan wants that for you, too. So there is no difference — no points of separation, no alienation — between what the plan wants for you and what you want for yourself. Where you get into difficulties with it is in what we might call the divine timing.

One quality that all of you need a little more of, or perhaps need to recognize that you need a little more of, is patience: patience with yourself, patience with others, patience with the working out of issues coming through old patterns of behavior. Let us say you have an intimate relationship with someone. It may be a polarity relationship or simply a close friend whom you love very much and whom you have known long enough to be intimate with (not sexually, perhaps, but emotionally). There are times in that relationship when something occurs that makes you feel that, if it isn't resolved, you might not want to keep that relationship; it's just too difficult, too deep an area.

Now, you know that communication is very important, and you feel (and this occurs in about 80% of relationships) that your relationship partner won't communicate with you — they simply will not, no matter what you do. So as you attempt to communicate, you feel that the other person is blocking that communication.

Is that really what is happening? On one level it is — on the least important level it is. But on the most important level, *you*, my friend, are blocking that communication. Through the mirrors it is showing you that a part of you that you are very close to, a part that you love and admire and are intimate with (which part that is will be different for each of you) is not communicating. There is a frustration in regard to that lack of communication and a sense of "I'll run away. I will not, I cannot. There is nothing I can do. I am victimized by this relationship unless I get away from it. Getting away is all that I can do because the communication doors have been closed."

On the physical level that may certainly seem to be true. Marriages break up, old friends will not talk to each other. The reason is that each of you comes in contact with an area within you, a pattern of behavior within you, that is so caught, so stuck and many times so difficult that you can't face it. You turn off the communication. What happens subconsciously is, it becomes shocky. There is no way to contact it. If I, Vywamus, try to bring you anything in this area, we get into convolution that takes a great deal of time and effort to get out of. If we look at it as a path we might seek to clear, we find that there are false paths and there are dead-end paths and there are paths of illusion and there are overlays of other patterns of behavior. There are many, many, many points of resistance that impact one of these large areas.

What to do? Well, at this point (and this is being dictated in 1990), what I am doing is bringing you these areas anyway, when you ask me. I am bringing the ones that are difficult, that are basic. The reason is, this gives you an opportunity to look through the Earth's strengths at the next step for you. By that I mean, as I said earlier, that the New Age is an age of groups. So built into the plan is a strength level; yes, it's a future strength level, but it is spiritual.

The future is as valid as the present and the past. It's all part of this opportunity. But because we do know how to work with that and energize that, we bring that strength of the future — the clear use of groups in the future — and we overlay it onto your present experience so that as you struggle within this relationship, you can begin to draw on your future clarity in relationship with groups.

Isn't that interesting? Is it possible? Not only is it possible, but you are doing it — beginning to — and I, Vywamus, am helping you to do so. There are angels, archangels, spiritual teachers and many others among us who are beginning to see that this might be the *key* to the New Age as you seek to live it: to bring your future strengths to the present, build a bridge to them and use them to clear these very basic deep areas of resistance where the communication breaks down and where, when we go into patterns of behavior, it is so convoluted that we almost get lost in our attempt to clear it.

The future strength can hold a focus for us in this area, allowing your future understanding of group relationships to be a strength in resolving present relationships. This is not a new idea. It's not one that hasn't been tried on your Earth. It has been tried and has been used somewhat successfully in the past. But in my opinion there were other, older patterns of behavior which got in the way and didn't allow as clear a use of that method as now becomes available here on the Earth.

We will be discussing this in many ways. My advice is to clear the group area as extensively as possible by "hanging in there" in your group experiences, whether they be two, ten, twenty or thirty, if you feel the purpose of the group is compatible with you and your soul, even if you can't see yet how that can be achieved.

Your choice to keep that group experience will allow the strengths that are being bridged to now to energize a clearer solution into your life.

◇ S I X ◇

Integrating within the Plan

INTEGRATION IS NOT SOMETHING THAT IS COMPLICATED, SOMETHING THAT needs to be difficult. It is an understanding that is only partially mental. The place where integration takes place is in your heart. As much as you can, I'd like you to feel that, because with integration comes a sense of peace and a feeling of clarity. There comes an awareness of the divine presence within you — a sense of "Yes, this is what speaks to me." This is integration.

You all have very busy lives; you are trying to do so many things that you are like a juggler keeping ten balls in the air at the same time. How do you keep from dropping one? How do you get everything to fit together? Sometimes it is necessary to become very quiet, to reach deeply into who you are and listen to that "still, small voice within." It is necessary to say to it, "I am ready."

Are you ready to find that integrated self? I think you are. You might say to me, "That sounds nice, and perhaps as you speak to us I can find a little in my heart, but how in the world is that going to affect my everyday life? How am I going to understand integration all of the time?"

Let's talk about that. Integration takes place through the process of communication. It comes through sorting the things you really want to keep in your life from the things you have but no longer want. As you begin sorting, you come across an old habit pattern that says, "I must adhere to this pattern. This pattern is who I am." In this acceptance an illusion is woven into how you live your life. You're wearing old garments, old habit patterns, that don't belong to who you really are. When you are trying to integrate those, you can't, because they don't fit in — they don't belong and were never meant to belong to what you truly are.

Perhaps it is necessary, then, to define what sort of life you really want. I don't think many of you do define what you want in life. In personal appointments with me, one of the questions you bring to me, one of the most important, is "What are my soul's purposes? Why am I here?"

You literally are a point of integration within the Source Itself. Your role is to allow information and feelings and energy — the life force — to flow through you so that you can develop and grow. This is the integrative process at work within the Divine Plan. There is no rigid application of integration — not anywhere! I have noticed that sometimes, when you are part of a group, some of you find the group process "interesting." You join a group of twelve people and find there are twelve different opinions about how that group should function. Is that bad? No, it's good — it's how the process is meant to be. That's the process of integration working out. Is it meant to come together so only one opinion is dominant? Not at all! Through communication, the process works within a group environment, within a group of people or within the group that you know as self with all its aspects.

One of the most profound activities in which you are all engaged is having your feelings (emotional body) talk to your thinking process (mental body). Is the goal to have your feelings "think" or your thinking process "feel"? Not at all. But an alignment takes place between feeling and thought, and this is the process of integration.

Integration is a point that, when you reach it, you know and you feel within your heart area. You say, "Aha! I get it; I understand; yes, that's it!" This is also called a point of realization, a point where you realize on every level who you are. A group on the physical level can reach that point too. The members of a group can come together and communicate until they understand how to allow each perspective to be there. You may have friends who are working toward integration but who have old patterns of behavior that you don't like — perhaps a habit of constantly interrupting someone else who is attempting to express their viewpoint. Well, as they work on themselves, they'll lose it — they'll see that they don't want to wear that pattern and they will, through the process of integration and transformation, discard it, just as you have discarded old patterns that were unprofitable and disliked by others. After all, it isn't always the other person who is burdened with old patterns that limit their growth. Allowing for growth in oneself and others is one of the most important aspects that can be used to reach an alignment or a point of integration.

Let's put it on what you call a mundane level, what I call a manifested creative effort on the physical plane: let's say you are driving a car. You come to a four-way stop sign; everyone has to stop. What you usually do is trust that everyone is going to stop. You stop, and when it's clearly your turn, you move on. What if someone ignores the instruction to stop and goes right through? There will be a collision or a jarring stop for the other cars in order to avoid a collision. There is an obvious disruption in the flow of traffic. There are other guidelines besides traffic signs given to help you live profitably on this Earth. Some of you call it a code of ethics and some of you call it being honest or using common sense or being true to yourself. When you are manifesting any or all of these, you are on the most direct route leading to the integration you are seeking. Every time you must make a decision, say to yourself, "Is this in the best interest of who I am? Is this in the best interest of others and the Cosmic Plan?"

Do you believe there is a Cosmic Plan? Or do you believe that all that is occurring is the result of an accident? Do you believe that suddenly this happens in the universe, then that happens, and there is no rhyme or reason working it out? There is a plan, and you are part of it.

How many of you ever ask that plan to assist you? How many of you have said, "I have a decision to make and I need some help and I don't know where to get it"? Well, how about saying to the universal plan, "Help me now; I seek your help." That's an invocation to the divine, isn't it? The divine comes through to you by a process that is called a plan, and what we are really talking about when we speak of integration is a flowing within the plan. When you are flowing within the plan, there are no sudden interruptions, no stop signs, no fear of collision. Is this possible? Yes, it is. It is not only possible, it is your divine destiny. What you are fated to experience eventually is your ability to flow within this plan unlimitedly. There is nothing more practical in the fullest sense than to be able to say, "Yes, I trust that there is a plan. That plan comes not only through me but through everyone; it is woven through each of us here and through everyone."

Every time you stop and think about that, something wonderful happens — there is an opening, there is a surrendering process. "Surrender" is what I call a charged word. There is another term that is important to all of you, and it is called "personal freedom." Freedom is a universal law. You are free to make your choices. You are almost entirely free to live the type of life you want, although you probably don't feel that you are. In the fullest sense, however, you are.

I say to you, at a specific point you are going to say, "I want to give that freedom up." Why were you given it in the first place? I seek to tell you that you were given it so you could give it up, so you would have something to surrender. Your unique creativity: are you ever going to lose that? No! You are not! You're going to gain something much greater. You're going to gain an integrative perspective, because integration truly includes all levels of creativity coming together, working together and cooperating together to make one life — your life, or a group expression, or perhaps a freer Earth, an Earth that can share. Poland can perhaps be tuned in to China, and China to North America, and North America to Iceland, and Brazil to Australia. The needs of each country can be met, and there is an integrative response to life that allows you to govern the planet from a united level. I believe that in 150 years or less you will have that planetary government, a government that speaks for the whole planet. You will have planetary council members, and you or your friends could be those members. It's possible because the aging process is being solved right now, and that is also a part of integration.

Integration can be seen as bringing potentialities into that "nowness" that you are experiencing, rather than having it somewhere in the past or in the future. Many of your potentials were expressed quite well in Egypt, but some of you closed down those potentials, some of that divine power. The point is, you can bring integration by allowing those potentialities to be not in the past or future, but right now. Together, then, you can express this more creatively free life.

You have to recognize what it means to be free so that you see what it is you surrender in the act of giving up that which has been to you your freedom. Once you do, you will find it is an unlocking process or, let's say, a key that really gives you a lot more than you give up. Surrender is always a key. Many of you try to force something: you try to force a relationship to work by saying, "I need something from you. I need your love, your affection. I need you to be supportive of me. I need that." I think the relationship will work only when you say to another, "I wish to be supportive of you. I love and admire you and I know that coming together we can be supportive of one another." No, I'm not saying that your needs can't be met, that you are wrong to need. But when you approach it from need, you are trying to force it, through emotion, to come to you. Force just doesn't accomplish what you desire. Allowing, trusting and surrendering opens the flow from the heart area and allows the response you seek to come through.

For some of you, what I am saying is an awakening. For others there will be a future awakening. It doesn't matter, because integration awaits you. It awaits you until you are ready to accept it. It is a point that you step into. You step into it, however, by *allowing* it to happen. Integration is really the plan moving through you. Trying to force the connection inhibits it and does not work.

Let us say you have two children; one is four years old and the other is seven. They are playing together and one day you hear screams, and one of them says, "That's my toy!" The other says, "No, it's mine, and you can't have it!" You go in and tell the children they must learn to share. You suggest that each choose a toy to share with the other and they play for a while. Well, there may be tears and resistance, but when they really get the idea and try it, something wonderful happens. You'll notice that they are more aware that the feelings they have about life are satisfied by that giving, that willingness to share.

What is sharing? Love? Loving yourself? How does one do that — how does one share oneself? By being aware of another's viewpoint, being aware of what they are looking for and sharing, and communicating the fact that we are aware. Often we are so busy thinking of our own needs and desires that we don't think; we don't understand that what someone else is really looking for is a communicative link. They seek the sharing of your time, your caring, your understanding, your love: things that don't cost anything — or do they? What are you giving up when you share yourself? Your time? Ego? Well, perhaps, but these are just limitations you've accepted for yourself, and isn't that all right? I think giving these up is fine, and it doesn't depend upon circumstance.

It's always true: When you are willing to share, you're going to be releasing some of those patterns of behavior that you've worn over eons. You've tried to push them away, and they always come back again. Do you really understand that? You see, there is a focus created through sharing, and that focus enlarges your perspective and your understanding. When you give yourself to others, many times what you get in return, at least partially, is part of someone else. Isn't that true? That allows growth to take place.

You can't grow all by yourself; it just doesn't work that way. The cosmos doesn't create just one of you at a time; you are all in this process together. That is probably one of the very most important things that you are learning. The evolution of each one of you is tied up with the evolution of your family members, business associates and friends. As one person reaches a point of realization, a point of integration, the whole networking of consciousness evolves. You can literally feel that — it's like an energy ignition that goes right to the core of All That Is. An expansion takes place, and from that expansion there is more energy available to you, there is more heart energy, there is more allowingness, and you can access it. An ignition has taken place, and it comes through sharing and caring and trusting.

Trust is one of the more important things you are learning. Have you ever played that game in which you stand in front of another person and allow yourself to fall backwards in total trust that you will be caught and upheld by the one behind you? If you try this, first look to the practical, physical elements. If you are large and the other person is not big enough to catch you, then, no matter how completely you trust their intent, you know it would be impractical to try it. But if it is physically feasible, it's a good exercise in trusting. It gives a strong feeling of what it is to trust.

When you need to do so, you can totally relax and let go and trust that the cocreator level will support you. It's a grand feeling. As you begin to develop trust what comes up is a bit of fear. You launch forth, not quite sure, concerned that you might repeat a past experience in which you didn't relax, let go and trust, and therefore took a tumble.

A wonderful thing has happened on your planet. In past lessons I have spoken of 35 avatars sent to Earth who embodied the Christ consciousness. Through them an anchoring of certain heart qualities comes forth. So at all times the process, the plan, watches over you, and what you need is brought to you. Your needs are fulfilled, and in one sense you needn't worry about them. I'm a very practical being, so I'm not saying you shouldn't look objectively, that you shouldn't use your mental body as you look at your lives.

There comes a time, however, when your mental body just can't do it all. The mental body is only one fourth of what we call the four-body system and isn't meant to be in total control. There is a difference between being practical in your life through evaluation and being *in control* of it.

There is a controlling aspect that you have put into your life. When you trust another person to catch and uphold you, as in our exercise in trusting, that controlling aspect lets go. It says, "I can trust." What are you trusting when you trust the cocreator level? You are trusting the cocreator level to uphold your creativity as a cocreator with Source. Suppose in your creative visualization you make some violet balls. You create one and throw it to, we'll say, John. So you caught it, John; what are you going to do with it? Oh, you threw it to someone else! You allowed that process to keep moving by sharing it. Integration again brings together all potentials on a conscious level by sharing.

Can you be integrated and yet not conscious of it? Not entirely, but somewhat. A good example is your physical structure. Many of you are quite well coordinated. You can ride a bicycle; you can rub your stomach and pat your head at the same time. You have learned to coordinate the basic functions so that they flow well and are quite integrated. But you can use these basic strengths on a much wider base.

Let's say you enjoy painting. Can you also be a writer, a dancer, a computer whiz and a mathematician? Can you integrate all of these abilities and skills? Yes, you could have all of them in your life; you'd be a bit busy, but you could. There is no limit to the number of focuses you could learn to integrate. In the fullest sense that is what you are doing right now. You remember only this life, but your soul level, which is not in sequential time, is integrating perhaps 1500 to 2000 lives. In your different lives you have been an explorer, a writer, a yogi in contemplation, a good housewife and mother, a space explorer — yes, a space explorer — because there are other levels of experience that you are also integrating. You can refer to the discussion of the Galactic Core. I feel this is the level Earth has now opened, and it is ready to explore that point of integration. There is a physical Galactic Core, but there is also a spiritual Galactic Core, a creative Galactic Core and an energy Galactic Core. All of these are part of the integrative process that you are putting together.

You are not aware of all the levels of self. Some of you enjoy moving around from planet to planet. It's no big deal, you do it all the time. You may be one who mines particular ores on asteroids; you may be an interplanetary council member traveling from one place to another. Am I making this up? No, I'm not; they are real. There is a level of you, then, that is much more broad-based creatively than your experience in this life. Integration in the fullest sense is putting together all of these things and understanding them. In my opinion you are ready to recognize these other levels that literally shine on your physical life now. It is like a sun that is shining:

there is that energy, that spiritual perspective, available for you to recognize and absorb on these other levels and integrate them.

Think about the Sun. What does it do? It provides energy and heat for your planet? Well, it doesn't, really, though that's what the scientists have said. There is a spiritual sun behind that, but we'll go with this example for a while. See that sun shining on your Earth; see yourselves absorbing it. Some of you like to sunbathe, to absorb that energy and warmth. Why? Why do you enjoy lying on the beach in the Sun? It feels good. Yes, but why? What happens when you lie there and surrender to that Sun? You feel relaxed, it makes you feel alive. Oh, I like that! The reason you feel alive is that in the cells there is literally a blending of the life force – an integration process that you are going through. When you are truly alive you are moving toward a point of life and realization that is so tremendous, so cosmic, so wonderful that it cannot be put into words.

What you can do is begin to *feel* it working through your heart energy, or through your physical body, through your trust area, through your allowing. You say, "Yes, what I am surrendering to now, this next opportunity, is something I have never known before. It is an aliveness of energy, of life force, that is magnified beyond my dreams, beyond my present understanding." Yet it's there for you – it's your goal; it's coming closer; it's the point of integration that you are seeking. It is the point where anything you want can be manifested, but you will only want what is integrated to the plan, because that will be the level of reality from which you function. It will be instant manifestation because you will have moved beyond time. You will have the tools, the resources, of the whole creative process instantly available to you. You will have them because you will have learned how to use them.

I sometimes put things in story form to help clarify. Suppose the Source said to you, "I want you to create a universe for me." You'd say, "Fine, I'll go into the place where we outline them and get a model and I'll go from there. I'm glad to do it; I'll do it immediately."

You see, when you function on that level you will have learned to integrate, and in order to integrate you have to know all the pieces. You have to have understood each piece enough to know where it fits with every other piece. The pieces are not the same. You yourself are unique, and all your pieces are unique, but they all fit together very well. This is not a mental exercise, nor a physical exercise, even though you are learning about it on the physical level. It is a spiritual exercise. Your emotions are what can connect you now into the next level of it. Think about this: even the emotions you might not like will help. They create a focus. To me this is most interesting. I do not advocate having fears, but suppose you are afraid to become a channel for some reason. When you have the courage to try anyway, the fear gathers up your programming and there is a flow past your fears because you can function beyond your fears.

Certainly it will be necessary to look at the cause of the fears and release them. Let's say you are standing in front of an audience for the first time. There are all those faces out there, all that solid energy. Perhaps your subconscious remembers other lifetimes when you rose to speak and were ridiculed or even stoned. You notice the face of a friend, or at least a face that looks friendly, and you sense that there are those who are with you and that you and the individuals in the audience are all parts of a common process. Then you can allow an integration and you begin to speak without fear. You just need to allow an integration into whatever activity or intent or purpose you choose in your life.

When you come to me individually and ask me to tell you of your purposes in life, I single out one part, because you think of them as separate. That one purpose will, however, develop and grow until you see it as a flow of purposes. To expand and allow means effort, and to allow your efforts to be integrated you must become a part of everything in the flow. You can't stand back and say, "All right, this is what I do, and I do it, but I have another part of me over there that's not involved." There needs to be a surrender of the whole to the purpose itself. Can you do this all at once? Well, most of you probably will do it in a step-by-step manner. You will keep bringing more of who you really are — more of your warmth, your love, your understanding and your time — into the effort. Get involved fearlessly with your purpose.

SEVEN

Time and Space

IME IS NOT NECESSARILY THE SAME ON EVERY LEVEL, AND IT IS NOT REFER-
enced the same in every dimension. I think you know that. But the
fact that the Earth is shifting from the third to the fourth dimension causes
a change in time-sequencing. If you would look at that as a vibration and
consider a certain number of vibrations to be gone through in order to have
one second, and a certain number to have one moment, what is occurring?
Well, as life moves into a higher, finer vibration, there is a parallel occurence
with time that plugs it in differently.

To give you an example, if we have something rotating at a certain rate,
and the speed of rotation is increased and also becomes excited magnetically
by another level of creativity, then the nowness, which has an eternal focus,
attracts the time-sequencing so that it isn't as inflexible. It becomes more
creative. It responds to the creative flow of the Source Itself.

Flexible Time

So let us say that the Source is considering something and learning about
something. It extends an area of Itself into time and space. It takes as long
as It needs to absorb and learn about that idea. Now, the higher the
vibration, the more in tune it is with taking as long as It takes; there is not
an inflexibility about time. So time begins to shrink and to expand or,
perhaps we could say, to be flexible to the creative sparking of the Source
Itself.

Let us say you all are powerful enough to get in tune with this. You
want to create in your life something important to you — for example, to
travel and meet everyday expenses. This is a specific creativity focus. As you
begin to consider it on this level in the nowness, you can hook it into the
responsiveness of the Source-level creativity, and that removes the pressure

of time-sequencing. It allows the creative effort to be hooked directly into the nowness. The trick is for you to function in the nowness, too, in order to utilize it. It isn't very difficult at this stage of your evolution for you to hook what you want to create into the nowness. But sometimes the difficulty lies in hooking yourself into it continually so that you can respond to what is responding to you. Does that make sense? At this point you need to realize that time is responding to you. When you recognize what is occurring, then you don't look for it to be sequencing as it has before.

With the Harmonic Convergence we wiped out the premise that time sequenced as it had before. Some of you are still keeping that old pattern about sequential time, and you could say that mass consciousness still has that idea rather deeply ingrained. But it is going to fade gradually, like an idea whose time is long gone but which you remember and hold on to through your memories.

There is a need, then, as you create, to recognize that there is enough time to use that creative idea. Until you really understand that, you can say to yourself, "I'm going to use the time that I have, and I know that I will eventually have all the time that I need." You can put it into that type of format first, where you recognize that there is time, and then use another block of time later. Ideally, however, if you had all been able to create time, it would have simply flowed into the ability to use it. Part of the problem you had today in waiting to be served at the restaurant was your inability to get in touch yet with the creative sparking, which is what time is for.

Time is a stepping-up process of the creative effort. I have often equated it to the soul. The soul stops and takes a picture of your creative effort each second (it's not quite as often as that). Then it takes a look at what's being created, and if the creative effort isn't what it wants, then it makes another effort and takes another picture. So the sequencing is there in order to get the picture. As you become stronger in your understanding of your ability to create on the physical level, you learn to use the ability to maintain that focus in the eternal nowness, which means grasping it through your creative strength. Then your efforts will remain focused. In this case we are discussing the goal of having enough money to travel and use. This goal will become more strongly focused; you will be able to grasp it, and it will flow to the nowness where you will need it. It is not the other way around.

Time is not an arbitrator that takes you away from something. There is the need to see that you have to go where time has, let's say, become flexible enough to be. That is an interesting way to look at it: You don't need more time; what you need is to become as flexible as time has become. This means that whatever the goal is, you can ask the universe to provide the time for it, and then believe or trust the universe. That's the first step. You know that's taken care of. You've asked the universe; the time is now there. But then you have to take yourself into that eternal now. That's where most of you get yourselves into a little bit of trouble, through the emotional responses or through a level of illusion in which you think you don't have the ability to have enough of abundance such as by remembering that you are a woman. The belief that most women are limited is very strong in the mass consciousness. If you have accepted that, then that bars the door to the eternal nowness, because any such limitation doesn't belong in the nowness. It is not actually in the nowness; it's in an arbitrarily controlled sense of sequencing. It is a part of the step-by-step releasing process that all of you are going through.

Time As a Hook

So if you can begin to think of time as a hook, that will focus for you whatever it is you want it to bring you, and it will hold it there. But it will be stretchable and flexible enough to allow you to grasp it when you are ready. Let's say you've decided that you want to be 21 years old again, and you tell that to the universe. What happens? Well, there is a step-by-step process that the universe goes through. It looks at you and then it looks at your goal (because, remember, to the universe you are a creator; and as cocreators you create in connection with others — there is a return flow). The universe picks up on that goal (or any goal, whether it is positive or "negative"). It picks up on what you have creatively focused upon and it looks at that and plugs in the wholeness. It may say to you, as it did especially before the Harmonic Convergence, that your goal doesn't quite fit into the sequencing of time (unless you have some very special abilities — which, although you're growing well, you haven't got yet).

When the Harmonic Convergence arrived, it wiped out that sequencing that was locked into your planet. In April [1989] it began to move in a way that it hadn't before. So now when you tell the universe, "I want to be 21 years old again," the universe looks at the Source level and says, "This is how to do it. Now we'll create that." And back comes to you the means to create it.

Can you see the difference? There is a creative response that is going to flow to you. I am not saying exactly what will be mirrored to you — it depends on the beliefs you have. If there are deep beliefs or resistances, then you will have mirrored to you something about stopping, or "I can't do it," or whatever. But if there is a belief that says, "Yes, that is a good age, and I can be 21 again," then the universe is going to start bringing you the way to do it.

A universe sometimes has a voice through others as they talk to you — but I'm talking about a creative voice that will speak to the cells within you. This is one of the most important things about aging. You don't need these complicated techniques that many are using; you simply need a creative sense of how to contact the universe, to be in that eternal-now space with it, and receive what the creative input of the universe is attempting to bring back to you.

If you are too blocked, what will happen? You won't receive it in the eternal now, and you will get what the universe would have sent you before the Harmonic Convergence. Your consciousness will take you back to that point where you used to be. Thus the time factor becomes hooked into your arbitrary use of time and keeps you from contacting that higher level of creativity that says, "This is what you wanted, and this is how to get it!" It is like an old pattern that says, "I'm going around and around, and I'm going nowhere." Because, in a sense, time does that. Have you ever noticed? It goes around and around and around and it doesn't spiral. That is the difference between the progression of consciousness as it recognizes itself as consciousness, and the rather sleeplike state (you call it not being awakened yet) that exists when you are on the physical level and think that the physical level is all there is. That's when you go around and around in time and believe you are fated to experience old age and illness.

Let's say you discover one day that you have an illness, and you are told that this illness, a type of kidney dysfunction, could be serious if you don't take care of yourself. What can you do? Certainly I would suggest physical remedies such as drinking plenty of water and perhaps looking at some acupuncture treatments. Beyond that, how about asking the universe to hook into that time before the illness was created and then bring that state into the eternal nowness? Remember, you have to be there to greet it. You have to be there exactly when it arrives, because it comes out of your programmed state and into the eternal nowness. Some of you have had that. It is like a state of realization when you say, "Aha, I've got it! I've got it!"

What have you got? You have brought your realized concept into the nowness, and your creative effort, which has been sequencing around here in those old patterns of behavior, has met you there and become perfect — whether it is perfect health, an alignment of the four bodies, a realization of who you are, the ability to manifest money, or the ability to be 21 again. No matter what it is, there is a perfect alignment, because it has gone from a circular sequencing, where it seemed to go faster and faster, to a spiral woven into the nowness.

The Evolving of Nowness and Source

Perhaps there is a misunderstanding about the nowness. The nowness is evolving, but it is not sequential. Can you conceive that? It is sometimes difficult on the physical level to conceive how the nowness could be moving outside sequential time, but the nowness knows who it is. I want to emphasize that the purpose of sequential time is simply to discover and release those misperceptions that you have from the past. The Source doesn't have any of those misperceptions; It knows who It is, and It is always discovering more about Itself. Nor does It have any illusions to release. There is only a greater understanding of love, a greater understanding of joy, a greater sense of appreciation and gratitude. All of the heart qualities are progressing, are expanding within that nowness. The effort is going in many, many directions, and I would say that curiosity is one of the more important attributes that our Source has.

I have taught that there are many levels of Source, and our Source is always merging into another, greater Source. There is almost always a coming together of levels of Sourceness, which then expands the creativity of All That Is. But this is not a sequencing of time. This is an expansion of creative knowingness, of the ability to integrate, of the sense of proportion, of the sense of dynamic and receptive interaction. It is a source of understanding, of wisdom, a source of a new beginning that fits proportionally into what is ending. In other words, it is difficult to talk about time without referring to sequence. But when one level of a spiral is ending and another is beginning, what does that show you? Well, that our Source is learning these things, but they are not programmed areas or levels of illusion.

I am not saying that physical existence contains only levels of illusion or programming, because it contains joy, your association with each other, and the ability to transcend what you felt was true for you in the past. You may have a life that is very good, but you are always transcending it, so it gets even better. The point is that the Source evolves and you evolve with It.

The Source level of clarity is yours for the asking. That is true, but you have heard it so many times that for some of you it almost doesn't register, it doesn't seem to enter the creative mode as widely as you would like. Why? Because of the nature of the subconscious mind. That is why in our work with the subconscious we go into the negative as well as the positive parts of it. For every time that you have heard "you are love" in your lives, you have experienced a dozen occasions of feeling guilty or unloved. So when you affirm or when you hear over and over again "you are love," all of these "buts" come up from the subconscious and get your attention. There is a lot of energy in these "buts," and that is what keeps you circling in physical existence. Certainly that doesn't mean that you're not moving — you are! But imagine how it would feel if, one of these days, when you hear the words "I am love," you could look at it from the level of the Source and say to the universe: "I want to plug into the understanding of that level. I want that to be mirrored back to me. I want to be in a creative space that is hooked into the eternal now enough that when that mirror says to me, 'I love you,' I can receive it in a space where I can recognize what that means."

I am not saying that every one of you will get this right tonight, but maybe you can accept that you are not at the mercy of time. Many of you have dropped illusions and now assume self-responsibility. But one of the last illusions to go is that of time and space. What many of you haven't yet understood is that it is time to utilize that eternal now to let go of this sequencing you have responded to over and over and over again.

Your Summary Life

One thing that happens, as many of you know, is that as you finish up physical existence, you summarize everything. This is a summary life – you know this. That means that at every physical age you go through in this life, you also experience what you went through in every other life at that age – everything that you haven't completely integrated into your understanding.

Let us say that you are 40 years old and that you have had 1500 lives on Earth. Let us further say that in 10% to 20% of those lives you didn't live to be 40 years old, so they don't hook in. In 80% of your lives you did, so let's look at those. Creatively, two or three months before you reach your 40th birthday, some anxieties begin to come up about it. On both the inner and outer levels you start running the gamut of what needs to be absorbed, what needs to be integrated in the 40th year. You may go into a life in which you had a spear in your side, and suddenly you have a pain there and you don't know why. Certainly you don't remember being speared there, but it hurts just the same. Or perhaps your neck is sore for a few days and you think, "I need to have it adjusted; it's killing me!" (Interesting term, isn't it?) So then you begin to work your way through that.

Perhaps in another life you were a woman, and at age 40 your dancing career was suddenly over. They told you, "You're too old to be a dancer any longer." Suddenly your legs begin to hurt; maybe you even find that one knee swells up with arthritis, or perhaps one day you trip and break a leg or you turn your ankle. Within your physical structure and within your emotional body you are running the gamut of those experiences that you haven't yet understood within physical existence. Now you can begin to understand that time has done something. Think about it. You took a whole life to reach that point of 40 and have that experience; and now, within about three months of your 40th year, you are going to look at the 80% of your lives and all those experiences you haven't yet absorbed. No wonder it gets intense!

The good news is that some of them are levels of the same thing. You may have 200 lives where this neck has been a problem in one way or another. Three years ago someone broke her ankle, and I told her that she had done it twice in this lifetime as well as 28 times in other lives on the Earth plane. You see, the same patterns of behavior occur over and over until you finally absorb the lesson, until you really understand. When you come into the summary life, time is different. You can bring together the many levels and layers in that one experience and resolve it. That is, in a sense, the beginning of understanding how to go beyond sequential time. In the summary life you get all the seeds of those abilities that are going to lead you beyond the physical plane. You can get a glimpse of bringing several things in – not sequentially, but gathering them together – and if you can do it consciously, that helps. This is an analogy of Sourceness gathering all

Its children, but it is also an analogy of you as a creator gathering up those little wandering aspects that are lost because you haven't yet built them into the heart process.

The Heart Is the Key

The heart is the key, and many of you know that. This key can be important as you go beyond time-sequencing. The heart qualities are the principal ingredients of Sourceness. Certainly we could look at the Source in many, many ways, but the heart qualities are the main ingredients, so the deeper you allow yourself to go into the heart qualities, the more nonsequential time will be for you. That is important for you.

Let us say that something has happened and you become angry or upset. First of all, forgive yourself. Then go immediately into the heart and allow it to connect you again. The reaction is the disconnector. The heart quality of forgiveness is the connector. Everytime you are connected, it stops time as you know it. Time will continue to seem to move. It is holding a connection and allowing an expansion of consciousness within that connection.

When you say to the Creator, "I grasp, I invoke, I demand my potentiality," that is not selfish, because you are doing it in the name of the creative process. You are doing it as a creator. It is not, in a sense, individualized; it is as an administrator of this creativity that you represent. If you selfishly ask the universe to send you something, the results are interesting. You might say, "I want to be a dictator on the Earth; I want all the power that the Earth contains. I want that!" Believe me, if you look at your history, there have been those who tried that. What happens to them? Well, at first it may seem to work; the connection is made, the universe listens as it always listens. And then something seems to go wrong. It doesn't seem to work very well after a while. Why not?

Well, the universe is run by a plan, and that plan has divided the power, or the creativity, proportionately. If you demand of the universe more than your portion, it will dish out your portion and then that's it, because there isn't any more of it for you. If you try to take it from other people, it might seem to work for a while because some people don't know how to hold on to their power and they'll give it away. But the universe is a great equalizer, and if you give away your power, the universe is going to redistribute it — not necessarily among people on the physical level, but it may use it to build new universes, another kind of use. It is not going to give it to someone else — not ever!

You may say, "I can tell you about this person and that person — they have a great deal of power." If we were to analyze that, I could tell you how they got it. They did not — *did not* — get more than their share from the universe. What may have happened is that they gave away their power for a long time and then all of a sudden got it back. That's how some people win the lottery or get a lot of money. Maybe for 50 lifetimes in a row they had piled up credits, then suddenly they found out how to call it in; they got this windfall. But it is something that they have earned. You can be very sure that there is a process of equalization within physical existence and beyond. I think most of you believe that it works that way on the spiritual level, but you have not seen that it can also work that well on the physical level.

Some of you may ask, "What about the conquerors on Earth — Alexander the Great, William the Conqueror, Napoleon, Hitler, Kublai Khan?" These beings had great power. But if they tried to manipulate power against the plan, they would not have piled up credits; they would have piled up debits. They borrowed against their future. Some of them have done that, and they're still paying it back. It's like a cosmic bank. The important point is that they aren't really taking it away from anyone else unless someone else allows them to. And even then the universe will equal that out. I think this is helpful to know, because sometimes life doesn't seem fair, does it?

When a great disaster wipes out a thousand children or when people are killed in an airplane crash, I know it seems unfair to many of you, and you ask why the universe has permitted that. First of all, it is an individual choice. For some people it is their exit gate: time-sequencing seems to have brought them to the point where this life is to be completed. But perhaps more importantly, in the area of power, within the area of creativity, they may have used up the power or credits available for that life. The Chinese have a name for it — when it is gone the life seems to be over.

But there is a renewal process, and that process is certainly within the heart. When you have faith in the Creator, when you have faith or trust in the Plan and believe that it is not unfair, that it will work for you and others, then something begins to happen. There is an enthusiasm built within you that says, "Yes! I can see that it is working, that things are happening! I can trust it."

When an airplane crashes, and hundreds of people are killed, I notice that there is a shock wave that goes all over your planet. This shock affects the creativity on the planet. It causes a separation in the ability to trust the process. Some people begin to wonder if they should fly in airplanes. "Look at that DC-10; its tail fell off. I don't want to get in one of those!" The whole process is seen as unsafe, whether it is an airplane, ship, dirigible or whatever. Many times in your past the vehicles that were supposed to be the safest, like the Titanic and the Hindenburg, went down. It is the system that you are using. It is important for you to communicate; when an accident like this happens, it is important to help the mass consciousness get over it. Your media has a tendency to sensationalize that sort of event. Why? Because sensation gives you a thrill in the area of creativity.

Some of you bury your emotions, and many mental people like sensationalism. Not every person likes sensationalism, but it allows mental people to get in contact with emotions they can't contact in any other way. Sensationalism is used to contact the creative process. But it doesn't get them anywhere because it goes around and around, and then they need more sensationalism. It begins to become rather addictive. You need more sensationalism to get the sense of being creative. Remember, my friends, there is certainly mental creativity, but in the fullest holistic sense, creativity needs emotional involvement.

You can't bury the emotions and still be fully conscious in the nowness. The very fact that you bury the emotions means that they are triggers to past experiences, and they continue to move you in this endless circle. You have to release the illusion that sensationalism, this thrill, is an emotion and is something you want to have. This is what lies behind the teenage game of "chicken" that was popular at one time, and it is the basis of movies in the United States such as *Friday the 13th*, movies that use women as victims. Why is it that a sense of sensationalism is used to substitute for a clear use of creativity? When you grow up a little creatively you begin to release the need to have this. You begin to see that the eternal nowness that you're trying to plug into can't use it. You have to get rid of that first or else you stay in that circling, that level of illusion, that teenage use of creativity.

The Awakening of Mass Consciousness

There is, then, an awakening on this planet, but it needs to go deeper. It needs to be reflected now into the mass consciousness. That is the next opportunity that is here. The plan is beginning to open up the mass consciousness. You might have noticed it. In certain areas of your world 20% of the people are ready for more conscious understanding of who they are. That is called transformation. This awakening of the mass conscious-ness is really accelerating. Why? Because the Earth is three-quarters of the way through its evolution. It's the same age as the cosmic day and is thus, in a sense, beginning to summarize who and what it is. Mass consciousness is getting ready to be more integrated in response to the cosmic day's integration; it is maturing with the planet. It's beginning to see that these things will not be necessary.

You may look at the material in mass consciousness and say, "It seems to me to be getting worse." But it is only getting more visible. Instead of being buried and hidden, as happened in your Victorian Age, it is coming up to the surface to be cleansed. It's a much freer age. In the Victorian Age it was a disgrace if a woman's ankle was seen, and there has since been a letting go of having to cover up. Becoming visible is not always comfortable; sometimes you would like to sweep things under the carpet — things like the drug problems that have been with you since the planet was created. There have been periods in your history when they were worse. But these and other symptoms are just more visible, and that's not necessarily bad.

As you reach the core of an issue, which is the most important, you may think it is the most difficult because you are pushing against all these things you are trying to summarize, to put together. It isn't so much that it is more; it's just that it is coming at you from every direction and you're trying to put it all together. This point was reached by the Earth two years ago, during the Harmonic Convergence. Thus we've come over the hump and there is now an ease that only just since April is finally beginning to manifest.

There is now a new level of creative freedom. Remember what freedom is – it is not running away from something but being willing to enter into something greater. The personality level often misunderstands freedom, so you have to reeducate it. A summary process is taking place on both the individual and the planetary levels. Whether we look at it as an individual or as a planetary process, we are talking about an integrative period where all of you in your religious beliefs allow each other, and it fits together very well.

Space Is Malleable

There are many ways of looking at space. Some have said that space is only here in the third dimension, that there is no space in the fourth dimension. I don't agree with that; it is just that space is a flow and the fourth dimension is a flow, so space is different in the fourth dimension. I also don't agree that space is an illusion. Space is a specific within a larger concept, and we are trying to see it fit in here. But space is as malleable now as time. This is why all of you are ready to learn teleportation – you're ready to move your physical body within your lightbody, wherever you want it to move. Space and time are not limiting now. Let us say that some of you who are from Europe want to return home, but it's a long, expensive trip. How about teleportation? It would certainly simplify it.

The key, of course, is realizing that you've got a support system. Many of you are familiar with this. There is an energy grid system that supports your planet, but it's not a fixed grid system. It used to be, but it's not anymore. It is responsive to the creative effort of the Source.

I would say that knowing a little astrology could be very helpful for you in learning to teleport. There are times during the phases of the Moon and the alignment of the planets where it's going to be much easier to teleport, where it's going to be easier to make that connection, because the grid system will reflect a particular alignment of the aspects (what are called planets in astrology are simply aspects of consciousness that exist on your planet). As they line up in periods of low resistance, or at particular triggering points – I would say to watch Neptune and Pluto – or when they are especially responsive to some of the more mundane planets (in relation to Venus, Jupiter and Mars, where there are good alignments or a trine of that planet with Earth, particularly a grand trine), then this can trigger something like a collapse of space until there is an overlay of certain areas. And then you have to trust the plan.

That's the hardest part for all of you: recognizing that you can plug in. When this time and this space collapses, it isn't any farther from here to Germany than it is from this chair to the one over there. But you must trust and balance whatever little space there seems to be. There is a need to be so focused into that eternal now that the universe keeps flashing to you a wider and wider band of your creativity, which you keep grasping, saying, "It's mine; I can hold on to that, and I can flow on it now. I can trust that in alignment with the plan." It's almost as if the plan has a band of light here; it's not space. It's a creative effort. Certainly we could call it a focus; let's say we'll make that focus align from here to that chair.

Now, let's say that in the planetary alignments, the space has integrated and is going to re-form in a way that is not as arbitrary as before. It is more malleable, more flexible. In the great inbreath and outbreath of the Source, which is not sequential, this is difficult to conceive. As the creative effort blends here, this is where you want to teleport before it breathes out again — that motion where the creative effort in its polarity interchange, in its receiving and dynamic flow, comes together, acknowledging its part's efforts. Perhaps that's the best way of putting it. It has to be aligned where you are acknowledging your creative part's effort. You come together this way [claps], with the universe balancing its inbreath and you balancing your creative inbreath, recognizing each other and then quickly flowing on that. That flow is not sequential; it is simply that you're here and then you're in Berlin, Munich, Stuttgart, Vienna, Zurich, anywhere. Later you'll be able to do it without that precise collapse of space, but at first it will be easier if you do that.

You can practice it through the breath. You can first of all sense the grid system that is flowing on the Earth, and you can say, "All right, now it is coming together. Now my physical body is focused so well in my lightbody — my mental body, my emotional body, my physical body, my spiritual body are within this light focus. You would do that all in advance so that you would touch into it just as that creative breath collapsed the space for you. Then you would use your dynamic energy to move into that wider connection, and you would find yourself in the next city.

It would be important, especially when you're practicing, to have a visual example of where you want to go. You don't want to end up in a fountain or in a wall. If you don't know anyone in the city you want to go, get someone to try to find a picture that shows you a place where you could land — perhaps a garden or outside a building. You can practice on someone's home if you've been there and land on their couch or something. I don't think it would be too comfortable for your physical cells to rematerialize inside a wall — they don't like being inside walls. I think it would be fun to be in a wall — I did that a couple of times; actually, I got quite a sore knee. I learned to teleport that way. That's why I can tell you: I did it once; that's how I learned it. I lost a leg and had to regrow it. Now, that taught me a lesson, because I had to learn to regrow it right then.

Another thing that is important in teleportation and space collapse is that the cells of your body fit into and literally cling to and become a part of that light beam. It is like hooking on to a wire. It is important to recognize this and allow the cells to be full of light. That's one reason I give you these meditations where you fill the cells with light. As you become more comfortable and confident in yourself as light, you become aware that that light can move anywhere. If you can have light here, you can see the light over there, so why can't you go over there? So you gain confidence in the fact that you are light and a part of light everywhere.

There is a being at the Galactic Core — Melchior — who is ready to help all of you with teleportation. Why don't you ask him for assistance? Meet him in the heart area; that connector can be very helpful for you. You can ask the angelic kingdoms, too, for help in this area. You might ask to have an angel who could become a light being; and perhaps you could feel comfortable walking on an angel. Why not? The angelic kingdom will assist you as you wish.

Or ask this ascended tree out here. You could ask the plant kingdom — believe me, your plant kingdom knows how to teleport! You might not have thought about that, but do you think those plants always stay where they are? No, they do not. You have plants here that have been in other parts of the world. Do they appear always to be there? Yes, but you've never watched them teleport. They know how to teleport. They move around your planet, but you don't see it. Perhaps they've learned not to let you see them do it. Why? Because they don't think you understand it. If a tree suddenly disappears when someone is looking, and they tell you about it, you might think they're nuts. Trees have a different time sequence.

Think about teleportation and space and time-sequencing. It is very important for you to recognize that time and space are not the way they were before. In fact, nothing exists as it did before the Harmonic Convergence. One of the most important things to recognize is that you have a more malleable existence. Because you have learned enough so that the universe is recognizing you again as a creator. Previously, the universe only recognized the Earth as the creator. Then there was an arbitrary law set up. Why? When you have a bunch of small children, you set up rules and guidelines so the children won't burn themselves. But when they grow up a little, you don't have to have those restrictions and rules. You've outgrown some of the need to have those restrictions now. I think that can be important. Let's do a final meditation now.

Meditation

❦ *I'd like to offer gratitude to each of you. I come to you, each one of you, and ask that you receive this gratitude. It is my gratitude; but perhaps beyond that it is the gratitude of many of us. Each one of you has given so much,* and we truly are very grateful. You are very strong; you are very loving beings who cared enough to come to the Earth. I hope you can sense how much we appreciate this, and perhaps in your return flow you can send your gratitude down to the Planetary Logos who made this possible for you – the beautiful being called Sanat Kumara. In our attunement to him let us feel the great love, and if you will allow, his love will flood you. If you will permit it, he will be there supporting you. There is now as much love there as you can allow, and more. This being is always there, always supportive, always allowing, always compassionately aware of you and your needs. I ask that you give thanks. I ask that you show your love, your appreciation, now.

🐝 Now let us look deeply at Sanat Kumara's physical structure. We enter deeply now, and what we find at the core is again love. Let us enter that focus of love and be responsive to it. Put it on now; wear it as a garment, a garment of light. Because love is light. Feel it now, a beautiful light that you are wearing. I thank you. Goodnight.

✧ E I G H T ✧

Cocreator University

T HE COCREATOR COUNCIL IS A DIRECTED LEVEL OF THE MANIFESTED SOURCE.
once you are through expressing your individuality at the cocreator
level — "cocreator university" — your aspects function on and share a level of
responsibility equal to directors and members of the Council. Your consciousness literally focuses in one of eleven areas, and that is the responsibility level you assume. Through a process of recognizing and growing into
that level, you assume a sense of wholeness within the Council circle. That
is what I am trying to convey as I discuss these eleven areas.

This cocreator university is a vast training ground, and within it are
many levels. Some cocreators are freshmen, and others are doing postgradu-
ate work. All levels are stepping into their fully manifested divine responsibilities within one of these positions.

When a cosmic day is created, the Creator decides upon one theme.
Courage is the theme of this cosmic day. There are eleven beings plus you
representing Sourceness. Number twelve is your I Am Presence. Remember, this is the manifested Source, not beingness without manifestation.

Our circle represents the conceptual framework of courage. At the
beginning of a cosmic day, the circle says, "We are going to explore courage
as fully as we can. Courage will be explored in this exercise of Sourceness."
Eleven beings take their place to administer this exercise. We could call
them connectors.

There is the basic level of physicality, the cocreator level, and all levels
in between. Each cocreator focuses a little differently and holds that focus.
They are the means, the pillars, upon which that day is explored.

Each of you has a future of holding a focus yourself. At one point there
will be a cosmic day in which you are a fully realized pillar on the cocreator
level. This will precede your ability to understand yourself as a full creator

— perhaps it is the last step before realizing yourself as all of creation.

You move into full creatorship one step at a time. Being a member of this council does not mean you will go through all eleven positions. Some have; others have held just one position. More fully, you sense what the Creator is by holding a position of responsibility in the overall scheme of things, the overall day, from every point of you. Eventually, you will probably explore this very vast concept on every level.

Each of the eleven beings has a focus. My point for bringing this in now is to give you their focus and your connection to each one. You have a mentor on this very high level who is educating your monadic level and viewing all your growth and learning.

Many of you ask me, "What is my purpose? Why am I here? What am I to do on the Earth?" What you are really asking is how to more clearly connect into one of these cocreators. You are looking for the point of focus that is going to help you integrate everything else. Your goal on Earth is to integrate your understanding of all you learn and go beyond. This leads to a new beginning and a new understanding to integrate at the next level, and again at the next level, and so on until you enter the cocreator university and become a freshman.

As a freshman you will actually help implement the day. This is not an individual focus; there is a being who directs it. Perhaps I'll generalize here and say there are one billion souls or monadic-level beings or more involved in each one of these focuses. Keep in mind that there is an unlimited number of beings in the many universes, and not every one is active in every cosmic day. In fact, only about 10% of all the Source's potentiality is active in a cosmic day.

You are interested in support because about 90% is supportive. You have often been a part of support, and you want to feel it again. About 90% of Source's potentiality is supportive (receptive) and 10% is active (dynamic). This is one reason why many of you understand your receptive side better than your dynamic side. You have explored the receptive, supportive side many more times than the dynamic.

Allow your intuition to put you in touch with the concepts I am giving you. Your intuition is aware in a way your mental, emotional and physical bodies is not. So sit and let this information flow in. Let your male body get as much as it can — that will help you understand the concepts. We are stimulating something beyond mental concepts that is difficult to put into words. We will do the best we can with the very limiting language called English. (It would be easier if you went back to Sanskrit, for it certainly could better express these concepts.)

Let me equate you, a support of Source, to a snowflake. The movement (dynamic) of a snowflake is equal to 10% of the snowflake. The other 90% is the support — the snowflake itself. Life force is held within that 90%. Each snowflake is unique because there are many points of consciousness within a snowflake. It is within groups of snowflakes that consciousness is held in a supportive way. When the snowflake moves, it is pulled through or driven by the active or the dynamic 10%.

Again, we might equate movement and support to a train which has a locomotive engine pulling along many cars. The cars (90%) are the support system and the locomotive (10%) the means to move them. In your active state you have a tendency to pull back to your supportive state because you are not yet balanced enough to use them both. The basic reason the Source gave us polarities is so that we could understand the difference between the supporting role and the active role. In a sense they are the same. Source has taken existence apart and shown you that there are parts so you can understand how they fit together.

The activity, the 10%, is what we are going to talk about. It's the active role of the cocreators saying, "All right, I will take responsibility for one phase of what is currently a long day. This one is 4.3 billion of your years, and you are three-quarters through it. You can see things are functioning very well, because there is a good basic understanding of everybody's role and how they fit together. In the last quarter of a cosmic day, there is always much more integration than before. Your Earth is a manifestation of the cosmic day, so it is in this same last quarter. Therefore it is integrating, it's learning its function and how it fits into the greater scheme.

You are all approaching this point of awakening. Do you have neighbors? How do you contact them? How do you allow them to come to the Earth? Equally important, how do you recognize that many are already here? Rather than have them hide for fear that humanity, in its warlike state, will harm them, how do you welcome them? The point is, your Earth now represents something much more cosmic.

There are eleven groups, departments or areas of expertise in the cocreator university. The following schematic diagram shows their areas and organization.

Department One I have termed **utilization**. In my book about dimensions [*Scopes of Dimensions*], I talk about the Source coming forth, manifesting as a wholeness and beginning to explore a new level. In this sense, Department One is the group that turns manifestation on. This is the first level of expression of a cosmic day. The learning at this level will be in the area of **courage**. This being, the mentor of this group, inspires others through courage because that is the function of everyone in this group. Many times they make contact with new frontiers. Often you don't see them because it is a lesson by which they learn and receive greater understanding.

This department of the cosmic day brings in everything about the theme of courage. It gathers together all the bits and pieces of what courage represents. Courage is the theme; there is a lot going on besides courage, but it all comes through the tone of courage. When you make a realization you use courage, then this department says, "Ah, there is one that's ours,"

THE COCREATOR COUNCIL

and a cosmic paper, a memo, is filed in Department One. They record your utilization of what you realized and defined through the theme of the day. Anyone focused with this first mentor will find it very difficult to escape from the recurring theme of courage; it will be there all the time.

In a very positive way, those focusing with the first mentor become great leaders because they get the full brunt of learning all that courage means as they get in basic contact with this theme. Others with different mentors don't yet see that you become what you think you are. They don't yet know that you have to believe you have courage and use what you really understand. Those with the first mentor are always in touch with courage, whether they know it on not.

Those of you who are focused on Department One (or anyone, for that matter) can reach these cocreator beings of utilization by contacting the being *La-mo-nay-go*. Of course, you are already in contact with them, but your goal is to be very conscious of every contact you have on every level.

Department Two has some correspondence with numerology. Its focus is **balance**, stability and centeredness. Many beings who have this mentor are world mediators or mediators of existence. Much of the time, these mediators see both sides of situations. They will say, "Yes, but on the other hand," and, "Yes, but I can see this point of view also." Through who they are, they are attempting to balance the whole wheel, to balance everything.

Say you are in a group. Everyone is talking, there are four or five opinions and it kind of heats up. Generally, there is someone who has a conceptual understanding and sees the whole big picture. They begin to smooth the waters by giving support to one opinion as well as another opinion, and yet another opinion, and because they seem to be supporting everyone, the discussion comes to a resolution.

Some at this level are just learning the ability to balance. Resolution doesn't mean they have learned to integrate everything, but they are balancing. This is an important point. They are balancing the level that is being activated in the cosmic day. There are infinite levels being activated. When one level is being expressed and experienced, this department's role is to help balance, stabilize and center that level.

Those associated with this second group are generally caught up in how much is going on, and they take it very well. They are generally very optimistic because they have a degree of sense about wholeness on an overall level. One life might not, but the overall view does.

The monad expresses; that expression goes to the soul level, which in turn expresses, and it is extended into physicality. So we are not talking about one part — we are talking about overall wholeness, that spark of Creator Itself.

If you are on this path, you may be an extension of a monad that needs the part you are learning in the area of balance. A monad might say, "I need someone in the South American jungle area" or "I need one who will explore the Arctic" or "I need one over here doing this and that." The monadic level directs souls. Sometimes people try to bypass the soul level. When I find that, I always help those people work with it. Level two is in quite direct contact with the monadic level, which fosters balance, stability and centeredness. The being who heads the monadic level, *Kom-go-ma-hay*, is truly magnificent.

Department Three I call *Ha-ha-ha*. This is **creativity**, open-ended flow. The chief focus in this cocreator section is clearing the path for the flow of creativity. It seeks a very open-ended, unrestricted, clear flow from the cocreator level to allow humanity and others to totally tune into and grasp this flow that indicates the Creator's plans for creation. This flow allows the pieces of the puzzle to be put together to create what is anticipated for this cosmic day.

This creativity must come from all the awarenesses of all the billions of beings on this third path. It ties in, or utilizes, all their former experiences and myriad ways of solving a creative problem. The group finds what is necessary for bringing into being the creative potential, the creative plan, for this universe for this cosmic day.

Many, many are involved in this, and you who are on this level find yourself constantly seeking for new and better solutions, better ways of making life interesting, exciting, purposeful, comfortable and joyous.

This creativity flow tries to maximize all of these happy emotions to bring forth the kind of cosmic day the Creator has envisioned. This group is looking for complete fulfillment through the use of courage. So, of course, it is also concerned with the creative aspect of the infinite number of ways courage can be tested, brought forth and used as a tool.

The creativity of each one blends into the whole, allowing for the many agendas of the billions of beings in this area. As in a university, the importance given to a certain phase of this exploration depends on the point of view of the graduate students and the director of that area. Their judgment is not negative; it is an evaluation, discrimination or decision that is more appropriate than any other. Ego is not there. There is a broad base of paradigms to be considered before something can be decided, for there is an infinite number of ways to go.

This group is very dynamic, very flowing with change. It is constantly in change and constantly introducing something new. There isn't a lot of reflection; there is more movement and doing. As cocreator ideas filter in and act upon this group, there is emotion and blending. Level Three uses the receptive and the dynamic, and polarity is very much involved.

At a beginning level, the movement is constant, and the creativity being utilized is not evaluated. Creativity is utilizing all it can push through, all it can allow to flow. In a later phase can come more selection of the correct, useful and appropriate level.

Department Four is called the **structure of existence** on all levels. Actually, it is a result of the third level. When it has been established what the creativity is going to be on all levels, it is necessary to have something holding that creativity, allowing it to be structured. There must be a basic foundation in the dimensions to allow them a certain type of creativity. Without structure there cannot be manifested creativity. All structures set up here are determined by what is needed for the creativity that has been decided upon and produced in this cosmic day. In this way, dimensions are determined on the basis of what it takes to support each level of creativity being used this cosmic day. This requires and allows for a structure that will support everything that needs to be, wants to be or can be created for the exploration of courage.

Everyone knows there is no water without a container to hold it in. Anything that flows through is gone rapidly, but if there is a structure to contain it, it can be worked with. This is the job of the cocreators of Level Four. I call this level An-mo-nee-na. Structures can be bodies, planets, solar systems or any of the kingdoms. Each little animal, each little bug, each star is a structure that can produce an exploration in courage. Their structures allow the creativity of Level Three to attain its potential.

There are many working on these structures all the time. Many angels are in charge of working on new structures, along with many elementals. Creating structures is a constant on this planet and within the Earth. Those workers are inspired by the cocreators of Department Four. They work constantly on changing and improving the structures here on Earth to allow new experiences. So allow them to change. Let the structures no longer needed here move off the Earth and be used where they are needed. Change is part of the whole wheel and cannot be ruled out of anything.

Once we have structures, we go on to Department Five, which I call **conceptual overview**. This looks at all the pieces, the creative potentials and all the structures designed to fit creative urges. Department Five looks at ways structures can fit together to make an appropriate, reasonable and lovable cosmic day.

The relationship of structures is crucial, *vital*. You cannot put Lilliputians and dinosaurs in the same place, unless you give the small ones a great deal more mental power than you give the great big ones. You cannot have a species that needs to maintain a temperature of 100° living with a species that needs a temperature of 0°. You must take into account any limitations of these structures – how they fit together, the relationship possible for the consciousnesses of these structures – to see how to put together structures that interact appropriately, lovingly. You need to allow courage to manifest without wiping out all the structures. That happens frequently, and it takes a very acute, analytical sense of relationships in this fifth cocreator level. It is the job of Level Five to bring everyone's purposes together through certain structures into a unified whole where they will fit together without clashing or squelching each other. That harmonious relationship must exist between all structures, all kingdoms, all physical existence, planets and universes.

This is a very delicate job and requires a very resourceful and knowledgeable being to do it. Perhaps more than any other, this job requires one who has a great deal of general information about a great deal of livingness. I am calling this one *Pa-ha-mop-?* The question mark indicates the question that is always present: It may look all right, but is it going to work?

Through their relationships, number-fives develop sensitivity, helping to identify more and more the overall view of all existence. It shows your part in the whole and your alignment within in the Plan so you can see how it fits together. The emphasis is on identifying relationships and your part in them so you can see the conceptual overview.

Department Six I call **expansive Source directive**, *Pha-ha-mop*. I find Level Six tremendously interesting because it was my original focus. (I have recently changed my focus; that is possible. When you know enough to know what you are transferring in and out of, you can transfer. I was studying to be. I desired to and was allowed to move.)

But Six was my original focus – expansive Source directive. I have added the bridging process. It might help you to know that from the time I was first on the physical level, I was always interested in Source. I wanted to know what It was, how It learned, how It was growing. I wanted to understand more and more about It, I wanted to identify with Source. With all my questions, I must have driven crazy any teacher I had on any level. I always wanted to know in what direction the Source was moving – "How will that go and what does that mean and what will come from that?" I would say, "Project your understanding a step further and show me how that will expand." I was always into the expansiveness of the Source level.

And this is the role of the eighth dimension. It is a laboratory for experimenting with many things. The beings on Level Six are the directors of that eighth-dimension laboratory. Not all cosmic days work out well; some are pulled back. It is not fair to have them go nowhere, so they are put into a laboratory and miniaturized on the eighth dimension, and there they get finished.

Not only are things finished on the eighth dimension, but things are being thought of, like "Where next?" Unlimited projections are made: "What if we do this? What if that is done? How could we do this? Well, let's just try this." You could call it a think tank directed by cocreator number six. Some of you to whom I gave number six may be stretched because ultimately it is your role to be part of such a process, and it is very exciting. The being in charge here is one of the most dynamic, intellectually stimulating and spiritually expansive beings I have ever had the privilege of meeting. I changed my focus because I realized my role could be used on Level Six and elsewhere by going into another focus. That was the only reason I moved.

Po-em-pay. Department Seven: **Integration through links of opportunity,** joining of levels, spontaneity through identification of creative linkage. I want to pull that together for you. We will call it relation through links of opportunity. You may ask, "Vywamus, what in the world does that mean?" Perhaps this I had the most difficulty understanding. I kept saying, "What do you mean, 'links of opportunity'?"

I have often said that opportunities don't knock on your door and tell you, "I'm an opportunity." They come in more than one at a time. There will be an opportunity, and you might say, "Oh, isn't that wonderful," and then another one will come in and you will have to decide which one to choose. When you were looking for one, it wasn't there, and now that you have more than one you have to make a decision.

The bunching or linking of opportunities is meant to teach you discernment. It teaches you which opportunities are openings and which are not or are invoked from your past and perhaps not the clearest way to go now. Some opportunities may keep reiterating the level of creativity you are on. Such opportunities are not terrible, but they won't lead you closer to the career level of creativity you want or fulfill your purposes here. So spontaneity is important.

We have talked about the Violet Flame. It is very much associated with Department Seven, and this is where it fits. I link the Violet Flame to spontaneity and all of this. It links levels of opportunities or shows you how to take the next step for yourself through discernment. Those associated with Level Seven yearn for the number seven and the Violet Flame. You wear a lot of violet. You might not be focused on this number, but you might be working through many opportunities that are beginning to link together. You are learning discernment, the spontaneity of opportunity which creates an integrative process. You take a step and go to a dance; that is one opportunity. You had decided not to take some opportunities, but here comes another. You say yes and here comes another, and pretty soon you are able to dance along, moving spontaneously. One yes to an opportunity triggers another through the transformational process of your consciousness.

This process allows evolution to take place. You have to have a cleansing process or you might get a little stuck as you move. Number seven is closely related to number four in an esoteric sense. On Earth, which is civilized through Level Four, many have tried to bring in either number three or number seven.

You have someone here called St. Germain. The "Ger" is our connection: *Ger-ha-ba*. This nice one is Department Eight. **Power**, as seen through the mirroring process, comes from Level Eight. Another word for Level Eight is **mirror**. The being *Ger-ha-ba* directs the mirroring process. This is an awesome concept.

At the Source level, every part of the cosmic day is mirroring to every other part. It is directed from and contains unlimited universes that are right here. Physical existence makes up only 10% of existence. The other 90% is more vast than you know. But even on the physical level there are unlimited universes, and yours is but one. This is a tremendously vast concept level.

Department Eight clearly reflects power. Those associated with this level are always learning about power, Many times they are clear about power but not necessarily all of the time. However, they have always been in league with divine power. We never find anyone focused on Level Eight who has misused power. They may have been confused, but they have never misused it because they have the strength to draw on their clear understanding of power. Each time you focus on a level, there will be a powerful learning for you. You will be very sensitive to issues common to that level.

At certain points, Level Eleven aspects are even more intimately linked with knowledge about power. This holds true when the physical environment, whether it is Earth or another planet, is opening its eyes to see that another level of power can be used instead of the limited one they have.

This happens when it is opening up to mirror another level.

Level Eight is represented by a very great being. Part of it is the ability to put any puzzle together very rapidly. When that is complete, number-eights have the ability to recognize it for what it is. There is power association.

How is power defined? Divine power is always heart-centered. If we look at it as always directed from the heart, then what is it? I am trying to get away from the negative charge often associated with the word "power." I want you to see beyond the misuse of power and beyond your present conscious understanding of power. Power is not something you turn on. I don't equate it with the dynamic energy, although the dynamic energy is a part of power. The word "power" helps you understand the Divine Essence and Its choices. Perhaps it helps you see beyond self and into the Self the Creator represents. This takes you beyond the sense that life force is only in the active stage, because power can be in the supportive, receptive or nonmanifested state, too.

Department Nine is *Bach-hoop-la*, or **invocation**. Invocation can mean different things to each of you. What I mean by the invocational process is the invoking of the next level of creativity. We have talked about how different levels integrate and open to the next one and how they affect the whole process, but this invocation is very specific. It says, "All right, now we are ready for the next step — let's do it." This is the ready-to-go syndrome.

Picture the spiral of this cosmic day moving and coming to this point. Level Nine says, "All right, we are ready to go now to another level." Then it starts drawing up the process so the next level is active. I have called it a spiral of creativity — levels that affect and reflect the creative process through invocation of the next level of creativity — but the keyword here is "invocative." It is a specific invocation. It isn't concerned with the whole multileveled process. It wants to go ahead with the next step, to proceed one step at a time. It is the focus that brings in the next step. In this sense you don't need time — you need a focus, and that focus is realization. When the realization of the next step comes in, it focuses here, and thus begins the expansion to the next level.

Department Ten: *Fa-am-zop*, or **beauty's flow**. Certainly this reminds one of heart energy. It is a connecting linkage to the heart. To think of it sequentially, by the time you get to Level Ten you are beginning to put everything together. You are beginning to sense the flow. You are reminded over and over again to flow. There is a sense of a mirroring that emphasizes the flow. There is a sense of connection, a structural understanding. The whole process is working well and it is time to lock in an appreciation, to express gratitude. In part, I wanted to use beauty because it becomes clear to you that this is more than just a feeling; at the same time, it is a feeling. It is connection into appreciation of all the gifts given and all that is being expressed here within this wholeness. It brings a sense of awe, appreciation, gratitude and grace that you have been given this — you haven't earned it.

You have been given this — yes, perhaps you have partaken in it because you chose to, but it is not an earned thing. It is a special sense of "Look what is there," and from it come the beauty and appreciation of it all.

In the mystery of all existence, your role has always been there. The wonder of existence brought your part to you. You were created from Source essence, and you are molded to fit into that. It always fits because that is the way the Creator creates: so that things fit together. The system is open-ended, and I would say one of the changes occurs when you are becoming conscious enough to recognize you are in one support system, functioning on one level. It is beginning to prepare you for the next level, whatever your role will be. At that time, you sometimes can make a change in your focus. There are some who go through the whole circle, some who stay on one level, some who go on to two. This is my second assignment, and this is where I am. I am also speaking about planning beyond this cosmic day. I am speaking about the fact that another mentor is beginning to help me understand what lies ahead of this cosmic day.

Department Eleven: *No-ing-nes* — **leadership**. This is the focus of all creativity for the group process at the cocreator level. This department is president of the Cocreator Council — the understanding of maturity of the cocreator council. Here is leadership, but it is not separate from anything — it is not ahead of anything nor behind anything; it is equal to everything. Its responsibility is leadership, as with the president of a university. The cocreator university oversees the whole thing. Many of these other positions report and say, "All right, this is what we need here and this is what we need there." We talked about an advisor in one of the other cocreator positions, but that is not what I mean. It isn't an advisorship role; it is assuming responsibility stepped down from the Creator level. We could say it is the most mature understanding among the cocreators. This is relative, because all of these beings are fully mature, but until we actually enter the cocreator level it is difficult to distinguish the various levels of maturity.

For example, if you are standing on Earth and there is a pole fifty feet high with two people standing on it, can you tell from the ground which of them is taller? Until we reach or enter the cocreator university, we trust, and we decide for ourselves as we enter. I am sure that will be true. One who has entered it recently is Lenduce. One who is a fully developed cocreator, not one of the eleven, is Atlanto. The teacher Atlanto, the one who is channeled, is on Level Eleven. Lenduce is one of the beginning cocreators within the university. I, Vywamus, have not reached that level of maturity yet, and it will be a while before I do. We are talking about different levels of maturity and understanding. One cannot be called better than another, just more conscious than another. Leadership, the chairing of the council, the chairing of the university, perhaps making decisions when there is a tie vote — anything you can think of as a responsibility of a corporate chairman — is what we are talking about in this position.

Anyone having number eleven is in training for such a position. This may be very interesting for those of you on this number. You might not recognize it in yourself yet, but that doesn't mean it isn't there.

These are extremely lofty concepts that explain one-billionth or less of that consciousness. You are getting just a bit because it is so vast. That does not negate doing it and it doesn't mean you are less than. I am just trying to show you the levels of which I am speaking.

Moving on to the I Am Presence, how is the twelfth position relative to these other focuses? It is a divine mystery. The "I Am" in which each of you are centered is itself always centered in the center of creation – in the center of the active process of the Source. Now, if it isn't active, if it is just the essence, there isn't any point asking where you are, because you are everywhere. In the spiraling of the consciousness of Source Itself, there is a center, and that center is everything that exists everywhere. It isn't space, it isn't time – it isn't anything but an essence. It is the transfer of the Wholeness into something that becomes a center, then becomes processed through the activity levels surrounding it. Thus you are a co-representative of Wholeness, centered in that space. It centers you in the learning process, centers you in the stillness, surrounded by the spiral of creation itself.

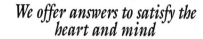

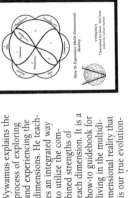

♦ BOOKS BY LYNN BUESS

CHILDREN OF LIGHT, CHILDREN OF DENIAL

In his fourth book Lynn calls upon his decaces of practice as counselor and psychotherapist to explore the relationship between karma and the new insights from ACOA/ Co-dependency writings.

$8.95 Softcover 150p   ISBN 0-929385-15-2

NUMEROLOGY FOR THE NEW AGE

An established standard, explicating for contemporary readers the ancient art and science of symbol, cycle, and vibration. Provides insights into the patterns of our personal lives. Includes life and personality numbers.

$11.00 Softcover 262p   ISBN 0-929385-31-4

NUMEROLOGY: NUANCES IN RELATIONSHIPS

The foremost spokesman for numerology and human behavior focuses on relationships. With clear and direct style he identifies the archetypal patterns of each numerical combination. By providing clues to conscious and unconscious issues, Lynn gives the reader choices of behavior in relationships.

$13.75 Softcover 310p   ISBN 0-929385-23-3

♦ BOOKS by WES BATEMAN

KNOWLEDGE FROM THE STARS

A telepath with contact to ETs, Bateman has provided a wide spectrum of scientific information. A fascinating compilation of articles surveying the Federation, ETs, evolution and the trading houses, all part of the true history of the galaxy.

$11.95 Softcover 171p   ISBN 0-929385-39-X

DRAGONS AND CHARIOTS

An explanation of spacecraft, propulsion systems, gravity, the Dragon, manipulated Light and interstellar and intergalactic motherships by a renowned telepath who details specific technological information received from ETs.

$9.95 Softcover 65p   ISBN 0-929385-26-8

♦ GABRIEL H. BAIN

LIVING RAINBOWS

A fascinating "how-to" manual to make experiencing human, astral, animal and plant auras an everyday event. Series of techniques, exercises and illustrations guide the reader to see and hear aural energy. Spiral-bound workbook.

$14.95 Softcover 134p   ISBN 0-929385-42-X

SOUL EVOLUTION FATHER

Lord God Jehovah through Arthur Fanning Jehovah is back with others, to lead humanity out of its fascination with density into an expanding awareness that each human is a god with unlimited power and potential.

$12.95 Softcover 200p

ISBN 0-929385-33-0

SIMON

A compilation of some of the experiences Arthur has had with the dolphins, which triggered his opening and awakening as a channel.

$9.95 Softcover 56p

ISBN 0-929385-32-2

ON BECOMING

Knowing the power of the light that you are. Expansion of the pituitary gland and strengthening the physical structure. Becoming more of you.   F101 $10

HEALING MEDITATIONS/ KNOWING SELF

Knowing self is knowing God. Knowing the pyramid of the soul is knowing the body. Meditation on the working of the soul and the use of the gold light within the body   F102 $10

MANIFESTATION & ALIGNMENT with the POLES

Alignment of the meridians with the planet's grid system. Connect the root chakra with the center of the planet.   F103 $10

THE ART OF SHUTTING UP

Gaining the power and the wisdom of the quiet being that resides within the sight of thy Father.   F104 $10

CONTINUITY OF CONSCIOUSNESS

Trains you in the powerful state of waking meditation.
(3-tape set) F105 $25

MERGING THE GOLDEN LIGHT REPLICAS OF YOU

The awakening of the Christ consciousness.   F107 $10

UNIFICATION OF THE TANTRIC YOU'S

Learning to love GOD! The essence of the lovingness of you is directly related to your love of God, your understanding of God. The understanding of God in the mate. The movement of God in the mate.   (6-tape set) F108 $60

THOUGHT UNIFIED

Moving into superconsciousness. Everyone will become telepathic. Meditation to balance both hemispheres of the brain.
(6-tape set) F109 $60

UNCONDITIONAL LOVE

The thoughts that each of you have has a wave effect around the planet and back to you. This is called the application of thought through the body. Meditations for the understanding of the application of thought.   (6-tape set) F110 $60

THE NATURAL PLANET

Each human chose to be on Earth now because of the union of the energies. The soul and spiritual consciousness are in a mating season; the physical vehicle is the place of the union. Meditations for experiential understanding.   (5-tape set) F111 $55

WHERE HUMANS ASSIST THE ANGELS

Each of the races holds a secret for humanity to understand.

When all of the pieces of the secret puzzle are put together humanity will understand the union with the divine. Humanity needs to get together to complete the puzzle. Everything is consciousness and everything is God. Humanity has been given the opportunity to live as God in the human vehicle and to know it. The process, however, is the lesson. Meditations for the completion of the puzzle.   (6-tape set) F112 $60

INTRODUCTION TO ID

YHWH explains working with yourself and others toward enlightenment to become much more than the body human. The soul is electrical and an insulator for the light because the physical body is not adapted to the strong force of the light as yet. Meditations to strengthen the physical body for the light.
(7-Tape Set) F113 $65

CONSCIOUSNESS AND THE ELECTRICAL BODY

The God Spark within all of us is altering itself to hold more light. For the physical vehicle to become more enlightened. Several meditations to prepare ourselves for the dimensional shifting taking place. Assisting in overcoming the fears.
(7-tape set) F114 $65

PEBBLES IN THE RIVER OF THOUGHT

YHWH explains the emotional experience as a polishing of the spiritual forces so that we may align unto our true spiritual power. Meditations for alignment and letting go of old patterns.
(6-tape set) F115 $60

RETRAINING THE MONKEY MIND

Working with the pure energy of your being. YHWH provides meditations that allow the inner truths to come out so that the brain can observe the truth and the power of the inner godhood. Retraining the self to speak with the inner power of the light.
(6-tape set) F116 $60

THE EGO AND ITS UNION WITH GOD

Meditations to experience the physical senses as lenses of perception for the soul in this dimension. Development of the inner senses through the 7 chakras.   (5-tape set) F117 $55

SYMBOLS OF THE CREATOR GODS — CONTEMPLATION OF GOD SELF

Meditations for the God Self. Within this system there are creator gods working with other creator gods within the concept of the denial of GOD. The stepping into the wisdom of the God self.
(5-tape set) F118 $55

BOOK MARKET

A reader's guide to the extraordinary books we publish, print and market for your enLightenment.

ORDER NOW!
1-800-450-0985
or Fax 1-800-393-7017
Or use order form at end

6

◆ BOOKS by ROYAL PRIEST RESEARCH

PRISM OF LYRA

Traces the inception of the human race back to Lyra, where the original expansion of the duality was begun, to be finally integrated on earth. Fascinating channeled information with inspired pen and ink illustrations for each chapter.

$11.95 Softcover 112p   ISBN 0-9631320-0-8

VISITORS FROM WITHIN

Explores the extra-terrestrial contact and abduction phenomenon in a unique and intriguing way. Narrative, precisely focused channeling & firsthand accounts.

$12.95 Softcover 171p   ISBN 0-9631320-1-6

PREPARING FOR CONTACT

Contact requires a metamorphosis of consciousness, since it involves two species who meet on the next step of evolution. A channeled guidebook to ready us for that transformation. Engrossing.

$12.95 Softcover 188p   ISBN 0-9631320-2-4

◆ EDITH BRUCE

THE KEYS TO THE KINGDOM

This little book is spiritually rich in wisdom and timely in terms of current world changes. Assembled from a series of channeled readings given by The Great Brother/Sisterhood of Light. The author has touched and lifted the lives of thousands with her powerful healing influence and gentle loving guidance.

$14.95 Softcover 136p   ISBN 0-929385-94-2

◆ MARY FRAN KOPPA

MAYAN CALENDAR BIRTHDAY BOOK

An ephemeris and guide to the Mayan solar glyphs, tones and planets, corresponding to each day of the year. Your birthday glyph represents your souls purpose for this lifetime, and your tone energy, which affects all that you do, influences your expression.

$12.95 Softcover 140p   ISBN 1-889965-03-0

MAYAN CALENDAR COLORING BOOK

Text by Scott Amun
The solar glyph found in each picture, derived from an original painting, holds the energy for the day. Mary studied art in Europe and the U.S., and after a near-death experience, began channeling energy paintings.

$8.95 Softcover 48p   ISBN 1-889965-02-2

BOOK MARKET

A reader's guide to the extraordinary books we publish, print and market for your enLightenment.

◆ NANCY FALLON

ACUPRESSURE FOR THE SOUL

A revolutionary vision of emotions as sources of power, rocket fuel for fulfilling our purpose. A formula for awakening transformation with 12 beautiful illustrations.

ACUPRESSURE FOR THE SOUL

BIOLOGICAL SPIRITUALITY and The Gifts of the Emotions

NANCY FALLON, Ph.D.

ISBN 0-929385-49-7

$11.95 Softcover 150p

◆ BOOKS by RUTH RYDEN

THE GOLDEN PATH

"Book of Lessons" by the master teachers explaining the process of channeling. Akashic Records, karma, opening the third eye, the ego and the meaning of Bible stories. It is a master class for opening your personal pathway.

THE GOLDEN PATH

RUTH RYDEN

ISBN 0-929385-43-8

$11.95 Softcover 200p

LIVING THE GOLDEN PATH

Practical Soul-utions to Today's Problems

Guidance that can be used in the real world to solve dilemmas, to strengthen inner resolves and see the Light at the end of the road. Covers the difficult issues of addictions, rape, abortion, suicide and personal loss.

LIVING THE GOLDEN PATH

CHANNELED BY RUTH RYDEN

ISBN 0-929385-65-9

$11.95 Softcover 186p

◆ PETE SANDERS JR.

ACCESS YOUR BRAIN'S JOY CENTER

An M.I.T.-trained scientist's discovery of how to self-trigger the brain's natural mood-elevation mechanisms as an alternative to alcohol, nicotine, drugs or overeating to cope with life's pressures and challenges.

Access Your Brain's Joy Center
The Free Soul Method

An M.I.T.-Trained Scientist's Stunning New Discovery for Greater Success and Happiness

Pete A. Sanders Jr.

ISBN 0-96419 11-2-1

$14.95 Softcover 214p

◆ JERRY MULVIN

OUT-OF-BODY EXPLORATION

Techniques for traveling in the Soul Body to achieve absolute freedom and experience truth for oneself. Discover reincarnation, karma and your personal spiritual path.

OUT-OF-BODY EXPLORATION

ISBN 0-941464-01-6

$8.95 Softcover 87p

◆ CHARLES H. HAPGOOD

VOICES OF SPIRIT

The author discusses 15 years of work with Elwood Babbit, the famed channel. Will fascinate both the curious sceptic and the believer. Includes complete transcripts.

Voices of Spirit

Through the Psychic Experience of Elwood Babbitt
by Charles H. Hapgood

ISBN 1-881343-00-6

$13.00 Softcover 350p

BOOK MARKET

A reader's guide to the extraordinary books we publish, print and market for your enLightenment.

— A DIVISION OF LIGHT TECHNOLOGY PUBLISHING

STARCHILD PRESS

1-800-450-0985
or Fax:
1-800-393-7017
Or use order
form at end

VISA   MasterCard

9

◆ BRIAN GOLD

CACTUS EDDIE

Imaginative and colorful, charmingly illustrated with 20 detailed paintings by the artist author. The tale of a small boy who when separated from his family has more adventures than Pecos Bill. Printed in large 8½" by 11" format.

$11.95 Softcover 62p
ISBN 0-929385-74-8

◆ TONI SIEGEL

SPIRIT OF THE NINJA

Returning as a dog, a Spiritual Warrior gains love and peace with a young woman in Sedona. Profoundly moving tale for all ages.

$7.95 Softcover 67p

ISBN 0-9627746-0-X

◆ LOU BADER

THE GREAT KACHINA

A warm, delightful story that will help children understand Kachina energy. With 20 full-color illustrations, printed in 8½" by 11" format to dramatize the artwork.

$11.95 Softcover 62p
ISBN 0-929385-60-8

◆ DOROTHY McMANUS

SONG OF SIRIUS

A truthful view of modern teens who face drugs and death, love and forgiveness. Guided by Eckrita of Sirius, they each find their destiny and desires.

$8.00 Softcover 155p

ISBN 0-929686-01-2

IN THE SHADOW OF THE SAN FRANCISCO PEAKS

FRONTIER ADVENTURES
LOU BADER

Collection of tales about those who shaped the frontier and were changed by it. A young boy's experiences with people and the wilderness is fascinating reading for all ages.

$9.95 Softcover 152p
ISBN 0-929385-52-7

◆ ALOA STARR

I WANT TO KNOW

Inspiring responses to the questions of Why am I here? Who is God? Who is Jesus? What do dreams mean? and What do angels do? Invites contemplation, sets values and delights the young.

$7.00 Softcover 87p

ISBN 0-929686-02-0

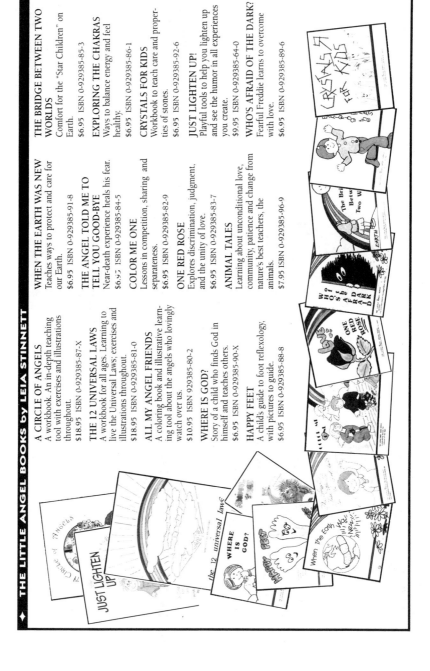

BOOK MARKET 12

A reader's guide to the extraordinary books we publish, print and market for your enLightenment.

◆ EILEEN ROTA

THE STORY OF THE PEOPLE

An exciting history of our coming to Earth, our traditions, our choices and the coming changes. It can be viewed as a metaphysical adventure, science fiction or the epic of all of us brave enough to know the truth. Beautifully written and illustrated.

$11.95 Softcover 209p   ISBN 0-929385-51-9

◆ GABRIEL HUDSON BAIN

AURAS 101

A Basic Study of Human Auras and the Techniques to See Them

An excellent, easy-to-read guide to seeing and understanding auras, the subtle energy fields that are part of every living being. This well-illustrated little book leads one easily through simple exercises and explanations into seeing auras.

$6.95 Softcover 4¼" by 5¾" 60p   ISBN 1-891824-07-4

◆ GUIDE BOOK

THE NEW AGE PRIMER

Spiritual Tools for Awakening

A guidebook to the changing reality, it is an overview of the concepts and techniques of mastery by authorities in their fields. Explores reincarnation, belief systems and transformative tools from astrology to crystals.

$11.95 Softcover 206p   ISBN 0-929385-48-9

◆ RAYMOND MARDYKS

SEDONA STARSEED

There is a boundary between the dimensions humans experience as reality and the beyond. Voices from beyond the veil reveal a series of messages. The stars and constellations will guide you to the place inside where infinite possibilities exist.

$14.95 Softcover 146p   ISBN 0-9644180-0-2

◆ MICHAEL FARKAS

1-800-GOD-HELP-ME

A Love Story

This is one man's story of light, love, ecstasy and creation to help those who need God's direct toll-free line for guidance and instruction on how to make the transition from a life of crisis, filled with drama and difficulty, to a life of constant bliss and evolution.

ISBN 1-891824-08-2

$15.95 Softcover 435p

◆ JONATHAN GOLDMAN

SHIFTING FREQUENCIES

Gives techniques and meditations to learn to shift our frequency, thus avoiding the effects of daily bombardments and enhancing the effects of the incoming assistance. Ultimately we can assist our response to new encodements of light and love coming to our planet now.

ISBN 1-891824-04-X

$14.95 Softcover 140p

BOOKS PUBLISHED BY LIGHT TECHNOLOGY PUBLISHING

	No. Copies	Total
1-800-GOD-HELP-ME	$15.95	$
ACUPRESSURE FOR THE SOUL	$11.95	$
ARCTURUS PROBE	$14.95	$
AURAS 101	$ 6.95	$
BEHOLD A PALE HORSE	$25.00	$
CACTUS EDDIE	$11.95	$
CHANNELING: EVOLUTIONARY...	$ 9.95	$
COLOR MEDICINE	$11.95	$
FOREVER YOUNG	$ 9.95	$
GUARDIANS OF THE FLAME	$14.95	$
GREAT KACHINA	$11.95	$
I'M OK, I'M JUST MUTATING	$ 6.00	$
KEYS TO THE KINGDOM	$14.95	$
LEGEND OF THE EAGLE CLAN	$12.95	$
LIVING RAINBOWS	$14.95	$
MAHATMA I & II	$19.95	$
MILLENNIUM TABLETS	$14.95	$
NEW AGE PRIMER	$11.95	$
PATH OF THE MYSTIC	$11.95	$
POISONS THAT HEAL	$14.95	$
PRISONERS OF EARTH	$11.95	$
SEDONA VORTEX GUIDE BOOK	$14.95	$
SHADOW OF SAN FRANCISCO PEAKS	$ 9.95	$
SHIFTING FREQUENCIES	$14.95	$
THE SOUL REMEMBERS	$14.95	$
STORY OF THE PEOPLE	$11.95	$
THIS WORLD AND THE NEXT ONE	$ 9.95	$
WELCOME TO PLANET EARTH	$14.95	$

ROBERT SHAPIRO/ARTHUR FANNING

	No. Copies	Total
SHINING THE LIGHT	$12.95	$
SHINING THE LIGHT — BOOK II	$14.95	$
SHINING THE LIGHT — BOOK III	$14.95	$
SHINING THE LIGHT — BOOK IV	$14.95	$
SHINING THE LIGHT — BOOK V	$14.95	$

ROBERT SHAPIRO

	No. Copies	Total
THE EXPLORER RACE	$25.00	$
ETs AND THE EXPLORER RACE	$14.95	$
EXPLORER RACE: ORIGINS...	$14.95	$
EXPLORER RACE: PARTICLE...	$14.95	$
EXPLORER RACE: CREATOR...	$19.95	$
EXPLORER RACE AND BEYOND	$14.95	$

ARTHUR FANNING

	No. Copies	Total
SOUL, EVOLUTION, FATHER	$12.95	$
SIMON	$ 9.95	$

WESLEY H. BATEMAN

	No. Copies	Total
DRAGONS & CHARIOTS	$ 9.95	$
KNOWLEDGE FROM THE STARS	$11.95	$

LYNN BUESS

	No. Copies	Total
CHILDREN OF LIGHT, CHILDREN...	$ 8.95	$
NUMEROLOGY: NUANCES...	$13.75	$
NUMEROLOGY FOR THE NEW AGE	$11.00	$

RUTH RYDEN

	No. Copies	Total
THE GOLDEN PATH	$11.95	$
LIVING THE GOLDEN PATH	$11.95	$

DOROTHY ROEDER

	No. Copies	Total
CRYSTAL CO-CREATORS	$14.95	$
NEXT DIMENSION IS LOVE	$11.95	$
REACH FOR US	$14.95	$

HALLIE DEERING

	No. Copies	Total
LIGHT FROM THE ANGELS	$15.00	$
DO-IT-YOURSELF POWER TOOLS	$25.00	$

JOSHUA DAVID STONE, PH.D.

	No. Copies	Total
COMPLETE ASCENSION MANUAL	$14.95	$
HIDDEN MYSTERIES	$14.95	$
BEYOND ASCENSION	$14.95	$
SOUL PSYCHOLOGY	$14.95	$
ASCENDED MASTERS LIGHT THE WAY	$14.95	$
COSMIC ASCENSION	$14.95	$
BEGINNERS GUIDE TO ASCENSION	$14.95	$
GOLDEN KEYS TO ASCENSION	$14.95	$
MANUAL FOR PLANETARY LEADERSHIP	$14.95	$
YOUR ASCENSION MISSION	$14.95	$
REVELATIONS OF A MELCHIZEDEK...	$14.95	$
HOW TO TEACH ASCENSION CLASSES	$14.95	$

VYWAMUS/JANET MCCLURE

	No. Copies	Total
AHA! THE REALIZATION BOOK	$11.95	$
LIGHT TECHNIQUES	$11.95	$
SANAT KUMARA	$11.95	$
SCOPES OF DIMENSIONS	$11.95	$
THE SOURCE ADVENTURE	$11.95	$
PRELUDE TO ASCENSION	$29.95	$

StarChild Press ★ ★ ★

LEIA STINNETT

	No. Copies	Total
A CIRCLE OF ANGELS	$18.95	$
THE TWELVE UNIVERSAL LAWS	$18.95	$
ALL MY ANGEL FRIENDS	$10.95	$
ANIMAL TALES	$ 7.95	$
WHERE IS GOD?	$ 6.95	$
JUST LIGHTEN UP!	$ 9.95	$
HAPPY FEET	$ 6.95	$
WHEN THE EARTH WAS NEW	$ 6.95	$
THE ANGEL TOLD ME...	$ 6.95	$
COLOR ME ONE	$ 6.95	$
ONE RED ROSE	$ 6.95	$
EXPLORING THE CHAKRAS	$ 6.95	$
CRYSTALS R FOR KIDS	$ 6.95	$
WHO'S AFRAID OF THE DARK	$ 6.95	$
BRIDGE BETWEEN TWO WORLDS	$ 6.95	$

BOOKS PRINTED OR MARKETED BY LIGHT TECHNOLOGY PUBLISHING

ACCESS YOUR BRAIN'S JOY CENTER	$14.95		STALKING THE WILD PENDULUM	$12.95
AN ASCENSION HANDBOOK	$11.95		THE SEDONA VORTEX EXPERIENCE	$ 4.95
ATLANTIS CONNECTION	$14.95		SONG OF SIRIUS	$ 8.00
AWAKEN TO THE HEALER WITHIN	$16.50		SOUL RECOVERY AND EXTRACTION	$ 9.95
BRINGERS OF THE DAWN	$12.95		TEMPLE OF THE LIVING EARTH	$16.00
EARTH IN ASCENSION	$14.95		TOUCHED BY LOVE	$ 9.95
GOD THIS IS A GOOD BOOK	$16.50		THE ARMSTRONG REPORT	$11.95
I WANT TO KNOW	$ 7.00		THE ONLY PLANET OF CHOICE	$16.95
JANE ROBERTS A VIEW FROM THE...	$14.95		THE TRANSFORMATIVE VISION	$14.95
LIFE IS THE FATHER WITHIN	$19.75		VOICES OF SPIRIT	$13.00
LIFE ON THE CUTTING EDGE	$14.95		WE ARE ONE	$14.95
M.A.S.S. 101	$ 9.95		**LEE CARROLL**	
MAYAN CALENDAR BIRTHDAY BOOK	$12.95		KRYON—BOOK I, THE END TIMES	$12.00
MAYAN CALENDAR COLORING BOOK	$ 8.95		KRYON—BOOK II, DON'T THINK LIKE.	$12.00
MEDICAL ASTROLOGY	$29.95		KRYON—BOOK III, ALCHEMY OF...	$14.00
MIRACLES & OTHER ORDINARY THINGS	$19.95		KRYON—THE PARABLES OF KRYON	$19.95
OUR COSMIC ANCESTORS	$ 9.95		KRYON—THE JOURNEY HOME	$14.95
OUT-OF-BODY EXPLORATION	$ 8.95		KRYON—PARTNERING WITH GOD	$14.00
PERFECT HEALTH	$15.95		**TOM DONGO**	
REFLECTIONS ON ASCENSION	$12.95		MYSTERIES OF SEDONA — BOOK I	$ 6.95
SEDONA STARSEED	$14.95		ALIEN TIDE — BOOK II	$ 7.95
SOUL RECOVERY AND EXTPACTION	$ 9.95		QUEST — BOOK III	$ 9.95

UNSEEN BEINGS, UNSEEN WORLDS	$ 9.95
MERGING DIMENSIONS	$14.95
SEDONA IN A NUTSHELL	$ 4.95
RICHARD DANNELLEY	
SEDONA POWER SPOT/GUIDE	$11.00
SEDONA: BEYOND THE VORTEX	$12.00
MSI	
ASCENSION!	$11.95
FIRST THUNDER	$12.95
SECOND THUNDER	$17.95
ENLIGHTENMENT	$15.95
PRESTON B. NICHOLS WITH PETER MOON	
MONTAUK PROJECT	$15.95
MONTAUK REVISITED	$19.95
PYRAMIDS OF MONTAUK	$19.95
ENCOUNTER IN THE PLEIADES...	$19.95
THE BLACK SUN	$19.95
MONTAUK: THE ALIEN CONNECTION	$19.95
LYSSA ROYAL AND KEITH PRIEST	
PREPARING FOR CONTACT	$12.95
PRISM OF LYRA	$11.95
VISITORS FROM WITHIN	$12.95

ASCENSION MEDITATION TAPES

JOSHUA DAVID STONE, PH.D.

ASCENSION ACTIVATION MEDITATION	S101	$12.00
TREE OF LIFE ASCENSION MEDITATION	S102	$12.00
MT. SHASTA ASCENSION ACTIVATION MEDITATION	S103	$12.00
KABBALISTIC ASCENSION ACTIVATION	S104	$12.00
COMPLETE ASCENSION MANUAL MEDITATION	S105	$12.00
SET OF ALL 5 TAPES		$49.95

VYWAMUS/BARBARA BURNS

THE QUANTUM MECHANICAL YOU (6 TAPES)	B101-6	$40.00

TAKA

MAGICAL SEDONA THROUGH THE DIDGERIDOO	T101	$12.00

BRIAN GRATTAN

SEATTLE SEMINAR RESURRECTION 1994 (12 TAPES)	M102	$79.95

YHWH/ARTHUR FANNING

ON BECOMING	F101	$10.00
HEALING MEDITATIONS/KNOWING SELF	F102	$10.00
MANIFESTATION & ALIGNMENT W/ POLES	F103	$10.00
THE ART OF SHUTTING UP	F104	$10.00
CONTINUITY OF CONSCIOUSNESS	F105	$25.00
MERGING THE GOLDEN LIGHT REPLICAS OF YOU	F107	$10.00
UNIFICATION OF THE TANTRIC YOU'S	F108	$60.00
THOUGHT UNIFIED	F109	$60.00
UNCONDITIONAL LOVE	F110	$60.00
THE NATURAL PLANET	F111	$55.00
WHERE HUMANS ASSIST THE ANGELS	F112	$60.00
INTRODUCTION TO ID	F113	$65.00
CONSCIOUSNESS AND THE ELECTRICAL BODY	F114	$65.00
PEBBLES IN THE RIVER OF THOUGHT	F115	$60.00
RETRAINING THE MONKEY MIND	F116	$60.00
THE EGO AND ITS UNION WITH GOD	F117	$55.00
SYMBOLS OF THE CREATOR GODS...	F118	$55.00

KRYON/LEE CARROLL

SEVEN RESPONSIBILITIES OF THE NEW AGE	K101	$10.00
CO-CREATION IN THE NEW AGE	K102	$10.00
ASCENSION AND THE NEW AGE	K103	$10.00
NINE WAYS TO RAISE THE PLANET'S VIBRATION	K104	$10.00
GIFTS AND TOOLS OF THE NEW AGE	K105	$10.00

JAN TOBER

CRYSTAL SINGER	J101	$12.00

BOOKSTORE DISCOUNTS HONORED — SHIPPING 15% OF RETAIL

NAME/COMPANY _____

ADDRESS _____

CITY/STATE/ZIP _____

PHONE _____ FAX _____

E-MAIL _____

SUBTOTAL: $ _____

SALES TAX: $ _____
(8.5% – AZ residents only)

SHIPPING/HANDLING: $ _____
($4 Min.; 15% of orders over $30)

CANADA S/H: $ _____
(20% of order)

TOTAL AMOUNT ENCLOSED: $ _____

All prices in US$. Higher in Canada and Europe. Books are available at all national distributors as well as the following international distributors:

CANADA: Dempsey (604) 683-5541 Fax (604) 683-5521 • ENGLAND/EUROPE: Windrush Press Ltd. 0608 652012/652025 Fax 0608 652125

AUSTRALIA: Gemcraft Books (03) 888-0111 Fax (03) 888-0044 • NEW ZEALAND: Peaceful Living Pub. (07) 571-8105 Fax (07) 571-8513

☐ CHECK ☐ MONEY ORDER

CREDIT CARD: ☐ MC ☐ VISA

_____

Exp. date: _____

Signature: _____

(U.S. FUNDS ONLY) PAYABLE TO:
LIGHT TECHNOLOGY
PUBLISHING

P.O. BOX 1526 • SEDONA • AZ 86339
(520) 282-6523 Fax: (520) 282-4130
1-800-450-0985
Fax 1-800-393-7017

BOOKSTORE DISCOUNTS HONORED — SHIPPING 15% OF RETAIL

NAME/COMPANY _____

ADDRESS _____

CITY/STATE/ZIP _____

PHONE _____ FAX _____

E-MAIL _____

SUBTOTAL: $ _____

SALES TAX: $ _____
(8.5% – AZ residents only)

SHIPPING/HANDLING: $ _____
($4 Min.; 15% of orders over $30)

CANADA S/H: $ _____
(20% of order)

TOTAL AMOUNT ENCLOSED: $ _____

All prices in US$. Higher in Canada and Europe. Books are available at all national distributors as well as the following international distributors:

CANADA: Dempsey (604) 683-5541 Fax (604) 683-5521 • ENGLAND/EUROPE: Windrush Press Ltd. 0608 652012/652025 Fax 0608 652125

AUSTRALIA: Gemcraft Books (03) 888-0111 Fax (03) 888-0044 • NEW ZEALAND: Peaceful Living Pub. (07) 571-8105 Fax (07) 571-8513

☐ CHECK ☐ MONEY ORDER

CREDIT CARD: ☐ MC ☐ VISA

_____

Exp. date: _____

Signature: _____

(U.S. FUNDS ONLY) PAYABLE TO:
LIGHT TECHNOLOGY
PUBLISHING

P.O. BOX 1526 • SEDONA • AZ 86339
(520) 282-6523 Fax: (520) 282-4130
1-800-450-0985
Fax 1-800-393-7017

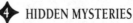

 **A BEGINNER'S GUIDE
TO THE PATH OF ASCENSION**

This volume covers the basics of ascension clearly and completely, from the spiritual hierarchy to the angels and star beings, in Dr. Stone's easy-to-read style. From his background in psychology he offers a unique perspective on such issues as karma, the transcendence of the negative ego, the power of the spoken word and the psychology of ascension.

$14.95   Softcover 166p   ISBN 1-891824-02-3

 **GOLDEN KEYS TO ASCENSION AND HEALING
REVELATIONS OF SAI BABA
AND THE ASCENDED MASTERS**

This book represents the wisdom of the ascended masters condensed into concise keys that serve as a spiritual guide. These 420 golden keys present the multitude of methods, techniques, affirmations, prayers and insights Dr. Stone has gleaned from his own background in psychology and life conditions and his thorough research of all the ancient and contemporary classics that speak of the path to God realization.

$14.95   Softcover 206p   ISBN 1-891824-03-1

 MANUAL FOR PLANETARY LEADERSHIP

Here at last is an indispensible book that has been urgently needed in these uncertain times. This book lays out, in an orderly and clear fashion the guidelines for leadership in the world and in one's own life. It serves as a reference manual for moral and spiritual living and offers a vision of a world where strong love and the highest aspirations of humanity triumph.

$14.95   Softcover 284p   ISBN 1-891824-05-8

 **YOUR ASCENSION MISSION
EMBRACING YOUR PUZZLE PIECE**

This book shows how each person's puzzle piece is just as vital and necessary as any other. Fourteen chapters explain in detail all aspects of living the fullest expression of your unique individuality.

$14.95   Softcover 248p   ISBN 1-891824-09-0

 REVELATIONS OF A MELCHIZEDEK INITIATE

Dr. Stone's spiritual autobiography, beginning with his ascension initiation and progression into the 12th initiation, is filled with insight, tools and information. It will lift you into wondrous planetary and cosmic realms.

$14.95   Softcover   ISBN 1-891824-10-4

 HOW TO TEACH ASCENSION CLASSES

This book serves as an ideal foundation for teaching ascension classes and presenting workshops. The inner-plane ascended masters have guided Dr. Stone to write this book, using his Easy-to-Read-Encyclopedia of the Spiritual Path as a foundation. It covers an entire one- to two-year program of classes.

$14.95   Softcover 136p   ISBN 1-891824-15-5

Former U.S. Naval Intelligence Briefing Team Member reveals information kept secret by our government since the 1940s. UFOs, the J.F.K. assassination, the Secret Government, the war on drugs and more by the world's leading expert on UFOs.

Behold A Pale Horse

About the Author

Bill Cooper, former United States Naval Intelligence Briefing Team member, reveals information that remains hidden from the public eye. This information has been kept in top-secret government files since the 1940s.

In 1988 Bill decided to "talk" due to events then taking place worldwide. Since Bill has been "talking," he has correctly predicted the lowering of the Iron Curtain, the fall of the Berlin Wall and the invasion of Panama, all of record well before the events occurred. His information comes from top-secret documents that he read while with the Intelligence Briefing Team and from over 17 years of thorough research.

by
William Cooper

$25^{00}

$25.00
Softcover 500p
ISBN 0-929385-22-5

Excerpt from pg. 94

"I read while in Naval Intelligence that at least once a year, maybe more, two nuclear submarines meet beneath the polar icecap and mate together at an airlock. Representatives of the Soviet Union meet with the Policy Committee of the Bilderberg Group. The Russians are given the script for their next performance. Items on the agenda include the combined efforts in the secret space program governing Alternative 3. I now have in my possession official NASA photographs of a moon base in the crater Copernicus."

Table of Contents

LIGHT TECHNOLOGY PUBLISHING

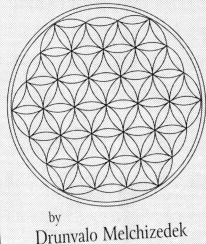